Danby Pickering

The Statutes at large from Magna Charta to the end of the eleventh Parliament of Great Britain

Vol. XXVI.

Danby Pickering

The Statutes at large from Magna Charta to the end of the eleventh Parliament of Great Britain
Vol. XXVI.

ISBN/EAN: 9783742899453

Manufactured in Europe, USA, Canada, Australia, Japa

Cover: Foto ©Suzi / pixelio.de

Manufactured and distributed by brebook publishing software
(www.brebook.com)

Danby Pickering

The Statutes at large from Magna Charta to the end of the eleventh Parliament of Great Britain

THE

Statutes at Large,

FROM

MAGNA CHARTA

To the END of the

Eleventh Parliament of GREAT BRITAIN,

Anno 1761.

CONTINUED.

VOL. XXVI.

By DANBY PICKERING, of Gray's-Inn, Esq;
Reader of the Law Lecture to that Honourable Society.

CAMBRIDGE,
Printed by JOSEPH BENTHAM, Printer to the UNIVERSITY;
for CHARLES BATHURST, at the Cross-Keys, opposite St. Dunstan's
Church in Fleet-Street, London. 1764.

CUM PRIVILEGIO.

A

TABLE

Containing the TITLES of all the

STATUTES

PUBLICK and PRIVATE,

Passed *Anno quarto*

GEORGII III. *Regis.*

Being the Third Session of the Twelfth Parliament of GREAT BRITAIN.

PUBLICK ACTS.

AN act for continuing and granting to his Majesty certain duties upon malt, mum, cyder, and perry, for the service of the year one thousand seven hundred and sixty four.

II. An act for granting an aid to his Majesty by a land tax to be raised in *Great Britain*, for the service of the year one thousand seven hundred and sixty four.

III. An act for punishing mutiny and desertion; and for the better payment of the army and their quarters.

IV. An act for exhibiting a bill in this present parliament, for naturalizing his highness the hereditary prince of *Brunswick Lunenburg*.

V. An act for naturalizing his highness *Charles William Ferdinand*, hereditary prince of *Brunswick Lunenburg*.

VI. An act to continue, for a limited time, the free importation of tallow, hogs lard, and grease, from *Ireland*.

VII. An act to explain and amend such part of an act made in the last session of parliament, (intituled, *An act for granting to his Majesty several additional duties upon wines imported into this kingdom, and certain duties upon all cyder and perry, and for raising the sum of three millions five hundred thousand pounds, by way of annuities and lotteries to be charged on the said duties*) as relates to cyder and perry made in this kingdom.

VIII. An act for the regulation of his Majesty's mar while on shore.

IX. An act for repealing the duties now payable up skins imported, and for granting other duties in lieu and for granting certain duties upon the exportation skins and bever wool; and for taking off the drawbac on the exportation of such skins.

X. An act for the more easy discharge of recogni streated into his Majesty's court of Exchequer.

XI. An act for continuing certain laws therein ment lating to *British* sail cloth, and to the duties payable c sail cloth, and to the allowance upon the exportation made gunpowder, and for giving further encourageme importation of naval stores from the *British* colonies in

XII. An act to continue several laws for the better r of pilots for the conducting of ships and vessels fro *Deal*, and *Isle of Thanet*, up the rivers of *Thames* and relating to the landing of rum or spirits of the *British* s tations before the duties of excise are paid thereon; a further punishment of persons going armed or disguise fiance of the laws of customs or excise; and to the re officers of the customs in informations upon seizures granting a liberty to carry sugars of the growth, pr manufacture of any of his Majesty's sugar colonies, di to foreign parts, in ships built in *Great Britain*, and according to law; and for punishing persons who sha or destroy any banks, flood-gates, sluices, or other w longing to the rivers and streams made navigable by a liament.

XIII. An act for granting to his Majesty a certa money out of the sinking fund, for the service of the thousand seven hundred and sixty four; and for preve certain cases, the obtaining of allowances in respect of age of wines imported into this kingdom; and for mal duplicates of Exchequer bills, tickets, certificates, rec nuity orders, and other orders, lost, burnt, or othe stroyed.

XIV. An act for the better regulating of building prevent mischiefs that may happen by fire within the w of mortality, and other places therein mentioned.

XV. An act for granting certain duties in the *Briti* and plantations in *America*; for continuing, amenc making perpetual, an act passed in the sixth year of th his late majesty King *George* the Second, (intituled, *the better securing and encouraging the trade of his Majesty lonies in* America); for applying the produce of su and of the duties to arise by virtue of the said act, to fraying the expences of defending, protecting, and sec said colonies and plantations; for explaining an act m twenty fifth year of the reign of King *Charles* the Sec tuled, *An act for the encouragement of the* Greenland *an trades, and for the better securing the plantation trade)*; and for altering and disallowing several drawbacks on exports from this kingdom, and more effectually preventing the clandestine conveyance of goods to and from the said colonies and plantations, and improving and securing the trade between the same and *Great Britain*.

XVI. An act to enable infants who are seised of lands, tenements, or hereditaments, within the duchy of *Lancaster*, or the counties palatine of *Chester*, *Lancaster*, or *Durham*, or the principality of *Wales*, in fee, or for the life or lives of one or more other person or persons, in trust, or by way of mortgage, to make conveyances of such estates by order of the court of the duchy chamber of *Lancaster*, of the court of *Exchequer* of the county palatine of *Chester*, the court of chancery of the county palatine of *Lancaster*, of the court of chancery of the county palatine of *Durham*; and of the courts of the great sessions in the principality of *Wales*.

XVII. An act to explain and amend an act passed in the second year of the reign of his present Majesty, intituled, *An act to explain, amend, and reduce into one act of parliament, the several laws now in being, relating to the raising and training the militia within that part of* Great Britain *called* England.

XVIII. An act for charging on the sinking fund certain annuities granted by an act passed in the first year of the reign of his present Majesty; and for carrying the duties therein mentioned, to the said fund; and also for consolidating such of the said annuities as are granted for a certain term of years, irredeemable, with other annuities granted by an act passed in the second year of his present Majesty's reign.

XIX. An act for importing salt from *Europe* into the province of *Quebec* in *America*, for a limited time.

XX. An act for vesting the fort of *Senegal*, and its dependencies, in the company of merchants trading to *Africa*.

XXI. An act for taking and swearing affidavits to be made use of in any of the courts of the county palatine of *Durham*.

XXII. An act for continuing several acts of parliament made for the encouragement of the whale fishery carried on by his Majesty's subjects.

XXIII. An act for raising a certain sum of money by loans or Exchequer bills; and for applying certain monies remaining in the Exchequer, for the service of the year one thousand seven hundred and sixty four; and for application of certain savings of publick monies, and of monies arisen by the sale of military stores; and for further appropriating the supplies granted in this session of parliament; and for relief of persons who have omitted to insert in indentures, or other writings the full sum agreed to be paid with clerks, apprentices, and other servants.

XXIV. An act for preventing frauds and abuses in relation to the sending and receiving of letters and packets free from the duty of postage.

XXV. An act for establishing an agreement with the governor and company of the bank of *England*, for raising certain sums of money towards the supply for the service of the year one thousand seven hundred and sixty four; and for more effectually preventing the forging powers to transfer such stock, or receive such dividends or annuities as are therein mentioned, and the fraudulent personating the owners thereof.

XXVI. An act for granting a bounty upon the importation of hemp, and rough and undressed flax, from his Majesty's colonies in *America*.

XXVII. An act for granting, for a limited time, a liberty to carry rice from his Majesty's provinces of *South Carolina* and *Georgia*, directly to any part of *America* to the southward of the said provinces, subject to the like duty as is now paid on the exportation of rice from the said colonies, to places in *Europe* situate to the southward of *Cape Finisterre*.

XXVIII. An act to enable his Majesty, with the advice of his privy council, to order the importation of provisions from *Ireland*, during the next recess of parliament, under certain restrictions and regulations therein mentioned.

XXIX. An act for the encouragement of the whale fishery in the gulph and river of *Saint Lawrence*, and on the coasts of his Majesty's colonies in *America*.

XXX. An act for applying the money granted in this session of parliament, for defraying the charge of the pay and cloathing of the militia of that part of *Great Britain* called *England*, for one year, beginning the twenty fifth day of *March*, one thousand seven hundred and sixty four.

XXXI. An act to indemnify such persons as have omitted to qualify themselves for offices and employments; and to indemnify justices of the peace, deputy lieutenants, and officers of the militia, or others, who have omitted to register or deliver in their qualifications within the time limited by law, and for giving further time for those purposes; and to indemnify members and officers in cities, corporations, and borough towns, whose admissions have been omitted to be stamped according to the several acts of parliament now in force for that purpose, or, having been stamped, have been lost or mislaid, and for allowing them time to provide admissions duly stamped; and to prevent the destruction of trees and underwoods growing in forests and chases.

XXXII. An act to impower the high court of chancery to lay out, upon proper securities, a further sum of money, not exceeding a sum therein limited, out of the common and general cash in the bank of *England* belonging to the suitors of the said court; and for applying the interest arising therefrom, towards answering the charges of the office of the accountant general of the said court.

XXXIII.. An act for preventing inconveniencies arising in cases of merchants, and such other persons as are within the description

scription of the statutes relating to bankrupts, being intitled to privilege of parliament, and becoming insolvent.

XXXIV. An act to prevent paper bills of credit, hereafter to be issued in any of his Majesty's colonies or plantations in *America*, from being declared to be a legal tender in payments of money; and to prevent the legal tender of such bills as are now subsisting, from being prolonged beyond the periods limited for calling in and sinking the same.

XXXV. An act for making compensation to the proprietors of such lands and hereditaments as have been purchased upon the sea coasts in the counties of *Kent*, *Sussex*, and *Southampton*, on which forts and batteries have been erected for defence of the said coasts, in pursuance of an act passed in the second year of the reign of his present Majesty, and for other purposes therein mentioned.

XXXVI. An act to continue an act made in the fifth year of the reign of his late majesty King *George* the Second, intituled, *An act to prevent the committing of frauds by bankrupts*; and for extending the laws, relating to hackney coaches, to the counties of *Kent* and *Essex*.

XXXVII. An act for the better establishing a manufactory of cambricks and lawns, or goods of the kind usually known under those denominations, now carrying on at *Winchelsea*, in the county of *Sussex*; and for improving, regulating, and extending the manufacture of cambricks and lawns, or goods of the kind usually known under those denominations, in that part of *Great Britain* called *England*.

XXXVIII. An act for allowing further time for inrollments of deeds and wills made by papists; and for relief of protestant purchasers.

XXXIX. An act to explain, amend, and render more effectual, two several acts of parliament, made in the second and third years of his present Majesty, for paving, cleansing, and lighting, the squares, streets, and lanes, within the city and liberty of *Westminster*, and other places therein mentioned, and for preventing annoyances therein; and for other purposes therein mentioned.

XL. An act for the more easy and speedy recovery of small debts within the borough and soke of *Doncaster*, in the county of *York*; and for lighting the streets, lanes, and other open passages and places, within the said borough.

XLI. An act for the more easy and speedy recovery of small debts in the town and parish of *Kirkby in Kendal*, in the county of *Westmorland*.

XLII. An act for repairing and widening the road from *Shillingford*, in the county of *Oxford*, through *Wallingford* and *Pangborne*, to *Reading*, in the county of *Berks*; and for building a bridge over the river *Thames*, at or near *Shillingford Ferry*.

XLIII. An act for maintaining, regulating, and employing the poor within the parish of *Saint John* at *Hackney*, in the county ty of *Middlesex*; and for lighting the said parish, and establishing a regular nightly watch therein.

XLIV. An act for repairing and widening the roads from *Horsham*, in the county of *Sussex*, through the parishes of *Shipley*, *West Grinsted*, *Ashurst*, *Steyning*, *Bramber*, and *Breeding*, in the said county.

XLV. An act to amend and render more effectual several acts of parliament, for repairing the roads from *Sherbrooke Hill*, near *Buxto* and *Chappel in the Frith*, in the county of *Derby*, through the town of *Stockport*, in the county of *Chester*, to *Manchester*, in the county of *Lancaster*, and other roads in the said acts mentioned, and for turning and diverting the roads from *Whaley Bridge* to *Chappel in the Frith*, and to *Sparrow Pit Gate*; and from *Whaley Bridge*, to the western end of *Longside Common*, in the county of *Chester*.

XLVI. An act to continue an act passed in the tenth year of the reign of his late majesty King *George* the Second, for continuing an act, passed in the fifth year of the reign of his late majesty King *George* the First, intituled, *An act for laying a duty of two pennies* Scots, *or one sixth part of a penny* Sterling, *upon every pint of ale or beer, that shall be vended or sold within the town of* Dunbar, *for improving and preserving the harbour, and repairing the town house, and building a school, and other publick buildings there; and for supplying the said town with fresh water.*

XLVII. An act for repairing and widening the roads, from the end of *Stanbridge Lane*, near a barn in the parish of *Romsey*, to the turnpike road at *Middle Wallop*, and from the turnpike road between *Stanbridge Lane* aforesaid, and *Great Bridge*, to the turnpike road at *Stockbridge*, and from the garden of *Henry Hattat*, at *Awbridge*, to the garden wall of *Denys Rolle*, esquire, at *East Tuderley*, and from *Lotkerley Mill Stream*, to *East Dean Gate*, and from the said garden wall to the turnpike road leading from *Stockbridge* aforesaid, in the county of *Southampton*, to *Salisbury*.

XLVIII. An act for repairing and widening several roads leading from *Calington* in the county of *Cornwall*.

XLIX. An act to enable the governor and company of the bank of *England* to purchase houses and ground for opening a passage for carriages, from *Cornhill* to the bank; and making more commodious several other passages leading thereto; and for enlarging the buildings of the said bank, and making the same more commodious.

L. An act for the relief of the bond and other creditors of the wardens and commonalty of the mystery of *Mercers* of the city of *London*.

LI. An act for continuing and enlarging the term and powers of an act, made in the twenty sixth year of the reign of his late majesty King *George* the Second, intituled, *An act for repairing and widening the road from the west end of the town of* Burton upon Trent, *in the county of* Stafford, *through the said town, to the south end of the town of* Derby, *in the county of* Derby.

LII. An

LII. An act for repairing and widening the road from *Workſop*, in the county of *Nottingham*, through the towns of *Gateſorth*, *Auſton*, *Aſton*, *Handſworth*, and *Darnall*, to the north eaſt end of *Attercliffe*, in the county of *York*, where the ſame joins the turnpike road from *Bawtry* to *Sheffield*.

LIII. An act for repairing and widening the roads from the *High Bridge* in *Spalding*, to a certain place called *Tydd Goat*, in the county of *Lincoln*; and from *Sutton Saint Mary's*, to *Sutton Waſh*, in the ſaid county.

LIV. An act for enlarging the term and powers granted by an act, paſſed in the twenty fourth year of the reign of his late Majeſty, intituled, *An act for making, widening, and keeping in repair, ſeveral roads in the ſeveral pariſhes of* Lambeth, Newington, Saint George Southwark, *and* Bermondſey, *in the county of* Surrey, *and* Lewiſham, *in the county of* Kent; and for repairing *Lambeth Back Lane*, and for lighting and watching the ſaid roads.

LV. An act for eſtabliſhing a regular and nightly watch, and for maintaining, regulating, and employing the poor within the pariſh of *Saint Clement Danes*, in the liberty of *Weſtminſter*, and county of *Middleſex*.

LVI. An act for the better relief and employment of the poor in the hundred of *Blything*, in the county of *Suffolk*.

LVII. An act for the better relief and employment of the poor in the hundred of *Boſmere* and *Claydon*, in the county of *Suffolk*.

LVIII. An act to amend and render more effectual an act paſſed in the twenty ninth year of the reign of his late majeſty King *George* the Second, intituled, *An act for the better relief and employment of the poor in the hundreds of* Colnies *and* Carlford, *in the county of* Suffolk.

LIX. An act for the better relief and employment of the poor, in the hundred of *Samford*, in the county of *Suffolk*.

LX. An act for the more effectual relief and employment of the poor, within the city of *Glouceſter*, and for lighting the ſtreets of the ſaid city.

LXI. An act for repairing and widening the road from *Derby* to *Mansfield*, in the county of *Nottingham*, and ſeveral other roads therein mentioned.

LXII. An act for continuing the terms of, and amending, the acts for repairing ſeveral roads leading from *Ledbury*, in the county of *Hereford*; and for widening and amending the road through the pariſh of *Bromeſberrow*, in the county of *Glouceſter*, and through *Corſe Lawn*, till it meets the road from *Glouceſter* to *Worceſter*.

LXIII. An act for amending and widening the road from a place near the village of *Milford*, through *Haſlemere*, to the *Portſmouth* road, between *Lippock* and *Rake*, in the ſeveral counties of *Surrey*, *Suſſex*, and *Southampton*.

LXIV. An act for amending and widening the road from *Tinſley* in the county of *York*, to the town of *Doncaſter* in the ſaid county.

LXV. An act for amending and widening the road from the south end of the town of *Rotherham* in the county of *York*, to the present turnpike road, near *Pleasley*, in the county of *Derby*, and also the road from the north end of the said town of *Rotherham*, into the present turnpike road on the east side of *Tankersley Park*, in the said county of *York*.

LXVI. An act to continue the term, and enlarge the powers, of an act passed in the seventeenth year of the reign of his late Majesty, for repairing the road between the town of *Kingston upon Hull*, and the town of *Beverley*, in the east riding of the county of *York*; and for repairing the road from *Newland Bridge*, to the west end of the town of *Cottingham*, in the said riding.

LXVII. An act for repairing, widening, and keeping in repair, the high roads leading from *Alfreton* in the county of *Derby*, through *Carters Lane*, to a certain place in the town of *Mansfield*, called *Stockwell*, and from the *Bridle Gate* at the division of the liberties of *Blackwell* and *Hucknall*, through the town of *Sutton* in *Ashfield*, to the *Mansfield* and *Newark* turnpike, at or near *Python Hill*, in the forest of *Sherwood*, in the county of *Nottingham*.

LXVIII. An act for continuing and enlarging the term and powers of an act made in the twenty eighth year of the reign of his late majesty King *George* the Second, intituled, *An act for repairing and widening the road from* Rochdale *to* Burnley, *in the county of* Lancaster.

LXIX. An act for repairing and widening the road from the west end of *Baxter Gate*, in the town of *Whitby*, to the south end of *Lockton Lane*, in the parish of *Middleton*, in the county of *York*.

LXX. An act for enlarging the term and powers of two acts of the twelfth of King *George* the First, and of the third of his late Majesty, for repairing several roads therein mentioned, in the county of *Salop*; and also for amending and widening the road, from the sign of the *Horse Shoe*, in *Uckington*, to *Longnor Green*; and also from the west end of *Hatcham Bridge*, to the *Cross Houses* upon the *Bridgenorth* turnpike road, in the said county.

LXXI. An act for extending the provisions of an act, passed in the twenty fifth year of his late Majesty, for repairing the roads from the north end of *Malling Street*, near *Lewes*, and other roads in *Sussex*, to the road leading from the north end of *Offham*, to the *Spital Barn* in *Lewes* aforesaid.

LXXII. An act for continuing one moiety of the duties, granted by an act of the eleventh and twelfth year of King *William* the Third, for the repair of *Dover Harbour*, and which have been by several other acts, continued till the twelfth day of *May*, one thousand seven hundred and sixty five; and for applying the same to compleating and keeping in repair the harbour of *Rye*, in the county of *Sussex*, and for more effectually compleating and keeping in repair the said harbour.

LXXIII. An act for paving, repairing, and cleansing, the streets,

ſtreets, lanes, alleys, and publick paſſages, within the town of *Whitby*, in the county of *York*; and for preventing incroachments and annoyances therein; and for regulating the carriages, cartmen, and porters there.

LXXIV. An act for amending and ſupplying the deficiencies of an act paſſed in the ſecond year of the reign of his preſent majeſty King *George* the Third, intituled, *An act to amend and render more effectual, ſeveral acts made for cleanſing and enlightning the ſtreets of the town of* Kingſton upon Hull, *and for preventing annoyances therein.*

LXXV. An act for ſupplying the borough and town of *Wigan*, in the county of *Lancaſter*, with freſh and wholſome water.

LXXVI. An act for repairing and widening the road from *Beverley* to *Kexby Bridge*, in the county of *York*.

LXXVII. An act for continuing and enlarging the term and powers of an act made in the twenty ſixth year of the reign of his late Majeſty, intituled, *An act for repairing and widening the road leading from* Piper's Inn, *in the pariſh of* Aſhcott, *in the county of* Somerſet, *to and through* Glaſtonbury *and* Wells *to the* White Poſt, *in the great weſtern road, to the city of* Bath, *and from* Wells *to* Ruſh Hill, *leading to the city of* Briſtol; and for repairing and widening ſeveral other roads leading from the city of *Wells*.

LXXVIII. An act for explaining and amending an act made in the twenty ſixth year of the reign of his late majeſty King *George* the Second, intituled, *An act for amending, widening, and repairing the road leading from* Dover *to* Barham Downs, *in the county of* Kent; and alſo for amending, widening, and repairing the road leading from *Cowgate* and *Archcliffe Fort*, in *Dover*, through *Folkſtone*, to the town of *Hythe*, in the ſaid county.

LXXIX. An act to enlarge the term and powers of ſo much of an act of the twenty ninth year of the reign of his late Majeſty, for repairing and widening ſeveral roads therein deſcribed, leading from the town of *Tewkeſbury*, in the county of *Glouceſter*, as relates to the firſt diſtrict of roads therein mentioned; and for amending the road from *Comb Hill*, to a bridge near *Norton Mill*, in the county of *Glouceſter*, and from *Eckington Bridge*, to join the turnpike road which leads from *Upton on Severn* to *Perſhore*, in the county of *Worceſter*.

LXXX. An act for repairing and widening the roads from *Spalding High Bridge*, to the market place in *Donington*, and from the tenth mile ſtone, in the pariſh of *Goſbertown*, to the eighth mile ſtone, in the pariſh of *Wigtoft*, in the county of *Lincoln*.

LXXXI. An act for amending, widening, and keeping in repair, ſeveral roads leading from the *Bucks-Head* at *Watling Street*, to *Beckbury*, and the *New Inn*; and from the *Birches Brook* to the *Hand Poſt*, in the pariſh of *Kemberton*, in the county of *Salop*.

LXXXII. An act for widening and repairing the road leading from *Aſhborne*, in the county of *Derby*, over *Belpar Bridge*, to the preſent turnpike road from *Sheffield* and *Cheſterfield* to *Derby*, at or near a place called *Openwood Gate*, and from *Belpar Bridge* to *Ripley*, in the county of *Derby*.

LXXXIII. An

LXXXIII. An act for repairing and widening the road from *Bramcott Odd House*, in the county of *Nottingham*, to the *Cross Post* upon *Smalley Common*, in the county of *Derby*, and from *Ilkeston* to the towns of *Heanor* and *Shipley*, in the said county of *Derby*, and from *Trowell*, in the county of *Nottingham*, to the town of *Nottingham*.

LXXXIV. An act for repairing and widening the roads from *Melton Mowbray*, in the county of *Leicester*, to the *Guide Post* in *Saint Margaret's Field*, *Leicester*, and from the town of *Leicester*, to the town of *Lutterworth*, in the said county, and other roads therein mentioned.

LXXXV. An act for repairing and widening the road from *Scots Dyke*, in the county of *Dumfries*, by or through the villages of *Langholm* and *Hawick* to *Haremoss*, in the county of *Roxburgh*.

LXXXVI. An act to amend and render more effectual two several acts passed in the twenty fourth and twenty eighth years of the reign of his late Majesty, for repairing the high roads in the county of *Edinburgh*, to and from the city of *Edinburgh*, and from *Cramond Bridge* to the town of *Queensferry*, in the county of *Linlithgow*.

LXXXVII. An act for repairing several roads leading from the town of *Bideford*, in the county of *Devon*.

LXXXVIII. An act for amending, widening, and keeping in repair, several roads leading from the town of *Cardiff*, and several other towns and places in the county of *Glamorgan*.

LXXXIX. An act for the better relief and employment of the poor, in the hundred of *Mutford* and *Lothingland*, in the county of *Suffolk*.

XC. An act for the better relief and employment of the poor in the hundreds of *Loddon* and *Clavering*, in the county of *Norfolk*.

XCI. An act for the better relief and employment of the poor in the hundred of *Wangford*, in the county of *Suffolk*.

XCII. An act for the better paving of the streets and lanes, and for preventing nuisances and other annoyances, in that part of the parish of *Portsea*, in the county of *Southampton*, commonly called *Portsmouth Common*.

XCIII. An act for the better supplying the town of *Knaresborough*, and that part of the township of *Scriven with Tenter Gate* adjoining upon the said town, with water.

PRIVATE ACTS.

AN act for naturalizing *Govert Cassau*.

2. An act for naturalizing *Andrew Solinus*.

3. An act for naturalizing *Peter Hasenclever*, *Johann Peter Rucker*, *John Francis Blaebe*, *Andrew Vezian*, *James Charles Granges*, and *Jacob Muller*.

4. An act for naturalizing *William Dunant*, *John Christian Schrieber*, *Jonas Dael*, and *Charles Henry Thalbitzer*.

5. An act for dividing and inclosing the open common fields, common

common meadows, and other commonable lands, in the parish of *Heckington*, in the county of *Lincoln*.

6. An act for dividing and inclosing the open and common fields, common meadows, common grounds, heath grounds, lanes, and waste ground, within *Guilsborough*, *Coton*, and *Nortoft*, in the county of *Northampton*.

7. An act for dividing and inclosing certain open common fields and grounds, in the manor and parish of *Staiuton in the Hole*, in the county of *Lincoln*.

8. An act for dividing and inclosing the common fields, common and waste grounds, in the parish of *Scarby*, in the county of *Lincoln*.

9. An act for dividing and inclosing the open and common fields, and commons, or waste grounds, in the parish of *Chilver's Coton*, in the county of *Warwick*.

10. An act for inclosing and dividing so much of the moor or common, called *Badley Moor*, as lies within the manors of *North Tuddenham*, alias *Saint Clares*, *Mattishall Tuddenham*, on the part of *North Tuddenham*, and *Bell-house Hall*, and in the parish of *North Tuddenham*, in the county of *Norfolk*, and certain other commons and wastes within the said manors and parish.

11. An act for dividing and inclosing the open and common fields, meadows, and common fen, in the parish of *Horbling*, in the county of *Lincoln*, and for draining and improving the said fen.

12. An act for dividing and inclosing the open fields, and commonable places, of and in *Billesdon*, in the county of *Leicester*.

13. An act for establishing and confirming the inclosure and division of certain lands in *Sudcoates*, in the parish of *Drypool*, in the county of *York*, and for other purposes.

14. An act for dividing and inclosing several common and open fields and meadows, in the parish of *Saint Margaret*, near the borough of *Leicester*, in the county of *Leicester*.

15. An act for dividing and inclosing the open and common fields of *Wartnaby*, in the county of *Leicester*, and all the lands and grounds within the same fields.

16. An act for dividing and inclosing the open and common fields, meadows, and pastures of *North Cave*, in the east riding of the county of *York*.

17. An act for confirming articles of agreement for inclosing and dividing several open fields, and several pieces or parcels of arable, meadow, and pasture ground, within the township of *Skipsea*, in the county of *York*.

18. An act for dividing and inclosing the open and common fields and grounds in the township and parish of *Skeffling* in *Holderness*, in the county of *York*.

19. An act for extinguishing the right of common, in, over, and upon, certain commonable lands and grounds, within the manor and parish of *Bromley*, in the county of *Kent*.

20. An act for exempting *Batchacre Grange*, in the counties of *Stafford* and *Salop*, or one of them, from payment of tythes, and other ecclesiastical dues, and for settling other tythes in lieu thereof.

21. An act for draining certain fen lands and wet grounds, in the parish of *Helgay*, in the county of *Norfolk*.

22. An act for draining and preserving certain marsh lands and low grounds, within the township of *Thorngumbald*, in the county of *York*.

23. An act for establishing and carrying into execution certain articles of agreement therein mentioned, for a division of certain real estates in the county of *York*, late of Sir *Hungerford Bland*, baronet, deceased, and for other purposes therein mentioned.

24. An act for empowering the committee or committees, for the time being, of the estate of *John Newport* esquire, a lunatick, to make leases of his estates during his lunacy.

25. An act for carrying into execution, an agreement between the governors and guardians of the hospital for the maintenance and education of exposed and deserted young children, and *Robert Nedham* esquire, deceased, relating to an estate in the island of *Jamaica*, devised by the will of *Henry Nedham* esquire, deceased.

26. An act for annexing the rectory of *East Lockinge*, in the county of *Berks*, to the office of warden of the college of the *Souls of all Faithful People deceased*, of *Oxford*.

27. An act for sale of the freehold and leasehold estates of *John Tregenna* clerk, deceased, in the county of *Cornwall*, given and devised by his will, in trust for his children, and for paying and applying the money to arise by such sales, in manner therein mentioned.

28. An act to enable the vicar of the parish of *Rochdale*, in the county of *Lancaster*, to grant a lease or leases of the glebe lands belonging to the said vicarage.

29. An act to enable the rector of the parish and parish church of *Bury*, in the county of *Lancaster*, for the time being, to grant leases of the glebe belonging to the said rectory.

30. An act for making the exemplification of the will of *Thomas King* esquire, deceased, evidence in all courts of law and equity, in *Great Britain* and *Ireland*.

31. An act to enable *Richard Symons*, an infant, (lately called *Richard Peers*) and the heirs of his body, to take and use the sirname of *Symons*, pursuant to the will of *Richard Symons* esquire, deceased.

32. An act for naturalizing *William Dingman* and *John Reincke*.

33. An act for naturalizing *John Marteilhe* of *London*, merchant.

34. An act for naturalizing *Egbert Nonnen*.

35. An act for dividing and inclosing the common and open fields, and commonable places of *Sharnford*, in the county of *Leicester*.

36. An act for dividing and inclosing the open and common fields, common pastures, common meadows, and other commonable lands and grounds, in *Whetstone*, in the county of *Leicester*.

37. An act for dividing and inclosing the open and common fields, common meadows, lammas grounds, and other commonable lands and grounds in the parish of *Fotherby*, in the county of *Lincoln*.

38. An

38. An act for dividing and inclosing the open fields, and commonable places in the parish of *Stony Stanton*, in the county of *Leicester*, and the lands, meadows, and commonable places, in the lordship of *Potters Marston*, in the said county, belonging to and used with the said fields of *Stoney Stanton*.

39. An act for dividing, allotting, and inclosing, the open fields and pasture ground, in the lordship of *Aldborough*, in *Holdernesse*, in the county of *York*.

40. An act for dividing and inclosing the several open and common fields, and ings, within the township and parish of *Houghton in the Marsh*, otherwise *Holton in the Clay*, in the county of *Lincoln*.

41. An act for dividing and inclosing the open and common fields, lying, in the manor and parish of *Stoke Albany*, in the county of *Northampton*.

42. An act for dividing and inclosing the common fields, common pastures, common meadows, common grounds, and waste grounds, of and in the manor and parish of *Newnham*, in the county of *Northampton*.

43. An act for dividing and inclosing the common fields, common pastures, common meadows, common grounds, and waste grounds, of and in the manor and parish of *Everdon*, otherwise *Great Everdon* and *Little Everdon*, in the county of *Northampton*.

44. An act for dividing and inclosing the common fields, common pastures, common grounds, and waste grounds, in the parish of *Ledger's Ashby*, in the county of *Northampton*.

45. An act for dividing and inclosing a certain moor or common, in the township of *Crook* and *Billyrow*, within the parish of *Brancepeth*, in the county of *Durham*.

46. An act for dividing and inclosing the open and common fields of *Atherstone*, in the county of *Warwick*, and all the lands, meadows, and grounds, within the same.

47. An act for draining, preserving, and improving, the low grounds, and carrs, lying and being in the parishes, townships, hamlets, lordships, precincts, and territories of *Sutton*, *Gainstead*, *Swine*, *Benningholme*, *Benningholme Grange*, and *Fairholme*, *North Skirlaugh*, *Rowton*, *Arnold*, *Long-Riston*, *Leven*, *Heigholme*, and *Hallytree-Holme*, *Brandes-Burton*, and *Bursall*, *Eske*, *Tickton*, *Weel*, *Routh*, *Meaux*, and *Waghen*, otherwise *Wawn*, in *Holderness*, in the east riding of the county of *York*.

48. An act to impower the right honourable *John* lord viscount *Spencer*, to make leases of the manor of *Battersea* and *Wandsworth* and of lands and grounds in *Battersea* and *Wandsworth*, in the county of *Surrey*, purchased in pursuance of the will of the most noble *Sarah* late dutchess dowager of *Marlborough*, in order for building upon and improving the same.

49. An act for confirming a partition of several estates, late of *Thomas Horton*, in the counties of *Wilts* and *Gloucester*, between *William Blanch*, *John Roberts*, *Richard Brereton*, and others, and for vesting and settling the premisses to the several uses therein mentioned.

50. An act for vesting the estate late of *Edmund Hungate Beagban*, esquire, deceased, in the counties of *Kent* and *Sussex*, in trustees, in trust, to sell and convey the same to *Edward Louisa Mann* esquire, or as he shall appoint, pursuant to an agreement for that purpose, and for applying the money arising by such sale, for the benefit of *George Edmund Beagban*, his only son and heir, an infant.

51. An act for vesting divers messuages and hereditaments in the city of *London*, the settled estate of *Elizabeth Brett*, wife of *Charles Brett* esquire, in the said *Charles Brett*, and his heirs, discharged from the uses of his marriage settlement, and for settling another estate, in the county of *Middlesex*, of greater value, in lieu thereof, to the uses limited of the said settled estate.

52. An act for discharging the uses and trusts of certain manors, lands, and hereditaments, in the county of *Norfolk*, settled upon, and for the benefit of, *William Wiggett Bulwer*, and *Mary* his wife, and their issue, and for substituting and settling other estates and hereditaments, in the same county, of greater value, in lieu thereof, to the like uses.

53. An act for vesting two shares in *Ranelagh House*, gardens, and premisses, late the estate of *James Delaune*, deceased, in *John Ferrett* and *Robert Edmeston*, and their heirs, in trust, to sell the same, and apply the money arising from such sale, to the several charitable purposes, as is directed by the will of the said *James Delaune*.

54. An act for vesting the settled estate of *William Young* esquire, in the county of *Wilts*, in trustees, to be sold, and for laying out the money arising thereby, together with other money of the said *William Young*, in the purchase of other hereditaments, of greater value, to be settled in lieu thereof.

55. An act to enable *John Pollard* esquire (lately called *John Carter*) and his heirs male, to take and use the surname and arms, of *Pollard*, pursuant to the will of *Elizabeth Pollard*, deceased.

56. An act for naturalizing *James Nabou de Bervillee*, *Johann Jacob Uckermann*, and *John Hauser*.

57. An act for naturalizing *James Alric*.

58. An act for dividing and inclosing the open and common fields, common pastures, common meadows, common grounds, heath and waste ground in the manor and parish of *West Haddon* in the county of *Northampton*.

59. An act for dividing and inclosing a waste ground, called *The Marsh*, in the township of *Newport*, in the county of *Salop*; and applying the produce thereof to the several purposes therein mentioned.

60. An act to enable *Lucy Knightley* esquire, to inclose several open and common fields, in the parish of *Haversham*, in the county of *Bucks*; and for vesting certain glebe lands, and the tythes belonging to the rectory of *Haversham*, aforesaid, in the said *Lucy Knightley*, and his heirs, and for making a compensation to the rector of the said parish in lieu thereof.

61. An act for dividing and inclosing the open and common fields, common meadows, common pastures, common grounds, and

and commonable lands, within the manor, parish, and liberties of *Westbury*, in the county of *Buckingham*.

62. An act for dividing and inclosing the common fields, common meadows, and common pastures, in the parish of *Nether Broughton*, in the county of *Leicester*.

63. An act for dividing and inclosing a moor, or common, called *Staindrop Moor*, within the township of *Staindrop*, in the county of *Durham*.

64. An act for dividing and inclosing the open and common fields, in the parish of *Great Wigston*, in the county of *Leicester*.

65. An act for dividing and inclosing the open and common fields, common pastures, common meadows, common grounds, and waste grounds, in the parish of *Husbands Bosworth*, otherwise *Boresworth*, in the county of *Leicester*.

66. An act for dividing and inclosing the common or waste grounds within the manor of *Wombwell*, in the county of *York*.

67. An act for dividing and inclosing the open and common field, common meadows, common pastures, common grounds, and commonable lands, lying within the township, hamlets, and liberties of *Warkworth*, in the county of *Northampton*.

68. An act for vesting divers manors, lands, and hereditaments, in the counties of *Bedford*, *Dorset*, and *Lancaster*, comprized in the marriage settlement of *John* earl of *Ashburnham*, in him the said earl, in fee simple, discharged of the uses and trusts of that settlement, and for substituting and settling other lands and hereditaments, in the dominion of *Wales*, in lieu thereof, and to the like uses.

69. An act to impower the guardians of *George* earl of *Egremont*, an infant, to enfranchise certain customary lands and hereditaments, in the county of *Cumberland*, part of the settled estates of the earl; and also to impower the guardians of the said earl, and his infant brothers, to make leases of part of the said estate, in the county of *Cumberland*, and to make leases and copyhold grants of the several estates limited and devised to them respectively by *Charles* earl of *Egremont* their late father, deceased, and for other the purposes therein mentioned.

70. An act for vesting lands and hereditaments in *Great Britain* and *Ireland*, part of the estate of *James* earl of *Barymore*, in trustees, for raising money towards paying and discharging the debts and incumbrances affecting his real estates.

71. An act for settling the estate of *Henrietta Rosa Peregrina Townsend*, wife of *James Townsend*, esquire, according to certain articles of agreement executed before her intermarriage with the said *James Townsend*, but subject to the charges and incumbrances affecting the same.

72. An act for enlarging the charitable uses, extending the objects, and regulating the application of the rents and profits of the estates given by Sir *William Harpur* knight, and dame *Alice* his wife, for the benefit of the poor, and other objects of charity, of the town of *Bedford*.

73. An act to enable the warden and fellows of the college of *Christ*, in *Manchester*, in the county palatine of *Lancaster*, for the

the time being, to grant leases of the glebe lands belonging to the said college.

74. An act to impower the honourable *George Lane Parker*, to shut up a road or way now used over certain inclosed lands, in the parish of *Gamblingay*, in the county of *Cambridge*, and for extinguishing all right to a certain toll which he now is intitled to in two lanes, near the said road or way, and for obliging him to keep the said lanes in repair.

75. An act for enlarging the time given to trustees therein named, to execute certain trusts vested in them, in and by an act of parliament made in the sixteenth year of the reign of his late Majesty, intituled, *An act for vesting the remainder in fee of several lands in* Ireland, *the estate of* Arthur Plunkett *esquire, in trustees, in order to sell such lands to protestant purchasers*; and also by another act of parliament made in the thirty second year of the reign of his said late Majesty, intituled, *An act for giving further time to trustees therein named, to execute certain trusts vested in them, in and by the said act of parliament made in the said sixteenth year of the reign of his said late Majesty.*

76. An act for divesting out of the crown, the reversion in fee, of certain lands in *Ireland*, late the estate of *Matthew Dowdall*, a papist, deceased, expectant upon the death of his three grandsons, without issue male; and for vesting the same in *Anthony Ladeveze*, of the city of *Dublin* esquire, a protestant and his heirs.

77. An act for divesting out of the crown, and to vest in *Gerald Fitzgerald*, of *Rathorne*, in the county of *Meath*, in the kingdom of *Ireland*, esquire, and his heirs, the reversion in fee of and in several lands in *Ireland*.

78. An act to enable the mayor and aldermen of the town of *Saffron Walden*, in the county of *Essex*, the guardians or trustees of King *Edward* the Sixth's alms-houses there, and other the feoffees thereof, to convey part of the lands, revenues, and possessions, of the said alms-houses, to Sir *John Griffin Griffin*, and his heirs, in exchange for other lands of greater value, to be conveyed to, and held by, them, to the uses, and upon the trusts therein mentioned; and for vesting part of the lands of *Thomas Fuller*, an infant, in *Saffron Walden* aforesaid, in the said Sir *John Griffin Griffin*, and his heirs, in exchange for other lands of greater value, to be conveyed to the said infant, and his heirs; and for other purposes therein mentioned.

79. An act for vesting certain messuages, lands, tenements, and hereditaments, in the town and county of *Northampton*, devised by the will of *Edward Bayly*, deceased, in trustees, to be sold, and for laying out the money, arising by such sale, in the purchase of other lands, to be settled to the like uses.

80. An act to dissolve the marriage of *John Weller* esquire, with *Charlotte Wilson*, his now wife, and to enable him to marry again: and for other purposes therein mentioned.

81. An act for naturalizing *Peter Pohlmann*, and *David Godin*.

82. An act for naturalizing *Henry Kock*.

83. An act for naturalizing *Alexander Joseph Poittier*.

THE STATUTES at Large, &c.

Anno quarto GEORGII III. Regis.

CAP. I.

An act for continuing and granting to his Majesty certain duties upon malt, mum, cyder, and perry, for the service of the year one thousand seven hundred and sixty four.

Most Gracious Sovereign,

WE *your Majesty's most dutiful and loyal subjects, the commons of* Great Britain, *in parliament assembled, towards raising the necessary supplies to defray your Majesty's public expences, have freely and voluntarily resolved to give and grant unto your Majesty, the rates, duties, and impositions herein after mentioned; and do most humbly beseech your Majesty, That it may be enacted; and* be it enacted by the King's most excellent majesty, by and with the advice and consent of the lords spiritual and temporal, and commons, in this present parliament assembled, and by the authority of the same, That within and throughout that part of *Great Britain* called *England*, *Wales*, and town of *Berwick upon Tweed*, &c. &c. Preamble.

Malt act of 1 *Geo.* iii. further continued to 24th *June* 1765.——— Malt in Scotland to pay 3d. per bushel. Mum 10 s. per barrel. Cyder and perry made for sale, 4 s. per hogshead. How these duties are to be raised. ———20,000 l. to be raised in Scotland. Surplus to be added to the fisheries, &c.——— This act to relate to the same day and time, as the act 1 *Geo.* iii. did.——— Malt brought from Scotland by sea, to be entered at the port of landing: brought by land, to be entered at *Berwick* or *Carlisle*. ——— Cyder for distilling not chargeable. Distiller to give notice to the officer when he distils cyder.——— Allowances for exportation of malt. 1 W. and M. On certificate of malt being exported, and security, allowance to be paid. Penalty on relanding, over and above the penalty of the bond, all the malt and treble the value forfeited.——— Malt steeping for exportation to be kept separate till measured. Malsters to give notice to officers, &c.——— Penalty on opening the locks, &c. after malt is measured, &c.——— Malsters, on 24th *June* 1764, to clear out of their warehouses all malt within fifteen months. And so all future malsters.——— Clauses in act 12 *Anne* and 6 *Geo.* i. 5 s. per bushel penalty on all corn steeping or steeped for malt, which shall be found in the cistern or couch, so hard and compact as it could not be, unless the same had been forced together to prevent the rising.——— 100l. penalty on fraudulently conveying from the cistern any steeping of corn, and mixing the same with other corn charged with duty in the couch; or fraudulently conveying the same away, so that no gauge of such corn can be taken in the couch. ——— Penalties how to be recovered.———Buyers of cyder or perry for their private use not to be charged.———Persons selling less than 20 gallons, to be deemed retailers.——— Clause of loan at 4l. per cent. Tallies of loan to be ſtruck, &c. Orders regiſtered and paid in courſe. No fee for regiſtering, &c. Penalty for undue preference. No undue preference, where tallies are dated or brought the ſame day; nor if ſubſequent orders be paid before ſuch as were not demanded in courſe. Orders aſſignable. ——— Commiſſioners of the treaſury impowered to prepare any number of Exchequer bills of one common ſum, or different ſums, in the principal monies.———Bills to bear intereſt at 4l. per cent. per annum. Theſe bills to be numbered arithmetically. Treaſury to direct the courſe of payment for loans or Exchequer bills, and to appoint cheques &c.—— The bills to be placed as caſh in the Exchequer, and to be iſſued thereout in common with other monies, and to be current in the revenue. Receivers to exchange bills for ready money. ——— Tallies to be levied for bills lent into the Exchequer.———Intereſt to continue till payment.——— Intereſt to ceaſe whilſt the bills are in the hands of receivers, &c.———Bills paid to receivers, &c. to be ſigned and dated. Intereſt to be allowed to the ſaid days.———The bills may be reiſſued, both for principal and intereſt.——— Receivers to keep a book. ——— Bills filled up by indorſements, or defaced, to be exchanged. ——— Bills not exceeding 5000l. each to be made forth at the Exchequer.——— Forging Exchequer bills, felony.——— How the monies ariſing by this act ſhall be applied.——— Treaſury on 29 *Sept.* 1765, to take an account of all monies raiſed and diſcharged.———Unſatisfied monies to be paid out of the next aid, or out of the ſinking fund.———Commiſſioners to appoint perſons to pay off principal ſums, which ſhall from time to time be in courſe of payment upon Exchequer bills.———Money, as brought in, to be paid to the paymaſters.———Bills to be regiſtered in courſe.———When intereſt to ceaſe. Paymaſters liable to the controul of the treaſury.———Treaſury to ſettle ſalaries of clerks, &c. and to contract with perſons to circulate bills, &c. ——— Contractors not diſabled from being members of parliament: may lower or raiſe the intereſt with conſent of the treaſury.——— Contractors how to be paid. ——— No fee to be taken. No intereſt for leſs than one penny. Charges to be paid out of the ſinking fund: to be replaced out of the firſt ſupplies.——— Clauſe of relief for bills loſt or deſtroyed. ——— Bills diſcharged to be cancelled.——— Sinking fund appropriated to diſcharge national debts incurred before 25 *Dec.* 1716.——— Deficiency of malt tax 2 *Geo.* iii. how to be ſupplied. ——— Arrears of former duties to be applied in aid of the ſupplies granted for the year 1764.

CAP. II.

An act for granting an aid to his Majeſty by a land tax to be raiſed in Great Britain, *for the ſervice of the year one thouſand ſeven hundred and ſixty four.*

Moſt Gracious Sovereign,

Preamble.

WE *your Majeſty's moſt dutiful and loyal ſubjects, the commons of* Great Britain, *in parliament aſſembled, taking into our ſerious conſideration ſuch expences as are abſolutely neceſſary for ſupporting your Majeſty's government, and being reſolved to ſupply the ſame, have for that end and purpoſe cheerfully and voluntary given and granted, and do by this act give and grant unto your Majeſty, the ſeveral and reſpective rates and aſſeſſments hereafter mentioned; and we do moſt humbly beſeech your Majeſty that it may be enacted; and* be it enacted by the King's moſt excellent majeſty, by and with the advice and conſent of the lords ſpiritual and temporal, and commons, in this preſent parliament aſſembled, and by the authority of the ſame, That the ſum of two millions thirty ſeven thouſand eight hundred fifty four pounds, nineteen ſhillings,

2,037,854l. 19s. and 11d. to be raiſed in Great Britain

shillings, and eleven pence, shall be raised, levied, and paid unto his Majesty, within the kingdom of *Great Britain*, by such proportions, and in such manner and form, as hereafter in this act are expressed.

And it is hereby declared and enacted by the authority aforesaid, That, &c. &c.

1,989,900l. 18s. and 9d. to be raised in England in one year from 25th *March* 1764. — Personal estates (except desperate debts, stock on land, household goods, and loans to his Majesty) to pay 4s. in the pound. — Employments of profit (except military officers of the army or navy) to pay 4s. per pound. — Pensions and annuities out of the Exchequer, &c. to pay, &c. — Lands, tenements, mines, &c. to be charged with equality and indifference, &c. — Lands, &c. subject to rent-charges, annuities, &c. — Commissioners of the land tax for the year 1763, to put this act in execution. — Commissioners to meet on or before the 30th of *April*, 1764, as by the act 4 W. and M. and may subdivide themselves, &c. — A list of the commissioners to act in each division, to be given to the receivers-general. — Commissioners, to summon fit persons to be assessors, who are to appear before them in eight days; and then to give them a charge. Persons absenting, or refusing to serve, forfeit, not exceeding 5l. nor less than 40s. Assessors to be two at least, and sufficient inhabitants —— Assesments to be brought in at a day and place prefixed. —— The full sum charged to be assessed. —— A certificate of the assessment to be brought in with the collectors names. —— Assessors, &c. neglecting their duty to be fined not above 40l. —— Assessors to deliver one copy of the assessments to the commissioners. —— Duplicates thereof to be signed, &c. and one delivered to the collectors, &c. with warrant for collecting. —— Commissioners required to give collectors notice at what time and place the appeal of any person who shall think himself aggrieved by being over-rated, may be heard and determined. —— A duplicate in parchment to be delivered, together with the names of the assessors and collectors, to the receiver-general; and one to the remembrancer's office, by 8th *August* 1764, or twenty days after (all appeals first determined) —— Remembrancer to give receipts gratis on penalty of 10l. —— The rates to be levied on the parties, or premisses; and to be paid to the receivers-general, &c. —— The money collected to be paid to the receiver-general, or deputies; and they to give commissioners notice. —— Collectors not obliged to travel above ten miles. —— Removal or death of receiver-general to be notified to the commissioners. —— 497,475l. 4s. and 8d. 1. q. for the first quarterly payment, to be paid to the receivers by 24th *June* 1764. the second payment by 29th *September* 1764. the third payment by 25th *December* 1764. the last payment by the 25th *March* 1765. —— Receiver-general within a month after receiving the full sum charged, to give the commissioners a receipt: which shall be a full discharge for payment. Receivers-general within twenty days to pay the monies into the Exchequer; and to be allowed 2d. in the pound. —— Collectors to have 3d. in the pound. Commissioners clerks to have three half pence in the pound. —— Collectors may levy by distress, in case of refusal of payment. Distress to be kept four days at the owner's charge; then appraised and sold, and the over-plus returned, &c. Commissioners to determine differences about distress. For want of distress offender may be committed (except a peer or peeress of *Great Britain*) —— Tenants to pay the tax, and deduct so much out of the rents. —— Tenants discharged for what they so pay. Commissioners to settle differences between landlord and tenant. Commissioners to cause all deficiencies to be reassessed, and made good. —— Assessor refusing to serve, to forfeit not exceeding 40l. fine; not to be discharged but by commissioners who imposed it; and levied by distress or imprisonment, and paid into the Exchequer, and inserted in the duplicates. —— Collectors detaining the money, to be imprisoned, their estates seized and sold, &c. —— Commissioners to examine whether the sums assessed be duly collected, &c. —— In case of controversies in assessing commissioners, the com-

commissioners concerned to withdraw: in default to be fined, not above 20l. —— No privileged place or person exempt from this tax. Fee-farm rents, &c. to be taxed. Tenants to pay the rates. —— Colleges, &c. in the universities, &c. not chargeable: nor the houses or lands, which before the 25th of *March* 1693. did belong to Christ's-hospital, &c. nor corporation of clergymen's sons, *Bromley* college, or any other hospital or almshouse. —— No tenants of hospitals, &c. to claim any exemption. —— Such tenants not discharged, who by leases are obliged to pay taxes. —— Commissioners to determine how far lands, &c. belonging to hospitals, &c. not exempted by name, ought to be charged. —— All hospital lands &c. assessed by 4 W. and M. liable to this aid, and no other. —— Receivers of fee-farm rents, &c. to allow 4s. per pound to the parties, without fee, on penalty of 20l. Auditors, &c. setting tenants *insuper* for what ought to be allowed, or refusing allowance, to forfeit 100l. —— Such fee-farm rents only to have an allowance of 4s. per pound, as are answerable to the crown, or were purchased according to 22 and 23 *Car.* ii. The owners to allow the same to the party paying. —— Lists of pensions &c. to be delivered gratis to the assessors. Taxes on pensions, &c. not paid, to be stopt in the Exchequer. A true account to be kept of the money stopt. —— Persons to be taxed in the parish where they dwell. —— No proviso to lessen the full sum by this act to be levied. —— Contracts between landlord and tenant, touching taxes, not to be avoided. —— All places to pay, where usually assessed. —— *West Barnfield* to be assessed in the lathe of *Skray*, Com. *Kent*, *Northmore*, Com' *Oxon*, in *Brampton*. *Charlbury*, &c. in *Chadlington*, *Leeds*, com' *Ebor.* in *Skyrac*. *Ombersley*, &c. com' *Worcester* in *Oswaldslow* hundred. Parish of *Yardley*, in *Halfshire* hundred. Forest of *Chute*, where the first 4s. aid was assessed. *Upton*, in *Pershore* hundred. *Calder* and *Ayre*, at *Wakefield* and *Leeds*. —— Inhabitants of appartments, &c. in *Somerset* house, to be assessed in the same proportion with those in *Lancaster* liberty. —— General issue. Treble costs. —— Where lands &c. are unoccupied, and no distress found, collectors may distrain at any time after. —— Wood may be cut down, and sold for distress (Timber-trees excepted) —— Tithes, tolls, &c. not paid within six days after demand, &c. may be seized and sold. —— Receiver general returning persons, who have paid the tax, to be in arrear, forfeits treble damages to the party grieved, and to his Majesty double the sum so returned. —— Commissioners to assess the assessors. —— None compelled to be assessors out of the limits of the city, &c. —— Assessments on foreign ministers houses to be paid by the landlords. —— In places extraparochial commissioners to nominate assessors and collectors, &c. —— No commissioner, &c. liable to any other penalties than such as are inflicted by this act. —— Commissioners not to act without taking the oaths by 1 *Geo.* i. &c. — acting before oaths taken forfeit 200l. —— Officers to pay, where employed, &c. —— Officers in chancery to be assessed in the rolls liberty. Annuities where rated. Pensions, where payable. Personal estates, where persons resident, &c. Persons not householders, where resident. Absent persons to be rated where they were last resident. —— Goods, &c. to be assessed where they shall be. —— Persons doubly rated, discharged on certificate. —— Not to extend to *Scotland*, *Ireland*, *Jersey*, or *Guernsey*. —— Persons avoiding the tax, charged treble. —— Householders to give an account of their lodgers, on forfeiture of 5l. —— Shares in the New river, &c. to pay 4s. per pound. Shares in the Fire offices, and in the lights, and the King's printing-house to pay 4s. per pound. Merchants, bank of *England*, post office, &c. to be paid by the governors. —— Governors, &c. of the river-waters, and water-works refusing to pay, the collectors impowered to levy the sum by distress and sale. —— Papists 18 years of age not taking the oaths 1 W. and M. to pay double: unless taken within ten days after the commissioners first meeting. —— Persons of 18 years of age refusing the oath, to pay double. —— Commissioners to summon suspected persons, &c. —— Quakers to subscribe the declaration 1 W. and M. —— Commissioners to double assess papists, where assessors omit. —— Tenants discharged from double rates. —— King's bench, Marshalsea prison, &c. to be assessed in St. George's parish, &c. —— Officers of the Marshalsea court refusing to pay, &c. collectors by warrant from commissioners may distrain. If no goods sufficient, officers to be imprisoned. —— Fleet prison to be assessed in St. *Bride's*. —— Officers at *Stoke Damrel*, near *Plymouth*, to be assessed within the town of *Plymouth*, &c. —— Officers of the hospital at *East Stonehouse*, to be assessed also within the town of *Plymouth*. 20l. to be paid out of the sum assessed on the said officers, in aid of the assessment on *East Stonehouse*. —— Water-works in *Southwark* to be assessed in *Surry*. —— Water-works in *Westminster* to be assessed there. Offices, &c. in *Whitehall* and St. *James's* to be there assessed. —— Collectors of the water-works in *Colchester* chargeable. Collectors for the water-works in *New Windsor*, chargeable. —— Patent officers to bishopricks to pay where assessed in 1693. —— Commissioners appointed to act, without subdividing the parish of St. *Andrew Holborn*, in *Middlesex*. The parish of St. *George Hanover-square* to be charged with distinct *Quota* from the parish of St. *Martin's* in the fields. Debates arising concerning the joint *Quota*, the commissioners who are inhabitants of either parish to withdraw, or to be fined a sum not exceeding 20l. —— The parishes of St. *John*, St. *Peter*, and *Berchington*, to be charged in *Dover* liberty, according to the assessment 4 W. and M. —— Lands not worth 20s. per annum not chargeable. —— Collectors keeping monies in their hands, to forfeit 40l. —— Receiver-general misapplying the monies to forfeit 500l. —— Commissioners of the treasury, &c. not to divert the payments into the Exchequer. — No *Noli prosequi*, &c. in any suit against this act. —— Commissioners to abate, where lands are over charged, and to re-assess, &c. or raise it on persons undercharged. —— Receiver-general answerable for deputies. Sub collector not to travel above ten miles, &c. Receivers not nominating deputies, &c. to forfeit 100l. —— Commissioners for the county at large may act for any city, &c. —— Mayors, bailiffs &c. to act as commissioners specially appointed. —— Members of parliament to be taxed at their mansion-houses. —— First meeting for the West riding of *York* at *Pontefract*; North riding, at *Thirsk*; East riding at *Beverley*. —— No commissioner capable to act in any county at large, unless rated at 100l. per annum (*Merioneth*, *Cardigan*, &c. excepted) Commissioners for *Anglesea*, &c. to act, if rated at 60l. per annum. —— Commissioners, may act for any city, being inhabitants, or inns of court, &c. Attornies &c. not to be commissioners, without possessing 100l. per annum. No commissioner of the city of *London*, or liberty of St. *Martin le grand* to act, unless rated at 20l. per annum of his own estate, &c. —— No commissioner of the city, &c. of *Westminster* to act, unless rated at 20l. per annum of his own estate. —— Persons disabled presuming to act, to forfeit 50l. —— Collectors of the new water-works in *Exon*, chargeable. —— Her Majesty the Queen not chargeable; nor her royal Highness the Princess dowager of *Wales*; nor his royal Highness the Duke of *Cumberland*, nor the princess *Amelia*. —— Superannuated sea-officers not to pay, &c. nor poor knights of *Windsor*. —— Residentiaries, in what cases not chargeable: nor 100l. per annum to the poor clergy of the isle of *Man*: nor pages of honour. —— Receivers-general to give notice of failures in payment of the taxes. —— Commissioners for *Lincoln* to act in *Lincoln-close*; and, for the county, in St. *Martin* in *Stamford* baron. —— Auditor to keep a register, &c. —— Deputies to pay for principals, and on nonpayment liable to distress. —— Receiver-general to give a list of money received by him, at the time and place appointed. On refusal to forfeit any sum not exceeding 20l. —— Collectors may keep so much money as any two commissioners judge reasonable. —— No receiver to return an *insuper* upon any county, &c. after three years for monies in arrear; but the same to be a debt on him and his securities. —— Sheriff, on writs of *distringas*, to return issues after the rate of 5l. *per cent*. of the sum set an *insuper*: and process to issue thereupon, &c. —— Water-works in Shrewsbury chargeable. —— Who shall have the benefit only of overplus sums uncharged. —— Clause for the ease of protestants, to whom lands, &c. have come, which have been doubly taxed. Where lands doubly taxed are liable only to a single assessment; commissioners on complaint to examine into the truth thereof, and to certify the same to the barons of the Exchequer, before 29th *September*, 1764; who are to discharge the overplus before the last day of *November* 1764. Certificates of the sums discharged to be produced to the commissioners at their next meeting. ——— Commissioners may summon collectors, who have converted land tax monies to their own use, or their heirs, &c. and on examination may issue their warrants for paying such monies to his Majesty's use. ——— The payments made according to the commissioners warrants, &c. shall be discharges to the collectors, or their heirs, &c. ——— Collectors not paying, may be imprisoned, and their estates seized and sold. ——— Arrears of former land-taxes to be levied by the present commissioners. ——— No receiver-general, or his agents, may sue the county for a robbery, unless the persons carrying the money be in company, and three at least in number. ——— Tolls or duties on turnpikes, not chargeable by this or any former act. ——— Commissioners may, before 29th *September* 1764, summon assessors; who have not charged their estates since 6th *May* 1717, and examine them upon oath, and award satisfaction, to be levied and paid to the collectors. ——— Commissioners, &c. to distinguish and set down the gross sums assessed for double taxes, to be transmitted in the Exchequer. ——— Assessments on the town of *Cambridge* to be raised on manors, &c. and on fishings, &c. on the river Cam. ——— On whom and when, yearly assessments on fairs, &c. to be collected. Distress on default of payment how to be levied. Tenants of booths, &c. to pay the rates, and deduct them out of their rents, &c.

47,954 l. 1 s. 2 d. to be raised in *Scotland*, by an 8 months cess of 5,994 l. 5 s. 1 d. 3 q. per mensem, to be rated as the tax roll now is, or shall be settled by themselves. ——— The first two months cess to be paid by 24th of *June* 1764, second, 29th *September* 1764, third 25th *December* 1764, fourth 25th *March* 1765. ——— Commissioners for putting this act in execution in *Scotland*, the same as for the act 2 *Geo.* iii. &c. And execution to be done as by the said act. First meeting to be at the head burghs on 30th *April* 1764. ——— All clauses in former acts relating to the bringing in the cess, &c. to be in full force. ——— No persons in *Scotland* holden to produce their receipts after 3 years. ——— Debtor owing money in *Scotland* at 6 per cent. to retain a 6th part of 6 per cent. from 11th *Nov.* 1763, to 11th *Nov.* 1764. 47,954 l. 1 s. 2 d. to be raised free of all charges, and to be paid at *Edinburgh*. ——— No person to be a commissioner of the land tax in *Scotland*, who is not enfeoft of 100 l. Scots, per annum real rent in the county where he acts. Exception. Commissioners in Scotland to take the oaths, and subscribe the assurance. ——— Provost, &c. of any royal borough may act as a commissioner. ——— Clause of loan at 4 l. per cent. ——— Tallies of loan to be struck, &c. Orders registered and paid in course. No fee for registering, &c. Penalty for undue preference. ——— No undue preference, where tallies are dated or brought the same day: nor if subsequent orders be paid before such as were not demanded in course. ——— Orders assignable. ——— Commissioners of the treasury impowered to prepare any number of Exchequer bills of one common sum, or different sums, in the principal monies. Bills to bear interest at 4 l. *per cent. per annum*. These bills to be numbered arithmetically. ——— Treasury to direct the course of payment for loans or Exchequer bills, and to appoint cheques, &c. ——— Land tax. The bills to be placed as cash in the Exchequer. ——— Clauses in the malt tax act relating to Exchequer bills extended to this. ——— How the monies arising by this act shall be applied. ——— Treasury on the 29 *Sept.* 1765, to take an account of all monies raised and discharged. ——— Unsatisfied monies to be paid out of the next aid, or out of the sinking fund. The monies to be replaced out of the first supplies. ——— Deficiency of the land tax 2 *Geo.* iii. how to be supplied.

CAP. III.

An act for punishing mutiny and desertion; and for the better payment of the army and their quarters.

Preamble. WHEREAS *the raising or keeping a standing army within this kingdom, in time of peace, unless it be with consent of par-*

parliament, is against law: and whereas it is judged necessary by his Majesty, and this present parliament, that a body of forces should be continued for the safety of this kingdom, the defence of the possessions of the crown of Great Britain, *and the preservation of the balance of power in* Europe; *and that the whole number of such forces should consist of seventeen thousand five hundred and thirty two effective men, including two thousand seven hundred and thirty nine invalids: and whereas, during the late just and necessary war in which his Majesty has been engaged against* France *and* Spain, *some part of his Majesty's forces, exceeding the number aforesaid, has been employed in distant parts beyond the seas, which must render the time when such forces may return home uncertain; some of which are intended to be broke, and others reduced, as soon after such arrival as conveniently may be: and whereas no man can be fore-judged of life or limb, or subjected in time of peace to any kind of punishment within this realm, by martial law, or in any other manner than by the judgment of his peers, and according to the known and established laws of this realm; yet nevertheless, it being requisite for the retaining all the before-mentioned forces in their duty, that an exact discipline be observed, and that soldiers who shall mutiny, or stir up sedition, or shall desert his Majesty's service within this realm, or the kingdom of* Ireland, Jersey, Guernsey, Alderney, *and* Sark, *or the islands thereto belonging, be brought to a more exemplary and speedy punishment than the usual forms of the law will allow*; be it therefore enacted by the King's most excellent majesty, by and with the advice and consent of the lords spiritual and temporal, and commons, in this present parliament assembled, and by the authority of the same, That from and

Number of forces, 17,532, including 2,739 invalids.

After 24 *March* 1764, during the continuance of this act, every officer and private man, who shall mutiny or desert, &c. or list in any other regiment, &c. or shall be found sleeping on, or shall desert his post, or hold illegal correspondence with the enemies of his Majesty, or shall strike, or disobey, his superior officer; shall suffer death, or such punishment as a court-martial shall inflict.——The King may grant commission to hold a court-martial, &c.——Court-martial may inflict corporal punishment for immoralities, &c.——General court-martial not to consist of less than 13; and the president to be a field officer, or officer next in seniority, not under the degree of a captain.——May administer an oath to witnesses.——Officers to be sworn. The oaths.——The judge-advocate to be sworn. The oath.——In sentences of death, nine officers to concur, &c. Hours of trial.——The party tried, intitled to a copy of the sentence and proceedings of the court-martial.——Original proceedings, &c. of courts-martial to be transmitted to the judge-advocate general in London, &c.——None to be tried a second time for the same offence, except in case of appeal.——This act not to exempt soldiers from ordinary process.——Penalty on false certificates to excuse soldiers from musters.——Penalty on officers making false musters, &c.——Fictitious names allowed by his Majesty's order upon the muster-rolls for the maintenance of officers widows, not to be construed a false muster.——Muster-master to give notice of muster to a mayor, &c. Penalty on neglect. Muster-rolls to be signed by the mayor, &c.——Penalty on persons offering themselves to be falsly mustered.——Horses falsly mustered, to be forfeited, &c.——Forfeiture how to be levied.——Officer embezzelling, &c. military stores, to be cashiered, and forfeit 100l. and the damage to be made good by sale of his goods and chattels; for want of distress the person to be committed. Application of the forfeiture.——Muster-master taking a muster, to make oath. The oath.——Muster-rolls though transmitted without

without the oath indorsed to the pay-masters general, to be good vouchers to the auditor. —— Penalty on agents, &c. detaining officers or soldiers pay. Weekly rates. Penalty on agents disobeying orders. —— Surgeon, &c. within ten miles of *London*, &c. to certify who are sick; and commanding officers, who are employed in raising recruits. —— Penalty on officers mustering persons by wrong names. —— Constables, &c. to quarter officers and men in inns, alehouses, &c. but in no distillers houses, or shopkeepers, or in any private houses. Penalty on constables, &c. quartering soldiers in private houses, &c. and on officers quartering soldiers contrary to this act, &c. Persons aggrieved by being quartered on, may complain to any justices and be relieved. —— No justice having any military office, to be concerned in billeting his soldiers. —— Officers and soldiers to pay rates for their provisions. —— What inn-holders may allow men quartered on them instead of meat. —— Penalty on officers taking money to excuse the quartering. —— Dragoons, &c. and their horses to be billeted in the same house. —— Manner of changing men and horses. —— Clause relating to a soldier's settlement for his wife and children. —— Officers, &c. to be quartered in *Scotland*, as the laws in force at the union direct. —— No pay-master, &c. to make deductions out of officers or soldiers pay. —— Exceptions. —— Treasury may issue out the money due for clothing every two months. Pay-masters to deduct the off-reckonings. —— Officers to give notice to inn-keepers of subsistence-money in their hands. Rates of subsistence to be paid to inn-keepers, &c. for soldiers quarters. Penalty on officers not paying subsistence-money. —— On non-payment of quarters the officer to make up accounts, &c. —— No muster in *Westminster*, &c. but in the presence of two or more justices. —— Constables, &c. may billet soldiers in *Westminster*, &c. Petty constables, &c. to quarter soldiers in their respective divisions. —— Constables, &c. to deliver lists at quarter-sessions, on oath, of inhabitants, and soldiers quartered in their respective divisions; to be inspected without fee. Copies of such lists to be wrote by the clerk at 2d. per sheet, containing 150 words. Penalty on default. Penalty on giving defective lists. How to be levied. —— This act to extend to *Jersey*, &c. —— Muster-rolls to be closed on day of muster, and returned to the pay-master of the forces, &c. Penalty. —— Justices may order constables to provide carriages. Rates for carriages. Penalty on officers forcing waggons to travel more than one day's journey, &c. —— Penalty on constables, &c. neglect. —— Treasurers of the county to repay the constables extraordinary charges. —— The money for those purposes how to be raised. —— No waggon, &c. to carry above 30 hundred weight. —— Carriages in *Scotland* how to be provided. —— Soldiers wives, &c. not to be quartered without consent. Penalty. —— Penalty on officers or soldiers destroying the game. —— How the account of every regiment shall be kept. —— Penalty on pay-master, &c. —— Penalty on colonels. —— Non-commission officer embezzelling the soldiers pay, &c. to be reduced, &c. —— Justices may commit deserters. —— Reward for taking-up deserters. —— Penalty on persons concealing deserters, or buying their arms, clothes, &c. —— Penalty on officer breaking open house without warrant. —— His Majesty empowered to make articles of war. —— None to be adjudged of life or limb, but for crimes expressed to be so punishable by this act. —— Deserters beyond sea, &c. may be tried here or in *Ireland*. —— This act to extend to deserters, &c. in *Ireland*, &c. —— Persons acquitted by the civil magistrate may only be cashiered by a court-martial. —— Persons accused of capital crimes, &c. to be delivered over to the civil magistrate, &c. —— Pay-masters, &c. to account with executors. —— Persons sued may plead the general issue. Treble costs. —— All suits to be brought in some of the courts of record at *Westminster*, or *Dublin*, or the court of session in *Scotland*. —— Continuance of this act. —— Penalties against the act 1 *Geo.* i. where to be sued for. —— No volunteer liable to process, unless for some criminal matter, or unless for a real debt of the value of 10l. Oath of the debt to be made before a judge, and marked on the back of the process. Plaintiff may file a common appearance. —— Penalty on taking money to excuse any person from quartering; or victuallers refusing to quarter soldiers. —— Justices may order constables to give an account of the number of soldiers quartered, &c. —— How

troops

troops are to pay in passing over ferries in *Scotland*. —— Clause for relief of persons hastily enlisting themselves. Persons refusing the said relief to be proceeded against, as if duly listed. ——— Offences against former mutiny acts punishable by this act. ———None liable to be tried or punished for offences against former acts, unless committed within three years; except for desertion. ——Officers, &c. of the train of artillery subject to this act.—*American* troops acting in conjunction with *British* forces, liable to the same martial laws. —— Officers and soldiers of the *American* troops sent over to *Great Britain* to be quartered and billetted as the *British* forces, and under the same regulations and penalties. ——— This act not to extend to the militia farther than is directed by the militia laws.

CAP. IV.

An act for exhibiting a bill in this present parliament, for naturalizing his highness the hereditary prince of Brunswick Lunenburg.

WHEREAS *the King's most excellent majesty (whom God long preserve) hath been pleased to the universal joy and satisfaction of his people, and for the better strengthening the protestant interest in* Europe, *to give his eldest sister, her royal highness the princess* Augusta, *possessing the most exalted virtues, and adorned with all possible accomplishments, in marriage to his highness the hereditary prince of* Brunswick Lunenburgh, *distinguished by the most heroick qualities, which have, from his early youth, rendered him illustrious over all* Europe, *and endeared him to this nation: and whereas a more grateful proof of the esteem and affection of this kingdom cannot be given to his highness, than, by an act of naturalization, to make him capable of enjoying those rights and liberties which are enjoyed in these kingdoms: and whereas by an act made in the seventh year of the reign of King* James *the First, every person is required to receive the sacrament of the Lord's supper, within one month before any bill for naturalization be exhibited, and also to take the oaths of supremacy and allegiance in the parliament house, before his or her bill be twice read: and whereas by an act passed in the first year of his majesty King* George *the First, it was enacted, That no person shall be naturalized, unless, in the bill exhibited for that purpose, a clause, or particular words, be inserted, to declare that such person shall not thereby be enabled to be of the privy council, or a member of either house of parliament, or to take any office or place of trust, either civil or military, or to have any grant of lands, tenements, or hereditaments, from the crown, to himself, or any other person in trust for him; and that no bill should, from thenceforth, be received in either house of parliament, unless such clause, or words, be first inserted or contained therein*; be it enacted by the King's most excellent majesty, by and with the advice and consent of the lords spiritual and temporal, and commons, in parliament assembled, and by the authority of the same, That a bill for the naturalization of his highness the hereditary prince of *Brunswick Lunenburg*, without the clause, or particular words, directed by the said last recited act to be inserted, and without his receiving the sacrament, or taking the oaths by the first recited act required, shall and may be exhibited and brought into this parliament, and twice read; the

Preamble.

Clauses in act 7 Jac. 1.

and 1 Geo. 1.

Leave given for exhibiting a bill for naturalizing his highness the hereditary prince of Brunswick Lunenburg, without inserting the clause, &c. in

the said recited acts, or any other law, statute, matter, or thing whatsoever, to the contrary notwithstanding.

the last recited act, or otherwise qualifying himself according to the first recited act.

CAP. V.

An act for naturalizing his highness, Charles William Ferdinand, *hereditary prince of* Brunswick Lunenburg.

Preamble.

WHEREAS *the King's most excellent majesty, whom God long preserve, has been pleased, to the universal joy and satisfaction of his people, and for the better strengthening the protestant interest in* Europe, *to give his eldest sister, her royal highness the princess* Augusta, *possessing the most exalted virtues, and adorned with all possible accomplishments, in marriage to his highness* Charles William Ferdinand, *hereditary prince of* Brunswick Lunenburg, *distinguished by the most heroic qualities, which have, from his early youth, rendered him illustrious over all* Europe, *and endeared him to this nation: and whereas a more grateful proof of the esteem and affection of this kingdom cannot be given to his highness, than, by an act of naturalization, to make him capable of enjoying those rights and liberties which are enjoyed in these kingdoms:* We therefore, your Majesty's most dutiful and loyal subjects, the lords spiritual and temporal, and commons, in parliament assembled, do most humbly beseech your Majesty that it may be enacted; and be it enacted by the King's most excellent majesty, by and with the advice and consent of the lords spiritual and temporal, and commons, in this present parliament assembled, and by the authority of the same, That his said highness *Charles William Ferdinand*, hereditary prince of *Brunswick Lunenburg*, be, to all intents and purposes whatsoever, deemed, taken, and esteemed, a natural-born subject of this kingdom, as if the said prince had been born within this realm; any law, statute, matter, or thing whatsoever, to the contrary notwithstanding.

His highness Charles William Ferdinand, hereditary prince of Brunswick Lunenburg, deemed a natural-born subject.

CAP. VI.

An act to continue, for a limited time, the free importation of tallow, hogs lard, and grease, from Ireland.

Preamble.

WHEREAS *the permitting the free importation of tallow, hogs lard, and grease, from* Ireland, *into this kingdom, hath been found useful and beneficial, and that the time allowed for that purpose is near expiring, and it is expedient that the same should be prolonged*; May it therefore please your Majesty, that it may be enacted; and be it enacted by the King's most excellent majesty, by and with the advice and consent of the lords spiritual and temporal, and commons, in this present parliament assembled, and by the authority of the same, That an act made in the thirty second year of the reign of his late majesty King *George* the Second, intituled, *An act to discontinue, for a limited time, the duties payable upon tallow imported from* Ireland; and also an act made in the first year of his present Majesty's reign, for extending the said first-mentioned act to hogs lard and grease; which have continuance till the first day of *May*, one thousand seven hun-

Act 32 Geo. II. & 1 Geo. III. farther continued to 1 May, 1769.

hundred and sixty four, and to the end of the next session of parliament, shall be, and the same are hereby further continued, from the expiration thereof, until the first day of *May*, one thousand seven hundred and sixty nine, and to the end of the next session of parliament.

CAP. VII.

An act to explain and amend such part of an act made in the last session of parliament, (intituled, An act for granting to his Majesty several additional duties upon wines imported into this kingdom, and certain duties upon all cyder and perry, and for raising the sum of three millions five hundred thousand pounds, by way of annuities and lotteries to be charged on the said duties) *as relates to cyder and perry made in this kingdom.*

Preamble, reciting clauses in the cyder act of the last session.

WHEREAS *by an act made in the last session of parliament, intituled,* An act for granting to his Majesty several additional duties upon wines imported into this kingdom, and certain duties upon all cyder and perry, and for raising the sum of three millions five hundred thousand pounds, by way of annuities and lotteries to be charged on the said duties; *a duty of four shillings* per *hogshead was, from and after the fifth day of* July, *one thousand seven hundred and sixty three, granted upon all cyder and perry which should be made in* Great Britain, *to be paid by the maker thereof, over and above all other duties then payable for cyder or perry: and it was thereby directed, that the amount of the said duty should be paid within the space of six weeks, to be computed from the time of making the charge, in manner therein mentioned, by the officer or officers of excise; and all makers of cyder and perry were thereby authorized to compound for the said duty, after the rate therein mentioned, in respect of the cyder and perry to be consumed in their own private families only, in such manner, with such exemptions, privileges, and advantages, and under such regulations, as are in the said act allowed and provided: and whereas it would be a great relief to the persons subject to the said duty, or to the composition in lieu thereof, many of whom are industrious persons with large families, if the time for payment of the said duty were enlarged, and the composition of five shillings, authorized to be made by the said act, were lowered;* be it therefore enacted by the King's most excellent majesty, by and with the advice and consent of the lords spiritual and temporal, and commons, in this present parliament assembled, and by the authority of the same, That from and after the fifth day of *July*, one thousand seven hundred and sixty four, in lieu and instead of the time of six weeks, limited by the said act for the payment of the said duty on cyder and perry, the space of six calendar months shall be and is hereby allowed for the payment of the said duty, to be computed from the time of making the charge thereof; and the said duty shall, from and after the expiration of the said six months, be recovered and levied in such manner, as the same could or might have been recovered and

The time limited by the former act for payment of the duties, extended to 6 months; when they may be recovered and levied, as thereby directed.

and levied by virtue of the said former act, at or after the expiration of the said time therein limited for payment thereof.

In lieu of the former composition,

II. And be it further enacted by the authority aforesaid, That from and after the fifth day of *July*, one thousand seven hundred and sixty four, when any person, being a maker of cyder or perry within this kingdom, shall be desirous of compounding for the said duty on cyder and perry to be consumed in the private family of such person only, it shall be lawful for the commissioners of excise for the time being in *England* and *Scotland* respectively, as the case may be, or the major part of such respective commissioners, or such person or persons as they, or the major part of them, shall respectively appoint for that purpose, and, in default of such appointment, then for the collector and supervisor for the district and division within which the person desiring to make such composition doth or shall inhabit (and the said commissioners of excise, and the persons so to be appointed by them, and in default thereof such collector and supervisor as aforesaid, are hereby respectively required) upon receiving from such person an exact list, signed by him or her, of the several persons of the age of eight years and upwards whereof his or her family consists (specifying their christian and surnames therein) to compound and agree with every person so delivering in such list, for and in lieu of the duty of four shillings granted by the said act on cyder and perry to be consumed in his or her own private family only, at the rate of two shillings *per annum* for each person which shall be mentioned in such list, in lieu and instead of the composition of five shillings authorized to be made by the said act; which composition, after the rate of two shillings as aforesaid, shall last for one year, and be renewed annually; and the money arising thereby shall be paid down at the respective times of making the composition: and in case the family of any person making the composition shall be increased at any time during the year compounded for, then every person whose family shall be so increased shall deliver in an additional list, containing the names of the several persons of the age of eight years and upwards added to the family, and shall then also pay down a proportionable composition for the persons so added; *videlicet*, two pence for each calendar month that shall be unexpired of the year for which his or her composition was made, for each and every person so added; and in like manner fresh lists shall be delivered, and compositions made accordingly every year; and that the monies arising by the said compositions shall be applied in such manner, and for such purposes, as the duties granted by the said act were thereby directed to be applied: and all parts of the said act (not hereby altered) relating to the compositions thereby authorized to be made for the said duty, and also to the persons compounding in pursuance of the power thereby given, and for preventing and punishing all frauds with respect to the said compositions, and for securing the said duty, shall take effect, and be in full force, applied, and put in execution, with respect to the composition hereby allowed to be made,

Officers of excise are authorized to compound with prviate families,

at the rate of 2s. per head per annum, for each person of 8 years old and upwards, in the lists delivered in to them.

Composition to be renewed annually;

and in case of an increase in the family during the year, an additional list is to be given in, and 2d. per month paid for every person added, during the subsisting unexpired term of such year.

Compositions to be applied as the duties.

Other parts of the recited act relating to compositions, continued in force.

made, and to all persons compounding under the authority of this act, and for preventing and punishing all frauds in relation thereto, and for securing the said duty, as fully and effectually, to all intents and purposes, as if such parts of the said act were herein specially repeated, re-enacted, and applied to this present act.

III. And be it further enacted by the authority aforesaid, That from and after the fifth day of *July*, one thousand seven hundred and sixty four, all and every person and persons, not being a compounder or compounders, who shall intend to make any cyder or perry at or with any mill, press, or other utensil whatsoever, not being the property of such person or persons, but of any other person or persons, whether compounding or not compounding for the said duty, shall, ten days at the least before he, she, or they shall begin to make cyder or perry, make a true and particular entry in writing, at the office of excise next to the place where such cyder or perry shall be intended to be made, of his, her, or their respective name or names; and of every mill, press, and other utensil so intended to be employed; and of the name or names of the owner or owners thereof; and also of every storehouse, warehouse, cellar, or other place wherein such maker or makers intend to lay or keep such cyder or perry: and if any such maker or makers shall make use of any other mill, press, utensil, storehouse, warehouse, cellar, or other place whatsoever, either for the making, laying, or keeping, any cyder or perry, without having made such entry as aforesaid, or an entry thereof, in pursuance of the said former act, he, she, or they shall respectively forfeit and lose the sum of twenty five pounds for every such offence: and all and every the officers of excise shall, at all times in the day-time, be permitted, upon their request, to enter the millhouse, storehouse, warehouse, cellar, and all other places whatsoever used by any such maker or makers as aforesaid, either for the making, laying, or keeping of cyder or perry, of which notice shall or ought to have been given in pursuance of this act; and to gauge and take an account of all the cyder or perry which shall be there found, and shall thereof make return or report in writing to the respective commissioners of excise in *Great Britain*, or such other person or persons as they shall respectively appoint to receive the same, leaving a true copy of such report in writing under his or their hand or hands, with or for such maker or makers of cyder or perry; and such report or return of the said officer or officers shall be a charge upon such maker or makers of cyder or perry; and the amount of the duties thereby charged shall be paid by such maker or makers respectively, within such time as is by this act appointed.

Makers of cyder at other presses than their own, not being compounders, are to enter their names at the next office of excise, 10 days previous to such making; together with the mills, and owners thereof; and the cellars or storehouses for keeping such cyder. Penalty of their using any unentered mill, storehouse, &c. 25l. Officers to have free access to the said mills, storehouses, &c. in the day-time, to gauge the cyder, &c. to make and report the charge, leaving a copy with the maker; who is to pay the duty according to such charge.

IV. Provided always, and be it further enacted by the authority aforesaid, That from and after the said fifth day of *July*, no owner or proprietor whatsoever of any mill, press, or other utensil for the making of cyder or perry, which shall be let out or lent to any other person for the purpose of making cyder or perry, shall be obliged to give any notice of the letting or lending

Proprietors of cyder mills, &c. so lent out, not obliged to give notice thereof.

ing

ing ſuch mill, preſs, or other utenſil, or of the making cyder or perry therewith, by the perſon to whom the ſame ſhall be ſo let or lent; any thing in the ſaid former act contained to the contrary thereof in any wiſe notwithſtanding.

Where the compounder intends to ſell or diſpoſe of cyder, &c. immediately from the mill, the officer is to deliver to him blank certificates and counterparts for the purpoſe, to be filled up occaſionally; which ſhall protect the removal of ſuch cyder.

V. And, for the better accommodation of ſuch makers of cyder or perry, who ſhall compound for the duty on cyder and perry granted by the ſaid recited act; be it further enacted by the authority aforeſaid, That from and after the fifth day of *July*, one thouſand ſeven hundred and ſixty four, when any ſuch maker ſhall intend to ſell or diſpoſe of any cyder or perry immediately from the mill pound's mouth, or place where the ſame ſhall be made, the officer of exciſe of the diviſion or place where ſuch makers ſhall reſide, ſhall, and he is hereby required, during the time of making cyder or perry only, and at no other time, to deliver to, and leave with ſuch maker, if demanded, in writing, a ſufficient quantity of blank certificates, numbered one, two, three, and ſo on in an arithmetical progreſſion, to be filled up by ſuch maker, and ſubſcribed by him or her, who ſhall expreſs in each of the ſaid certificates that ſhall be filled up, the exact number of gallons of cyder or perry intended to be ſent therewith, and the number of caſks or package containing the ſame, and the place to which, and the name and place of abode of the perſons to whom, ſuch cyder or perry is to be ſent, and the time when ſuch certificate is filled up; which certificate (provided it accompanies the quantity of cyder or perry mentioned therein) ſhall be a ſufficient protection for the removal of ſuch cyder or perry, immediately from the mill pound's mouth, or place where the ſame ſhall be made; and that the officer of exciſe, at the ſame time that he delivers any quantity of blank certificates to any ſuch maker as aforeſaid, ſhall alſo deliver to ſuch maker a like quantity of blank counterparts of ſuch certificates, bearing the ſame numbers with the certificates; and ſuch maker is hereby required, whenever he fills up the blanks of any certificate for the removal of cyder or perry, as aforeſaid, at the ſame time to fill up and ſubſcribe the blanks of the counterpart thereof, in all particulars agreeable to the certificate; and ſuch maker ſhall, at the time of the delivery of the ſaid blank certificates and counterparts, give a receipt to the officer of exciſe, delivering the ſame, acknowledging that he or ſhe hath received ſo many blank certificates and the counterparts thereof numbered as aforeſaid; which counterparts ſo filled up ſhall be returned by ſuch maker to the reſpective officer of exciſe whenever he ſhall require the ſame; and ſuch maker ſhall then alſo ſhew to the officer all the certificates and counterparts not uſed or filled up, to the end the officer may then know what number of certificates have been filled up; and ſuch maker ſhall, at the reſpective times when he or ſhe ſhall deliver up ſuch counterparts ſo filled up, from time to time declare upon oath (or affirmation if a *quaker)* to be adminiſtered by the ſupervisor of exciſe of the diviſion or diſtrict where ſuch maker reſides, that the ſeveral quantities of cyder and perry ſpecified in the ſeveral counterparts

The counterpart to be filled up and ſigned, at the ſame time with the certificate; and to be returned to the officer. Receipt to be given for the certificates.

The certificates and counterparts not uſed, to be produced when called for.

The quantities ſold, &c. and certified for, to be verified on oath.

parts so directed to be delivered up, contain the whole quantities of cyder and perry which he or she shall have sold or disposed of, from his or her mill pound's mouth, or place where the same was made: and the respective officers of excise within their several divisions are hereby required, from time to time, from the several counterparts of such certificates so filled up, sworn to, and delivered as aforesaid, to make returns or reports in writing, of the several quantities of cyder and perry sold or disposed of as aforesaid by every such maker respectively, to the respective commissioners of excise in *Great Britain*, or such other person or persons as they shall respectively appoint to receive the same, leaving true copies of such report in writing, under his or their hand or hands, with or for such respective maker; and such returns or reports of the said officer or officers, shall be the charges upon such respective makers of cyder or perry; and the amount of the duties thereby charged, shall be paid respectively by such makers to the respective collectors of excise, within whose collection such makers shall dwell and inhabit, or to such other person or persons as the said respective commissioners of excise shall respectively appoint to receive the same, within the space of six calendar months, to be computed from the time of making such charge: and if any such maker of cyder or perry shall neglect or refuse to deliver to the officer of excise, when required, all the counterparts of certificates then filled up, or to declare upon oath or affirmation as aforesaid, or to shew to the officer all the certificates and counterparts not used or filled up, or shall sell or dispose of more cyder or perry from the mill pound's mouth or place of making, than is mentioned in such counterparts so delivered up, or shall fraudulently insert in the blank of either counterpart or certificate, a greater or less quantity of cyder or perry than is really sent with such certificate; every such maker offending in any of the said cases, for every such offence shall respectively forfeit and lose the sum of twenty five pounds; and that no certificate to be filled up by any such maker, shall be in force for the removal of cyder or perry immediately from the mill pound's mouth or place of making, but between the first day of *September* and the thirty first day of *December*, in each year; and that every such maker shall, every year, within ten days next after the thirty first day of *December* in each year, deliver, or cause to be delivered, to the officer of excise of the division or place where he or she resides, all the blank certificates and counterparts thereof which have not been filled up by such maker; and if any such maker of cyder or perry shall neglect or refuse, by the space of ten days next after the thirty first day of *December*, in any year, to deliver, or cause to be delivered, to the proper officer of excise, all the blank certificates and counterparts thereof which have not been filled up by such maker, every such maker shall, for every such offence respectively forfeit and lose the sum of twenty five pounds.

Returns to be made, and duties charged, from the counterparts.

Copy to be left with the maker,

who is to pay the duty accordingly within 6 months from thence.

Maker not complying with these regulations, or being guilty of any fraud,

to forfeit 25l.

Certificates for removal of cyder from the mill, to be in force, but between 1 Sept. & 31 Dec. yearly.

Blank certificates and counterparts to be delivered up within 10 days after,

on penalty of 25l.

VI. And be it further enacted by the authority aforesaid, That if, from and after the said fifth day of *July*, any person or per-

Penalty of obstructing an officer in his duty 50l.

persons whatsoever shall assault, oppose, molest, or hinder, any officer or officers of excise in the due execution of any of the powers or authorities given and granted by this act; all and every the party or parties so offending shall, for every such offence respectively, forfeit and lose the sum of fifty pounds.

Officers not doing their duty in any of the premisses,

VII. And be it further enacted by the authority aforesaid, That if any officer of excise shall refuse or wilfully neglect to leave a true copy of his report in writing, with the maker or makers of cyder and perry, as this or the said former act direct, or to grant a certificate for the removal of any cyder or perry, upon reasonable request made for that purpose; or if any maker of cyder and perry authorized and impowered by this present act to compound and agree for and in lieu of the duty granted by the said former act, shall offer to make such composition and agreement, and if such officer of excise, shall refuse or wilfully neglect to accept such composition and agreement as this present act directs; every such officer of excise so refusing or wilfully neglecting, shall, for each refusal or neglect, forfeit and pay the sum of forty shillings; which forfeiture and penalty shall and may be sued for, levied, recovered, and applied, in like manner as the other forfeitures and penalties imposed by this or the said former act, may be sued for, levied, recovered, and applied.

forfeit 40s.

Recovery and disposition of the penalties.

VIII. And be it further enacted by the authority aforesaid, That the several penalties imposed by this act, shall and may be sued for, recovered, levied, mitigated, and disposed of, by the same ways, means, and methods, and in the same proportions as any penalty imposed by the said recited act may be sued for, recovered, levied, mitigated, or disposed of.

IX. And be it further enacted by the authority aforesaid, That if any person or persons shall at any time or times be sued, molested, or prosecuted for any thing by him, her, or them done or executed in pursuance of or by colour of this act, or of any matter or thing in this act contained, such person or persons shall and may plead the general issue, and give this act, and the special matter, in evidence, in his, her, or their defence or defences; and if afterwards a verdict shall pass for the defendant or defendants, or the plaintiff or plaintiffs shall become nonsuited, or discontinue his, her, or their action or prosecution, or judgment shall be given against him or them upon demurrer, or otherwise; then such defendant or defendants shall have treble costs awarded to him, her, or them, against such plaintiff or plaintiffs.

General issue.

Treble costs.

CAP. VIII.

An act for the regulation of his Majesty's marine forces while on shore.

Preamble.

WHEREAS *it may be necessary for the safety of this kingdom, and the defence of the possessions of the crown of* Great Britain, *that a body of marine forces should be employed in his Majesty's fleet and naval service, under the direction of the lord high admiral, or commissioners for executing the office of lord high admiral of* Great

image

not

available

as under this act, provided no person be liable to be tried for offences committed three years before issuing the warrant for trial, except in cases of desertion only. No volunteer liable to process, unless for some criminal matter, or unless for a real debt of the value of 10 l. Oath of the debt to be made before a judge, and a memorandum thereof marked on the back of the process; otherwise prisoner to be discharged with costs.—— Plaintiff giving notice, may file a common appearance, and proceed to judgment and execution. —— Penalty on constables, &c. neglecting to quarter marines. Penalty on taking money to excuse any person from quartering, and on victuallers refusing to receive marines.—— To prevent abuses in quartering, justices may order constables to give an account of the number of officers, and private men, and where quartered. —— Clause for relief of persons hastily listing themselves.——As often as it shall be necessary, officers of the marine and land forces may sit in conjunction upon courts-martial; taking rank according to the seniority of their commissions.—— Marine forces being borne as part of the complement of any ships of war, are liable to be governed by the rules established by act 22 *Geo.* II.

CAP. IX.

An act for repealing the duties now payable upon bever skins imported, and for granting other duties in lieu thereof; and for granting certain duties upon the exportation of bever skins and bever wool; and for taking off the drawback allowed on the exportation of such skins.

Preamble.

WHEREAS *the duties now payable upon the importation of bever skins, and the drawback allowed upon the exportation of such skins, are great discouragements to the manufacture of hats in this kingdom; therefore we, your Majesty's most dutiful and loyal subjects, the commons of* Great Britain, *being desirous to promote and encourage the manufactures of this kingdom, do most humbly beseech your Majesty that it may be enacted*; and be it enacted by the King's most excellent majesty, by and with the advice and consent of the lords spiritual and temporal, and commons, in this present parliament assembled, and by the authority of the same, That from and after the seventh day of *April*, which shall be in the year of our Lord one thousand seven hundred and sixty four, the several rates, duties, subsidies, and impositions payable upon the importation of bever skins, imported into *Great Britain* from any of his Majesty's dominions in *America*, shall cease, determine, and be no longer paid.

After 7 April, 1764, the former duties payable upon bever skins imported, to cease;

II. And be it further enacted by the authority aforesaid, That from and after the said seventh day of *April*, the following duties shall be paid to his Majesty, his heirs and successors, that is to say,

and other duties to be paid in lieu thereof, viz.

For every bever skin imported into *Great Britain* from any of his Majesty's dominions in *America*, the sum of one penny; and

For every bever skin, or piece of bever skin, exported from *Great Britain*, the sum of seven pence; and

For every pound weight averdupoise of bever wool or wombs exported from *Great Britain*, the sum of one shilling and six pence.

III. And

III. And be it further enacted by the authority aforesaid, That the several duties and impositions by this act granted, shall be laid, levied, collected, paid, and applied, in such manner, and for the same purposes, as the several rates and duties by this act repealed as aforesaid, and now respectively raised, levied, collected, and paid, and applied: and all the provisions of or in every act or law now in force for raising, levying, collecting, paying, and applying the duties and impositions hereby repealed as aforesaid, shall be in full force, and shall be put in execution, for raising, levying, collecting, paying, and applying, the duties and impositions by this act granted, as fully and effectually, to all intents and purposes, as if the said provisions were particularly repeated and re-enacted in the body of this present act.

The new duties to be paid, and applied as the former; and the provisions in former acts respecting the same, to be in force, and extended to the duties of this act;

IV. Provided always, and be it further enacted by the authority aforesaid, That from and after the said seventh day of *April*, no drawback shall be allowed on the exportation of any bever skin from *Great Britain*.

and no drawback to be allowed on the exportation of bever skins.

CAP. X.

An act for the more easy discharge of recognizances estreated into his Majesty's court of Exchequer.

Preamble.

WHEREAS *many recognizances have been estreated into his Majesty's court of Exchequer, against persons for not appearing as parties or witnesses in his Majesty's courts of record at* Westminster, *or at the assizes and general quarter sessions, or other courts of record in that part of* Great Britain *called* England, *or for not prosecuting indictments there, or otherwise not performing the conditions in such recognizances contained; many of which neglects of duty have happened by the inattention of ignorant people, some of whom are imprisoned, and a great number of others liable to be so, by the process constantly issued against them out of the courts of Exchequer, and directed to the sheriffs, though no other prosecution be subsisting but merely for such forfeitures of their recognizances, from which there are no easy means at present, for poor persons especially, to procure any discharge:* for remedy whereof, be it enacted by the King's most excellent majesty, by and with the advice and consent of the lords spiritual and temporal, and commons, in this present parliament assembled, and by the authority of the same, That from and after the fifth day of *May*, one thousand seven hundred and sixty four, it shall be lawful for the barons of his Majesty's court of Exchequer, upon affidavit and petition to be presented to them by or on the behalf of the person or persons imprisoned, or liable to be imprisoned, on the forfeiture of any such recognizances, to discharge such person or persons, by order from the said barons, without any *quietus* to be sued out for that purpose; for which order no more than one pound and one shilling shall be taken by the officer appointed to give out the same: provided that no discharge shall be given on such petitions where any debt is due to the crown, other than by the recognizances so prayed to be discharged; nor in any cases of defrauding his Majesty's revenue by contraband trade, or assaulting

After 1 May, 1764, the barons of the Exchequer impowered to discharge, upon affidavit and petition, and without *quietus* sued, recognizances of persons estreated into the Exchequer; Fee payable upon such order, 1 l. 1 s. Debts due to the crown;

cases of frauds by contraband trade; and assaulting officers of the revenue; excepted.

ing his Majesty's officers of the customs or excise in the execution of their duty, or any person or persons lawfully assisting them therein.

CAP. XI.

An act for continuing certain laws therein mentioned relating to British *sail cloth, and to the duties payable on foreign sail cloth, and to the allowance upon the exportation of* British *made gunpowder, and for giving further encouragement for the importation of naval stores from the* British *colonies in* America.

WHEREAS *the laws herein after-mentioned are found to be very useful and beneficial, and are near expiring*; may it therefore please your Majesty, that it may be enacted; and be it enacted by the King's most excellent majesty, by and with the advice and consent of the lords spiritual and temporal, and commons, in this present parliament assembled, and by the authority of the same, That an act made in the ninth year of the reign of his late majesty King *George* the Second, intituled, *An act for further encouraging and regulating the manufacture of* British *sail cloth, and for the more effectual securing the duties now payable on foreign sail cloth imported into this kingdom*, which was to continue in force from the twenty fourth day of *June*, one thousand seven hundred and thirty six, for the term of five years, and from thence to the end of the then next session of parliament; and which, by several subsequent acts made in the thirteenth, twenty fourth, and thirty first, years of his said Majesty's reign, was further continued until the twenty ninth day of *September*, one thousand seven hundred and sixty four, and from thence to the end of the then next session of parliament; shall be, and the same is hereby further continued from the expiration thereof, until the twenty ninth day of *September*, one thousand seven hundred and seventy one, and from thence to the end of the then next session of parliament.

Act 9 Geo. II. relating to British sail cloth, &c.

further continued to 29 Sept. 1771.

II. And be it further enacted by the authority aforesaid, That an act made in the fourth year of the reign of his late majesty King *George* the Second, intituled, *An act for granting an allowance upon the exportation of* British *made gunpowder*, which was to continue in force for five years from the twenty fourth day of *June*, one thousand seven hundred and thirty one, and from thence to the end of the then next session of parliament; and which, by several subsequent acts made in the tenth, sixteenth, twenty fourth, and thirty first, years of his said Majesty's reign, was further continued until the twenty ninth day of *September*, one thousand seven hundred and sixty four, and from thence to the end of the then next session of parliament; shall be, and the same is hereby further continued from the expiration thereof, until the twenty ninth day of *September*, one thousand seven hundred and seventy one, and from thence to the end of the then next session of parliament.

Act 4 Geo. II. relating to the allowance upon the exportation of British made gunpowder,

further continued to 29 Sept. 1771.

III. And

III. And be it further enacted by the authority aforesaid, That so much of an act made in the eighth year of the reign of King *George* the First, intituled, *An act for giving further encouragement for the importation of naval stores, and for other purposes therein mentioned*, as relates to the importation of wood and timber, and of the goods commonly called *Lumber*, therein particularly enumerated, from any of his Majesty's *British* plantations or colonies in *America*, free from all customs and impositions whatsoever; which was to be in force for twenty one years, from the twenty fourth day of *June*, one thousand seven hundred and twenty two; and which, by several subsequent acts made in the sixteenth, twenty fourth, and thirty first, years of the reign of his late majesty King *George* the Second, was further continued until the twenty ninth day of *September*, one thousand seven hundred and sixty four, and from thence to the end of the then next session of parliament; shall be, and the same is hereby further continued from the expiration thereof, until the twenty ninth day of *September*, one thousand seven hundred and seventy one, and from thence to the end of the then next session of parliament.

So much of act 8 Geo. I. as relates to the importation of wood, timber, and lumber, from the British plantations in America,

further continued to 29 Sep. 1771.

CAP. XII.

An act to continue several laws for the better regulating of pilots for the conducting of ships and vessels from Dover, Deal, *and* Isle of Thanet, *up the rivers of* Thames *and* Medway; *relating to the landing of rum or spirits of the* British *sugar plantations before the duties of excise are paid thereon; and to the further punishment of persons going armed or disguised, in defiance of the laws of customs or excise; and to the relief of the officers of the customs in informations upon seizures; and for granting a liberty to carry sugars of the growth, produce, or manufacture, of any of his Majesty's sugar colonies, directly into foreign parts, in ships built in* Great Britain, *and navigated according to law; and for punishing persons who shall damage or destroy any banks, flood-gates, sluices, or other works, belonging to the rivers and streams made navigable by act of parliament.*

Preamble.

WHEREAS *the laws herein after mentioned have, by experience, been found useful and beneficial, and are near expiring*; may it therefore please your Majesty, that it may be enacted; and be it enacted by the King's most excellent majesty, by and with the advice and consent of the lords spiritual and temporal, and commons, in this present parliament assembled, and by the authority of the same, That an act made in the third year of the reign of King *George* the First, intituled, *An act for the better regulating of pilots for the conducting of ships and vessels from* Dover, Deal, *and the* Isle of Thanet, *up the rivers of* Thames *and* Medway, which was

Act 3 Geo. I. for regulating pilots of vessels from Dover, &c. up the Thames and Medway;

to continue in force for seven years, and from thence to the end of the end of the then next session of parliament; and also a clause for further regulating the pilots of *Dover*, *Deal*, and the *Isle of Thanet*, in an act passed in the seventh year of his said Majesty's reign, which was to be in force during the continuance of the said act of the third year of his said Majesty's reign; which said act, together with the said clause, were, by several subsequent acts, made in the tenth year of his said Majesty's reign, and of the eighth and twenty third years of the reign of his late majesty King *George* the Second, further continued until the twenty fifth day of *March*, one thousand seven hundred and sixty four, and from thence to the end of the then next session of parliament; shall be, and the same are hereby further continued from the expiration thereof until the twenty fifth day of *March*, one thousand seven hundred and seventy eight, and from thence to the end of the then next session of parliament.

and clause in act 7. Geo. I. for further regulating the pilots of Dover, Deal, and Thanet, &c.

further continued to 25 March, 1778.

So much of act 15 & 16 Geo. II. as relates to the landing of rum or spirits, of the British sugar plantations, before duties paid,

II. And be it further enacted by the authority aforesaid, That so much of an act made in the fifteenth and sixteenth years of the reign of his late majesty King *George* the Second, intituled, *An act to impower the importers or proprietors of rum or spirits of the* British *sugar plantations, to land the same before payment of the duties of excise charged thereon, and to lodge the same in warehouses at their own expence; and for the relief of* Ralph Barrow, *in respect to the duty on some rock salt, lost by the overflowing of the rivers* Weaver *and* Dane; as relates to the landing of rum or spirits of the *British* sugar plantations before payment of the duties of excise, and to the lodging of the same in warehouses at the expence of the importers or proprietors thereof; which was to continue in force until the twenty ninth day of *September*, one thousand seven hundred and forty nine, and from thence to the end of the then next session of parliament; and which, by an act made in the twenty third year of his said late Majesty's reign, was further continued from the expiration thereof until the twenty ninth day of *September*, one thousand seven hundred and fifty seven, and from thence to the end of the then next session of parliament; and which, by an act made in the thirty first year of his said late Majesty's reign, was amended, and further continued until the twenty ninth day of *September*, one thousand seven hundred and sixty four, and from thence to the end of the then next session of parliament; shall be, and the same is hereby further continued from the expiration thereof until the twenty ninth day of *September*, one thousand seven hundred and seventy one, and from thence to the end of the then next session of parliament.

further continued to 29 Sept, 1771.

So much of act 19 Geo. II. as relates to persons going armed or disguised in defiance of the laws of customs and excise;

III. And be it further enacted by the authority aforesaid, That so much of an act made in the nineteenth year of the reign of his late majesty King *George* the Second, intituled, *An act for the further punishment of persons going armed or disguised in defiance of the laws of customs or excise; and for indemnifying offenders against those laws upon the terms therein mentioned; and for relief of officers of the customs in informations upon seizures*; as relates to the further

further puniſhment of perſons going armed or diſguiſed in defiance of the laws of cuſtoms or exciſe, and to the relief of officers of the cuſtoms in informations upon ſeizures; which act was to continue in force for the ſpace of ſeven years, and from thence to the end of the then next ſeſſion of parliament; and which, by ſeveral ſubſequent acts, made in the twenty ſixth and thirty ſecond years of his ſaid Majeſty's reign, was further continued until the twenty ninth day of *September*, one thouſand ſeven hundred and ſixty four, and from thence to the end of the then next ſeſſion of parliament; ſhall be, and the ſame is hereby further continued from the expiration thereof until the twenty ninth day of *September*, one thouſand ſeven hundred and ſeventy one, and from thence to the end of the then next ſeſſion of parliament.

and to the relief of officers of the cuſtoms in informations upon ſeizures;

further continued to 29 Sept. 1771.

IV. And be it further enacted by the authority aforeſaid, That an act made in the twelfth year of the reign of his late majeſty King *George* the Second, intituled, *An act for granting a liberty to carry ſugars of the growth, produce, or manufacture, of any of his Majeſty's ſugar colonies in* America, *from the ſaid colonies directly to foreign parts, in ſhips built in* Great Britain, *and navigated according to law*; which was to continue in force for five years from the twenty ninth day of *September*, one thouſand ſeven hundred and thirty nine, and from thence to the end of the then next ſeſſion of parliament; and which, by ſeveral ſubſequent acts made in the ſeventeenth, twenty fourth, and thirty firſt years of his ſaid Majeſty's reign, was further continued until the twenty ninth day of *September*, one thouſand ſeven hundred and ſixty four, and from thence to the end of the then next ſeſſion of parliament; ſhall be, and the ſame is hereby further continued, from the expiration thereof, until the twenty ninth day of *September*, one thouſand ſeven hundred and ſeventy one, and from thence to the end of the then next ſeſſion of parliament.

Act 12 Geo. II. granting liberty to carry ſugars of the growth of the Britiſh plantations in America, directly to foreign parts, &c.

further continued to 29 Sept. 1771.

V. And whereas the laws now in being are not ſufficient for the preſervation of the banks, flood-gates, ſluices, and other works, belonging to rivers and ſtreams made navigable by act of parliament, and for the maintaining the navigation of ſuch rivers and ſtreams; be it therefore enacted by the authority aforeſaid, That from and after the paſſing of this act, if any perſon or perſons ſhall wilfully or maliciouſly break, throw down, damage, or deſtroy, any banks, flood-gates, ſluices, or other works, or open or draw up any flood-gate or flood-gates, or do any other wilful hurt or miſchief to any ſuch navigation, ſo as to obſtruct, hinder, or prevent, the carrying on, compleating, ſupporting, or maintaining, ſuch navigation; every ſuch perſon or perſons ſhall be adjudged guilty of felony; and the court before whom ſuch perſon or perſons ſhall be tried and convicted, ſhall and hereby have power and authority to order ſuch perſon or perſons to be tranſported for ſeven years.

Perſons who ſhall damage any banks, flood-gates, or other works belonging to rivers, &c. made navigable by act of parliament, ſhall be adjudged guilty of felony, and be tranſported for 7 years.

CAP. XIII.

An act for granting to his Majesty a certain sum of money out of the sinking fund, for the service of the year one thousand seven hundred and sixty four; and for preventing, in certain cases, the obtaining of allowances in respect of the leakage of wines imported into this kingdom; and for making forth duplicates of Exchequer bills, tickets, certificates, receipts, annuity orders, and other orders, lost, burnt, or otherwise destroyed.

Most gracious Sovereign,

Preamble.

WE, *your Majesty's most dutiful and loyal subjects, the commons of* Great Britain, *in parliament assembled, towards raising the necessary supplies which we have chearfully granted to your Majesty, in this session of parliament, have resolved to give and grant to your Majesty the sum herein after mentioned*; and do therefore most humbly beseech your Majesty, that it may be enacted; and be it enacted by the King's most excellent majesty, by and with the advice and consent of the lords spiritual and temporal, and commons, in this present parliament assembled, and by the authority of the same, That

Towards raising the supplies granted, there may be issued out of the sinking fund a sum not exceeding 2,000,000 l. —— Clause of loan for raising the aforesaid sum of 2,000,000 l. —— Tallies of loan may be struck for the same. Orders to be registred, and paid in course. No fee to be paid for registring, &c. Penalty of undue preference; how to be recovered. —— It shall be deemed no undue preference, where tallies are dated, or brought the same day; —— nor if subsequent orders be paid before such as were not demanded in course. —— Orders assignable toties quoties. —— Commissioners of the treasury, if they shall think it more adviseable to raise the said sum, or any part thereof, by Exchequer bills, may make out any number of new Exchequer bills for the same, in like manner and form as is prescribed by the malt act of this session. —— Clauses in the said act relating to Exchequer bills, extended to those to be made out in pursuance of this act. —— The said bills, interest, premium, and charges, payable out of the sinking fund. —— The bank impowered to advance, on the said credit of loan, any sum or sums, not exceeding 2,000,000 l. the act 5 & 6 W. & M. notwithstanding. —— Clause of relief for Exchequer bills, lottery tickets, certificates, annuity orders, &c. lost, burnt, or otherwise destroyed.

XI. And whereas by the eighth rule annexed to the book of rates referred to in the act of tonnage and poundage, passed in the twelfth year of the reign of King *Charles* the Second, every merchant bringing in any sort of wines into this kingdom by way of merchandize, and making due entries thereof, is allowed twelve *per cent.* for leakage: and whereas it is of late years become a practice for several merchants to lodge *Spanish*, *Portugal*, and other wines at the islands of *Guernsey* and *Jersey*, and after they have filled up the casks there, to import such wines into this kingdom, and demand the before mentioned allowances for leakage, notwithstanding the casks are quite full; to the lessen-

ing

ing of his Majesty's revenue, and the prejudice of other merchants who import wines directly from the place of their growth: for remedy whereof, and in order to put all merchants upon a more equal footing; be it enacted by the authority aforesaid, That from and after the first day of *May*, one thousand seven hundred and sixty four, no merchant shall be allowed twelve *per centum*, or have any allowance for leakage upon any wine imported into this kingdom, unless such wine be imported directly from the country or place of the growth of the said wine, or the usual port or place of its first shipping, except only *Madeira* wines imported into this kingdom from any of the *British* colonies or plantations in *America*, or from the *East Indies*; any thing in the said recited rule, or any law, custom, or usage to the contrary notwithstanding.

The former allowance of 12 l. per cent. for leakage upon wines imported, taken off, with respect to all such wines as shall not be imported directly from the place of their growth; Madeira wines excepted.

CAP. XIV.

An act for the better regulating of buildings; and to prevent mischiefs that may happen by fire within the weekly bills of mortality, and other places therein mentioned.

Preamble, reciting clause in act 11 Geo. I.

WHEREAS *so much of the act, passed in the eleventh year of the reign of his late majesty King* George *the First, intituled,* An act for the better regulating of buildings; and to prevent mischiefs that may happen by fire within the weekly bills of mortality, and other places therein mentioned; *as relates to pulling down or rebuilding of partitions or party walls, between house and house, is confined to cases where one of the houses is to be erected or built; and it may happen that party walls within the said city and liberty of* Westminster, *and the parishes, precincts, and places comprised within the weekly bills of mortality, and within the several parishes of* Saint Mary Le Bone, *and* Paddington, *and within the parishes of* Chelsea, *and* Saint Pancras, *or either of them, in the county of* Middlesex *(except the city of* London, *and the liberties thereof; and also, except houses on* London Bridge, *and on the river of* Thames *below bridge) may be so far out of repair, as to render it necessary to pull down and rebuild the same, although neither of the adjoining houses, to which such party walls belong, require to be rebuilt; and it may happen, that party walls, within the limits aforesaid, may be so far defective and bad, by falling out of the perpendicular, as to become unsafe for the builder of the next adjoining house to rest timbers thereupon, or oblige such builder to run or place his timbers quite through such defective party walls, in order to preserve their just lengths, whereby fire may be more readily communicated from house to house, contrary to the intent of the said act: and whereas the workmen appointed, by virtue of the said recited act, to examine party walls, are often equally divided in opinion about the necessity of pulling down and rebuilding such party walls, whereby a certificate from the major part of such workmen, as by the said recited act is required, cannot be obtained, and the purposes of the said act, in many instances, have been evaded;* wherefore, may it therefore please your most excellent Majesty that it may be enacted; and

and be it enacted by the King's most excellent majesty, by and with the advice and consent of the lords spiritual and temporal, and commons, in this present parliament assembled, and by the authority of the same, That so much of the said recited act as relates to party walls within the said city and liberty of *Westminster*, or any parish, precinct, or place, comprised within the weekly bills of mortality, or within the several parishes of *Saint Mary le Bone* and *Paddington*, or within the parishes of *Chelsea*, and *Saint Pancras*, or either of them, in the county of *Middlesex* (except the city of *London*, and the liberties thereof; and also, except the party walls of houses on the river of *Thames* below bridge) shall, from and after the passing of this present act, extend, and be construed, deemed, and taken to extend, to all cases whatsoever within the said city and liberty of *Westminster*, and the several parishes, precincts, and limits aforesaid, where it is or shall be necessary to pull down and rebuild any party wall, whether either of the adjoining houses shall or shall not be, or require to be, rebuilt, or new built.

So much of the recited act as relates to party walls within the city and liberty of Westminster, &c. extended to all cases, where necessary to pull down and rebuild any party wall; whether either of the adjoining houses shall be to be rebuilt or not.

II. And be it further enacted by the authority aforesaid, That from and after the passing of this present act, in case the major part of the workmen appointed, in manner by the said recited act prescribed, to view the party wall of any house or houses within the said city of *Westminster*, and the several parishes, precincts, and limits aforesaid, intended to be pulled down, shall not, within the space of one calendar month next after such appointment, sign a certificate in writing, as by the said act is required; then, and in every such case, it shall and may be lawful to and for any two or more of his Majesty's justices of the peace for the city or county, residing within or near the parish, liberty, or precinct, where the house or houses, having such party wall or walls intended to be pulled down, shall stand, and such two or more justices are hereby authorized and required, upon application to them, for that purpose, made, by the owner or occupier of either of the houses between which the party wall, so proposed to be pulled down, shall be, to name and appoint one other able workman, to be added to the workmen appointed by virtue or in pursuance of the said recited act; and the workmen so appointed by virtue and in pursuance of the said former act, and of this present act, or the major part of them who shall meet for that purpose (ten days notice having been given to, or left at the dwelling house of, each and every of them, of such intended meeting) shall view the party wall so proposed to be pulled down; and in case the major part of such workmen, shall certify in writing, under their hands, that such party wall is defective and bad, and ought to be pulled down, then, and in such case, it shall and may be lawful to and for the owner or occupier of either of the said adjoining houses, to cause such party wall to be pulled down and rebuilt; and he or she shall have such remedy for recovering a moiety of the expences thereof, as in and by the said recited act is given or provided; subject

Where a majority of the workmen, appointed in pursuance of the recited act to view any party wall to be pulled down, shall not sign a certificate, as required, Two neighbouring justices, upon application, may name another, to be added to them; and the majority then agreeing in a report of such wall being defective, the same may be pulled down and rebuilt; and a moiety of the expen-

ſubject nevertheleſs to ſuch appeal to, and determination by, the juſtices of the peace, as by the ſame act is directed.

ces recovered accordingly.

And whereas it would tend greatly to prevent the fatal conſequences of fire ſpreading and communicating to adjoining houſes, within the ſaid city, pariſhes, precincts, and other the limits aforeſaid, if party walls between houſe and houſe, within the ſame, were to be made of greater thickneſs than is preſcribed by the act paſſed in the ſeventh year of the reign of her late majeſty Queen *Anne*, intituled, *An act for making more effectual an act made in the ſixth year of her ſaid Majeſty's reign, for the better preventing of miſchiefs that may happen by fire*; and if no timbers, except the timbers of the girders, binding joiſts, and the templets under the ſame, were laid into the party walls; and if no timbers of the roof be laid into ſuch party walls (except the purloins or kerb thereof) and if the ends of the girders or binding joiſts, lying within the ſaid party walls, did not exceed one foot; and if none of the ends of the girders or binding joiſts, in adjoining houſes, met, or were laid oppoſite to each other, and the ſides thereof were laid at leaſt fourteen inches diſtant from each other; and if there ſhould be nine inches, at leaſt, of ſolid brick-work left at or between the ends of all lentils, wall plates, and bond timbers, which may or ſhall be laid in or upon the walls of the fore and back fronts of all houſes which ſhall adjoin to each other; be it therefore enacted by the authority aforeſaid, That all party walls which, from and after the expiration of three calendar months next after the paſſing of this act, ſhall be erected or built within the ſaid city or liberty of *Weſtminſter*, and the pariſhes, precincts, and limits aforeſaid, ſhall be two bricks and an half thick at the leaſt in the cellar, and two bricks thick upwards to the garret floor, and from thence one brick and an half thick at leaſt eighteen inches above the roofs or gutters which adjoin to ſuch party walls; and that the ſame ſhall be built of ſtone, or of good ſound burnt bricks, and none other.

Act 7 Annæ.

Thickneſs for the future of party walls, in the cellar, to the garret floor, and from thence upwards; and to be 18 inches high above the roofs.

III. And be it further enacted by the authority aforeſaid, That from and after the expiration of the ſaid three calendar months, no timbers, except the timbers of the girders, binding joiſts, and the templets under the ſame, ſhall be laid into the party walls erected or built, or to be erected or built, within the ſaid city or liberty of *Weſtminſter*, and the pariſhes, precincts, and limits aforeſaid; and that no timbers of the roof be laid into ſuch party walls (except the purloins or kerb thereof) and that the ends of girders, and binding joiſts, lying within ſuch party walls, ſhall not exceed nine inches; and that none of the ends of the girders, or binding joiſts, in adjoining houſes, ſhall meet, or be laid oppoſite to each other; and that the ſides thereof ſhall be, at leaſt, fourteen inches diſtant from each other; and that there ſhall be nine inches, at leaſt of ſolid brick-work left at or between the ends of all lentils, wall plates, and bond timber, which may or ſhall be laid in or upon the walls of the fore and back fronts of all houſes which ſhall adjoin to each other: and if any head builder, maſter bricklayer, or

No timbers to be laid into the party walls, except what are herein particularly allowed.

Rules to be obſerved in placing the ends of the girders, and joiſts;

lentils, wall plates, and bond timbers.

Builder, &c. not conforming to these directions,

or workman, shall erect and build, or cause to be erected and built, any party wall within the said city and liberty of *Westminster*, and the parishes, precincts, and limits aforesaid, contrary to the directions, true intent, and meaning of this act; or shall use, in the building thereof, any bricks, other than good sound burnt bricks; or shall lay any timber in any party wall erected or built, or which shall be erected or built, within the said city or liberty of *Westminster*, and the parishes, precincts, and limits aforesaid, contrary to the directions, true intent and meaning of this act; then such head builder, master bricklayer, or workman, shall, for every such offence, forfeit and pay the sum of fifty pounds, to be equally divided, one moiety thereof to the informer, and the other moiety to the poor of the parish where such building shall be; to be levied, by warrant under the hands and seals of two or more of his Majesty's justices of the peace, by distress and sale of the offenders goods, upon conviction upon oath of one or more credible witness or witnesses, or upon his or their own confession, rendring the overplus (if any be) to the owner or owners; and, for want of such distress, the offender shall be imprisoned for the space of six months, unless the said penalty shall be sooner paid, by warrant under the hands and seals of the said two or more justices, who are hereby required and impowered to issue such warrant accordingly; or that it shall and may be lawful to and for all and every person and persons whomsoever, to sue for and recover all and every or any the aforesaid penalty and penalties, given or imposed by this act, by action of debt, bill, plaint, suit, or information, in any of his Majesty's courts of record at *Westminster*, wherein no essoin, protection, privilege, or wager of law, or more than one imparlance, shall be allowed; and that every the person and persons, suing or prosecuting for any such penalty or penalties, shall, in all cases where he or they shall recover the same in manner herein last mentioned, be intitled to, and shall recover double costs of suit, over and above all and every such penalty and penalties; and one moiety of every such penalty and penalties, when recovered, shall be immediately paid, by the person or persons recovering the same, to the churchwardens or overseers of the poor for the time being of the parish, liberty, or precinct, in which such penalty or penalties shall arise, and for which such action shall be commenced, for the use of the poor of such parish, liberty, or precinct, and the other moiety thereof shall be for the use of the person or persons who shall inform, sue for, and recover the same.

or using bricks not duly burnt, or laying timber in party walls otherwise than prescribed, to forfeit 50 l. to be levied by distress and sale; and for want of distress offender to be committed for 6 months; or the penalty may be sued for and recovered in any the courts at Westminster, with double costs. Application of the penalty.

IV. And be it enacted by the authority aforesaid, That from and after the first day of *July*, one thousand seven hundred and sixty four, no timber or timbers whatsoever shall be laid or placed under the hearth or hearths of any room or rooms, or within nine inches of any funnel or flew of any chimney or chimnies of any house or houses within the limits aforesaid; and that no timber buildings whatsoever shall be built adjoining to any house or houses, so as the timbers thereof shall be laid into the wall of

Rules to be observed with respect to hearths and chimnies; and to timber buildings.

of any ſuch houſe or houſes already built, or hereafter to be built, within the limits aforeſaid, under the penalty of fifty pounds; to be recovered, levied, and applied, againſt the workman offending therein, or the inhabitant or perſon cauſing ſuch building to be erected or built, in like manner as any other penalty or forfeiture is, in and by this act, directed to be recovered, levied, and applied.

Penalty of not conforming thereto, 50 l.

V. And be it further enacted by the authority aforeſaid, That after any party wall or party walls ſhall be erected or built purſuant to the directions of this act, no perſon or perſons whatſoever, who ſhall build againſt ſuch party wall or party walls, ſhall, on any pretence whatſoever, cut into or wound the ſame, for the conveniency of making a chimney or chimnies, or for any other purpoſe whatſoever: nor ſhall lay into the ſame any other timbers than are allowed by this act to be laid into new party walls, under the penalty of fifty pounds, to be recovered againſt the party or perſon offending, in the manner herein before directed.

Party walls not to be cut into or wounded, by adjoining buildings, nor other timbers to be laid therein, than is here allowed, on penalty of 50 l.

VI. And be it further enacted by the authority aforeſaid, That every maſter builder who ſhall, after the firſt day of *July*, one thouſand ſeven hundred and ſixty four, erect or build any houſe within the limits above mentioned, ſhall, within fourteen days after the ſame ſhall be covered in, cauſe the ſame to be ſurveyed by one or more ſurveyor or ſurveyors; and ſuch ſurveyor or ſurveyors ſhall make oath, before one of his Majeſty's juſtices of the peace for the ſaid county of *Middleſex*, or city of *Weſtminſter* (which oath ſuch juſtice is hereby impowered and required to adminiſter) that the ſame hath been (to the beſt of his or their judgment and belief) built and erected agreeable to the ſeveral directions in this act contained; which affidavit ſhall be filed with the clerk of the peace for the ſaid county of *Middleſex*, within ten days after the making thereof; and the ſaid clerk of the peace ſhall, for his trouble therein, be intitled to and receive the ſum of one ſhilling, and no more: and if any maſter builder ſhall make default in the premiſſes, by neglecting to cauſe ſuch ſurvey to be made, or ſuch affidavit to be made and filed as aforeſaid, ſuch maſter builder ſhall, for every ſuch neglect or default, forfeit the ſum of fifty pounds; to be recovered and applied in the ſame manner, as any penalties or forfeitures are, by this act, directed to be recovered and applied.

Builders to cauſe the houſes to be ſurveyed;

Surveyors to make oath of the ſame being built according to the directions of this act.

Oath to be filed with the clerk of the peace:

His fee.

Builder not complying, to forfeit 50 l.

VII. And be it further enacted by the authority aforeſaid, That the pariſhioners and inhabitants of the pariſh, liberty, or precinct, where any offence againſt this act ſhall be committed (except perſons receiving alms) ſhall be admitted and allowed to be competent witneſſes, notwithſtanding his, her, or their being a pariſhioner or pariſhioners, inhabitant or inhabitants, in ſuch pariſh, liberty, or precinct.

Pariſhioners, &c. deemed competent witneſſes.

VIII. And whereas ſome part or parts of houſes already pulled down, or that ſhall hereafter be pulled down, in order to be rebuilt, may be ſo intermixed with adjoining houſes over or under each other, in ſuch manner, that a party wall or party walls,

of

of brick or ſtone, cannot be effectually built upon the old foundations, perpendicular quite through all the ſtories, in order to prevent miſchiefs by fire, without pulling down ſome part or parts of the one, and laying the ſame to the other: for preventing diſputes thereupon, or determining any ſubſiſting diſputes, be it enacted by the authority aforeſaid, That in all caſes where any diſpute or controverſy hath ariſen, or ſhall ariſe, between the owner or owners of any houſe or houſes already pulled down, or that ſhall be pulled down in order to be rebuilt, and the owner or owners of any houſe adjoining on either ſide to ſuch houſe or houſes, within the ſaid city or liberty of *Weſtminſter*, and the pariſhes, precincts, and limits aforeſaid, concerning any part or parts thereof intermixed over or under each other, in ſuch manner that a party wall or party walls of brick or ſtone cannot be effectually built upon the old foundations, perpendicular quite through all the ſtories of the ſaid houſe or houſes, in order to prevent miſchiefs by fire, without pulling down ſome part or parts of one or more of the ſaid adjoining houſes, and laying ſome part or parts of one or more of the ſaid adjoining houſe or houſes or ground to the other or others thereof, it ſhall and may be lawful to and for the juſtices of the peace, in the general or quarter ſeſſions to be holden for the ſaid city and liberty of *Weſtminſter*, or the county of *Middleſex*, and they are hereby authorized and required, upon application made to them by the perſon or perſons deſirous to pull down or rebuild any houſe or houſes as aforeſaid, to examine into ſuch diſpute or controverſy, and aſcertain the property, and fix the value, of what may be found neceſſary to be wanted for erecting perpendicular party walls upon the old foundations as aforeſaid; and for that purpoſe, to iſſue their order to the ſheriffs or bailiffs, or other proper officer of the city or county wherein any ſuch diſpute or controverſy hath ariſen or ſhall ariſe, to ſummon a jury to view the premiſſes, try the facts, and fix the value of any damages that may ariſe, on their verdict; and, upon ſuch verdict, the ſaid juſtices ſhall and may, and are hereby authorized and required to make ſuch order or orders in the ſaid premiſſes as they, in their diſcretions, ſhall think to be juſt and reaſonable; and the determinations of the ſaid juſtices ſhall be final and concluſive to all parties, without any appeal from the ſame.

Diſputes about damage, by erecting new perpendicular party walls upon the old foundations, where parts of the adjoining houſes intermix, are to be referred to the juſtices at their quarter ſeſſions, who are to ſummon a jury to fix the value; and the order made upon ſuch verdict.

IX. And, for the better preventing miſchiefs that may happen by fire, and to deter and hinder ill-minded perſons from wilfully ſetting their houſe or houſes, or other buildings, on fire, with a view of gaining to themſelves the inſurance money, whereby the lives and fortunes of many families are loſt; be it further enacted by the authority aforeſaid, That it ſhall and may be lawful to and for the reſpective governors or directors of the ſeveral inſurance offices, within the cities of *London* and *Weſtminſter*, for inſuring houſes and other buildings againſt loſſes by fire, and they are hereby authorized and required, upon the application and requeſt of any perſon or perſons intereſted in, or intitled unto, any houſe or houſes, or other buildings, within the

Caſes, wherein inſurance offices may lay out the inſurance money, towards rebuilding, &c. houſes burnt, or damnified by fire.

the limits by this act prescribed, which hereafter shall or may be burnt down, demolished, or damnified by fire; or upon any grounds of suspicion that the owner or owners, occupier or occupiers, or other person or persons who shall have insured such house or houses, or other buildings, have been guilty of fraud, or of wilfully setting their house or houses, or other buildings, on fire; to cause the insurance money to be laid out and expended, as far as the same will go, towards rebuilding, reinstating, or repairing such house or houses, or other buildings, so burnt down, demolished, or damnified by fire; unless the party or parties claiming such insurance money shall, within sixty days next after such claim shall be adjusted, give a sufficient security to the governors or directors of the insurance office where such house or houses, or other buildings, are insured, that the same insurance money shall be so laid out and expended as aforesaid; or unless the said insurance money shall be in that time settled and disposed of to and amongst all the contending parties, to the satisfaction and approbation of such governors or directors of such insurance offices respectively.

Orders of justices not liable to be quashed for want of form, nor to be removed by *Certiorari*.

X. And be it further enacted by the authority aforesaid, That no order which shall be made by any justice or justices of the peace, by virtue of or under this act, or any other proceedings to be had touching the conviction or convictions of any offender or offenders against this act, shall be quashed or vacated for want of form only, or be removed or removeable by *Certiorari*, or any other writ or process whatsoever, into any of his Majesty's courts of record at *Westminster*.

Limitation of actions.

XI. And be it further enacted by the authority aforesaid, That if any action shall be brought, or suit commenced, against any person or persons, for any thing done in pursuance of this act, such action or suit shall be laid or brought within six months next after the fact done, and not afterwards; and shall be laid or brought in the county or place where the fact was committed, and not elsewhere; and the defendant or defendants in such action may plead the general issue, and give this act and the special matter in evidence, at any trial to be had thereupon, and that the same was done in pursuance and by authority of this act: and if the same shall appear to have been so done, or if any action or suit shall not be brought within the time before limited, or shall be brought in any other county or place than as aforesaid, then the jury shall find for the defendant or defendants; or if the plaintiff or plaintiffs shall become nonsuited, or suffer a discontinuance of his, her, or their action or actions; or if a verdict shall pass against the plaintiff or plaintiffs; or if, upon demurrer, judgment shall be given against the plaintiff or plaintiffs; the said defendant or defendants shall have treble costs, and shall have such remedy for recovering the same as any defendant or defendants hath or have, for costs, in any other cases by law.

General issue.

Treble costs.

Expence of party walls pulled down and rebuilt, in pursuance of the recited act,

XII. Provided always, and be it enacted by the authority aforesaid, That in all cases where any party wall within the said city or liberty of *Westminster*, and the parishes, precincts, and limits aforesaid, shall, by virtue of the said recited act of the eleventh

to be estimated between the parties, at the rate of 6 l. 10 s. per rod;

eleventh year of his majesty King *George* the First, and of this present act, be pulled down and rebuilt, agreeable to the directions of this present act, by the owner or occupier of one of the adjoining houses, the expence of such party wall shall be estimated and computed at and after the rate of six pounds and ten shillings *per* rod; any thing in the said former act to the contrary thereof in any wise notwithstanding.

and in like manner those built in pursuance of this act.

XIII. Provided also, and be it enacted by the authority aforesaid, That in all cases where any party wall shall be erected or built, agreeable to the directions of this present act, in execution of any contract or contracts entered into with the builder or workman before the first day of *July*, one thousand seven hundred and sixty four, the expence of such party wall shall be estimated and computed at and after the rate of six pounds and ten shillings *per* rod; any thing in such contract or contracts to the contrary thereof in any wise notwithstanding.

Back and fore fronts of all future buildings to be of stone, or good brick, from the breast summer upwards, as also the party walls. Height of the breast summer.

XIV. And be it further enacted by the authority aforesaid, That for the further and better preventing the spreading of fires, all houses or other buildings which, from and after the expiration of three calendar months next after the passing of this act, shall be erected or built within the said city or liberty of *Westminster*, and the parishes, precincts, and limits aforesaid, shall be built of stone, or of good sound hard well burnt bricks, and none other, both in the fore front, and back front thereof, from the breast summer upwards (and likewise the party wall thereof) and that such breast summer, in all such houses or other buildings, shall not be higher than the floor of the one pair of stairs.

Act 6 Annæ.

XV. And whereas, by an act made in the sixth year of the reign of her late majesty Queen *Anne*, a reward of ten shillings is to be paid to the turn cock belonging to any water work where water shall be found on, or first come into, the main or pipe where the first plug shall be opened at any fire; thirty shillings to the first engine keeper, who brings in any parish engine to help to extinguish any fire; twenty shillings to the keeper of the second parish engine, that shall be next brought to a fire; and to the third, ten shillings; by the churchwardens of the parish where such fire shall happen; be it further enacted by the authority aforesaid, That in all cases where any of the said rewards shall be claimed, by reason of any fire happening within the said city of *Westminster*, or within the parishes, precincts, liberties, or places aforesaid, such rewards shall be paid and payable in the same manner to the keeper of any other large engine (though not a parish engine) who shall bring in such engine in good order and complete, to help to extinguish such fire, in the same manner as if such engine was a parish engine.

In cases of fire, the keepers of other large engines are equally intitled with the parish engines to the rewards granted by act 6 Annæ.

Publick act.

XVI. And it is hereby further enacted, That this act shall be deemed, and taken to be a publick act, and shall be judicially taken notice of as such by all judges, justices, and all other persons whatsoever, without specially pleading the same.

CAP.

CAP. XV.

An act for granting certain duties in the Britiſh *colonies and plantations in* America; *for continuing, amending, and making perpetual, an act paſſed in the ſixth year of the reign of his late majeſty King* George *the Second, (intituled,* An act for the better ſecuring and encouraging the trade of his Majeſty's ſugar colonies in *America*;) *for applying the produce of ſuch duties, and of the duties to ariſe by virtue of the ſaid act, towards defraying the expences of defending, protecting, and ſecuring the ſaid colonies and plantations; for explaining an act made in the twenty fifth year of the reign of King* Charles *the Second, (intituled,* An act for the encouragement of the *Greenland* and *Eaſtland* trades, and for the better ſecuring the plantation trade;) *and for altering and diſallowing ſeveral drawbacks on exports from this kingdom, and more effectually preventing the clandeſtine conveyance of goods to and from the ſaid colonies and plantations, and improving and ſecuring the trade between the ſame and* Great Britain.

Preamble.

WHEREAS *it is expedient that new proviſions and regulations ſhould be eſtabliſhed for improving the revenue of this kingdom, and for extending and ſecuring the navigation and commerce between* Great Britain *and your Majeſty's dominions in* America, *which, by the peace, have been ſo happily enlarged: and whereas it is juſt and neceſſary, that a revenue be raiſed, in your Majeſty's ſaid dominions in* America, *for defraying the expences of defending, protecting, and ſecuring the ſame; we, your Majeſty's moſt dutiful and loyal ſubjects, the commons of* Great Britain, *in parliament aſſembled, being deſirous to make ſome proviſion, in this preſent ſeſſion of parliament, towards raiſing the ſaid revenue in* America, *have reſolved to give and grant unto your Majeſty the ſeveral rates and duties herein after-mentioned*; and do moſt humbly beſeech your Majeſty that it may be enacted; and be it enacted by the King's moſt excellent majeſty, by and with the advice and conſent of the lords ſpiritual and temporal, and commons, in this preſent parliament aſſembled, and by the authority of the ſame, That from and after the twenty ninth day of *September*, one thouſand ſeven hundred and ſixty four, there ſhall be raiſed, levied, collected, and paid, unto his Majeſty, his heirs and ſucceſſors, for and upon all white or clayed ſugars of the produce or manufacture of any colony or plantation in *America*, not under the dominion of his Majeſty, his heirs and ſucceſſors; for and upon indico, and coffee of foreign produce or manufacture; for and upon all wines (except *French* wine;) for and upon all wrought ſilks, bengals, and ſtuffs, mixed with ſilk or herba, of the manufacture

From and after 29 Sept. 1764, the following rates and duties to take place on the ſeveral ſpecies of foreign goods here enumerated, imported into any of his Majeſty's plantations in America;

nufacture of *Persia*, *China*, or *East India*, and all callico painted, dyed, printed, or stained there; and for and upon all foreign linen cloth called *Cambrick* and *French Lawns*, which shall be imported or brought into any colony or plantation in *America*, which now is, or hereafter may be, under the dominion of his Majesty, his heirs and successors, the several rates and duties following; that is to say,

On foreign white or clayed sugars, 1 l. 2 s. per C. wt. For every hundred weight avoirdupois of such foreign white or clayed sugars, one pound, two shillings, over and above all other duties imposed by any former act of parliament.

Indico 6 d. per lb. For every pound weight avoirdupois of such foreign indico, six pence.

Coffee 2 l. 19 s. 9 d. per C. wt. For every hundred weight avoirdupois of such foreign coffee, which shall be imported from any place, except *Great Britain*, two pounds, nineteen shillings, and nine pence.

Madeira wines 7 l. per ton. For every ton of wine of the growth of the *Madeiras*, or of any other island or place from whence such wine may be lawfully imported, and which shall be so imported from such islands or places, the sum of seven pounds.

Portugal and Spanish wines 10 s. per ton. For every ton of *Portugal*, *Spanish*, or any other wine (except *French* wine) imported from *Great Britain*, the sum of ten shillings.

Wrought silks, bengals, and stuffs, mixt with silk or herba, 2 s. per lb. For every pound weight avoirdupois of wrought silks, bengals, and stuffs, mixed with silk or herba, of the manufacture of *Persia*, *China*, or *East India*, imported from *Great Britain*, two shillings.

Callicoes 2 s. 6 d. per piece. For every piece of callico painted, dyed, printed, or stained, in *Persia*, *China*, or *East India*, imported from *Great Britain*, two shillings and six pence.

Cambricks 3 s. per piece. For every piece of foreign linen cloth, called *Cambrick*, imported from *Great Britain*, three shillings.

French lawns 3 s. per piece. For every piece of *French* lawn imported from *Great Britain*, three shillings.

And after those rates for any greater or lesser quantity of such goods respectively.

Duties on coffee and pimento of the growth of the British colonies, imported from thence to other places, except Great Britain, viz. II. And it is hereby further enacted by the authority aforesaid, That from and after the said twenty ninth day of *September*, one thousand seven hundred and sixty four, there shall also be raised, levied, collected, and paid, unto his Majesty, his heirs and successors, for and upon all coffee and pimento of the growth and produce of any *British* colony or plantation in *America*, which shall be there laden on board any *British* ship or vessel, to be carried out from thence to any other place whatsoever, except *Great Britain*, the several rates and duties following; that is to say,

Coffee 7 s. per C. wt. III. For every hundred weight avoirdupois of such *British* coffee, seven shillings.

Pimento 2 q. per lb. For every pound weight avoirdupois of such *British* pimento, one halfpenny.

And after thoſe rates for any greater or leſſer quantity of ſuch goods reſpectively.

IV. And whereas an act was made in the ſixth year of the reign of his late majeſty King *George* the Second, intituled, *An act for the better ſecuring and encouraging the trade of his Majeſty's ſugar colonies in* America, which was to continue in force for five years, to be computed from the twenty fourth day of *June*, one thouſand ſeven hundred and thirty three, and to the end of the then next ſeſſion of parliament, and which, by ſeveral ſubſequent acts made in the eleventh, the nineteenth, the twenty ſixth, and twenty ninth, and the thirty firſt years of the reign of his ſaid late Majeſty, was, from time to time, continued; and, by an act made in the firſt year of the reign of his preſent Majeſty, was further continued until the end of this preſent ſeſſion of parliament; and although the ſaid act hath been found in ſome degree uſeful, yet it is highly expedient that the ſame ſhould be altered, enforced, and made more effectual; but, in conſideration of the great diſtance of ſeveral of the ſaid colonies and plantations from this kingdom, it will be proper further to continue the ſaid act for a ſhort ſpace, before any alterations and amendments ſhall take effect, in order that all perſons concerned may have due and proper notice thereof; be it therefore enacted by the authority aforeſaid, That the ſaid act made in the ſixth year of the reign of his late majeſty King *George* the Second, intituled, *An act for the better ſecuring and encouraging the trade of his Majeſty's ſugar colonies in* America, ſhall be, and the ſame is hereby further continued, until the thirtieth day of *September*, one thouſand ſeven hundred and ſixty four.

Act 6 Geo. II. further continued to 30 Sept. 1764.

V. And be it further enacted by the authority aforeſaid, That from the twenty ninth day of *September*, one thouſand ſeven hundred and ſixty four, the ſaid act, ſubject to ſuch alterations and amendments as are herein after contained, ſhall be, and the ſame is hereby made perpetual.

The ſaid act made perpetual, ſubject to the alterations made herein.

VI. And be it further enacted by the authority aforeſaid, That in lieu and inſtead of the rate and duty impoſed by the ſaid act upon melaſſes and ſyrups, there ſhall, from and after the ſaid twenty ninth day of *September*, one thouſand ſeven hundred and ſixty four, be raiſed, levied, collected, and paid, unto his Majeſty, his heirs and ſucceſſors, for and upon every gallon of melaſſes or ſyrups, being the growth, product, or manufacture, of any colony or plantation in *America*, not under the dominion of his Majeſty, his heirs or ſucceſſors, which ſhall be imported or brought into any colony or plantation in *America*, which now is, or hereafter may be, under the dominion of his Majeſty, his heirs or ſucceſſors, the ſum of three pence.

Foreign melaſſes and ſyrups imported into the Britiſh colonies to pay 3d. per gallon.

VII. And it is hereby further enacted by the authority aforeſaid, That the ſaid rates and duties hereby charged upon ſuch foreign white or clayed ſugars, foreign indico, foreign coffee, wines, wrought ſilks, bengals, and ſtuffs, mixed with ſilk or herba, callico, cambricks, *French* lawns, and foreign melaſſes or ſyrups, imported into any *Britiſh American* colony or plantation,

The duties on the enumerated goods here mentioned to be raiſed and paid as by the recited act of 6 Geo. II.

ſhall be raiſed, levied, collected, and paid, in the ſame manner and form, and by ſuch rules, ways, and means, and under ſuch penalties and forfeitures (not otherwiſe altered by this act) as are mentioned and expreſſed in the ſaid act of parliament, made in the ſixth year of the reign of his late majeſty King *George* the Second, with reſpect to the raiſing, levying, collecting, and payment, of the rates and duties thereby granted; and that the aforeſaid duties hereby charged upon *Britiſh* coffee and pimento, exported from any *Britiſh* colony or plantation, ſhall be raiſed, levied, collected, and paid, in the ſame manner and form, and by ſuch rules, ways, and means, and under ſuch penalties and forfeitures, as are mentioned and referred unto in an act of parliament, made in the twenty fifth year of the reign of King *Charles* the Second, intituled, *An act for the encouragement of the* Greenland *and* Eaſtland *trades, and for the better ſecuring the plantation trade*, with reſpect to the raiſing, levying, collecting, and payment, of the rates and duties thereby granted upon the ſeveral goods therein particularly enumerated: and that all powers, penalties, proviſions, articles, and clauſes, in thoſe acts reſpectively contained and referred unto (except in ſuch caſes where any alteration is made by this act) ſhall be obſerved, applied, practiſed, and put in execution, for the raiſing, levying, collecting, and anſwering, the reſpective rates and duties granted by this act, as fully and effectually, as if the ſame were particularly and at large re-enacted in the body of this preſent act, and applied to the rates and duties hereby impoſed; and as fully and effectually, to all intents and purpoſes, as the ſame could have been at any time put in execution, for the like purpoſes, with reſpect to the rates and duties granted by the ſaid former acts.

Thoſe upon coffee and pimento, as by act 25 Car. II.

VIII. Provided always, and it is hereby further enacted by the authority aforeſaid, That if the importer of any wines ſhall refuſe to pay the duties hereby impoſed thereon, it ſhall and may be lawful for the collector, or other proper officer of the cuſtoms where ſuch wines ſhall be imported, and he is hereby reſpectively required to take and ſecure the ſame, with the caſks or other package thereof, and to cauſe the ſame to be publickly ſold, within the ſpace of twenty days at the moſt after ſuch refuſal made, and at ſuch time and place as ſuch officer, ſhall, by four or more days publick notice, appoint for that purpoſe; which wine ſhall be ſold to the beſt bidder, and the money ariſing by the ſale thereof ſhall be applied, in the firſt place, in payment of the ſaid duties, together with the charges that ſhall have been occaſioned by the ſaid ſale; and the overplus, if any, ſhall be paid to ſuch importer, or any other perſon authorized to receive the ſame.

Importer refuſing to pay the duties on wines, officer may ſeize the ſame, and publickly ſell them to the beſt bidder, and deduct the duties and charges.

IX. Provided alſo, That if the money offered for the purchaſe of ſuch wine, ſhall not be ſufficient to diſcharge the duty and charges aforeſaid, then, and in every ſuch caſe, the collector, or other proper officer, ſhall cauſe the wine to be ſtaved, ſpilt, or otherwiſe deſtroyed, and ſhall return the caſks or other package wherein the ſame was contained to ſuch importer.

If they ſhall not bring ſufficient to pay the duty and charges, they are to be ſtaved and ſpilt.

X. And

X. And it is hereby declared and enacted, That every piece of callico intended to be charged with the duty herein before-mentioned, if of the breadth of one yard and a quarter or under, shall not exceed in length ten yards; and if above that breadth, shall not exceed six yards in length; and that every piece of cambrick and *French* lawn shall contain thirteen ells each, and shall pay duty for the same in those proportions for any greater or lesser quantity, according to the sum herein before charged upon each piece of such goods respectively.

Limited length and breadth of callicoes, and of cambricks, and French lawns.

XI. And it is hereby further enacted by the authority aforesaid, That all the monies which, from and after the twenty ninth day of *September*, one thousand seven hundred and sixty four, shall arise by the several rates and duties herein before granted; and also by the duties which, from and after the said twenty ninth day of *September*, one thousand seven hundred and sixty four, shall be raised upon sugars and paneles, by virtue of the said act made in the sixth year of the reign of his said late majesty King *George* the Second (except the necessary charges of raising, collecting, levying, recovering, answering, paying, and accounting for the same) shall be paid into the receipt of his Majesty's Exchequer, and shall be entered separate and apart from all other monies paid or payable to his Majesty, his heirs or successors: and shall be there reserved, to be, from time to time, disposed of by parliament, towards defraying the necessary expences of defending, protecting, and securing, the *British* colonies and plantations in *America*.

Monies arising by the several duties before granted; and upon sugars, &c. to be paid into the Exchequer; and to be reserved towards defraying the charges of protecting the British colonies in America.

XII. And it is hereby further enacted by the authority aforesaid, That from and after the tenth day of *September*, one thousand seven hundred and sixty four, upon the exportation of any sort of wine (except *French* wines) from this kingdom to any *British* colony or plantation in *America*, as merchandize, the exporter shall be paid, in lieu of all former drawbacks, a drawback or allowance of all the duties paid upon the importation of such wine, except the sum of three pounds ten shillings *per* ton, part of the additional duty of four pounds *per* ton, granted by an act made in the last session of parliament (intituled, *An act for granting to his Majesty several additional duties upon wines imported into this kingdom, and certain duties upon all cyder and perry, and for raising the sum of three millions five hundred thousand pounds, by way of annuities and lotteries, to be charged on the said duties)* and also except such part of the duties paid upon wines imported by strangers or aliens, or in foreign ships, as exceeds what would have been payable upon such wines, if the same had been imported by *British* subjects and in *British* ships; any law, custom, or usage, to the contrary notwithstanding; which drawback or allowance shall be made in such manner, and under such rules, regulations, penalties, and forfeitures, in all respects, as any former drawback or allowance, payable out of the duties of customs upon the exportation of such wine, was, could, or might be made, before the passing of this act.

Exporter of wines from this kingdom to the British colonies in America, to be paid a drawback of the duties on importation; except 3 l. 10s. per ton granted by an act of the last session; and also the aliens duty:

He firſt giving bond and ſecurity

XIII. Provided always, and it is hereby further enacted, That upon the entry of any ſuch wine for exportation to any *Britiſh* colony or plantation in *America*, and before any debenture ſhall be made out for allowing the drawback thereon, the exporter ſhall give bond, with ſufficient ſecurity, to his Majeſty, his heirs and ſucceſſors, to be approved of by the collector, or other principal officer of the cuſtoms at the port of exportation, in treble the amount of the drawback payable for the goods, that the

for the due exportation and landing of the ſame;

ſame, and every part thereof, ſhall (the dangers of the ſeas and enemies excepted) be really and truly exported to, and landed in, ſome *Britiſh* colony or plantation in *America*, and that the ſame ſhall not be exported, or carried to any other place or country whatſoever, nor relanded in any part of *Great Britain*,

conditioned to produce a certificate thereof from the proper officer, within 18 months.

Ireland, or the iſlands of *Guernſey*, *Jerſey*, *Alderney*, *Sark*, or *Man*, or either of them: and ſuch bonds ſhall not be delivered up nor diſcharged, until a certificate ſhall be produced, under the hands and ſeals of the collector or other principal officer of the cuſtoms at the port or place where ſuch goods ſhall be landed, teſtifying the landing thereof: and the condition of ſuch bond ſhall be, to produce ſuch certificate in eighteen months from the date of the

No part of the old ſubſidy to be repaid for any foreign goods exported as aforeſaid;

bonds (the dangers of the ſeas and enemies excepted.) And it is hereby further enacted by the authority aforeſaid, That from and after the firſt day of *May*, one thouſand ſeven hundred and ſixty four, no part of the rate or duty, commonly called *The old ſubſidy*, ſhall be repaid or drawn back for any foreign goods of the growth, production, or manufacture, of *Europe*, or the

except for wines, white callicoes, and muſlins:

Eaſt Indies, which ſhall be exported from this kingdom to any *Britiſh* colony or plantation in *America* (wines, white callicoes, and muſlins, only excepted;) any law, cuſtom, or uſage, to the contrary notwithſtanding.

And upon the exportation of white callicoes or muſlins, neither the moiety of the old ſubſidy, nor the third part of the net duties thereon, granted by

XIV. And it is hereby further enacted by the authority aforeſaid, That from and after the tenth day of *September*, one thouſand ſeven hundred and ſixty four, upon the exportation of any ſort of white callicoes or muſlins, except as herein after is mentioned, from this kingdom to any *Britiſh* colony or plantation in *America*, beſides the one half of the rate or duty commonly called *The old ſubſidy*, which now remains, and is not drawn back for the ſame, there alſo ſhall not be repaid or drawn back the further ſum of four pounds fifteen ſhillings for every hundred pounds of the true and real value of ſuch goods, according to the groſs price at which they were ſold at the ſale of the united company of merchants trading to the *Eaſt Indies*, being the third part of the net duties granted thereon reſpectively

Act 11 and 12 Will. III.

by two ſeveral acts of parliament, the one made in the eleventh and twelfth year of the reign of King *William* the Third, intituled, *An act for laying further duties upon wrought ſilks, muſlins, and ſome other commodities of the* Eaſt Indies, *and for enlarging the*

and 3 and 4 Annæ, ſhall be repaid;

time for purchaſing certain reverſionary annuities therein mentioned; and the other made in the third and fourth year of the reign of Queen *Anne*, intituled, *An act for continuing duties upon low wines, and upon coffee, tea, chocolate, ſpices, and pictures, and upon hawkers, pedlars,*

pedlars, and petty chapmen, and upon muslins; *and for granting new duties upon several of the said commodities, and also upon callicoes, China-ware, and drugs*; any law, custom, or usage to the contrary notwithstanding.

XV. Provided always, and be it further enacted by the authority aforesaid, That until the first day of *March*, one thousand seven hundred and sixty five, upon the exportation from this kingdom, to any *British* colony or plantation in *America*, of such white callicoes or muslins only as were sold on or before the twenty fifth day of *March*, one thousand seven hundred and sixty four, at the sale of the united company of merchants trading to the *East Indies*, such and the same drawbacks shall be allowed as are now payable upon the exportation of the said goods.

but until 1 March, 1765, upon exportation of such white callicoes and muslins as were sold on or before 25 March preceding, at the India House, the same drawbacks shall be allowed as are now payable.

XVI. And be it further enacted by the authority aforesaid, That if any merchant or other person shall, from and after the said first day of *May*, one thousand seven hundred and sixty four, enter any goods for exportation to parts beyond the seas, other than to the said *British* colonies or plantations in *America*, in order to obtain any drawback not allowed by this act upon the exportation of such goods to the said *British* colonies or plantations, and the said goods shall nevertheless be carried to any *British* colony or plantation in *America*, and landed there, contrary to the true intent and meaning hereof, that then, and in such case, the drawback shall be forfeited, and the exporter of such goods, and the master of the ship or vessel on board which the same were loaden and exported, shall forfeit double the amount of the drawback paid or to be paid for the same, and also treble the value of the said goods.

Where goods entered for exportation to parts beyond the seas, in order to obtain a drawback not allowed by this act, shall be carried to any British plantation in America, such drawback shall be forfeited, and double the amount thereof; with treble the value of the goods.

XVII. And it is further enacted by the authority aforesaid, That from and after the said first day of *May*, one thousand seven hundred and sixty four, if any goods, not allowed to draw back any part of the old subsidy, or any other duty by this act, shall be entered for exportation from this kingdom to any other place beyond the seas, except to some *British* colony or plantation in *America*, in every case where the exporter is required, by any law now in force, to swear that such goods are not landed or intended to be landed in *Great Britain*, *Ireland*, or the isle of *Man*, there shall also be added to, and included in, the oath upon the debenture for such goods, "*any* British *colonies or plantations in* America."

Addition to the oath upon debentures, for such goods as shall be entered for exportation to other places beyond the seas, than to the British American plantations.

XVIII. And be it further enacted by the authority aforesaid, That from and after the twenty ninth day of *September*, one thousand seven hundred and sixty four, no rum or spirits of the produce or manufacture of any of the colonies or plantations in *America*, not in the possession or under the dominion of his Majesty, his heirs or successors, shall be imported or brought into any of the colonies or plantations in *America* which now are, or hereafter may be, in the possession or under the dominion of his

Foreign rum or spirits imported into any of the British plantations in America, liable to be forfeited, together with vessel, &c.

Majesty, his heirs or successors, upon forfeiture of all such rum or spirits, together with the ship or vessel in which the same shall be imported, with the tackle, apparel, and furniture thereof; to be seized by any officer or officers of his Majesty's customs, and prosecuted in such manner and form as herein after is expressed; any law, custom, or usage, to the contrary notwithstanding.

No sugars may be imported into Ireland, but such as shall be shipped in Great Britain, and carried directly from thence.

XIX. And it is hereby further enacted and declared by the authority aforesaid, That from and after the twenty ninth day of *September*, one thousand seven hundred and sixty four, nothing in the before-recited act made in the sixth year of the reign of his late majesty King *George* the Second, or any other act of parliament, shall extend, or be construed to extend, to give liberty to any person or persons whatsoever to import into the kingdom of *Ireland*, any sort of sugars, but such only as shall be fairly and *bona fide* loaden and shipped in *Great Britain*, and carried directly from thence in ships navigated according to law.

Exporter of rum, spirits, paneles, molasses or syrups, from the British colonies in America, as of the growth thereof, to produce and deliver to the proper officer before clearing, an affidavit of the quality of the goods, and denomination of the packages, &c.

XX. And, for the better preventing frauds in the importation of foreign sugars and paneles, rum and spirits, molasses and syrups, into any of his Majesty's dominions, under pretence that the same are the growth, produce, or manufacture, of the *British* colonies or plantations, it is further enacted by the authority aforesaid, That from and after the twenty ninth day of *September*, one thousand seven hundred and sixty four, every person or persons loading on board any ship or vessel, in any of the *British* colonies or plantations in *America*, any rum or spirits, sugars or paneles, molasses or syrups, as of the growth, product, or manufacture, of any *British* colony or plantation, shall, before the clearing out of the said ship or vessel, produce and deliver to the collector or other principal officer of the customs at the loading port, an affidavit signed and sworn to before some justice of the peace in the said *British* colonies or plantations, either by the grower, maker, or shipper, of such goods, or his or their known agent or factor, expressing, in words at length and not in figures, the quality of the goods so shipped, with the number and denomination of the packages, and describing the name or names of the plantation or plantations, and the name of the colony where the same grew or were produced and manufactured; which affidavit shall be attested, under the hand of the said justice of the peace, to have been sworn to in his presence; who is hereby required to do the same without fee or reward: and the collector or other principal officer of the customs to whom such affidavit shall be delivered, shall thereupon grant to the master, or other person having the charge of the ship or vessel, a certificate under his hand and seal of office (without fee or reward) of his having received such affidavit pursuant to the directions of this act; which certificate shall express the quality of the goods shipped on board such ship or vessel, with the number and denomination of the packages: and such collector or other principal officer of the customs shall also (without fee or reward) within thirty days after the sailing of the ship or vessel, transmit an exact copy of the said affidavit to the secretary's of-

Officer to grant the master of the vessel a certificate thereof;

and to transmit a copy of such affidavit to the secretary's office

fice for the reſpective colony or plantation where the goods were ſhipped, on forfeiture of five pounds.

for the colony, on penalty of 5 l.

XXI. And it is further enacted, That upon the arrival of ſuch ſhip or veſſel into the port of her diſcharge, either in *Great Britain* or any other port of his Majeſty's dominions, where ſuch goods may be lawfully imported, the maſter or other perſon taking the charge of the ſhip or veſſel ſhall, at the time he makes his report of his cargo, deliver the ſaid certificate to the collector or other principal officer of the cuſtoms, and make oath before him, that the goods ſo reported are the ſame that are mentioned in the ſaid certificate, on forfeiture of one hundred pounds; and if any rum or ſpirits, ſugars or paneles, molaſſes or ſyrups, ſhall be imported or found on board any ſuch ſhip or veſſel, for which no ſuch certificate ſhall be produced, or which ſhall not agree therewith, the ſame ſhall be deemed and taken to be foreign rum and ſpirits, ſugar and paneles, molaſſes and ſyrups, and ſhall be liable to the ſame duties, reſtrictions, regulations, penalties, and forfeitures, in all reſpects, as rum, ſpirits, ſugar, paneles, molaſſes, and ſyrups, of the growth, produce, or manufacture, of any foreign colony or plantation, would reſpectively be liable to by law.

On arrival of the veſſel at the port of diſcharge, the maſter is to deliver the certificate to the proper officer, and make oath of the identity of the goods, on penalty of 100 l.

and goods found on board not certified for, &c. are to pay foreign duties.

XXII. Provided always, That if any rum or ſpirits, ſugar or paneles, molaſſes or ſyrups, ſhall be imported into *Great Britain* from any *Britiſh* colony or plantation in *America*, without being included in ſuch certificate as is herein before directed, and it ſhall be made to appear, to the ſatisfaction of the commiſſioners of his Majeſty's cuſtoms at *London* or *Edinburgh* reſpectively, that the goods are really and truly the produce of ſuch *Britiſh* plantation or colony, and that no fraud was intended, it ſhall and may in ſuch caſe be lawful for the ſaid reſpective commiſſioners to permit the ſaid goods to be entered, upon payment of the like duties as ſuch goods would be liable to if this law had not been made.

Where any ſuch goods, not included in the certificate, ſhall be imported without intending a fraud, they may be admitted to entry, paying the uſual duties.

XXIII. And whereas by an act of parliament made in the twelfth year of the reign of King *Charles* the Second, intituled, *An act for encouraging and increaſing of ſhipping and navigation*, and ſeveral ſubſequent acts of parliament which are now in force, it is, amongſt other things, directed, that for every ſhip or veſſel that ſhall load any commodities, in thoſe acts particularly enumerated, at any *Britiſh* plantation, being the growth, product, or manufacture thereof, bonds ſhall be given with one ſurety, to the value of one thouſand pounds, if the ſhip be of leſs burthen than one hundred tons, and of the ſum of two thouſand pounds; if the ſhip be of greater burthen, that the ſame commodities ſhall be brought by ſuch ſhip or veſſel to ſome other *Britiſh* plantation, or to ſome port in *Great Britain*; notwithſtanding which, there is great reaſon to apprehend ſuch goods are frequently carried to foreign parts, and landed there: and whereas great quantities of foreign molaſſes and ſyrups are clandeſtinely run on ſhore in the *Britiſh* colonies, to the prejudice of the revenue, and the great detriment of the trade of this kingdom, and it's *American* plantations: to remedy which practices for the future, be it further enacted

Clauſe in act 12 Car. II.

Bond and security to be given pursuant to the recited act, in case of lading any enumerated goods, that any foreign molasses and syrups, on board, shall be brought to some of the British plantations in America, or to Great Britain; of which report is to be made at the port of arrival.

enacted by the authority aforesaid, That from and after the twenty ninth day of *September*, one thousand seven hundred and sixty four, bond and security, in the like penalty, shall also be given to the collector or other principal officer of the customs at any port or place in any of the *British American* colonies or plantations, with one surety besides the master of every ship or vessel that shall lade or take on board there any goods not particularly enumerated in the said acts, being the product or manufacture of any of the said colonies or plantations, with condition, that, in case any molasses or syrups, being the produce of any of the plantations, not under the dominion of his Majesty, his heirs or successors, shall be laden on board such ship or vessel, the same shall (the danger of the seas and enemies excepted) be brought, without fraud or wilful diminution, by the said ship or vessel to some of his Majesty's colonies or plantations in *America*, or to some port in *Great Britain*; and that the master or other person having the charge of such ship or vessel, shall, immediately upon his arrival at every port or place in *Great Britain*, or in the *British American* colonies and plantations, make a just and true report of all the goods laden on board such ship or vessel under their true and proper denominations; and if any such non-enumerated goods shall be laden on board any such ship or vessel before such bond shall be given, the goods so laden together with the ship or vessel and her furniture shall be forfeited, and shall and may be seized by any officer of the customs, and prosecuted in the manner herein after directed.

Non-enumerated goods laden on board without bond given, are forfeited, with the vessel.

Master before sailing from the port of lading, is to take a certificate of his having given bond;

XXIV. And it is hereby further enacted by the authority aforesaid, That every master or person having the charge of any ship or vessel shall, before he departs from any *British* colony or plantation where he receives his lading, take a certificate under the hands and seals of the collector or other principal officer of the customs there (which certificate such officers are hereby required to grant without fee or reward) that bond hath been given, pursuant to the directions of this or any other act of parliament, as the case shall require; and the master or person having the charge of such ship or vessel, shall keep such certificate in his custody till the voyage is compleated, and shall then deliver the same up to the collector or other chief officer of the customs at the port or place where he shall discharge his lading, either in *Great Britain* or any *British American* colony or plantation, on forfeiture of one hundred pounds for each and every offence.

which, upon compleating his voyage, he is to deliver up at the port of discharge, on penalty of 100 l.

British vessels with any British American goods, or foreign molasses or syrups, discovered near the British American coasts, not producing a certificate

XXV. And it is hereby further enacted, That if any *British* ship or vessel laden, as aforesaid, with any goods of the produce or manufacture of any *British* colony or plantation in *America*, or having on board any molasses or syrups the produce of any foreign colony or plantation, shall be discovered by any officer of his Majesty's customs within two leagues of the shore of any *British* colony or plantation in *America*, and the master or person taking charge of such ship or vessel shall not produce a certificate that bond has been given, pursuant to the directions of this or any other act of parliament, as the case may require; or if if he ſhall not produce ſuch certificate to the collector or other chief officer of the cuſtoms where he ſhall arive, either in *Great Britain* or any *Britiſh American* colony or plantation, ſuch ſhip or veſſel, with her tackle, apparel, and furniture, and all the goods therein laden, ſhall be forfeited, and ſhall and may be ſeized and proſecuted as herein after is directed.

as required by law; or not producing one at the port of arrival, are liable to be forfeited.

XXVI. And it is hereby further enacted by the authority aforeſaid, That the ſaid bond directed to be given by this act, with reſpect to ſuch non-enumerated goods, ſhall continue in force for one year from and after the completion of the voyage; and in caſe no fraud ſhall appear within that time, it ſhall be lawful for the commiſſioners of his Majeſty's cuſtoms, or any four or more of them, to direct the ſaid bond to be delivered up.

Bond for non-enumerated goods to be in force for 1 year after the voyage; when, if no fraud appear, it is to be given up.

XXVII. And it is hereby further enacted by the authority aforeſaid, That from and after the twenty ninth day of *September*, one thouſand ſeven hundred and ſixty four, all coffee, pimento, cocoa nuts, whale fins, raw ſilk, hides, and ſkins, pot and pearl aſhes, of the growth, production, or manufacture, of any *Britiſh* colony or plantation in *America*, ſhall be imported directly from thence into this kingdom, or ſome other *Britiſh* colony or plantation, under the like ſecurities, penalties, and forfeitures, as are particularly mentioned in two acts of parliament made in the twelfth and twenty fifth years of the reign of King *Charles* the Second, the former intituled, *An act for the encouraging and increaſing of ſhipping and navigation*, and the latter intituled, *An act for the encouragement of the* Greenland *and eaſt-land trades, and for the better ſecuring the plantation trade*, or either of them, with reſpect to the goods in thoſe acts particularly enumerated; any law, cuſtom, or uſage, to the contrary notwithſtanding.

Coffee, and other enumerated goods of the Britiſh American plantations, to be imported under like ſecurities and penalties, as thoſe in acts 12 & 25 Car. II.

XXVIII. And it is hereby further enacted by the authority aforeſaid, That from and after the twenty ninth day of *September*, one thouſand ſeven hundred and ſixty four, no iron, nor any ſort of wood, commonly called *Lumber*, as ſpecified in an act paſſed in the eighth year of the reign of King *George* the Firſt, intituled, *An act for giving further encouragement for the importation of naval ſtores, and for other purpoſes therein mentioned*, of the growth, production, or manufacture, of any *Britiſh* colony or plantation in *America*, ſhall be there loaden on board any ſhip or veſſel to be carried from thence, until ſufficient bond ſhall be given, with one ſurety beſides the maſter of the veſſel, to the collector or other principal officer of the cuſtoms at the loading port, in a penalty of double the value of the goods, with condition, that the ſaid goods ſhall not be landed in any part of *Europe* except *Great Britain*; which bonds ſhall be diſcharged in the manner hereafter mentioned; that is to ſay, for ſuch of the ſaid goods as ſhall be entered for, or landed in, *Great Britain*, the condition of the bonds ſhall be, to bring a certificate in diſcharge thereof within eighteen months from the date of the bond; and within ſix months for ſuch of the ſaid goods as ſhall be entered for, or landed in, any of the *Britiſh* colonies or plantations

Bond and ſecurity to be given before lading any iron or lumber of the Britiſh American plantations,

condition to land the ſame, if for Europe, in Great Britain; and to produce a certificate thereof within 18 months; and if for any of the Britiſh American plantations, within 6 months;

tations in *America*; which refpective certificates fhall be under the hands and feals of the collector or other principal officer of the cuftoms refident at the port or place where fuch goods fhall be landed, teftifying the landing thereof; and for fuch of the faid goods as fhall be entered for, or landed at, any other place in *America*, *Africa*, or *Afia*, to bring the like certificate within twelve months, under the common feal of the chief magiftrate, or under the hands and feals of two known *Britifh* merchants refiding there; or fuch bond or bonds fhall be difcharged, in either of the faid cafes, by proof upon oath made by credible perfons, that the faid goods were taken by enemies, or perifhed in the feas.

and if for any other place in America, Africa, or Afia, within 12 months.

Where the goods perifh, or are taken, the bond is difcharged.

XXIX. And, for the better preventing frauds in the importation or exportation of goods that are liable to the payment of duties, or are prohibited, in the *Britifh* colonies or plantations in *America*, it is further enacted by the authority aforefaid, That from and after the twenty ninth day of *September*, one thoufand feven hundred and fixty four, no goods, wares, or merchandizes, of any kind whatfoever, fhall be fhipped or laden on board any fhip or veffel in any of the *Britifh* colonies or plantations in *America*, to be carried from thence to any other *Britifh* colony or plantation, without a fufferance or warrant firft had and obtained from the collector or other proper officer of the cuftoms at the port or place where fuch goods fhall be intended to be put on board; and the mafter of every fuch fhip or veffel fhall, before the fame be removed or carried out from the port or place where he takes in his lading, take out a cocket or cockets expreffing the quantity and quality of the goods, and marks of the package, fo laden, with the merchants names by whom fhipped and to whom configned; and if they are goods that are liable to the payment of any duty, either upon the importation into, or upon the exportation from, the faid colonies or plantations, the faid cocket or cockets fhall likewife diftinctly fpecify that the duties have been paid for the fame, referring to the times or dates of entry and payment of fuch duties, and by whom they were paid; which cocket or cockets fhall be produced by the mafter of fuch fhip or veffel, to the collector or other principal officer of the cuftoms at the port or place where fuch fhip or veffel fhall arrive in any of the *Britifh* colonies or plantations in *America*, before any part of the goods are unladen or put on fhore: and if any goods or merchandizes fhall be fhipped as aforefaid without fuch fufferance, or the veffel fhall depart and proceed on her voyage without fuch cocket or cockets, or the goods fhall be landed or put on fhore before fuch cocket or cockets are produced at the port or place of difcharge, or if the goods do not agree in all refpects therewith, the goods, in any or either of thofe cafes, fhall be forfeited and loft; and any officer of his Majefty's cuftoms is hereby impowered to ftop any fuch fhip or veffel, bound as aforefaid, which fhall be difcovered within two leagues of the fhore of any of the faid *Britifh* colonies or plantations in *America*, and to feize and take from thence all the goods

No goods to be fhipped in one Britifh colony to be carried to another, without a fufferance;

and taking out a proper cocket;

which is to be produced at the port of difcharge;

on forfeiture of the goods.

Goods alfo to be forfeited if they do not agree with the cocket.

Veffel difcovered near the

goods which ſhall be found on board ſuch ſhip or veſſel for which no ſuch cocket or cockets ſhall be produced to him.

coaſt may be ſtopt; and the goods, for which no cocket is produced, may be ſeized.

XXX. And whereas *Britiſh* veſſels arriving from foreign parts at ſeveral of the out ports of this kingdom, fully or in part laden abroad with goods that are pretended to be deſtined to ſome foreign plantation, do frequently take on board ſome ſmall parcels of goods in this kingdom which are entred outwards for ſome *Britiſh* colony or plantation, and a cocket and clearance thereupon granted for ſuch goods, under cover of which the whole cargoes of ſuch veſſels are clandeſtinely landed in the *Britiſh American* dominions, contrary to ſeveral acts of parliament now in force, to the great prejudice of the trade and revenue of this kingdom; for remedy whereof, be it further enacted by the authority aforeſaid, That from and after the firſt day of *May*, one thouſand ſeven hundred and ſixty four, no ſhip or veſſel ſhall, upon any pretence whatſoever, be cleared outwards from any port of this kingdom, for any land, iſland, plantation, colony, territory, or place, to his Majeſty belonging, or which ſhall hereafter belong unto or be in the poſſeſſion or under the dominion of his Majeſty, his heirs, or ſucceſſors, in *America*, unleſs the whole and entire cargo of ſuch ſhip or veſſel ſhall be *bona fide*, and without fraud, laden and ſhipped in this kingdom; and any officer of his Majeſty's cuſtoms is hereby impowered to ſtop any *Britiſh* ſhip or veſſel arriving from any part of *Europe*, which ſhall be diſcovered within two leagues of the ſhore of any of the ſaid *Britiſh* colonies or plantations in *America*, and to ſeize and take from thence, as forfeited, any goods (except as herein after mentioned) for which the maſter or other perſon taking the charge of ſuch ſhip or veſſel ſhall not produce a cocket or clearance from the collector or proper officer of his Majeſty's cuſtoms, certifying that the ſaid goods were laden on board the ſaid ſhip or veſſel in ſome port of *Great Britain*.

No veſſel to be cleared out for any of the Britiſh colonies in America, unleſs the whole cargo be ſhipped in this kingdom;

and where any European veſſel is diſcovered near ſuch coaſts, the goods for which no ſuch cocket is produced, may be ſeized;

XXXI. Provided always, That this act ſhall not extend, nor be conſtrued to extend, to forfeit, for want of ſuch cocket or clearance, any ſalt laden in *Europe* for the fiſheries in *New England*, *Newfoundland*, *Penſylvania*, *New York*, and *Nova Scotia*, or any other place to which ſalt is or ſhall be allowed by law to be carried; wines laden in the *Madeiras*, of the growth thereof; and wines of the growth of the *Weſtern Iſlands*, or *Azores*, and laden there; nor any horſes, victuals, or linen cloth, of and from *Ireland*, which may be laden on board ſuch ſhips or veſſels.

Salt,

Madeira wines, &c.

Horſes, proviſions, or linens from Ireland, excepted.

XXXII. And it is hereby further enacted, That if any perſon or perſons ſhall counterfeit, raſe, alter, or falſify, any affidavit, certificate, ſufferance, cocket, or clearance, required or directed by this act, or ſhall knowingly or willingly make uſe of any affidavit, certificate, ſufferance, cocket, or clearance, ſo counterfeited, raſed, altered, or falſified, ſuch perſon or perſons ſhall, for every ſuch offence, forfeit the ſum of five hundred pounds; and ſuch affidavit, certificate, ſufferance, cocket, or clearance, ſhall be invalid and of no effect.

Penalty on counterfeiting, &c. any affidavit or certificate, 500 l. &c.

XXXIII. And

Clause in act 9 Geo. 2.

XXXIII. And whereas by an act of parliament, made in the ninth year of the reign of his late majesty King *George* the Second, intituled, *An act for indemnifying persons who have been guilty of offences against the laws made for securing the revenue of customs and excise, and for enforcing those laws for the future*, and by other acts of parliament since made, which are now in force, in order to prevent the clandestine landing of goods in this kingdom from vessels which hover upon the coasts thereof, several goods and vessels, in those laws particularly mentioned and described, are declared to be forfeited, if such vessels are found at anchor, or hovering within two leagues of the shore of this kingdom, without being compelled thereto by necessity or distress of weather; which laws have been found very beneficial to the publick revenue: and whereas, if some provision of that sort was extended to his Majesty's *American* dominions, it may be a means of preventing an illicit trade therewith, and tend to enforce an act made in the twelfth year of the reign of King *Charles* the Second, intituled, *An act for the encouraging and increasing of shipping and navigation*, and another act made in the seventh and eighth years of the reign of King *William* the Third, intituled, *An act for preventing frauds, and regulating abuses in the plantation trade*, so far as those laws do prohibit any goods or commodities to be imported into or exported out of any *British* colony or plantation in *America*, in any foreign ship or vessel; to which end therefore, be it enacted by the authority aforesaid, That from and after the twenty ninth day of *September*, one thousand seven hundred and sixty four, if any foreign ship or vessel whatsoever shall be found at anchor, or hovering within two leagues of the shore of any land, island, plantation, colony, territory, or place, which shall or may be in the possession or under the dominion of his Majesty, his heirs or successors, in *America*, and shall not depart from the coast, and proceed upon her voyage to some foreign port or place, within forty eight hours after the master or other person taking the charge of such ship or vessel shall be required so to do by any officer of his Majesty's customs, unless in case of unavoidable necessity and distress of weather, such ship or vessel, with all the goods therein laden, shall be forfeited and lost, whether bulk shall have been broken or not; and shall and may be seized and prosecuted by any officer of his Majesty's customs, in such manner and form as herein after is expressed.

12 Car. II. and 7 & 8 Will. 3.

Foreign vessels found at anchor, or hovering on the coasts of any of the British American dominions, and not departing, unless distressed, within 48 hours after notice, are liable to be forfeited, together with the goods.

Except French fishing vessels off Newfoundland.

XXXIV. Provided always, That nothing herein contained shall extend, or be construed to extend, to any ship or vessel belonging to the subjects of the *French* king, which shall be found fishing, and not carrying on any illicit trade, on that part of the island of *Newfoundland*, which stretches from the place called *Cape Bonavista* to the northern part of the said island, and from thence running down to the western side, reaches as far as the place called *Point Riche*.

XXXV. And, in order to prevent any illicit trade or commerce between his Majesty's subjects in *America*, and the subjects

jects of the crown of *France* in the islands of *Saint Pierre* and *Miquelon*, it is hereby further enacted by the authority aforesaid, That from and after the twenty ninth day of *September*, one thousand seven hundred and sixty four, if any *British* ship or vessel shall be found standing into, or coming out from, either of those islands, or hovering or at anchor within two leagues of the coasts thereof, or shall be discovered to have taken any goods or merchandizes on board at either of them, or to have been there for that purpose; such ship or vessel, and all the goods so taken on board there, shall be forfeited and lost, and shall and may be seized and prosecuted by any officer of his Majesty's customs; and the master or other person having the charge of such ship or vessel, and every person concerned in taking any such goods on board, shall forfeit treble the value thereof.

British vessels found standing into, or coming out from the isles of St. Pierre and Miquelon, or hovering, &c. on the coasts, or with goods on board from thence, &c. are forfeited, together with the goods; and the master, &c. forfeits also treble value.

XXXVI. And, to prevent the concealing any goods in false packages, or private places, on board any ship or vessel arriving at any of the *British* colonies or plantations in *America*, with intent to their being clandestinely landed there, be it further enacted by the authority aforesaid, That from and after the twenty ninth day of *September*, one thousand seven hundred and sixty four, all goods which shall be found concealed in any place whatsoever on board any such ship or vessel, at any time after the master thereof shall have made his report to the collector or other proper officer of the customs, and which shall not be comprized or mentioned in the said report, shall be forfeited and lost, and shall and may be seized and prosecuted by any officer of the customs; and the master or other person having the charge or command of such ship or vessel (in case it can be made appear, that he was any wise consenting or privy to such fraud or concealment) shall forfeit treble the value of the goods so found.

Concealed goods found on board, after report made by the master, and not comprised in his report, are forfeited; and the master, being privy to the fraud, forfeits treble the value.

XXXVII. And it is hereby further enacted by the authority aforesaid, That from and after the twenty ninth day of *September*, one thousand seven hundred and sixty four, if any goods or merchandizes whatsoever, liable to the payment of duties in any *British* colony or plantation in *America* by this or any other act of parliament, shall be loaden on board any ship or vessel outward bound, or shall be unshipped or landed from any ship or vessel inward bound, before the respective duties due thereon are paid, agreeable to law; or if any prohibited goods whatsoever shall be imported into, or exported out of, any of the said colonies or plantations, contrary to the true intent and meaning of this or any other act of parliament; every person who shall be assisting, or otherwise concerned, either in the loading outwards, or in the unshipping or landing inwards, such goods, or to whose hands the same shall knowingly come after the loading or unshipping thereof, shall, for each and every offence, forfeit treble the value of such goods, to be estimated and computed according to the best price that each respective commodity bears at

If customed goods be either laden on board, or landed, before the duties are paid, or prohibited goods be imported into, or exported out of, any of the British colonies in America, the persons concerned therein forfeit treble the value;

at the place where such offence was committed; and all the boats, horses, cattle, and other carriages whatsoever, made use of in the loading, landing, removing, carriage, or conveyance, of any of the aforesaid goods, shall also be forfeited and lost, and shall and may be seized and prosecuted, by any officer of his Majesty's customs, as herein after mentioned.

together with the boats, carriages, and cattle employed.

XXXVIII. And it is hereby further enacted by the authority aforesaid, That from and after the twenty ninth day of *September*, one thousand seven hundred and sixty four, if any officer of his Majesty's customs shall, directly or indirectly, take or receive any bribe, recompence, or reward, in any kind whatsoever; or connive at any false entry, or make any collusive seizure or agreement; or do any other act or deed whatsoever by which his Majesty, his heirs or successors, shall or may be defrauded in his or their duties, or whereby any goods prohibited shall be suffered to pass either inwards or outwards, or whereby the forfeitures and penalties inflicted by this or any other act of parliament relating to his Majesty's customs in *America* may be evaded; every such officer therein offending shall, for each and every offence, forfeit the sum of five hundred pounds, and be rendered incapable of serving his Majesty in any office or employment civil or military: and if any person or persons whatsoever shall give, offer, or promise to give, any bribe, recompence, or reward, to any officer of the customs, to do, conceal, or connive at, any act, whereby any of the provisions made by this or any other act of parliament relating to his Majesty's customs in *America* may be evaded or broken, every such person or persons shall, for each and every such offence (whether the same offer, proposal, or promise, be accepted or performed, or not) forfeit the sum of fifty pounds.

Officer receiving any bribe, &c. conniving at a false entry; making a collusive seizure; or guilty of other fraud in his office; forfeits 500l. and is disabled: And persons giving, or promising, any bribe, &c. to such officer, in order to betray his trust, forfeit 50l.

XXXIX. And whereas by an act of parliament made in the seventh and eighth year of the reign of King *William* the Third, intituled, *An act for preventing frauds, and regulating abuses, in the plantation trade*, all governors or commanders in chief of any of his Majesty's colonies or plantations, are required to take a solemn oath, to do their utmost that all the clauses, matters, and things, contained in that act, and several other acts of parliament therein referred to, relating to the said colonies and plantations, be punctually and *bona fide* observed, according to the true intent and meaning thereof: and whereas divers other good laws have been since made, for the better regulating and securing the plantation trade: be it further enacted by the authority aforesaid, That all the present governors or commanders in chief of any *British* colony or plantation shall, before the twenty ninth day of *September*, one thousand seven hundred and sixty four, and all who hereafter shall be made governors or commanders in chief of the said colonies or plantations, or any of them, before their entrance into their government, shall take a solemn oath, to do their utmost that all the clauses, matters, and things, contained in any act of parliament heretofore made, and now in force, relating to the said colonies and

Clause in act 7 & 8 Will. 3.

Governors, or commanders in chief of the British colonies, are to take an oath for the due execution of their duty in this and all other acts re-

and plantations, and that all and every the clauses contained in this present act, be punctually and *bona fide* observed, according to the true intent and meaning thereof, so far as appertains unto the said governors or commanders in chief respectively, under the like penalties, forfeitures, and disabilities, either for neglecting to take the said oath, or for wittingly neglecting to do their duty accordingly, as are mentioned and expressed in the said recited act made in the seventh and eighth year of the reign of King *William* the Third; and the said oath, hereby required to be taken, shall be administered by such person or persons as hath or have been, or shall be, appointed to administer the oath required to be taken by the said act made in the seventh and eighth year of the reign of King *William* the Third.

lating to the said colonies, &c.

under the penalties in the recited act of 7 & 8 Will. 3.

XL. And be it further enacted by the authority aforesaid, That all penalties and forfeitures herein before mentioned, which shall be incurred in *Great Britain*, shall and may be prosecuted, sued for, and recovered, in any of his Majesty's courts of record at *Westminster*, or in the court of Exchequer in *Scotland*, respectively; and (all necessary charges for the recovery thereof being first deducted) shall be divided and applied, one moiety to and for the use of his Majesty, his heirs and successors, and the other moiety to the seizor or prosecutor.

Penalties and forfeitures incurred in Great Britain where to be recovered; and how to be divided and applied.

XLI. And it is hereby further enacted and declared, That from and after the twenty ninth day of *September*, one thousand seven hundred and sixty four, all sums of money granted and imposed by this act, and by an act made in the twenty fifth year of the reign of King *Charles* the Second, intituled, *An act for the encouragement of the* Greenland *and* Eastland *trades, and for the better securing the plantation trade*, as rates or duties; and also all sums of money imposed as penalties or forfeitures, by this or any other act of parliament relating to the customs, which shall be paid, incurred, or recovered, in any of the *British* colonies or plantations in *America*; shall be deemed, and are hereby declared to be sterling money of *Great Britain*, and shall be collected, recovered, and paid, to the amount of the value which such nominal sums bear in *Great Britain*; and that such monies shall and may be received and taken according to the proportion and value of five shillings and six pence the ounce in silver; and that all the forfeitures and penalties inflicted by this or any other act or acts of parliament relating to the trade and revenues of the said *British* colonies or plantations in *America*, which shall be incurred there, shall and may be prosecuted, sued for, and recovered in any court of record, or in any court of admiralty, in the said colonies or plantations where such offence shall be committed, or in any court of vice admiralty which may or shall be appointed over all *America* (which court of admiralty or vice admiralty are hereby respectively authorized and required to proceed, hear, and determine the same) at the election of the informer or prosecutor.

The money granted by this act, and act 25 Car. 2. as rates or duties;

and the penalties and forfeitures relating to the customs, in America, are to be deemed sterling money of Great Britain, at the rate of 5s. 6d. per ounce, in silver.

Penalties and forfeitures in America, may be recovered in the courts of record there, or court of vice admiralty;

XLII. And it is hereby further enacted, That all penalties and forfeitures so recovered there, under this or any former act of

and the net produce is to be paid,

of parliament, ſhall be divided, paid, and applied, as follows; that is to ſay, after deducting the charges of proſecution from the groſs produce thereof, one third part of the net produce ſhall be paid into the hands of the collector of his Majeſty's cuſtoms at the port or place where ſuch penalties or forfeitures ſhall be recovered, for the uſe of his Majeſty, his heirs and ſucceſſors; one third part to the governor or commander in chief of the ſaid colony or plantation; and the other third part to the perſon who ſhall ſeize, inform, and ſue for the ſame; excepting ſuch ſeizures as ſhall be made at ſea by the commanders or officers of his Majeſty's ſhips or veſſels of war duly authorized to make ſeizures; one moiety of which ſeizures, and of the penalties and forfeitures recovered thereon, firſt deducting the charges of proſecution from the groſs produce thereof, ſhall be paid as aforeſaid to the collector of his Majeſty's cuſtoms, to and for the uſe of his Majeſty, his heirs and ſucceſſors, and the other moiety to him or them who ſhall ſeize, inform, and ſue for the ſame; any law, cuſtom, or uſage, to the contrary notwithſtanding; ſubject nevertheleſs to ſuch diſtribution of the produce of the ſeizures ſo made at ſea, as well with regard to the moiety herein before granted to his Majeſty, his heirs and ſucceſſors, as with regard to the other moiety given to the ſeizor or proſecutor, as his Majeſty, his heirs and ſucceſſors, ſhall think fit to order and direct by any order or orders of council, or by any proclamation or proclamations, to be made for that purpoſe.

One third to the King, One third to the governor, and one third to the proſecutor. But ſeizures made at ſea by the King's ſhips are to go, One moiety to the King and the other to the proſecutor; ſubject nevertheleſs to ſuch diſtribution, as his Majeſty by order of council, or proclamation, ſhall make.

XLIII. Provided always, and it is hereby further enacted by the authority aforeſaid, That if the produce of any ſeizure made in *America*, ſhall not be ſufficient to anſwer the expences of condemnation and ſale; or if, upon the trial of any ſeizure of any ſhip or goods, a verdict or ſentence ſhall be given for the claimant, in either of thoſe caſes, the charges attending the ſeizing and proſecuting ſuch ſhip or goods ſhall and may, with the conſent and approbation of any four of the commiſſioners of his Majeſty's cuſtoms, be paid out of any branch of the revenue of cuſtoms ariſing in any of the *Britiſh* colonies or plantations in *America*; any thing in this or any other act of parliament to the contrary notwithſtanding.

Where the ſeizure ſhall not anſwer the expence of condemnation and ſale, or a verdict be given for the claimant, the charges, with approbation of the commiſſioners, may be defrayed out of the cuſtoms in America.

XLIV. And it is hereby further enacted by the authority aforeſaid, That from and after the ſaid twenty ninth day of *September*, one thouſand ſeven hundred and ſixty four, no perſon ſhall be admitted to enter a claim to any ſhip or goods ſeized in purſuance of this or any other act of parliament, and proſecuted in any of the *Britiſh* colonies or plantations in *America*, until ſufficient ſecurity be firſt given, by perſons of known ability, in the court where ſuch ſeizure is proſecuted, in the penalty of ſixty pounds, to anſwer the coſts and charges of proſecution; and, in default of giving ſuch ſecurity, ſuch ſhip or goods ſhall be adjudged to be forfeited, and ſhall be condemned.

No claim to be admitted, till ſecurity to anſwer coſts be given, to the amount of 60 l. and in default, ſhip and goods to be condemned.

XLV. And it is hereby further enacted by the authority aforeſaid, That from and after the twenty ninth day of *September*, one thouſand ſeven hundred and ſixty four, if any ſhip or goods

Where ſhip or goods are ſeized for any cauſe of for-

goods ſhall be ſeized for any cauſe of forfeiture, and any diſpute ſhall ariſe whether the cuſtoms and duties for ſuch goods have been paid, or the ſame have been lawfully imported or exported, or concerning the growth, product, or manufacture, of ſuch goods, or the place from whence ſuch goods were brought, then, and in ſuch caſes, the proof thereof ſhall lie upon the owner or claimer of ſuch ſhip or goods, and not upon the officer who ſhall ſeize or ſtop the ſame; any law, cuſtom, or uſage, to the contrary notwithſtanding.

feiture, the owner is to prove the matter in diſpute.

XLVI. And be it further enacted by the authority aforeſaid, That from and after the twenty ninth day of *September*, one thouſand ſeven hundred and ſixty four, in caſe any information ſhall be commenced and brought to trial in *America*, on account of any ſeizure of any ſhip or goods as forfeited by this or any other act of parliament relating to his Majeſty's cuſtoms, wherein a verdict or ſentence ſhall be given for the claimer thereof; and it ſhall appear to the judge or court before whom the ſame ſhall be tried, that there was a probable cauſe of ſeizure, the judge or court before whom the ſame ſhall be tried ſhall certify on the record or other proceedings, that there was a probable cauſe for the proſecutors ſeizing the ſaid ſhip or goods; and, in ſuch caſe, the defendant ſhall not be intitled to any coſts of ſuit whatſoever; nor ſhall the perſons who ſeized the ſaid ſhip or goods, be liable to any action, or other ſuit or proſecution, on account of ſuch ſeizure: and in caſe any action, or other ſuit or proſecution, ſhall be commenced and brought to trial againſt any perſon or perſons whatſoever, on account of the ſeizing any ſuch ſhip or goods, where no information ſhall be commenced or brought to trial to condemn the ſame, and a verdict or ſentence ſhall be given upon ſuch action or proſecution againſt the defendant or defendants, if the court or judge before whom ſuch action or proſecution, ſhall certify in like manner as aforeſaid that there was a probable cauſe for ſuch ſeizure, then the plaintiff, beſides his ſhip or goods ſo ſeized, or the value thereof, ſhall not be intitled to above two pence damages, nor to any coſts of ſuit; nor ſhall the defendant in ſuch proſecution be fined above one ſhilling.

In trials upon information, in America, where a probable cauſe of ſeizure appears, the judge ſhall certify the ſame on the record; and the defendant ſhall have no coſts, nor action; and in ſuits, where no information ſhall be commenced and brought to trial, and the court ſhall certify there was a probable cauſe of ſeizure, the plaintiff ſhall have but 2 d. damages, and no coſts; and the defendant be fined not more than 1 s.

XLVII. And be it further enacted by the authority aforeſaid, That if any action or ſuit ſhall be commenced, either in *Great Britain* or *America*, againſt any perſon or perſons for any thing done in purſuance of this or any other act of parliament relating to his Majeſty's cuſtoms, the defendant or defendants in ſuch action or ſuit may plead the general iſſue, and give the ſaid acts, and the ſpecial matter, in evidence at any trial to be had thereupon, and that the ſame was done in purſuance and by the authority of ſuch act; and if it ſhall appear ſo to have been done, the jury ſhall find for the defendant or defendants; and if the plaintiff ſhall be non-ſuited, or diſcontinue his action after the defendant or defendants ſhall have appeared, or if judgment

General iſſue.

Treble costs.

ſhall be given upon verdict or demurrer againſt the plaintiff, the defendant or defendants ſhall recover treble coſts, and have the like remedy for the ſame as defendants have in other caſes by law.

CAP. XVI.

An act to enable infants who are ſeized of lands, tenements, or hereditaments, within the duchy of Lancaſter, *or the counties palatine of* Cheſter, Lancaſter, *or* Durham, *or the principality of* Wales, *in fee, or for the life or lives of one or more other perſon or perſons, in truſt, or by way of mortgage, to make conveyances of ſuch eſtates by order of the court of the duchy chamber of* Lancaſter, *of the court of* Exchequer *of the county palatine of* Cheſter, *the court of* Chancery *of the county palatine of* Lancaſter, *of the court of* Chancery *of the county palatine of* Durham, *and of the courts of the great ſeſſions in the principality of* Wales.

Preamble reciting clauſe in act 7 Ann.

WHEREAS *by an act of parliament made in the ſeventh year of the reign of her late majeſty Queen* Anne, *intituled,* An act to enable infants who are ſeiſed or poſſeſſed of eſtates in fee, in truſt, or by way of mortgage, to make conveyances of ſuch eſtates, *perſons under the age of one and twenty years, having eſtates in lands, tenements, or hereditaments, only in truſt for others, or by way of mortgage, are enabled and compellable, by the direction and order of the high court of* Chancery, *or the court of* Exchequer, *to convey and aſſure ſuch lands, tenements, or hereditaments, in ſuch manner as the ſaid court of* Chancery, *or the court of* Exchequer, *ſhall, by ſuch order in purſuance of the ſaid act, direct: and whereas the benefit intended by the ſaid act will be manifeſtly extended, by giving to, and veſting in, the proper reſpective courts of the duchy of* Lancaſter, *and the courts in the ſeveral counties palatine of* Cheſter, Lancaſter, *and* Durham, *and the courts of the great ſeſſions in* Wales, *ſuch and the like power, juriſdiction, and authority, reſpecting infants who are or ſhall be ſeiſed of lands, tenements, or hereditaments, within the ſaid duchy of* Lancaſter, *and the ſeveral counties palatine of* Cheſter, Lancaſter, *and* Durham, *and the principality of* Wales *reſpectively, in fee, or for the life or lives of one or more other perſon or perſons, as by the ſaid act is given to, and veſted in, the high court of* Chancery, *and the court of* Exchequer: be it therefore enacted by the King's moſt excellent majeſty, by and with the advice and conſent of the lords ſpiritual and temporal, and commons, in this preſent parliament aſſembled, and by the authority of the ſame, That from and after the firſt day of *June*, one thouſand ſeven hundred and ſixty four, it ſhall and may be lawful to and for any perſon or perſons under the age of one and twenty years, having ſuch eſtate or eſtates in lands, tenements, or hereditaments, within the duchy of *Lancaſter*, or the counties palatine of *Cheſter*, *Lancaſter*, and *Durham* reſpectively, or in the principality of *Wales*, by the direction of the court of the

Infants ſeiſed of lands, tenements, or hereditaments, may, by order of the court,

the duchy chamber of *Lancaster*, of the court of *Exchequer* of the county palatine of *Chester*, of the court of *Chancery* of the county palatine of *Lancaster*, of the court of *Chancery* of the county palatine of *Durham*, and of the ſeveral courts of the great ſeſſions in *Wales* reſpectively, ſignified by an order made upon hearing all parties concerned on the petition or motion of the perſon or perſons for whom ſuch infant or infants ſhall be ſo ſeized as aforeſaid, in truſt, or of the mortgagor or mortgagors, or guardian or guardians, of ſuch infant or infants, or perſons intitled to the monies ſecured by or upon any ſuch lands, tenements, or hereditaments, whereof any infant or infants are or ſhall be ſeiſed, in truſt, or by way of mortgage, or of the perſon or perſons intitled to the redemption thereof, to convey and aſſure any ſuch lands, tenements, or hereditaments, in ſuch manner as the ſaid ſeveral courts of the ſaid duchy, counties palatine, and great ſeſſion in *Wales*, wherein ſuch lands, tenements, or hereditaments, ſhall lie, by ſuch order ſo to be obtained, direct, to any other perſon or perſons; and ſuch conveyance or aſſurance ſo to be had and made as aforeſaid, ſhall be as good and effectual in law, to all intents and purpoſes whatſoever, as if the ſaid infant or infants was or were at the time of making ſuch conveyance or aſſurance of the full age of one and twenty years; any law, cuſtom, or uſage, to the contrary in any wiſe notwithſtanding.

upon petition, or motion made, make conveyances of ſuch eſtates; which ſhall be deemed good in law.

II. And be it further enacted by the authority aforeſaid, That all and every ſuch infant or infants, being only truſtee or truſtees, mortgagee or mortgagees, as aforeſaid, ſhall and may be compelled, by ſuch order as aforeſaid to be obtained, to make ſuch conveyance or conveyances, aſſurance or aſſurances, as aforeſaid, in like manner as truſtees or mortagees of full age are compellable to convey or aſſign their truſt eſtates or mortgages.

Infants being only truſtees, or mortgagees, may be compelled by ſuch order, to make ſuch conveyances and aſſurances accordingly.

CAP. XVII.

An act to explain and amend an act, paſſed in the ſecond year of the reign of his preſent Majeſty, intituled, An act to explain, amend, and reduce into one act of parliament, the ſeveral laws now in being, relating to the raiſing and training the militia within that part of *Great Britain* called *England*.

Preamble.

WHEREAS *the laws now in force, for the raiſing and training the militia, within that part of* Great Britain *called* England, *are in ſome reſpects defective: and whereas frequent delays, and many difficulties have occured in the execution of the acts now in force for raiſing and training the militia, from the manner in which the whole execution of the acts is made to depend in all counties, ridings, and places, where the militia has been or ſhall be raiſed, upon holding a general meeting, on either the laſt* Tueſday *in* October, *or the laſt* Tueſday *in* May, *in each year; and doubts have ariſen, whether, in ſuch caſe, any ſubſequent general meetings can now be called for the purpoſes of the ſaid acts, unleſs there ſhall have been a previous general meeting on one of the days before ſpecified*; may it therefore pleaſe

please your Majesty, that it may be enacted; and be it enacted by the King's most excellent majesty, by and with the advice and consent of the lords spiritual and temporal, and commons, in this present parliament assembled, and by the authority of the same, That it shall and may be lawful for his Majesty's lieutenant of every county, riding, and place, where the militia has been or shall be raised, together with any two or more deputy lieutenants, and on the death or removal, or in the absence of his Majesty's lieutenant, any three or more deputy lieutenants, whenever and as often as they shall find necessary, to summon, or cause to be summoned, a general meeting, according to the directions of the act, passed in the second year of the reign of his present Majesty, for summoning general meetings in counties where the militia has not been raised; which general meetings herein directed, shall have the same powers as if such general meetings had been held on the last *Tuesday* in *May*, or on the last *Tuesday* in *October*, in each year, in pursuance of the said act.

In counties where the militia has been or shall be raised, general meetings may be summoned in the same manner as in counties where the militia has not been raised, and shall have the same power as meetings held on the last Tuesday in May, or the last Tuesday in October.

II. And whereas the raising the militia has, in some counties, been delayed by the vacancy of lord lieutenants in particular counties, and it is essential to the good of the service, and the establishment of a militia, which, to be effectual, should be general, that such local difficulties should be removed for the future; be it therefore enacted, and it is hereby enacted, That in every county, riding, and place, where the office of lord lieutenant is, or shall be vacant, it shall and may be lawful for his Majesty, his heirs and successors, to appoint three persons out of the deputy lieutenants of any such county, riding, or place, to execute the office of lord lieutenant of such county, riding, or place, so far as the same relates to the executing the several powers and authorities vested in lieutenants, in and by the several acts of parliament for the raising and training the militia, during such vacancy.

In every county, &c. where the office of lord lieutenant is vacant his Majesty to appoint 3 deputy lieutenants, to execute that office so far as relates to the acts for raising and training the militia.

III. And whereas many inconveniencies have arisen in the service, from the want of some description of the men who shall be accepted as volunteers, offered by parishes as parochial substitutes, or of men tendered to serve as substitutes by persons chosen by ballot; be it enacted, That no such volunteer or substitute shall be admitted and sworn to serve in the militia who shall not be five feet four inches in height, and able and fit for service.

No volunteer or substitute to be admitted and sworn, who shall not be 5 feet 4 inches high.

IV. And whereas it is become necessary to prevent the militia men of one county from inrolling themselves in the militia of another; be it therefore enacted, That if any person, after being inrolled in the militia of one county, riding, or place, shall, during such service, engage and be inrolled to serve in the militia of any other county, riding, or place, he shall, upon conviction thereof before any one justice of the peace of the county in which he shall last enter into the said militia, forfeit and pay any sum not exceeding the sum of ten pounds; and in case such person shall not immediately pay such penalty, such justice of the peace shall, by warrant under his hand and seal, commit such person

A person being inrolled to serve in the militia of one county, and who shall engage and be inrolled to serve in the militia of another county,

Perſon to the common gaol of the county, riding, or place, where he ſhall have been ſo convicted, there to remain without bail or mainprize, for any time not exceeding three months, or unleſs he ſhall ſooner pay the penalty aforeſaid.

forfeits 10l. if not immediately paid, to be committed for any time not exceeding 3 months.

V. And whereas the proviſions in the ſaid act, paſſed in the ſecond year of the reign of his preſent Majeſty, for reimburſing officers of pariſhes the monies by them expended for the relief of militia men, who on their march, or at the place where they ſhall be called out to annual exerciſe, ſhall, by ſickneſs or otherwiſe, want ſuch relief, have been found inſufficient for the purpoſes thereby intended; be it therefore enacted, That in caſe any man ſerving in the militia ſhall, on the march, or at the place where he ſhall be called out to annual exerciſe, be diſabled by ſickneſs or otherwiſe, it ſhall and may be lawful for any one juſtice of the peace of the county, riding, or place, or any mayor or chief magiſtrate of any city, town, or place, where ſuch man ſhall then be, by warrant under his hand and ſeal, to order him ſuch relief as he ſhall think reaſonable; and the officers of the pariſh, tything, or place, where ſuch militia man ſhall be ſo relieved, ſhall, upon producing an account of the expences occaſioned thereby, allowed under the hand of a juſtice of the peace, to the treaſurer of the county, riding, or place, for which ſuch militia man ſhall ſerve, ſhall be reimburſed ſuch expences by the treaſurer of ſuch county, out of the county ſtock, and ſuch treaſurer ſhall, upon producing ſuch account allowed as aforeſaid, be allowed the ſame in his accounts.

A militia man on the march, or at the place of exerciſe, diſabled by ſickneſs, or otherwiſe, to be relieved by the officers of the pariſh where he ſhall then be, and pariſh officers to be reimburſed the expences occaſioned thereby, out of the county ſtock, upon producing accounts thereof allowed by a juſtice of the peace.

VI. And whereas, as the laws for regulating the militia now ſtand, no power is given of puniſhing ſuch militia men as ſhall, after having joined their corps, deſert during the time of annual exerciſe, and not be taken till after the expiration of the time of ſuch annual exerciſe, and conſequently of the period now fixed for the continuance of martial law; be it therefore enacted, That if any militia man ſhall ſo offend, and not be apprehended during the time of ſuch annual exerciſe, every ſuch militia man, being thereof convicted upon oath, before one juſtice of the peace, of any county where ſuch militia man ſhall be apprehended, ſhall incur the penalty, and be ſubject to the puniſhment, inflicted by the ſaid act of the ſecond year of his preſent Majeſty upon militia men not joining their corps.

Militia men who after having joined their corps, ſhall deſert, during the time of annual exerciſe, and ſhall not be taken till after the expiration of the time of annual exerciſe, ſhall incur the ſame penalty as militia men not joining their corps.

VII. And whereas it would be very conducive to the preſervation of order and diſcipline, during the time of annual exerciſe, of great convenience to the corporals and private militia men in the ſupplying them with neceſſaries, and of eſſential utility to their reſpective families, if the captains or commanding officers were enabled to ſtop a limited part of the daily pay of ſuch corporals and private men when called out to annual exerciſe; be it therefore enacted, That it ſhall and may be lawful for every captain or commanding officer of the militia, to put the corporals

A captain or commanding officer may put corporals and

porals and private militia men of his company under ſtoppages, not exceeding ſix pence a day, for the purpoſes aforeſaid: provided always, That every captain and commanding officer ſhall account with each corporal or private militia man for the ſaid ſtoppages, before ſuch corporal or private man ſhall be diſmiſſed from the ſaid annual exerciſe, having firſt deducted what ſhall have been laid out for them for neceſſaries and repair of arms damaged by their neglect.

private men under ſtoppages, not exceeding 6 d. a day, and ſhall account with them for ſuch ſtoppages before they are diſmiſſed from annual exerciſe.

VIII. And whereas no powers are granted by the ſaid act, paſſed in the ſecond year of the reign of his preſent Majeſty, for puniſhing drummers for miſbehaviour during the time the militia to which they belong is not called out to annual exerciſe (except by their being diſplaced by their captain) which defect in the law has been found inconvenient to the ſervice of the militia; be it therefore enacted, That if any drummer ſhall be negligent in his duty, or diſobedient to the orders of the adjutant, or other his ſuperior officers, and be thereof convicted upon the oath of the adjutant, or other ſuperior officer, or other credible witneſs, before one or more juſtice or juſtices of the peace of the county in the militia of which ſuch drummer ſerves, ſuch drummer ſhall forfeit and pay any ſum not exceeding forty ſhillings, at the diſcretion of ſuch juſtice or juſtices; and if ſuch drummer ſhall not immediately pay ſuch penalty, it ſhall and may be lawful for the captain, or commanding officer of the company of militia to which ſuch drummer ſhall belong, and he is hereby required to ſtop the pay of ſuch drummer, until the ſame ſhall amount to the ſum of money aſcertained by ſuch juſtice or juſtices, as the penalty inflicted upon ſuch drummer; and the ſaid captain, or commanding officer, ſhall pay the ſame to the clerk of the regiment or battalion, to be applied and accounted for as part of the common ſtock of ſuch regiment or battalion; and the receipt of the clerk for ſuch ſum ſhall be a diſcharge to the captain, or commanding officer for the ſame; and the money ſo paid, ſhall be deemed as ſo much money paid to ſuch drummer for his ſervice in the militia.

A drummer negligent in his duty, or diſobedient to the orders of the adjutant, or other ſuperior officer, to forfeit not exceeding 40s. if not immediately paid, the captain of the company to ſtop the pay of ſuch drummer, to pay the penalty: penalty to be applied as part of the common ſtock of the regiment or battalion.

IX. And whereas by the ſaid act, paſſed in the ſecond year of the reign of his preſent Majeſty, it is enacted, That in all counties and places where the militia has not, or ſhall not be raiſed, by virtue of the ſeveral acts made for raiſing the militia forces, that the ſum of five pounds ſhall be annually paid for and in lieu of every private man therein directed to be raiſed within each reſpective county, riding, and place; which ſaid ſum and ſums of five pounds *per* man, the juſtices of the peace of each reſpective county, riding, and place, aſſembled at their general or quarter ſeſſions, are directed to rate and aſſeſs on the county; and that the ſaid ſum and ſums ſhall be rated and aſſeſſed in ſuch and the ſame manner, and according to ſuch and the ſame proportions, upon every town, pariſh, and place, within each reſpective county or riding, and ſhall be collected, received, levied, paid, and accounted for, by the perſons making ſuch collection, in ſuch manner, and by ſuch means, as the county rates

rates have been usually, or may, by an act made in the twelfth year of the reign of his late Majesty, intituled, *An act for the more easy assessing, collecting, and levying of county rates*, be assessed, collected, received, levied, paid, and accounted for: and whereas there are several cities, towns, and places, in many counties and ridings, which do not contribute to the payment of the said rate, called the *County Rate*, by reason whereof doubts have arisen, whether such cities, towns, and places can be legally rated or assessed towards the payment of the said sum and sums of five pounds *per* man, in pursuance of the directions of the said act of the second year of the reign of his present Majesty: and whereas it is just and reasonable, that all such cities, towns, and places, should bear an equal share and proportion of the said payment of five pounds *per* man with each county or riding within which such cities, towns, and places, may happen to lie; be it therefore enacted, That in all cases where the militia has not been raised, or shall not at any time hereafter be raised, for any county or riding, within which any city, town, or place, shall not be rated to the said rate called the *County Rate*, the payment of the said sum of five pounds *per* man, upon the whole number of private militia men directed to be raised within every county or riding, shall be divided and apportioned between each respective county or riding, and each such respective city, town, and place within the same, as shall not contribute to the said rate, called the *County Rate*, in such proportion as the respective quotas paid to the land tax by each respective county or riding, and by each such respective city, town, and place, bear to each other, and the respective sum and sums so ascertained and apportioned shall be rated, levied, and paid, out of the rates for the relief of the poor, to be collected within each such respective city, town, and place, not rated to the said rate, called the *County Rate*, by such ways and means, and with such powers and regulations for levying, collecting, and keeping the same distinct, as are prescribed in the said act passed in the second year of the reign of his present Majesty, for each respective county or riding; and the churchwardens and overseers of the poor of each such respective city, town, and place, shall, from time to time, pay over the same to the treasurer or treasurers of every county or riding within which any such city, town, and place as aforesaid lies, in order that the said treasurer or treasurers may pay over the same to the receiver general of the said county or riding, together with the proportion of the said sum of five pounds *per* man, directed to be rated, levied, and paid, by each county or riding, by the said act passed in the second year of the reign of his present Majesty.

Where the militia shall not be raised for any county within which any city shall not be rated to the county rate, the payment of 5 l. *per* man shall be apportioned between such county and city as the respective quotas paid to the land tax bear to each other; and the sums so apportioned shall be paid out of the poors rate collected in such city by the churchwardens and overseers of the poor, to the treasurer of the county, to be by him paid to the receiver general, together with the proportion of the said sum of 5 l. to be paid by such county.

X. And be it further enacted, That in such cities, towns, and places, as are counties of themselves, and yet have no such rate or assessment as is called the *County Rate*, nor any powers or directions for rating, levying, or collecting the proportion of the said sum of five pounds *per* man, to be raised by the county to which the said cities, towns, or places are, by the said act passed in

The same method to be followed in such cities as are counties of themselves.

in the second year of the reign of his present Majesty, united for the purposes of the said act, the directions herein before given for rating, levying, and collecting the proportion of the said sum of five pounds *per* man, within such cities, towns, and places, as do not contribute to the county rate, shall be pursued and followed in all such cities, towns, or places, as are counties of themselves.

Where a town lies in two counties they are to contribute their quota, in lieu of raising the militia, for that county in which their church stands; the county in

XI. And whereas, in some parts of this kingdom there are towns which lie in two counties, and doubts have arisen, whether such towns are obliged to pay to both counties the sum of five pounds in lieu of every private militia man which shall not be raised by such counties; be it therefore enacted by the authority aforesaid, That where any town lies in two counties, it shall be lawful for the said town to contribute their quota, for and in lieu of raising the militia, for that county only where the church of the said town is situate; and the deficiencies of the other county rate, which the said town would have paid, shall be made up by the county in general, and not by the division or hundred where the said town is situated.

and the deficiencies of the other county rates, are to be made up by general.

CAP. XVIII.

An act for charging on the sinking fund certain annuities granted by an act passed in the first year of the reign of his present Majesty; and for carrying the duties therein mentioned, to the said fund; and also for consolidating such of the said annuities as are granted for a certain term of years, irredeemable, with other annuities granted by an act passed in the second year of his present Majesty's reign.

Preamble, reciting clauses in act 1 Geo. III.

WHEREAS, *in pursuance of an act of parliament made in the first year of the reign of his present Majesty, intituled,* An act for granting to his Majesty an additional duty upon strong beer and ale; and for raising the sum of twelve millions, by way of annuities and a lottery, to be charged on the said duty; and for further encouraging the exportation of strong beer and ale; *several persons, bodies politic or corporate, have advanced and lent the sum of twelve millions upon the credit of the several duties upon strong beer and ale by the said act granted, for the purchase of annuities transferrable at the bank of* England, *after the rate of three pounds* per centum per annum, *upon the said sum of twelve millions; and also of an annuity after the rate of one pound, two shillings, and six pence,* per annum, *for every hundred pounds of the sum of eleven millions four hundred thousand pounds, part of the said sum of twelve millions so subscribed as aforesaid, for a certain term of ninety nine years, to be computed from the fifth day of* January, *one thousand seven hundred and sixty one: and whereas in pursuance of*

2 Geo. III.

an act of parliament made in the second year of the reign of his present

sent Majesty, intituled, An act for raising by annuities, in manner therein mentioned, the sum of twelve millions to be charged on the sinking fund; and for applying the surplus of certain duties on spirituous liquors, and also the monies arising from the duties on spirituous liquors, granted by an act of this session of parliament; *several persons, bodies politic or corporate, have advanced and lent the sum of twelve millions upon the credit of the surplus of the several duties on spirituous liquors, granted by two acts of parliament of the twenty fourth and thirty third years of the reign of his late majesty King* George *the Second, and on the credit of the several duties on spirituous liquors, granted by an act of the second year of his present Majesty, for the purchase of annuities transferrable at the bank of* England, *at the rates following; that is to say, for every sum of eighty pounds by them advanced towards the sum of nine millions six hundred thousand pounds, part of the said twelve millions, to be intitled to one hundred pounds capital, being an interest of four pounds* per centum per annum, *during the term of nineteen years; and after the expiration thereof, to an annuity of three pounds* per centum per annum *on every hundred pounds of such capital, redeemable by parliament; and for every twenty pounds of the sum of two millions four hundred thousand pounds, remainder of the said twelve millions, to an annuity of one pound* per annum, *for a certain term of ninety eight years, to be computed from the fifth day of* January, *one thousand seven hundred and sixty two: and whereas it is thought necessary that the said annuities granted for the term of ninety nine years from the fifth of* January, *one thousand seven hundred and sixty one, by the said act of the first year of the reign of his present Majesty, and transferrable at the bank of* England, *should be, with the consent of the proprietors thereof, added to, and made a joint stock with, the said annuities granted by the said act of the second year of the reign of his present Majesty, for the term of ninety eight years, from the fifth day of* January, *one thousand seven hundred and sixty two, also transferrable at the bank of* England; *and that the charges and expences of the said annuities granted in the first year of the reign of his present Majesty, be charged upon and paid out of the sinking fund, in the same and like manner as those of the said annuities granted in the second year of the reign of his present Majesty are paid and payable: and whereas it is thought necessary that the said principal sum of twelve millions borrowed on the credit of the said act of the first year of the reign of his present Majesty, together with the charges and expences attending the same, should be, with the consent of the proprietors thereof to be signified within the time herein after-mentioned, charged upon, and paid out of, the fund commonly called* The Sinking Fund; *and that the several duties upon strong beer and ale, which by the said act were made a fund for the payment of the said three pounds* per centum per annum *annuities, should be carried to and made part of the said fund;* may it therefore please your most excellent Majesty, that it may be enacted; and be it enacted by the King's most excellent majesty, by and with the advice and consent of the lords spiritual and temporal, and commons, in this present parliament assembled,

The long annuities granted by the recited act of 1 Geo. III. with consent of the proprietors, to be added to, and made a joint stock with, those granted by act 2 Geo. III. and to be charged upon and payable out of the Sinking Fund.

bled, and by the authority of the same, That from and after the fifth day of *January*, one thousand seven hundred and sixty four, the said annuities granted by the said act of the first year of the reign of his present Majesty, for the term of ninety nine years, from the fifth day of *January*, one thousand seven hundred and sixty one, shall be, with the consent of the several proprietors, added to, and made a joint stock with, the annuities which were granted by the said act of the second year of the reign of his present Majesty, for the term of ninety eight years, from the fifth day of *January*, one thousand seven hundred and sixty two, transferrable at the bank of *England*; and that the charges and expences thereof be charged upon, and paid out of, the fund commonly called *The Sinking Fund*, in the same and like manner as those of the said annuities granted for ninety eight years, in the second year of the reign of his present Majesty, are paid and payable; any thing in the said act made in the first year of the reign of his present Majesty to the contrary thereof in any wise notwithstanding.

The principal sum of 12,000,000l. borrowed on the credit of act 1 Geo. III. with the charges attending to be charged, with consent of the proprietors, on the Sinking Fund, and paid thereout, till redeemed.

II. And be it further enacted by the authority aforesaid, That from and after the fifth day of *January*, one thousand seven hundred and sixty four, the said principal sum of twelve millions borrowed on the credit of the said act of the first year of the reign of his present Majesty, carrying an interest after the rate of three pounds *per centum per annum*, together with the charges and expences attending the same, shall be, with the consent of the proprietors, charged upon, and paid out of, the fund commonly called *The Sinking Fund*, until redemption thereof by parliament; any thing in the said act made in the first year of his present Majesty's reign to the contrary thereof in any wise notwithstanding.

Annuitants not entering their dissent on or before 1 June, 1764. to the charging their respective annuities on the Sinking Fund, deemed to assent thereto.

III. And be it further enacted by the authority aforesaid, That such proprietors of the said annuities for ninety nine years, and also such proprietors of the said annuities on the capital sum of twelve millions redeemable by parliament, granted by the said act of the first year of the reign of his present Majesty, who shall not on or before the first day of *June*, one thousand seven hundred and sixty four, signify their dissent to the charging their respective annuities on the sinking fund in books to be opened at the bank of *England* for that purpose, shall be deemed and taken to assent thereto; any thing to the contrary thereof in any wise notwithstanding.

The monies arising by the duties, made a fund for payment of the said annuities and principal sums,

IV. And be it further enacted by the authority aforesaid, That all the monies which have arisen since the fifth day of *January*, one thousand seven hundred and sixty four, or that shall or may hereafter arise of the several duties upon strong beer and ale, which were made a fund for the payment of three pounds *per centum per annum*, in manner above mentioned, on twelve millions; and also of the said annuities for ninety nine years, by virtue of the said act made in the first year of the reign of his present Majesty (which sum of twelve millions was granted towards the supply of the year one thousand seven hundred and

sixty

ſixty one) ſhall be carried to, and made part of, the fund commonly called *The Sinking Fund*; and the ſame ſhall be deemed and taken to be part of the ſame ſinking fund; and ſhall be iſſued and applied to ſuch uſes and purpoſes as the ſeveral exceſſes, ſurpluſſes, or overplus monies compoſing the ſinking fund, are or may be iſſued and applied; any thing in the ſaid act of the firſt year of the reign of his preſent Majeſty to the contrary thereof in any wiſe notwithſtanding.

to be carried to the Sinking Fund, and applied accordingly.

CAP. XIX.

An act for importing ſalt from Europe *into the province of* Quebec *in* America, *for a limited time.*

Preamble.

WHEREAS *the rivers, bays, and coaſts, of the colony of* Quebec *in* America, *and the ſeas adjoining, are commodiouſly ſituated for carrying on a very advantageous fiſhery, to the great benefit of the inhabitants of the ſaid colony, and to the extending the commerce and increaſing the riches of theſe kingdoms: and whereas it would be of great advantage to the ſaid fiſhery, if his Majeſty's ſubjects were permitted to import ſalt into the ſaid colony directly from foreign parts, in like manner as is allowed with reſpect to the fiſheries of* New England, Nova Scotia, *and* Newfoundland, *by ſeveral laws now in being:* may it pleaſe your moſt excellent Majeſty, that it may be enacted; and be it enacted by the King's moſt excellent majeſty, by and with the advice and conſent of the lords ſpiritual and temporal, and commons, in this preſent parliament aſſembled, and by the authority of the ſame, That from and after the twenty fourth day of *June*, one thouſand ſeven hundred and ſixty four, it ſhall and may be lawful to and for any of his Majeſty's ſubjects to carry and import ſalt from any part of *Europe* into the ſaid province of *Quebec* in *America*, in *Britiſh* ſhips and veſſels manned and navigated according to the act of parliament made in the twelfth year of the reign of King *Charles* the Second, intituled, *An act for encouraging and increaſing of ſhipping and navigation*, and in the ſame manner as ſalt may be imported from *Europe* into *New England* and *Newfoundland* by an act made in the fifteenth year of the reign of the ſaid King *Charles* the Second, intituled, *An act for the encouragement of trade*; any law, ſtatute, uſage, or cuſtom, to the contrary in any wiſe notwithſtanding.

From and after 24 June 1764, ſalt may be imported in Britiſh veſſels, manned and navigated according to act 12 Car. II. from any port of Europe into the province of Quebec; in like manner as into New England, &c. by virtue of act 15 Car. II.

II. And be it further enacted by the authority aforeſaid, That this act ſhall continue and be in force from and after the ſaid twenty fourth day of *June*, for the term of one year, and from thence to the end of the then next ſeſſion of parliament.

Act to be in force for one year from 24 June 1764.

CAP. XX.

An act for vesting the fort of Senegal, *and its dependencies, in the company of merchants trading to* Africa.

Preamble, reciting clauses in act 23 Geo. II.

WHEREAS *by an act made in the twenty third year of the reign of his late majesty King* George *the Second, intituled,* An act for extending and improving the trade to *Africa, all the* British *forts, settlements, and factories, on the coast of* Africa, *and all other the regions, countries, dominions, territories, continents, coasts, ports, bays, rivers, and places, within the limits of the said act described, were vested in the company by the said act established, and called* The company of merchants trading to *Africa, and their successors, to the intent and purpose, that the said forts, settlements, and premisses, should be employed at all times thereafter, only for the protection, encouragement, and defence, of the said trade: and whereas the fort of* Senegal *and its dependencies were, by the late treaty of peace, ceded to* Great Britain, *and are now subject thereto: and whereas it would be of advantage to* Great Britain, *and to the trade to* Africa, *if the said fort and its dependencies were also vested in the said company:* may it therefore please your Majesty that it may be enacted; and be it enacted by the King's most excellent majesty, by and with the advice and consent of the lords spiritual and temporal, and commons, in this present parliament assembled, and by the authority of the same, That from and after the passing of this act, the fort of *Senegal*, and its dependencies, shall be, and the same, and every part thereof, are hereby declared to be, vested in the company of merchants trading to *Africa*, to be employed at all times hereafter for the protection, encouragement, and defence of the *African* trade, in the same manner, and under the same regulations, and subject to the same rules, orders, directions, governments, limitations, restrictions, powers, and authorities, as the other forts and settlements on the coast of *Africa* are now vested in the said company, and subject to, by virtue of the said recited act, in as full, ample, and effectual manner, as the same could or would have been, if the said fort and dependencies had been mentioned in the said act, or all the clauses, provisoes, authorities, powers, directions, limitations, restrictions, matters, and things, contained in the said recited act, were herein again repeated and enacted.

The fort of Senegal, and its dependencies, vested in the African company.

Clause in the recited act.

II. And whereas by the said recited act, the committee for the time being having the direction and management of the affairs of the said company, are impowered, out of the monies they shall receive, to deduct annually a sum not exceeding eight hundred pounds, for paying salaries, house-rent, and other charges, and for the other purposes mentioned in the said act; which sum will now be inadequate to the expences of the said committee, and the intention of the said act; be it therefore further enacted by the authority aforesaid, That the said committee shall deduct annually out of the monies they shall receive, a further sum not exceeding four hundred pounds, for the purpose of paying

The committee having the direction and management of the affairs of the company, impower-

paying the salaries of their clerks and agents at *London*, *Bristol*, and *Liverpoole*, the house-rent of their office in *London*, and all charges of management, commission, or agency, in *England*, and as a further compensation for their trouble and attendance in the said office as committee-men.

ed to deduct, annually, a further sum of 400l. for salaries, house-rent, &c.

III. And be it further enacted by the authority aforesaid, That this act shall be deemed, and taken to be a publick act, and shall be taken notice of as such by all judges, justices, and other persons whatsoever, without specially pleading the same.

Publick act.

CAP. XXI.

An act for taking and swearing affidavits to be made use of in any of the courts of the county palatine of Durham.

WHEREAS *it hath been found very inconvenient, that no person or persons is or are impowered to grant commissions for the taking and swearing of affidavits to be read and made use of in the court of chancery of and for the county palatine of* Durham, *and in the court of session of pleas held in and for the said county palatine of* Durham, *before his Majesty's justices as well of pleas of the crown as of common pleas, and all manner of pleas whatsoever within the said county palatine of* Durham, *in the several matters and causes depending in the said courts respectively*; for remedy whereof, be it enacted by the King's most excellent majesty, by and with the advice and consent of the lords spiritual and temporal, and commons, in this present parliament assembled, and by the authority of the same, That the chancellor of the county palatine of *Durham* for the time being, the justices of the court of pleas in and for the said county palatine for the time being, or any two of them in their session of pleas, shall and may, by one or more commission or commissions under the several seals of the said respective courts of chancery and court of pleas in and for the said county palatine of *Durham*, from time to time, as need shall require, impower what and as many persons as shall be thought fit and necessary, to take and swear all and every such affidavit and affidavits as any person or persons shall be willing and desirous to make before any of the persons so impowered, in or concerning any cause, matter, or thing, depending, or hereafter to be depending, or any wise concerning any of the proceedings to be in either of the said courts of chancery, or court of pleas, in and for the said county palatine of *Durham*, as masters in chancery in extraordinary do use to do; which said affidavits, taken as aforesaid, shall be filed in the several and respective offices of the said court of chancery, and the court of pleas, in and for the said county palatine of *Durham*; and the same shall and may be read and made use of in the said respective courts, to all intents and purposes, as other affidavits taken in the said courts now are: and that all and every affidavit and affidavits, taken as aforesaid, shall be of the same force as affidavits taken in the said respective courts now are: and all and every person and persons forswearing him, her, or themselves, in

Preamble.

The chancellor, and justices of the court of pleas, impowered to issue commissions to proper persons to take and swear affidavits in causes depending in their respective courts.

The affidavits to be filed in the proper courts, and read in evidence.

Penalty of forswearing;

in ſuch affidavit or affidavits, ſhall incur and be liable unto the ſame penalties, as if ſuch affidavit or affidavits had been made and taken in open court: which ſaid ſeveral commiſſions ſhall be made out by the curſitor of the ſaid county palatine of *Durham*, upon a fiat or warrant from the ſaid chancellor of the ſaid county palatine of *Durham*, for taking affidavits in the ſaid court of chancery; and upon a fiat or warrant from any two of the juſtices of the pleas, in their ſeſſion of pleas, in and for the ſaid county palatine of *Durham*, for taking affidavits in the ſaid court of pleas: and the ſaid curſitor ſhall cauſe an entry to be made, in a book to be kept for that purpoſe, of the names of the perſons to whom ſuch commiſſions are from time to time granted, and the reſpective times when iſſued: and the following fees ſhall be paid for each commiſſion, and no more, (to wit) the ſum of two ſhillings for the fiat or warrant; the ſum of four ſhillings for making out the ſaid commiſſion, beſides the King's duty, and value of the parchment; and the ſum of four ſhillings for ſealing the ſame: and every commiſſioner or perſon ſo impowered ſhall take and receive, for the ſwearing of every affidavit before him in the ſaid court of chancery of *Durham*, the ſum or fee of two ſhillings, and no more; and for the ſwearing of every affidavit before him in the ſaid court of pleas, in and for the ſaid county palatine of *Durham*, the ſum or fee of one ſhilling, and no more.

Curſitor to make out the commiſſions, upon a fiat from the chancellor; and fiat from 2 juſtices of the pleas; and make an entry thereof: His fees for each commiſſion. Commiſſioners fees for ſwearing affidavits.

II. Provided always, and it is hereby declared, That ſuch officers of the ſaid reſpective courts of chancery and court of pleas, in the ſaid county palatine of *Durham*, as have heretofore taken or ſworn affidavits, ſhall and may continue ſo to do, in the ſame manner as if this act had not been made.

Officers of the reſpective courts impowered to take affidavits as heretofore.

CAP. XXII.

An act for continuing ſeveral acts of parliament made for the encouragement of the whale fiſhery carried on by his Majeſty's ſubjects.

Preamble.

WHEREAS *divers acts of parliament have been made for the encouragement of his Majeſty's ſubjects to carry on and improve the whale fiſhery, which, by the bounties given by the ſaid acts, did, till checked by the late war, greatly increaſe, and by the continuance thereof, will ſtill further increaſe, to the great advantage of the trade and navigation of theſe kingdoms*; be it therefore enacted by the King's moſt excellent majeſty, by and with the advice and conſent of the lords ſpiritual and temporal, and commons, in this preſent parliament aſſembled, and by the authority of the ſame, That an act made in the fifth year of the reign of his late majeſty King *George* the Second, intituled, *An act for encouraging the* Greenland *fiſhery*, which was to continue in force for nine years from the twenty fifth day of *December*, one thouſand ſeven hundred and thirty one; and which act, by an act of parliament made in the thirteenth year of his ſaid late Majeſty's reign, intituled, *An act for continuing ſeveral laws therein mentioned relating to the premiums upon the importation of maſts, yards*

Act 5 Geo. II. which was continued by ſeveral ſubſequent acts of 13 Geo. II.

yards, and bowsprits, tar, pitch, and turpentine; to British *made sail cloth, and the duties payable on foreign sail cloth; to the* Greenland, *and to the whale fishery; for granting a further bounty for all ships employed in the whale fishery during the present war; for exempting harpooners and others employed in the* Greenland *fishery trade, from being impressed; and for giving further time for the payment of duties omitted to be paid for the indentures and contracts of clerks and apprentices*; was continued unto the twenty fifth day of *December*, one thousand seven hundred and fifty, and from thence to the end of the then next session of parliament; and which act, by an act of parliament made in the twenty second year of his said late Majesty's reign, intituled, *An act for the further encouragement and enlargement of the whale fishery, and for continuing such laws as are therein mentioned relating thereto; and for the naturalization of such foreign protestants as shall serve, for the time therein mentioned, on board such ships as shall be fitted out for the said fishery*, was further continued unto the twenty fifth day of *December*, one thousand seven hundred and fifty seven, and from thence to the end of the then next session of parliament; and which act, by an act of parliament made in the twenty eighth year of his said late Majesty's reign, intituled, *An act for continuing, explaining, and amending, the several acts of parliament made for the further encouragement of the whale fishery carried on by his Majesty's subjects, and to authorize the payment of the bounty to* Thomas Hood *and others, upon three ships fitted out for the said fishery, and lost in the* Greenland Seas, was further continued unto the twenty fifth day of *December*, one thousand seven hundred and sixty four, and from thence to the end of the then next session of parliament; shall be, and the same is hereby further continued, from the time in the said last-mentioned act limited for the expiration thereof, unto the twenty fifth day of *December*, one thousand seven hundred and sixty seven, and from thence to the end of the then next session of parliament.

22 Geo. II.

28 Geo. II.

further continued to 25 Dec. 1767.

II. And be it further enacted by the authority aforesaid, That an act made in the sixth year of the reign of his said late Majesty, intituled, *An act for the further encouragement of the whale fishery carried on by his Majesty's subjects*, which was to be in force during the continuance of the act of the fifth year of his said late Majesty's reign, intituled, *An act for encouraging the* Greenland *fishery*; and which was, by the said act of the thirteenth year of his said late Majesty's reign, continued unto the said twenty fifth day of *December*, one thousand seven hundred and fifty, and from thence to the end of the then next session of parliament; and which act was, by the said act of the twenty second year of his said Majesty's reign, continued unto the twenty fifth day of *December*, one thousand seven hundred and fifty seven, and from thence to the end of the then next session of parliament; and which act was, by the said act of the twenty eighth year of his said late Majesty's reign, further continued unto the twenty fifth day of *December*, one thousand seven hundred and sixty four, and from thence to the end of the then next

Act 6 Geo. II. continued by several subsequent acts before recited, further continued to 25 Dec. 1767.

ſeſſion of parliament; ſhall be, and the ſame is hereby further continued, from the time in the ſaid laſt mentioned act limited for the expiration thereof, unto the twenty fifth day of *December*, one thouſand ſeven hundred and ſixty ſeven, and from thence to the end of the then next ſeſſion of parliament.

Act 22 Geo. II. which was continued by a ſubſequent act of 28 Geo. II.

III. And be it further enacted by the authority aforeſaid, That the ſaid act of the twenty ſecond year of his ſaid Majeſty's reign, intituled, *An act for the further encouragement and enlargement of the whale fiſhery, and for continuing ſuch laws as are therein mentioned relating thereto, and for the naturalization of ſuch foreign proteſtants as ſhall ſerve, for the time therein mentioned, on board ſuch ſhips as ſhall be fitted out for the ſaid fiſhery*, which was to be in force from the twenty ninth day of *September*, one thouſand ſeven hundred and forty nine, until the twenty fifth day of *December*, one thouſand ſeven hundred and fifty ſeven, and from thence to the end of the then next ſeſſion of parliament; and which was, by the ſaid act of the twenty eighth year of his ſaid late Majeſty's reign, continued unto the twenty fifth day of *December*, one thouſand ſeven hundred and ſixty four, and from thence to the end of the then next ſeſſion of parliament; ſhall be, and the ſame is hereby further continued, from the time in the ſaid laſt mentioned act limited for the expiration thereof, unto the twenty fifth day of *December*, one thouſand ſeven hundred and ſixty ſeven, and from thence to the end of the then next ſeſſion of parliament.

further continued to 25 Dec. 1767.

CAP. XXIII.

An act for raiſing a certain ſum of money by loans or Exchequer bills; and for applying certain monies remaining in the Exchequer, for the ſervice of the year one thouſand ſeven hundred and ſixty four; and for application of certain ſavings of publick monies and of monies ariſen by the ſale of military ſtores; and for further appropriating the ſupplies granted in this ſeſſion of parliament; and for relief of perſons who have omitted to inſert in indentures, or other writings, the full ſum agreed to be paid with clerks, apprentices, and other ſervants.

Moſt gracious Sovereign,

Preamble.

WE, *your Majeſty's moſt dutiful and loyal ſubjects, the commons of* Great Britain *in parliament aſſembled, for raiſing the reſidue of the neceſſary ſupplies which we have chearfully granted to your Majeſty in this ſeſſion of parliament, have reſolved to give and grant unto your Majeſty the ſums herein after mentioned*; and do therefore moſt humbly beſeech your Majeſty, that it may be enacted; and be it enacted by the King's moſt excellent majeſty, by and with the advice and conſent of the lords ſpiritual and temporal, and commons, in this preſent parliament aſſembled, and by the authority of the ſame, That

Treasury impowered to take in loans, or issue Exchequer bills, for any sum not exceeding 800,000 l. in like manner as is prescribed by the malt act of this session, concerning loans and Exchequer bills, thereby authorized to be taken and made. —— Clauses, &c. in the said act relating to loans or Exchequer bills, extended to this act. —— Exchequer bills so issued not to be tendred or received in payment of any of the publick taxes, before 6 *April* 1765; unless the same shall be in course of payment before the said day. —— The same to be repaid out of the first supplies which shall be granted in the next session; or out of the sinking fund, if no supplies be granted before 5 *July*, 1765. —— Monies issued for that purpose out of the sinking fund, to be replaced out of the next supplies. — The bank impowered to advance on the credit of the said loan, any sum or sums not exceeding 800,000 l. the act 5 & 6 *W. & M.* notwithstanding. —— And they are further impowered to issue the sum of 3,497 l. 9 s. 9d. surplus of the duties upon beer, &c. granted by act 1 *Geo.* 3. to 5 *Jan.* 1764; and surplus of 150,000 l. granted the last session, for paying and cloathing of the militia; remaining in the Exchequer. Also the sum of 102,469 l. 19 s. 3 d. 3 q. savings of the grant last session, for pay of the *Brunswick* troops, subsidies, and former grants, &c. and 61,088 l. 4 s. other savings; and by sale of stores in *Germany* and *Portugal*, to be applied towards the extraordinary expences of the land forces, &c. incurred to 5 *Dec.* 1763, not provided for. 170,906 l. 2 s. 8 d. savings upon the non-effective accounts of several regiments; to be applied towards the unsatisfied claims in *Germany*, reported to be due. —— The monies arising by the malt act, land tax, with the sum of 2,000,000 l. charged on the *sinking fund*; and the sum of 1,110,000 l. to be raised by the bank; and also the aforesaid sum of 3,497 l. 9 s. 9 d. surplus remaining in the Exchequer of the duties on beer and ale; and also the savings on 150,000 l. granted last session for pay and cloathing of the militia; and 800,000 l. granted by this act; together with the money arising by sale of *French* prizes taken before the war; are appropriated, *viz.* 80,000 l. for the marriage portion of the princess *Augusta*, 1,430,568 l. 11 s. 9 d. towards naval services in general; 3,000 l. for building 4 houses for the officers of the hospital at *Plymouth*. 10,000 l. upon account, to the commissioners of *Greenwich* hospital, for out pensioners. 650,000 l. towards paying off the debt of the navy. 1,231 l. 17 s. 6 d. for paying a bounty for the year 1764, to the oldest chaplains of the navy, who have served 4 years on board in the late war, and have not preferment of 50 l. *per ann.* value, *viz.* to 15 such 2 s. 6 d. *per diem*, and to 15 others 2 s. *per diem*. 173,080 l. 8 s. 6 d. charge of the office of ordnance for land service. 52,359 l. 8 s. 1 d. charge of the office of ordnance for land service not provided for in 1763. 2,610,745 l. 10 s. 7 d. 3 q. for pay, &c. of the land forces in general; whereof 617,704 l. 17 s. 10 d. 3 q. charge of 17,532 effective men, including invalids, for guards and garrisons, &c. 372,774l. 6s. 4d. 3q. for the forces and garrisons in the plantations, and in *Minorca* and *Gibraltar*; and for provisions for them; 11,322 l. 7 s. 3 d. for pay of the general and general staff officers. 80,000 l. on account, for pay and cloathing of the militia; 30,188 l. 18 s. to the reduced officers of the land forces and marines, for the year 1764; 115,455 l. 13 s. to the reduced officers of the land forces disbanded in 1763, and such as are to be reduced for the year 1764. 2,605 l. 15 s. to the officers and private gentlemen of the two troops of horse guards, and regiment of horse reduced, and superannuated gentlemen of the four troops of horse guards; 1,696l. for pensions to officers widows. 103,794l. 2s. for out-pensioners of *Chelsea* hospital; 18,331l. 17s. 11d. deficiency in the grant of the last year for out-pensioners of the said hospital in 1763; 43,901l. 3s. 7d. 3q. subsidy to the duke of *Brunswick*, pursuant to treaty; 50,000l. on account, to the landgrave of *Hesse Cassel*, pursuant to treaty; 823,876l. 12s. 2d. 3q. extraordinary expences of land forces, &c. incurred in 1763, not provided for; 319,093l. 17s. 4d. upon account, towards satisfying the claims in *Germany*, reported to be due. 1,800,000l. for paying off Exchequer bills made out by virtue of an act of the last session; 5,703l. 14s. 11d. for supporting the civil establishment in *Nova Scotia*; 4,031l. 8s. 8d. for charges of the civil establishment in *Georgia*; 5,700l. for charges of the civil establishment in *East Florida*; 5,700l. for charges of the civil establishment in *West Florida*; 1,818l. for charges of the general surveys in *North America*; 20,000l. for supporting the forts and settlements on the coast of *Africa*; 38,347l. 10s. to the foundling hospital, to be issued without fee; 7,150l. to make good to his Majesty the like sum issued by him, pursuant to the address of the commons; 10,000l. to enable the commissioners for paving, &c. the streets of *Westminster*, to perform the trusts reposed in them; whereof 5,000 l. to be paid by 5 *April* 1764; and 5,000l. by 5 *April* 1765; 2,000l. to the trustees of the *British Museum*; 2,500l. to *J. Blake* esquire, for carrying on his fish scheme; 545l. 15s. compensations for lands purchased, &c. under act 2 *Geo. 1.* for erecting forts on the sea coasts; 103l. 13s. 9d. 1q. for interest of principal money for lands purchased under the recited act of 2 *Geo.* 3. 7,000 to *Samuel Touchet* merchant, expences incurred in fitting out vessels in the expedition against *Senegal*, &c. 69,671l. 1s. 2d. to replace to the sinking fund the like sum issued thereout, for the half year's payment due 29 *Sept.* 1763. on the annuities granted on the navy and victualling bills; 41,123l. 1s. 6d. to make good the deficiency on 5 *July*, 1763. of the duties on offices and pensions, and upon houses and lights; 36,699l. 15s. 4d. 2q. to make good the deficiency on 10 *Oct.* 1763. of the additional duties upon wines imported, and duties upon cyder and perry; 129,489l. 0s. 3d. to make good the deficiencies of the grants for the year 1763.——These aids to be applied to no other uses.——Rules to be observed in the application of the half-pay.—Clause in the act of 3 *Geo.* 3.——Application of the savings of the several sums of 33,351l. 17s. 6d. and 88,704l. 3s. 4d. granted the last session towards half-pay.——Clause for relief of persons who have omitted to insert in indentures, or other writings, the full sum agreed to be paid with clerks, apprentices, or servants. The duties to be paid by 29 *Sept.* 1764.

CAP. XXIV.

An act for preventing frauds and abuses in relation to the sending and receiving of letters and packets free from the duty of postage.

WHEREAS, *under colour of the privilege of sending and receiving post letters by members of parliament, free from the duty of postage, many great and notorious frauds have been and still are frequently practised, as well in derogation of the honour of parliament, as to the detriment of the publick revenue; divers persons having presumed to counterfeit the hand, and otherwise fraudulently to make use of the names, of members of parliament, upon letters and packets to be sent by the post, in order to avoid the payment of the duty of postage: and whereas the allowance of sending and receiving letters and packets free from the duty of postage, heretofore granted to, or customarily exercised by, certain persons not being members of parliament, in respect of their offices, has not been sufficiently confined to such letters and packets only as relate to the business of their respective offices, and may therefore, if continued without further restrictions and limitations, be liable to great abuse:* in order, therefore, to put the more effectual stop to these and the like frauds and abuses, and at the same time to ascertain, for the better guidance and direction of his Majesty's post master general, and the officers to be employed under him, in the performance of their duty, by what persons only, and under what regulations or restrictions, the privilege or allowance of sending and receiving letters and packets free from the duty of postage shall thenceforth be enjoyed and

exercised

exercised, may it please your Majesty that it may be enacted; and be it enacted by the King's most excellent majesty, by and with the advice and consent of the lords spiritual and temporal, and commons, in this present parliament assembled, and by the authority of the same, That from and after the first day of *May*, one thousand seven hundred and sixty four, so long as the revenue arising in the general letter office or post office, or office of post master general, shall continue to be carried to, and made part of the aggregate fund, no letters or packets sent by the post, to or from any place whatsoever, shall be exempted from paying the duty of postage, according to the rates established by the several acts of parliament now in force; other than and except such letters and packets as are herein after excepted, and in such manner, and under such restrictions, as are herein after declared and enacted concerning the same; that is to say, Except all such letters and packets as shall be sent from or to the King's most excellent majesty; all letters and packets, not exceeding the weight of two ounces, sent from and to any places (within the kingdoms of *Great Britain* or *Ireland*) during the sitting of any session of parliament, or within forty days before or forty days after any summons or prorogation of the same, which shall be signed, on the outside thereof, by any member of either of the two houses of parliament of *Great Britain*, and whereof the whole superscription shall be of the hand writing of such member, or which shall be directed to any member of either house of the parliament of *Great Britain*, at any of the places of his usual residence, or at the place where he shall actually be at the time of the delivery thereof, or at the house of parliament, or the lobby of the house of parliament of which he is a member; all letters and packets, not exceeding the weight of two ounces, sent from and to any places within the kingdom of *Ireland*, during the sitting of any session of parliament of *Ireland*, or within forty days before or forty days after any summons or prorogation thereof, which shall be signed, on the outside thereof, by any member of either of the two houses of the parliament of *Ireland*, and whereof the whole superscription shall be of the hand writing of such member, or which being sent, during such time as aforesaid, from any part of *Great Britain* or *Ireland* to any part of *Ireland*, shall be directed to any member of either house of the parliament of *Ireland*, at any of the places of his usual residence, or at the place where he shall actually be at the time of the delivery thereof, or at the house of parliament, or the lobby of the house of parliament of which he is a member; all letters and packets directed to the lord high treasurer, or commissioners of the treasury, or the secretaries to the treasury; to the lord high admiral, or commissioners of the admiralty, or the secretaries of the admiralty; to his Majesty's principal secretaries of state, or their under secretaries; to the commissioners for trade and plantations, or their secretary; to his Majesty's secretary at war, or the deputy secretary at war; or to his Majesty's lieutenant general, or other chief governor or governors of

From and after 1 May, 1764, while the revenue of the post office shall continue to be carried to the aggregate fund; no letters or packets shall be exempted from postage, but such as shall be sent from or to the King; and such, not exceeding two ounces in weight, as shall be sent during the session of parliament, or within 40 days before or after summons or prorogation, and be signed on the outside by a member of either house, and the whole of the superscription to be of such member's writing; or, directed to a member, at his usual residence, or place where he shall then be, or at the house, &c. of parliament: and in like manner, letters and packets sent from and to places in Ireland, during the session there, or within 40 days before or after summons or prorogation, signed and directed as aforesaid: also all letters and packets to the lord high

of *Ireland*, and his or their chief ſecretary, his or their ſecretary for the provinces of *Ulſter* and *Munſter* in that kingdom, his or their ſecretary reſiding always in *Great Britain*, the under ſecretary and firſt clerk in the office in *Ireland* of the ſaid chief ſecretary, the firſt clerk in the office in *Ireland* of the ſaid ſecretary for the provinces of *Ulſter* and *Munſter*; or to his Majeſty's poſtmaſter general, or to the deputy of the poſtmaſter general, for that part of *Great Britain* called *Scotland*, for the kingdom of *Ireland*, or for his Majeſty's dominions in *America* reſpectively; or to the ſecretary of ſuch poſtmaſter general, or deputy of the poſtmaſter general, or to the farmer of the bye and croſs road letters, or to any of the ſurveyors of the poſt office; all for the time being; and all letters and packets ſent from any of the ſaid officers for the time being, which ſhall be ſigned, on the outſide thereof, by ſuch officer, and whereof the whole ſuperſcription ſhall likewiſe be of the hand writing of ſuch officer; and alſo except all letters and packets ſent from the treaſury, the admiralty office, the office of his Majeſty's principal ſecretaries of ſtate, the plantation office, the war office, or from the general poſt office at *London*, or from any of the chief offices at *Edinburgh*, at *Dublin*, or in *America*, and which ſhall appear, by an indorſement made thereupon by ſome perſon properly authorized as herein after mentioned to make the ſame, to be upon his Majeſty's ſervice, and ſhall be ſealed with the ſeal of the office, or with the ſeal of the principal officer in the office or department from which they are ſent.

treaſurer, or commiſſioners, and ſecretaries to the treaſury; lord high admiral, commiſſioners and ſecretaries to the admiralty; principal ſecretaries of ſtate, and their under ſecretaries; commiſſioners for trade and plantations, or their ſecretary; ſecretary at war, or his deputy; lieutenant general, or other chief governor or governors of Ireland; or their chief ſecretary, or ſecretary for the provinces of Ulſter and Munſter; their ſecretary reſiding in Great Britain; the under ſecretary, and firſt clerk, in the office in Ireland of the chief ſecretary, and the firſt clerk in the office of the ſecretary for Ulſter and Munſter, the poſtmaſter general, or deputy for Scotland, Ireland, and America; the ſecretary, or deputy of the poſtmaſter general; farmer of the bye and croſs road letters; ſurveyors of the poſt office; and letters and packets ſent from any of the ſaid offices, ſigned by them on the outſide, and the whole ſuperſcription of their writing: and letters and packets from the treaſury, admiralty office, office of the ſecretaries of ſtate, plantation office, war office, general poſt office at London, chief offices at Edinburgh, Dublin, and America, indorſed for the King's ſervice, and ſealed with the ſeal of office, or of the principal officer in the department.

Commiſſioners of the treaſury, and admiralty, the ſecretaries of ſtate, commiſſioners for trade and plantations, ſecretary at war, poſtmaſter general, and his deputies, impowered to authorize certain perſons in their reſpec- offices, of whom liſts to be tranſmitted to the general

II. And, for more effectually preventing all ſuch frauds and abuſes as might otherwiſe be practiſed under colour of the allowance hereby granted and continued, of ſending letters and packets from the ſeveral offices and officers herein before mentioned free from the duty of poſtage; be it further enacted by the authority aforeſaid, That it ſhall and may be lawful for the lord high treaſurer, or commiſſioners of the treaſury, the lord high admiral, or commiſſioners of the admiralty, his Majeſty's principal ſecretaries of ſtate, the commiſſioners for trade and plantations, his Majeſty's ſecretary at war, his Majeſty's poſtmaſter general, and the deputies of the poſtmaſter general herein before mentioned, all for the time being, to authorize and direct certain perſons in each of their offices or departments reſpectively, a liſt of whoſe names ſhall be from time to time tranſmitted, by the principal officer or officers authorizing the ſame, to the general poſt office in *London*, to make and ſubſcribe an indorſement upon each letter or packet which ſhall concern the

publick

publick business of their respective offices, signifying that such letter or packet is upon his Majesty's service, and to seal the same with the seal of such office or officer respectively; all which persons are hereby strictly forbid so to indorse and seal any letter or packet whatsoever, unless such only concerning which they shall receive the special direction of their superior officer, or which they shall themselves know to concern the business of their respective offices; and if any person employed in any of the said offices, shall knowingly make and subscribe such indorsement, or procure the same to be made upon any letter or packet which does not really concern the business of the office in respect of which he is authorized to make the same, he shall, for the first offence, forfeit and pay the sum of five pounds, to be recovered and applied in such manner as, by the act of the ninth year of the reign of Queen *Anne* for establishing a general post office, is directed, with respect to the penalties inflicted by the said act; and, for the second offence, shall be dismissed from his office.

post office, London, to indorse the letters and packets upon the King's service, and seal the same with the seal of office, &c. None to be so indorsed and sealed, but by direction of their superior officer, or which concerns the business of the office, on forfeiture of 5 l. for the first offence, to be recovered and applied as by act 9 Annæ is directed, and for the second offence, the offender to be dismissed

III. Provided always, That the number of persons so to be appointed, in each of the offices above mentioned, to make and subscribe such indorsement as aforesaid, shall not exceed two in any one office or department, except only in the admiralty office and the war office; and that the number so to be appointed in the admiralty office shall not exceed eight in time of peace, or twelve in time of war; and that the number so to be appointed in the war office shall not exceed six in time of peace, or ten in time of war.

Persons appointed to make such indorsements, not to exceed 2 in any office, admiralty and war offices excepted; and in the admiralty not to exceed 8 in time of peace, and 12 in time of war; and in the war office, not to exceed 6 in time of peace, and 10 in time of war.

IV. Provided also, and be it further enacted by the authority aforesaid, That in case any person intitled to send letters or packets free of the duty of postage, being, by bodily infirmity, disabled from writing the whole superscription of such letters or packets, shall chuse to authorize and appoint some one person, on his behalf, and in his stead, to sign his name upon, and write the superscription of, such letters and packets, and shall cause notice thereof in writing, under his hand and seal, to be transmitted to his Majesty's postmaster general, all letters and packets, so signed and superscribed by the person so authorized and appointed, shall be allowed to pass free of the duty of postage, and shall in all respects, be proceeded with, as if the whole superscription had been of the hand writing of the person by whom such authority was given as aforesaid.

Where any privileged person, disabled from writing the whole superscription, shall authorize some person to sign his name upon, and write the superscription, and give notice thereof under his hand and seal to the postmaster general, letters and packets so signed and superscribed, shall go free.

V. Provided always, and it is hereby further enacted, That nothing herein contained shall extend to charge with the duty of postage, any printed votes, or proceedings in parliament, or printed news papers, being sent without covers, or in covers open at the sides, which shall be signed, on the outside thereof, by

Printed votes and proceedings in parliament, and news papers, sent without covers, or in covers open at

by the hand of any member of parliament, in ſuch manner as hath been heretofore practiſed, or which ſhall be directed to any member of parliament, at any place whereof he ſhall have given notice in writing to the poſtmaſter general, or to his deputy at *Edinburgh* or *Dublin* reſpectively, but that all ſuch votes, proceedings, and news papers, ſo ſent and ſigned or directed as aforeſaid, ſhall be received free of the duty of poſtage; any thing in this or any former act to the contrary notwithſtanding.

the ſides, and ſigned on the outſide by a member, or directed to a member, according to notice given by him to the poſtmaſter general, or his deputy at Edinburgh or Dublin, are to go free.

Clerks in the offices of the ſecretaries of ſtate and poſt office, being duly licenſed, may continue to frank the votes, and proceedings in parliament, and news papers, as heretofore; ſending the ſame without covers, or in covers open at the ſides.

VI. And foraſmuch as it hath been uſual for the clerks in the offices of his Majeſty's principal ſecretaries of ſtate, and alſo for certain officers in the office of his Majeſty's poſtmaſter general, to frank printed votes, and proceedings in parliament, and printed news papers, to be ſent by the poſt; be it therefore enacted by the authority aforeſaid, That it ſhall and may be lawful for ſuch clerks and officers as aforeſaid, being thereunto licenſed by his Majeſty's principal ſecretaries of ſtate, or his Majeſty's poſtmaſter general reſpectively, to continue to frank ſuch printed votes, and proceedings in parliament, and printed news papers, in ſuch manner as they have heretofore been accuſtomed to frank the ſame; provided that ſuch printed votes, proceedings, and news papers, ſhall be ſent without covers, or in covers open at the ſides.

Poſtmaſter general, and officers under him, may ſearch any packet ſent without a cover, or in a cover open at the ſides; and if they ſhall find any other paper or thing incloſed therein, or there ſhall be any writing, other than the ſuperſcription upon the printed paper, or cover, the whole of ſuch packet is to be charged with the poſtage.

VII. And be it further enacted by the authority aforeſaid, That it ſhall and may be lawful for his Majeſty's poſtmaſter general, or any of the officers employed under him, to examine and ſearch any packet ſent without a cover, or in a cover open at the ſides, in order to diſcover whether any other paper or thing whatſoever be incloſed or concealed in or with ſuch printed paper, as is hereby permitted to be ſent free of poſtage without a cover, or in a cover open at the ſides; and in caſe any ſuch other paper or thing whatſoever ſhall be found to be incloſed or concealed in or with ſuch printed paper as aforeſaid, or in caſe there ſhall be any writing, other than the ſuperſcription upon ſuch printed paper, or upon the cover thereof, the whole of ſuch packet ſhall be charged with the duty of poſtage, according to the rates eſtabliſhed by the ſeveral acts of parliament now in force for that purpoſe.

If any perſon ſhall, after 1 June, 1764, counterfeit the writing of any perſon in the ſuperſcription of any letter or packet, to avoid the poſtage, he ſhall be adjudged guilty of felony, and be tranſported for 7 years.

VIII. And be it further enacted by the authority aforeſaid, That if any perſon ſhall, after the firſt day of *June*, one thouſand ſeven hundred and ſixty four, counterfeit the hand writing of any perſon whatſoever, in the ſuperſcription of any letter or packet to be ſent by the poſt, in order to avoid the payment of the duty of poſtage, every perſon, ſo offending, ſhall be deemed guilty of felony, and ſhall be tranſported for ſeven years.

CAP.

CAP. XXV.

An act for establishing an agreement with the governor and company of the bank of England, *for raising certain sums of money towards the supply for the service of the year one thousand seven hundred and sixty four; and for more effectually preventing the forging powers to transfer such stock, or receive such dividends or annuities as are therein mentioned, and the fraudulent personating the owners thereof.*

WHEREAS *by an act of parliament made in the seventh year of the reign of her late majesty, Queen* Anne, *intituled,* An act for enlarging the capital stock of the bank of *England,* and for raising a further supply to her Majesty for the service of the year one thousand seven hundred and nine; *it was declared and enacted, That the governor and company of the bank of* England, *and their successors for ever, should continue and be one body corporate and politic, and should for ever have, receive, and enjoy, the entire yearly fund of one hundred thousand pounds therein mentioned, out of certain rates and duties of excise therein described, and such abilities, capacities, powers, authorities, franchises, exemptions, privileges, profits, and advantages, as are therein expressed, subject nevertheless to a power and condition of redemption in that act contained in that behalf; and it was thereby provided and enacted, That at any time, upon twelve months notice, after the first day of* August *which should be in the year of our Lord one thousand seven hundred and thirty two, and not before, and upon repayment by parliament to the said governor and company of the bank of* England, *or their successors, of the several sums amounting to one million six hundred thousand pounds therein mentioned, without any deduction, discount, or abatement whatsoever, to be made out of the said sum of one million six hundred thousand pounds, or any part thereof, and upon payment to the said governor and company, and their successors, of all arrears of the said one hundred thousand pounds* per annum, *and all the principal and interest money which should be owing unto them upon all such tallies, Exchequer orders, or parliamentary funds, which the said governor and company, or their successors, should have remaining in their hands, or be intitled to, at the time of such notice to be given as aforesaid (such funds for redemption whereof other provision was made in the same act, only excepted) then, and in such case, and not till then, the said yearly fund of one hundred thousand pounds should cease and determine, as by the said act (relation being thereunto had) may more plainly appear: and whereas by an act of parliament made in the twelfth year of her said late Majesty's reign, (intituled,* An act to raise twelve hundred thousand pounds for public uses, by circulating a further sum in Exchequer bills; and for enabling her Majesty to raise five hundred thousand pounds on the revenues appointed for uses of her civil government, to be applied for or towards payment of such debts, and arrears owing to

Preamble, reciting clauses in act 7 Annæ,

12 Annæ,

to her servants, tradesmen, and others, as are therein mentioned) *the before recited proviso or condition, for determining the said yearly fund of one hundred thousand pounds, upon twelve months notice after the said first day of* August, *one thousand seven hundred and thirty two, upon such payments as aforesaid, was thereby repealed and made void; and it was thereby provided and enacted, That at any time, upon twelve months notice, after the first day of* August, *which should be in the year of our Lord one thousand seven hundred and forty two, and not before, and upon repayment by parliament to the said governor and company of the bank of* England, *or their successors, of the said sum of sixteen hundred thousand pounds, without any deduction, discount, or abatement whatsoever, and upon payment to the said governor and company, and their successors, of all arrears of the said one hundred thousand pounds* per annum, *and all the principal and interest money, which should be owing to them upon all such tallies, Exchequer orders, or parliamentary funds, which the said governor and company, or their successors, should have remaining in their hands, or be intitled to, at the time of such notice to be given as aforesaid (such funds for redemption whereof other provision is made in the said former acts, or any of them, or in the said recited act, always excepted) then, and in such case, and not till then, the said yearly fund of one hundred thousand pounds should cease and determine: and it is also further provided and enacted, That from and after such redemption of the said one hundred thousand pounds* per annum, *and from and after redemption should be made by parliament of the annuity of one hundred and six thousand five hundred and one pounds, thirteen shillings, and five pence, by the said recited act, of the seventh year of her said late Majesty's reign, settled and payable to the said governor and company, in the manner therein mentioned, and from and after redemption should likewise be made of the fund established by the said recited act, in relation to the Exchequer bills therein mentioned, then, and not till then, the said corporation of the governor and company of the bank of* England *should cease and determine; but till then the said governor and company should continue a corporation, and should have and enjoy all the powers and privileges they were intitled to, as by the same act (relation being thereunto had) may more fully appear: and whereas by an act of parliament made in*
15 Geo. II. *the fifteenth year of the reign of his late majesty King* George *the Second (intituled,* An act for establishing an agreement with the governor and company of the bank of *England,* for advancing the sum of one million six hundred thousand pounds, towards the supply for the service of the year one thousand seven hundred and forty two) *the said governor and company, and their successors, were directed to advance and pay into the receipt of his Majesty's Exchequer, for his Majesty's use, the full sum of one million six hundred thousand pounds, on or before such time, and in such manner, and under such conditions, as in the said act are mentioned: and it was thereby declared and enacted, That the several and respective provisoes, contained in the said acts of the seventh and twelfth years of the reign of her late majesty Queen* Anne, *and each of them, and all other provisoes contained in any other act or acts of parliament for deter-*

determining the said fund of one hundred thousand pounds per annum, *and the said corporation of the governor and company of the bank of* England, *upon the respective notices and payments in the same respective acts mentioned, should be, and were thereby repealed and made void; and that the said governor and company of the bank of* England, *so enlarged as aforesaid, and their successors for ever, should remain, continue, and be, one body corporate and politic, by the name aforesaid, and should for ever have, receive, and enjoy, the said entire yearly fund of one hundred thousand pounds, out of the said rates and duties of excise, together with a perpetual succession, and privilege of exclusive banking, as therein after was mentioned, and all other abilities, capacities, powers, authorities, franchises, exemptions, privileges, profits, and advantages whatsoever, whereunto the governor and company of the bank of* England, *before the making of the said act, were intitled by the said acts of the seventh and twelfth years of the reign of her said late majesty Queen* Anne, *or either of them, or by any other act or acts of parliament, grants or charters whatsoever, then in force; all which were by the said act ratified and confirmed to the said governor and company, and their successors, freed and discharged of and from the said provisoes and conditions of redemption thereby repealed, or intended to be repealed, as aforesaid, and all other provisoes, powers, acts, matters, and things whatsoever, theretofore had, made, done, or committed, for redeeming, determining, or making void, the said corporation, or yearly fund of one hundred thousand pounds, and the said privilege of exclusive banking, and all other their abilities, capacities, powers, authorities, franchises, exemptions, privileges, profits, and advantages, or any of them; subject nevertheless to such restrictions, rules, and directions, and also to such other agreements, matters, and things, as in the said acts and charters, or any of them then in force, were contained or prescribed, and also subject to the power and condition of redemption thereafter in the said act contained in that behalf; and it was thereby also provided and enacted, That at any time, upon twelve months notice, after the first day of* August, *which should be in the year of our Lord one thousand seven hundred and sixty four, and not before, and upon the re-payment by parliament to the said governor and company of the bank of* England, *or their successors, as well of the said sum of one million six hundred thousand pounds formerly advanced, as of the sum of one million six hundred thousand pounds before mentioned then to be advanced, amounting, in the whole, to the sum of three millions two hundred thousand pounds, without any deduction, discount, or abatement whatsoever, to be made out of the said sum of three millions two hundred thousand pounds, or any part thereof, and upon payment to the said governor and company, and their successors, of all the arrears of the said one hundred thousand pounds* per annum, *and all the principal and interest money which should be owing unto them upon all such tallies, Exchequer orders, Exchequer bills, or parliamentary funds, which the said governor and company, or their successors, should have remaining in their hands, or be intitled to, at the time of such notice to be given as aforesaid (such funds for redemption whereof other provision was made in and by the acts of parliament therein mentioned;*

always

always and only excepted) then, and in such case, and not till then, the said yearly fund of one hundred thousand pounds should cease and determine: and whereas the said governor and company of the bank of England *are willing and contented to advance, towards the supply granted to your Majesty for the service of the year one thousand seven hundred and sixty four, the sum of one million, on Exchequer bills bearing interest at the rate of three pounds* per centum per annum, *the said interest to be paid quarterly, and the said Exchequer bills to be charged upon, and repaid out of, the first aids or supplies which shall be granted by parliament for the service of the year one thousand seven hundred and sixty six, and in case sufficient aids or supplies shall not be granted for that purpose before the fifth day of* April, *one thousand seven hundred and sixty six, the same to be charged upon, and repaid out of, the sinking fund; and also to pay into his Majesty's Exchequer, towards the said supply, the sum of one hundred and ten thousand pounds, without any repayment of the principal, or allowance of interest for the same, provided that the privilege of exclusive banking, and all other the abilities, capacities, powers, authorities, franchises, exemptions, privileges, profits, and advantages, in this or any former act contained, be granted and confirmed to the said governor and company, in such manner as is herein after mentioned:* now we, your Majesty's most dutiful and loyal subjects, the commons of *Great Britain* in parliament assembled, being desirous to raise, with as much ease and advantage as possible to your subjects, the necessary supplies, and to encourage the said governor and company to advance the said sums of one million, and of one hundred and ten thousand pounds, in the manner herein after appointed, do most humbly beseech your Majesty, that it may be enacted; and be it enacted by the King's most excellent majesty, by and with the advice and consent of the lords spiritual and temporal, and commons, in this present parliament assembled, and by the authority of the same, That it shall and may be lawful to and for the commissioners of his Majesty's treasury now on for the time being, or any three or more of them, or the high treasurer for the time being, at any time or times before the fifth day of *January*, one thousand seven hundred and sixty five, to cause or direct any number of Exchequer bills to be made out for any sum or sums of money not exceeding in the whole the sum of one million, in the same or like manner, form, and order, and according to the same or like rules and directions, as in and by an act of this present session of parliament (intituled, *An act for continuing and granting to his Majesty certain duties upon malt, mum, cyder, and perry, for the service of the year one thousand seven hundred and sixty four)* are enacted and prescribed concerning the Exchequer bills to be made in pursuance of the said act.

Commissioners of the treasury impowered at any time before 5 Jan. 1765, to direct Exchequer bills to be made out for any sum not exceeding 1,000,000 l. in like manner as is prescribed by the malt act of this session, concerning Exchequer bills thereby authorized to be made out.

II. And be it further enacted by the authority aforesaid, That all and every the clauses, provisoes, powers, privileges, advantages, penalties, forfeitures, and disabilities, contained in the said last mentioned act, relating to the Exchequer bills authorized to be made by the same act (except such clauses as do charge

Clauses, &c. in the said act extended to the Exchequer bills to be made in pur-

charge the ſame on the taxes granted by the ſame act, and ſuch claufes as limit or relate to the aſcertaining the rate of intereſt to be paid for the forbearance of money lent on the credit of the ſaid act, and alſo except as herein after mentioned) ſhall be applied and extended to the Exchequer bills to be made in purſuance of this act, as fully and effectually, to all intents and purpoſes, as if the ſame had been originally authorized by the ſaid laſt mentioned act, or as if the ſaid ſeveral clauſes or proviſoes had been particularly repeated and re-enacted in the body of this act. suance of this act.

III. And be it further enacted by the authority aforeſaid, That the ſaid Exchequer bills ſhall bear an intereſt after the rate of three pounds *per centum per annum*. Bills to carry 3 l. per cent. intereſt.

IV. Provided always, and be it further enacted by the authority aforeſaid, That no Exchequer bill or bills to be made out by virtue of this act, ſhall, after the ſame hath or have been iſſued at the Exchequer, be afterwards, at any time before the fifth day of *April*, one thouſand ſeven hundred and ſixty ſix, received or taken, or paſs or be current to any receiver or collector in *Great Britain* of the cuſtoms, exciſe, or any revenue, ſupply, aid, or tax whatſoever, due or payable to his Majeſty, his heirs, or ſucceſſors, or at the receipt of the Exchequer, from any ſuch receiver or collector, or from any other perſon or perſons, bodies politic or corporate, otherwiſe, or on any other account, than for the diſcharge and cancelling of ſuch bills, in caſe the ſame ſhall be in due courſe or order of payment, before the ſaid fifth day of *April*, one thouſand ſeven hundred and ſixty ſix; nor ſhall any ſuch receiver or collector exchange, at any time before the ſaid fifth day of *April*, one thouſand ſeven hundred and ſixty ſix, for any money of ſuch revenues, aids, taxes, or ſupplies, in his hands, any Exchequer bill or bills which ſhall have been iſſued as aforeſaid by virtue of this act; nor ſhall any action be maintained againſt any ſuch receiver or collector, for neglecting or refuſing to exchange any ſuch bill or bills for ready money before the ſaid fifth day of *April*, one thouſand ſeven hundred and ſixty ſix; any thing in the ſaid act made in this preſent ſeſſion of parliament, intituled, *An act for continuing and granting to his Majeſty certain duties upon malt, mum, cyder, and perry, for the ſervice of the year one thouſand ſeven hundred and ſixty four*, or this act, contained to the contrary notwithſtanding. Exchequer bills ſo iſſued not to be tendered or received in payment of any of the publick taxes, before 5 April, 1766, unleſs the ſame be in courſe of payment before the ſaid day.

V. And be it further enacted by the authority aforeſaid, That all ſuch Exchequer bills, together with the intereſt and charges incident to or attending the ſame, ſhall be and are hereby charged and chargeable upon, and ſhall be repaid or borne by or out of, the firſt aids or ſupplies which ſhall be granted by parliament for the ſervice of the year one thouſand ſeven hundred and ſixty ſix; and in caſe ſufficient aids or ſupplies for that purpoſe ſhall not be granted before the fifth day of *April*, one thouſand ſeven hundred and ſixty ſix, then all the ſaid Exchequer bills, with the intereſt and charges incident to or attending the ſame, ſhall be and are hereby charged and chargeable upon ſuch The ſaid bills to be repaid out of the firſt ſupplies which ſhall be granted for the year 1766;

such monies as, at any time or times at or after the said fifth day of *April*, shall be or remain in the receipt of the Exchequer, of the surplusses, excesses, overplus monies, and other revenues, composing the fund commonly called *The Sinking Fund* (except such monies of the said sinking fund as shall then be appropriated to any particular use or uses by any act or acts of parliament in that behalf) and such monies of the said sinking fund shall and may be issued and applied, as soon as the same can be regularly stated and ascertained, for and towards paying off, cancelling, and discharging, such Exchequer bills, interest, and charges, until the whole of them shall be paid off, cancelled, and discharged, or money sufficient for that purpose be kept and reserved in the Exchequer, to be payable on demand to the respective proprietors thereof.

or out of the sinking fund, if no supplies be granted before 5 April of that year.

VI. Provided always, and be it enacted by the authority aforesaid, That whatever monies shall be so issued out of the said surplusses, excesses, overplus monies, or other revenues composing the sinking fund, shall from time to time be replaced by and out of the first supplies to be then after granted in parliament; any thing herein contained to the contrary notwithstanding.

Monies issued for that purpose out of the sinking fund, to be replaced out of the first supplies after.

VII. And it is hereby further enacted by the authority aforesaid, That the said governor and company of the bank of *England*, and their successors, shall and are hereby required to exchange for ready money, from time to time, all such of the said Exchequer bills as shall, at any time or times before the said fifth day of *April*, one thousand seven hundred and sixty six, be tendered or produced to them, or their cashier or cashiers, for that purpose, by any person or persons; and shall pay or cause to be paid to such person or persons, in ready money, the sum for which every such bill, so tendered or produced, was issued, together with the interest, after the said rate of three pounds *per centum per annum*, which shall be then due thereupon; and shall exchange, in manner as aforesaid, such of the said bills as shall have been, from time to time, paid away or circulated by or on the behalf of the said governor and company, or their successors, and shall before the said fifth day of *April*, one thousand seven hundred and sixty six, be tendered or produced as aforesaid, as often as such case shall happen; and the said governor and company, or their successors, or their agents or servants, shall not be intitled to or receive any premium, rate, or allowance whatsoever, for or in respect of the exchanging or circulating the said Exchequer bills; any thing herein, or in any other act of parliament to the contrary notwithstanding.

Bank to exchange for ready money such of the said bills, as shall be tendered them before the said 5 April, with the interest due thereupon; and no allowance is to be made to the bank for the same.

VIII. And be it further enacted by the authority aforesaid, That in case the said governor and company of the bank of *England*, or their successors, or their cashier or cashiers, shall neglect or refuse to exchange any such Exchequer bill or bills for ready money as aforesaid, contrary to the true intent and meaning of this act, upon demand thereof made at their chief office within the city of *London*, for the space of twenty four hours,

Bank refusing to discharge such bills,

hours, then the person or persons demanding the same, or the person or persons for and on whose behalf such demand shall be made, shall and may recover such money to his, her, or their own use, by action of debt or upon the case, bill, suit, or information, in any of his Majesty's courts of record at *Westminster*, wherein no essoin, protection, privilege, or wager of law, shall be allowed, or any more than one imparlance; in which action, bill, suit, or information, it shall be lawful to declare, that the said governor and company, or their successors, are indebted to the plaintiff or plaintiffs, the money demanded upon the said bill or bills, according to the form of this statute, and have not paid the same, which shall be sufficient; and the plaintiff or plaintiffs in such action, bill, suit, or information, shall recover against the said governor and company, and their successors, not only the money so neglected or refused to be paid, but also damages after the rate of fifteen pounds *per centum per annum*, on such money, together with full costs of suit; and the said governor and company, and their successors, and their said stock and funds, shall be, and are hereby made subject and liable thereunto.

the money may be recovered in any of the courts at Westminster,

with damages, after the rate of 15l. per cent. and full costs.

IX. And be it further enacted by the authority aforesaid, That the clauses, powers, and provisions, in the said act, made in this present session of parliament, intituled, *An act for continuing and granting to his Majesty certain duties upon malt, mum, cyder, and perry, for the service of the year one thousand seven hundred and sixty four*, relating to such person or persons, body or bodies politick or corporate, as should contract by virtue of that act with the high treasurer, or any three or more of the commissioners of the treasury for the time being, for the circulating and exchanging for ready money the Exchequer bills by the said act authorized to be issued (except the clause for altering the rate of interest, and such other parts as are varied by this act) shall extend to and operate with respect to the said governor and company of the bank of *England*, and their successors, in relation to the Exchequer bills to be made out, exchanged, and circulated, by virtue of this act, in as full and ample manner, to all intents and purposes, as if a contract in writing had been made for that purpose in the manner prescribed by the said act, and as if the said clauses, powers, and provisions, were herein specially re-enacted, and applied to the purposes of this act.

Clauses in the malt act of this session relating to the circulating Exchequer bills,

extended to the bills to be issued by virtue of this act.

X. And be it further enacted by the authority aforesaid, That the said governor and company of the bank of *England*, and their successors, shall advance and pay into the receipt of his Majesty's Exchequer, for his Majesty's use, the full sum of one hundred and ten thousand pounds, on or before the twenty third day of *April*, one thousand seven hundred and sixty four; and that the said governor and company of the bank of *England*, or their successors, shall not be intitled to any repayment of the principal, or allowance of any interest for or in respect of all or any part of the said sum of one hundred and ten thousand pounds;

Bank to pay into the Exchequer 110,000l. by 23 April, 1764;

and no repayment to be made of principal or interest for the same. pounds; and in case the said governor and company of the bank of *England*, or their successors, shall make failure in the said payment so by this act appointed to be made into his Majesty's Exchequer as aforesaid, the said sum of one hundred and ten thousand pounds, or any part thereof, remaining unpaid, after the said twenty third day of *April* one thousand seven hundred and sixty four, shall and may be recovered to his Majesty's use by action of debt, or upon the case, bill, suit, or information, in any of his Majesty's courts of record at *Westminster*, wherein no essoin, protection, privilege, or wager of law, shall be allowed, or any more than one imparlance: in which action, bill, suit, or information, it shall be lawful to declare, that the said governor and company, or their successors, are indebted to his Majesty the money of which they shall have made default in payment according to the form of this statute, and have not paid the same, which shall be sufficient; and in or upon such action, bill, suit, or information, there shall be further recovered to his Majesty's use against the said governor and company of the said bank of *England*, or their successors, damages after the rate of twelve pounds *per centum* for the money so unpaid contrary to this act, together with full costs of suit; and the said governor and company and their successors, and their said stock and funds, shall be, and are hereby made subject and liable thereunto.

Bank making failure, the money may be recovered in any of the courts at Westminster; with damages after the rate of 12 l. per cent. and full costs.

In consideration of the bank's complying with the premisses,

XI. And for the encouragement of the said governor and company of the bank of *England*, and their successors, to exchange and circulate the said Exchequer bills, in the manner and during the time herein before mentioned, and to pay into the receipt of his Majesty's Exchequer the said sum of one hundred and ten thousand pounds on or before the day above limited; and to the end the said governor and company, and their successors, may have a competent recompence and consideration for so doing; it is hereby declared and enacted by the authority aforesaid, That such part of the said recited provision contained in the said act, made in the fifteenth year of the reign of his late majesty King *George* the Second, as relates to the determining the said fund of one hundred thousand pounds *per annum*, and the said corporation of the governor and company of the bank of *England*, upon the notice and payments therein mentioned, shall be, and is hereby repealed and made void; and that the said governor and company of the bank of *England*, and their successors for ever, shall remain, continue, and be, one body corporate and politick, by the name aforesaid, and shall for ever have, receive, and enjoy, the said intire yearly fund of one hundred thousand pounds out of the said rates and duties of excise, together with a perpetual succession, and privilege of exclusive banking, as herein after is mentioned, and all other abilities, capacities, powers, authorities, franchises, exemptions, privileges, profits, and advantages whatsoever, whereunto the governor and company of the bank of *England* are, or, before the making of this act, were intitled, by the said acts of the seventh and twelfth years of the reign of her said late majesty Queen

Part of the provision in the recited act of 15 Geo. II. relating to the determining their fund, &c. is repealed; and they are continued a body corporate, &c. with all their former abilities, privileges, and advantages.

Queen *Anne*, and the ſaid act of the fifteenth year of the reign of his late majeſty King *George* the Second, or any of them, or by any other act or acts of parliament, grants or charters whatſoever now in force; all which are by this act ratified and confirmed to the ſaid governor and company, and their ſucceſſors, freed and diſcharged of and from the ſaid proviſo and conditions of redemption hereby repealed or intended to be repealed as aforeſaid, and all other proviſoes, powers, acts, matters, and things whatſoever, heretofore had, made, done, or committed, for redeeming, determining, or making void, the ſaid corporation or yearly fund of one hundred thouſand pounds, and the ſaid privilege of excluſive banking, and all other their abilities, capacities, powers, authorities, franchiſes, exemptions, privileges, profits, and advantages, or any of them; ſubject nevertheleſs to ſuch reſtrictions, rules, and directions, and alſo to ſuch other agreements, matters, and things, as in the ſaid acts and charters, or any of them now in force, are contained or preſcribed, and alſo ſubject to the power and condition of redemption hereafter in this act contained in this behalf.

XII. Provided always, and it is hereby further enacted by the authority aforeſaid, That at any time, upon twelve months notice after the firſt day of *Auguſt*, which ſhall be in the year of our Lord one thouſand ſeven hundred and eighty ſix, and not before, and upon repayment by parliament to the ſaid governor and company of the bank of *England*, or their ſucceſſors, of the ſaid ſum of three millions two hundred thouſand pounds advanced by virtue of the ſaid in part recited acts, without any deduction, diſcount, or abatement whatſoever, to be made out of the ſaid ſum of three millions two hundred thouſand pounds, or any part thereof; and upon payment to the ſaid governor and company, and their ſucceſſors, of all the arrears of the ſaid one hundred thouſand pounds *per annum*, and all the principal and intereſt money which ſhall be owing unto them upon all ſuch tallies, Exchequer orders, Exchequer bills, or parliamentary funds, which the ſaid governor and company, or their ſucceſſors, ſhall have remaining in their hands, or be intitled to, at the time of ſuch notice to be given as aforeſaid; ſuch funds, for redemption whereof other proviſion is made in and by one act of parliament made in the eighth year of the reign of his majeſty King *George* the Firſt, intituled, *An act to enable the* South Sea *company to diſpoſe of the effects in their hands by way of lottery, or ſubſcription, or to ſell part of their fund or annuity payable at the Exchequer, in order to pay the debts of the ſaid company, and for relief of ſuch who were intended to have the benefit of a late act touching payment of ten* per centum *therein mentioned*; and in and by one other act of parliament made in the firſt year of the reign of his late majeſty King *George* the Second, intituled, *An act for granting an aid to his Majeſty by ſale of annuities to the bank of* England, *at four pounds* per centum, *redeemable by parliament, and charged upon the duties on coals and culm; and for further applying the produce of the ſinking fund; and for enlarging the time for ex*-

Clauſe of redemption, with reſpect to monies advanced by the bank on the parliamentary funds, &c. by virtue of the recited acts, &c. on the terms and conditions here mentioned.

Act 8 Geo. I.

1 Geo. II.

 chang-

changing Nevis *and* Saint Christophers *debentures for annuities at three* per centum; *and for applying the arrears of his late Majesty's civil list revenues*; and by one other act of parliament, made in

2 Geo. II. the second year of the reign of his said late Majesty, intituled, *An act for raising the sum of one million two hundred and fifty thousand pounds, by sale of annuities to the bank of* England, *after the rate of four pounds* per centum per annum, *redeemable by parliament*; *and for applying the produce of the sinking fund*; and by

Act 19 Geo. II. one other act of parliament made in the nineteenth year of the reign of his said late Majesty, intituled, *An act for establishing an agreement with the governor and company of the bank of* England, *for cancelling certain Exchequer bills upon the terms therein mentioned, and for obliging them to advance the sum of one million upon the credit of the land tax and malt duties granted to his Majesty for the service of the year one thousand seven hundred and forty six*; always and only excepted, then, and in such case, and not till then, the said yearly fund of one hundred thousand pounds shall cease and determine.

Privilege of exclusive banking granted to the bank by former acts, confirmed to them; subject to the clause of redemption before mentioned.

XIII. And, to prevent any doubts that may arise concerning the privilege or power given by former acts of parliament to the said governor and company of exclusive banking, and also in regard to the erecting any other bank or banks by parliament, or restraining other persons from banking during the continuance of the said privilege granted to the governor and company of the bank of *England* as before recited, it is hereby further enacted and declared by the authority aforesaid, That it is the true intent and meaning of this act, that no other bank shall be erected, established, or allowed by parliament; and that it shall not be lawful for any body politic or corporate whatsoever erected or to be erected, or for any other persons united or to be united in covenants or partnership, exceeding the number of six persons, in that part of *Great Britain* called *England*, to borrow, owe, or take up, any sum or sums of money, on their bills or notes payable at demand, or at any less time than six months from the borrowing thereof, during the continuance of such said privilege to the said governor and company, who are hereby declared to be and remain a corporation, with the privilege of exclusive banking as before recited, subject to redemption on the terms and conditions before-mentioned; that is to say, on one year's notice after the first day of *August*, one thousand seven hundred and eighty six, and repayment of the three millions two hundred thousand pounds, and all arrears of the one hundred thousand pounds *per annum*, and all the principal and interest money that shall be owing them on all such tallies, Exchequer orders, Exchequer bills, or parliamentary funds (such funds as are before mentioned only and always excepted) which the said governor and company, or their successors, shall have remaining in their hands, or be intitled to, at the time of such notice to be given as aforesaid, and not otherwise; any thing in this act, or any former act or acts of parliament, to the contrary in any wise notwithstanding.

 XIV. And

XIV. And it is hereby alſo enacted and declared by the authority aforeſaid, That any vote or reſolution of the houſe of commons, ſignified by the ſpeaker of the ſaid houſe in writing, and delivered at the publick office of the ſaid governor and company, or their ſucceſſors, ſhall be deemed and adjudged to be a ſufficient notice, within the words or meaning of this act; any thing herein contained to the contrary notwithſtanding.

Vote of the houſe of commons ſignified by the ſpeaker, deemed ſufficient notice.

XV. And whereas it is neceſſary that proviſion ſhould be made for more effectually preventing the forging powers to transfer any ſuch ſtock, or to receive ſuch dividends or annuities, as are herein after mentioned, and the fraudulent perſonating the owners thereof, be it further enacted by the authority aforeſaid, That if any perſon or perſons whatſoever, from and after the firſt day of *May*, one thouſand ſeven hundred and ſixty four, ſhall forge or counterfeit, or procure to be forged or counterfeited, or knowingly and wilfully act or aſſiſt in the forging or counterfeiting, any letter of attorney, or other authority or inſtrument, to transfer, aſſign, ſell, or convey, any ſhare or ſhares, or any part of any ſhare or ſhares, of and in any capital ſtock or ſtocks of any body or bodies politic or corporate, which now are, or hereafter ſhall be, eſtabliſhed by any act or acts of parliament; or any ſhare or ſhares, or any part of any ſhare or ſhares, of and in any annuities in reſpect whereof the proprietors of ſuch annuities have or ſhall have transferrable ſhares in any capital ſtock or ſtocks now eſtabliſhed, or which ſhall hereafter be eſtabliſhed by any act or acts of parliament, in proportion to their reſpective annuities; or any ſhare or ſhares, or any part of any ſhare or ſhares, of or in any other transferrable annuities which now are, or hereafter ſhall be, eſtabliſhed by any act or acts of parliament; or to receive any ſuch annuity or annuities, or any dividend or dividends attending ſuch ſhares, or any of them, or any part thereof; or ſhall forge or counterfeit, or procure to be forged or counterfeited, or knowingly and wilfully act or aſſiſt in the forging or counterfeiting, any the name or names of any the proprietors of any ſuch ſhare or ſhares in ſtock, or of any the perſons intitled to any ſuch annuity or annuities, dividend or dividends, as aforeſaid, in or to any ſuch pretended letter of attorney, inſtrument, or authority; or ſhall knowingly and fraudulently demand, or endeavour to have, any ſuch ſhare or ſhares in ſtock or annuities, or any part thereof, transferred, aſſigned, ſold, or conveyed, or ſuch annuity or annuities, dividend or dividends, or any part thereof, to be received by virtue of any ſuch counterfeit or forged letter of attorney, authority, or inſtrument; or ſhall falſly and deceitfully perſonate any true and real proprietor of the ſaid ſhares in ſtock, annuities, and dividends, or any of them, or any part thereof, and thereby transferring, or endeavouring to transfer, the ſtock or annuities, or receiving, or endeavouring to receive, the money of ſuch true and lawful proprietor, as if ſuch offender were the true and lawful owner thereof; then, and in every or any ſuch caſe, all and every ſuch perſon and perſons (being thereof lawfully con-

Penalty of forging power to transfer any ſtock; or to receive any dividends or annuities thereon; or the fraudulent perſonating the owners thereof;

is felony, without benefit of clergy.

 victed

victed in due form of law) shall be adjudged guilty of felony, and shall suffer as in cases of felony, without benefit of clergy.

Publick act.

XVI. And be it further enacted by the authority aforesaid, That this act shall be deemed, adjudged, and taken to be a publick act, and be judicially taken notice of by all judges, justices, or other persons whatsoever, without specially pleading the same.

CAP. XXVI.

An act for granting a bounty upon the importation of hemp, and rough and undressed flax, from his Majesty's colonies in America.

Preamble.

WHEREAS *the encouragement of the importation of hemp, and rough and undressed flax, from his Majesty's colonies and plantations in* America, *will be a means of furnishing this kingdom with sail cloth and cordage (so essentially necessary for the supply of his Majesty's royal navy, as well as for ships employed in the merchants service) at more reasonable rates than at present, and will also tend to make the supply of the said materials cheaper and less precarious, and be a means of employing and enriching his Majesty's subjects within the said colonies and plantations:* may it therefore please your most excellent Majesty, that it may be enacted; and be it enacted by the King's most excellent majesty, by and with the advice and consent of the lords spiritual and temporal, and commons, in this present parliament assembled, and by the authority of the same, That from and after the twenty fourth day of *June*, one thousand seven hundred and sixty four, every person or persons who shall, within the time appointed by this act, import or cause to be imported into this kingdom, directly from any of his Majesty's *English* colonies or plantations in *America*, in any ship or ships that may lawfully trade to his Majesty's plantations, manned as by law is required, any hemp, water rotted, bright, and clean, or any rough and undressed flax, shall have and enjoy as a reward or premium for such importation, the following sum; that is to say,

Bounty allowed upon the importation of hemp, and rough and undressed flax, from the British American plantations,

viz. 8l. per ton for all imported between 24 June, 1764, and 24 June, 1771;

For every ton of such hemp, or rough or undressed flax, so imported from the twenty fourth day of *June*, one thousand seven hundred and sixty four, to the twenty fourth day of *June*, one thousand seven hundred and seventy one, the sum of eight pounds sterling.

6l. per ton for all imported between 24 June, 1771, and 24 June, 1778;

For every ton of such hemp, or rough or undressed flax, so imported from the twenty fourth day of *June*, one thousand seven hundred and seventy one, to the twenty fourth day of *June*, one thousand seven hundred and seventy eight, the sum of six pounds sterling.

and 4l. per ton for all imported between 24 June, 1778, and 24 June, 1785;

And for every ton of such hemp, or rough or undressed flax, imported from the twenty fourth day of *June*, one thousand seven hundred and seventy eight, to the twenty fourth day of *June*, one thousand seven hundred and eighty five, the sum of four pounds sterling.

To

To be paid upon demand to the importer of ſuch hemp or flax, by the collector of the port where the ſame ſhall be imported, out of the cuſtoms: and in caſe the collector of the port where the ſame ſhall be imported, ſhall not have money ſufficient in his hands, he is hereby required to certify the ſame to the commiſſioners of the cuſtoms, who ſhall cauſe the ſame to be paid by the receiver general of his Majeſty's cuſtoms; the bounty of the hemp and flax imported into *England*, to be paid by the receiver general of the cuſtoms in *England*, and of that imported into *Scotland*, to be paid by the receiver general there.

to be paid by the collector at the port of importation; or upon his want of money, then by the receiver general of the cuſtoms.

II. And to the end a particular benefit may accrue hereby to his Majeſty's royal navy, and for the better ſupply of the ſame with naval ſtores, be it further enacted, That upon the importation of any ſuch hemp or rough and undreſſed flax from his Majeſty's ſaid colonies and plantations, for which a reward or premium is hereby granted, the pre-emption or refuſal of ſuch hemp or flax ſhall be offered and tendered to the commiſſioners of his Majeſty's navy, upon landing the ſame; and if within the term of twenty days after ſuch tender the ſaid commiſſioners ſhall not contract or bargain for the ſame, it ſhall and may be lawful for the importer or importers, owner or owners, of the ſaid hemp or flax, otherwiſe to diſpoſe of the ſame for his or their beſt profit and advantage.

The pre-emption or refuſal of ſuch hemp or flax to be tendered to the commiſſioners of the navy; if they ſhall not contract for the ſame within 20 days, importer is at liberty to diſpoſe of it otherwiſe.

III. And, in order to intitle the importer of ſuch hemp and flax to the premium granted by this act, and to prevent frauds by importing foreign hemp and flax, be it further enacted by the authority aforeſaid, That all and every perſon or perſons importing any ſuch hemp or flax into *Great Britain*, ſhall produce to the chief officer or officers of the cuſtoms a certificate or certificates under the hand and ſeal of the governor, lieutenant governor, collector of his Majeſty's cuſtoms, and naval officer, or any two of them, reſiding and being within any of his Majeſty's colonies and plantations, that before the departure of ſuch ſhip or veſſel, ſhips or veſſels, the perſon or perſons, merchant, trader, or factor, loading the ſame, had made oath before them, that the ſaid hemp or flax ſo ſhipped on board (expreſſing in the ſaid certificate, the number, marks, and packages of ſuch hemp and flax) were truly and *bona fide* of the growth and produce of his Majeſty's ſaid colonies and plantations; which oath the ſaid governor, lieutenant governor, collector of his Majeſty's cuſtoms, and naval officer, or any two of them are hereby authorized to adminiſter; as likewiſe upon oath to be made in any port of *Great Britain*, by the maſter or maſters of ſuch ſhip or veſſel, ſhips or veſſels, importing ſuch hemp and flax, that the ſame were truly laden on board ſuch ſhip or veſſel, ſhips or veſſels, within ſome of his Majeſty's colonies or plantations in *America*, and that he or they know or believe that the ſaid hemp and flax were the produce of the ſaid colonies or plantations.

Certificate to be produced at the port of importation of ſuch hemp or flax being the growth and produce of the Britiſh colonies, &c.

Oaths to be adminiſtered upon that occaſion.

IV. And, that the officers of the cuſtoms may be the better able to diſcover any frauds intended for receiving the aforeſaid premium, be it further enacted by the authority aforeſaid, That it

Officers of the customs to examine whether such hemp and flax is good and merchantable.

it shall and may be lawful for the said officers, and they are hereby required before they make out any such certificate, to examine the said hemp and flax, by opening each package, and shifting the same, in such manner as to see the whole contents, or by such other means as they shall think proper, to find out and discover whether the said hemp is water rotted, bright, and clean, and the said flax is good and merchantable, and free from any false mixture.

In case of doubt about the quality of such as shall be imported into London, Commissioners of the customs may call in two skilful persons, who shall give their opinion upon oath; and upon like doubts in the out ports, samples to be sent up to London, or Edinburgh, to be inspected and adjudged there.

V. Provided always, That in case any doubt or dispute shall arise between the surveyors or officers of the customs, and the owners or importers of such hemp or flax as is imported into the port of *London*, as to the quality of the same, it shall and may be lawful for the commissioners of his Majesty's customs to call two or more merchants, manufacturers, or others well skilled in the commodity, who shall declare upon oath, if required, their opinion, as to the quality of the same, and according to the best of their judgment determine whether the said hemp or flax is intitled to the premium hereby granted, or not: and if any doubt or dispute shall arise as to the quality of any hemp or flax imported into any of the out ports in *England*, samples thereof shall be taken, and sent up to the commissioners of the customs in *London*; and into the out ports in *Scotland*, to the commissioners of the customs at *Edinburgh*; in such manner as the respective commissioners shall direct, in order to be inspected and adjudged there as before mentioned.

Officers to take no fee for doing their duty, on penalty of being incapacitated, and forfeiting 100l.

VI. And be it further enacted by the authority aforesaid, That no fee, gratuity, or reward, shall be demanded, taken, or received, by any officer of his Majesty's customs, for examining, viewing, or delivering such hemp or flax, with respect to the premium or reward allowed by this act; or for the signing any of the certificates in order to the receiving such premium or reward, or for paying the same; and any such officer demanding or taking such fee or reward, shall, for such offence, forfeit his office, and such officer shall also be incapable of serving his Majesty, his heirs and successors, and shall forfeit the sum of one hundred pounds.

Premium allowed on the importation, to be repaid on the exportation thereof;

VII. And be it further enacted by the authority aforesaid, That if any such hemp or flax of the growth of the *British* colonies or plantations in *America*, shall, after the twenty fourth day of *June*, one thousand seven hundred and sixty four, be exported from *Great Britain*; that then, and in every such case, the person or persons so exporting the same shall, before the entry thereof, pay unto the collector of the customs at the port where the same shall be exported, or to the chief officer of the customs there, the full sum which is by this act allowed as a premium on all such hemp or flax as he intends to export, over and above any duty the same is now by law subject to pay at exportation by any act.

VIII. Provided always, That the said collector or chief officer

cer of the cuſtoms, upon receiving of ſuch premium from the exporter of ſuch hemp or flax as aforeſaid, charge himſelf with the money ſo received, or with the ſaid premium; and the commiſſioners of his Majeſty's cuſtoms are to take particular care that the ſame be duly brought to the account of his Majeſty, by ſuch collector or chief officer as aforeſaid.

and officer to make himſelf debtor for the ſame, and the commiſſioners to ſee the ſame brought to account.

IX. And be it further enacted by the authority aforeſaid, That if any perſon or perſons, their agents, or aſſigns, ſhall be found fraudulently to export ſuch hemp or flax without paying ſuch premium to the collector or chief officer of the cuſtoms in manner aforeſaid, ſuch perſon or perſons ſhall forfeit and loſe all ſuch hemp and flax, and double the value thereof; one moiety whereof ſhall be to the uſe of his Majeſty, his heirs and ſucceſſors, and the other moiety to the informer or proſecutor; to be proſecuted in any of his Majeſty's courts of record at *Weſtminſter*, or in the court of Exchequer in *Scotland* reſpectively, wherein no eſſoin, protection, or wager of law, or more than one imparlance ſhall be allowed.

Such hemp and flax as ſhall be fraudulently exported without paying the premium, is forfeited, with double value.

X. Provided always, That if any doubt or diſpute ſhall ariſe, whether any of the hemp or flax, or any part thereof ſo to be exported, are of the growth, product, or manufacture, of his Majeſty's plantations in *America*, or of foreign growth, product, or manufacture, the *Onus probandi* ſhall lie on the owner or claimer thereof, and not on the informer or proſecutor; any law, cuſtom, or uſage, to the contrary notwithſtanding.

In caſe of doubt with reſpect to the place of growth of any hemp or flax to be exported, proof to lie on the owner.

XI. And be it further enacted by the authority aforeſaid, That if the maſter or owner of any ſhip or veſſel ſhall clandeſtinely import, or receive in ſuch ſhip or veſſel to be imported, into *Great Britain*, any hemp or flax, knowing the ſame to be foreign hemp or flax, and ſhall demand or receive for any ſuch foreign hemp or flax the reward or premium hereby granted, ſuch maſter or owner ſhall forfeit the ſum of one hundred pounds, to be ſued for and recovered in manner as aforeſaid; and the ſhip or veſſel in which ſuch foreign hemp or flax ſhall be ſo fraudulently imported, with all her guns, tackle, apparel, and furniture, ſhall be forfeited to the King's majeſty, his heirs and ſucceſſors.

Maſter receiving foreign hemp or flax on board, and demanding, &c. the premium, forfeits 100l. and the veſſel.

XII. And be it further enacted by the authority aforeſaid, That the ſeveral directions and proviſions in this act ſhall commence and take effect from and after the twenty fourth day of *June*, one thouſand ſeven hundred and ſixty four, and ſhall continue and be in force, from the ſaid twenty fourth day of *June*, for the term of twenty one years, and no longer.

Commencement and continuance of this act.

CAP. XXVII.

An act for granting, for a limited time, a liberty to carry rice from his Majesty's provinces of South Carolina *and* Georgia, *directly to any part of* America *to the southward of the said provinces, subject to the like duty as is now paid on the exportation of rice from the said colonies, to places in* Europe *situate to the southward of* Cape Finisterre.

Preamble, reciting clauses in act 3 & 4 Annæ,

WHEREAS *by an act made in the third and fourth years of the reign of her late majesty Queen* Anne, *intituled,* An act for granting to her Majesty a further subsidy on wines and merchandizes imported, *all rice of the growth or production of the* English *plantations in* America, Asia, *or* Africa, *is obliged to be imported into* England, Wales, *or* Berwick *upon* Tweed, *or to some other of the said plantations, under such securities and penalties as other enumerated goods or commodities of the growth, production, or manufacture, of the said plantations, are subject to, by an act made in the twelfth year of the reign of the late King* Charles *the Second,* (12 Car. II.) *intituled,* An act for encouraging and encreasing of shipping and navigation, *or by another act made in the five and twentieth year of the reign of the said late King,* (25 Car. II.) *intituled,* An act for the encouragement of the *Greenland* and *Eastland* trades, and for the better securing the plantation trade: *and whereas an act was made in the third year of the reign of his late majesty King* George *the Second,* (3 Geo. II.) *intituled,* An act for granting liberty to carry rice from his Majesty's province of *Carolina* in *America*, directly to any part of *Europe* southward of *Cape Finisterre*: *and whereas by an act made in the eighth year of the reign of his said Majesty the liberty* (8 Geo. II.) *granted by the said act of the third year of his said Majesty was extended to his Majesty's province of* Georgia *in* America: *and whereas very great advantages have arisen from the powers given by the said acts; and there is great reason to apprehend, that not only the produce of rice in those parts, but that also the exportation thereof would be greatly increased, for the mutual benefit of this kingdom and the said provinces, if, notwithstanding the laws relating to navigation and trade to and from the plantations, liberty or licence was granted for ships built in* Great Britain, *or in any of his Majesty's colonies in* America, *to load rice in either of the said provinces, and to carry the same directly to any part of* America, *to the southward of the said provinces of* Carolina *or* Georgia, *without bringing the same first to* Great Britain, *as the laws now require; whereby the same will arrive at such places, in a seasonable condition, for the consumption thereof:* for this end, and for providing proper securities for your Majesty's duties, and for preventing any prejudice or damage to this nation which might happen thereby, from any unlawful commerce between the plantations and any other foreign countries, as to any other enumerated commodities, or otherwise, may it therefore please your most excellent Majesty that it may be enacted; and be it enacted by the King's most excellent majesty, by and with the advice and consent of the lords spiritual

ſpiritual and temporal, and commons, in this preſent parliament aſſembled, and by the authority of the ſame, That the ſaid act, paſſed in the third and fourth years of the reign of her ſaid late Majeſty, ſo far as the ſame extends to the making of rice, of the growth and produce of his Majeſty's plantations in *America*, an enumerated commodity, ſhall be, and is hereby ratified and confirmed, as to all perſons, ſhips, veſſels, or places, in all reſpects whatſoever; except as to ſuch of the ſaid rice, as, by the ſaid acts of the third and eighth years of his ſaid majeſty King *George* the Second, and by this act, are and ſhall be permitted or allowed to be exported from his Majeſty's provinces of *South Carolina* and *Georgia* in *America*, by ſuch perſons, and in ſuch ſhips and veſſels, and to ſuch foreign countries and places, and under ſuch entries, ſecurities, reſtrictions, regulations, limitations, penalties, and forfeitures, as are herein after particularly deſcribed, appointed, limited, and enacted for that purpoſe.

Act 3 & 4 Annæ, with reſpect to making rice of the Britiſh American colonies an enumerated commodity, confirmed; except as to ſuch as by acts 3 & 8 Geo. II. and by this act, are permitted to be exported from S. Carolina and Georgia, &c.

II. And be it further enacted by the authority aforeſaid, That from and after the twenty ninth day of *June*, one thouſand ſeven hundred and ſixty four, it ſhall and may be lawful, notwithſtanding any of the acts aforeſaid, or any other act of parliament, for any of his Majeſty's ſubjects, in any ſhip or veſſel built in *Great Britain*, or in his Majeſty's colonies in *America*, or belonging to any of his Majeſty's ſubjects, and navigated according to law, that ſhall clear outwards in any part of the ſaid provinces of *South Carolina* or *Georgia*, to ſhip or load rice in the ſaid provinces, and to carry the ſame directly to any parts of *America* ſouthward of *South Carolina* or *Georgia*, without carrying the ſame to any other of his Majeſty's plantations in *America*, or to *Great Britain*; the maſter or other perſon having or taking charge of ſuch ſhip or veſſel, before ſhe clears outwards, firſt taking a licence, under the hand of the governor of the reſpective province for the time being, for the carrying the ſame from the ſaid provinces reſpectively to ſome part of *America* ſouthward of the ſaid provinces, as aforeſaid; which licence the ſaid governors reſpectively are hereby authorized and required to grant, upon a certificate from the collector or comptroller of the port where ſuch licence ſhall be deſired, certifying that bond has been given (which bonds ſuch collector or comptroller reſpectively is hereby authorized and required to take) with one or more ſufficient ſecurity, in the ſum of one thouſand pounds if the ſhip be of leſs burthen than one hundred tons, and the ſum of two thouſand pounds if the ſhip ſhall be of that or a greater burthen, that no tobacco, ſugars, cotton wool, indigo, ginger, fuſtick, or other dying wood, molaſſes, tar, pitch, turpentine, hemp, maſts, yards, bowſprits, copper ore, beaver ſkins, or other furs, of the growth, production, or manufacture, of any *Britiſh* plantation in *America*, ſhall be loaden or taken on board ſuch ſhip or veſſel at *South Carolina* or *Georgia*, or any other of his Majeſty's plantations in *America*, unleſs it be for the neceſſary proviſions of the ſhip in their voyage, and that ſuch ſhip or veſſel,

Rice may be loaded on board ſhips navigated according to law, and belonging to Britiſh ſubjects, in any part of South Carolina and Georgia, and carried directly to any parts of America ſouthward of the ſaid colonies; the maſter firſt taking out a licence; which is to be granted, upon a certificate that bond has been given, that no enumerated goods ſhall be taken on board,

unleſs for neceſſary proviſions of the ſhip;

and that the vessel shall return to some of the British colonies within 4 months. vessel, after landing the said rice by virtue of such licence, shall return to the said provinces of *South Carolina* or *Georgia*, or proceed to some port in any of his Majesty's colonies or plantations in *America*, within the space of four calendar months from the time of clearing out of such port respectively; and that every master or other person taking charge of such ship or vessel, for which such licence shall be obtained for carrying rice to any parts of *America* southward of the said provinces of *South Carolina* or *Georgia*, shall produce such licence to the collector or comptroller, or other proper officer at such port as he shall arrive at in any of his Majesty's colonies or plantations in *America*; which said collector or comptroller, or other proper officer, is and are hereby authorized and required to give to the said master a certificate, certifying the arrival of such ship or vessel at such port within the time herein before limited and appointed; and that in case the said certificate be produced to the collector or comptroller of the said provinces respectively within twelve calendar months, the bond taken as aforesaid shall be cancelled and given up, otherwise such bond shall be forfeited to his Majesty, and shall and may be sued and prosecuted in any court of record in the said provinces respectively.

Licence to be produced at the port of arrival; and a certificate of arrival to be thereupon granted the master; upon producing whereof within 12 months, the bond is to be discharged.

III. And, in order to ascertain the true quantity of rice exported from the said provinces, pursuant to such licence, and the liberty granted by this act, be it enacted by the authority aforesaid, That before the same shall be shipped or put on board, the merchant, or other person exporting the same, shall make an entry thereof in writing with the collector of his Majesty's customs, and the naval officer, and also with the comptroller (where there is such an officer) and thereupon there shall be payable to his Majesty so much as the half subsidy of the rice so shipped in *South Carolina* or *Georgia* shall amount unto, which would have remained in case the said rice had been first imported into *Great Britain*, and afterwards re-exported; and the collector of the port in which such ship shall be entered to sail, may and shall demand the full sum due for the half subsidy for all the rice mentioned in such entry; which said payment shall be well and truly made to the collector of such port respectively, at or before the said ship or vessel obtains the clearance; and the merchant or other person exporting such rice shall also take out a certificate or coquet of such entry, and shall, before the rice be shipped or put on board, indorse on the back of such coquet or certificate the true quantity intended to be shipped, mentioning the marks, number, and contents of each cask; and shall deliver the coquet, so indorsed, to the searcher or other officer appointed for examining and shipping thereof; and if, upon the weighing and examining the rice brought or intended to be shipped by virtue of such coquet or certificate, before or after the shipping thereof, the quantity shall appear to be greater than is indorsed thereon; or if any rice shall be laden or put on board any ship or vessel having liberty to trade by virtue of this act, or any hoy, lighter, bottom, boat, or other vessel, in order to be put

Exporter to make an entry of the rice before shipping;

and pay the half subsidy before clearance.

Coquet of such entry to be taken out, and the quantity to be shipped to be indorsed thereon, which is to be delivered to the searcher.

If the quantity be found greater than what is so indorsed,

put on board ſuch ſhip or veſſel before ſuch entry, or taking out ſuch coquet, and indorſing and delivering the ſame as aforeſaid, contrary to the true intent and meaning hereof; all ſuch rice, ſo ſhipped or intended to be ſhipped, ſhall be forfeited, as alſo the hoy, lighter, bottom, boat, or other veſſel, employed in ſhipping the ſame; and the owner of ſuch rice, or other perſon employed in ſhipping the ſame, ſhall alſo forfeit treble the value thereof, to be recovered in the court of vice admiralty held in any of his Majeſty's plantations in *America*, or in any court of record in any of his Majeſty's plantations in *America*, at the election of the informer or proſecutor; one third part thereof to be to the uſe of his Majeſty, his heirs, and ſucceſſors, one third part to the governor of the ſaid provinces reſpectively, and the other one third to the informer or proſecutor.

or rice be put on board before entry, or in any other veſſel, in order to be fraudulenty ſhipped; ſuch rice, together with veſſel employed therein, to be forfeited, and alſo treble the value. Recovery and application of the forfeiture.

IV. And be it further enacted by the authority aforeſaid, That this act ſhall continue for five years from the twenty fourth day of *June*, one thouſand ſeven hundred and ſixty four, and from thence to the end of the then next ſeſſion of parliament.

Act to be in force for 5 years from 24 June, 1764.

V. And whereas great quantities of foreign molaſſes and ſyrups are clandeſtinely run on ſhore in the *Britiſh* colonies, to the prejudice of the revenue, and the great detriment of the trade of this kingdom, and its *American* plantations; to remedy which practices for the future, be it further enacted by the authority aforeſaid, That from and after the twenty ninth day of *September*, one thouſand ſeven hundred and ſixty four, bond and ſecurity, in the like penalty, ſhall alſo be given to the collector or other principal officer of the cuſtoms, at any port or place in any of the *Britiſh American* colonies or plantations, with one ſurety beſides the maſter of every ſhip or veſſel that ſhall lade or take on board there any goods particularly enumerated in the ſaid acts, being the product or manufacture of any of the ſaid colonies or plantations, or rice, by virtue of the licence under this preſent act, with condition, that, in caſe any molaſſes or ſyrups, being the produce of any of the plantations not under the dominion of his Majeſty, his heirs, or ſucceſſors, ſhall be laden on board ſuch ſhip or veſſel, the ſame ſhall (the danger of the ſeas and enemies excepted) be brought, without fraud or wilful diminution, by the ſaid ſhip or veſſel, to ſome of his Majeſty's colonies or plantations in *America*, or to ſome port in *Great Britain*; and that the maſter or other perſon having the charge of ſuch ſhip or veſſel ſhall, immediately upon his arrival at any port or place in *Great Britain*, or in the *Britiſh American* colonies and plantations, make a juſt and true report of all the goods laden on board ſuch ſhip or veſſel, under their true and proper denominations; and if any ſuch non-enumerated goods, or rice, as before-mentioned, ſhall be laden on board any ſuch ſhip or veſſel before ſuch bond ſhall be given, the goods ſo laden, together with the ſhip or veſſel, and her furniture, ſhall be forfeited, and ſhall and may be ſeized by any officer of the cuſtoms, and proſecuted, ſued for, and recovered, in any court of record, or in any court of admiralty in the ſaid colonies or plantations

From and after 29 Sept. 1764, where any enumerated goods or rice ſhall be ſhipped, bond and ſecurity is to be given,

that any foreign molaſſes or ſyrups on board ſhall be brought without fraud to ſome of the Britiſh colonies, or to Great Britain; of which report is to be made at the port of arrival.

Non-enumerated goods, and rice, laden before giving bond, are forfeited, together with the veſſel.

where

where ſuch offence ſhall be committed, or in any court of vice admiralty which may or ſhall be appointed over all *America* (which court of admiralty, or vice admiralty, are hereby reſpectively authorized and required to proceed, hear, and determine the ſame) at the election of the informer or proſecutor.

Diviſion and application of the penalties.

VI. And it is hereby further enacted, That all penalties and forfeitures ſo recovered there, under this or any former act of parliament, ſhall be divided, paid, and applied, as follows; that is to ſay, after deducting the charges of proſecution from the groſs produce thereof one third part of the nett produce ſhall be paid into the hands of the collector of his Majeſty's cuſtoms at the port or place where ſuch penalties or forfeitures ſhall be recovered, for the uſe of his Majeſty, his heirs, and ſucceſſors, one third part to the governor or commander in chief of the ſaid colony or plantation, and the other third part to the perſon who ſhall ſeize, inform, and ſue for the ſame.

CAP. XXVIII.

An act to enable his Majeſty, with the advice of his privy council, to order the importation of proviſions from Ireland, *during the next receſs of parliament, under certain reſtrictions and regulations therein mentioned.*

Preamble.

WHEREAS *the price of proviſions is at preſent high, and may become higher; that it greatly affects the poor people, and will tend to hurt the trade and manufactures of this kingdom, if not timely prevented*; may it therefore pleaſe your Majeſty that it may be enacted; and be it enacted by the King's moſt excellent majeſty, by and with the advice and conſent of the lords ſpiritual and temporal, and commons, in this preſent parliament aſſembled, and by the authority of the ſame, That it ſhall and may be lawful for his Majeſty, during the next receſs of parliament, by and with the advice of his privy council, from time to time, to order, permit, and authorize, the free importation of ſalted beef, ſalted pork, bacon, and butter, from *Ireland* into this kingdom, as his Majeſty, in his great wiſdom, ſhall think convenient and needful, and as the neceſſity of the times may require, and in ſuch manner as his Majeſty ſhall think fit to direct; any thing in any act or acts of parliament to the contrary notwithſtanding.

His Majeſty enabled with, advice of his privy council, to order the importation of ſalt proviſions from Ireland, during the receſs of parliament;

II. And be it further enacted by the authority aforeſaid, That all perſons ſhall be and are hereby exempted, freed, and diſcharged, from the payment of all ſubſidies, cuſtoms, rates, duties, and other impoſitions, and alſo from all penalties, forfeitures, payments, and puniſhments, for or upon account of importing or bringing ſuch proviſions from *Ireland* into this kingdom, for ſuch time or times as his Majeſty, by and with the advice of his privy council, ſhall, by his royal proclamation, think fit to order, permit, and authorize, to be imported; any act or acts of parliament to the contrary notwithſtanding.

and all perſons are exempted from payment of duties, and from penalties, &c. on account of ſuch importation;

III. And,

III. And, to the intent that the revenue may not be prejudiced by the importation of salted provisions from *Ireland*, be it enacted by the authority aforesaid; That there shall be paid to such officer as the commissioners for the duties on salt for the time being shall appoint, at the port in *England* into which any salted beef, pork, bacon, or butter, shall, in pursuance of his Majesty's royal proclamation, be imported from *Ireland* as aforesaid, and before any part thereof shall be delivered out to the person or persons to whom the same shall belong or be consigned, the sum of three shillings and four pence for every barrel or cask of salted beef or pork, to be imported during the continuance of this act, containing thirty two gallons, and so in proportion for any greater or lesser quantity; and for every hundred weight of salted beef, called *dried beef*, or dried neats tongues, or dried hogsmeat, the sum of one shilling and three pence; and the sum of four pence for every hundred weight of all such salted butter, and so in proportion for any greater or less quantity than an hundred weight; as or for custom, or for duty, on or in respect thereof; the money so arising by the importation of the said salted beef, pork, or butter, to be paid into his Majesty's Exchequer as part of the duties on salt, laid on by an act in the fifth year of the reign of his late majesty King *George* the Second, and continued by several subsequent acts.

other than the following duties to the commissioners for the duties on salt; viz. 3s. 4d. per barrel for beef or pork; 1s. 3d. per C. wt. for all dried beef, neats tongues, and hogmeat; and 4 d. per C. wt. for all salted butter; which is to be paid over into the Exchequer as part of the duties on salt.

IV. And be it further enacted by the authority aforesaid, That if any person or persons shall, during the next recess of parliament, land any such salted beef, pork, or butter, or any salt beef called *dried beef*, or dried neat tongues, or dried hogsmeat, into this kingdom from *Ireland*, before payment of the duty or duties by this act specified and directed, the same shall be forfeited and lost, and twenty shillings *per* barrel for every barrel thereof, and so in proportion for any greater or less quantity, to be recovered of the importer or proprietor thereof; and that it shall and may be lawful to and for any person or persons, being an officer or officers of the customs, or of his Majesty's duties upon salt, to take and seize all such commodities as shall be imported and landed, contrary to the true intent and meaning of this act, together with the casks, vessels, and package containing the same; and that all such penalties and forfeitures shall be distributed in manner following; that is to say, one moiety thereof to the King, his heirs and successors, and the other moiety thereof to the person or persons who shall seize, sue, or inform for the same; to be recovered by action of debt, bill, plaint, or information, in any of his Majesty's courts of record at *Westminster*.

Any of the said provisions being landed without duty is first paid, are forfeited, with 20s. per barrel.

Recovery and application of the penalties.

V. Provided always, That no drawback shall be allowed or paid for any such salted beef or pork, so imported into this kingdom from *Ireland*, and which shall be exported from hence elsewhere.

No drawback to be allowed on exportation elsewhere.

VI. And be it further enacted by the authority aforesaid, That if any action or suit shall be commenced against any person or persons for any thing done in pursuance of this act, the defendant or defendants, in any such action or suit, may plead the general

General issue. general issue, and give this act and the special matter in evidence, at any trial to be had thereupon; and that the same was done in pursuance and by the authority of this act: and if it shall appear so to have been done, the jury shall find for the defendant or defendants; and if the plaintiff shall be nonsuited, or discontinue his action after the defendant or defendants shall have appeared, or if judgment shall be given upon any verdict or demurrer against the plaintiff, the defendant or defendants shall and may recover treble costs, and have the like remedy for the same as any defendant or defendants hath or have in other cases by law. Treble costs.

Restrictions with respect to the granting importation of provisions from Ireland.

VII. Provided always, and it is hereby declared to be the true intent and meaning of this act, That nothing herein contained shall extend to authorize the free importation of salted beef, salted pork, bacon, or butter, from *Ireland*, unless when the price of the best ox beef in *Smithfield* market shall exceed three pence *per* pound for the four quarters, and unless the price of the best pieces of such beef shall exceed four pence *per* pound at *Leaden Hall* market, and unless the price of the best pork shall exceed four pence *per* pound, the best bacon seven pence *per* pound, and of the best butter shall exceed nine pence *per* pound, at *Leaden Hall* market aforesaid.

No order, &c. for importation to take place, before 1 June, 1764.

VIII. Provided always, and be it enacted by the authority aforesaid, That no order, permission, or authority, for the importation of butter from *Ireland* into this kingdom, shall be given or granted, till after the first day of *June*, one thousand seven hundred and sixty four.

CAP. XXIX.

An act for the encouragement of the whale fishery in the gulph and river of Saint Lawrence, *and on the coasts of his Majesty's colonies in* America.

Preamble.

WHEREAS *a considerable whale fishery has been discovered in the gulph and river of* Saint Lawrence, *and has been carried on with success, but is still capable of improvement: and whereas it would contribute greatly to the encouragement of the said fishery, if the duty now payable on the importation of whale fins, taken from whales caught in the said gulph and river of* Saint Lawrence, *or in any seas on the coasts of any of his Majesty's colonies in* America, *were, for a competent time, lessened and reduced*; we your Majesty's most dutiful and loyal subjects, the commons of *Great Britain* in parliament assembled, desirous to improve the advantages that have accrued to your Majesty's subjects from the cessions made by the late peace, most humbly beseech your Majesty that it may be enacted; and be it enacted by the King's most excellent majesty, by and with the advice and consent of the lords spiritual and temporal, and commons, in this present parliament assembled, and by the authority of the same, That it shall and may be lawful to and for any person or persons, from and after the passing of this act, at any time before the twenty fifth day of *December*,

From the passing this act, to 25 Dec. 1770, &c. Whale fins, taken from whales caught by British sub-

December, one thousand seven hundred and seventy, and from thence to the end of the then next session of parliament, to import in ships belonging to his Majesty's subjects (whereof the captain or master, and three fourth parts of the mariners, are his Majesty subjects) whale fins taken from whales caught by any of his Majesty's subjects in the gulph or river of *Saint Lawrence*, or in any seas on the coasts of any of his Majesty's colonies in *America*, without paying any custom, subsidy, or duty, for the same, other than and except the rate or duty commonly called *The old subsidy*, granted by an act made in the twenty fifth year of the reign of King *Charles* the Second, intituled, *An act for the encouragement of the* Greenland *and* Eastland *trades, and for the better securing the plantation trade*, for and during the said term; any law or statute to the contrary thereof notwithstanding.

jects in the gulph or river of Saint Lawrence, or on the coasts of the British colonies, may be imported in British ships, duly navigated, paying no other duty, than the old subsidy granted by act 25 Car. II.

II. Provided always, and be it enacted by the authority aforesaid, That nothing in this act contained shall extend, or be construed to extend, to allow the importation of whale fins without paying any custom, subsidy, or duty, other than and except the said rate or duty commonly called *The old subsidy*, unless the captain, master, or other commanding officer of the ship or vessel, or the person importing the same, shall first make oath before one of the principal officers of the customs in the port or ports of importation (who is and are hereby authorized and required to administer such oath) that all the whale fins imported in such ship or vessel were, to the best of his knowledge and belief, really and *bona fide* the fins of whales caught and taken in the gulph or river of *Saint Lawrence*, or in the seas on the coasts of some of his Majesty's colonies in *America*, by the crew of such ships and vessels only, whereof the owner or owners, the captain or master, and three fourth parts of the mariners, were his Majesty's subjects.

the master first making oath, at the port of importation, of the truth of the premisses.

CAP. XXX.

An act for applying the money granted in this session of parliament, for defraying the charge of the pay and cloathing of the militia of that part of Great Britain *called* England, *for one year, beginning the twenty fifth day of* March, *one thousand seven hundred and sixty four.*

Preamble.

WHEREAS *the sum of eighty thousand pounds has been granted to his Majesty for defraying the charge of pay and cloathing for the militia, for one year, from the twenty fifth day of* March, *one thousand seven hundred and sixty four*: in order therefore that the charge of pay and cloathing for such militia may be duly and properly defrayed and satisfied; be it enacted by the King's most excellent majesty, by and with the advice and consent of the lords spiritual and temporal, and commons, in this present parliament assembled, and by the authority of the same, That

Where the militia is or shall be raised, the receiver general of the county is to issue 4 months pay in advance, according to the establishment of pay here set down; with half a year's salary to the regimental and battalion clerks;

clerks; and the allowances to the clerks of the general and sub-division meetings; and pay for cloathing the militia.—— The above sums are not to be paid, if pay has not before been issued, till the lord lieutenant or deputies shall have certified to the treasury and receivers general the inrollment of three fifths of the men and officers.—— The money is to be paid by the receiver general to the clerk of the regiment or battallion (except the allowances to the clerks of the meetings) upon producing the warrant of his appointment; and for independent companies, to the respective captains, or to their order; according to the establishment laid down in the militia act of 2 *Geo.* iii.—— A second payment is also to be made within three months after the first; and a third within three months after the second. Receipts of the persons, to whom the monies shall be so paid, discharge to the receivers general.——The regimental and battallion clerks are to pay in advance one month's pay to the adjutant; and two months pay to each captain, for the serjeants, drummers, and contingent expences of the said company; Captains to pay for each man 1 *d. per* month out of the contingent money, towards charges of the hospital; and for the serjeant-major, and drum-major; to be paid to the commanding officer of the company, to which they belong: Captains to distribute the pay accordingly; and account for the same yearly to the clerk or receiver general, if an independent company; and pay back the surplus monies in his hands, except the contingent expences, which is to be accounted for, and applied to the general use of the regiment, &c. Captains of independent companies to distribute the pay to their men, and apply the money allowed for contingent expences.——Clerk to retain money in his hands for his own salary; and discharge the cloathing bills.——When the lords lieutenants or deputies shall have fixed the days of exercise, they are to certify the same to the receiver general, specifying the number of men, and days they shall be absent from home. Receiver general to issue thereupon pay for officers and men to the regimental clerk, &c. Where there shall be independent companies only, the receiver general is to issue pay to the captains, according to the rate here set down. Regimental clerk to pay over the money to the respective captains. Captains to make up their account, to be signed by them, and countersigned by the commanding officer, and delivered with ballance, to the clerk or receiver general. Accounts allowed sufficient vouchers.——During the time the troops are embodied, and called out into actual service, and receive pay as the King's other forces, all pay and allowances from the receivers general is to cease. Receiver general to pay the clerk of the general meetings upon producing an order from the lieutenant, or three deputy lieutenants assembled. And the clerks of the sub-division meetings upon producing a like order from one deputy lieutenant. Orders to discharge receivers general.——Regimental and battallion clerks to give security for paying and accounting for the monies received by them; the bonds to be lodged with the receivers general, and put in suit by them on non-performance of the condition; and they are intitled thereupon to full costs and charges; and 5 l. *per cent.* of the money recovered; the residue to be accounted for to the auditor.——The regimental and battallion clerks, and captains of independent companies, are to deliver in accounts of their receipts and disbursements, and pay over the ballance to the receivers general; who are to transmit the accounts into the auditor's office.——Recovery of penalties, &c.——No fee payable for any warrant or sum of money issued in pursuance of this act.——Officers in half pay serving in the militia, may receive the subsistence money payable to captains, lieutenants, or ensigns; they taking oath before a justice, that during such period of time they have not had any other place or employment of profit civil or military under his Majesty.

CAP.

CAP. XXXI.

An act to indemnify such persons as have omitted to qualify themselves for offices and employments; and to indemnify justices of the peace, deputy lieutenants, and officers of the militia, or others, who have omitted to register or deliver in their qualifications within the time limited by law, and for giving further time for those purposes; and to indemnify members and officers in cities, corporations, and borough towns, whose admissions have been omitted to be stamped according to the several acts of parliament now in force for that purpose, or, having been stamped, have been lost or mislaid, and for allowing them time to provide admissions duly stamped; and to prevent the destruction of trees and underwoods growing in forests and chases.

WHEREAS *divers persons, who, on account of their offices, places, employments, or professions, or any other cause or occasion, ought to have taken and subscribed the oaths, or the assurance, respectively appointed to be by such persons taken and subscribed, in and by an act made in the first year of the reign of his late majesty King* George *the First, of glorious memory, intituled,* An act for the further security of his Majesty's person and government, and the succession of the crown in the heirs of the late princess *Sophia*, being protestants; and for extinguishing the hopes of the pretended prince of *Wales*, and his open and secret abettors; *or to have qualified themselves according to an act made in the thirteenth year of the reign of King* Charles *the Second, intituled,* An act for the well governing and regulating corporations; *or to have qualified themselves according to another act made in the twenty fifth year of the reign of King* Charles *the Second, intituled,* An act for preventing the dangers which may happen from popish recusants, *by receiving the sacrament of the Lord's supper according to the usage of the church of* England, *and making and subscribing the declaration against transubstantiation therein mentioned; or according to another act made in the thirtieth year of the reign of King* Charles *the Second, intituled,* An act for the more effectual preserving the King's person and government, by disabling papists from sitting in either house of parliament; *or according to another act made in the eighteenth year of the reign of his late majesty King* George *the Second, intituled,* An act to amend and render more effectual an act passed in the fifth year of his present Majesty's reign, intituled, *An act for the further qualification of justices of the peace; or according to another act made in the second year of the reign of his present Majesty, intituled,* An act to explain, amend, and reduce into one act of parliament, the several laws now in being relating to the raising and training the militia within that part of *Great Britain* called *England*; *have, through ignorance of the law, absence, or some unavoidable accident, omitted to take and subscribe the said oaths and assurance, or otherwise to qualify themselves as aforesaid*, within such time, and in such manner, as in and by the said

Preamble, reciting the several qualifying acts of 1 Geo. I.

13 Car. II.

25 Car. II.

30 Car. II.

18 Geo. II.

and 2 Geo. III.

acts respectively, or by any other act of parliament in that behalf made and provided, is required, whereby they may be in danger of incurring divers penalties and disabilities: for quieting the minds of his Majesty's subjects, and for preventing any inconveniencies that might otherwise happen by means of such omissions, be it enacted by the King's most excellent majesty, by and with the advice and consent of the lords spiritual and temporal, and commons, in this present parliament assembled, and by the authority of the same, That all and every person or persons, who shall, on or before the twenty eighth day of *November*, one thousand seven hundred and sixty four, take and subscribe the said oaths and assurance respectively, in such cases wherein by law the said oaths and assurance ought to have been taken or subscribed, in such manner and form, and such place and places, as are appointed in and by the said act made in the first year of the reign of his said late majesty King *George* the First, or by any other act or acts of parliament in that behalf made and provided; and also receive the sacrament of the Lord's supper, according to the usage of the church of *England*, and make and subscribe the said declaration against transubstantiation, in such cases wherein the said sacrament ought to have been received, and the said declaration ought to have been made and subscribed; and take and subscribe the oath directed by the said act made in the eighteenth year of the reign of his late majesty King *George* the Second, in such cases wherein the said oath ought to have been taken and subscribed, in such manner as by the said act is directed; and also, being a deputy lieutenant or officer of the militia, shall, on or before the first day of *August*, one thousand seven hundred and sixty four, leave his qualification in writing with the clerk of the peace, with whom he is, by the said act made in the second year of his present Majesty's reign, required to leave the same; shall be and are hereby indemnified, freed and discharged, from and against all penalties, forfeitures, incapacities, and disabilities, incurred or to be incurred, for or by reason of any former neglect or omission of taking or subscribing the said oaths or assurance, or receiving the sacrament, or making or subscribing the said declarations, or taking and subscribing the said oath, or leaving his qualification in writing with the clerk of the peace respectively, according to the above-mentioned acts, or any of them, or any other act or acts, is and are and shall be fully and actually recapacitated and restored to the same state and condition as such person or persons were before such neglect or omission, and shall be deemed and adjudged to have duly qualified him, her, or themselves, according to the above-mentioned acts, and every of them; and that all acts done or to be done by any such person or persons, or by authority derived from him, her, or them, are and shall be of the same force and validity, as the same or any of them would have been, if such person or persons respectively had taken the said oaths or assurance, and received the sacrament of the Lord's supper, and made and subscribed the said declaration, and taken and subscribed

Further time to 28 Nov. 1764, allowed to persons who have omitted to qualify themselves, as the said laws direct.

Persons qualifying themselves in manner, and within the time, appointed, recapacitated and indemnified.

ſcribed the ſaid oath, and left his qualification in writing with the clerk of the peace, according to the direction of the ſaid acts, and every of them; and that ſuch perſon or perſons qualifying themſelves in manner, and within the time, appointed by this act, ſhall be, to all intents and purpoſes, as effectual, as if ſuch perſon or perſons had reſpectively taken the ſaid oaths and aſſurance, and received the ſacrament, and made and ſubſcribed the ſaid declaration, and taken and ſubſcribed the ſaid oath, and left his qualification in writing with the clerk of the peace within the time, and in the manner appointed by the ſeveral acts before mentioned.

Offices, &c. already avoided by judgment of a court, and filled up, confirmed.

II. Provided always, That this act, or any thing herein contained, ſhall not extend, or be conſtrued to extend, to reſtore or intitle any perſon or perſons to any office or employment, benefice, matter, or thing, whatſoever, already actually avoided by judgment of any of his Majeſty's courts of record, already filled up or enjoyed by any other perſon; but ſuch office, employment, benefice, matter, or thing, ſo avoided, or filled up and enjoyed, ſhall be and remain in and to the perſon or perſons who is or are now intitled to the ſame, as if this act had never been made.

None indemnified where final judgment hath been given for the penalty incurred.

III. Provided alſo, That this act, or any thing herein contained, ſhall not extend, or be conſtrued to extend, to indemnify any perſon againſt whom final judgment ſhall have been given in any action of debt, bill, plaint, or information, in any of his Majeſty's courts of record, for any penalty incurred by having neglected to qualify himſelf within the time limited by law, or any perſon who ſhall have omitted to qualify himſelf within the time limited by any act or acts of parliament made during the reign of his late majeſty King *George* the Second, for indemnifying perſons who have omitted to qualify themſelves for offices and employments.

IV. And whereas admiſſions of divers members and officers of cities, corporations, and borough towns, which, by ſeveral acts of parliament, are directed and required to be ſtamped, may not have been provided, or the ſame not duly ſtamped, or may have been loſt or miſlaid; be it further enacted by the authority aforeſaid, That for the relief of ſuch perſons whoſe admiſſions may not have been provided, or not duly ſtamped as aforeſaid, or where the ſame have been loſt or miſlaid, it ſhall and may be lawful to and for ſuch perſons, on or before the ſaid twenty eighth day of *November*, one thouſand ſeven hundred and ſixty four, to provide, or cauſe to be provided, admiſſions duly ſtamped, and ſuch perſons ſo providing admiſſions duly ſtamped as aforeſaid, are and ſhall be hereby confirmed and qualified to act as member or members, officer or officers, of ſuch cities, corporations, and borough towns reſpectively, to all intents and purpoſes, and ſhall and may hold, enjoy, and execute the ſame, or any other office or offices into which he or they hath or have been elected, notwithſtanding his or their omiſſion, or the omiſſion of any of their predeceſſors in ſuch cities, corporations, or borough towns, as aforeſaid, and ſhall be indemnified and diſ-

Such perſons whoſe admiſſions may not have been provided, or not duly ſtampt, or which have been loſt, or miſlaid, are allowed to 28 Nov. 1764, to provide, &c. the ſame;

and they are thereupon indemnified, &c.

charged of and from all incapacities, disabilities, forfeitures, penalties, and damages, by reason of any such omission, and none of his or their acts shall be questioned or avoided by reason of the same.

Where any shall desire to have their admissions renewed,

V. Provided always, and be it further enacted by the authority aforesaid, That when and as often as any member or members, officer or officers of any city, corporation, or borough town, shall desire to have his, her, or their admissions, renewed or confirmed in manner aforesaid, the mayor or other chief magistrate of such city, corporation, or borough town, shall, and he is hereby required in every such case, upon notice given to him by any one or more member or members, officer or officers, of any city, corporation, or borough town, to summon a hall, common council, or other proper publick meeting, within ten days after such notice given to him, for the purpose of admitting or granting copies, and confirming the admissions of such person or persons as aforesaid.

a hall is to be summoned for granting copies, and confirming such admissions.

Officers and keepers of woods and chases, &c. may seize any saw or other instrument used in unlawfully cutting any trees, &c. therein.

VI. And whereas the laws in being are found to be ineffectual for preventing the destruction of timber trees, and other trees, underwood and covert, growing upon the forests and chases within this kingdom; be it further enacted by the authority aforesaid, That from and after the passing of this act, it shall and may be lawful for every surveyor of his Majesty's woods, and his lawful deputy, and also for the officers and keepers of any forest or chase, to seize and take away, for his and their own use, any saw, axe, hatchet, bill-hook, or other instrument, used by any person or persons whom they shall find unlawfully stocking up, sawing, cutting down, topping, lopping, or destroying, any timber tree, or other tree, underwood or covert, within such forest or chase.

CAP. XXXII.

An act to impower the high court of chancery to lay out, upon proper securities, a further sum of money, not exceeding a sum therein limited, out of the common and general cash in the bank of England *belonging to the suitors of the said court; and for applying the interest arising therefrom, towards answering the charges of the office of the accountant general of the said court.*

Preamble, reciting clause in act 12 Geo. II.

WHEREAS *by an act of parliament passed in the twelfth year of the reign of his late majesty King* George *the Second, intituled,* An act to impower the high court of chancery to lay out, upon proper securities, any monies not exceeding a sum therein limited, out of the common and general cash in the bank of *England* belonging to the suitors of the said court, for the ease of the said suitors, by applying the interest arising therefrom for answering the charges of the office of accountant general of the said court, *a provision is made for the support and maintenance of the office of accountant general of the court of chancery, by directing certain*

tain payments to be made, in the manner therein mentioned, to the ſaid accountant general and his two clerks, for their ſalaries, in lieu of, and in recompence for, all fees whatſoever that would be due and payable to the ſaid office by the ſuitors: and whereas ſince the paſſing the ſaid act, the money and effects belonging to the ſuitors of the ſaid court, under the care and direction of the ſaid accountant general, are greatly increaſed; by reaſon whereof the neceſſary buſineſs of the ſaid office is grown ſo extenſive and laborious, that the proviſion made by the ſaid act is become inſufficient to anſwer the charges attending the execution of the ſaid office: wherefore, in order to provide for the further ſupport of the ſaid office, be it enacted by the King's moſt excellent majeſty, by and with the advice and conſent of the lords ſpiritual and temporal, and commons, in this preſent parliament aſſembled, and by the authority of the ſame, That out of the caſh that now lies, or ſhall hereafter lie dead and unemployed in the bank of *England*, belonging to the ſuitors of the ſaid court of chancery, a ſum not exceeding five thouſand pounds ſhall and may, by virtue of any order or orders of the ſaid court to be made for that purpoſe, from time to time be placed out in one intire ſum, or in parcels, on ſuch government or parliamentary ſecurities as in and by ſuch order or orders ſhall be directed, to the intent that the intereſt and annual profits ariſing from the money ſo to be placed out as aforeſaid, may be applied for the purpoſes herein after mentioned; and that the ſaid court of chancery may, from time to time, change the ſecurity or ſecurities on which the ſaid monies ſhall be ſo placed out, as the ſaid court ſhall think expedient.

Court of chancery authorized to direct the placing out at intereſt, on government ſecurities, 5000 l. of the caſh lying dead in the bank, belonging to the ſuitors of the court; and to change the ſecurities as the court ſhall think proper.

II. And be it further enacted, That the intereſt and annual profits ariſing and to be produced from the ſaid ſecurities ſhall, from time to time, be received by the governor and company of the bank of *England*, and placed to the credit of the ſame account as was raiſed in the books kept there for the ſuitors of the ſaid court, by virtue of the ſaid act herein before mentioned, of intereſt ariſing from money placed out in purſuance of the ſaid act; and that out of ſuch intereſt money and annual profits, there ſhall be paid, by quarterly payments, by the governor and company of the bank of *England*, by virtue of an order or orders of the court of chancery to be made for that purpoſe, the annual ſum of one hundred and twenty pounds to the ſaid accountant general's third clerk; which ſaid ſalary ſhall commence from the eighth day of *April* in the year of our Lord one thouſand ſeven hundred and ſixty four, and ſhall, together with the ſalaries appointed by the ſaid act herein before mentioned, be in lieu of, and in recompence and ſatisfaction for, all fees whatſoever, which, from that time ſhall or would be due or payable to the ſaid office, by the ſuitors; and that the reſidue of the intereſt and annual profits, ariſing and to be produced from the ſaid ſecurities, ſhall be accounted for and taken as part of the common and general caſh of and belonging to the ſuitors of the ſaid court of chancery, and ſhall be iſſued and applied purſuant and according to the directions of an act of parliament, paſſed in the

The bank to receive the intereſt and profits thereof, and to pay thereout, upon an order from the court, 120 l. per ann. by quarterly payments, to the accountant general's third clerk; the ſalary to commence from 8 April, 1764, and to be in lieu of all fees. Reſidue of the intereſt, &c. to be accounted for as part of the general caſh belonging to the suitors, and to be applied pursuant to act 12 Geo. I.

the twelfth year of the reign of his late majesty King George the First, intituled, *An act for the relief of the suitors of the high court of chancery.*

If the whole, or any part of the said sums of 5000 l. shall be wanted to pay the suitors, the court may direct the calling in thereof.

III. Provided always, and be it further enacted and declared, That if at any time hereafter the whole, or any part of the said sum of five thousand pounds, shall be wanted to answer any of the demands of the suitors of the said court of chancery, then, and in such case, the said court may and shall direct the same, or any part thereof, to be called in, or the securities on which the same shall be placed to be disposed of, in order that the suitors of the said court may at all times be paid their respective demands, out of the common and general cash belonging to such suitors.

CAP. XXXIII.

An act for preventing inconveniencies arising in cases of merchants, and such other persons as are within the description of the statutes relating to bankrupts, being intitled to privilege of parliament, and becoming insolvent.

Preamble.

WHEREAS, *merchants, bankers, brokers, factors, scriveners, and traders, within the description of the statutes relating to bankrupts, having privilege of parliament, are not compellable to pay their just debts, or to become bankrupts, by reason of the freedom of their persons from arrests upon civil process; and some doubts have also arisen, whether, in cases of bankruptcy, a commission can be sued out during the continuance of such privilege*: to remedy which inconveniencies, and to support the honour and dignity of parliament and good faith and credit in commercial dealings, which require, that in such cases, the laws should have their due course, and that no such merchants, bankers, brokers, factors, scriveners, or traders, in case of actual insolvency, should, by any privilege whatever, be exempted from doing equal justice to all their creditors; be it enacted by the King's most excellent majesty, by and with the advice and consent of the lords spiritual and temporal, and commons, in this present parliament assembled, and it is hereby enacted by the authority of the same, That from and after the eleventh day of *May*, one thousand seven hundred and sixty four, it shall be lawful for any single creditor, or two or more creditors, being partners, whose debt or debts shall amount to one hundred pounds or upwards, and for any two creditors whose debts shall amount to one hundred and fifty pounds or upwards, or any three or more creditors whose debts shall amount to two hundred pounds or upwards, of any person or persons deemed a merchant, banker, broker, factor, scrivener, or trader or traders, within the description of the acts of parliament relating to bankrupts, having privilege of parliament, at any time, upon affidavit or affidavits being made and filed of record in any of his Majesty's courts at *Westminster* by such creditor or creditors, that such debt or debts is or are justly due to him or them respectively, and that every such debtor, as he or they verily believe, is a merchant, banker, broker, factor, scrivener

From and after 11 May, 1764, creditors, to a certain value, of any merchant, &c. within the description of the laws relating to bankrupts, having privilege of parliament, may, upon affidavit made of the debt, and filed in any of the courts at Westminster,

vener, or trader, within the deſcription of the ſtatutes relating to bankrupts, to ſue out of the ſame court a ſummons, or an original bill and ſummons, againſt ſuch merchant, banker, broker, factor, ſcrivener, or trader, and ſerve him with a copy thereof; and if ſuch merchant, banker, broker, factor, ſcrivener, or trader, ſhall not within two months after perſonal ſervice of ſuch ſummons (affidavits of the debt or debts having been duly made and filed as aforeſaid) pay, ſecure, or compound for, ſuch debt or debts, to the ſatisfaction of ſuch creditor or creditors, or enter into a bond in ſuch ſum, and with two ſuch ſufficient ſureties, as any of the judges of that court out of which ſuch ſummons ſhall iſſue ſhall approve of, to pay ſuch ſum as ſhall be recovered in ſuch action or actions, together with ſuch coſts as ſhall be given in the ſame, he ſhall be accounted and adjudged a bankrupt from the time of the ſervice of ſuch ſummons; and any creditor or creditors may ſue out a commiſſion againſt any ſuch perſon, and proceed thereon in like manner as againſt other bankrupts.

ſue out a ſummons, or original bill, &c. againſt ſuch debtor: and if he ſhall not, within 2 months, pay, ſecure, or compound for the debt, he ſhall be adjudged a bankrupt; and a commiſſion may be accordingly ſued out againſt him.

II. Provided always, and it is hereby declared, That this act ſhall not extend, or be deemed or conſtrued to extend, to any ſuch debt or debts as aforeſaid contracted before the eighth day of *March*, one thouſand ſeven hundred and ſixty four; any thing herein before contained to the contrary thereof in any wiſe notwithſtanding.

But this act is not to extend to ſuch debts as were contracted before 8 March, 1764.

III. And be it further enacted by the authority aforeſaid, That if any merchant, banker, broker, factor, ſcrivener, or trader, ſhall, after the laſt day of this ſeſſion of parliament, commit any act of bankruptcy, that then, and in ſuch caſe, any creditor or creditors as aforeſaid may ſue out a commiſſion of bankrupt againſt ſuch merchant, banker, broker, ſcrivener, or trader; and the commiſſioners in ſuch commiſſion, and other perſons, may proceed thereon in like manner as againſt other bankrupts; any privilege of parliament to the contrary notwithſtanding.

But any merchant, &c. committing an act of bankruptcy after the laſt day of this ſeſſion, the creditors may ſue out a commiſſion againſt him, and the commiſſioners proceed therein, as againſt other bankrupts, notwithſtanding his privilege.

IV. Provided nevertheleſs, and be it enacted, That nothing in this act ſhall ſubject any perſon intitled to privilege of parliament to be arreſted, or impriſoned, during the time of ſuch privilege, except in caſes made felony by the acts relating to bankrupts, or any of them.

Perſons intitled to privilege not ſubject to arreſt, &c. except in caſes made felony.

CAP. XXXIV.

An act to prevent paper bills of credit, hereafter to be iſſued in any of his Majeſty's colonies or plantations in America, *from being declared to be a legal tender in payments of money; and to prevent the legal tender of ſuch bills as are now ſubſiſting, from being prolonged beyond the periods limited for calling in and ſinking the ſame.*

WHEREAS *great quantities of paper bills of credit have been created and iſſued in his Majeſty's colonies or plantations in* America,

Preamble.

America, *by virtue of acts, orders, resolutions, or votes of assembly, making and declaring such bills of credit to be legal tender in payment of money: and whereas such bills of credit have greatly depreciated in their value, by means whereof debts have been discharged with a much less value than was contracted for, to the great discouragement and prejudice of the trade and commerce of his Majesty's subjects, by occasioning confusion in dealings, and lessening credit in the said colonies or plantations:* for remedy whereof, may it please your most excellent Majesty, that it may be enacted; and be it enacted by the King's most excellent majesty, by and with the advice and consent of the lords spiritual and temporal, and commons, in this present parliament assembled, and by the authority of the same, That from and after the first day of *September*, one thousand seven hundred and sixty four, no act, order, resolution, or vote of assembly, in any of his Majesty's colonies or plantations in *America*, shall be made, for creating or issuing any paper bills, or bills of credit of any kind or denomination whatsoever, declaring such paper bills, or bills of credit, to be legal tender in payment of any bargains, contracts, debts, dues, or demands whatsoever; and every clause or provision which shall hereafter be inserted in any act, order, resolution, or vote of assembly, contrary to this act, shall be null and void.

After 1 Sept. 1764, all future acts of assembly, &c. for creating, &c. paper bills of credit, declaring them to be a legal tender in payment of money; are void,

II. And whereas the great quantities of paper bills, or bills of credit, which are now actually in circulation and currency in several colonies or plantations in *America*, emitted in pursuance of acts of assembly declaring such bills a legal tender, make it highly expedient that the conditions and terms, upon which such bills have been emitted, should not be varied or prolonged, so as to continue the legal tender thereof beyond the terms respectively fixed by such acts for calling in and discharging such bills; be it therefore enacted by the authority aforesaid, That every act, order, resolution, or vote of assembly, in any of the said colonies or plantations, which shall be made to prolong the legal tender of any paper bills, or bills of credit, which are now subsisting and current in any of the said colonies or plantations in *America*, beyond the times fixed for the calling in, sinking, and discharging of such paper bills, or bills of credit, shall be null and void.

as are also all acts, &c. which shall be made to prolong the legal tender of such bills now subsisting, beyond the periods limited for calling in and sinking the same.

III. And be it further enacted by the authority aforesaid, That if any governor or commander in chief for the time being, in all or any of the said colonies or plantations, shall, from and after the said first day of *September*, one thousand seven hundred and sixty four, give his assent to any act or order of assembly contrary to the true intent and meaning of this act, every such governor or commander in chief shall, for every such offence, forfeit and pay the sum of one thousand pounds, and shall be immediately dismissed from his government, and for ever after rendered incapable of any public office or place of trust.

Governor, giving his assent to any such act, forfeits 1000l, and is incapacitated,

IV. Provided always, That nothing in this act shall extend to alter or repeal an act passed in the twenty fourth year of the reign

This act not to alter or re-

reign of his late majesty King *George* the Second, intituled, *An act to regulate and restrain paper bills of credit in his Majesty's colonies or plantations of* Rhode Island *and* Providence *plantations,* Connecticut, *the* Massachuset's Bay, *and* New Hampshire, *in* America, *and to prevent the same being legal tenders in payments of money.* peal the act 24 Geo. II.

V. Provided also, That nothing herein contained shall extend, or be construed to extend, to make any of the bills now subsisting in any of the said colonies a legal tender. nor to make any bills now subsisting a legal tender.

CAP. XXXV.

An act for making compensation to the proprietors of such lands and hereditaments as have been purchased upon the sea coasts in the counties of Kent, Sussex, *and* Southampton, *on which forts and batteries have been erected for defence of the said coasts, in pursuance of an act passed in the second year of the reign of his present Majesty, and for other purposes therein mentioned.*

WHEREAS *in pursuance of an act of parliament passed in the second year of his Majesty's reign, intituled,* An act for vesting certain lands, tenements, and hereditaments upon the sea coasts in the counties of *Kent*, *Sussex*, and *Southampton*, on which forts and batteries have been erected for the defence of the said coasts, in trustees, for certain uses, and for other purposes therein mentioned; *his Majesty was most graciously pleased to issue a commission by his letters patent under the great seal of* Great Britain, *bearing date at* Westminster *the nineteenth day of* July, *in the second year of his reign, to impower and authorize certain persons therein named to be commissioners for putting in execution the said act, and did give to them, or any five or more of them, full power and authority to do, perform, and execute all and every the matters and things whatsoever, which by the said act such commissioners were authorized and required to do, perform, and execute, thereby willing them, or any five or more of them, from time to time, to proceed and act according to the rules and directions of the said act of parliament: and whereas by virtue of the said commission, and in pursuance of the said act, eleven of the said commissioners, in the said commission named, did, on the sixth day of* September, *in the said second year of his Majesty's reign, meet, pursuant to notice thereof given and fixed up at the door of the Guild hall of the city of* Canterbury *in the said county of* Kent, *and at the principal gates of, and entrances into, the respective forts and batteries at* Folkestone *and* Hyth, *and likewise published in the* London Gazette, *thirty days and more before such meeting, at the* Old Castle *of* Canterbury *aforesaid; and did then and there, in a summary manner, proceed and act by and upon the testimony of witnesses, inspection and examination of deeds, writings, and records, and by and upon the inquest of seventeen good and lawful men qualified to serve upon juries at the assizes for the said county of* Kent, *impanelled, summoned, and returned by* George Kelly *esquire, sheriff of the said county, to take the inquest, who, upon their oaths duly administered,* Preamble, reciting clauses in act 2 Geo. III.

nistered, did inquire into and present the true and real value of the lands, tenements, and hereditaments, mentioned in the said act to be situate at Folkestone *and* Hyth *in the said county of* Kent, *and of every part and parcel thereof, and who respectively were the owners and proprietors thereof, and their respective estates and interest therein; and thereupon the said commissioners then present did adjudge and determine who respectively were the owners and proprietors of the said lands, tenements, and hereditaments at* Folkestone *and* Hyth *aforesaid, and their respective estates and interest therein, and in every part and parcel thereof, and what each respective owner and proprietor thereof was intitled to for his respective estates and interest therein, amounting together to the sum of ninety pounds of lawful money of* Great Britain: *and whereas by virtue of the said commission, and in pursuance of the said act, ten of the said commissioners in the said commission named, did, on the thirteenth day of* September, *in the said second year of his Majesty's reign, meet at the town hall of the borough of* Lewes *in the said county of* Sussex, *pursuant to notice given and fixed up at the town hall of the borough of* Lewes *aforesaid, and at the principal gates of, and entrances into, the respective forts and batteries at* Little Hampton, Brighthelmstone, Newhaven, Blotchington, Seaford, Hasting, *and at the* Upper Battery *and* Lower Battery *at* Rye, *and likewise published in the* London Gazette *thirty days and more before such meeting; and did then and there, in a summary manner, by and upon the testimony of witnesses, inspection and examination of deeds, writings, and records, and by and upon the inquest of nineteen good and lawful men qualified to serve upon juries at the assizes for the said county of* Sussex, *impanelled, summoned, and returned by* Thomas Grainger *esquire, sheriff of the said county of* Sussex, *to take the inquest, who, upon their oaths, did enquire into and present the true and real value of the said lands, tenements, and hereditaments, in the said act mentioned to be situate in* Climpton, Brighthelmstone, Newhaven, Blotchington, Seaford, Hasting, *and* Rye, *in the said county of* Sussex, *and of every part and parcel thereof, and who respectively were the owners and proprietors thereof, and their respective estates and interest therein, and thereupon the said commissioners then present, did adjudge and determine who respectively were the owners and proprietors of the said lands and hereditaments in the said county of* Sussex, *and their respective estates and interest therein, and in every part and parcel thereof, and what each respective owner and proprietor thereof was intitled to, for his, her, and their respective estates and interest therein, amounting together to the sum of one hundred twenty one pounds, thirteen shillings, of like lawful money of* Great Britain: *and the said commissioners then present at the said town hall of the said borough of* Lewes, *upon the complaint of several persons owners of lands, adjoining to part of the lands by the said act vested, that they had respectively received damage by making the fortifications there, did certify and estimate the respective damages done to the respective lands of the several persons complaining, amounting together to the sum of thirty two pounds, and seventeen shillings, of like lawful money of* Great Britain: *and whereas by virtue of the said commission, and in pursuance of the said act, six of the com-*

commissioners in the said commission named did, on the twenty seventh day of September, *in the said second year of his Majesty's reign, meet at the town hall of the borough of* Portsmouth, *in the said county of* Southampton, *pursuant to notice given and fixed up at the door of the town hall of the said borough of* Portsmouth *aforesaid, and at the principal gates of, and entrances into, the respective forts and batteries at* Lumps and Eastney, *and likewise published in the* London Gazette, *thirty days and more before such meeting; and did then and there, in a summary manner, by and upon the testimony of witnesses, inspection and examination of deeds, writings, and records, and by and upon the inquest of two and twenty good and lawful men qualified to serve upon juries at the assizes for the said county of* Southampton, *impanelled, summoned, and returned, by Sir* Thomas Gatehouse *knight, sheriff of the said county of* Southampton, *to take the inquest, who, upon their oaths, did enquire into and present the true and real value of the said lands, tenements, and hereditaments, in the said act mentioned to be situate in the parish of* Portsea, *in the said county of* Southampton, *and of every part and parcel thereof, and who respectively were the owners and proprietors thereof, and their respective estates and interest therein, and thereupon the said commissioners then present did adjudge and determine who respectively were the owners and proprietors of the said lands, tenements, and hereditaments, in the said parish of* Portsea, *and their respective estates and interest therein, and in every part and parcel thereof, and what each respective owner and proprietor thereof was intitled to, for his respective estate and interest therein, amounting together to the sum of three hundred and one pounds, five shillings, of like lawful money of* Great Britain: *and whereas it is just and reasonable the owners and proprietors of the respective lands, tenements, and hereditaments should be paid the respective sums to them adjudged, for their estates and interest in the said lands, tenements, and hereditaments, in and by the said recited act mentioned and vested in the said trustees therein named, together with interest for the same, after the rate of four pounds* per centum per annum, *from the time the said lands were first made use of for the purposes in the said act mentioned, to the time of payment of their principal money;* for which purpose, and for the more effectual carrying the said act into execution, may it please your Majesty that it may be enacted; and be it enacted by the King's most excellent majesty, by and with the advice and consent of the lords spiritual and temporal, and commons, in this present parliament assembled, and by the authority of the same, That out of all or any the aids or supplies granted to his Majesty, for the service of the year one thousand seven hundred and sixty four, there shall and may be issued and applied any sum or sums of money, not exceeding the sum of six hundred forty nine pounds, eight shillings, and nine pence farthing, for and towards making a reasonable and just compensation and satisfaction to all and every person and persons, bodies politic and corporate, ecclesiastical and civil, who, at the time of making the said recited act, were the several and respective owners and proprietors of the lands, tenements, and hereditaments, in the said recited

A sum not exceeding 649 l. 8 s. 9 d. 1 q. to be issued out of the supplies granted for the service of the current year, towards making satisfaction to the respective proprietors and persons interested in the premisses.

recited act mentioned, according to their several estates and interest therein, in possession, reversion, remainder, or otherwise.

II. And to the intent that all and singular the proprietors aforesaid may be paid for their respective estates and interests, all and every such sum and sums of money as they have been adjudged and determined by the said commissioners to be respectively intitled unto, together with interest for the same after the rate of four pounds *per centum per annum*, from the time the respective lands were first made use of for the purposes in the said recited act mentioned, to the time of payment of the said principal sums; be it further enacted by the authority aforesaid, That it shall and may be lawful for the surveyor general of the ordnance for the time being to make out and allow one or more bill or bills to the respective person or persons, bodies politic or corporate, for such sum and sums of money as is or are to them respectively adjudged, together with interest for the same after the rate of four pounds *per centum per annum*; which bill or bills, so made out and allowed, shall express the respective lands, and the number of acres, together with the name of the person or persons, bodies politic or corporate, and the respective sum or sums of money he, she, or they is or are to receive; and thereupon one or more debenture or debentures shall be prepared for the several and respective sums as aforesaid by the clerk of the ordnance for the time being, and signed by three or more of the principal officers of the ordnance for the time being; which debenture or debentures is and are hereby required to be paid by the treasurer of the ordnance for the time being, who shall take acquittances from the parties indorsed thereon.

Bills to be made out at the office of ordnance for the sums due to the respective proprietors, &c. and debentures to be granted thereupon, which are to be paid by the treasurer of the ordnance.

III. And be it further enacted by the authority aforesaid, That if any person or persons, bodies politic or corporate, shall wilfully refuse to accept of or receive such debenture or debentures as aforesaid, that then, and in such case, it shall and may be lawful for the clerk of the ordnance for the time being, to leave and deposit such debenture or debentures with the clerk of the peace of the respective counties where the lands, tenements, or hereditaments do lie, in respect whereof such sum of money is to be paid, and to take his acquittance or acquittances for the same; which such clerk of the peace is hereby required to give without any fee or reward, and which shall be taken and deemed to be valid; and the lands, tenements, and hereditaments, of such person or persons, bodies politic or corporate, so refusing to accept such debenture or debentures, shall be vested to the use of his Majesty, his heirs and successors for ever, as if he, she, or they had received such debenture or debentures, and the money thereon due had been fully satisfied and paid.

Debentures refused to be accepted, may be left with the clerk of the peace of the county wherein the lands lie, and acquittance to be taken for the same;

Lands to vest thereupon in his Majesty.

IV. And whereas, the money respectively adjudged to the several person and persons, bodies politic and corporate, are, taken distributely, so minute and inconsiderable, that were the same to be paid into the hands of the deputy of the King's remembrancer of his Majesty's court of Exchequer at *Westminster*, to be disposed of, subject to, and by the orders and direction of the

the ſaid court, the ſeveral owners and proprietors of the lands would have no ſatisfaction for the ſame; but the whole or greater part of the money, would neceſſarily be expended in diſcharging the fees of the ſaid court; for remedy whereof, be it further enacted, That the ſeveral ſum and ſums of money due and owing to any impropriator, appropriator, parſon, or vicar, in right of his church, ſhall, and lawfully may be paid into the hands of ſuch impropriator, appropriator, parſon, or vicar; and all ſum and ſums of money due and owing to any body or bodies politic or corporate, or any truſtees for their uſe, ſhall, and lawfully may be paid into the hands of the mayor, bailiff, or other chief officer of ſuch body or bodies politic or corporate; and all ſuch ſum or ſums of money of any perſon or perſons whatſoever, who by reaſon of any diſability, by nonage, or under any ſettlement, is or are not capable by law to take and diſpoſe of the ſeveral ſums which ſhall be due and payable to them as aforeſaid, ſhall, and lawfully may be paid into the hands of the guardians of ſuch infants, or the truſtees under ſuch ſettlement, for the uſe of ſuch body or bodies politic or corporate, eccleſiaſtical and civil, and the reſpective perſons intereſted therein as aforeſaid; which ſeveral ſums of money ſo to be paid, ſhall by ſuch impropriators, appropriators, parſons, vicars, mayors, bailiffs, or other chief officer, of any body politic or corporate, guardians and truſtees, be, with all convenient ſpeed, reſpectively laid out in the purchaſe of other lands, tenements, or hereditaments, in places moſt convenient for the parties intereſted, their heirs and ſucceſſors; any law, ſtatute, or cuſtom, to the contrary thereof notwithſtanding: and the eſtate or eſtates, ſo to be purchaſed, ſhall be conveyed and ſettled to the ſame uſes, intents, and purpoſes, as the former eſtates were ſettled, at ſuch time as they became veſted in the truſtees appointed by the ſaid recited act; and that, until ſuch purchaſes can be made, it ſhall and may be lawful for ſuch impropriator, appropriator, parſon, vicar, mayor, bailiff, or other chief officer of ſuch body politic or corporate, guardians and truſtees, to place ſuch monies out at intereſt on parliamentary funds, or other good ſecurities, declaring the truſt thereof in the ſame manner, as the eſtate or eſtates, ſo to be purchaſed, are to be conveyed and ſettled; and the intereſt thereof ſhall, from time to time, as the ſame ſhall grow due, be paid to the ſeveral and reſpective parties who would be reſpectively intitled to the rents and profits of the eſtate or eſtates, ſo to be purchaſed, in caſe the ſame were purchaſed.

The money adjudged due to impropriators, &c. to be paid into their hands; that due to bodies politic or corporate, or truſtees for their uſe, to be paid to the mayor or other chief officer; that to infants, &c. to be paid to the guardians or truſtees;

and to be laid out in the purchaſe of other lands, &c.

to be ſettled to the ſame uſes;

and till ſuch purchaſes be made, the monies are to be placed out in the publick funds, &c.

and the intereſt to be paid the reſpective parties.

CAP.

CAP. XXXVI.

An act to continue an act made in the fifth year of the reign of his late majesty King George *the Second, intituled,* An act to prevent the committing of frauds by bankrupts; *and for extending the laws, relating to hackney coaches, to the counties of* Kent *and* Essex.

Preamble.

WHEREAS *the law hereafter mentioned hath, by experience, been found useful and beneficial, and is near expiring;* may it therefore please your Majesty, that it may be enacted; and be it enacted by the King's most excellent majesty, by and with the advice and consent of the lords spiritual and temporal, and commons, in this present parliament assembled, and by the authority of the same, That an act made in the fifth year of the reign of his late majesty King *George* the Second, intituled, *An act to prevent the committing of frauds by bankrupts*, which was to continue in force for three years from the twenty fourth day of *June*, one thousand seven hundred and thirty two, and from thence to the end of the then next session of parliament; and which, by several subsequent acts, made in the ninth and sixteenth years of his said Majesty's reign, was further continued until the twenty ninth day of *September*, one thousand seven hundred and fifty; and which, by another act made in the twenty fourth year of his said Majesty's reign, was amended, and further continued until the first day of *September*, one thousand seven hundred and fifty seven, and from thence to the end of the then next session of parliament; and which, by another act made in the thirty first year of his said Majesty's reign, was further continued until the twenty ninth day of *September*, one thousand seven hundred and sixty four, and from thence to the end of the then next session of parliament; shall be, and the same is hereby further continued from the expiration thereof, until the twenty ninth day of *September*, one thousand seven hundred and seventy one, and from thence to the end of the then next session of parliament.

Act 5 Geo. II. which was continued by several subsequent acts,

further continued to 29 Sept, 1771.

II. And whereas by the several laws now in being, for licensing and regulating the owners and drivers of hackney coaches within the cities of *London* and *Westminster*, and the suburbs thereof, and the parishes and places comprized within the weekly bills of mortality, the said drivers are subjected to certain penalties and punishments for exactions or misbehaviour, but the cognizance thereof is, by the said laws, consigned to the commissioners for licensing the said coaches, the aldermen of *London*, and the justices of the peace for the city of *Westminster*, and the counties of *Middlesex* and *Surrey* (into which counties the limits comprized within the said bills of mortality do in part extend:) and whereas the counties of *Essex* and *Kent* lie but at a small distance from the city of *London*, and the said licensed hackney coaches often travel into those counties through a small part

part of the said county of *Middlesex* or *Surrey*, but the drivers thereof are subject to no jurisdiction of the justices of the peace after they pass the said counties of *Middlesex* or *Surrey*; be it therefore further enacted by the authority aforesaid, That from and after the first day of *May*, one thousand seven hundred and sixty four, every justice or justices of the peace of or for the counties of *Kent* and *Essex* shall have the same power and authority, within his or their respective jurisdiction or jurisdictions, to put the said laws, or any of them, in execution against the drivers of the said licensed hackney coaches, for any offence committed against the said laws, or any of them, to all intents and purposes, as the said commissioners, aldermen, and justices of *London*, *Westminster*, *Middlesex*, and *Surrey*, now have by law, within their respective jurisdictions.

Justices for the counties of Kent and Essex authorized to put the laws relating to hackney coaches in execution within their respective jurisdictions.

CAP. XXXVII.

An act for the better establishing a manufactory of cambricks and lawns, or goods of the kind usually known under those denominations, now carrying on at Winchelsea, *in the county of* Sussex; *and for improving, regulating, and extending the manufacture of cambricks and lawns, or goods of the kind usually known under those denominations, in that part of* Great Britain *called* England.

Preamble.

WHEREAS *the establishing a manufacture of linens in* England, *of the kind usally known under the denomination of cambricks and* French *lawns, will be of great utility to this kingdom, as well by the employment of a great number of poor, as by preventing the illegal importation of foreign cambricks and* French *lawns: and whereas a manufactury of cambricks and lawns hath been already set up at* Winchelsea *in the county of* Sussex, *and large quantities of such goods have been made there, and may be made in other parts of this kingdom, equal, if not superior, in quality to those made in foreign parts; and many persons are desirous of subscribing large sums towards the support and extension of the said manufactury (for the effectual carrying on of which a large fund will be necessary) but are apprehensive that difficulties may arise, as well in recovering debts which may grow due to the proprietors of the said manufactury, as in defending suits or actions which may be brought or commenced against them, for any matter or thing relative thereto, as, by law, all the several proprietors or subscribers to the said manufactury must, in such cases both sue and be sued, implead and be impleaded, by their several and distinct names and descriptions; and therefore, for the more easily carrying on the manufacture, and avoiding the difficulties aforesaid, are desirous of being incorporated and having a common seal and name by which they may sue and be sued; and many persons are desirous of subscribing large sums thereto, but are deterred from so doing, lest they may thereby become liable, in case the said manufactury should not be successful, to pay large sums of money over and above the sums by them subscribed, to make good the debts to be incurred therefrom; and many persons who are not now liable to become bankrupts,* with-

within the intent and meaning of any of the laws now in force concerning bankrupts are likewise fearful of subscribing money to carry on the said manufacture, as, by becoming subscribers to and part owners thereof, they may be liable to have commissions of bankrupt issued against them as traders: and whereas some doubts have arisen, whether such cambricks and lawns, so made and fabricated in England, *can, consistent with the laws now in being relating to cambricks and* French *lawns, be legally sold, disposed of, and used in* Great Britain; may it therefore please your Majesty that it may be enacted; and be it enacted by the King's most excellent majesty, by and with the advice and consent of the lords spiritual and temporal, and commons, in this present parliament assembled, and by the authority of the same, That it shall and may be lawful to and for any person or persons whomsoever, to make and vend, or cause to be made and vended, all such linen goods called *Cambricks* or *Lawns*, or goods of the kind usually known by or under either of those denominations, as shall be made in this kingdom, and stamped in the manner herein after directed; and that such lawns or cambricks, or other such like goods so made and stamped, may be exposed to sale, and worn by any person or persons in this kingdom; any law, usage, or custom, to the contrary notwithstanding.

Any person may make and sell cambricks and lawns in this kingdom.

II. And whereas the sole right and prerogative of granting charters of incorporation (not being such as are repugnant to any law or statute of this kingdom) doth belong to your Majesty; be it therefore enacted by the authority aforesaid, That it shall and may be lawful to and for his Majesty, his heirs, and successors, by one charter, indenture, or letters patent, under the great seal of *Great Britain*, to declare and grant, That the right honourable the earl *Verney* in the kingdom of *Ireland*, the right honourable *Charles Townshend*, Sir *George Colebrooke* baronet, Sir *Lawrence Dundas* baronet, *Arnold Nesbitt* esquire, *Peregrine Cust* esquire, *George Prescott* esquire, *Barlow Trecothick* esquire, *Gilbert Heathcote* esquire, *Moses Franks* esquire, master *Edward Bridgen*, master *Benjamin Barnett*, master *William Grace*, master *Thomas Bidwell*, and every other person or persons who shall hereafter, either in their own right, or as executors, administrators, successors, or assigns, in right of any other person or persons, become proprietors of, or interested in, any part or share of the joint capital stock or fund herein after mentioned, shall be one distinct and separate body politick and corporate, in deed and in name, by the name and stile of *The* English *Linen Company*, or such other name as his Majesty shall think proper; and that such corporation shall have perpetual succession, subject to such power of revocation as to his Majesty shall seem meet; and that such corporation shall have power, from time to time, to chuse ten directors, and all proper officers and servants, for the better management of the affairs of the said corporation, in such manner, and under such restrictions and qualifications, as are herein after directed, or such as shall be prescribed in that behalf in and by such charter; nevertheless the first directors of the said cor-

The King may incorporate the persons herein named (the present subscribers)

by the name of The English Linen Company, with such power of revocation as to his Majesty shall seem meet:

They may chuse directors, &c.

corporation ſhall and may be appointed by his Majeſty in and by the ſame charter; and that the ſaid firſt directors ſhall continue in their reſpective offices from the time of their appointment by his Majeſty, until the firſt *Wedneſday* in *March* next after ſuch appointment; and all ſubſequent directors ſhall continue in their reſpective offices for one year from the time of their reſpective appointments; and in caſe of death, removal, or diſqualification, be ſupplied in ſuch manner as herein after is directed; and that the ſaid corporation ſhall and may have and uſe a common ſeal for the buſineſs only of the ſaid corporation; and ſuch ſeal, from time to time, may break, change, make new, or alter, as ſhall be found moſt expedient; and that the ſaid corporation ſhall be able and capable in law, to purchaſe, take, and enjoy, meſſuages, lands, tenements, or hereditaments, not exceeding the value of five hundred pounds *per annum*, and to grant, alien, demiſe, or diſpoſe of, the ſame, or any part thereof, at their free wills and pleaſures; and in their corporate name, ſhall be able and capable in law, to ſue and implead, be ſued and impleaded, anſwer and be anſwered, in any court of record, or elſewhere, in all cauſes and actions whatſoever, for, touching or concerning, ſuch corporation, or the manufactury by them carried on as aforeſaid.

and purchaſe lands, &c. not exceeding the value of 500l. per annum;

may ſue and be ſued;

III. And be it further enacted by the authority aforeſaid, That it ſhall and may be lawful to and for ſuch corporation, when conſtituted, to raiſe a capital joint ſtock, to be applied for the carrying on the ſaid manufacture, and effecting the purpoſes of the ſaid charter, not exceeding one hundred thouſand pounds of lawful money of *Great Britain*, at ſuch times, and in ſuch proportions, as at any general court or courts of ſuch corporation, to be holden purſuant to the directions of this act, or of ſuch charter, ſhall be directed, either by taking ſubſcriptions from particular perſons (being or not being members of ſuch corporation) for advancing money for that purpoſe, according to the orders of ſuch general courts reſpectively, or by calls of money from the members of the ſaid corporation for the time being, or ſuch other methods as the ſaid general courts ſhall think expedient for making up the ſaid capital; and that all and every perſon or perſons, by or from whom any ſubſcriptions ſhall be accepted, or payment made, purſuant to any order or orders of the ſaid general courts, towards raiſing the ſaid capital ſtock, their executors, adminiſtrators, and aſſigns, ſhall be intitled to a ſhare of the ſaid capital ſtock, in proportion to the money which they ſhall contribute, and to ſuch intereſt thereon, and alſo to ſuch ſhare of the profits and advantages attending the ſaid capital ſtock, and payable at ſuch times, and in ſuch proportions, as ſhall be directed and agreed upon by the ſaid corporation at any of their general courts; and ſuch ſubſcriber or ſubſcribers, not being then a member or members of ſuch corporation, upon making their ſeveral ſubſcriptions and payments in manner herein-after directed, ſhall be admitted, and are hereby declared to be, members thereof; which ſaid ſub-

and may raiſe a capital, not exceeding 100,000l.

Subſcribers intitled to a ſhare of capital, in proportion to their ſubſcriptions,

and to be members of the corporation.

subscriptions and all other subscriptions to the said capital stock or fund of the said corporation, shall be distinctly and separately entered in a proper book or books to be provided for that purpose, and signed by the respective person or persons making such subscriptions; and the sums subscribed shall be entered in such book or books, in words at length, and also in figures, together with the day of the month and year on which such subscriptions shall respectively be made; and all and every such subscription and subscriptions shall be made in the presence of, and attested by, one or more witness or witnesses, who shall, by order of the said directors, have the custody of the said book.

Subscriptions to be entered, signed, and attested.

IV. Provided always, and be it enacted by the authority aforesaid, That it shall and may be lawful to and for his Majesty, his heirs, and successors, by warrant under his or their sign manual, from time to time, to impower such corporation to enlarge the capital stock of such corporation, from time to time, as the affairs of the said corporation shall require, on the like terms and conditions with the original capital.

The King may grant power to enlarge the capital.

V. And be it further enacted by the authority aforesaid, That all and every person and persons who shall subscribe any sum or sums of money for or towards raising such capital stock as aforesaid, shall answer and pay all such sum and sums of money, which he or they shall so subscribe, unto the directors of the said corporation for the time being, or to the cashier of the said corporation for the time being, or to such other person or persons who shall be authorized to receive the same in manner following; that is to say, one fourth part (the whole in four equal parts being divided) of every such sum so subscribed, shall be paid down at the time of making each subscription; and the remaining three fourth parts thereof at such times, and in such proportions, as any court or courts of directors of the said corporation shall think proper to call for or demand the same; notice of every such call or demand having been first published in the *London Gazette*, ten days at least before the day limited and appointed for the making of any payment, pursuant to any such call or demand: and if any person or persons, who shall have so subscribed as aforesaid, do not pay down one full fourth part of all such sum or sums as he or they shall subscribe, upon or at the time of his or their subscription, then every such subscription, without such payment, shall be utterly void and of none effect; and if any person or persons, who shall have subscribed, as aforesaid, his or their executors, administrators, or assigns, having paid, in manner aforesaid, any part or parts of the sum or sums so by him or them subscribed, shall make default in any of the subsequent payments which shall be called for or demanded, in manner aforesaid, for the space of ten days after the time or times, in such notice or notices, as aforesaid, limited and appointed for the payment of such calls respectively; then, and in every such case, one moiety or half part of the first sum paid by such person or persons, on his or their respective subscription, shall be lost and forfeited to the said corporation;

Subscribers to pay a fourth at the time of subscribing, and the remainder at such calls as the directors shall appoint.

10 days notice of every call to be published in the London Gazette.

On neglect of first payment, subscription to be void; and on neglect of subsequent payments, one half of the first to be forfeited, &c.

tion; and the share or interest of all and every such person or persons so making default of and in the capital stock of the said corporation, and the interest and profits which he or they would otherwise have been intitled to receive therefrom, shall be reduced, lessened, or proportioned, according to the money actually paid upon every such subscription respectively, after an abatement or deduction of one moiety or half part of the first payment to be forfeited as aforesaid.

Directors to appoint a house in or near London or Westminster to transact their business.

VI. And be it further enacted by the authority aforesaid, That it shall and may be lawful to and for his Majesty, in and by such charter, to impower the court of directors of the said company or corporation for the time being, and such court of directors shall and may, from time to time, fix upon and appoint a proper place or house in or near the cities of *London* or *Westminster*, for the transacting the affairs and business of the said company; and that the directors in the said charter named, and their successors, or any five or more of them, shall be and be called a court of directors, and have full power and authority to act as such; and that it shall and may be lawful to and for the said court of directors to meet as often as they shall think necessary or proper; and they are hereby authorized and impowered to nominate and appoint such officers and servants, or other persons, as shall be any ways necessary to be employed in the management and carrying on the affairs of the said company, and from time to time to dismiss such officers and servants from their employ, and nominate and appoint new ones in their stead or steads, or to encrease or lessen their number, as such court of directors shall from time to time think proper, and to give such orders and directions for the management of the affairs of the said corporation as they shall think proper, and are consistent with the general rules and orders made by the said corporation; and to take, from time to time, any number of apprentices to be employed in the manufactury carried on by the said company, upon such terms and conditions, and for such number of years, as to them shall seem meet; and to affix the common seal of the said corporation to a counter-part of the articles of agreement, or indentures of apprenticeship, made with such apprentices respectively, their parents, guardians or other persons authorized to put out and bind such apprentices respectively.

Directors to be a court, and nominate all officers and servants;

and to take apprentices.

A general annual court to be held the first Wednesday in March, for electing directors.

VII. And be it further enacted by the authority aforesaid, That there shall be one general annual court of the said corporation, held on the first *Wednesday* in *March* in every year, and as many other general courts as shall be necessary; which said general courts shall be held at any house or place in the cities of *London* or *Westminster*, which shall be appointed by the said court of directors; of which said general court, or any other general courts to be called by any court of directors of the said company, and which general courts such directors are hereby authorized to hold and call as often as such court of directors shall think the same necessary, ten days notice at the least shall be given in the *London Gazette*; and that the said general court, held on the first *Wednesday* in *March* yearly, shall be chosen out of and from the members of the said corporation, by the majority of votes of all the members then present.

Qualifications of directors,

VIII. And be it further enacted by the authority aforesaid, That no person shall be capable of being elected into or exercising the office of a director of the said corporation but under the qualification following (that is to say) that the directors of the said corporation shall severally be possessed of a share or interest in the said stock in their own right respectively, not less than five hundred pounds capital; and that the directors shall not continue in their respective offices any longer than they shall respectively continue to be possessed of the said share and interest in the said capital stock, in his or their own name and right respectively; and that no person shall be qualified to vote at any general court, who shall not then be possessed of a share or interest in the said capital stock, to the amount of two hundred pounds at the least in his own right; and that such person who in his own right shall be possessed of five hundred pounds capital stock, shall have two votes at such general court; and that such person who shall be possessed in his own right of one thousand pounds capital stock, shall have three votes at such general court; but no person shall have more than three votes upon any account whatsoever; and if such share or interest of any proprietor in the said capital stock shall be at any time afterwards diminished from the proportion herein before ascertained, that then the same shall be no longer a qualification for voting at any general court.

and voters, and the number of votes they may have.

Members voting, to swear to their qualifications, if required.

IX. And be it further enacted by the authority aforesaid, That all proprietors shall (if required) before they vote at any court, take an oath in the form which shall be approved of by a general court, to be administered to them by one of the directors (who are hereby authorized and impowered to administer the same, or to direct such oath to be administered by any other person or persons in his or their presence) declaring their property, share, or interest in the capital stock of the said corporation, and the *Quantum* thereof, and that the same, or any part thereof, is not in trust for any other person or persons, and that no person shall be admitted to vote at any such court who shall refuse to take such oath; and all officers and servants of the said corporation shall, if required by the court of directors, before they enter on their respective offices, likewise take an oath in the form which for that purpose shall be approved by a general court of the said corporation, to be administered by the directors of the said corporation, or any one of them, for the due and faithful discharge of their respective offices; which oath such directors, or any one of them, are hereby authorized and impowered to administer, or direct the same to be administered by any other person or persons in his or their presence; and in case any such officer or servant shall refuse or neglect to take such oath for the space of ten days after he or they shall be chosen or ap-

Officers, &c. to be sworn according to the form approved by a general court;

refusing or neglecting to take such oath for 10 days, election void.

appointed to any ſuch office or offices as aforeſaid, if required, ſuch choice or appointment ſhall be void, and a new election or appointment made.

X. And be it further enacted by the authority aforeſaid, That the court of directors of the ſaid corporation for the time being ſhall be obliged, upon demand made to them by any ten or more members of the ſaid corporation, who ſhall in the whole, or together, be poſſeſſed of not leſs than five thouſand pounds in the capital or joint ſtock of the ſaid corporation, ſuch demand being made in writing, and ſigned by the members demanding the ſame, and delivered at a court of directors to any one member of ſuch court then preſent, to call a general court; and upon ſuch court of directors refuſing, or, for the ſpace of ten days, neglecting ſo to do, the members demanding ſuch court ſhall be at liberty to call and hold ſuch general court, upon the like notice as ſhould have been given by the ſaid court of directors; and any general court, either called by the court of directors of the ſaid corporation, or by any of the members or proprietors of the ſaid corporation, in manner aforeſaid, ſhall have full power and authority, and are hereby fully authorized and impowered, to remove or diſplace any director, for miſbehaviour, breach of truſt, or other juſt cauſe, and to elect a new director or directors in his or their ſtead, in the ſame manner as if he or they was or were dead, or had diſqualified himſelf or themſelves, or his or their office, truſt, or employ, was in any other manner become void.

General courts to be called on demand of certain ſubſcribers; on refuſal, they may call ſuch court themſelves. General court may diſplace directors.

XI. And be it further enacted by the authority aforeſaid, That no member or members of the ſaid corporation, or any perſon or perſons having the conduct or direction of the ſaid manufactury, his or their heirs, executors, or adminiſtrators, lands or hereditaments, goods, chattels, or effects, other than his or their ſhare or ſhares in the capital ſtock and effects of the ſaid corporation, ſhall be liable or ſubject to the payment of any debt or debts contracted by or on account of the ſaid corporation, or the manufactury carried on by the ſaid corporation, in any other manner than is herein after directed and provided.

No member liable to any debt of the corporation, further than his ſhare in the capital.

XII. Provided always, and be it enacted by the authority aforeſaid, That if the ſum total of all the debts which the ſaid corporation ſhall owe at any one time to any perſon or perſons, bodies politick or corporate, ſhall exceed the value of the principal or capital ſtock and effects of the ſaid company or corporation, which at ſuch time ſhall be and remain to the ſaid corporation undivided; or if the ſaid corporation, by any dividend or dividends whatſoever, either in the name of intereſt, or otherwiſe, to be made amongſt themſelves, or in their private or perſonal capacities, ſhall reduce or leſſen their joint ſtock, principal or capital, ſo that the value of their joint ſtock, principal, or capital ſhall not be ſufficient to anſwer their juſt debts then remaining unpaid; in every ſuch caſe the particular members of the ſaid corporation, and every of them reſpectively, who in their private or perſonal capacities ſhall receive any ſhare or dividend

If the corporate debts ſhall exceed the value of the capital undivided, or if they reduce their capital, ſo that their ſtock ſhall not be ſufficient to pay their debts; Perſons receiving any dividend by which the capital ſhall be reduced, are to be perſonally liable to make good ſuch deficiency, ſo far as the dividends they ſhall have received ſhall extend.

vidend of the capital or ſtock of the ſaid corporation, by which the capital ſtock of the ſaid corporation, ſhall be ſo reduced or leſſened, ſhall be ſeverally liable, and they are hereby made liable, ſo far as their reſpective ſhares ſo by them reſpectively received upon ſuch dividend or dividends ſhall extend, to pay and ſatisfy the debts which ſhall remain due and unpaid by the ſaid company or corporation; and the perſon or perſons, bodies politick or corporate, to whom ſuch debts ſhall be due and owing, ſhall and may ſue for and recover the ſame; any thing in this act contained to the contrary thereof in any wiſe notwithſtanding.

Members not liable to bankruptcy,

nor the effects of the company, or any member's ſhare, liable to foreign attachment.

XIII. And be it further enacted by the authority aforeſaid, That no perſon being or becoming a member of, or ſubſcriber to, the ſaid corporation, for carrying on the ſaid manufacture in purſuance of this act, ſhall, by means of becoming a member of, or ſubſcriber to, or in reſpect of his ſhare or intereſt in the capital ſtock of the ſaid corporation, be, or be adjudged liable to be, a bankrupt, within the intent or meaning of all or any of the ſtatutes made againſt or concerning bankrupts; nor ſhall the capital ſtock or effects of the ſaid corporation, or the ſhare or intereſt of any particular member therein, be liable to any foreign attachment whatſoever; any law, uſage, or cuſtom, to the contrary notwithſtanding.

Shares to be aſſignable; but not till ſeven years from the conſtitution of the corporation, unleſs in caſe of death or bankruptcy.

Members ſhares, &c. to be perſonal eſtates.

XIV. And be it further enacted by the authority aforeſaid, That the particular ſhare of every member in the capital ſtock or fund of the ſaid corporation; and all lands, tenements, hereditaments, and eſtates whatſoever, held by or in truſt for them or their ſucceſſors ſhall, from time to time, be aſſignable, tranſferrable, and deviſeable; but no member or members of the ſaid corporation ſhall be at liberty to ſell or aſſign his or their ſhare or intereſt therein, till after the expiration of ſeven years, from the time of the conſtitution of the ſaid corporation; but if ſuch member or members ſhall die or become bankrupt, then the ſhare and intereſt of ſuch member or members ſo dying or becoming bankrupt, of and in the capital ſtock of the ſaid corporation, ſhall and may be aſſigned and transferred by his or their executors or adminiſtrators, aſſignee or aſſignees, at any time within the ſaid term of ſeven years, in like manner as the ſame might have been done had the ſaid term of ſeven years been fully expired; and all the right, title, intereſt, claim, and demand, of each and every particular member of the ſaid corporation, in or to the capital ſtock and effects whatſoever of the ſaid corporation, and the gains and increaſe thereof, ſhall be, and be adjudged, taken, and accepted, in conſtruction of law, by all judges, and in all courts of law and juſtice, and in all places whatſoever, to be a perſonal and not a real eſtate, and ſhall go to the executors or adminiſtrators, or other legal repreſentatives intitled to the perſonal eſtate of the perſon or perſons dying poſſeſſed thereof, or intitled thereunto; and not to the heirs of ſuch perſon or perſons; any law, ſtatute, uſage, or cuſtom whatſoever, to the contrary notwithſtanding.

XV. And

XV. And be it further enacted by the authority aforesaid, That if any person or persons shall forge or counterfeit the common seal of the said corporation, to be established in pursuance of this act, or shall forge, counterfeit, or alter, any deed, bill, bond, or obligation, under the common seal of the said corporation, or shall offer to dispose of, or pay away any such forged, counterfeited, or altered bill, bond, or obligation, knowing the same to be such, or shall demand any money therein mentioned or pretended to be due thereon, or on any part thereof, of and from the said corporation, or any members, officers, or servants thereof, knowing such bill, bond, or obligation, to be forged, counterfeited, or altered, with intent to defraud the said corporation, or their successors, or any other person or persons whomsoever; every person so offending, and being convicted thereof in due form of law, shall be judged guilty of felony, and shall suffer as in cases of felony, without benefit of clergy.

Forging the seal, &c. of the corporation, felony.

XVI. And be it further enacted by the authority aforesaid, That if any person or persons shall by day or night break into any house, shop, cellar, vault, or other place or building, or by force enter into any house, shop, cellar, vault, or other place or building, with intent to steal, cut, or destroy, any linen yarn, or any linen cloth, or any manufacture of linen yarn belonging to any manufactury, or the looms, tools, or implements used therein; or shall wilfully or maliciously cut in pieces or destroy any such goods, either when exposed to bleach or dry; every such offender, being thereof lawfully convicted, shall be judged guilty of felony, and shall suffer as in cases of felony, without benefit of clergy.

Breaking into a shop, &c. with intent to steal or destroy, &c. any material or implements declared to be felony.

XVII. And be it further enacted by the authority aforesaid, That all cambricks and lawns, or goods of the kind usually known under either of those denominations, which from and after the tenth day of *May*, now next ensuing, shall be wove or fabricated in *England*, or the principality of *Wales*, shall be marked or sealed at each end of every piece with such mark or seal, and by such officer or officers, as the commissioners of excise in *England* shall direct or appoint for that purpose.

Cambricks and lawns made in England after 10 day of May, 1764, to be sealed at both ends.

XVIII. And, for the greater ease and convenience of the person or persons, who shall make, weave, or fabricate any such cambricks or lawns, or goods of the kind usually known by or under either of those denominations; be it enacted by the authority aforesaid, That it shall and may be lawful to and for the commissioners of excise for the time being, or the major part of them, from time to time, upon request made to them by any such person or persons, and at the expence of such person or persons, to provide such seal or marks as to them the said commissioners, or the major part of them, shall seem proper; and to direct or appoint one or more supervisor, or other officer or officers of the excise, of the district or division in which any such manufacture shall be carried on, to seal or mark each and every piece of such cambrick or lawn, or goods of the kind usual-

Commissioners of excise upon request, to provide seals, and appoint officers to mark the goods;

usually known under either of those denominations, which shall be made, wove, or fabricated, by such person or persons applying as aforesaid, with such seal or mark, or seals or marks, in manner herein after mentioned and directed; and the officer or officers of excise who shall be so appointed to mark or seal such goods, shall by the fabricator, maker, weaver, or proprietor of such goods, be paid for every piece of such goods, which he or they shall mark or seal in pursuance of this act, before the same shall be cut or taken out of the loom, such sum as the commissioners of excise for the time being, or the major part of them, shall direct and appoint.

who are to be paid for marking, &c. such goods before taken out of the loom.

XIX. And be it further enacted by the authority aforesaid, That all and every person and persons who shall weave, fabricate, or make any such cambricks or lawns, or goods of the kind usually known by or under either of those denominations, shall, before the same shall be taken or cut out of the loom, give notice in writing, of the finishing of every or any piece or pieces of such goods, to such supervisor or other officer as aforesaid, who, before any such piece of goods shall be cut out of the loom, shall mark or seal both the ends of every such piece of goods, with such stamp, mark, or seal, which shall be provided and appointed for that purpose, in manner aforesaid, upon pain that every person who shall weave, make, or fabricate such cambricks or lawns, or goods of the kind usually known by or under those denominations, and shall cut or take any piece of such goods out of the loom, after the same shall have been finished, or permit the same to be done without having first given such notice in writing, and having the ends thereof marked or sealed as aforesaid, shall, for every such offence, forfeit five pounds; and the goods so cut out of the loom without such notice being given, and such marks or seals being set thereon, in manner herein before directed, shall be forfeited, and shall and may be seized by any officer or officers of the customs or excise.

Manufacturer to give notice to officer of the finishing of every piece, who is to mark the ends before taken out of the loom.

Penalty on taking any piece out of the loom without giving such notice, and having the ends marked, 5l. and loss of the goods.

XX. And be it further enacted by the authority aforesaid, That every supervisor or other officer of excise, of the district in which any such manufacture of cambricks or lawns, or goods of the kind usually known by or under either of those denominations, shall be carried on, who shall be so as aforesaid appointed by the commissioners of excise, or the major part of them, to mark or seal such goods, upon reasonable notice given to him or them by any person or persons who shall make, weave, or fabricate any such goods, that any piece of such goods is finished, shall forthwith, or as soon as conveniently may be consistent with other the duty and business of his office, in manner herein before directed, mark or seal both ends of every such piece of goods with such mark or seal which shall be so as aforesaid appointed and provided for that purpose, and also fix or set a distinct and separate number to every piece of such goods before the same shall be taken out of the loom; and also make a just and true entry in writing, in proper books to be provided for that purpose at the expence of the manufacturer of such goods, of

Officer, on notice of the finishing any pieces of such goods, forthwith to mark the beginnings and ends, and set a number on each piece before taken out of the loom;

and to make a true entry of the numbers, lengths,

of the number ſet to each piece of ſuch goods, and of the number of yards which each piece of ſuch goods ſhall contain in length, and alſo of the number of threads contained in the warp of each piece of ſuch goods, upon pain that every ſupervisor, or other officer or officers ſo appointed as aforeſaid, who ſhall, upon reaſonable notice given as aforeſaid of the finiſhing of any piece of ſuch goods, neglect or refuſe to mark or ſeal the beginning and end of every piece of ſuch goods in manner herein before directed, or to fix or ſet a diſtinct and ſeparate number on each piece of ſuch goods, or to make a true and juſt entry in manner aforeſaid, of the number ſet or affixed to each piece of ſuch goods, and of the number of yards which each piece thereof ſhall contain in length, and alſo the number of threads contained in the warp of each piece of ſuch goods, ſhall, for every ſuch refuſal or neglect, forfeit the ſum of ten pounds.

and the number of threads in the warp of each piece on forfeiture of 10 l.

XXI. And be it further enacted by the authority aforeſaid, That if any ſuch ſupervisor, or other officer or officers of the exciſe, who ſhall be ſo appointed to mark or ſeal ſuch cambricks or lawns, or who ſhall have the cuſtody of any mark or ſeal which ſhall be ſo provided and appointed to mark or ſeal ſuch goods, ſhall therewith mark or ſeal any cambricks or lawns, or goods of the kind uſually known by or under either of thoſe denominations, which ſhall not have been made, wove, and fabricated in *England*, or the principality of *Wales*, or ſhall knowingly permit it to be done, or ſhall mark or ſeal any piece of ſuch goods after the ſame ſhall have been taken out of the loom, every ſuch ſupervisor, or other officer or officers ſo marking or ſealing any ſuch cambricks or lawns, or goods of the kind uſually known under either of thoſe denominations, or wilfully or knowingly permiting the ſame to be done, contrary to the true intent and meaning of this act, ſhall forfeit the ſum of fifty pounds for every piece of ſuch goods which he or they ſhall ſo mark or ſeal, or permit or ſuffer to be marked or ſealed, contrary to the true intent and meaning of this act, to be ſued for and recovered in any of his Majeſty's courts of record at *Weſtminſter*, by bill, plaint, or information, by any perſon or perſons who will inform or ſue for the ſame; and ſuch ſupervisor, or other officer or officers, upon being convicted of any or either of the offences aforeſaid, ſhall loſe his or their office or offices and employments under the exciſe, and is and are hereby declared and rendered ever after incapable of having, uſing, or enjoying any office or place of truſt under his Majeſty, his heirs and ſucceſſors.

Officers marking cambricks or lawns not made in England, or marking ſuch goods after taken out of the loom, to forfeit 50 l. and be incapacitated.

XXII. And be it further enacted by the authority aforeſaid, That if any perſon or perſons ſhall, by bribery, fraud, covin, deceit, or impoſition, or in any manner whatſoever prevail on or procure any officer or officers of the exciſe, or other perſon who ſhall be appointed to mark or ſeal any cambricks or lawns, or who ſhall have the cuſtody of any ſeal, ſtamp, or mark, provided and appointed for that purpoſe, in purſuance of this act, to ſet or affix ſuch mark, ſeal, or ſtamp, to any piece or pieces of

Penalty on bribing officers.

of cambrick or lawn, or of goods of the kind usually known under either of those denominations, which shall not have been actually and *bona fide* made, wove, or fabricated, in that part of *Great Britain* called *England*, or principality of *Wales*, or after the same shall have been cut or taken out of the loom, contrary to the true intent and meaning of this act; all and every such offender and offenders, and his and their aiders, abetters, and assistants (being thereof lawfully convicted) shall, for every such offence, forfeit and lose the sum of one hundred pounds, and be adjudged to stand in the pillory two hours; and if any person or persons shall give, pay, or secure, or offer to give, pay, or secure, to any such officer or officers, or other person as aforesaid, any bribe, recompence, or reward, of any kind whatsoever, in order to corrupt, persuade, or prevail on such officer or officers, or other person, to set or affix such mark, stamp, or seal, as aforesaid, to any piece or pieces of cambrick, lawn, or other goods directed by this act to be stamped or sealed, which shall not have been actually and *bona fide* made, wove, and fabricated, in that part of *Great Britain* called *England*, or the principality of *Wales*, or after the same shall have been taken out of the loom, such person or persons so offending shall, for every such offence, forfeit and lose the sum of fifty pounds.

Officers to transmit to the commissioners of excise an annual account of all goods they shall stamp, and a copy of all entries relating thereto.

XXIII. And be it further enacted by the authority aforesaid, That all and every supervisor or other officer or officers of excise, who shall in manner aforesaid be appointed to mark or seal any cambricks, lawns, or such kind of goods, in pursuance of this act, shall yearly and every year (while such officer or officers shall have the custody of any such seal provided or appointed for that purpose in manner aforesaid) in the month of *June*, transmit and send to the commissioners of excise in *London*, a full, true, and just account in writing of all and every piece and pieces of such goods, which he or they shall seal or stamp in pursuance of this act; and also a true copy of all and every entry or entries of any kind whatsoever, which he or they shall make in any such book or books provided for that purpose, in any wise relating thereto, for or during the twelve calendar months next preceding the said month of *June*; distinguishing in such accounts the several manufacturers or proprietors, if there shall be more than one such in such officer's district, who shall have made or be owners of such goods, upon pain of being dismissed from his or their employ as an officer or officers of excise; and all and every such officer or officers having the custody of any such stamp, mark, or seal as aforesaid, his or their executors or administrators, or such other person or persons in whose custody or power the same shall fall or come by the death of such officer or officers, or in any other manner shall, upon demand or order from or by the commissioners of excise, or the major part of them, deliver up to such commissioners, or such person or persons as they shall appoint to receive the same, all and every such seal or seals which shall have been delivered to such officer or officers, or by any other means

Officers, &c. to deliver up seals, &c. to commissioners of excise, on

come

come or fallen into the hands, custody or power of such officer or officers, or other persons whatsoever; upon pain that any such officer or officers, or other person or persons, refusing or neglecting so to do upon any such order or demand as aforesaid, shall forfeit and lose the sum of two hundred pounds, to be recovered and applied in like manner with the other penalties inflicted by this act, by any person or persons who will inform or sue for the same.

demand, on a penalty of 200l.

XXIV. And be it further enacted by the authority aforesaid, That if any cambrick or lawn, or goods of the kind usually known by or under either of those denominations, made, wove, or fabricated, in *England*, or the principality of *Wales*, after the said tenth day of *May* next ensuing, shall be found in any house, shop, warehouse, room, cellar, vault, or other place, in *England*, or principality of *Wales*, without being marked or sealed at each end of every whole and entire piece, and at one end of every remnant of such cambricks or lawns, or goods of the kind usually known by or under those denominations, all such goods shall be forfeited, and shall and may be seized by any supervisor or other officer or officers of the customs or excise, and such supervisor or other officer or officers is and are hereby indemnified for seizing such goods; and all such goods so seized shall and may be deposited in the customhouse warehouse, or in the excise office next to the place where the same shall be seized, and, after condemnation thereof by due course of law, shall be publickly sold to the best bidder; and that one moiety of the produce arising by the sale thereof, after deducting the charges and expences attending the condemnation and sale of such goods, shall be to the use of his Majesty, his heirs, and successors, and the other moiety thereof to such supervisor or other officer or officers as aforesaid, who shall seize or sue for the same; and all and every person or persons who shall sell or expose to sale, or have in his or their custody for that purpose, any cambricks or lawns, or goods of the kind usually known by or under either of those denominations, made and fabricated in *England*, or the principality of *Wales*, and not marked or sealed at both ends of every entire piece, and at one end of every remnant of such goods, in manner by this act directed, shall, for every such offence, forfeit the sum of two hundred pounds, to be recovered and divided in manner herein after directed.

Cambricks and lawns made in England after 10 May, 1764, found unstampt, may be seized.

Persons exposing to sale, or having in their custody for sale, such goods unstamped, to forfeit 200l.

XXV. And be it further enacted by the authority aforesaid, That no cambricks or lawns, or goods of the kind usually known by or under either of those denominations, which after the said tenth day of *May*, one thousand seven hundred and sixty four, shall be seized and condemned by virtue of this act, shall be consumed or worn in this kingdom, but shall be exported, and not sold otherwise than on condition to be exported, and shall not be delivered out of the warehouse where the same shall have been secured, until sufficient security by bond, to be approved of by the collector of the port from whence such goods shall be exported, in the penalty of double the value of the goods

Goods condemned by virtue of this act, not to be worn here, but sold for exportation, and the buyers to give security.

to be given by the exporter thereof, that the ſame, and every part thereof, ſhall be exported, and not relanded in any part of *Great Britain*.

Perſons counterfeiting the ſeal, &c. or ſelling goods with a counterfeit ſeal, &c. guilty of felony.

XXVI. And be it further enacted by the authority aforeſaid, That if any perſon or perſons ſhall, at any time or times hereafter, forge or counterfeit any ſtamp, mark, or ſeal, to reſemble any ſtamp, mark, or ſeal, which ſhall be provided or uſed in purſuance of this act, or ſhall forge, reſemble or counterfeit the impreſſion of any ſuch mark, ſtamp, ſeal, upon any goods required by this act to be ſtamped, marked, or ſealed, or ſhall import or bring into *England* any foreign cambricks or lawns, or goods of the kind uſually known by or under either of thoſe denominations, having any ſuch counterfeit mark, ſeal, ſtamp, or impreſſion thereon, or ſell or expoſe to ſale any cambricks or lawns, or goods of the kind uſually known by or under either of thoſe denominations, with ſuch counterfeit mark, ſeal, ſtamp, or impreſſion thereon, knowing ſuch ſtamp, mark, or ſeal, to be counterfeited; every ſuch perſon ſo offending, being thereof lawfully convicted, ſhall be judged guilty of felony, and ſhall ſuffer as in caſes of felony, without benefit of clergy.

Cambricks or lawns made or begun in England before commencement of this act, to be ſealed.

XXVII. Provided always, and be it enacted by the authority aforeſaid, That it ſhall and may be lawful to and for the commiſſioners of exciſe in *England* for the time being, or the major part of them, at any time within two months next after the commencement of this act, to order and direct all ſuch cambricks and lawns, or goods of the kind uſually known by or under either of thoſe denominations, which ſhall have been made, or begun to be made, wove, and fabricated in *England* or *Wales*, at any time before the commencement of this act, to be ſealed or marked at both ends of every piece thereof with ſuch mark or ſeal which ſhall be provided and appointed as aforeſaid, notwithſtanding the ſame ſhall have been taken out of the loom (proof being firſt made upon oath to the ſatisfaction of the ſaid commiſſioners, that all ſuch goods were really and *bona fide* made, or begun to be made, wove and fabricated, in *England* or *Wales*, before the commencement of this act) which goods ſo marked or ſealed, and numbered, in purſuance of ſuch directions, ſhall and may be ſold, diſpoſed of, and uſed, in like manner as if the ſame had been made or wrought after the commencement of this act, and all the directions thereof fully complied with; any thing in this act contained to the contrary thereof, in any wiſe notwithſtanding; and the ſupervisor, or other officer or officers of the exciſe who ſhall be directed to mark or ſeal and number ſuch goods, ſhall make the like entry of the number of yards in length, and number of threads contained in the warp of each piece of ſuch goods, and the number ſet thereon, in like manner and under the like penalties as herein before directed, with reſpect to cambricks or lawns made after the commencement of this act.

Seizures and penalties, how

XXVIII. And be it further enacted by the authority aforeſaid, That all ſuch goods which ſhall be ſeized or condemned

in

in pursuance of this act, and all pecuniary penalties and forfeitures by this act inflicted, shall and may be sued for, prosecuted, and recovered, in any of his Majesty's courts of record at *Westminster*, by action of debt, bill, plaint, or information, in the name of his Majesty's attorney general, or in the name or names of any such supervisor or other officer or officers of the customs or excise as aforesaid, except in such cases where it is otherwise provided by this act; and that one moiety of the clear produce arising from the sale of all such goods, and of all the pecuniary penalties and forfeitures inflicted by this act, after all charges deducted, shall be to his Majesty, his heirs, and successors, and the other moiety thereof to the officer or officers, or such other person who, pursuant to the directions of this act, shall seize, inform, or prosecute for the same.

to be recovered and applied.

XXIX. And be it further enacted by the authority aforesaid, That upon every action, bill, plaint, or information, entered or filed as aforesaid, for any pecuniary penalty imposed by this act, a *Capias* in the first process shall and may issue, specifying the sum of the penalty sued for; and the defendant or defendants shall be obliged to give sufficient bail or security by natural-born subjects, persons naturalized, or denizens, to the person or persons to whom such *Capias* shall be directed, to appear in the court out of which such *Capias* shall issue, at the day of the return of such writ, to answer such suit or prosecution; and shall likewise, at the time of such appearance, give sufficient bail or security, by such persons as aforesaid, in the said court, to answer and pay all the forfeitures and penalties incurred for such offence or offences, in case he, she, or they shall be convicted thereof, or to yield his, her, or their body or bodies to prison.

A *Capias* to issue for the penalties in the first process.

Defendants to give bail.

XXX. And be it further enacted by the authority aforesaid, That if any action or suit shall be commenced against any person or persons, for recovery of any of the pecuniary penalties inflicted by this act, such action or suit shall be brought or commenced within twelve calendar months next after the cause of action shall arise, and not afterwards, and shall be laid and brought in the county or place where the cause of action shall arise, and not elsewhere; and the defendant or defendants in such action or suit shall and may plead the general issue, and give this act, and the special matter in evidence, at any trial to be had thereon, and that the same was done by the authority of this act: and if it shall appear to have been so done, then the jury shall find for the defendant or defendants; and if the plaintiff or plaintiffs shall become nonsuited, or discontinue his, her, or their action or suit, after the defendant or defendants shall have appeared; or if, upon verdict or demurrer, judgment shall be given against the plaintiff or plaintiffs; the defendant or defendants shall recover treble costs, and have such remedy for the same as any defendant or defendants hath or have in other cases by law.

Limitation of actions.

General issue.

Treble costs.

XXXI. And be it further enacted by the authority aforesaid, That if any cambricks or lawns, or goods of the kind usually known

Onus probandi to lie on the claimer.

known by or under either of those denominations, shall be seized by virtue or in pursuance of this or any other act now in force; or if any action shall be brought by the owner or claimer of such goods, against any officer of the customs or excise, or any other person, for any thing done in pursuance of this or any other act now in force, and any doubt or question shall arise where such goods were manufactured, the proof thereof shall lie upon the owner or claimer of such goods, and not on the person who seized the same, or against whom such action shall be brought; any law, usage, or custom, to the contrary notwithstanding.

Act not to extend to Scotland or Ireland.

XXXII. Provided always, and be it enacted, That nothing in this act contained shall be extended, or construed, deemed, or taken, to prevent the sale of, or lay any kind of restriction on, any linen goods whatsoever, really and *bona fide* made, wove, or fabricated in *Scotland* or *Ireland*; but that all such goods shall and may be lawfully sold and used in *England*, in the same manner as if this act had not been made.

Publick act.

XXXIII. And be it further enacted by the authority aforesaid, That this act shall be adjudged, deemed, and taken to be, a public act, and be judicially taken notice of as such, by all judges, justices, and other persons whatsoever, without specially pleading the same.

CAP. XXXVIII.

An act for allowing further time for inrollments of deeds and wills made by papists; and for relief of protestant purchasers.

Preamble, reciting the acts 3 Geo. I.

WHEREAS *by a clause in an act of parliament passed in the third year of the reign of his late majesty King* George *the First, intituled,* An act for explaining an act passed in the last session of parliament, intituled, *An act to oblige papists to register their names and real estates, and for enlarging the time for such registering; and for securing purchases made by protestants; it was enacted, That from and after the twenty ninth day of* September, *in the year of our Lord one thousand seven hundred and seventeen, no manors, lands, tenements, hereditaments or any interest therein, or rent or profit thereout, should pass, alter, or change, from any papist, or person professing the popish religion, by any deed or will, except such deed, within six months after the date, and such will, within six months after the death of the testator, should be inrolled in one of the King's courts of record at* Westminster, *or else within the same county or counties wherein the manors, lands, and tenements, lie, in such manner as therein for that purpose is particularly directed: and*

10 Geo. II. & 3, 6, 9, 11, 12, 16, & 19 Geo. II.

whereas by several acts of parliament made in the tenth year of his said late Majesty's reign, and in the third, sixth, ninth, eleventh, twelfth, sixteenth, and nineteenth years of the reign of his late majesty King George *the Second, it was enacted, That every deed and will which had been then made since the twenty ninth day of* September, *one thousand seven hundred and seventeen, in order to pass,*

alter,

alter, or change, any manors, lands, tenements, or hereditaments, or any interest therein, or rent or profit thereout, from any papist or person professing the popish religion, though not then inrolled, should be as good and effectual in the law, as the same would have been in case the said deeds and wills had been inrolled within the time limited, by the said clause in the said first-mentioned act, for inrollment thereof, provided the said deeds and wills should be inrolled on or before the respective times in the said several acts respectively mentioned, in such manner as by the said first-mentioned act was directed: and whereas by another act made in the twenty sixth year of the reign of his late majesty King George the Second, it was enacted, That every deed and will made since the first day of December, one thousand seven hundred and forty six, in order to pass, alter, or change, any manors, lands, tenements, or hereditaments, or any interest therein, or any rent or profit thereout, from any papist or person professing the popish religion, to any protestant or protestants, or by or by reason of which deed or will any protestant or protestants may claim or derive any legal, equitable, or other interest whatsoever, to his, her, or their use, for his, her, or their benefit, or to the use or benefit of any other protestant or protestants, though not inrolled, or not inrolled in due time, should be as good and effectual in the law, as the same would have been in case the said deeds and wills had been inrolled within the times limited by the said clauses in the said acts for the inrollment thereof, provided the same deeds and wills should be inrolled on or before the first day of January, one thousand seven hundred and sixty four, in such manner as by the said clause in the said first-mentioned act is directed: and whereas by an act made in the twenty eighth year of the reign of his late majesty King George the Second, it was enacted, That every deed and will made since the twenty ninth day of September, one thousand seven hundred and seventeen, in order to pass, alter, or change, any manors, lands, tenements, or hereditaments, or any interest therein, or any rent or profit thereout, from any papist or person professing the popish religion, to any protestant or protestants, or by or by reason of which deed or will, any protestant or protestants may claim or derive any legal, equitable, or other interest whatsoever, to his, her, or their use, for his, her, or their benefit, or to the use or benefit of any other protestant or protestants, though not inrolled in due time, should be as good and effectual in the law, as the same would have been in case the said deeds and wills had been inrolled within the times limited by the said clauses in the said acts for the inrollment thereof, provided the same deeds and wills should be inrolled on or before the first day of January, one thousand seven hundred and fifty six, in such manner as by the said clause in the said first-mentioned act is directed: and whereas by an act made in the thirty first year of the reign of his late majesty King George the Second, it was enacted, That every deed and will made since the twenty ninth day of September, one thousand seven hundred and seventeen, in order to pass, alter, or change, any manors, lands, tenements, or hereditaments, or any interest therein, or any rent or profits thereout, from any papist or person professing the popish religion, to any protestant or protestants, or by or by reason of which deed or will any pro-

26 Geo. II.

28 Geo. II.

31 Geo. II.

protestant or protestants may claim or derive any legal, equitable, or other interest whatsoever, to his, her, or their use, for his, her, or their benefit, or to the use or benefit of any other protestant or protestants, though not inrolled, or not inrolled in due time, should be as good and effectual in the law, as the same would have been in case the same deeds and wills had been inrolled within the times limited by the said clauses in the said acts for the inrollment thereof, provided the said deeds and wills should be inrolled on or before the first day of January, *one thousand seven hundred and fifty nine, in such manner as by the said clause in the said first-mentioned act is directed: and whereas by an act passed in the thirty third year of his said late Majesty's reign, it was enacted, That every deed and will made since the twenty ninth day of* September, *one thousand seven hundred and seventeen, in order to pass, alter, or change, any manors, lands, tenements, or hereditaments, or any interest therein, or any rent or profit thereout, from any papist or person professing the popish religion, to any protestant or protestants, or by or by reason of which deed or will any protestant or protestants may claim or derive any legal, equitable, or other interest whatsoever, to his, her, or their use, for his, her, or their benefit, or to the use or benefit of any other protestant or protestants, though not inrolled, or not inrolled in due time, shall be as good and effectual in the law, as the same would have been in case the said deeds and wills had been inrolled within the times limited by the said clauses in the said acts for the inrollment thereof, provided the same deeds and wills should be inrolled on or before the twenty fifth day of* December, *one thousand seven hundred and sixty, in such manner as by the said clause in the said first-mentioned act is directed: and whereas by an act made in the second year of his present Majesty's reign, it was enacted, That every deed and will made since the twenty ninth day of* September, *one thousand seven hundred and seventeen, in order to pass, alter, or change, any manors, lands, tenements, or hereditaments, or any interest therein, or any rent or profit thereout, from any papist or person professing the popish religion, to any protestant or protestants, or by or by reason of which deed or will, any protestant or protestants, may claim or derive any legal, equitable, or other interest whatsoever, to his, her, or their use, for his, her, or their benefit, or to the use or benefit of any other protestant or protestants, though not inrolled, or not inrolled in due time, shall be as good and effectual in the law, as the same would have been in case the said deeds and wills had been inrolled within the times limited by the said clauses in the said acts for the inrollment thereof, provided the same deeds and wills should be inrolled on or before the twenty fifth day of* December, *one thousand seven hundred and sixty two, in such manner as by the said clause in the said first-mentioned act is directed*; be it enacted by the King's most excellent majesty, by and with the advice and consent of the lords spiritual and temporal, and commons in this present parliament assembled, and by the authority of the same, That every deed and will made since the twenty ninth day of *September*, one thousand seven hundred and seventeen, in order to pass, alter, or change, any manors, lands, tenements, or hereditaments, or any interest therein, or any rent or

33 Geo. II.

& 2 Geo. III.

Further time given for inrolling deeds and wills of papists, till 1 Jan. 1765.

or profit thereout, from any papist or person professing the popish religion, to any protestant or protestants, or by reason of which deed or will, any protestant or protestants may claim or derive any legal, equitable, or other interest whatsoever, to his, her, or their use, for his, her, or their benefit of any other protestant or protestants, though not inrolled, or not inrolled in due time, shall be as good and effectual in the law, as the same would have been in case the said deeds and wills had been inrolled within the times limited by the said clauses in the said acts for the inrollment thereof, provided the same deeds and wills shall be inrolled on or before the first day of *January*, one thousand seven hundred and sixty five, in such manner as by the said clause in the said first mentioned act is directed.

No deed, will, or lease, made good hereby, whereof advantage has been taken of the non-inrollment thereof, before 1 Jan. 1764.

II. Provided always, That nothing herein contained shall extend, or be construed to extend, to make good any such deed, will, or lease, already made and not inrolled, of the want of inrollment whereof advantage shall have been taken on or before the first day of *January*, one thousand seven hundred and sixty four, but every such deed, will, or lease, shall remain of such force and effect only, as the same would have had if this act had never been made, and of none other force and effect.

Purchases made by protestants shall stand good, if no advantage has been taken for non-inrollment.

III. And whereas many purchases made by protestants, may be in danger of being impeached or called in question, in regard that some deeds or wills, through which the title thereto is derived, ought to have been inrolled according to the said acts, but have not been so inrolled; be it therefore further enacted by the authority aforesaid, That no purchase made for full and valuable consideration of any manors, messuages, lands, tenements, or hereditaments, or of any interest therein, by any protestant or protestants, and merely and only for the benefit of the protestants, shall be impeached or avoided, for or by reason that any deed or will through which the title thereto is derived, hath not been inrolled as required by the said acts, so as no advantage was taken of inrollment thereof, before such purchase was made, and so as no decree or judgment have been obtained for want of the inrollment of such deeds or wills.

No grant, lease, or mortgage of the advowson, or right of presentation to a living, &c. made by any papist in trust, &c. to be hereby deemed good.

IV. Provided also, That nothing herein contained shall extend, or be construed to extend, to make good any grant, lease, or mortgage, of the advowson, or right of presentation, collation, nomination, or donation, of and to any benefice, prebend, or ecclesiastical living, school, hospital, or donative, or any avoidance thereof, made by any papist or person professing the popish religion, in trust, directly or indirectly, mediately or immediately, by or for any such papist or person professing the popish religion, whether such trust hath been declared by writing or not.

CAP. XXXIX.

An act to explain, amend, and render more effectual, two several acts of parliament, made in the second and third years of his present Majesty, for paving, cleansing, and lighting, the squares, streets, and lanes, within the city and liberty of Westminster, *and other places therein mentioned, and for preventing annoyances therein; and for other purposes therein mentioned.*

Preamble.

WHEREAS *an act was made in the second year of the reign of his present Majesty, intituled,* An act for paving, cleansing, and lighting, the squares, streets, and lanes, within the city and liberty of *Westminster*, the parishes of *Saint Giles in the Fields*, *Saint George the Martyr*, *Saint George Bloomsbury*, that part of the parish of *Saint Andrew's Holbourn* which lies in the county of *Middlesex*, the several liberties of the *Rolls* and *Savoy*, and that part of the dutchy of *Lancaster* which lies in the county of *Middlesex*, and for preventing annoyances therein; and for other purposes therein mentioned: *and whereas another act was made in the last session of parliament, to explain, amend, and render more effectual, the last mentioned act: and whereas the commissioners for putting the said two several acts in execution, have made some further progress in the trusts thereby reposed in them, but find that both the said acts are defective with respect to some of the powers thereby given; nor can the said acts be effectually put in execution, so as to answer the good purposes thereby intended, unless some new powers are granted, and the said acts, in other respects, amended, and made more effectual*; may it therefore please your Majesty, that it may be enacted; and be it enacted by the King's most excellent majesty, by and with the advice and consent of the lords spiritual and temporal, and commons, in this present parliament assembled, and by the authority of the same, That if at any time or times, from and after the passing of this act, it shall happen, that there shall not appear at any meeting which shall be appointed to be had or held by the said commissioners, a sufficient number of commissioners, as provided for by the said recited acts, to act at such meeting, and to adjourn to another day, that then, in such case, it shall and may be lawful to and for the clerk to the said commissioners for the time being, and he is hereby required to summon the said commissioners to meet at the place where the last meeting was appointed to be held, within six days next after the day on which such last meeting was appointed to be held; such summons to be in writing, and signed by the clerk, and to be delivered at the usual or last place of abode of the said commissioners, at least four days before such next meeting; and in case the said clerk shall happen to die before such summons issued, or shall neglect to issue such summons in manner aforesaid, then the treasurer to the said commissioners for the time being shall and may, and he is hereby required to issue such summons in manner aforesaid.

Where a sufficient number of commissioners shall not meet to act and adjourn, Clerk is to summon another meeting; and the summons is to be delivered 4 days before, at the commissioners houses. Clerk dying, or neglecting, the treasurer is to summon such meeting.

II. And

II. And be it further enacted by the authority aforesaid, That all and every the powers, authorities, directions, provisions, regulations, clauses, matters, and things whatsoever, contained in the said recited former acts, and this act, or either of them, shall extend to all places, not thoroughfares, within the said parishes, precincts, and places, comprized in the said former acts, in such and the same manner as they already extend, or are hereby intended to extend, to places which are thoroughfares, as effectually, to all intents and purposes, as if the respective powers, authorities, directions, provisions, regulations, clauses, matters, and things, in the said acts, or either of them, contained, were herein repeated and specially enacted.

Powers and clauses in the present and former acts, extended to all places comprized in the said acts.

III. And whereas by the said act of the second year of his present Majesty, the commissioners for putting the said act in execution, are directed to cause the works done, under the authority of the said act, to be inspected by their surveyor or surveyors, or other person or persons appointed by them for that purpose, who are to report to the commissioners, in case the said works shall not be performed according to the true sense of the contract or contracts entered into for that purpose, before the said commissioners can cause the person or persons, so contracting, to be sued for nonperformance of their contract, which method has been found inconvenient; wherefore, be it further enacted by the authority aforesaid, That so much of the said act as requires and directs a report to be made by the surveyor or surveyors, or other person or persons appointed by the commissioners for that purpose, before any action shall be brought against any person so contracting, shall be, and the same is hereby declared to be repealed.

Clause in act 2 Geo. III. requiring a report to be made by the surveyor, of any non-performance of contract, before the commissioners bring an action for the same, repealed.

IV. And be it further enacted by the authority aforesaid, That it shall and may be lawful for the receiver or receivers of the rates, or assessments appointed or to be appointed by the said commissioners, or any or either of such receiver or receivers, or for any other person or persons authorized by the said commissioners, or any three or more of them, at all convenient times (first having an order under the hands of the said commissioners, or any three or more of them, for that purpose, to inspect the books or rates made for raising money for the relief and maintenance of the poor of all or any of the parishes or places comprehended within the said recited acts, or either of them, in order to ascertain the rates and assessments to be raised by virtue of this and the said two recited acts, and also to take copies thereof, or make extracts therefrom, and likewise to inspect and take copies of, or extracts out of or from, any book or books kept by any parish officer or officers, or other officer or officers appointed by authority of parliament, within the cities of *London* or *Westminster*, or county of *Middlesex*, for the paving, cleansing, or lighting, any square, street, lane, place, or district, in *London*, *Westminster*, or *Middlesex*; which inspection, copies, and extracts, the vestry clerk or vestry clerks, or other officer or officers of the respective parishes and places, or other officer or

Receivers, or other persons authorized by the commissioners are to be allowed to inspect and take copies of, or extracts from the books of poors rates in the several parishes gratis, in order to ascertain the assessments to be made by virtue of the recited acts.

officers,

officers, person or persons, having the custody of such book and rate books and rates, are hereby required to permit and suffer to be made, without fee or reward, by such receiver or receivers, or other person or persons appointed as aforesaid, on their producing an order under the hands of the said commissioners, or any three or more of them, for that purpose; and in case any such vestry clerk, or other such officer or officers, or person or persons, shall neglect or refuse so to do, within three days after such order shall be produced and shewn to him or them, or a copy thereof left at his or their last or most usual place of abode, then, and in every such case, he or they so refusing or neglecting, shall, for the first offence, forfeit the sum of twenty shillings; for the second offence, the sum of forty shillings; and for the third, and every other offence, the sum of three pounds.

Penalty of such refusal.

Commissioners allowed to compound for penalties in breach of contract.

V. And be it further enacted by the authority aforesaid, That it shall and may be lawful to and for the said commissioners, or any five or more of them, from time to time, and at all times hereafter, to compound and agree with any person or persons against whom the said commissioners, or any five or more of them, shall bring or cause to be brought any action or actions, suit or suits, for any penalty or penalties, contained in any contract or contracts already entered into, or hereafter to be entered into, on account of any breach or nonperformance of any such contract or contracts, for such sum or sums of money as they, or any five or more of them, shall think proper, so as the sum so compounded and agreed for, be not less than the injury or damage sustained by the breach or nonperformance of any such contract or contracts, and all the costs, charges, and expences, which shall be occasioned thereby.

Dead walls, void spaces of ground, and buildings, &c. belonging to any such land, house, shop, &c. how to be rated and assessed.

VI. And, for the more effectual and proportional rating dead walls, void spaces of ground, and other buildings and erections belonging to any land, house, shop, warehouse, cellar, vault, or other tenement; be it further enacted, That it shall and may be lawful to and for the said commissioners, or any five or more of them, and they are hereby required, when and at such time and times as the rates and assessments hereby and in the said recited acts, or either of them, are directed to be made, to rate and assess all such dead walls, void spaces of ground, and other buildings and erections, belonging to any such land, house, shop, warehouse, cellar, vault, or other tenement, situate, standing, lying, and being within the said parishes and places, comprehended within the said recited acts, or this act, or either of them, at a rate not exceeding six pence for every square yard, belonging to such dead wall, void space of ground, building, or other erection, over and above what such land, house, shop, warehouse, cellar, vault, or other tenement, to which such dead wall, void space of ground, building, or erection belongs, shall, by virtue of the said recited acts, or this present act, or either of them, be rated at the said rates or assessments, to be laid, received, recovered, and applied, in such manner as other rates

and

and assessments are directed to be laid, received, recovered, and applied, by the said former acts, or this act, or either of them.

VII. And be it further enacted by the authority aforesaid, That when any defective or bad pavement shall be mended, altered, or repaired, by the order or direction of the said commissioners, or any three or more of them, by virtue of the powers given by the act passed in the third year of his present Majesty's reign; the charges and expences thereof shall be reimbursed and paid by the tenant or tenants, occupier or occupiers, of the respective lands, houses, shops, warehouses, cellars, vaults, or other tenements, to which such pavements shall adjoin, appertain, or belong; and such tenant or tenants, occupier or occupiers, of lands, houses, shops, warehouses, cellars, vaults, or other tenements, are and shall be liable to pay the whole of such charges and expences; and in case such tenant or tenants, occupier or occupiers, shall not within ten days after the same shall be demanded, by a notice thereof in writing given to him, her, or them, or left at his, her, or their last or most usual place of abode, pay or cause to be paid, the said charges and expences to the said commissioners, or any three or more of them, or to such person or persons as they shall appoint to receive the same (which said notice shall be in writing, and signed by the clerk to the commissioners for the time being, by order of the said commissioners, or any three or more of them, and annexed to the bill containing an account of the expence of such repairs) it shall and may be lawful for the person or persons so to be appointed by the said commissioners to receive the same, to make complaint thereof to any one or more justice or justices of the peace for the county or place where such person or persons so refusing or neglecting shall be and reside; and such justice or justices may, and is and are hereby authorized and required to issue a warrant under his or their hand and seal, or hands and seals, to cause the party or parties to be brought before him or them, and upon the party or parties appearing, or not being to be found after due enquiry, and proof thereof by the oath of the party making such enquiry (which oath the said justice or justices is and are hereby impowered and required to administer) to hear and determine the matter in a summary way; and if upon the confession of the party or parties, or by the oath of one or more credible witness or witnesses (which oath such justice or justices is and are hereby impowered and required to administer) it shall appear to such justice or justices, that such charges and expences have been incurred by the said commissioners, and not paid or satisfied by the party or parties as aforesaid, then such justice or justices may, and he or they is and are hereby authorized and required to issue a warrant or warrants under his and their hand and seal, or hands and seals, for the levying the same, by distress and sale of the goods and chattels of such party or parties; and if after full payment thereof, together with all charges attending such distress and sale, there shall be an over-

Charges of altering or repairing defective or bad pavements, to be paid by the tenant or occupier;

and if not paid after due notice given,

any justice for the county, &c. upon complaint thereof, may issue his warrant for bringing the offender before him;

and may afterwards levy the expence by distress and sale.

plus, then the ſame ſhall be paid to the owner or owners of ſuch goods and chattels, upon demand.

Contracts between landlord and tenant concerning keeping pavements in repair not altered by this act.

VIII. Provided always, That nothing herein contained ſhall be deemed or taken to make void any contract, covenant, or agreement, between landlord and tenant, touching or concerning the keeping in repair ſuch pavement.

Defective or bad pavements belonging to lands or houſes, &c. untenanted, to be repaired by the commiſſioners at the expence of the owners; and if not paid after due notice given, the treaſurer may bring an action for the ſame.

IX. And be it further enacted by the authority aforeſaid, That when any defective or bad pavement adjoining or belonging to any land, houſe, ſhop, warehouſe, cellar, vault, or other tenement, or to any part or parts thereof, which ſhall then be untenanted or unoccupied, ſhall, by the direction of the ſaid commiſſioners, or any three or more of them, be mended, altered, or repaired, then, and in every ſuch caſe, the expence of mending, repairing, or altering ſuch pavement ſhall be paid by the owner or owners, proprietor or proprietors of ſuch land, houſe, ſhop, warehouſe, cellar, vault, or other tenement reſpectively; and in caſe of non-payment thereof within ten days next after notice in writing, to be ſigned by the clerk to the ſaid commiſſioners for the time being, by order of the ſaid commiſſioners, or any three or more of them, given or left at the laſt or moſt uſual place of abode of ſuch owner or owners, proprietor or proprietors, or of the known agent or agents, ſteward or ſtewards, to ſuch owner or owners, proprietor or proprietors, to pay the ſame; and in caſe ſuch reſpective place of abode ſhall not be known, and, upon inquiry, not to be found, ſuch inquiry to be verified upon oath before one or more juſtice or juſtices of the peace, who is and are hereby authorized to adminiſter the ſame to the perſon or perſons making ſuch inquiry, then, within ten days next after notice in writing, ſigned as aforeſaid, ſhall be affixed on ſome conſpicuous part of ſuch land, houſe, ſhop, warehouſe, cellar, vault, or other tenement reſpectively; in every ſuch caſe, the ſaid commiſſioners, or any three or more of them, ſhall and may, if they ſhall think proper, bring, or cauſe to be brought, any action or actions in the name of their treaſurer for the time being, againſt any ſuch owner or owners, proprietor or proprietors, for the money at any time ſo due; in which action or actions no eſſoin, protection, or wager of law, or more than one imparlance, ſhall be allowed.

Penalty of running, driving or drawing any wheel, ſledge, wheel-barrow, or other carriage, on any of the foot pavements.

X. And be it further enacted, That if any perſon or perſons ſhall, for the future, run, drive, draw, or cauſe to be run, driven, or drawn, on any of the foot pavements of any of the ſaid ſquares, ſtreets, lanes, courts, alleys, yards, paſſages, or places, which ſhall be begun to be paved by virtue of the ſaid former acts, or either of them, or of this act, any wheel or wheels, ſledge, wheel-barrow, or any carriage whatſoever, ſuch perſon or perſons ſhall forfeit, for the firſt offence, the ſum of ten ſhillings; for the ſecond offence, the ſum of twenty ſhillings; and for the third and every other offence, the ſum of forty ſhillings.

Notice to be given to the commiſſioners

XI. And be it further enacted by the authority aforeſaid, That when and ſo often as any part of the pavements of any of the

the ſquares, ſtreets, lanes, courts, alleys, yards, paſſages, or places, which ſhall be begun to be paved by virtue of this or the ſaid two recited acts, ſhall be taken up by any perſon or perſons, for the purpoſe of making, repairing, or altering, any vault or drain, or for any other purpoſe whatſoever; the perſon or perſons ſo taking up ſuch pavement or pavements, ſhall immediately give notice thereof to the ſurveyor or ſurveyors employed by the commiſſioners for putting this and the ſaid recited acts in execution, in order that the ſame may, with all convenient ſpeed, be laid down and repaired, under the inſpection of the ſaid ſurveyor or ſurveyors; and the charges and expences thereof ſhall be paid by the ſaid commiſſioners, and they ſhall be reimburſed the ſame by the perſon or perſons, companies of water-works, or commiſſioners of ſewers, who ſhall take up, or cauſe or procure to be taken up, the ſaid pavement or pavements, or any part or parts thereof; and in caſe ſuch perſon or perſons, companies of water-works, or commiſſioners of ſewers reſpectively, ſhall neglect or refuſe to pay what the ſaid commiſſioners ſhall have ſo paid and diſburſed, within ten days next after notice thereof, to be left, by the receiver or receivers appointed, or to be appointed, by the ſaid commiſſioners, at the dwelling-houſe, or laſt place of abode of ſuch perſon or perſons, or of the ſecretary or ſecretaries, clerk or clerks, of ſuch companies of water-works, or commiſſioners of ſewers reſpectively; which notice ſhall be in writing, and ſigned by the clerk to the commiſſioners for putting this and the ſaid recited acts into execution, by order of the ſaid commiſſioners, or any three or more of them, and annexed to the bill containing an account of the expence of ſuch repair; it ſhall and may be lawful to and for the ſaid laſt mentioned commiſſioners, or any three or more of them, and they are hereby authorized and impowered to bring, or cauſe to be brought, any action or actions, in the name or names of their treaſurer or treaſurers for the time being, for the recovery of ſuch ſum or ſums of money as they ſhall have ſo expended, for the relaying and repairing ſuch pavement or pavements taken up in manner aforeſaid; and in caſe ſuch perſon or perſons hereby directed to give ſuch notice to the ſurveyor or ſurveyors, as is before directed, ſhall neglect ſo to do, for the ſpace of twenty four hours after ſuch pavement or pavemetns be ſo taken up, ſuch perſon or perſons ſhall, for every ſuch offence, forfeit and pay the ſum of twenty ſhillings.

surveyor, of the taking up any pavements for the purpoſe of making, repairing, or altering, any vault or drain, &c. in order that the ſame may be relaid under his inſpection.

Commiſſioners to pay the expence, and they are to be reimburſed by the perſons taking up ſuch pavements: on their neglect or refuſal, after due notice given,

an action may be brought for the money in the treaſurer's name.

Penalty of not giving due notice of the taking up ſuch pavements,

XII. And be it further enacted by the authority aforeſaid, That when and ſo often as there ſhall be occaſion, after the paſſing of this act, to make new, or additional, or repair, or alter, any of the old grates belonging to the commiſſioners of ſewers, in any of the ſquares, ſtreets, lanes, courts, yards, alleys, paſſages, or places, which have been, or ſhall be, begun to be paved by virtue of this and the ſaid two former acts, the ſame ſhall be made new, repaired, or altered, at the expence of the ſaid commiſſioners of ſewers; and the ſame, when ſo made new, repaired, or altered, ſhall be laid down in ſuch places, and at ſuch diſtance

Where it ſhall be neceſſary to make new grates, or to repair or alter old ones, the commiſſioners of ſewers are to pay the expence; and the grates are to be laid down as the surveyors under this act shall direct.

If the commissioners of sewers neglect, &c. the commissioners under this act may order the same to be done, and they are to be reimbursed by the commissioners of sewers.

distance from each other, and in such manner and form, as shall be directed by the surveyor or surveyors to the commissioners appointed by the said recited acts, or either of them, at the expence of the said commissioners of sewers; and in case the said commissioners of sewers shall neglect or refuse so to do, for the space of ten days next after notice given, or left with their clerk or clerks for the time being, it shall and may be lawful to and for the said commissioners appointed by the said recited acts, or any three or more of them, or their surveyor or surveyors, to cause such grate or grates as shall be necessary to be made new, repaired, altered, and laid down, to be so made new, repaired, altered, and laid down; the expence whereof shall be reimbursed and paid by the said commissioners of sewers.

Commissioners impowered to remove and alter all steps projecting into the foot ways, steps, and doors, going down out of the foot ways, into cellars, shew-glasses, and other matters, causing an obstruction or nuisance in the common passages.

XIII. And whereas several of the streets, lanes, and other places, comprehended within the said two recited acts, or this act, or either of them, are in some parts thereof very narrow, and are greatly obstructed and made dangerous to foot passengers, by steps being brought out from several houses into the streets; steps, and doors, going down into cellars, vaults, and other places, belonging to such houses; and by shew-glasses, shew-boards, or other matters or things projecting from shops or houses, over and beyond the area belonging to such houses, or into the foot ways; be it therefore enacted by the authority aforesaid, That from and after the passing of this act, all such steps projecting into the foot ways of the streets, all steps, and doors, going down out of the foot ways into any cellars, vaults, or other places, belonging to any house, shop, warehouse, or tenement, as likewise all shew-glasses, or shew-boards, projecting over and beyond the areas, or into the foot ways; and all and every other material, matter, or thing, belonging to any houses, warehouses, shops, cellars, or other buildings, which cause or occasion any nuisance, annoyance, incroachment, or obstruction, in any of the squares, streets, lanes, courts, alleys, yards, passages, or other places (either in the foot or carriage ways thereof) which shall be begun to be paved by virtue of this and the said two former acts, shall be, at the expence of the said commissioners, removed, fixed, placed, or altered, in such manner and form as shall be approved of by the said commissioners, or any five or more of them, or their surveyor or surveyors by their direction.

Penalty of obstructing any officer, or other person, in the execution of his duty.

XIV. And be it further enacted by the authority aforesaid, That if any person or persons shall, at any time or times hereafter, obstruct, hinder, or molest, any surveyor or surveyors, or other officer or officers, person or persons whatsoever, who are or shall be employed to put this and the said two former acts, or either of them, in execution, in the performance or execution of their duty; every such person and persons so offending shall, for the first offence, forfeit the sum of twenty shillings; for the second offence, the sum of forty shillings; and for the third and every other offence, the sum of three pounds.

XV. And

XV. And whereas all that part of a certain ſtreet or place called *Swallow Street* (which is ſituate in the two ſeveral pariſhes of *Saint James* and *Saint George Hanover Square*, within the liberty of *Weſtminſter*; and extends from the weſt end of a publick way or paſſage called *Major Foubert's paſſage*, in the ſaid pariſh of *Saint James*; and from the eaſt end of *Conduit Street* in the ſaid pariſh of *Saint George Hanover Square*, northwards, to a certain ſtreet, or place called *Oxford Road*) hath for ſeveral years paſt been, and ſtill is, in all reſpects compleatly paved as a ſtreet, with houſes of habitation, and other buildings regularly erected and built on each ſide thereof: and whereas the ſaid part of *Swallow Street* above deſcribed, was not a ſtreet (at the time of paſſing an act of parliament in the ſecond year of the reigns of the late King *William* and Queen *Mary*, made (amongſt other things) for paving and cleanſing the ſtreets in the cities of *London*, *Weſtminſter*, and ſuburbs and liberties thereof) but was then, and for ſeveral years after, uſed as a common graveled lane or highway, not built upon as a ſtreet, and was called *Marybone Lane*; and therefore ſome doubts have lately ariſen, whether the ſaid part of *Swallow Street* above deſcribed, is or is not now a ſtreet within the meaning of the ſaid laſt mentioned act of parliament, with reſpect to the paving thereof, and keeping the ſame in repair; for the obviating of which doubts, be it enacted by the authority aforeſaid, That the ſaid part of *Swallow Street* herein before deſcribed, ſhall at all times hereafter be, and be deemed and taken to be, a publick ſtreet, and part of *Swallow Street* aforeſaid, to all intents, conſtructions, and purpoſes whatſoever, and within the meaning of the ſaid act of parliament, made in the ſaid ſecond year of the reign of King *William* and Queen *Mary*; any thing in this or in any former act or acts of parliament contained, or any other law, uſage, or cuſtom, to the contrary in any wiſe notwithſtanding.

The whole of Swallow Street above deſcribed, declared to be a publick ſtreet, and to be within the meaning of the act of 2 W. & M.

XVI. And be it further enacted by the authority aforeſaid, That the ſaid commiſſioners, or any ſeven or more of them, may, and they are hereby impowered to make, or cauſe to be made, any paſſage or paſſages, through any ſquare or place within the pariſhes and places comprized in the ſaid recited acts or this preſent act, with the conſent of the owner or owners, proprietor or proprietors, and at the expence of ſuch owner or owners, proprietor or proprietors thereof; and if any ſuch new paſſage or paſſages ſhall be made, the ſaid commiſſioners may pave, repair, cleanſe, and light the ſame, in like manner, and under the ſame powers, proviſions, rules, regulations, and authorities, as is herein and in the ſaid two ſeveral recited acts provided, in reſpect of the ſquares, ſtreets, lanes, courts, alleys, yards, paſſages, and places before mentioned.

Commiſſioners impowered, with conſent of the proprietors, and at their expence, to make any new paſſages, and to pave, cleanſe, and light the ſame.

XVII. Provided always, That no part of the monies that ſhall be given by parliament for the purpoſes of this and the ſaid two recited acts, nor any part of the monies that ſhall be raiſed by the rates to be made and levied by virtue of this and the ſaid two recited acts, ſhall be applied to the purpoſe of purchaſing the

No part of the monies granted by parliament, or raiſed by the rates, to be applied in purchasing houses or ground for the above purpose.

the said lands or houses, or either of them, or the ground or soil thereof.

In order to make a new passage, or open the old one, at the Devil's gap near Long Acre, the commissioners are impowered, upon such money as shall be agreed on being paid, or satisfaction made to the owners, to take down such houses as shall be necessary for that purpose:

XVIII. And whereas by the said recited act of the second year of his present Majesty, power is given to the said commissioners, or any seven or more of them, to make a new passage, or widen the old one, from *Drury Lane* into *Great Queen Street*, in the parish of *Saint Giles in the Fields*, in the county of *Middlesex*, at or near a certain place called *The Devil's Gap*, and near adjoining to the east end of *Long Acre*, in manner, and upon the terms and conditions, in the said act mentioned; be it therefore further enacted by the authority aforesaid, That upon payment of such sum or sums of money as shall be agreed to be paid for the premisses mentioned in the said first recited act, or such part thereof as shall be necessary to be purchased for that purpose; or if no agreement or contract shall be made, then upon making satisfaction, in manner herein after mentioned, to the owners of, and persons interested in, such premisses, it shall and may be lawful to and for the said commissioners, or any seven or more of them, to take down, or cause or procure to be taken down, all such house or houses, with the appurtenances, on the south side of the said gap, or any part or parts of all of such of the said houses as shall be necessary for the purpose (not exceeding in the whole six such houses) and to cause the materials thereof to be removed and taken away.

And where the persons interested in such lands and houses,

XIX. And be it further enacted by the authority aforesaid, That if any body politick, corporate, or collegiate, corporation aggregate or sole, feoffees in trust, executors, administrators, guardians, committees, or other trustees, or any other person or persons whomsoever, in any wise interested in any such lands, tenements, buildings, houses, grounds, or hereditaments, upon ten days notice to them given or left in writing at the dwelling-house or houses, place or places of abode, of such person or persons, or of the head officer or officers of such body politick, corporate, or collegiate, aggregate or sole, or at the house of the tenant in possession of such lands, tenements, houses, buildings, grounds, and hereditaments, shall neglect or refuse to treat, or shall not agree for the sale of any such lands, tenements, houses, buildings, grounds, or hereditaments, or any part or parts thereof, or for their interest therein, or, by reason of absence, or otherwise, shall be prevented from treating as aforesaid; then, and in any such case, the said commissioners, or any seven or more of them, shall cause it to be enquired into, and ascertained, by and upon the oath of a jury of twelve indifferent men of the county of *Middlesex* (which oath the said commissioners, or any three or more of them, are hereby impowered and required to administer) what damages will be sustained by, and what recompence and satisfaction shall be made to, such owners, occupiers, proprietors, or other person or persons interested for such lands, tenements, houses, buildings, grounds, and hereditaments, or any part or parts thereof, which the said commissioners shall want to purchase: and in order thereunto,

shall refuse to treat or agree for the sale thereof,

the damage and recompence is to be ascertained by a jury.

the

the said commissioners, or any seven or more of them, are hereby impowered and required, from time to time, as there shall be occasion, to summon and call before the said jury, and examine upon oath, all persons whatsoever, who shall be thought necessary or proper to be examined as witnesses touching or concerning the premisses (which oath the said commissioners, or any two or more of them, are hereby impowered and required to administer) and if any of the parties interested shall request the same, or the said commissioners, or any seven or more of them, shall think it necessary, shall also cause the said jury to view the place or places in question, and shall use all other lawful ways and means as well for their own, as for the said jury's better information in the premisses, in such manner as they the said commissioners, or any seven or more of them, shall think fit: and after the said jury shall have so inquired of, ascertained, and settled, such damage and recompence, they the said commissioners, or any seven or more of them, shall thereupon order and adjudge the sum or sums of money so assessed by the said jury for such purchases as aforesaid, to be paid to the persons interested in such lands, tenements, buildings, houses, grounds, or hereditaments, or any part or parts thereof, according to the verdict or inquisition of the said jury; which said verdict or inquisition, and the order or adjudication so had and made, shall be final and conclusive to all intents and purposes against all parties or persons whatsoever, claiming in possession, reversion, remainder, or otherwise, their heirs, executors, or administrators, and successors respectively, as well absent as present, infants, femes covert, lunaticks, idiots, and persons under any other disability whatsoever, bodies politick, corporate, or collegiate, aggregate or sole, as well as other person or persons whomsoever; and all and every such owners, occupiers, and proprietors, and all and every person and persons in any wise interested in such lands, tenements, buildings, houses, grounds, or hereditaments, or any part or parts thereof so purchased as aforesaid, shall thereby be, from and after the money so contracted and agreed for, or so assessed and adjudged for such purchases as aforesaid, shall be paid, tendered, or left as herein directed, to all intents and purposes divested of all right, claim, interest, or property, of, in, to, or out of, the same; and the said commissioners, or any seven or more of them, shall have full power, by virtue of this act, by deed indented and inrolled, within three months after the making thereof, in some of his Majesty's courts of record at *Westminster*, to grant, bargain, sell, and convey such lands, tenements, buildings, houses, grounds, or hereditaments, or such parts thereof as shall be purchased as aforesaid, to such person or persons, and their heirs and assigns, as the said commissioners, or any seven or more of them, shall nominate and appoint, in trust for the said commissioners and their successors, for the purposes of the said recited acts, and of this act, or either of them; which said grant, bargain, sale, and conveyance, shall be good and available in the law to such person or persons, and their

And the commissioners are impowered to summon a jury accordingly, and examine witnesses on oath touching the premisses;

and to adjudge the sum assessed to be paid accordingly.

The verdict of the jury, and order thereupon made, to be final;

and the parties to be divested of all property in the premisses,

which may be sold and conveyed by the commissioners,

in trust for the purposes mentioned in this and the recited acts.

their heirs, in trust as aforesaid, against all persons whomsoever, their heirs, executors, administrators, or assigns, whether under abilities or disabilities as aforesaid, or in any wise interested in, or claiming, any estate, right, title, or interest, in such lands, tenements, buildings, houses, grounds, or hereditaments, and every part or parts thereof so purchased as aforesaid.

If the sums awarded shall not be duly paid, &c.

XX. Provided always, That in case the said sum or sums so assessed by the said jury, and ordered and adjudged by the said commissioners to be paid, as a satisfaction to the owners, incumbrancers, occupiers or others, for their respective interests in the said premisses, shall not be paid, tendered, or left, as herein mentioned, according to the true intent and meaning of this act, within one calendar month after the same shall have been so assessed, ordered, and adjudged; then, and in such case, the verdict of the said jury, and order and adjudication of the said commissioners, shall not be binding upon the said parties; any thing herein contained to the contrary notwithstanding: and, for the summoning and returning of such jury or juries, the said commissioners, or any five or more of them, are hereby impowered, from time to time, to issue their warrant or warrants to the sheriff of the said county, thereby requiring him to impanel, summon, and return, an indifferent jury of twenty four persons, to appear before the said commissioners, or any five or more of them, at such time and place as in such warrant shall be appointed; of which time and place all parties interested shall have ten days notice given or left in manner herein last before-mentioned; and the said sheriff, or his deputy or deputies, is and are hereby required to impanel, summon, and return such twenty four persons accordingly; and out of the persons so impanelled, summoned, and returned, or out of such of them as shall appear according to or upon such summons, the said commissioners, or any five or more of them, shall cause to be sworn twelve, who shall be the jury for the purposes aforesaid; and for default of a sufficient number of jurymen, the said sheriff, or his deputy or deputies, shall return so many of the standers-by as shall be necessary to make up the number of twelve, to serve on such jury.

the said verdict and adjudication to be void.

Commissioners impowered to issue their warrant to the sheriff for summoning a jury,

Sheriff to return a jury accordingly;

and in default of a sufficient number appearing, standers-by may be returned.

Jury may be challenged.

XXI. Provided always, and be it further enacted by the authority aforesaid, That all persons concerned shall, from time to time, have their lawful challenges (but not to challenge the array of the panel) against any of the said jurymen, when they come to be sworn; and the said commissioners, or any seven or more of them, acting in the premisses, shall have power, from time to time, to impose any reasonable fine or fines on such sheriff, his deputy or deputies, bailiffs, or agents, making default in the premisses; and on any of the persons that shall be summoned and returned on such jury, and shall not appear, or refuse to be sworn on the said jury, or to give their verdict, or in any manner wilfully neglecting their duty therein, contrary to the true intent and meaning of this act; and on any of the persons who, being required to give evidence touching the

Power given to the commissioners to fine the sheriff, his agents, and jury, and persons summoned to give evidence,

the premisses, shall refuse to be examined or to give evidence; and, from time to time, to levy such fine or fines in such manner as any penalties in the said recited acts are directed to be levied and recovered, so as that no such fine shall exceed the sum of ten pounds upon any one person for any one offence.

making default in the premisses.

Limitation of such fines.

XXII. And be it further enacted by the authority aforesaid, That in case such person or persons, to whom such sum or sums of money shall be so assessed or due as aforesaid, cannot be found, or if by reason of disputes depending in any court of law or equity, or for defect of evidence, or otherwise, it shall not appear to the said commissioners what person or persons is or are intituled; or if any mortgagee or mortgagees shall refuse to take in his, her, or their mortgage money due on the premisses, after notice given to him, her, or them, for that purpose; then, and in all and every such case and cases, it shall and may be lawful to and for the said commissioners, or any seven or more of them, to order the sum or sums so assessed and awarded, as aforesaid, or as shall be due on such mortgage, to be paid into the bank of *England*, in the name of the treasurer to the said commissioners for the time being, and of any five or more of the said commissioners, for the use of the parties interested in the said premisses, to be paid to them, and every of them, according to their respective estates and interests in the said premisses, as the said commissioners, or any five or more of them, shall, by any order to be made by them, direct.

If the parties to whom the consideration money shall be awarded cannot be found, or there be any dispute in law, or defect of evidence, or mortgagees refuse to take in their mortgage money;

the sums assessed to be paid into the bank, for the use of the parties.

XXIII. And whereas several noblemen, gentlemen, and others, residing near and passing through the said gap, have, by voluntary subscription among themselves, agreed to raise a considerable sum of money towards purchasing the said houses and ground, but it may so happen that the said fund may not be quite sufficient to pay the purchase-money; and in order to compleat the said design, other persons may be induced to lend and advance money towards the said purchase: and whereas by reason of such purchases as aforesaid, the commissioners may be possessed of one or more house or houses, or some piece or parcel of ground, over and above what may be necessary for the opening and widening the said gap; be it therefore further enacted, That it shall and may be lawful to and for the said commissioners, or any three or more of them, to let, sell, or dispose of such house or houses, or such piece or parcel of ground, either together, or separately and in parcels, as they shall think most advantageous and convenient, to such person or persons as shall be willing to contract for and purchase the same; and to design and lay out in what manner the houses to be built thereon shall be erected and built, and of what breadth and extent the said street or gap, so intended to be widened, shall be; and also to sell and dispose of the materials of such house or houses as the said commissioners shall purchase and cause to be pulled down as aforesaid; and apply the money arising by such sale as aforesaid, to reimburse and pay the person and persons who shall have advanced any sum or sums of money, over and besides

Commissioners may let or sell such houses and old materials, or the ground so purchased, which shall be more than sufficient for their purpose; and lay out the manner of building thereon; and the breadth and extent of the street; and apply the money arising by the ſale to the contributors. ſides the money raiſed by ſuch voluntary ſubſcription as aforeſaid.

Such of the powers, &c. granted by the former act, as are altered by this, are repealed.

XXIV. And be it further enacted by the authority aforeſaid, That ſuch of the powers, proviſions, and authorities, contained in the ſaid former acts, or either of them, as are varied or altered by this act, ſhall be, and the ſame are hereby declared to be repealed.

Clauſes in act 6 Geo. I. 3 Geo. II. and 19 Geo. II.

XXV. And whereas by an act made in the ſixth year of the reign of his majeſty King *George* the Firſt, for preventing the carriage of exceſſive loads of meal, malt, bricks, and coals, within ten miles of *London* and *Weſtminſter*, it is provided, That no perſon ſhall carry, at one load, within the ſaid limits, in any waggon or cart having the wheels thereof ſhod or bound with tire or ſtreaks of iron, more than one chaldron of coals: and whereas by an act made in the third year of the reign of his late majeſty King *George* the Second, for the better regulation of the coal trade, proviſion is made for inflicting a penalty on all perſons who ſhall ſell any quantity of coals as and for pool meaſure including the ingrain, and ſhall not deliver to the buyer of ſuch coals the full quantity of coals ſo ſold, as the ſame were meaſured from on ſhipboard, together with the ingrain thereof: and whereas by an act made in the nineteenth year of the reign of his ſaid majeſty King *George* the Second, for preventing frauds and abuſes in the admeaſurement of coals, it is declared, That all agreements for coals to be delivered within the limits aforeſaid, directly from any lighter or other craft, to the conſumer, not being a leſs quantity than five chaldrons, ſhall be deemed and underſtood to be for pool meaſure, including the ingrain of one chaldron for every twenty chaldrons: and whereas many perſons have, to their great prejudice, ſuffered the penalty inflicted by the ſaid act made in the ſixth year of the reign of his majeſty King *George* the Firſt, by carrying the ingrain belonging to each chaldron in the ſame cart with the coals: therefore, for preventing ſuch hardſhips for the future, be it further enacted by the authority aforeſaid, That from and after the paſſing of this act, it ſhall be lawful for any perſon or perſons to carry at one load, within the limits deſcribed by the ſaid act of the ſixth of King *George* the Firſt, in any waggon or cart, any quantity of coals not exceeding the quantity of one chaldron, and the ingrain thereunto belonging, after the rate of one chaldron in every twenty chaldrons, without being liable to any penalty for the ſame; any thing in the ſaid act of the ſixth year of the reign of his ſaid majeſty King *George* the Firſt, or any other act or acts, to the contrary thereof in any wiſe notwithſtanding.

Any quantity of coals, not exceeding 1 chaldron, with the ingrain, may be carried at one load, without being liable to any penalty.

Recovery and application of penalties.

XXVI. And be it further enacted by the authority aforeſaid, That all penalties and forfeitures by this act impoſed (the manner of levying and recovering whereof is not hereby otherwiſe particularly directed) ſhall be levied and recovered by diſtreſs and ſale of the offender's goods and chattels, by warrant under the hand and ſeal of ſome juſtice of the peace for the ſaid county of of *Middlesex*, or the city or liberty of *Westminster*, as the case may be; which warrant such justice is hereby impowered and required to grant, upon the confession of the party or parties, or upon the information of any one or more credible witness or witnesses upon oath (which oath such justice is hereby impowered to administer) and the penalties and forfeitures when recovered, after rendering the overplus, if any be, upon demand to the party or parties whose goods and chattels shall be so distrained and sold (the charges of such distress and sale being first deducted) shall be paid to the treasurer to the said commissioners for the time being, and be applied towards the purposes of the said former acts, and this act; and in case sufficient distress cannot be found, and such penalties or forfeitures shall not be paid, it shall and may be lawful for such justice, and he is hereby authorized and required, by warrant under his hand and seal, to commit such offender or offenders to the house of correction, for any time not exceeding two months.

XXVII. And be it further enacted by the authority aforesaid, That no proceeding to be had touching the conviction of any offender or offenders against this act, or any order made, or other matter or thing to be done or transacted, in or relating to the execution of this act, shall be vacated or quashed for want of form, or be removed by *Certiorari*, or any other writ or process whatsoever, into any of his Majesty's courts of record at *Westminster*; any law or statute to the contrary notwithstanding.

Proceedings touching the conviction of offenders, not to be quashed for want of form, or removed by *Certiorari*.

XXVIII. And be it further enacted by the authority aforesaid, That no action or suit shall be commenced against any person or persons for any thing done in pursuance of this act, until eight clear days notice shall be thereof given in writing to the clerk or treasurer to the said commissioners, or after sufficient satisfaction, or tender thereof, hath been made to the party or parties aggrieved, or after six calendar months next after the fact committed, for which such action or actions, suit or suits, shall be so brought; and every such action shall be brought, laid, and tried, in the county or place where such matters and things respectively shall be committed or done, and not in any other county or place; and that the defendant or defendants in such actions and suits, and every of them, may plead the general issue, and give this act, and the special matter, in evidence, at any trial or trials which shall be had thereupon, and that the matter or thing for which such action or actions, suit or suits, shall be so brought, was done in pursuance and by the authority of this act: and if the said matter or thing shall appear to have been so done, or if it shall appear that such action or suit was brought before eight clear days notice thereof given as aforesaid, or that sufficient satisfaction was made or tendered as aforesaid, or if any such action or suit shall not be commenced within the time before for that purpose limited, or shall be laid in any other county or place than as aforesaid, then the jury or juries shall find for the defendant or defendants therein; and if a verdict or verdicts

Limitation of actions.

General issue.

verdicts ſhall be found for ſuch defendant or defendants, or if the plaintiff or plaintiffs in ſuch action or actions, ſuit or ſuits, ſhall become nonſuited, or ſuffer a diſcontinuance of ſuch action or actions, or if, upon any demurrer or demurrers any ſuch action or actions, judgment ſhall be given for the defendant or defendants therein, then, and in either of the caſes aforeſaid, ſuch defendant or defendants ſhall have treble coſts; and ſhall have ſuch remedy for recovering the ſame, as any defendant or defendants may have for his, her, or their coſts in any other caſes by law.

Treble coſts.

CAP. XL.

An act for the more eaſy and ſpeedy recovery of ſmall debts within the borough and ſoke of Doncaſter, *in the county of* York; *and for lighting the ſtreets, lanes, and other open paſſages and places, within the ſaid borough.*

Preamble.

WHEREAS *the borough of* Doncaſter *in the county of* York, *is large and populous, has a navigable river, and is a great thoroughfare between the ſouth and northern parts of this kingdom, by means whereof a conſiderable trade is carried on in the ſaid borough and ſoke thereof: and whereas there are many perſons to whom the traders of the ſaid borough and ſoke are obliged to give credit for ſmall ſums of money, who frequently refuſe, although able, to pay the ſame, preſuming on the diſcouragements which creditors lie under, from the expence which they are unavoidably put to, and the delays they meet with in ſuing for ſuch debts: and whereas a more eaſy and ſpeedy method of recovering ſmall debts, within the ſaid borough and ſoke, would greatly tend to promote induſtry, and ſupport uſeful credit therein: and whereas the lighting, in a proper manner, the ſtreets, lanes, and other open paſſages and places, within the ſaid borough, would be of great benefit and ſafety to the inhabitants thereof, as well as to all perſons reſorting thereto:* may it therefore pleaſe your Majeſty that it may be enacted; and be it enacted by the King's moſt excellent majeſty, by and with the advice and conſent of the lords ſpiritual and temporal, and commons, in this preſent parliament aſſembled, and by the authority of the ſame, That

Commiſſioners appointed. They are conſtituted a court of requeſts. Three or more impowered to hold a court on *Thurſday* in every other week. Firſt meeting. Buſineſs of other courts not to be impeded by their meetings. Power and buſineſs of this court. Caſting vote, on equality, to lie in the mayor, ſenior alderman, or commiſſioner who ſtands firſt on the liſt. —— Method of electing new commiſſioners. — The order, in which the commiſſioners are to be ſummoned. —— Any commiſſioner, though not ſummoned, &c. may ſit in the court. —— Commiſſioners to take oath for faithful impartial, and honeſt diſcharge of the truſt; to be adminiſtred by the clerk, and regiſtred. —— *Richard Shepherd* conſtituted clerk of the court; with power to appoint a deputy. —— Serjeants at mace appointed ſerjeants of the court. —— Creditors may ſue for any debt under 40 s. in the ſaid court. And on application to the clerk, who ſhall ſummon the debtor, and proof of ſervice of the ſummons, the commiſſioners are to enquire into the demand, and paſs final judgment thereupon: and may adminiſter an oath to witneſſes and officers. —— Debtor not appearing, court may hear the cauſe on the part of the plaintiff, and paſs judgment.

ment thereon, with costs. — Plaintiff not appearing, or being nonsuited, costs to be awarded to the defendant. —— Upon order for payment of money, execution is to be awarded against the body or goods of the party. Confinement on execution not to exceed three months. If the execution be prevented, or evaded, the court may order another upon the first default of payment, the court may award execution for the whole debt with further costs. — Debt and costs to be marked on the back of the precept. On paying in the same to the clerk, before execution takes effect, with the fees due to the officers, &c. execution is to be superseded. —— Attornies and solicitors not exempted. —— Officer neglecting his duty, liable to pay the debt. Fees allowed to the clerk and serjeants. A table thereof to be hung up in the court. —— Penalty of demanding or taking greater or other fees, not exceeding 40 s. nor less than 10 s. Clerk or serjeants guilty of notorious misbehaviour, court may enquire into the same, and certify the particulars to the mayor, who shall summon a general meeting, who may remove the delinquent. —— A commissioner interested in any cause depending, is to withdraw, after being heard, till the same is determined: and officer being interested, the court is to appoint another person to act *pro tempore*. —— Persons insulting the court while sitting, or any members thereof going to or from the same, or interrupting the proceedings, may be punished by fine or imprisonment. Where fine cannot be levied, offender is to be committed. Application of the fines. Copy of this clause to be fixed up in the court. —— Actions for debt recoverable in this court, are not to be brought in any other. The registers of the court, or true copies thereof, deemed legal evidence. Proceedings, &c. not to be removed. —— Specification of debt, &c. not suable in this court. —— Penalty of wilful and corrupt perjury. —— Keepers of the common gaol are to receive and keep in safe custody, &c. all persons committed by order of the court; on penalty of forfeiting not exceeding 5 l. nor less than 40 s. to be levied by distress and sale of the offenders goods, and to be paid and applied as other fines. —— No attorney to speak in the court, where he is not a party or witness, on penalty of 20 l. nor to act as a commissioner. —— Witness duly summoned, refusing to appear and give evidence, may be fined not exceeding 50 s. nor less than 5 s. to be levied by distress and sale of the offenders goods, and paid over to the party injured. —— No writ may be sued out against any commissioner or officer, for any thing done in the execution of their respective offices, until they have been served with due notice. Attorney's fee for preparing and serving such notice. — Defendant tendering sufficient amends; verdict to be given for him. If none, or insufficient amends are tendered, &c. plaintiff to recover damages and costs. If notice has not been given, defendant to recover. Defendant may pay money into court before issue joined. No evidence to be given on the trial, but what is contained in the notice. —— Corporation at their own expence, to light the streets, &c. within the borough. Lamps, &c. vested in the mayor: penalty on persons injuring them. Limitation of actions. General issue. Treble costs. Publick act.

CAP. XLI.

An act for the more easy and speedy recovery of small debts in the town and parish of Kirkby in Kendal, *in the county of* Westmorland.

WHEREAS *a great trade is carried on in the town and parish of* Kirkby in Kendal, *in the county of* Westmorland, *and the inhabitants thereof have of late years greatly increased: and whereas many poor honest persons are obliged to contract small debts within the said town and parish, and limits of the same, and they being frequently rendered unable to pay the said debts in due time, their creditors do often bring suits and actions against them for recovery of the* — Preamble.

the ſame, and in conſequence thereof their goods and effects are ſeized and ſold, or their perſons imprisoned, to the utter ruin of themſelves and families, the loſs of their labour to the publick, and the great burthen and charge of the pariſh or townſhip to which they belong: for remedy whereof, and to the intent that ſome other eaſy and ſpeedy method may be provided for the recovery and payment of ſmall debts within the ſaid town and pariſh and the limits thereof: may it pleaſe your moſt excellent Majeſty that it may be enacted; and be it enacted by the King's moſt excellent majeſty, by and with the advice and conſent of the lords ſpiritual and temporal, and commons, in this preſent parliament aſſembled, and by the authority of the ſame, That

Commiſſioners named; and any three, or more, of them conſtituted a court of requeſts. Proviſo. Commiſſioners to aſſemble at a certain place: to be choſen in rotation. Commiſſioners to elect a clerk. —— Commiſſioners to iſſue a *Capias*. Penalty on perſons refuſing to obey ſubpænas of the court. Creditors may ſue for debts under 40 s. Commiſſioners to adminiſter oaths. —— Penalty on inſulting the commiſſioners, or being guilty of perjury. —— Commiſſioners to take an oath. Fees to be taken. 5 l. Penalty on demanding greater fees. —— Certain debts excepted. —— Plaintiffs not appearing, &c. Commiſſioners may award coſts to defendants. —— If debtors refuſe to appear, commiſſioners may hear and determine the cauſe. Application of penalties. —— Clerk to adjourn the court. —— Debts recoverable in this court, not to be ſued for in any other court. —— Proceedings not removeable by *Certiorari*. Limitation of actions. General iſſue. Treble coſts. Publick act.

CAP. XLII.

An act for repairing and widening the road from Shillingford, *in the county of* Oxford, *through* Wallingford *and* Pangborne, *to* Reading, *in the county of* Berks; *and for building a bridge over the river of* Thames, *at or near* Shillingford Ferry.

CAP. XLIII.

An act for maintaining, regulating, and employing the poor within the pariſh of Saint John *at* Hackney, *in the county of* Middleſex; *and for lighting the ſaid pariſh, and eſtabliſhing a regular nightly watch therein.*

CAP. XLIV.

An act for repairing and widening the roads from Horſham, *in the county of* Suſſex, *through the pariſhes of* Shipley, Weſt Grinſted, Aſhurſt, Steyning, Bramber, *and* Breeding, *in the ſaid county.*

CAP. XLV.

An act to amend and render more effectual ſeveral acts of parliament, for repairing the roads from Sherbrooke Hill, *near* Buxton *and* Chappel in the Frith, *in the county of* Derby, *through the town of* Stockport, *in the county of* Cheſter, *to* Mancheſter, *in the county of* Lancaſter, *and*

other roads in the said acts mentioned, and for turning and diverting the roads from Whaley Bridge, *to* Chappel in the Frith, *and to* Sparrow Pitt Gate; *and from* Whaley Bridge, *to the western end of* Longside Common, *in the county of* Chester.

CAP. XLVI.

An act to continue an act passed in the tenth year of the reign of his late majesty King George *the Second, for continuing an act, passed in the fifth year of the reign of his late majesty King* George *the First, intituled,* An act for laying a duty of two pennies *Scots*, or one sixth part of a penny *Sterling*, upon every pint of ale or beer, that shall be vended or sold within the town of *Dunbar*, for improving and preserving the harbour, and repairing the town house, and building a school, and other publick buildings there; and for supplying the said town with fresh water.

CAP. XLVII.

An act for repairing and widening the roads, from the end of Stanbridge Lane, *near a barn in the parish of* Romsey, *to the turnpike road at* Middle Wallop, *and from the turnpike road between* Stanbridge Lane *aforesaid, and* Great Bridge, *to the turnpike road at* Stockbridge, *and from the garden of* Henry Hattat, *at* Awbridge, *to the garden wall of* Denys Rolle, *esquire, at* East Tuderley, *and from* Lockerley Mill Stream, *to* East Dean Gate, *and from the said garden wall to the turnpike road leading from* Stockbridge *aforesaid, in the county of* Southampton, *to* Salisbury.

CAP. XLVIII.

An act for repairing and widening several roads leading from Callington *in the county of* Cornwall.

CAP. XLIX.

An act to enable the governor and company of the bank of England *to purchase houses and ground for opening a passage for carriages, from* Cornhill *to the bank, and making more commodious several other passages leading thereto; and for enlarging the buildings of the said bank, and making the same more commodious.*

CAP. L.

An act for the relief of the bond and other creditors of the wardens and commonalty of the mystery of Mercers *of the city of* London.

CAP. LI.

An act for continuing and enlarging the term and powers of an act, made in the twenty sixth year of the reign of his late majesty King George *the Second, intituled,* An act for repairing and widening the road from the west end of the town of *Burton upon Trent*, in the county of *Stafford*, through the said town, to the south end of the town of *Derby*, in the county of *Derby*.

CAP. LII.

An act for repairing and widening the road from Worksop, *in the county of* Nottingham, *through the towns of* Gateforth, Anston, Aston, Handsworth, *and* Darnall, *to the north east end of* Attercliffe, *in the county of* York, *where the same joins the turnpike road from* Bawtry *to* Sheffield.

CAP. LIII.

An act for repairing and widening the roads from the High Bridge *in* Spalding, *to a certain place called* Tydd Goat, *in the county of* Lincoln; *and from* Sutton Saint Mary's, *to* Sutton Wash, *in the said county.*

CAP. LIV.

An act for enlarging the term and powers granted by an act, passed in the twenty fourth year of the reign of his late Majesty, intituled, An act for making, widening, and keeping in repair, several roads in the several parishes of *Lambeth*, *Newington*, *Saint George Southwark*, and *Bermondsey*, in the county of *Surrey*, and *Lewisham*, in the county of *Kent*; *and for repairing* Lambeth Back Lane, *and for lighting and watching the said roads.*

CAP. LV.

An act for establishing a regular and nightly watch, and for maintaining, regulating, and employing the poor within the parish of Saint Clement Danes, *in the liberty of* Westminster, *and county of* Middlesex.

CAP. LVI.

An act for the better relief and employment of the poor in the hundred of Blything, *in the county of* Suffolk.

CAP. LVII.

An act for the better relief and employment of the poor in the hundred of Bosmere *and* Claydon, *in the county of* Suffolk.

CAP. LVIII.

An act to amend and render more effectual an act passed in the twenty ninth year of the reign of his late majesty King George *the Second, intituled,* An act for the better relief and employment of the poor in the hundreds of *Colneis* and *Carlsford*, in the county of *Suffolk*.

CAP. LIX.

An act for the better relief and employment of the poor, in the hundred of Samford, *in the county of* Suffolk.

CAP. LX.

An act for the more effectual relief and employment of the poor, within the city of Gloucester, *and for lighting the streets of the said city.*

CAP. LXI.

An act for repairing and widening the road from Derby *to* Mansfield, *in the county of* Nottingham, *and several other roads therein mentioned.*

CAP. LXII.

An act for continuing the terms of, and amending, the acts for repairing several roads leading from Ledbury, *in the county of* Hereford; *and for widening and amending the road through the parish of* Bromesberrow, *in the county of* Gloucester, *and through* Corse Lawn, *till it meets the road from* Gloucester *to* Worcester.

CAP. LXIII.

An act for amending and widening the road from a place near the village of Milford, *through* Haslemere, *to the* Portsmouth *road, between* Lippock *and* Rake, *in the several counties of* Surrey, Sussex, *and* Southampton.

CAP. LXIV.

An act for amending and widening the road from Tinsley *in the county of* York, *to the town of* Doncaster, *in the said county.*

CAP. LXV.

An act for amending and widening the road from the south end of the town of Rotherham *in the county of* York, *to the present turnpike road, near* Pleasley, *in the county of* Derby, *and also the road from the north end of the said town of* Rotherham, *into the present turnpike road on the east side of* Tankersley Park, *in the said county of* York.

CAP. LXVI.

An act to continue the term, and enlarge the powers, of an act passed in the seventeenth year of the reign of his late Majesty, for repairing the road between the town of Kingston upon Hull, *and the town of* Beverley, *in the east riding of the county of* York; *and for repairing the road from* Newland Bridge, *to the west end of the town of* Cottingham, *in the said riding.*

CAP. LXVII.

An act for repairing, widening, and keeping in repair, the high roads leading from Alfreton *in the county of* Derby, *through* Carters Lane, *to a certain place in the town of* Mansfield, *called* Stockwell, *and from the* Bridle Gate *at the division of the liberties of* Blackwell *and* Hucknall, *through the town of* Sutton *in* Ashfield, *to the* Mansfield *and* Newark *turnpike, at or near* Python Hill, *in the forest of* Sherwood, *in the county of* Nottingham.

CAP. LXVIII.

An act for continuing and enlarging the term and powers of an act made in the twenty eighth year of the reign of his late majesty King George *the Second, intituled,* An act for repairing and widening the road from *Rochdale* to *Burnley*, in the county of *Lancaster*.

CAP. LXIX.

An act for repairing and widening the road from the west end of Baxter Gate, *in the town of* Whitby, *to the south end of* Lockton Lane, *in the parish of* Middleton, *in the county of* York.

CAP. LXX.

An act for enlarging the term and powers of two acts of the twelfth of King George *the First, and of the third of his late Majesty, for repairing several roads therein mentioned, in the county of* Salop; *and also for amending and widening the road from the sign of the* Horse Shoe *in* Uckington, *to* Longnor Green; *and also from the west end of* Hatcham Bridge, *to the* Cross Houses *upon the* Bridgenorth *turnpike road, in the said county.*

CAP. LXXI.

An act for extending the provisions of an act, passed in the twenty fifth year of his late Majesty, for repairing the roads from the north end of Malling Street, *near* Lewes, *and other roads in* Suffex, *to the road leading from the north end of* Offham, *to the* Spital Barn *in* Lewes *aforesaid.*

CAP. LXXII.

An act for continuing one moiety of the duties, granted by an act of the eleventh and twelfth year of King William *the Third, for the repair of* Dover Harbour, *and which have been by several other acts, continued till the twelfth day of* May, *one thousand seven hundred and sixty five; and for applying*

applying the same to compleating and keeping in repair the harbour of Rye, *in the county of* Sussex, *and for more effectually compleating and keeping in repair the said harbour.*

CAP. LXXIII.

An act for paving, repairing, and cleansing, the streets, lanes, alleys, and publick passages, within the town of Whitby, *in the county of* York; *and for preventing incroachments and annoyances therein; and for regulating the carriages, cartmen, and porters there.*

CAP. LXXIV.

An act for amending and supplying the deficiencies of an act passed in the second year of the reign of his present majesty King George *the Third, intituled,* An act to amend and render more effectual, several acts made for cleansing and enlighting the streets of the town of *Kingston upon Hull*, and for preventing annoyances therein.

CAP. LXXV.

An act for supplying the borough and town of Wigan, *in the county of* Lancaster, *with fresh and wholsome water.*

CAP. LXXVI.

An act for repairing and widening the road from Beverley *to* Kexby Bridge, *in the county of* York.

CAP. LXXVII.

An act for continuing and enlarging the term and powers of an act made in the twenty sixth year of the reign of his late Majesty, intituled, An act for repairing and widening the road leading from *Piper's Inn*, in the parish of *Ashcot*, in the county of *Somerset*, to and through *Glastonbury* and *Wells* to the *White Post*, in the great western road, to the city of *Bath*, and from *Wells* to *Rush Hill*, leading to the city of *Bristol*; *and for repairing and widening several other roads leading from the city of* Wells.

CAP. LXXVIII.

An act for explaining and amending an act made in the twenty sixth year of the reign of his late majesty King George *the Second, intituled,* An act for amending, widening, and repairing the road leading from *Dover* to *Barham Downs*, in the county of *Kent*; *and also for amending, widening, and repairing the road leading from* Cowgate *and* Archcliffe Fort, *in* Dover, *through* Folkstone, *to the town of* Hythe, *in the said county.*

CAP. LXXIX.

An act to enlarge the term and powers of so much of an act of the twenty ninth year of the reign of his late Majesty, for repairing and widening several roads, therein described, leading from the town of Tewkesbury, *in the county of* Gloucester, *as relates to the first district of roads therein mentioned; and for amending the road from* Comb Hill, *to a bridge near* Norton Mill, *in the county of* Gloucester, *and from* Eckington Bridge, *to join the turnpike road which leads from* Upton on Severn *to* Pershore, *in the county of* Worcester.

CAP. LXXX.

An act for repairing and widening the roads from Spalding High Bridge, *to the market place in* Donington, *and from the tenth mile stone, in the parish of* Gosbertown, *to the eighth mile stone, in the parish of* Wigtoft, *in the county of* Lincoln.

CAP. LXXXI.

An act for amending, widening, and keeping in repair, several roads leading from the Bucks Head *at* Watling Street, *to* Beckbury, *and the* New Inn; *and from the* Birches Brook *to the* Hand Post, *in the parish of* Kemberton, *in the county of* Salop.

CAP. LXXXII.

An act for widening and repairing the road leading from Ashborne, *in the county of* Derby, *over* Belpar Bridge, *to the present turnpike road from* Sheffield *and* Chesterfield *to* Derby, *at or near a place called* Openwood Gate, *and from* Belpar Bridge *to* Ripley, *in the county of* Derby.

CAP. LXXXIII.

An act for repairing and widening the road from Bramcott Odd House, *in the county of* Nottingham, *to the* Cross Post *upon* Smalley Common, *in the county of* Derby, *and from* Ilkeston *to the towns of* Heanor *and* Shipley, *in the said county of* Derby, *and from* Trowell, *in the county of* Nottingham, *to the town of* Nottingham.

CAP. LXXXIV.

An act for repairing and widening the roads from Melton Mowbray, *in the county of* Leicester, *to the* Guide Post *in* Saint Margaret's Field, Leicester, *and from the town of* Leicester, *to the town of* Lutterworth, *in the said county, and other roads therein mentioned.*

CAP.

CAP. LXXXV.

An act for repairing and widening the road from Scots Dyke, *in the county of* Dumfries, *by or through the villages of* Langholm *and* Hawick *to* Haremoſs, *in the county of* Roxburgh.

CAP. LXXXVI.

An act to amend and render more effectual two ſeveral acts paſſed in the twenty fourth and twenty eighth years of the reign of his late Majeſty, for repairing the high roads in the county of Edinburgh, *to and from the city of* Edinburgh, *and from* Cramond Bridge *to the town of* Queensferry, *in the county of* Linlithgow.

CAP. LXXXVII.

An act for repairing ſeveral roads leading from the town of Bideford, *in the county of* Devon.

CAP. LXXXVIII.

An act for amending, widening, and keeping in repair, ſeveral roads leading from the town of Cardiff, *and ſeveral other towns and places in the county of* Glamorgan.

CAP. LXXXIX.

An act for the better relief and employment of the poor in the hundred of Mutford *and* Lothingland, *in the county of* Suffolk.

CAP. XC.

An act for the better relief and employment of the poor in the hundreds of Loddon *and* Clavering, *in the county of* Norfolk.

CAP. XCI.

An act for the better relief and employment of the poor in the hundred of Wangford, *in the county of* Suffolk.

CAP. XCII.

An act for the better paving of the ſtreets and lanes, and for preventing nuiſances and other annoyances, in that part of the pariſh of Portſea, *in the county of* Southampton, *commonly called* Portſmouth Common.

CAP. XCIII.

An act for the better ſupplying the town of Knareſborough, *and that part of the townſhip of* Scriven with Tenter Gate *adjoining upon the ſaid town, with water.*

ANNO REGNI

GEORGII III.

REGIS

Magnæ Britanniæ, Franciæ, & Hiberniæ,

QUINTO.

At the parliament begun and holden at *Westminster*, the Nineteenth Day of *May*, *Anno Dom.* 1761, in the First Year of the Reign of our Sovereign Lord *GEORGE* the Third, by the Grace of God, of *Great Britain*, *France*, and *Ireland*, King, Defender of the Faith, &c.

And from thence continued by several prorogations to the Tenth Day of *January* 1765, being the Fourth Session of the Twelfth Parliament of *Great Britain*.

CAMBRIDGE:

Printed by JOSEPH BENTHAM, Printer to the UNIVERSITY; for CHARLES BATHURST, opposite St. Dunstan's Church in Fleet-street, London. 1765.

A

TABLE

OF THE

STATUTES

PUBLICK and PRIVATE,

Passed *Anno quinto*

GEORGII III. *Regis*.

Being the Fourth Session of the Twelfth Parliament of GREAT. BRITAIN.

PUBLICK ACTS.

AN act for importation of salted beef, pork, bacon, and butter, from *Ireland*, for a limited time.

II. An act for continuing and granting to his Majesty certain duties upon malt, mum, cyder, and perry, for the service of the year one thousand seven hundred and sixty five.

III. An act for extending the time granted by an act passed in the third year of the reign of his present Majesty, for allowing his Majesty's subjects to import their goods and effects, being the produce of certain places ceded to *France* and *Spain* by the late treaty of peace, upon payment of the same duties as they would have been liable to if the same places had remained in his Majesty's possession.

IV. An act to indemnify such persons as have omitted to qualify themselves for offices and employments; and to indemnify justices of the peace, deputy lieutenants, officers of the militia, or others, who have omitted to register or deliver in their qualifications within the time limited by law, and for giving further time for those purposes.

V. An act for granting an aid to his Majesty by a land tax to be raised in *Great Britain*, for the service of the year one thousand seven hundred and sixty five.

VI. An act for the regulation of his Majesty's marine forces while on shore.

VII. An act for punishing mutiny and desertion; and for the better payment of the army and their quarters.

VIII. An act for the more easy and speedy recovery of small debts within the hundreds of *Blackheath*, of *Bromley* and *Beckenham*, of *Rokesly*, otherwise *Ruxley*, and of *Little* and *Lessness*, in the county of *Kent*.

IX. An act for the more easy and speedy recovery of small debts within the hundreds of *Chippenham*, *Calne*, and *Damerham North*, and lordship or liberty of *Corsham*, in the county of *Wilts*.

X. An act to permit the free importation of cattle from *Ireland*.

XI. An act for rendering more effectual an act made in the twelfth year of the reign of her late majesty Queen *Anne*, intituled, *An act for providing a publick reward for such person or persons as shall discover the longitude at sea*, with regard to the making experiments of proposals made for discovering the longitude.

XII. An act for granting and applying certain stamp duties, and other duties, in the *British* colonies and plantations in *America*, towards further defraying the expences of defending, protecting, and securing the same; and for amending such parts of the several acts of parliament relating to the trade and revenues of the said colonies and plantations, as direct the manner of determining and recovering the penalties and forfeitures therein mentioned.

XIII. An act for impowering the commissioners for putting in execution the several acts passed for paving, cleansing, and lighting, the squares, streets, and lanes, within the city and liberty of *Westminster*, and parts adjacent, to collect certain tolls on *Sundays*, upon the several roads therein mentioned, and apply the same for the purposes of the said acts.

XIV. An act for the more effectual preservation of fish in fish ponds and other waters; and conies in warrens; and for preventing the damage done to sea banks, within the county of *Lincoln*, by the breeding conies therein.

XV. An act for enlarging the times limited for executing and performing several provisions, powers and directions, in certain acts of this session of parliament.

XVI. An act for altering the times of payment of certain annuities, established by two acts made in the thirty third year of the reign of his late Majesty, and in the second year of the reign of his present Majesty.

XVII. An act to confirm all leases already made by archbishops and bishops, and other ecclesiastical persons, of tythes and other incorporeal hereditaments, for one, two, or three life or lives, or twenty one years; and to enable them to grant such leases, and to bring actions of debt for recovery of rents reserved and in arrear on leases for life or lives.

XVIII. An act for continuing an act, made in the thirty first year of his late Majesty's reign, for encouraging the growth and cultivation of madder in that part of *Great Britain* called *England*, by ascertaining the tythe thereof.

XIX. An act for raising a certain sum of money by loans or exchequer bills, for the service of the year one thousand seven hundred and sixty five.

XX. An act for explaining and rendering more effectual two acts, one made in the twelfth year of the reign of Queen *Anne*, intituled, *An act for providing a publick reward for such person or persons as shall discover the longitude at sea*; and the other in the twenty sixth year of the reign of King *George* the Second, intituled, *An act to render more effectual an act made in the twelfth year*

of

of the reign of her late majesty Queen Anne, *intituled*, An act for providing a publick reward for such person or persons as shall discover the longitude at sea, *with regard to the making experiments of proposals made for discovering the longitude; and to enlarge the number of commissioners for putting in execution the said act.*

XXI. An act for appointing commissioners to put in execution an act of this session of parliament, intituled, *An act for granting an aid to his Majesty by a land tax, to be raised in* Great Britain, *for the service of the year one thousand seven hundred and sixty five*, together with those named in two former acts for appointing commissioners of the land tax; and for indemnifying persons who have acted as commissioners of the land tax, by virtue of estates of or above a certain value, though the same were not rated or assessed at the value of one hundred pounds *per annum*; and for limiting a time within which suits and prosecutions shall be commenced, with respect to the qualifications of persons who shall act as commissioners of the land tax.

XXII. An act for the further encouragement of the *British* white herring fishery.

XXIII. An act for granting annuities, to be attended with a lottery, to satisfy and discharge certain navy, victualling, and transport bills; and for charging the payment of such annuities on the sinking fund.

XXIV. An act to oblige agents for prize money to account for such sums of money as remain in their hands unclaimed, the property of any of his Majesty's land forces; and for the application thereof.

XXV. An act to alter certain rates of postage, and to amend, explain, and enlarge, several provisions in an act made in the ninth year of the reign of Queen *Anne*, and in other acts relating to the revenue of the post office.

XXVI. An act for carrying into execution a contract made, pursuant to the act of parliament of the twelfth of his late majesty King *George* the First, between the commissioners of his Majesty's treasury and the duke and dutchess of *Atholl*, the proprietors of the *Isle of Man*, and their trustees, for the purchase of the said island and its dependencies, under certain exceptions therein particularly mentioned.

XXVII. An act to provide for the administration of the government, in case the crown should descend to any of the children of his Majesty, being under the age of eighteen years; and for the care and guardianship of their persons.

XXVIII. An act to impower the high court of *Chancery* to lay out, upon government securities, a sum of money therein mentioned, out of the common and general cash in the bank of *England* belonging to the suitors of the said court; and to apply the interest arising therefrom, towards augmenting the income of the masters of the said court.

XXIX. An act for repealing the duties now payable upon raw silk imported, and for granting other duties in lieu thereof; for allowing a drawback on the exportation of raw or thrown silk to *Ireland*, and for prohibiting the exportation of raw silk from *Ireland*.

 XXX. An

XXX. An act for more effectually supplying the export trade of this kingdom to *Africa*, with such coarse printed callicoes, and other goods of the product or manufacture of the *East Indies*, or other places beyond the *Cape of Good Hope*, as are prohibited to be worn and used in *Great Britain*; for encouraging the importation of bugles into this kingdom; for the better supply of the export trade thereof; and for discontinuing the bounty payable in *Great Britain*, and all bounties and allowances in *Ireland*, upon the exportation of corn, grain, malt, meal, and flour, from thence to the *Isle of Man*.

XXXI. An act to discontinue, for a limited time, the duties upon wheat and wheat flour imported; and also the bounty payable on the exportation of wheat and wheat flour.

XXXII. An act to enable his Majesty, with the advice of his privy council, to prohibit the exportation of wheat, wheaten meal, flour, bread, biscuit, and starch, during the next recess of parliament, at such time, and in such manner, as the necessity of the time may require, and he, in his wisdom, shall think convenient and needful.

XXXIII. An act to amend and render more effectual, in his Majesty's dominions in *America*, an act passed in this present session of parliament, intituled, *An act for punishing mutiny and desertion, and for the better payment of the army and their quarters.*

XXXIV. An act for applying the money granted in this session of parliament, for defraying the charge of the pay and cloathing of the militia of that part of *Great Britain* called *England*, for one year, beginning the twenty fifth day of *March*, one thousand seven hundred and sixty five; and for punishing militia men for neglecting their duty.

XXXV. An act for granting to his Majesty certain duties on the exportation of coals; and of several *East India* goods; and upon policies of assurance for retaining, upon the exportation of white callicoes and muslins, a further part of the duties paid on the importation thereof; and for obviating a doubt with respect to stamp duties imposed upon deeds by two former acts.

XXXVI. An act to explain, amend, and enforce the several laws now in being relating to the raising and training the militia within that part of *Great Britain* called *England*.

XXXVII. An act for laying certain duties upon *Gum Senega* and *Gum Arabic* imported into or exported from *Great Britain*, and for confining the exportation of *Gum Senega* from *Africa* to *Great Britain* only.

XXXVIII. An act to continue part of an act made in the thirtieth year of the reign of his late majesty King *George* the Second, intituled, *An act to render more effectual the several laws now in being, for the amendment and preservation of the publick highways and turnpike roads of this kingdom*; and for making further provisions for the preservation of the said roads.

XXXIX. An act for more effectually preventing the mischiefs arising to the revenue and commerce of *Great Britain* and *Ireland*, from the illicit and clandestine trade to and from the *Isle of Man*.

XL. An act for granting to his Majesty a certain sum of money

ney out of the ſinking fund; for applying certain monies therein mentioned for the ſervice of the year one thouſand ſeven hundred and ſixty five; for further appropriating the ſupplies granted in this ſeſſion of parliament; for allowing to the receivers general of the duties on offices and employments in *Scotland* a reward for their trouble; and for allowing further time to ſuch perſons as have omitted to make and file affidavits of the execution of indentures of clerks to attornies and ſolicitors.

XLI. An act for the relief of inſolvent debtors.

XLII. An act for redeeming one fourth part of the joint ſtock of annuities eſtabliſhed by an act made in the third year of his preſent Majeſty's reign, in reſpect of ſeveral navy, victualling, and tranſport bills, and ordnance debentures.

XLIII. An act for the better ſecuring, and further improvement, of the revenues of cuſtoms, exciſe, inland and ſalt duties; and for encouraging the linen manufacture of the *Iſle of Man*; and for allowing the importation of ſeveral goods the produce and manufacture of the ſaid iſland, under certain reſtrictions and regulations.

XLIV. An act for repealing the act made in the laſt ſeſſion of parliament, intituled, *An act for veſting the fort of* Senegal, *and its dependencies, in the company of merchants trading to* Africa; and to veſt as well the ſaid forts and its dependencies, as all other the *Britiſh* forts and ſettlements upon the coaſt of *Africa*, lying between the port of *Sallee* and *Cape Rouge*, together with all the property, eſtate and effects of the company of merchants trading to *Africa*, in or upon the ſaid forts, ſettlements and their dependencies, in his Majeſty; and for ſecuring, extending and improving the trade to *Africa*.

XLV. An act for more effectually ſecuring and encouraging the trade of his Majeſty's *American* dominions; for repealing the inland duty on coffee, impoſed by an act made in the thirty ſecond year of his late majeſty King *George* the Second; and for granting an inland duty on all coffee imported (except coffee of the growth of the *Britiſh* dominions in *America*); for altering the bounties and drawbacks upon ſugars exported; for repealing part of an act made in the twenty third year of his ſaid late Majeſty, whereby bar iron made in the ſaid dominions was prohibited to be exported from *Great Britain*, or carried coaſtwiſe; and for regulating the fees of officers of the cuſtoms in the ſaid dominions.

XLVI. An act for altering the ſtamp duties upon admiſſions into corporations or companies; and for further ſecuring and improving the ſtamp duties in *Great Britain*.

XLVII. An act for encreaſing the fund for payment of the ſums of money directed, by an act made in the thirty ſecond year of the reign of his late majeſty King *George* the Second, to be applied in augmentation of the ſalaries of the puiſne judges in the court of *King's Bench*, the judges in the court of *Common Pleas*, the barons of the coif in the court of *Exchequer* at *Weſtminſter*, and the juſtices of *Cheſter*, and the great ſeſſions for the counties of *Wales* for the time being; and for applying certain ſums in augmentation of the ſalaries of the ſaid judges and juſtices, and of the judges in the courts of ſeſſion and *exchequer* in

Scotland, for a certain time previous to the commencement of the augmentations established by the said act.

XLVIII. An act for prohibiting the importation of foreign manufactured silk stockings, silk mits and silk gloves into *Great Britain*, and the *British* dominions; and for rendering more effectual an act passed in the third year of the reign of his present Majesty, for explaining, amending and rendering more effectual an act made in the nineteenth year of the reign of King *Henry* the Seventh, intituled, *Silk works*.

XLIX. An act to prevent the inconveniencies arising from the present method of issuing notes and bills by the banks, banking companies, and bankers, in that part of *Great Britain* called *Scotland*.

L. An act to enlarge the powers of, and to render more effectual the several acts passed in the second, third and fourth years of his present Majesty's reign, for paving, cleansing, lighting and otherwise regulating, the squares, streets and other places, within the city and liberty of *Westminster*, and other parts in the said acts mentioned; and for extending the provisions of the said acts to the *Surry* side of *Westminster* bridge; and for enlarging the powers of the said acts with respect to squares.

LI. An act for repealing several laws relating to the manufacture of woollen cloth in the county of *York*; and also so much of several other laws, as prescribes particular standards of width and length of such woollen cloths; and for substituting other regulations of the cloth trade within the west riding of the said county, for preventing frauds in certifying the contents of the cloth; and for preserving the credit of the said manufacture at the foreign market.

LII. An act for repairing and widening the road leading from the town of *Wadhurst* in the county of *Sussex*, to the turnpike road at *Lamberhurst Pound* and *Pullen's Hill*, in the county of *Kent*; and from the top of *Pullen's Hill*, through the parishes of *Horsmonden*, *Marden*, *Yalden*, and *West Farley*, to *West Farley Street*, in the said county of *Kent*.

LIII. An act for continuing the terms of several acts, and for giving further powers for repairing the road from *Chatteris-Ferry*, to *Hammond's Eau* and *Somersham Bridge*, and for amending and widening the road from *Somersham Bridge* to the *Sheep-Market*, in *Saint Ives*; and also the road branching out of the said road near *Stocks Bridge* through *Needingworth*, to *Earith*, in the county of *Huntingdon*.

LIV. An act for repairing and widening the road from *Dunham-Ferry*, to the south end of *Great Markham Common*, in the county of *Nottingham*.

LV. An act to continue the term, and to vary and enlarge the powers, of an act passed in the twenty fifth year of his late Majesty, for repairing the road from *Wallingford* in the county of *Berks*, to *Wantage*, and from thence to *Farringdon*, and also from *Wantage* to *Idson*, in the said county, so far as the same relate to the road leading from *Wallingford* to *Wantage*, and from thence to *Farringdon*; and for discontinuing the said term and powers, so far as the same relate to the road leading from *Wantage* to *Idson*;

and for repairing the road leading from the north east corner of *Nuffield Common*, by the pariſh church of *Nuffield*, otherwiſe *Tuffield*, in the county of *Oxford*, to the commencement of the ſaid turnpike road leading from *Wallingford* to *Wantage*.

LVI. An act for repairing and widening the road leading from *Porthaethwy Ferry* to *Holyhead*, in the county of *Angleſey*.

LVII. An act for continuing the term, and altering and enlarging the powers of an act paſſed in the thirtieth year of the reign of his late majeſty, For amending, widening and keeping in repair the roads leading from the village of *Milford* in the county of *Surrey*, through *Petworth*, to the top of *Dunckton Hill*, and from *Petworth* to *Stopham Bridge*, in the county of *Suſſex*.

LVIII. An act for repairing, widening and keeping in repair, ſeveral roads in and near *Great Torrington*, in the county of *Devon*.

LIX. An act for repairing and widening ſeveral roads leading from the quay at *Lymington*, in the county of *Southampton*.

LX. An act for continuing and rendering more effectual, two acts paſſed in the twelfth year of King *George* the Firſt, and the twentieth of his late Majeſty, for repairing the ſeveral roads therein mentioned in the counties of *Eſſex* and *Suffolk*; and for repairing and widening ſeveral other roads in the counties of *Eſſex* and *Hertford*.

LXI. An act for repairing, widening and keeping in repair, ſeveral roads leading to and from *Crewkerne*, in the county of *Somerſet*.

LXII. An act for enlarging the term and powers of two acts of the thirteenth of *George* the Firſt, and of the ſixteenth of his late Majeſty, for repairing ſeveral roads leading from the town of *Warminſter*, in the county of *Wilts*; and for amending ſeveral other roads near the ſaid town; and for repealing ſo much of an act made in the firſt year of the reign of his preſent Majeſty, for repairing ſeveral roads therein mentioned, in the ſaid county, as relates to the road within the town of *Heyteſbury*; and for other purpoſes therein mentioned.

LXIII. An act for repairing and widening the roads leading from the turnpike road at *Kipping's Croſs* in the pariſh of *Brenchley*, in the county of *Kent*, through the pariſhes of *Brencnley*, *Horſmonſden* and *Goudhurſt*, by the left hand ſide of *Iden Green*, to the turnpike road on *Wilſley Green*, in the pariſh of *Cranbrooke*; and from a place near *Goudhurſt Gore*, through the pariſh of *Marden*, to *Stile Bridge* in the ſaid pariſh, and from *Underden Green*, in *Marden* aforeſaid, to *Wanſhutt's Green*, in the county of *Kent*.

LXIV. An act for repairing, widening, and keeping in repair, the road leading from the turnpike road on *Hurſt Green*, in the county of *Suſſex*, through *Etchingham* and *Burwaſh*, to the extent of the ſaid pariſh of *Burwaſh*, in the ſaid county.

LXV. An act for rebuilding the pariſh church of *Alhallows on the Wall*, in the city of *London*; and for rebuilding the houſe belonging to the rector of the ſaid pariſh; and for purchaſing ſeveral pieces of ground and tenements thereon, to render the paſſages to and from the ſaid church and houſe more commodious.

LXVI. An act to continue the term, and enlarge the powers, of an act paſſed in the ſecond year of the reign of his preſent

Majesty, for repairing and widening the road from *Mullens Pond*, in the county of *Southampton*, to the eighteen mile stone from the city of *Salisbury*, and several other roads in the said act mentioned; and also for repairing and widening several other roads leading out of the said roads, and for other purposes therein mentioned.

LXVII. An act for amending the road from the *Pinfold* in *Balby*, in the county of *York*, to *Workfop*, in the county of *Nottingham*.

LXVIII. An act for repairing, widening, and keeping in repair, the road leading from the turnpike road at *Wrotham Heath*, in the county of *Kent*, to the turnpike road leading from *Croydon* to *Godstone*, in the county of *Surrey*.

LXIX. An act for repairing and widening the roads from the south end of *Newton Abbott* to the passage way in *Kinswear*, opposite *Clifton Dartmouth Hardness*, and from the end of a lane leading out of the turnpike road between *Newton Abbott* and *Totnes*, towards *Abbotts Kerswell*, to *Five Lanes*; and from *Langvers Barn* to the said turnpike road, between *Newton Abbott* and *Totnes*; and from *Galmpton Warborough* to *Monks Bridge* and *Brixham Quay*; and from *Langvers Barn* to the north end of *Paington* town, all in the county of *Devon*.

LXX. An act for repairing and widening the roads from *Keyberry Bridge* to the passage at *Shalldon*; and from the said bridge to the pier or harbour of *Torkey*, in the county of *Devon*.

LXXI. An act for repairing and widening the road from *Tonbridge* to *Maidstone*, and from *Watts Cross* to *Cowden*, in the county of *Kent*.

LXXII. An act for amending and widening the road from the sign of the *Coach and Horses* in *Birstol*, to the turnpike road at *Nunbrook*; and from *Bradley Lane* to the town of *Huddersfield*, in the west riding of the county of *York*.

LXXIII. An act for repairing and widening the road from *Great Grimsby Haven*, at or near a place called the *Upper Sand End*, to *Wold Newton Church*; and from *Nuns Farm* to the *Mill Field*, in the parish of *Irby*, in the county of *Lincoln*.

LXXIV. An act for enlarging the powers of several acts for repairing the road from *Stump Cross* to *Newmarket Heath* and the town of *Cambridge*, and from *Foulmire* to *Cambridge*, and other roads adjoining thereto, so far as the same relate to the road from *Foulmire* to *Cambridge*, and the said other roads adjoining thereto.

LXXV. An act for enlarging the term and powers of so much of an act made in the twenty seventh year of the reign of his late majesty, for repairing several roads in the counties of *Dorset* and *Devon*, as relates to the road from *Penn Inn*, in the county of *Dorset*, to the work-house at the east end of the town of *Honiton*, in the county of *Devon*, and to the road from the intrenchment on *Askerwell Hill* to *Penn Inn*, and from *Bridport* to *Beamister*; and for repairing and amending several other roads therein mentioned in the counties of *Dorset* and *Devon*.

LXXVI. An act for repairing, widening and keeping in repair, several roads leading from *Kidwelly*, in the county of *Carmarthen*; and also several roads leading from *Llandilo*, in the said county.

LXXVII. An

LXXVII. An act for enlarging the terms and powers of several acts of the ninth and twelfth years of Queen *Anne*, and of the thirteenth of King *George* the First, and of the fourteenth of his late Majesty, for repairing the highways leading from *Royston*, in the county of *Hertford*, to *Wansford Bridge*, in the county of *Huntingdon*, so far as relates to the middle and south divisions of the road comprized in the said acts; and for amending the road from the town of *Huntingdon* to the causeway at or near the west end of the town of *Somersham*, in the said countyof *Huntingdon*.

LXXVIII. An act for repairing, widening and keeping in repair, the road from *Welford Bridge*, in the county of *Northampton*, through *Husband's Bosworth* and *Great Wigston*, to *Milston Lane*, in the town of *Leicester*.

LXXIX. An act to continue the term, and alter and enlarge the powers, of an act passed in the third year of his present Majesty, for repairing, widening, turning and keeping in repair, the road from the town of *Cambridge* to *Ely*, and from thence to *Soham*; and for building a bridge cross the river *Ouze*, at or near a place called *Stretham Ferry*, in the county of *Cambridge*; and for repairing and widening, and making several other roads, adjoining to the roads directed to be repaired and widened by the said act.

LXXX. An act for continuing the terms of several acts, and for giving further powers for repairing the road leading from *Chapel on the Heath*, in the county of *Oxford*, to *Bourton on the Hill*, in the county of *Gloucester*.

LXXXI. An act for cleansing and lighting the streets, lanes, and passages, within the towns of *Manchester* and *Salford*, in the county palatine of *Lancaster*; and for providing fire engines and fire-men; and for preventing annoyances within the said towns.

LXXXII. An act to enlarge certain powers granted by an act passed in the twenty second year of the reign of King *George* the Second, intituled, *An act for enlarging and maintaining the harbour of* Ramsgate, *and for cleansing, amending and preserving the haven of* Sandwich.

LXXXIII. An act for amending the road from *Chatterris Ferry*, through *Chatterris* and *Marsh*, to *Wisbech Saint Peters*; and from thence to *Tid Gote* in the *Isle of Ely*; and from *Wisbech* aforesaid, through *Outwell*, to *Downham Bridge* in the county of *Norfolk*; and for repealing the several acts for repairing the said road between *Wisbech* and *March*.

LXXXIV. An act for repairing and widening the road from *Newcastle under Line* to *Hassop*; and from *Middle Hills* to the *Macclesfield* turnpike road, near *Buxton*; and also the road branching out of the said first mentioned road at *Cobridge*, to *Burslem*; and to the *Uttoxeter* turnpike at *Shelton*, in the county of *Stafford*.

LXXXV. An act for repairing and widening the roads from *Bawtry Bridge*, in the county of *Nottingham*, to *Hainton*, in the county of *Lincoln*; and from *North Willingham* to the north end of the lane betwixt *Dexthorpe* and *Langton*, and from *West Raisin* to *Pilford Bridge*; and from the great road near *Bishop Bridge* to *Bishop Norton Common*; and from the hamlet of *Morton* to *Epworth*;

Epworth; and from *Haxey Field*, to the *Trent* at *Kinnald Ferry*, in the county of *Lincoln*.

LXXXVI. An act for enlarging the term and powers of an act made in the twenty fifth year of the reign of his late Majesty, for repairing the high road from the town of *Shrewsbury* through *Cressage*, *Harley*, *Much Wenlock*, by *Muckley Cross*, and through *Morville*, to *Bridgenorth*, in the county of *Salop*; and for amending several other roads near or adjoining thereto.

LXXXVII. An act to amend several acts passed in the fourth and sixth years of King *George* the First, and in the eleventh and twenty fourth years of King *George* the Second, for repairing several roads from the *Stones End* in *Kent Street*, and *Bermondsey Street*, *Southwark*, to *Dartford*, and to the extent of the parish of *Lewisham*, next *Bromley* and *Beckenham*, in the county of *Kent*; and for extending the said acts to the repair of the roads leading from the end of the present turnpike to the west end of *Stroud Green*, and to *Farnborough Well*, and to the *Stones End* in *London Street*, *Greenwich*, and to the north end of *Burnt Ash Lane*, in the parish of *Lee*, and from the west end of *Greenwich Park Wall* to *Woolwich Warren*; and for making an allowance out of the tolls arising by the said acts to the trustees for putting in execution an act of the twenty second year of King *George* the Second, *for opening and making a new road from the east end of* New Street, *in the parish of* Saint John, Southwark, *to and through the several places therein mentioned*; *and for keeping the said road in repair for the future.*

LXXXVIII. An act for repairing and widening the road from *Barton Waterside house*, to *Riseham Hedge Corner*, and several other roads in the county of *Lincoln*, therein mentioned.

LXXXIX. An act for the building a bridge over the river *Tay*, at or near the town of *Perth*, in the county of *Perth*.

XC. An act for repairing and widening the road from the *Alfreton* turnpike road, near a place called *Little Robbins*, in the parish of *Mansfield*, in the county of *Nottingham*, through *Woolley Moor*, to the *Nottingham* turnpike road, near *Tansley*, in the county of *Derby*, and from *Woolley Moor*, to the *Chesterfield* turnpike road at *Kelstidge*, in the county of *Derby*.

XCI. An act for vesting certain glebe lands, belonging to the rectory of the parish church of *Saint Christopher*, in the city of *London*, in the governor and company of the bank of *England*; and for making a recompence to the rector of the said parish, and his successors, in lieu thereof; and for obviating certain doubts in an act passed in the thirty third year of the reign of his late Majesty, for widening certain streets, lanes and passages, within the city of *London*.

XCII. An act for explaining and amending, and likewise for enlarging the term and powers granted by a certain act of parliament, passed in the twenty fifth year of the reign of his late majesty King *George* the Second intituled, *An act for amending several roads leading from the town of* Taunton, *in the county of* Somerset.

XCIII. An act for repairing, widening, turning, altering, and keeping in repair, the roads leading from the port town and borough

rough of *Minehead*, through *Dunstan* and *Timberscombe*, to *Hele Bridge*, and through the town of *Dulverton*, and by the river and *Brushford Green* to *Exbridge*, in the county of *Somerset*, and from thence to *Batham Bridge*, in the town of *Bampton*, in the county of *Devon*; and also the road leading from the said port town and borough of *Minehead*, through *Carhampton* and *Billbrooke* to *Harrow Gate*, in the parish of *Stogumber*, in the county of *Somerset*; and also the road leading from *Carhampton* aforesaid, through the town of *Watchet*, in the parish of *Saint Decumans*, in the county of *Somerset*, to or near the village of *Rydon*, and by *Long Cross Barn*, to the end of the *Bridgewater* turnpike road, in the town of *Nether Stowey*, in the county of *Somerset*; and also from the said town of *Watchet* to *Tower Hill*, in the village of *Williton*, in the parish of *Saint Decumans*, and from the said town of *Watchet*, by way of *Five Bells* to *Fair Cross*, and from thence to *Stickle Path*, over *Brendon Hill*, to *Robery Lane*, and to *Bampton*, in the said county of *Devon*.

XCIV. An act for repairing the church of the united parishes of *All Saints* and *Saint John*, in the town of *Hertford*.

XCV. An act for repairing and widening the road, leading from a street called *The Hundred*, at *Romsey*, through *Chilworth*, to the river at *Swathling*, in the county of *Southampton*, and for connecting the same with the road leading from the city of *Winchester*, through *Hursley*, to *Chandler's Ford*; and from *Hursley* aforesaid, to the turnpike road at *Romsey* aforesaid; and also for repairing and widening the road leading from the river at *Swathling* aforesaid, through *Botley*, to the turnpike road at *Sherril Heath*, in the said county of *Southampton*.

XCVI. An act for repairing and widening the road from *Alford* to *Boston*, and from thence to *Cowbridge*, in the county of *Lincoln*.

XCVII. An act for the better relief and employment of the poor, in the hundreds of *Loes*, and *Wilford*, in the county of *Suffolk*.

XCVIII. An act to enlarge the term and powers of an act made in the twenty fourth year of his late Majesty, for repairing the road from *Crossford Bridge* to *Manchester*, and for amending the road from *Crossford-Bridge* aforesaid, to a certain place in *Altrincham*, in the county palatine of *Chester*.

XCIX. An act for amending and widening the road, from the city of *York*, by *Grimston Smithy*, to *Kexby Bridge*, and from *Grimstone Smithy* aforesaid, to a certain gate, at the upper end *Garraby Hill*, in the county of *York*.

C. An act for repairing and widening the road from *Stockport*, in the county of *Chester*, to *Saxon's Lane End*, in the county of *Lancaster*, and from the cross, in *Ashton-Under-Line* in the said county of *Lancaster*, to *Doctor's-Lane-Head*, in the county of *York*; and also the road branching out of the first-mentioned road, in the township of *Bredbury*, to *Mottram*, in the said county of *Chester*.

CI. An act for repairing and widening the roads from the *Little Bridge*, over the end of the drain, next *Wisbeach River*, lying between *Roper's Fields*, and the *Bell Inn* in *Wisbeach*, in the *Isle of Ely*, to the sign of the *Bear* in *Walsoken*, in the county of *Norfolk*; and from *Walsoken Bridge*, lying over the same drain,

to

to the said sign of the *Bear*, and to *Lord's Bridge*, in *Islington*; and from thence to the west ends of *Maudlin Bridge* and *German's Bridge*, in the county of *Norfolk*; and from the east end of *German's Bridge* aforesaid, to the west end of *Long Bridge*, in *South Lynn*, in the borough of *King's Lynn*, in the said county of *Norfolk*; and from *Islington* aforesaid, to *Cross Keys Wash*, in the said county.

CII. An act for repairing and widening several roads, leading from between the second and third mile stones, on the turnpike road between the town and county of *Poole*, and *Winborn Minster*, in the county of *Dorset*, to *Bratton Corner*, in the county of *Somerset*.

CIII. An act to enlarge the term and powers of an act made in the twenty seventh year of his late Majesty, for opening, making, widening, and keeping in repair, a road from *Ratcliffe Highway*, through *Cannon Street*, in the county of *Middlesex*, and other roads in the said act mentioned; and for lighting, watching and watering the said roads.

CIV. An act for enlarging the term and powers granted by an act passed in the twenty sixth year of his late Majesty's reign, intituled *An act for repairing and widening the roads therein mentioned, leading to and from the towns of* Shepton Mallet *and* Ivelchester, *in the county of* Somerset; *and for repairing the roads from* Shepton Mallet *to* Leighton, *and from* Shepton Mallet *to* Long Cross Bottom.

CV. An act for repairing and widening the road, from the turnpike road in *Banbury*, in the county of *Oxford*, through *Daventre*, and *Cottesbach*, to the south end of *Mill Field*, in the parish of *Lutterworth*, in the county of *Leicester*.

CVI. An act to continue the term and render more effectual an act passed in the thirtieth year of the reign of his late Majesty, for repairing and widening the roads leading from *Spalding High Bridge*, through *Littleworth*, and by *Frognall*, and over *James Deeping Stone Bridge*, in the county of *Lincoln*, to *Maxey Outgang*, in the county of *Northampton*, adjoining to the high road there.

CVII. An act for repairing and widening the road from the *Great Bridge*, in the borough of *Warwick*, through *Southam* and *Daventry*, to the town of *Northampton*.

CVIII. An act for amending and widening the road, from the north end of *Old Malton Gate*, in the town and borough of *New Malton*, to the town of *Pickering*, in the county of *York*.

PRIVATE ACTS.

1. An act for dividing and inclosing the open and common fields, common meadows, common pastures, and commonable waste grounds, in the manor and parish of *Podington*, in the county of *Bedford*.

2. An act for dividing and inclosing the open common fields, common pastures, common meadows, common grounds, lanes, and waste ground, within the manors and parish of *Hardingstone* and *Cotton*, in the county of *Northampton*.

3. An act for naturalizing *John William Plauel*, *John James Long*, *Jacob Nadal*, and *Christopher Henry Beaumer*.

4. An act for naturalizing *Luder Lang.*

5. An act for naturalizing *Christian James Strackboven.*

6. An act for dividing and inclosing the open commons, common fields, meadows, and grounds, lying in the hamlet of *Donnington*, in the parish of *Stow on the Wold*, in the county of *Gloucester.*

7. An act for dividing and inclosing certain open and common fields, common pastures, common meadows, and commonable waste grounds, in the manor, hamlet, and tything, of *Westcote*, in the parish of *Waddesdon*, in the county of *Bucks.*

8. An act for dividing and inclosing the common fields, meadows, pastures, and waste grounds, in the manor of *Long Eaton*, in the parish of *Sawley*, in the county of *Derby.*

9. An act for dividing and inclosing the open and common fields, and grounds, within the township of *Ulrome*, otherwise *Owram* in *Holderness*, in the county of *York.*

10. An act for dividing and inclosing the open and common fields, common meadows, common pastures, common grounds, and waste grounds, in the parish of *North Kilworth*, in the county of *Leicester.*

11. An act for annexing the rectory of *Colerne*, in the county of *Wilts*, to the office of warden of the college of *Saint Mary*, of *Winchester*, in *Oxford.*

12. An act for vesting the settled estates of *Ann Wilson*, widow, and *Ann Wilson*, her daughter, an infant, in trustees, to be sold, for discharging the debts and incumbrances affecting the same.

13. An act to enable *Richard Duppa*, clerk (heretofore called *Richard Hancorn*) and his heirs male, to take and use the surname and arms of *Duppa*, pursuant to the will of *Baldwin Duppa* esquire, deceased.

14. An act to enable *William Ager*, and his issue, to take and use the surname of *Turner.*

15. An act to enable *John Jennings* esquire (now called *John Smith*) and his heirs, to take and use the surname of *Smith*, pursuant to the will of *Thomas Smith*, deceased.

16. An act to enable *William Marwood* esquire, lately called *William Metcalfe*, and his issue, to take, use, and bear, the surname and arms of *Marwood*, pursuant to the will of *Jane Turner*, widow, deceased.

17. An act to enable *William Nevile Blondeau* esquire, and his issue, to take and use the surname of *Hart.*

18. An act to enable *Benjamin Francis Tribe* esquire (and his heirs) to take and use the surname of *Poole*, pursuant to the will of *Elizabeth Ludwell*, deceased.

19. An act for naturalizing *Dirk Jager* of the city of *London*, merchant.

20. An act for naturalizing *Andrew Fuhrer*, and *Rene Labutte.*

21. An act for naturalizing *John Elias Jaquery*, *Peter Samuel Darbonnier*, *Daniel Henriod*, *John James Osvald*, and *John Francis Anthony Rivaz.*

22. An act for naturalizing *Peter Anthony Sapte*, and *David Francis Sapte.*

23. An act for dividing and inclosing the open and common arable

arable fields, meadows, paſtures, commons, and waſte grounds, in the lordſhip and pariſh of *Flamborough*, in the county of *York.*

24. An act for dividing and allotting the commons or waſtes, and the common fields, and ings, in the manor and townſhip of *Everingham*, in the county of *York*; and for other purpoſes therein mentioned.

25. An act for dividing and incloſing the open and common fields, common meadows, common paſtures, common grounds, and commonable lands, lying within the townſhips and hamlets of *Horley* and *Hornton*, in the pariſh of *Horley* aforeſaid, in the county of *Oxford*.

26. An act for dividing and allotting certain open fields, meadows, and ſtinted paſtures, in the townſhip of *Fenton*, in the pariſh of *Kettlethorp*, in the county of *Lincoln*, and a certain free common, called *The Eaſt Moor*, in the ſame pariſh.

27. An act for dividing and incloſing certain common fields, meadows, and common paſtures, in the townſhip and pariſh of *Newton*, in the county of *Lincoln*, and certain rights of paſture in *Kettlethorpe* in the ſaid county.

28. An act for dividing and incloſing the common fields, common meadows, common paſtures, common grounds, and waſte grounds, of and in the manor of *Wellingborough*, and of and in the manor of *Wellingborough*, formerly belonging to the college of *Irtlingborough*, and in the pariſh of *Wellingborough*, in the county of *Northampton*.

29. An act for dividing and incloſing the open common fields and meadows, common paſtures, and other commonable lands, lying within the pariſh of *Lowdham*, in the county of *Nottingham*.

30. An act for dividing and incloſing ſeveral open and common fields, lands, and grounds, in the pariſh of *Benton*, in the eaſt riding of the county of *York*.

31. An act for dividing and incloſing certain open common fields, lands, and grounds, in *Ellerker*, in the pariſh of *Brantingham*, in the eaſt riding of the county of *York*.

32. An act for dividing and incloſing certain open common fields, lands, and grounds, in *Brantingham*, and *Thorpe Brantingham*, in the pariſh of *Brantingham*, in the eaſt riding of the county of *York*.

33. An act for dividing and incloſing the open and common fields, heath, and waſte grounds, and commonable places, in the lordſhip and liberties of *Draycot*, in the pariſh of *Bourton*, in the county of *Warwick*.

34. An act for dividing and incloſing the common fields and common grounds, in the manor and pariſh of *Denford*, in the county of *Northampton*.

35. An act for dividing and incloſing the open and common fields, common meadows, common paſtures, and commonable waſte grounds, in the manor and pariſh of *Twywell*, in the county of *Northampton*.

36. An act for dividing and incloſing the open and common fields, common meadows, and other commonable lands, within the manor and pariſh of *Snitfield*, otherwiſe *Snitterfield*, in the county of *Warwick*.

37. An act for dividing and inclosing the open lands and grounds, lying in the pariſh of *Bretferton*, in the county of *Worceſter*.

38. An act for dividing and incloſing the common fields, commons, and waſte grounds, in the pariſh of *Rothwell*, in the county of *Lincoln*.

39. An act for dividing and incloſing the common fields and grounds, lying in the pariſh of *Lenchwick* and *Norton*, and the borough of *Eveſham*, in the county of *Worceſter*.

40. An act for dividing and incloſing certain pieces or parcels of land, in the pariſhes of *Doncaſter* and *Cantley*; and for draining and preſerving the ſaid lands; and alſo ſeveral other lands and grounds, in the ſeveral pariſhes of *Roſſington* and *Wadworth*, in the weſt riding of the county of *York*.

41. An act for confirming the allotments of, and for incloſing, the common and ſeveral waſte lands, in the manor and pariſh of *Sebraham*, otherwiſe *Sebergham*, in the county of *Cumberland*.

42. An act for dividing and incloſing the common called *Scarning Common*, and the greens called *Pound Green*, *Pope's Green*, and *Bett's Green*, lying within the ſeveral manors of *Scarning Hall*, *Drayton Hall*, and *Northern Hall*, *Scarning Parva*, *Guntons* and *Roughelme*, on the part of *Hoe*, or ſome or one of them, and in the pariſh of *Scarning*, in the county of *Norfolk*.

43. An act for dividing and incloſing the common fields, common paſtures, common meadows, common grounds, and waſte grounds, of and in the pariſh and liberties of *Spratton*, in the county of *Northampton*.

44. An act for dividing and incloſing the commons and waſte grounds within the manor of *Cropton*, in the county of *York*, and for other purpoſes therein mentioned.

45. An act for dividing, allotting, and incloſing, divers parcels of common or waſte grounds, within the manors of *Appleton* and *Lymm*, in the county of *Cheſter*.

46. An act for incloſing and dividing ſeveral lands and grounds, in the townſhip of *Kirkhammerton*, in the pariſh of *Kirkhammerton*, in the county of *York*.

47. An act for confirming and eſtabliſhing an exchange agreed to be made between *Thomas Holles* duke of *Newcaſtle*, and *Margaret Cavendiſh* dutcheſs dowager of *Portland*, of ſeveral parts of their ſettled eſtates, in the county of *Nottingham*; and for ſettling the lands given in exchange to each party, to ſuch uſes, as the lands for which the ſame are exchanged ſtood ſettled.

48. An act for veſting an eſtate, called *Woodlands*, in the county of *Wilts*, belonging to the maſter, fellows, and ſcholars, of the college called *Clare Hall*, in the univerſity of *Cambridge*, in *William* earl of *Shelburne*, and his heirs.

49. An act for confirming and eſtabliſhing an agreement, between the maſter, brethren, and ſiſters, of the hoſpital of the lord *Haſtings* of *Loughborough*, founded at *Stoke Poges*, in the county of *Bucks*, and *Thomas Penn* eſquire, for exchanging certain lands and premiſſes in *Stoke Poges* aforeſaid; and for rendering the ſaid agreement more effectual, for the purpoſes thereby intended.

50. An act to enable *Fanny Fowler*, ſpinſter, a minor, to convey,

vey, aſſign, and ſettle, her real and perſonal eſtate, in the manner therein mentioned, on her intended marriage with Sir *Brooke Bridges* baronet.

51. An act for ſale of certain lands in the county of *Kent*, ſettled upon the rector of the pariſh of *Saint George Bloomſbury*, in the county of *Middleſex*; and for applying the money ariſing thereby, in manner therein mentioned, for the benefit of the ſaid rector.

52. An act to apply a certain ſum of money ariſing by the ſale of a houſe in *Tetbury*, in the county of *Glouceſter*, and by donations of ſeveral perſons, for rebuilding the pariſh church and chancel of *Tetbury*, aforeſaid.

53. An act for the ſale of lands and tenements, in the county of *Cumberland*, late the eſtate of *William Dobinſon* genleman, deceaſed for the benefit of the children of *Joſeph Banks*, his nephew, deceaſed.

54. An act to diſſolve the marriage of *John Nixon*, with *Heſter Spencer*, his now wife, and to enable him to marry again; and for other purpoſes therein mentioned.

55. An act to enable *Brigg Price* eſquire, and his iſſue, to take and uſe the ſurname of *Fountaine*, and to bear the arms of Sir *Andrew Fountaine* knight, deceaſed.

56. An act for naturalizing *Henrietta Roſa Peregrina Townſend*, wife of *James Townſend* eſquire.

57. An act for naturalizing *John His*, *John Henry Ernſt*, *John Michael Platz*, and *Rudolph Lemann*.

58. An act for naturalizing *Charles Frederick Hempel*, *James Janot*, *Chriſtopher John Schultz*, *John Gottifried Klotz*, *Erdmann Chriſtopher Riemann*, and *Bernhard Johann Fleiſchmann*.

59. An act for for dividing and incloſing the open fields and commonable places, in the pariſh of *Houghton on the Hill*, in the county of *Leiceſter*.

60. An act for dividing and incloſing *Walkden Moor*, and a part of a parcel of moſs ground, called *Chatmoſs*, within the manor of *Worſley*, in the county palatine of *Lancaſter*.

61. An act for dividing and incloſing the open fields, common paſtures, and other commonable places, in *Burton Overy*, in the county of *Leiceſter*.

62. An act for dividing and incloſing ſeveral lands and grounds, in the pariſh of *Aukborough*, in the county of *Lincoln*.

63. An act for dividing and incloſing ſeveral common fields, common meadows, and waſte grounds, in the pariſh of *Emload*, in the county of *Worceſter*.

64. An act for dividing and incloſing certain moors orcommons, in the pariſh of *Wolſingham*, in the county palatine of *Durham*.

65. An act for dividing and incloſing ſeveral open and common fields, common meadows, commons, and waſte grounds, within the manor and pariſh of *Hartſhorn*, in the county of *Derby*.

66. An act for incloſing and dividing the open common fields, meadows, paſtures, and common grounds, in the manor and pariſh of *Tetford*, in the county of *Lincoln*.

67. An act for dividing and incloſing ſeveral open fields, meadows, and commons, within the lordſhip or liberty of *Wilford*, in the county of *Nottingham*.

68.

68. An act for dividing and inclosing the open and common fields, and all the commonable lands and grounds, in *Grimston*, in the county of *Leicester*.

69. An act for dividing and inclosing two moors, or commons, within the barony and manor of *Warke*, and parish of *Symondburn* in the county of *Northumberland*.

70. An act for dividing and inclosing certain open common arable fields, in the parishes of *North Cockerington* and *South Cockerington* in the county of *Lincoln*.

71. An act for dividing and inclosing certain open and common fields and grounds, within the several parishes of *Keelby* and *Stallingbrough*, in the county of *Lincoln*.

72. An act for dividing and inclosing the common fields, and common pasture, common meadow, common grounds, and waste grounds, in the manor and lordship of *Carlton upon Trent*, in the county of *Nottingham*.

73. An act for dividing and inclosing a certain common fen, in the parishes of *Aslackby* and *Dowsby*, in the county of *Lincoln*; and for draining and improving the said fen; and also certain inclosed low grounds adjoining to the said fen.

74. An act for dividing and inclosing the fen grounds, moors, sheep-walks, woodings, sike closes, open and common fields, and other commonable lands and grounds, in the parish of *Branston*, in the county of the city of *Lincoln*.

75. An act for dividing and inclosing the open and common fields, common pastures, common meadows, common grounds, and waste ground, in the lordship and liberties of *Granburrow*, in the county of *Warwick*.

76. An act for dividing and inclosing the common fields, common pastures, common meadows, common grounds, waste grounds, and commonable lands, of and in the manor, parish, and liberties, of *Long Buckby*, in the county of *Northampton*, exclusive of that part of the hamlet of *Murcot* which lies in the said parish.

77. An act for dividing and inclosing a certain common moor, or tract of waste land, within the barony or manor of *Bulbeck*, in the county of *Northumberland*.

78. An act for extinguishing certain rights of common, in the parish of *Lutcham*, alias *Litcham*, in the county of *Norfolk*.

79. An act for inclosing and dividing the high and low commons of *Austerfield*, in the county of *York*.

80. An act for dividing and inclosing the several open arable fields, undivided inclosures, commons, and wastes, lying and being within the parish of *Wadworth*, in the west riding of the county of *York*.

81. An act for dividing and inclosing the several fields, meadows, pastures, commons, and waste grounds, within the hamlets of *Ashford* and *Sheldon*, in the parish of *Bakewell*, and county of *Derby*.

82. An act for dividing and inclosing the common fields, common meadows, and other commonable lands and grounds, in the manor and parish of *Elford*, in the county of *Stafford*.

83. An act for dividing and inclosing a certain open common field, common pastures, common meadows, and waste grounds, in the manor and parish of *Somerton*, in the county of *Oxford*.

84. An act for dividing and inclosing the open and common field, common meadows, common pastures, common grounds, and commonable lands, lying within the township and hamlet of *Shutford*, in the parish of *Swalcliffe*, in the county of *Oxford*.

85. An act for dividing and inclosing certain commons, called *The High and Low Commons*, in the parish of *Tickhill*, in the counties of *York* and *Nottingham*.

86. An act for draining and improving certain low, marsh, and fen lands, lying between *Boston Haven* and *Bourn*, in the parts of *Kesteven* and *Holland* in the county of *Lincoln*.

87. An act for vesting part of the settled estates of *Dorothy* late countess dowager of *Burlington*, lying in the counties of *Middlesex*, *York*, and *Lincoln*, in trustees, to be sold and conveyed in manner therein mentioned; and for investing part of the money arising by such sale, in discharging a mortgage debt affecting the same premisses, and the residue thereof in the purchase of other manors, lands, and hereditaments, to be settled to the same uses as the said settled estates do now stand limited, or so many of them as shall be then existing.

88. An act for vesting certain undivided parts or shares belonging to the honourable *John Saint John*, an infant, and *Edward Dering*, also an infant, of and in several messuages, lands, and hereditaments, in the isle of *Thanet*, in the county of *Kent*, in trustees, to be sold; and for laying out the money arising by the sale thereof, in the purchase of other lands, to be conveyed to the use of the said *John Saint John* and *Edward Dering*, respectively, and their respective heirs; and for other purposes therein mentioned.

89. An act for making the portions provided by the marriage settlement of Sir *George Trevelyan* baronet, and dame *Julia* his wife, for their younger children, vested interests, so that the same may be raised and paid, notwithstanding the deaths of such children in the life-time of their father; and for other purposes therein mentioned.

90. An act for vesting the barony or manor of *Shipbrook*, in the county of *Chester*, part of the estate of *Henry Vernon* esquire, comprized in his marriage settlement, in trustees, to be sold, for raising money to discharge the debts and incumbrances charged upon and affecting the same, previous to the said settlement; and for other purposes therein mentioned.

91. An act for selling part of the settled estates of *Robert Dolman* esquire in *Pocklington*, and elsewhere, in the county of *York*, for discharging the debts and incumbrances of himself and *Robert Dolman* the younger, his eldest son, affecting the same; and for making provision for *Robert Dolman* the younger, and for the younger children of *Robert Dolman* the elder.

92. An act for vesting part of the settled estates of *Christopher Crowe* esquire, in the county of *York*, in him in fee simple; and

for settling other estates, in the same county, in lieu thereof.

93. An act for vesting the settled estate of *John Knowsley*, and *Elizabeth* his wife, in the county of *York*, in trustees, to be conveyed pursuant to certain articles for the purchase thereof; and for laying out the money thereby stipulated to be paid in the purchase of other lands, to be charged and settled in manner as therein mentioned.

94. An act for vesting certain estates, late of *Elizabeth Cary* widow, deceased, in the county of *Middlesex*, in trustees, in trust to sell and convey the same to *Robert Child* esquire, and for laying out the money arising by such sale in three *per centum* consolidated bank annuities, to be secured and transferred in manner therein mentioned; and for other purposes.

95. An act for divesting out of the heir at law, or other legal representative or representatives of *Edmund Neeler* deceased, the several freehold estates of the late *William Westbrook* esquire, deceased, in the counties of *Middlesex*, *Bucks*, *Kent*, and *Surrey*, and in the city of *London*; and for vesting the same in trustees, to be sold and conveyed to such persons as may already have contracted, or shall hereafter contract, to become the purchasers of any parts or shares thereof, under the directions of the court of *Chancery*.

96. An act for sale of the copyhold estates late of doctor *Robert Taylor*, deceased; and for laying out the money arising thereby, in the purchase of other lands and hereditaments, to be settled in lieu thereof; and for other the purposes therein mentioned.

97. An act to confirm and establish exchanges of land, at *Dorking* in *Surrey*, between *Charles Howard* esquire, and *Edward Walter* esquire; and between the said *Charles Howard*, and *Jonathan Tryes* esquire.

98. An act for vesting part of the real estate of *Mary Phelps* widow, deceased, given and devised by her will, in trustees, to be sold for payment of debts, legacies, and incumbrances.

99. An act for vesting several freehold and copyhold estates, in the several counties of *Essex*, *Suffolk*, *Bucks*, and *Middlesex*, and in the city of *London*, in trustees, for the sale thereof, in order to discharge the several legacies or portions bequeathed by the will of *William Hollingworth* esquire, deceased; and for other purposes therein mentioned.

100. An act for sale of the estates comprized in the marriage settlement of *John Bristow* esquire, in the county of *Norfolk*; and for applying the monies arising thereby in the purchase of other lands and hereditaments, to be settled to the uses contained in the said settlement.

101. An act for making a partition of divers lands and hereditaments, in the counties of *Lincoln* and *York*, late the estate of *Edward Ayscough* deceased, which, upon his death, belonged to his four daughters and co-heirs; and for settling the lands and hereditaments, to be allotted upon the said partition, to the

ſeveral uſes limited, of their ſeveral undivided ſhares thereof reſpectively.

102. An act for ſale of the freehold eſtate late of *Amie Broxolme* widow, deceaſed, in the pariſh of Saint *George Hanover Square*; and for laying out the money ariſing by ſuch ſale, in the purchaſe of other freehold lands and hereditaments, to be ſettled in lieu thereof.

103. An act for naturalizing *Louiſa Rudolphina Wale*, and *Greorgy Wale*.

104. An act to naturalize *Benedict Paul Wagner*.

105. An act for naturalizing *Sabine Louiſſe Winn*.

106. An act for dividing and incloſing ſeveral lands and grounds, undivided incloſures, commons, and waſtes, in or near the village or hamlet of *Marſborough*, in the townſhip of *Kimberworth*, and in the pariſh of *Rotherham*, in the county of *York*.

107. An act for dividing and incloſing the open and common fields, and common paſtures, of *Scalford*, in the county of *Leiceſter*, and all the lands and grounds within the ſame fields.

108. An act for dividing and incloſing the open and common fields, common meadows, common paſtures, and other commonable lands and grounds, in the pariſh of *Felmerſham*, in the county of *Bedford*.

109. An act for veſting divers manors, lands, and hereditaments, in the counties of *York*, *Cumberland*, *Northumberland*, and *Durham*, late the eſtate of *Henry* earl of *Carliſle*, deceaſed, in truſtees, to be ſold and diſpoſed of, in and for the payment of his debts, legacies, and incumbrances, and other the purpoſes in his will mentioned.

110. An act to enable *John* lord *Bellew*, baron of *Duleek*, in the kingdom of *Ireland*, more effectually to exerciſe his power, to raiſe certain ſums therein mentioned, out of his ſettled eſtates in the ſaid kingdom, for the portions of younger children.

111. An act for veſting the eſtate late of *Peter Wyche* eſquire, at *Goadby*, alias *Godeby Marwood*, in the county of *Leiceſter*; in truſt, to be conveyed to the moſt noble *John* marquis of *Granby*, or as he ſhall appoint; and for applying the purchaſe money in manner and for the porpoſes therein mentioned.

112. An act for dividing and incloſing the common fields, common paſtures, common meadows, common grounds, and commonable lands, within the manor or manors, and pariſh of *Syreſham*, otherwiſe *Siſeham*, in the county of *Northampton*.

113. An act for dividing and incloſing certain common fields and waſte ground, in the pariſh of *Braithwell*, in the county of *York*.

114. An act to enable *Jeremiah Rayment* the younger eſquire, and his iſſue, to take and uſe the ſurname and arms of *Hadſley*, purſuant to the will of *Robert Hadſley* eſquire, deceaſed.

115. An act for naturalizing *Henry de Miſſy*, and *Gabriel Le Royer*.

The END *of the* TABLE.

THE

STATUTES at Large, &c.

Anno quinto GEORGII III. *Regis.*

CAP. I.

An act for the importation of salted beef, pork, bacon, and butter, from Ireland, *for a limited time.*

WHEREAS *the permitting the importation of salted beef, pork, bacon, and butter, into the kingdom of* Great Britain, *from* Ireland, *for a limited time, may, at this time, be a great advantage to both kingdoms*; be it therefore enacted by the King's most excellent majesty, by and with the advice and consent of the lords spiritual and temporal, and commons, in this present parliament assembled, and by the authority of the same, That the importation of all salted beef, pork, bacon, and butter, into the kingdom of *Great Britain*, from *Ireland*, shall be, and is hereby permitted, allowed, and authorized, for and during the term of twelve months from the commencement of this act; and that all persons shall be, and are hereby exempted, freed, and discharged, from the payment of all subsidies, customs, rates, duties, or other impositions, and also from all penalties, forfeitures, payments, and punishments, for or upon account of importing or bringing salted beef, pork, bacon, or butter, into the kingdom of *Great Britain*, from *Ireland*, during the term aforesaid, other than such as herein after are mentioned in respect thereof; any act or acts of parliament to the contrary notwithstanding.

Preamble.

The importation of salted provisions allowed from Ireland for 12 months;

II. Provided always, and, to the intent that the revenue arising from salt may not be prejudiced by such importation of salted beef, pork, bacon, or butter, from *Ireland*, be it enacted, That from the commencement of this present act, during the continuance thereof, there shall be paid to such officer as the commissioners for the duties on salt for the time being shall appoint, at the port in *Great Britain* into which such salted beef, pork, bacon, or butter, shall, in pursuance of this act, be imported from *Ireland*, and before any part thereof shall be delivered out to the person or persons to whom the same shall belong, or be consigned, the sum of three shillings and four pence for every barrel or cask of salted beef or pork to be imported during the continuance of this act, containing thirty two gallons, and so in proportion for any greater or lesser quantity; and for every hundred weight of bacon, salted beef called *dried beef*,

upon payment of the following salt duties;

viz. 3s. 4d. per barrel for beef or pork;

beef,

1s. 3d. per 100 weight for all dried beef, neats tongues, and hog-meat; and 4d. per 100 weight for all ſalted butter; and ſo in proportion for all leſſer quantities.

beef, dried neats tongues, and dried hog-meat, the ſum of one ſhilling and three pence; and for every hundred weight of all ſuch ſalted butter, the ſum of four pence; and ſo in proportion for any greater or leſſer quantity than an hundred weight of any ſuch ſalted beef called *dried beef*, bacon, dried neats tongues, or dried hog-meat, as or for cuſtom or for duty, on or in reſpect thereof: the money ſo ariſing by the importation of the ſaid ſalted beef, pork, bacon, dried beef, dried neats tongues, dried hog-meat, or butter, to be paid into his Majeſty's exchequer, as part of the duties on ſalt, laid by an act of the fifth year of the reign of his late majeſty King *George* the Second, and continued by ſeveral ſubſequent acts.

The duties to be paid over into the exchequer as part of the duties on ſalt.

Proviſions landed without the ſaid duties being firſt paid, are forfeited; together with 20s. per barrel for all beef and pork, and 20s. per 100 weight for all dried meat and butter.

III. And be it further enacted by the authority aforeſaid, That if any perſon or perſons ſhall, after the commencement and during the continuance of this act, land any ſuch ſalted beef, pork, bacon, or butter, or any ſalted beef called *dried beef*, dried neats tongues, or dried hog-meat, into the kingdom of *Great Britain*, from *Ireland*, before payment of the duty or duties by this act ſpecified and directed, the ſame ſhall be forfeited and loſt, and twenty ſhillings *per* barrel for every barrel or caſk of ſuch ſalted beef or pork, and twenty ſhillings *per* hundred weight for every hundred weight of ſuch bacon, ſalted beef called *dried beef*, dried neats tongues, dried hog-meat, or ſalted butter, and ſo in proportion for any greater or leſſer quantity, to be recovered of the importer or proprietor thereof; and that it ſhall and may be lawful to and for any perſon or perſons, being an officer or officers of the cuſtoms, or of his Majeſty's duties upon ſalt, to take and ſeize all ſuch commodities as ſhall be imported and landed contrary to the true intent and meaning of this act, together with the caſks, veſſels, and package containing the ſame; and that all ſuch penalties and forfeitures ſhall be diſtributed in manner following; that is to ſay, one moiety thereof to the King, his heirs, and ſucceſſors, and the other moiety thereof, to the perſon or perſons who ſhall ſeize, ſue, or inform for the ſame; to be recovered by action of debt, bill, plaint, or information, in any of his Majeſty's courts of record at *Weſtminſter*, or in the court of *exchequer* in *Scotland*; or may be ſued for, recovered, and mitigated, as any forfeiture or penalty may be ſued for, recovered, and mitigated, by any of the laws relating to the duties on ſalt.

Recovery; mitigation, and application, of the penalties.

No drawback to be allowed on the exportation thereof elſewhere.

IV. Provided always, and be it hereby enacted, That no drawback ſhall be allowed or paid for any ſuch ſalted beef, pork, bacon, or butter, ſo imported into the kingdom of *Great Britain*, from *Ireland*, and which ſhall be exported from *Great Britain* elſewhere.

V. And be it further enacted by the authority aforeſaid, That if any action or ſuit ſhall be commenced againſt any perſon or perſons for any thing done in purſuance of this act, the defendant or efendants in any ſuch action or ſuit, may plead the general iſſue, and give this act, and the ſpecial matter, in evidence,

General iſſue.

at

at any trial to be had thereupon; and that the ſame was done in purſuance and by the authority of this act; and if it ſhall appear ſo to have been done, the jury ſhall find for the defendant or defendants: and if the plaintiff ſhall be nonſuited, or diſcontinue his action, after the defendant or defendants ſhall have appeared; or if judgement ſhall be given upon any verdict or demurrer againſt the plaintiff, the defendant or defendants ſhall and may recover treble coſts, and have the like remedy for the ſame, as any defendant or defendants hath or have in other caſes by law. Treble coſts.

CAP. II.

An act for continuing and granting to his Majeſty certain duties upon malt, mum, cyder, and perry, for the ſervice of the year one thouſand ſeven hundred and ſixty five.

Preamble. Malt act of 1 George III. further continued to 24 June, 1766. Malt in Scotland to pay 3d. per buſhel. Mum 10s. per barrel. Cyder and perry made for ſale, 4s. per hogſhead. How theſe duties are to be raiſed, &c. 20,000l. to be raiſed in Scotland. Surplus to be added to the fiſheries, &c. This act to relate to the ſame day and time as the act 1 Geo. III. did. Malt brought from Scotland by ſea, to be entered at the port of landing: brought by land, to be entered at Berwick or Carliſle. Cyder for diſtilling not chargeable. Diſtiller to give notice to officer when he diſtils cyder. Allowances for exportation of malt, 1 W. & M. On certificate of malt being exported, and ſecurity, allowance to be paid. Penalty on relanding. Malt ſteeping for exportation to be kept ſeparate till meaſured. Malſters to give notice to officers, &c. Penalty on opening the locks, &c. Malſters, on 24 June, 1765, to clear out of their warehouſes all malt within fifteen months. And ſo all future malſters. Clauſes in act 12 Annæ, & 6 Geo. 1. 5s per buſhel penalty on all corn ſteeping, or ſteeped for malt, which ſhall be found in the ciſtern or couch, ſo hard and compact as it could not be unleſs the ſame had been forced together to prevent the riſing. 100l. penalty on fraudulently conveying from the ciſtern, any ſteeping of corn, and mixing the ſame with other corn charged with the duty in the couch; or fraudulently conveying the ſame away, ſo that no gauge of ſuch corn can be taken in the couch. Penalties how to be recovered. Buyers of cyder or perry for their private uſe, not to be charged. Perſons ſelling leſs than 20 gallons to be deemed retailers. Clauſe of loan at 3l. 10s. per cent. Tallies of loan to be ſtruck, &c. Orders regiſtered and paid in courſe. No fee for regiſtering, &c. Penalty for undue preference. No undue preference, where tallies are dated or brought the ſame day: nor if ſubſequent orders be paid before ſuch as were not demanded in courſe. Orders aſſignable. Commiſſioners of the treaſury impowered to prepare any number of exchequer bills of one common ſum, or different ſums, in the principal monies. Bills to bear intereſt at 3l. 10s. per cent. per ann. Theſe bills to be numbered arithmetically. Treaſury to direct the courſe of payment for loans or exchequer bills, and to appoint cheques, &c. The bills to be placed as caſh in the exchequer, and to be iſſuable thereout in common with other monies, and to be current in the revenue. Receivers to exchange bills for ready money. Tallies to be levied for bills ſent into the exchequer. Intereſt to continue till payment. Intereſt to ceaſe whilſt the bills are in the hands of receivers, &c. Bills paid to receivers, &c. to be ſigned and dated. Intereſt to be allowed to the ſaid days. The bills may be re-iſſued both for principal and intereſt. Receivers to keep a book. Bills filled up by indorſements, or defaced, to be exchanged. Bills not exceeding 5000l. each, to be made forth at the exchequer. Forging exchequer bills, felony. How the monies ariſing by this act ſhall be applied. Treaſury on 29 Sept. 1766, to take an account of all monies raiſed and diſcharged. Unſatisfied monies to be paid out of the next aid, or out of the ſink-

ſinking fund. Commiſſioners to appoint perſons to pay off principal ſums which ſhall from time to time be in courſe of payment upon exchequer bills. Money, as brought in, to be paid to the paymaſters. Bills to be regiſtered in courſe. When intereſt to ceaſe. Paymaſters liable to the controul of the treaſury. Treaſury to ſettle ſalaries of clerks, &c. and to contract with perſons to circulate bills, &c. Contractors not diſabled from being members of parliament: may lower or raiſe the intereſt with conſent of treaſury. Contractors how to be paid. No fee to be taken. No intereſt for leſs than one penny. Charges to be paid out of the ſinking fund: to be replaced out of the firſt ſupplies. Clauſe of relief for bills loſt or deſtroyed. Bills diſcharged to be cancelled. Sinking fund appropriated to diſcharge national debts incurred before 25 Dec. 1716. Deficiency of malt tax, 3 Geo. 3. how to be ſupplied. Arrears of former duties to be applied in aid of the ſupplies granted for the year 1765.

CAP. III.

An act for extending the time granted by an act paſſed in the third year of the reign of his preſent Majeſty, for allowing his Majeſty's ſubjects to import their goods and effects, being the produce of certain places ceded to France *and* Spain *by the late treaty of peace, upon payment of the ſame duties as they would have been liable to if the ſame places had remained in his Majeſty's poſſeſſion.*

Preamble reciting act 3 Geo. 3.

WHEREAS *by an act of parliament paſſed in the third year of the reign of his preſent Majeſty, intituled,* An act for raiſing a certain ſum of money by loans or exchequer bills, for the ſervice of the year one thouſand ſeven hundred and ſixty three; and for further appropriating the ſupplies granted in this ſeſſion of parliament; and for allowing his Majeſty's ſubjects to import their goods and effects, being the produce of certain places ceded to *France* and *Spain* by the late treaty of peace, upon payment of the ſame duties as they would have been liable to if ſuch places had remained in his Majeſty's poſſeſſion; *reciting, That, by the definitive treaty of peace between his Majeſty and the crowns of* France *and* Spain, *ratified the tenth day of* March, *one thouſand ſeven hundred and ſixty three, the iſlands of* Guadeloupe, Marie Galante, Deſirade, Martinico, *and* Goree, *are ceded to* France, *and all that his Majeſty had conquered in the iſland of* Cuba *is ceded to* Spain; *and the term of eighteen months, to be computed from the day of the ratification of the ſaid treaty, is thereby allowed to* Britiſh *ſubjects to tranſport their effects from those iſlands; and alſo reciting, That the produce of thoſe places, imported into this kingdom after the reſtitution thereof to* France *and* Spain, *would be ſubject to higher duties than they were liable to during the time they remained in his Majeſty's poſſeſſion; and that to the end his Majeſty's ſubjects, having effects in the places before-mentioned, might have all due encouragement and opportunity to bring the ſame from thence, it is enacted, That it ſhould and might be lawful for any of his Majeſty's ſubjects to import into this kingdom, at any time before the firſt day of* November, *one thouſand ſeven hundred and ſixty four, and no longer, in* Britiſh *ſhips navigated according to law, directly from the places before-mentioned, any goods or effects being the* growth

growth or produce thereof respectively, upon payment of such and the like customs and duties only, as would be due and payable for the same if such places had remained and were in the possession of his Majesty; any law, custom, or usage, to the contrary notwithstanding: and whereas many of his Majesty's subjects, under sanction of the said act, sent out ships for the purpose of importing their goods and effects from the said places into this kingdom; which ships, from various circumstances, could not arrive in any of the ports of Great Britain *before the said first day of* November, *one thousand seven hundred and sixty four, the time limited by the said act: and whereas several of the said ships arrived in* Great Britain *since the said first day of* November, *one thousand seven hundred and sixty four, and the goods and effects therein imported, are now detained, being subject to further customs and duties than they would have been subject to if the said ships had arrived before the said first day of* November, *one thousand seven hundred and sixty four; and several other of the said ships are not yet arrived:* in order therefore that his Majesty's said subjects may have relief, agreeable to the good intentions of the said act, may it please your Majesty, that it may be enacted; and be it enacted by the King's most excellent majesty, by and with the advice and consent of the lords spiritual and temporal, and commons, in this present parliament assembled, and by the authority of the same, That the said goods and effects, so imported as aforesaid since the said first day of *November*, one thousand seven hundred and sixty four, shall be subject to such and the like customs and duties only, as they would have been subject and liable to if they had been imported into this kingdom any time before the said first day of *November*, one thousand seven hundred and sixty four; and it shall and may be lawful for any of his Majesty's subjects to import into this kingdom, at any time before the first day of *May*, one thousand seven hundred and sixty five, and no longer, in *British* ships navigated according to law, directly from the places beforementioned, any goods or effects being the growth or produce thereof respectively, upon payment of such and the like customs and duties only, as would be due and payable for the same if the same places had remained and were in the possession of his Majesty; any law, custom, or usage, to the contrary notwithstanding.

Goods and effects imported since 1 Nov. 1764, are to pay such duties only, as they would have been liable to, if imported before the said time; and such as shall be duly imported, in like manner, at any time before 1 May, 1765, are to be admited to like payment also.

CAP. IV.

An act to indemnify such persons as have omitted to qualify themselves for offices and employments; and to indemnify justices of the peace, deputy lieutenants, officers of the militia, or others, who have omitted to register or deliver in their qualifications within the time limited by law, and for giving further time for those purposes.

Preamble, reciting the several qualifying acts of 1 Geo. 1. 13 Car. 2, 25 Car. 2, 30 Car. 2, 18 Geo. 2, and 2 Geo. 3. Further time to 28 Nov. 1765, allowed to persons who have omitted to qualify themselves, as the said laws direct. Persons qualifying themselves in manner, and within the time appointed, recapacitated and indemnified. Offices, &c. already a. voided by judgement of a court, and filled up, confirmed. None indemnified where final judgement hath been given for the penalty incurred.

CAP. V.

An act for granting an aid to his Majesty by a land tax to be raised in Great Britain, *for the service of the year one thousand seven hundred and sixty five.*

2,037,854l. 19s. and 11d. to be raised in Great Britain. 1,989,900l. 18s. and 9d. to be raised in England, in one year, from 25 March, 1765. Personal estates (except desperate debts, stock on land, houshold goods, and loans to his Majesty) to pay 4s. in the pound. Employments of profit (except military officers of the army or navy) to pay 4s. per pound. Pensions and annuities out of the exchequer, &c. to pay, &c. lands, tenements, mines, &c. to be charged with equality and indifference, &c. Lands, &c. subject to rent-charges, annuities, &c. Commissioners of the land tax for the year 1763, to put this act in execution. Commissioners to meet on or before the 30th of April, 1765, as by the act 4 W. & M. and may subdivide themselves, &c. A list of the commissioners to act in each division, to be given to the receiver-general. Commissioners to summon fit persons to be assessors, who are to appear before them in 8 days; and then to give them a charge. Persons absenting, or refusing to serve, forfeit, not exceeding 5l. nor less than 40s. Assessors to be two at least, and sufficient inhabitants. Assessments to be brought in at a day and place prefixt. The full sum charged to be assessed. A certificate of the assessment to be brought in, with the collectors names. Assessors, &c. neglecting their duty, to be fined not above 40l. Assessors to deliver one copy of the assessments to the commissioners. Duplicates thereof to be signed, &c. and one delivered to the collectors, &c. with warrant for collecting. Commissioners required to give collectors notice at what time and place the appeal of any person who shall think himself aggrieved, by being over-rated, may be heard and determined. A duplicate in parchment to be delivered, together with the names of the assessors and collectors, to the receiver-general; and one to the remembrancer's office, by 8 August 1765, or 20 days after (all appeals first determined.) Remembrancer to give receipts gratis, on penalty of 10l. The rates to be levied on the parties, or premisses, and to be paid to the receivers-general, &c. The money collected to be paid to the receiver-general, or deputies; and they to give commissioners notice. Collectors not obliged to travel above 10 miles. Removal or death of receiver-general to be notify'd to the commissioners. 497,475l. 4s. and 8d. 1q. for the first quarterly payment, to be paid to the receivers by 24 June, 1765. The second payment by 29 Sept. 1765. The third payment by 25 Dec. 1765. The last payment by 25 March, 1766. Receiver-general within a month after receiving the full sum charged, to give the commissioners a receipt: which shall be a full discharge for payment. Receivers-general within 20 days to pay the monies into the exchequer. Receiver-general allowed 2d. in the pound. Collectors to have 3d. in the pound. Commissioners clerks to have three halfpence in the pound. Collectors may levy by distress in case of refusal of payment. Distress to be kept four days at the owner's charge; then appraised and sold, and overplus returned, &c. Commissioners to determine differences about distress. For want of distress, offender may be committed, (except a peer or peeress of Great Britain) tenants to pay the tax, and deduct so much out of the rents. Tenants discharged for what they so pay. Commissioners to settle differences between landlord and tenant. Commissioners to cause all deficiencies to be re-assessed, and made good. Assessor refusing to serve, to forfeit, not exceeding 40l. Fine not to be discharged but by commissioners who imposed it; and levied by distress or imprisonment, and paid into the exchequer, and inserted in the duplicates. Collectors detaining the money, to be imprisoned, ed, their estates seized and sold, &c. Commissioners to examine whether the sums assessed be duly collected, &c. In case of controversies in assessing commissioners, the commissioners concerned to withdraw. In default to be fined, not above 20 l. No privileged place or person exempt from this tax. Fee-farm rents, &c. to be taxed. Tenants to pay the rates. Colleges, &c. in the universities, &c. not chargeable: nor the houses or lands which before the [illegible]th of March, 1693, did belong to Christ's hospital, &c. Nor corporation of clergymens sons, Bromley college, or any other hospitals. No tenants of hospitals, &c. to claim any exemption. Such tenants not discharged, who by leases are obliged to pay taxes. Commissioners to determine how far lands, &c. belonging to hospitals, &c. not exempted by name, ought to be charged. All hospitals, lands, &c. assessed by 4 W. & M. liable to this aid, and no other. Receivers of fee-farm rents, &c. to allow 4 s. per pound to the parties, without fee, on penalty of 20 l. Auditors, &c. setting tenants *insuper* for what ought to be allowed, or refusing allowance, to forfeit 100 l. Such fee-farm rents only to have an allowance of 4 s. per pound, as are answerable to the crown, or were purchased according to 22 & 23 Car. 2. The owners to allow the same to the party paying. Lists of pensions, &c to be delivered gratis to the assessors. Taxes on pensions, &c. not paid, to be stopt in the exchequer. A true account to be kept of the money stopt. Persons to be taxed in the parish where they dwell. No proviso to lessen the full sum by this act to be levied. Contracts between landlord and tenant, touching taxes, not to be avoided. All places to pay where usually assessed. West Barnfield to be assessed in the lathe of Skray, Com' Kent. Northmore, Com' Oxon. in Bampton. Charlbury, &c. in Chadlington. Leeds, Com' Ebor. in Skyrack. Ombersley, Com' Worcester, in Oswaldslow hundred. Aldemaston, in Oswaldslow hundred. Parish of Yardley, in Halfshire hundred. Forest of Chute, where the first 4 s. aid was assessed. Upton, in Pershore hundred. Calder and Ayre, at Wakefield and Leeds. Inhabitants of apartments, &c. in Somerset House, to be assessed in the same proportion with those in Lancaster liberty. General issue. Treble costs. Where lands, &c. are unoccupied, and no distress found, Collectors may distrain at any time after. Wood may be cut down, and sold for distress. (Timber trees excepted) Tithes, tolls, &c, not paid within 6 days after demand, &c. may be seized and sold. Receiver-general returning persons, who have paid the tax, to be in arrear, forfeits treble damages to the party grieved, and to his Majesty double the sum so returned. Commissioners to assess the assessors. None compelled to be assessors out of the limits of the city, &c. Assessments on foreign ministers houses to be paid by the landlords. In places extraparochial commissioners to nominate assessors and collectors, &c. No commissioner, &c. liable to any other penalties than such as are inflicted by this act. Commissioners not to act without taking the oaths by 1 Geo. 1. &c. Acting before oaths taken, forfeit 200 l. Officers to pay where employed, &c. Officers in Chancery to be assessed in the rolls liberty. Annuities where rated. Pensions, where payable. Personal estates, where persons resident, &c. Persons not housholders, where resident. Absent persons to be rated where they were last resident. Goods, &c. to be assessed where they shall be. Persons doubly rated, discharged on certificate. Not to extend to Scotland, Ireland, Jersey, or Guernsey. Persons avoiding the tax charged treble. Housholders to give an account of their lodgers, on forfeiture of 5 l. Shares in the New River, &c. to pay 4 s. per pound. Shares in the Fire Offices, and in the Lights, and the King's Printing House to pay 4 s. per pound. Merchants, bank of England, post office, &c. to be paid by the governors. Governors, &c. of the river-waters, and water works, refusing to pay, the collectors impowered to levy the sum by distress and sale. Papists 18 years of age not taking the oaths 1 W. & M. to pay double: unless taken within 10 days after the commissioners first meeting. Persons 18 years of age refusing the oaths, to pay double. Commissioners to summon suspected persons, &c. Quakers to subscribe the declaration 1 W. & M. Commissioners to double assess Papists, where assessors omit. Tenants discharged from double rates. King's Bench,

Bench, Marshalsea prison, &c. to be assessed in Saint George's parish, &c. Officers of the Marshalsea court refusing to pay, &c. Collectors by warrant from commissioners may distrain. If no goods sufficient, officer to be imprisoned. Fleet prison to be assessed in St. Bride's. Officers at Stoke Damrel, near Plymouth, to be assessed within the town of Plymouth, &c. Hospital at East Stonehouse to be assessed also within the town of Plymouth, &c. 20l. to be paid out of the sum assessed on the said officers, in aid of the assessment on East Stonehouse. Water-works in Southwark to be assessed in Surrey. Water-works in Westminster to be assessed there. Offices, &c. in Whitehall and St. James's, to be there assessed. Collectors of the water-works in Colchester chargeable. Collectors for the water-works in New Windsor, chargeable. Patent officers to bishopricks to pay where assessed in 1693. Commissioners appointed to act, without subdividing the parish of St. Andrew Holborn, in Middlesex. The parish of St. George Hanover Square to be charged with a distinct quota from the parish of St. Martin in the fields. Debates arising concerning the joint quota; the commissioners who are inhabitants of either parish to withdraw, or to be fined a sum not exceeding 20 l. The parishes of St. John, St. Peter, and Berchington, to be charged in Dover liberty, according to the assessment 4 W. & M. Lands not worth 20s. per annum, not chargeable. Collectors keeping monies in their hands, to forfeit 40 l. Receiver-general misapplying the monies to forfeit 500 l. Commissioners of the treasury, &c. not to divert the payments into the exchequer. No *Noli prosequi*, &c. in any suit against this act. Commissioners to abate where lands are overcharged, and to re-assess, &c. or raise it on persons undercharged. Receiver-general answerable for deputies. Sub-collector not to travel above ten miles, &c. Receivers not nominating deputies, &c. to forfeit 100l. Commissioners for the county at large may act for any city, &c. Mayors, bailiffs, &c. to act as commissioners specially appointed. Members of parliament to be taxed at their mansion-houses. First meeting for the west riding of York at Pontefract; north riding at Thirsk; east riding at Beverley. No commissioner capable to act in any county at large, unless rated at 100 l. per ann. (Merioneth, Cardigan, &c. excepted.) Commissioners for Anglesea, &c. to act, if taxed at 60 l. per ann. Commissioners may act for any city, being inhabitants, or inns of court, &c. Attornies, &c. not to be commissioners, without possessing 100 l. per ann. No commissioner of the city of London, or liberty of St. Martin le Grand, to act, unless rated at 20 l. per ann. of his own estate, &c. No commissioner of the city, &c. of Westminster to act, unless rated at 20 l. per ann. of his own estate. Persons disabled, presuming to act, to forfeit 50l. Collectors of the new water-works in Exon, chargeable. Her Majesty the Queen not chargeable; nor her royal highness the princess dowager of Wales; nor his royal highness the duke of Cumberland, nor the princess Amelia. Superannuated sea-officers not to pay, &c. nor poor knights of Windsor. Residentiaries in what cases not chargeable. Nor 100l. per ann. to the poor clergy of the isle of Man. Nor pages of honour. Receivers-general to give notice of failures in payment of the taxes. Commissioners for Lincoln to act in Lincoln Close. And for the county, in St. Martin Stamford Baron. Auditor to keep a register, &c. Deputies to pay for principals, and on nonpayment liable to distress. Receiver-general to give a list of money received by him, at the time and place appointed. On refusal, to forfeit any sum not exceeding 20 l. Collectors may keep so much money as any 2 commissioners judge reasonable. No receiver to return an *Insuper* upon any county, &c. after 3 years, for monies in arrear; but the same to be a debt on him and his securities. Sheriff, on writs of *Distringas*, to return issues after the rate of 5 l. per cent. of the sum set *insuper*; and process to issue thereupon, &c. Water-works in Shrewsbury chargeable. Who shall have the benefit only of overplus sums uncharged. Clause for the ease of protestants, to whom lands, &c. have come, which have been doubly taxed. Where lands formerly doubly taxed are liable only to a single assessment; Commissioners, on complaint, to examine into the truth thereof, and to certify the same to the barons of the Exchequer, before 29 Sept. 1765; who are to discharge the overplus before the last day of Nov. 1765. Certificates of

the

the sums discharged to be produced to the commissioners at their next meeting. Commissioners may summon collectors, who have converted land tax monies to their own use, or their heirs, &c. and on examination may issue their warrants for paying such monies to his Majesty's use. The payments made according to the commissioners warrants, &c. shall be discharges to the collectors, or their heirs, &c. Collectors not paying, may be imprisoned, and their estates seized and sold. Arrears of former land taxes to be levied by the present commissioners. No receiver general, or his agents, may sue the county for a robbery, unless the persons carrying the money be 3 in company. Tolls or duties on turnpikes not chargeable by this or any former act. Commissioners may, before 29 Sept. 1765, summon assessors, who have not charged their estates since 6 May, 1717, and examine them upon oath, and award satisfaction, to be levied and paid to the collectors Commissioners, &c. to distinguish and set down the gross sums assessed for double taxes, to be transmitted in the exchequer. Assessments on the town of Cambridge to be raised on manors, &c. and on fishings, &c. on the river Cam. On whom, and when, yearly assessments on fairs, &c. to be collected. Distress on default of payment, how to be levied. Tenants of booths, &c. to pay the rates, and deduct them out of their rents, &c. 47,954 l. 1 s. 2 d. to be raised in Scotland, by an 8 months cess of 5,994 l. 5 s. 1 d. 3 q. per mensem; to be rated as the tax roll now is or shall be settled by themselves. The first two months cess to be paid by 24 June, 1765. Second 29 Sept. 1765. Third 25. Dec. 1765. Fourth 25 March, 1766. Commissioners for putting this act in execution in Scotland. And execution to be done as by the said acts. First meeting to be at the head burghs on 30 April, 1765. All clauses in former acts relating to the bringing in the cess, &c. to be in full force. No persons in Scotland holden to produce their receipts after 3 years. Debtor owing money in Scotland at 6 per cent. to retain a 6th part of 6 per cent. from 11 Nov. 1764, to 11 Nov. 1765. 47,954 l. 1 s. 2 d. to be raised free of all charges, and to be paid at Edinburgh. No person to be a commissioner of the land tax in Scotland, who is not infeoft of 100 l. Scots per ann. real rent, in the county where he acts. Exception. Commissioners in Scotland to take the oaths, and subscribe the assurance. Provost, &c. of any royal borough may act as a commissioner. Clause of loan at 3 l. 10 s. per cent. Tallies of loan to be struck. &c. Orders to be registered and paid in course. No Fee for registering, &c. Penalty for undue preference. No undue preference where tallies are dated or brought the same day: nor if subsequent orders be paid before such as were not demanded in course. Orders assignable. Commissioners of the treasury impowered to prepare any number of exchequer bills of one common sum, or different sums, in the principal monies. Bills to bear interest at 3 l. 10 s. per cent. per ann. These bills to be numbered arithmetically. Treasury to direct the course of payment for loans or exchequer bills, and to appoint cheques, &c. The bills to be placed as cash in the exchequer, Clauses in the malt tax act relating to exchequer bills, extended to this. How the monies arising by this act shall be applied. Treasury on 29 Sept. 1766, to take an account of all monies raised and discharged. Unsatisfied monies to be paid out of the next aid, or out of the sinking fund. The monies to be replaced out of the first supplies. Deficiency of the land tax, 3 Geo. 3. how to be supplied.

CAP. VI.

An act for the regulation of his Majesty's marine forces while on shore.

WHEREAS *it may be necessary for the safety of this kingdom, and the defence of the possessions of the crown of* Great Britain, *that a body of marine forces should be employed in his Majesty's fleet and naval service, under the direction of the lord high admiral, or commissioners for executing the office of lord high admira.*

of

of Great Britain: *and whereas the ſaid marine forces may frequently be quartered on ſhore, where they will not be ſubject to the laws relating to the government of his Majeſty's forces by ſea; yet nevertheleſs, it being requiſite for the retaining of ſuch forces in their duty, that an exact diſcipline be obſerved, and that marines who ſhall mutiny, or ſtir up ſedition, or ſhall deſert his Majeſty's ſervice, be brought to a more exemplary and ſpeedy puniſhment than the law will allow*; be it enacted, &c.

After 25 March 1765, during the continuance of this act, every marine officer and private man on ſhore, who ſhall mutiny or deſert, &c. or liſt in any other regiment, &c. or ſhall be found ſleeping on, or ſhall deſert, his poſt, or hold illegal correſpondence with the enemies of his Majeſty, or ſhall ſtrike, or diſobey his ſuperior officer; ſhall ſuffer death, or ſuch puniſhment as a court-martial ſhall inflict. The lord high admiral, or commiſſioners for executing that office, may grant a commiſſion to hold general courts-martial, &c. Courts-martial may inflict corporal puniſhment for immoralities, &c. Lords, &c. of the admiralty impowered to make articles for puniſhment of mutiny and deſertion, &c. and to conſtitute courts-martial. None to be adjudged of life or limb, but for crimes expreſſed to be ſo puniſhable by this act. General court-martial not to conſiſt of leſs than 13; and the preſident to be a field officer, or officer next in ſeniority, not under the degree of a captain. May adminiſter an oath to witneſſes. Officers to be ſworn. The oath. The oath. The judge advocate to be ſworn. The oath. In ſentences of death, nine officers to concur, &c. Hours of trial. The party tried, intitled to a copy of the ſentence and proceedings of the court martial. Original proceedings, &c. of courts-martial, to be tranſmitted to the ſecretary of the admiralty, &c. None to be tried a ſecond time for the ſame offence. Sentence not to be reviſed more than once. Deſerters beyond ſea, &c. may be tried here or in Ireland. This act not to exempt any on ſhore from ordinary proceſs. Perſons acquitted by the civil magiſtrate, may only be caſhiered by a court martial. Perſons accuſed of capital crimes, &c. to be delivered over to the civil magiſtrate, &c. Fictitious names allowed by his Majeſty's order upon the muſter-rolls, for the maintenance of officers widows, not to be conſtrued a falſe muſter. Paymaſter to pay the full pay of ſuch men to the receiver. Conſtables, &c. to quarter officers and men in inns, ale-houſes, &c. But in no diſtillers houſes, or ſhopkeepers, or in any private houſes. Penalty on officers quartering private men contrary to this act, &c. Perſons aggrieved by being quartered on, may complain to any juſtices, and be relieved. Officers and marines to be furniſhed at the rates herein ſet for their proviſions. What inn-holders may allow men quartered on them, inſtead of meat. Penalty on taking money to excuſe any perſon from quartering. Commanding officer may exchange marines in their quarters. Conſtables to billet the ſame accordingly. No paymaſter, &c. to make deductions out of officers or private mens pay. Exceptions. Officers to give notice to innkeepers of ſubſiſtence money in their hands. Rates of ſubſiſtence to be paid to innkeepers, &c. for marines quarters. Officers not giving notice of ſubſiſtence-money, and paying quarters, paymaſter to ſatisfy them out of the company's next pay, and officer to be caſhiered. On moving from quarters, the officer to make up accounts, and give certificates for money due, &c. Paymaſter to pay the ſum certified for. Officers, &c. to be quartered in Scotland, as the laws in force at the union direct. Juſtices to order conſtables to provide carriages for the marine forces on their march. Rates for carriages. Penalty on officers forcing waggons to travel more than one day's journey, &c. Penalty on conſtables, &c. neglect. Treaſurers of the county to repay the conſtable's extraordinary charges. The money for thoſe purpoſes how to be raiſed. No waggon, &c. to carry above 20 hundred weight. Carriages in Scotland how to be provided. Marines wives, &c. not to be quartered without conſent. Penalty. Penalty on officers and marines deſtroying the game.

Con-

Constables may apprehend deserters, and carry them before a justice. Justices to commit them, and transmit an account to the secretary of the admiralty. Gaol keeper to receive the subsistence of deserters. Reward for taking up deserters. Penalty on persons concealing deserters, or buying their arms, clothes, &c. This act to extend to deserters, &c. in Ireland. Continuance of this act. Offences against former acts may be enquired of and punished as under this act, provided no person be liable to be tried for offences committed 3 years before issuing their warrant for trial; except in cases of desertion only. No volunteer liable to process, unless for some criminal matter, or unless for a real debt of the value of 10l. Oath of the debt to be made before a judge, and a memorandum thereof marked on the back of the process; otherwise prisoner to be discharged, with costs. Plaintiff giving notice, may file a common appearance, and proceed to judgement and execution. Penalty on constables, &c. neglecting to quarter marines. Penalty on taking money to excuse any person from quartering, and on victuallers refusing to receive marines. To prevent abuses in quartering, justices may order constables to give an account of the number of officers, and private men, and where quartered. Clause for relief of persons hastily listing themselves. As often as it shall be necessary, officers of the marine and land forces may sit in conjunction upon courts-martial; taking rank according the seniority of their commissions. Marine forces being borne as part of the complement of any ships of war, are liable to be governed by the rules established by act 22 Geo. 2.

CAP. VII.

An act for punishing mutiny and desertion; and for the better payment of the army and their quarters.

Preamble.

WHEREAS *the raising or keeping a standing army within this kingdom, in time of peace, unless it be with consent of parliament, is against law: and whereas it is judged necessary by his Majesty, and this present parliament, that a body of forces should be continued for the safety of this kingdom, the defence of the possessions of the crown of* Great Britain, *and the preservation of the balance of power in* Europe, *and that the whole number of such forces should consist of seventeen thousand four hundred and twenty one effective men, including two thousand six hundred and twenty eight, invalids: and whereas, during the late just and necessary war in which his Majesty has been engaged against* France *and* Spain, *some part of his Majesty's forces, exceeding the number aforesaid, has been employed in distant parts beyond the seas, which must render the time when such forces may return home uncertain; some of which are intended to be broke, and others reduced, as soon after such arrival as conveniently may be: and whereas no man can be fore-judged of life or limb, or subjected in time of peace to any kind of punishment within this realm, by martial law, or in any other manner than by the judgement of his peers, and according to the known and established laws of this realm; yet nevertheless, it being requisite for the retaining all the before-mentioned forces in their duty, that an exact discipline be observed, and that soldiers who shall mutiny, or stir up sedition, or shall desert his Majesty's service within this realm, or the kingdom of* Ireland, Jersey, Guernsey, Alderney, *and* Sark, *or the islands thereto belonging, be brought to a more exemplary and speedy punishment than the usual forms of the law will allow;* be it therefore enacted, &c.

Number of forces 17,421 including 2,628 invalids

2 After

After 24 March 1765, during the continuance of this act, every officer and private man, who shall mutiny or desert, &c. or list in any other regiment, &c. or shall be found sleeping on, or shall desert, his post, or hold illegal correspondence with the enemies of his Majesty, or shall strike, or disobey his superior officer; shall suffer death, or such punishment as a court-martial shall inflict. The King may grant a commission to hold a court-martial, &c. Courts-martial may inflict corporal punishment for immoralities, &c. General courts-martial not to consist of less than 13; and the president to be field a officer, or officer next in seniority, not under the degree of a captain. May administer an oath to witnesses. Officers to be sworn. The oath. The oath. The judge advocate to be sworn. The oath. In sentences of death, nine officers to concur, &c. Hours of trial. The party tried, intitled to a copy of the sentence and proceedings of the court-martial. Original proceedings, &c. of courts-martial to be transmitted to the judge advocate general in London, &c. None to be tried a second time for the same offence, except in case of appeal. This act not to exempt soldiers from ordinary process. Penalty on false certificates to excuse soldiers from musters. Penalty on officers making false musters, &c. Fictitious names allowed by his Majesty's order upon the muster rolls, for the maintenance of officers widows, not to be construed a false muster. Muster-master to give notice of muster to mayor, &c. Penalty on muster-master neglecting so to do. Muster-rolls to be signed by the mayor, &c. Penalty on persons offering themselves to be falsly mustered. Horses falsly mustered, to be forfeited, &c. Forfeiture how to be levied. Officer embezilling, &c. military stores, to be cashiered and forfeit 100l. and the damage to be made good by sale of his goods and chattels; for want of distress, the person to be committed. Application of the forfeiture. Muster-master, &c. taking a muster to make oath. The oath. Muster-rolls, though transmitted without the oath indorsed to the paymasters general, to be good vouchers to the auditor. Penalty on agent, &c. detaining officer's or soldier's pay. Weekly rates. Penalty on agents disobeying of orders. Surgeon, &c. within ten miles of London, &c. to certify who are sick; and commanding officer, who are employed in raising recruits. Penalty on officer mustering persons by wrong names. Constables, &c. to quarter officers and men in inns, ale houses, &c. But in no distillers houses, or shopkeepers, or in any private houses. Penalty on constables, &c. quartering solders in private houses, &c. Penalty on officers quartering soldiers contrary to this act, &c. Persons aggrieved by being quartered on, may complain to any justices, and be relieved. No justice having any military office, to be concerned in billeting his soldiers. Officers and soldiers to pay rates for their provisions. What inn-holders may allow men quartered on them, instead of meat. Penalty on taking money to excuse any person from quartering. Dragoons, &c. and their horses, to be billeted in the same house. Manner of changing men and horses. Clause relating to a soldier's settlement for his wife and children. Officers, &c. to be quartered in Scotland, as the laws in force at the union direct. No paymaster, &c. to make deductions out of officers or private mens pay. Exceptions. Treasury may issue out the money due for cloathing, every two months. Paymasters to deduct the off reckonings. Officers to give notice to innkeepers of subsistence-money in their hands. Rates of subsistence to be paid to inn-keepers, &c. for soldiers quarters. Penalty on officers not paying subsistence-money. On nonpayment of quarters, the officer to make up accounts, &c. No muster in Westminster, &c, but in the presence of two or more justices. Constables, &c. may billet soldiers in Westminster, &c. Petty constables, &c. to quarter soldiers in their respective divisions. Constables, &c. to deliver lists at quarter sessions, on oath, of inhabitants, and soldiers quartered in their respective divisions; to be inspected without fee. Copies of such lists to be wrote by the clerk, at 2d. per sheet, containing 150 words. Penalty on default. Penalty on giving defective lists. How to be levied. This act to extend to Jersey, &c. Muster-rolls to be closed on the day of muster, and returned to the paymaster of the forces, &c. Penalty. Justices may order constables to provide carriages. Rates for carriages. Penalty on officers forcing waggons to travel more than 1 day's journey, &c. Penalty on constables, &c. neglect. Treasurers

ſurers of the county to repay the conſtable's extraordinary charges. The money for thoſe purpoſes how to be raiſed. No waggon, &c. to carry above 30 hundred weight. Carriages in Scotland how to be provided. Soldiers wives, &c. not to be quartered without conſent. Penalty. Penalty on officers or ſoldiers deſtroying the game. How the account of every regiment ſhall be kept. Penalty on paymaſters, &c. Penalty on colonels. Non-commiſſion officer embezelling ſoldier's pay to be reduced, &c. Juſtices may commit deſerters. Reward for taking up deſerters. Penalty on perſons concealing deſerters, or buying their arms, clothes, &c. Penalty on officer breaking open houſe without warrant. His Majeſty impowered to make articles of war. None to be adjudged of life or limb, but for crimes expreſſed to be ſo puniſhable by this act. Deſerters beyond ſea, &c. may be tried here or in Ireland. This act to extend to deſerters, &c. in Ireland, &c. Perſons acquitted by the civil magiſtrate, may only be caſhiered by a court-martial. Perſons accuſed of capital crimes, &c. to be delivered over to the civil magiſtrate, &c. Paymaſters, &c. to account with executors. Perſons ſued may plead the general iſſue. Treble coſts. All ſuits to be brought in ſome of the courts of record at Weſtminſter or Dublin, or the court of ſeſſion in Scotland. Continuance of this act. Penalties againſt the act 1 Geo. 1. where to be ſued for. No volunteer liable to proceſs, unleſs for ſome criminal matter, or unleſs for a real debt of the value of 10l. Oath of the debt to be made before a judge, and a memorandum thereof marked on the back of the proceſs; plaintiff may file a common appearance. Penalty on taking money to excuſe any perſon from quartering; or victuallers refuſing to quarter ſoldiers. Juſtices may order conſtables to give an account of the number of ſoldiers quartered, &c. How the troops are to pay in paſſing over ferries in Scotland. Clauſe for relief of perſons haſtily liſting themſelves. Perſons refuſing the ſaid relief, to be proceeded againſt as if duly liſted. Offences againſt former mutiny acts puniſhable by this act. None liable to be tried or puniſhed for offences againſt former acts, unleſs committed within 3 years; except for deſertion. Officers, &c. of the train of artillery ſubject to this act. American troops, acting in conjunction with Britiſh forces, liable to the ſame martial laws. Officers and ſoldiers of the American troops ſent over to Great Britain, to be quartered and billeted as the Britiſh forces, and under the ſame regulations and penalties. This act not to extend to the militia farther than is directed by the militia laws. As often as it ſhall be neceſſary, officers of the land and marine forces may ſit in conjunction upon courts-martial; taking rank according to the ſeniority of their commiſſions.

CAP. VIII.

An act for the more eaſy and ſpeedy recovery of ſmall debts within the hundreds of Blackheath, *of* Bromley *and* Beckenham, *of* Rokeſly, *otherwiſe* Ruxley, *and of* Little *and* Leſſneſs, *in the county of* Kent.

CAP. IX.

An act for the more eaſy and ſpeedy recovery of ſmall debts within the hundreds of Chippenham, Calne, *and* Damerham North, *and the lordſhip or liberty of* Corſham, *in the county of* Wilts.

CAP. X.

An act to permit the free importation of cattle from Ireland.

WHEREAS *an act, paſſed in the thirty ſecond year of the reign of his late majeſty King* George *the Second, intituled,* An act Preamble. Act 32 Geo. 2.

act to permit the free importation of cattle from *Ireland* for a limited time, *is near expiring*; be it therefore enacted by the King's moſt excellent majeſty, by and with the advice and conſent of the lords ſpiritual and temporal, and commons in this preſent parliament aſſembled, and by the authority of the ſame, That from and after the end of this ſeſſion of parliament, the free importation of all ſorts of cattle into this kingdom from *Ireland* ſhall be, and is hereby permitted, allowed, and authorized, for and during the ſpace of ſeven years, and from thence to the end of the then next ſeſſion of parliament; and that all perſons ſhall be, and are hereby, exempted, freed, and diſcharged, from the payment of all ſubſidies, cuſtoms, rates, duties, and other impoſitions, and alſo from all penalties, forfeitures, payments, and puniſhments, for or on account of importing or bringing cattle into this kingdom from *Ireland*; any act or acts of parliament to the contrary notwithſtanding.

The free importation of cattle from Ireland allowed for the term of 7 years; without payment of duties.

II. And be it further enacted by the authority aforeſaid, That if any action or ſuit ſhall be commenced againſt any perſon or perſons for any thing done in purſuance of this act, the defendant or defendants, in ſuch action or ſuit, may plead the general iſſue, and give this act and the ſpecial matter in evidence at any trial to be had thereupon, and that the ſame was done in purſuance and by the authority of this act; and if it ſhall appear ſo to have been done, the jury ſhall find for the defendant or defendants: and if the plaintiff ſhall be nonſuited, or diſcontinue his action after the defendant or defendants ſhall have appeared, or if judgement ſhall be given upon any verdict or demurrer againſt the plaintiff, the defendant or defendants ſhall and may recover treble coſts; and have the like remedy for the ſame, as any defendant or defendants hath or have in other cases by law.

General iſſue.

Treble coſts.

CAP. XI.

An act for rendering more effectual an act made in the twelfth year of the reign of her late majeſty Queen Anne, *intituled,* An act for providing a publick reward for ſuch perſon or perſons as ſhall diſcover the longitude at ſea; *with regard to the making experiments of propoſals made for diſcovering the longitude.*

WHEREAS *by an act of parliament made in the twelfth year of the reign of her late majeſty Queen* Anne, *intituled,* An act for providing a publick reward for ſuch perſon or perſons as ſhall diſcover the longitude at ſea, *the commiſſioners therein named or any five or more of them, have full power to hear and receive any propoſal or propoſals that ſhall be made to them for diſcovering the ſaid longitude: and in caſe the ſaid commiſſioners, or any five or more of them, ſhall be ſo far ſatisfied of the probability of any ſuch diſcovery, as to think it proper to make experiments thereof, they ſhall certify the ſame, under their hands and ſeals, to the commiſſioners of the navy for the time being, together with the perſons*

Preamble, reciting ſeveral clauſes in act 12 Annæ,

names who are authors of such proposals; and, upon producing such certificate, the said commissioners are hereby authorized and required to make out a bill or bills for any such sum or sums of money, not exceeding two thousand pounds, as the said commissioners for the discovery of the said longitude, or any five or more of them, shall think necessary for making the experiments, payable by the treasurer of the navy; which sum or sums the treasurer of the navy is by the said act required to pay immediately, to such person or persons as shall be appointed by the said commissioners to make those experiments, out of any money that shall be in his hands unapplied for the use of the navy: and whereas for a due and sufficient encouragement to any such person or persons as shall discover a proper method for finding the said longitude, it is likewise enacted by the said act, that the first author or authors, discoverer or discoverers, of any such method, his or their executors, administrators, or assigns, shall be intitled to, and have such reward, as in the said act is particularly mentioned: and whereas by another act of parliament made in the fourteenth year of of the reign of his late majesty King George *the Second, intituled,* An act for surveying the chief ports and head lands on the coasts of *Great Britain* and *Ireland*, and the islands and plantations thereto belonging, in order to the more exact determination of the longitude and latitude thereof, *it was enacted, that the said commissioners for discovering the said longitude, or any five or more of them, should have full power to apply such part of the said sum of two thousand pounds, mentioned in the said first recited act, as had not then been laid out in experiments, as they should think necessary for the making such survey, and determining the longitude and latitude of the chief ports and head lands on the coasts of* Great Britain and Ireland, *and the islands and plantations thereto belonging; and that such sum or sums, part of the said two thousand pounds, which the said commissioners, or any five or more of them, should think necessary, should be paid immediately, by the treasurer of the navy, to such person or persons as should be appointed by the said commissioners to make such survey and determine such longitude and latitude, out of the money that should be in the hands of such treasurer unapplied for the use of the navy: and whereas by an act made in the twenty sixth year of the reign of his late majesty King* George *the Second, intituled,* An act to render more effectual an act made in the twelfth year of the reign of her late majesty Queen *Anne*, intituled, *An act for providing a publick reward for such person or persons as shall discover the longitude at sea*, with regard to the making experiments of proposals made for discovering the longitude, and to enlarge the number of commissioners for putting in execution the said act, *the further sum of two thousand pounds was directed to be applied, in such manner as the commissioners for the discovery of the longitude should think necessary, for making further experiments: and whereas by an act in the second year of the reign of his present Majesty, intituled,* An act for rendering more effectual an act made in the twelfth year of the reign of her late majesty Queen *Anne*, intituled, *An act for providing a publick reward for such person or persons as shall discover the longitude at sea*, with regard to the making ex-

Act 14 Geo. 2.

Act 26 Geo. 2.

and act 2 Geo. 3.

 periments

periments of propoſals made for diſcovering the longitude, *the further ſum of two thouſand pounds was directed to be applied, in ſuch manner as the commiſſioners for the diſcovery of the longitude ſhould think neceſſary, for making further experiments: and whereas the ſaid commiſſioners have, by virtue of the powers veſted in them by the ſaid ſeveral acts before-mentioned, heard and received ſeveral propoſals made to them at different times for diſcovering the ſaid longitude, and have accordingly certified the ſame, from time to time, to the commiſſioners of the navy for the time being; whereupon bills have been made out for ſeveral ſums of money, amounting in the whole to ſix thouſand pounds; all which reſpective ſums have been paid to ſeveral perſons by the treaſurer of the navy, purſuant to the directions of the ſaid acts of parliament, which the ſaid commiſſioners for diſcovering the longitude thought neceſſary for making the ſaid experiments: and whereas, by reaſon of the ſeveral payments made by the treaſurer of the navy to the ſeveral perſons as aforeſaid, the ſaid commiſſioners have, by virtue of the ſaid acts of parliament, expended the whole of the ſums thereby granted for the purpoſes aforeſaid: and whereas from the experiments which have already been made, in purſuance of the powers veſted in the ſaid commiſſioners as aforeſaid, there is great reaſon to expect, that, by continuing to encourage ingenious perſons to invent and make further improvements and experiments in order to diſcover the ſaid longitude, ſuch diſcoveries may at length be produced as will effectually anſwer that end, and thereby contribute very much to the advantage of the trade and honour of this kingdom:* therefore, for enabling the ſaid commiſſioners to cauſe ſuch further experiments to be made as they ſhall think proper for the purpoſes aforeſaid, be it enacted by the King's moſt excellent majeſty, by and with the advice and conſent of the lords ſpiritual and temporal, and commons, in this preſent parliament aſſembled, and by the authority of the ſame, That the ſaid commiſſioners, conſtituted by the ſaid ſeveral acts of parliament before mentioned for the diſcovery of the longitude at ſea, and for examining, trying, and judging of all propoſals, experiments, and improvements, relating to the ſame, or any five or more of them, ſhall have full power to hear and receive any propoſal or propoſals that have been, or ſhall hereafter be made to them, for diſcovering the ſaid longitude at ſea; and in caſe the ſaid commiſſioners, or any five or more of them, ſhall be ſo far ſatisfied of the probability of any ſuch propoſal or diſcovery, as to think it proper to make experiment thereof, they ſhall certify the ſame, under their hands and ſeals, to the commiſſioners of the navy for the time being, together with the perſons names who ſhall be the authors of ſuch propoſals; and upon producing ſuch certificate, the ſaid commiſſioners of the navy, are hereby authorized and required to make out a bill or bills for any ſuch ſum or ſums of money, not exceeding two thouſand pounds, as the ſaid commiſſioners for the diſcovery of the ſaid longitude, or any five or more of them, ſhall think neceſſary for making any experiments in purſuance of this act, or any of the ſaid former acts above mentioned, payable by the treaſurer

The commiſſioners conſtituted by the recited acts are impowered to receive propoſals for diſcovering the longitude at ſea; and if ſatisfied of the probability of any ſuch propoſal, they are to certify the ſame, with the author's name, to the commiſſioners of the navy; who are thereupon to make out a bill for ſuch ſum, not exceeding 2000l. as ſhall be thought neceſſary for making the experiment;

of the navy; which sum or sums the treasurer of the navy, for the time being, is hereby required to pay immediately to such person or persons as shall be appointed by the commissioners for the discovery of the said longitude, to make those experiments, out of any money that shall be in his, the said treasurer's hands, unapplied for the use of the navy.

to be paid by the treasurer of the navy.

CAP. XII.

An act for granting and applying certain stamp duties, and other duties, in the British *colonies and plantations in* America, *towards further defraying the expences of defending, protecting, and securing the same; and for amending such parts of the several acts of parliament relating to the trade and revenues of the said colonies and plantations, as direct the manner of determining and recovering the penalties and forfeitures therein mentioned.*

Preamble.

WHEREAS *by an act made in the last session of parliament, several duties were granted, continued, and appropriated, towards defraying the expences of defending, protecting, and securing, the* British *colonies and plantations in* America: *and whereas it is just and necessary, that provision be made for raising a further revenue within your Majesty's dominions in* America, *towards defraying the said expences:* we, your Majesty's most dutiful and loyal subjects, the commons of *Great Britain* in parliament assembled, have therefore resolved to give and grant unto your Majesty the several rates and duties herein after mentioned; and do most humbly beseech your Majesty that it may be enacted, and be it enacted by the King's most excellent majesty, by and with the advice and consent of the lords spiritual and temporal, and commons, in this present parliament assembled, and by the authority of the same, That from and after the first day of *November*, one thousand seven hundred and sixty five, there shall be raised, levied, collected, and paid unto his Majesty, his heirs, and successors, throughout the colonies and plantations in *America* which now are, or hereafter may be, under the dominion of his Majesty, his heirs and successors,

The following stamp duties to take place from and after 1 Nov. 1765.

Viz. On all declarations, pleas, replications, rejoinders, demurrers, &c. in courts of law, 3 d. per sheet.

For every skin or piece of vellum or parchment, or sheet or piece of paper, on which shall be ingrossed, written or printed, any declaration, plea, replication, rejoinder, demurrer, or other pleading, or any copy thereof, in any court of law within the *British* colonies and plantations in *America*, a stamp duty of three pence.

Special bail and appearances, in the said courts, 2 s. per sheet.

For every skin or piece of vellum or parchment, or sheet or piece of paper, on which shall be ingrossed, written or printed, any special bail and appearance upon such bail in any such court, a stamp duty of two shillings.

Petitions, bills, answers, claims, pleas,

For every skin or piece of vellum or parchment, or sheet or piece of paper, on which shall be ingrossed, written, or printed, ed, any petition, bill, anſwer, claim, plea, replication, rejoinder, demurrer, or other pleading in any court of chancery or equity within the ſaid colonies and plantations, a ſtamp duty of one ſhilling and ſix pence.

replications, rejoinders, demurrers, &c. in courts of chancery or equity, 1s. 6d. per ſheet.

Copies of petitions, bills, &c. in the ſaid courts, 3d. per ſheet.

For every ſkin or piece of vellum or parchment, or ſheet or piece of paper, on which ſhall be ingroſſed, written, or printed, any copy of any petition, bill, anſwer, claim, plea, replication, rejoinder, demurrer, or other pleading in any ſuch court, a ſtamp duty of three pence.

Monitions, libels, anſwers, allegations, inventories, or renunciations, &c. in courts exercifing eccleſiaſtical jurisdiction, 1 s. per ſheet.

For every ſkin or piece of vellum or parchment, or ſheet or piece of paper, on which ſhall be ingroſſed, written, or printed, any monition, libel, anſwer, allegation, inventory, or renunciation in eccleſiaſtical matters in any court of probate, court of the ordinary, or other court exerciſing eccleſiaſtical juriſdiction within the ſaid colonies and plantations, a ſtamp duty of one ſhilling.

Copies of wills, monitions, &c. in the ſaid courts, 6 d. per ſheet.

For every ſkin or piece of vellum or parchment, or ſheet or piece of paper, on which ſhall be ingroſſed, written, or printed, any copy of any will (other than the probate thereof) monition, libel, anſwer, allegation, inventory, or renunciation in eccleſiaſtical matters in any ſuch court, a ſtamp duty of ſix pence.

Donations, preſentations, collations, inſtitutions, regiſters, entries, teſtimonials, certificates of degrees, 2 l. per ſheet.

For every ſkin or piece of vellum or parchment, or ſheet or piece of paper, on which ſhall be ingroſſed, written, or printed, any donation, preſentation, collation, or inſtitution of or to any benefice, or any writ or inſtrument for the like purpoſe, or any regiſter, entry, teſtimonial, or certificate of any degree taken in any univerſity, academy, college, or ſeminary of learning, within the ſaid colonies and plantations, a ſtamp duty of two pounds.

Monitions, libels, claims, anſwers, allegations, informations, letters of requeſt, executions, renunciations, inventories, &c. in courts of admiralty, 1 s. per ſheet.

For every ſkin or piece of vellum or parchment, or ſheet or piece of paper, on which ſhall be ingroſſed, written, or printed, any monition, libel, claim, anſwer, allegation, information, letter of requeſt, execution, renunciation, inventory, or other pleading, in any admiralty court within the ſaid colonies and plantations, a ſtamp duty of one ſhilling.

Copies of any ſuch monitions, libels, &c. 6 d. per ſheet.

For every ſkin or piece of vellum or parchment, or ſheet or piece of paper, on which any copy of any ſuch monition, libel, claim, anſwer, allegation, information, letter of requeſt, execution, renunciation, inventory, or other pleading ſhall be ingroſſed, written, or printed, a ſtamp duty of ſix pence.

Appeals, writs, of error and of dower, *Ad quod damnum*, certiorari, ſtatute mer-

For every ſkin or piece of vellum or parchment, or ſheet or piece of paper, on which ſhall be ingroſſed, written, or printed, any appeal, writ of error, writ of dower, *Ad quod damnum*, certiorari, ſtatute merchant, ſtatute ſtaple, atteſtation, or certificate, by any officer, or exemplification of any record or proceeding in any court whatſoever within the ſaid colonies and plantations (except appeals, writs of error, certiorari, atteſtations,

tions, certificates, and exemplifications, for or relating to the removal of any proceedings from before a single justice of the peace) a stamp duty of ten shillings.

hant, statute staple, attestations, certificates, exemplifications of records or proceedings in any of the courts (except appeals, &c. from proceedings before a single justice) 10 s. per sheet.

For every skin or piece of vellum or parchment, or sheet or piece of paper, on which shall be ingrossed, written, or printed, any writ of covenant for levying of fines, writ of entry for suffering a common recovery, or attachment issuing out of, or returnable into, any court within the said colonies and plantations, a stamp duty of five shillings.

Writs of covenant, or of entry, attachments, &c. in any of the said courts, 5 s. per sheet.

For every skin or piece of vellum or parchment, or sheet or piece of paper, on which shall be ingrossed, written, or printed, any judgement, decree, sentence, or dismission, or any record of *Nisi Prius* or *Postea*, in any court within the said colonies and plantations, a stamp duty of four shillings.

Judgements, decrees, sentences, dismissions, records of *Nisi prius* or *Postea*, in any of the courts, 4 s. per sheet.

For every skin or piece of vellum or parchment, or sheet or piece of paper, on which shall ingrossed, written, or printed, any affidavit, common bail or appearance, interrogatory deposition, rule, order, or warrant of any court, or any *Dedimus Potestatem*, *Capias*, *Subpœna*, summons, compulsory citation, commission, recognizance, or any other writ, process, or mandate, issuing out of, or returnable into, any court, or any office belonging thereto, or any other proceeding therein whatsoever, or any copy thereof, or of any record not herein before charged, within the said colonies and plantations (except warrants relating to criminal matters, and proceedings thereon or relating thereto) a stamp duty of one shilling.

Affidavits, common bail or appearance, interrogatory depositions, rules, orders, warrants of court, *Dedimus Potestatem*, *Capias*, *Subpœnas*, summonses, compulsory citations, commissions, recognizances, &c. in any of the said courts (except warrants, &c. relating to criminal matters, &c.) 1 s. per sheet.

For every skin or piece of vellum or parchment, or sheet or piece of paper, on which shall be ingrossed, written, or printed, any licence, appointment, or admission of any counsellor, sollicitor, attorney, advocate, or proctor, to practise in any court, or of any notary within the said colonies and plantations, a stamp duty of ten pounds.

Licences, appointments, admissions, of counsellors, sollicitors, &c. to practise in any court, 10l. per sheet.

For every skin or piece of vellum or parchment, or sheet or piece of paper, on which shall be ingrossed, written, or printed, any note or bill of lading, which shall be signed for any kind of goods, wares, or merchandize, to be exported from, or any cocket or clearance granted within the said colonies and plantations, a stamp duty of four pence.

Bills of lading, cockets, clearances, 4 d. per sheet.

For every skin or piece of vellum or parchment, or sheet or piece of paper, on which shall be ingrossed, written, or printed, letters of mart, or commission for private ships of war, within the said colonies and plantations, a stamp duty of twenty shillings.

Letters of mart, commissions for private ships war, 20 s. per sheet.

For every skin or piece of vellum or parchment, or sheet or piece of paper, on which shall be ingrossed, written or printed, any grant, appointment, or admission of or to any publick beneficial,

Grants, appointments, admissions to publick beneficial offices, &c. of 20 l. per ann. value, or upwards (army, navy, judges, and justices of peace excepted) 10 s. per sheet.

neficial office or employment, for the space of one year, or any lesser time, of or above the value of twenty pounds *per annum* sterling money, in salary, fees, and perquisites, within the said colonies and plantations, (except commissions and appointments of officers of the army, navy, ordnance, or militia, of judges, and of justices of the peace) a stamp duty of ten shillings.

Grants of liberties, privileges, or franchises, under the seal of any of the colonies, or sign manual of any governor, &c. or any exemplifications thereof, 6 l. per sheet.

For every skin or piece of vellum or parchment, or sheet or piece of paper, on which any grant of any liberty, privilege, or franchise, under the seal of any of the said colonies or plantations, or under the seal or sign manual of any governor, proprietor, or publick officer alone, or in conjunction with any other person or persons, or with any council, or any council and assembly, or any exemplification of the same, shall be ingrossed, written, or printed, within the said colonies and plantations, a stamp duty of six pounds.

Licences for retailing spirituous liquors, 20 s. per sheet.

For every skin or piece of vellum or parchment, or sheet or piece of paper, on which shall be ingrossed, written, or printed, any licence for retailing of spirituous liquors, to be granted to any person who shall take out the same, within the said colonies and plantations, a stamp duty of twenty shillings.

Licences for retailing wine only, 4 l. per sheet.

For every skin or piece of vellum or parchment, or sheet or piece of paper, on which shall be ingrossed, written, or printed, any licence for retailing of wine, to be granted to any person who shall not take out a licence for retailing of spirituous liquors, within the said colonies and plantations, a stamp duty of four pounds.

Licences for retailing wine, where a licence has been granted for retailing spirituous liquors, 3 l. per sheet.

For every skin or piece of vellum or parchment, or sheet or piece of paper, on which shall be ingrossed, written, or printed, any licence for retailing of wine, to be granted to any person who shall take out a licence for retailing of spirituous liquors, within the said colonies and plantations, a stamp duty of three pounds.

Probates of wills, letters of administration, or guardianship, &c. on the continent, and the islands of Bermuda and Bahama, 5 s. per sheet.

For every skin or piece of vellum or parchment, or sheet or piece of paper, on which shall be ingrossed, written or printed, any probate of a will, letters of administration, or of guardianship for any estate above the value of twenty pounds sterling money; within the *British* colonies and plantations upon the continent of *America*, the islands belonging thereto, and the *Bermuda* and *Bahama* islands, a stamp duty of five shillings.

Probates, letters of administration or guardianship, in other parts of America, 10 s. per sheet.

For every skin or piece of vellum or parchment, or sheet or piece of paper, on which shall be ingrossed, written or printed, any such probate, letters of administration or of guardianship, within all other parts of the *British* dominions in *America*, a stamp duty of ten shillings.

Bonds for any sum not exceeding 10 l.

For every skin or piece of vellum or parchment, or sheet or piece of paper, on which shall be ingrossed, written, or printed, any

any bond for securing the payment of any sum of money, not exceeding the sum of ten pounds sterling money, within the *British* colonies and plantations upon the continent of *America*, the islands belonging thereto, and the *Bermuda* and *Bahama* islands, a stamp duty of six pence.

on the continent, and islands of Bermuda and Bahama, 6 d. per sheet.

For every skin or piece of vellum or parchment, or sheet or piece of paper, on which shall be ingrossed, written, or printed, any bond for securing the payment of any sum of money above ten pounds, and not exceeding the sum of twenty pounds sterling money, within such colonies, plantations, and islands, a stamp duty of one shilling.

Bonds for any sum above 10 l. and not exceeding 20 l. within the said places, 1 s. per sheet.

For every skin or piece of vellum or parchment, or sheet or piece of paper, on which shall be ingrossed, written, or printed, any bond for securing the payment of any sum of money above twenty pounds, and not exceeding forty pounds sterling money, within such colonies, plantations, and islands, a stamp duty of one shilling and six pence.

Bonds for any sum above 20 l. and not exceeding 40 l. within the same places, 1 s. 6 d. per sheet.

For every skin or piece of vellum or parchment, or sheet or piece of paper, on which shall be ingrossed, written, or printed, any order or warrant for surveying or setting out any quantity of land, not exceeding one hundred acres, issued by any governor, proprietor, or any publick officer alone, or in conjunction with any other person or persons, or with any council, or any council and assembly, within the *British* colonies and plantations in *America*, a stamp duty of six pence.

Warrants for surveying or setting out any lands, not exceeding 100 acres, 6 d. per sheet.

For every skin or piece of vellum or parchment, or sheet or piece of paper, on which shall be ingrossed, written, or printed, any such order or warrant for surveying or setting out any quantity of land above one hundred, and not exceeding two hundred acres, within the said colonies and plantations, a stamp duty of one shilling.

Warrants for surveying or setting out any lands above 100 acres, and not exceeding 200, 1 s. per sheet.

For every skin or piece of vellum or parchment, or sheet or piece of paper, on which shall be ingrossed, written, or printed, any such order or warrant for surveying or setting out any quantity of land above two hundred, and not exceeding three hundred and twenty acres, and in proportion for every such order or warrant for surveying or setting out every other three hundred and twenty acres, within the said colonies and plantations, a stamp duty of one shilling and six pence.

Warrants for surveying or setting out any lands above 200 acres, and not exceeding 320, 1 s. 6 d. per sheet.

For every skin or piece of vellum or parchment, or sheet or piece of paper, on which shall be ingrossed, written, or printed, any original grant, or any deed, mesne conveyance, or other instrument whatsoever, by which any quantity of land not exceeding one hundred acres shall be granted, conveyed, or assigned, within the *British* colonies and plantations upon the continent of *America*, the islands belonging thereto, and the *Bermuda* and *Bahama* islands (except leases for any term not exceeding the term of twenty one years) a stamp duty of one shilling and six pence,

Original grants, or deeds, mesne conveyances, &c. of lands, not exceeding 100 acres upon the continent, or islands of Bermuda and Bahama, 1 s. 6 d. per sheet.

Original grants, &c. of lands above 100 acres, and not exceeding 200, within the ſaid places 2 s. per ſheet.

For every ſkin or piece of vellum or parchment, or ſheet or piece of paper, on which ſhall be ingroſſed, written, or printed, any ſuch original grant, or any ſuch deed, meſne conveyance or other inſtrument whatſoever by which any quantity of land above one hundred, and not exceeding two hundred acres, ſhall be granted, conveyed, or aſſigned, within ſuch colonies, plantations, and iſlands, a ſtamp duty of two ſhillings.

Original grants, &c. of lands above 200 acres, and not exceeding 320, and in proportion for every other 320 acres, in the ſaid places, 2s. 6d. per ſheet.

For every ſkin or piece of vellum or parchment, or ſheet or piece of paper, on which ſhall be ingroſſed, written, or printed, any ſuch original grant, or any ſuch deed, meſne conveyance, or other inſtrument whatſoever, by which any quantity of land above two hundred, and not exceeding three hundred and twenty acres, ſhall be granted, conveyed, or aſſigned, and in proportion for every ſuch grant, deed, meſne conveyance, or other inſtrument, granting, conveying, or aſſigning, every other three hundred and twenty acres, within ſuch colonies, plantations, and iſlands, a ſtamp duty of two ſhillings and ſix pence.

Original grants, &c. of lands not exceeding 100 acres, within all other parts of America, 3 s. per ſheet.

For every ſkin or piece of vellum or parchment, or ſheet or piece of paper, on which ſhall be ingroſſed, written, or printed, any ſuch original grant, or any ſuch deed, meſne conveyance, or other inſtrument whatſoever, by which any quantity of land not exceeding one hundred acres ſhall be granted, conveyed, or aſſigned, within all other parts of the *Britiſh* dominions in *America*, a ſtamp duty of three ſhillings.

Original grants, &c. of lands above 100 acres, and not exceeding 200, within the ſame parts, 4 s. per ſheet.

For every ſkin or piece of vellum or parchment, or ſheet or piece of paper, on which ſhall be ingroſſed, written, or printed, any ſuch original grant, or any ſuch deed, meſne conveyance, or other inſtrument whatſoever, by which any quantity of land above one hundred, and not exceeding two hundred acres, ſhall be granted, conveyed, or aſſigned, within the ſame parts of the ſaid dominions, a ſtamp duty of four ſhillings.

Original grants, &c. of lands above 200 acres, and not exceeding 320, and in proportion for every other 320 acres, within the ſaid parts, 5 s. per ſheet.

For every ſkin or piece of vellum or parchment, or ſheet or piece of paper, on which ſhall be ingroſſed, written, or printed, any ſuch original grant, or any ſuch deed, meſne conveyance, or other inſtrument whatſoever, whereby any quantity of land above two hundred, and not exceeding three hundred and twenty acres, ſhall be granted, conveyed, or aſſigned, and in proportion for every ſuch grant, deed, meſne conveyance, or other inſtrument, granting, conveying, or aſſigning, every other three hundred and twenty acres, within the ſame parts of the ſaid dominions, a ſtamp duty of five ſhillings.

Grants, appointments, or admiſſions, to any publick beneficial office, not before charged, above 20 l. per ann. value, or exemplifications

For every ſkin or piece of vellum or parchment, or ſheet or piece of paper, on which ſhall be ingroſſed, written, or printed, any grant, appointment, or admiſſion, of or to any publick beneficial office or employment, not herein before charged, above the value of twenty pounds *per annum* ſterling money in ſalary, fees, and perquiſites, or any exemplification of the ſame, within the *Britiſh* colonies and plantations upon the continent of *America*, the iſlands belonging thereto, and the *Bermuda* and *Bahama* iſlands (except commiſſions of officers of the army, navy, ordnance

nance, or militia, and of justices of the peace) a stamp duty of four pounds.

thereof (army, navy, and justices of the peace, excepted) upon the continent, or islands of Bermuda and Bahama, 4 l. per sheet.

For every skin or piece of vellum or parchment, or sheet or piece of paper, on which shall be ingrossed, written, or printed, any such grant, appointment, or admission, of or to any such publick beneficial office or employment, or any exemplification of the same, within all other parts of the *British* dominions in *America*, a stamp duty of six pounds.

Grants or admissions, &c. to any such offices in any other parts of America, 6 l. per sheet.

For every skin or piece of vellum or parchment, or sheet or piece of paper, on which shall be ingrossed, written, or printed, any indenture, lease, conveyance, contract, stipulation, bill of sale, charter party, protest, articles of apprenticeship, or covenant (except for the hire of servants not apprentices, and also except such other matters as are herein before charged) within the *British* colonies and plantations in *America*, a stamp duty of two shillings and six pence.

Indentures, leases, conveyances, contracts, stipulations, bills of sale, charter parties, protests, articles of apprenticeship, or covenant (except for the hire of servants, and other matters before charged) 2s. 6 d. per sheet.

For every skin or piece of vellum or parchment, or sheet or piece of paper, on which any warrant or order for auditing any publick accounts, beneficial warrant, order, grant, or certificate, under any publick seal, or under the seal or sign manual of any governor, proprietor, or publick officer alone, or in conjunction with any other person or persons, or with any council, or any council and assembly, not herein before charged, or any passport or let-pass, surrender of office, or policy of assurance, shall be ingrossed, written, or printed, within the said colonies and plantations (except warrants or orders for the service of the navy, army, ordnance, or militia, and grants of offices under twenty pounds *per annum* in salary, fees, and perquisites) a stamp duty of five shillings.

Warrant for auditing publick accounts, beneficial warrants, orders, grants, certificates, under the publick seal, or sign manual of a governor, &c. not before charged; passports, surrenders of offices, policies of assurance (warrants for the navy or army, and grants of offices under 20 l. per annum value, excepted) 5 s. per sheet.

For every skin or piece of vellum or parchment, or sheet or piece of paper, on which shall be ingrossed, written, or printed, any notarial act, bond, deed, letter of attorney, procuration, mortgage, release, or other obligatory instrument, not herein before charged, within the said colonies and plantations, a stamp duty of two shillings and three pence.

Notarial acts, bonds, deeds, letters of attorney, procuration, mortgage, release, or obligatory instrument, not charged before, 2 s. 3 d. per sheet.

For every skin or piece of vellum or parchment, or sheet or piece of paper, on which shall be ingrossed, written or printed, any register, entry, or inrollment of any grant, deed, or other instrument whatsoever herein before charged, within the said colonies and plantations, a stamp duty of three pence.

Registers, entries, or inrolments, of grants, deeds, &c. before charged, 3d. per sheet.

For every skin or piece of vellum or parchment, or sheet or piece of paper, on which shall be ingrossed, written, or printed, any register, entry, or inrollment of any grant, deed, or other instru-

Registers, entries, or inrolments of grants, deeds,

&c. not before charged, 2s. per sheet.

instrument whatsoever not herein before charged, within the said colonies and plantations, a stamp duty of two shillings.

Duties payable upon cards and dice. viz. on

And for and upon every pack of playing cards, and all dice, which shall be sold or used within the said colonies and plantations, the several stamp duties following (that is to say)

Cards, 1s. per pack.

For every pack of such cards, the sum of one shilling.

Dice, 10s. per pair.

And for every pair of such dice, the sum of ten shillings.

Duties payable upon pamphlets and news papers, viz.

And for and upon every paper, commonly called a *pamphlet*, and upon every news paper, containing publick news, intelligence, or occurrences, which shall be printed, dispersed, and made publick, within any of the said colonies and plantations, and for and upon such advertisements as are herein after mentioned, the respective duties following (that is to say)

On pamphlets of half a sheet, or less, ½d. on every printed copy; being larger than half a sheet, and not exceeding a whole sheet, 1d. for every printed copy;

For every such pamphlet and paper contained in half a sheet, or any lesser piece of paper, which shall be so printed, a stamp duty of one halfpenny, for every printed copy thereof.

For every such pamphlet and paper (being larger than half a sheet, and not exceeding one whole sheet) which shall be so printed, a stamp duty of one penny, for every printed copy thereof.

being larger than 1 whole sheet, and not exceeding 6, in octavo, or under; or not exceeding 12 sheets in quarto, or 20 sheets in folio, 1s. per sheet for one printed copy.

For every pamphlet and paper being larger than one whole sheet, and not exceeding six sheets in octavo, or in a lesser page, or not exceeding twelve sheets in quarto, or twenty sheets in folio, which shall be so printed, a duty after the rate of one shilling for every sheet of any kind of paper which shall be contained in one printed copy thereof.

For every advertizement in any gazette or other paper 2s.

For every advertisement to be contained in any gazette, news paper, or other paper, or any pamphlet which shall be so printed, a duty of two shillings.

For every almanack, &c. to serve for 1 year, and printed on one side of 1 sheet only, 2d.

For every almanack or calendar, for any one particular year, or for any time less than a year, which shall be written or printed on one side only of any one sheet, skin, or piece of paper parchment, or vellum, within the said colonies and plantations, a stamp duty of two pence.

For every other almanack, &c. for 1 year, 4d.

For every other almanack or calendar for any one particular year, which shall be written or printed within the said colonies and plantations, a stamp duty of four pence.

For every almanack to serve for several years, duties to the same amount respectively for each year.

And for every almanack or calendar written or printed within the said colonies and plantations, to serve for several years, duties to the same amount respectively shall be paid for every such year.

On instruments, proceedings, &c. aforesaid, ingrossed, writ-

For every skin or piece of vellum or parchment, or sheet or piece of paper, on which any instrument, proceeding, or other matter or thing aforesaid, shall be ingrossed, written, or printed, within the said colonies and plantations, in any other than the

English

English language, a stamp duty of double the amount of the respective duties before charged thereon.

ten, or printed, in any other than the English language, double the amount of the respective duties before charged thereon.

On fees paid with clerks or apprentices, not exceeding 50l. a duty of 6d, for every 20s. so paid;

And there shall be also paid in the said colonies and plantations, a duty of six pence for every twenty shillings, in any sum not exceeding fifty pounds sterling money, which shall be given, paid, contracted, or agreed for, with or in relation to any clerk or apprentice, which shall be put or placed to or with any master or mistress to learn any profession, trade, or employment.

and 1s. for every 20s. in any sum exceeding 50l.

II. And also a duty of one shilling for every twenty shillings, in any sum exceeding fifty pounds, which shall be given, paid, contracted, or agreed, for, with, or in relation to any such clerk, or apprentice.

What shall be deemed policies of assurance within the meaning of the act.

III. And be it further enacted by the authority aforesaid, That every deed, instrument, note, memorandum, letter, or other minument or writing, for or relating to the payment of any sum of money, or for making any valuable consideration for or upon the loss of any ship, vessel, goods, wages, money, effects, or upon any loss by fire, or for any other loss whatsoever, or for or upon any life or lives, shall be construed, deemed, and adjudged to be policies of assurance, within the meaning of this act: and if any such deed, instrument, note, memorandum, letter, or other minument or writing, for insuring, or tending to insure, any more than one ship or vessel for more than any one voyage, or any goods, wages, money, effects, or other matter or thing whatsoever, for more than one voyage, or in more than one ship or vessel, or being the property of, or belonging to, any more than one person, or any particular number of persons in general partnership, or any more than one body politick or corporate, or for more than one risque; then, in every such case, the money insured thereon, or the valuable consideration thereby agreed to be made, shall become the absolute property of the insured, and the insurer shall also forfeit the premium given for such insurance, together with the sum of one hundred pounds.

On what cases the insurance and premium are forfeited.

What shall be deemed a charter party.

IV. And be it further enacted by the authority aforesaid, That every deed, instrument, note, memorandum, letter, or other minument or writing, between the captain or master or owner of any ship or vessel, and any merchant, trader, or other person, in respect to the freight or conveyance of any money, goods, wares, merchandizes, or effects, laden or to be laden on board of any such ship or vessel, shall be deemed and adjudged to be a charter party within the meaning of this act.

Books, &c. serving chiefly for almanacks to pay duty as such only.

V. And be it further enacted by the authority aforesaid, That all books and pamphlets serving chiefly for the purpose of an almanack, by whatsoever name or names intituled or described, are and shall be charged with the duty imposed by this act on almanacks, but not with any of the duties charged by this act on pamphlets, or other printed papers; any thing herein contained to the contrary notwithstanding.

The aforesaid duties not to

VI. Provided always, That this act shall not extend to charge any bills of exchange, accompts, bills of parcels, bills of fees, or

extend to bills of exchange, &c. or any bills or notes not ſealed for payment of money at ſight, or upon demand, or at the end of certain days of payment.

or to probate of wills, or letters of adminiſtration, to common ſeamen or ſoldiers dying in the King's ſervice.

VII. Provided, That nothing in this act contained ſhall extend to charge the probate of any will, or letters of adminiſtration to the effects of any common ſeaman or ſoldier, who ſhall die in his Majeſty's ſervice; a certificate being produced from the commanding officer of the ſhip or veſſel, or troop or company in which ſuch ſeaman or ſoldier ſerved at the time of his death, and oath, or if by a quaker a ſolemn affirmation, made of the truth thereof, before the proper judge or officer by whom ſuch probate or adminiſtration ought to be granted; which oath or affirmation ſuch judge or officer is hereby authorized and required to adminiſter, and for which no fee or reward ſhall be taken.

The extraordinary duties on inſtruments, in any other than the Engliſh language, are not to take place within Quebec or Granada, for 5 years.

VIII. Provided always, and be it enacted, That until after the expiration of five years from the commencement of the ſaid duties, no ſkin or piece of vellum or parchment, or ſheet or piece of paper, on which any inſtrument, proceeding, or other matter or thing ſhall be ingroſſed, written, or printed, within the colonies of *Quebec* or *Granada*, in any other than the *Engliſh* language, ſhall be liable to be charged with any higher ſtamp duty than if the ſame had been ingroſſed, written, or printed in the *Engliſh* language.

Inſtruments for granting, &c. lands, made with any Indian nation, are not chargeable with duties;

IX. Provided always, That nothing in this act contained ſhall extend to charge with any duty, any deed, or other inſtrument, which ſhall be made between any *Indian* nation and the governor, proprietor of any colony, lieutenant governor, or commander in chief alone, or in conjunction with any other perſon or perſons, or with any council, or any council and aſſembly of any of the ſaid colonies or plantations, for or relating to the granting, ſurrendering, or conveying, any lands belonging to ſuch nation, to, for, or on behalf of his Majeſty, or any ſuch proprietor, or to any colony or plantation.

nor are proclamations, forms of prayer, votes of any houſes of aſſembly; School books, Books of piety or devotion; ſingle advertiſements printed ſolely; daily accounts of imports, and exports;

X. Provided always, That this act ſhall not extend to charge any proclamation, forms of prayer and thankſgiving, or any printed votes of any houſe of aſſembly in any of the ſaid colonies and plantations, with any of the ſaid duties on pamphlets or news papers; or to charge any books commonly uſed in any of the ſchools within the ſaid colonies and plantations, or any books containing only matters of devotion or piety; or to charge any ſingle advertiſement printed by itſelf, or the daily accounts or bills of goods imported and exported, ſo as ſuch accounts or bills do contain no other matters than what have been uſually comprized therein; any thing herein contained to the contrary notwithſtanding.

or certificates to receive parliamentary bounties.

XI. Provided always, That nothing in this act contained ſhall extend to charge with any of the ſaid duties, any vellum, parchment, or paper, on which ſhall only be engroſſed, written, or printed, any certificate that ſhall be neceſſary to intitle any perſon to receive a bounty granted by act of parliament.

XII. And

XII. And be it further enacted by the authority aforesaid, That the said several duties shall be under the management of the commissioners, for the time being, of the duties charged on stamped vellum, parchment, and paper, in *Great Britain*: and the said commissioners are hereby impowered and required to employ such officers under them, for that purpose, as they shall think proper; and to use such stamps and marks, to denote the stamp duties hereby charged, as they shall think fit; and to repair, renew, or alter the same, from time to time, as there shall be occasion; and to do all other acts, matters, and things, necessary to be done, for putting this act in execution with relation to the duties hereby charged.

The duties to be under the management of the commissioners for the stamp duties in Great Britain, who are to appoint proper officers, and stamps, &c.

XIII. And be it further enacted by the authority aforesaid, That the commissioners for managing the said duties, for the time being, shall and may appoint a fit person or persons to attend in every court or publick office within the said colonies and plantations, to take notice of the vellum, parchment, or paper, upon which any of the matters or things hereby charged with a duty shall be ingrossed, written, or printed, and of the stamps or marks thereupon, and of all other matters and things tending to secure the said duties; and that the judges in the several courts, and all other persons to whom it may appertain, shall, at the request of any such officer, make such orders, and do such other matters and things, for the better securing of the said duties, as shall be lawfully or reasonably desired in that behalf: and every commissioner and other officer, before he proceeds to the execution of any part of this act, shall take an oath in the words, or to the effect following (that is to say)

They are to appoint an officer to attend in every court, or publick office, to take care of all matters relating to the said duties. Judges and others to assist in securing the said duties. Commissioners and other officers, to take the following oath.

I A. B. *do swear, That I will faithfully execute the trust reposed in me, pursuant to an act of parliament made in the fifth year of the reign of his majesty King* George *the Third, for granting certain stamp duties, and other duties, in the* British *colonies and plantations in* America, *without fraud or concealment; and will from time to time true account make of my doing therein, and deliver the same to such person or persons as his Majesty, his heirs, or successors, shall appoint to receive such account; and will take no fee, reward, or profit, for the execution or performance of the said trust, or the business relating thereto, from any person or persons, other than such as shall be allowed by his Majesty, his heirs, and successors, or by some other person or persons under him or them to that purpose authorized.*

The oath.

Or if any such officer shall be of the people commonly called *Quakers*, he shall take a solemn affirmation to the effect of the said oath; which oath or affirmation shall and may be administered to any such commissioner or commissioners by any two or more of the same commissioners, whether they have or have not previously taken the same: and any of the said commissioners, or any justice of the peace, within the kingdom of *Great Britain*, or any governor, lieutenant governor, judge, or other magistrate,

Oath by whom to be administered.

within the ſaid colonies or plantations, ſhall and may adminiſter ſuch oath or affirmation to any ſubordinate officer.

Commiſſioners and officers under them, to obſerve ſuch rules as the treaſury ſhall preſcribe them.

XIV. And be it further enacted by the authority aforeſaid, That the ſaid commiſſioners, and all officers to be employed or entruſted by or under them as aforeſaid, ſhall, from time to time, in and for the better execution of their ſeveral places and truſts, obſerve ſuch rules, methods, and orders, as they reſpectively ſhall, from time to time, receive from the high treaſurer of *Great Britain*, or the commiſſioners of the treaſury, or any three or more of ſuch commiſſioners for the time being; and that the ſaid commiſſioners for managing the ſtamp duties ſhall take eſpecial care, that the ſeveral parts of the ſaid colonies and plantations ſhall, from time to time, be ſufficiently furniſhed with vellum, parchment, and paper, ſtamped or marked with the ſaid reſpective duties.

Care to be taken that the colonies be ſufficiently furniſhed with ſtamps.

Perſons ſigning, writing, printing, or ſelling any thing chargeable with the duties,

XV. And be it further enacted by the authority aforeſaid, That if any perſon or perſons ſhall ſign, ingroſs, write, print, or ſell, or expoſe to ſale, or cauſe to be ſigned, ingroſſed, written, printed, or ſold, or expoſed to ſale, in any of the ſaid colonies or plantations, or in any other part of his Majeſty's dominions, any matter or thing, for which the vellum, parchment, or paper, is hereby charged to pay any duty, before the ſame ſhall be marked or ſtamped with the marks or ſtamps to be provided as aforeſaid, or upon which there ſhall not be ſome ſtamp or mark reſembling the ſame; or ſhall ſign, ingroſs, write, print, or ſell, or expoſe to ſale, or cauſe to be ſigned, ingroſſed, written, printed, or ſold, or expoſed to ſale, any matter or thing upon any vellum, parchment, or paper, that ſhall be marked or ſtamped for any lower duty than the duty by this act made payable in reſpect thereof; every ſuch perſon ſo offending ſhall, for every ſuch offence, forfeit the ſum of ten pounds.

before the ſame ſhall be duly ſtampt, &c.

or which ſhall be ſtampt for a lower duty, forfeit 10 l.

No inſtrument chargeable with a duty to be admitted as evidence in any court, unleſs duly ſtampt:

XVI. And be it further enacted by the authority aforeſaid, That no matter or thing whatſoever, by this act charged with the payment of a duty, ſhall be pleaded or given in evidence, or admitted in any court within the ſaid colonies and plantations, to be good, uſeful, or available in law or equity, unleſs the ſame ſhall be marked or ſtamped, in purſuance of this act, with the reſpective duty hereby charged thereon, or with an higher duty.

But if any inſtrument not duly ſtampt at the execution or inrollment be produced to a chief diſtributor, and payment made of 10 l. and double duties, he is to ſign a certificate, and

XVII. Provided neverthele ſs, and be it further enacted by the authority aforeſaid, That if any vellum, parchment, or paper, containing any deed, inſtrument, or other matter or thing, ſhall not be duly ſtamped in purſuance of this act, at the time of the ſigning, ſealing, or other execution, or the entry or inrollment thereof, any perſon intereſted therein, or any perſon on his or her behalf, upon producing the ſame to any one of the chief diſtributors of ſtampt vellum, parchment, and paper, and paying to him the ſum of ten pounds for every ſuch deed, inſtrument, matter, or thing, and alſo double the amount of the duties payable in reſpect thereof, ſhall be intitled to receive from ſuch diſtributor, vellum, parchment, or paper, ſtamped purſuant

to

this act, to the amount of the money so paid; a certificate being first written upon every such piece of vellum, parchment, or paper, expressing the name and place of abode of the person by or on whose behalf such payment is made, the general purport of such deed, instrument, matter, or thing, the names of the parties therein, and of the witnesses (if any) thereto, and the date thereof, which certificate shall be signed by the said distributor; and the vellum, parchment, or paper, shall be then annexed to such deed, instrument, matter, or thing, by or in the presence of such distributor, who shall impress a seal upon wax, to be affixed on the part where such annexation shall be made, in the presence of a magistrate, who shall attest such signature and sealing; and the deed, instrument, or other matter or thing, from thenceforth shall and may, with the vellum, parchment, or paper, so annexed, be admitted and allowed in evidence in any court whatsoever, and shall be as valid and effectual as if the proper stamps had been impressed thereon at the time of the signing, sealing, or other execution, or entry or inrollment thereof: and the said distributor shall, once in every six months, or oftener if required by the commissioners for managing the stamp duties, send to such commissioners true copies of all such certificates, and an account of the number of pieces of vellum, parchment, and paper, so annexed, and of the respective duties impressed upon every such piece.

annex the same to the deed, &c.

after which it shall be admitted as evidence.

Copies of such certificates, &c. to be transmitted half yearly to the commissioners for stamps.

XVIII. And be it further enacted by the authority aforesaid, That if any person shall forge, counterfeit, erase, or alter, any such certificate, every such person so offending shall be guilty of felony, and shall suffer death as in cases of felony without the benefit of clergy.

The penalty of forging or altering any such certificate, is death.

XIX. And be it further enacted by the authority aforesaid, That if any person or persons shall, in the said colonies or plantations, or in any other part of his Majesty's dominions, counterfeit or forge any seal, stamp, mark, type, device, or label, to resemble any seal, stamp, mark, type, device, or label, which shall be provided or made in pursuance of this act; or shall counterfeit or resemble the impression of the same upon any vellum, parchment, paper, cards, dice or other matter or thing, thereby to evade the payment of any duty hereby granted; or shall make, sign, print, utter, vend, or sell, any vellum, parchment, or paper, or other matter or thing, with such counterfeit mark or impression thereon, knowing such mark or impression to be counterfeited; then every person so offending shall be adjudged a felon, and shall suffer death as in cases of felony without the benefit of clergy.

The penalty of counterfeiting or forging any of the stamps, or the impressions thereof; or making, signing, printing or entering, any thing with such counterfeit mark, knowingly, is death.

XX. And it is hereby declared, That upon any prosecution or prosecutions for such felony, the dye, tool, or other instrument made use of in counterfeiting or forging any such seal, stamp, mark, type, device, or label, together with the vellum, parchment, paper, cards, dice, or other matter, or thing having such counterfeit impression, shall, immediately after the trial or con-

Counterfeit stamps, &c. after conviction of the party, to be destroyed in open court.

conviction of the party or parties accuſed, be broke, defaced, o deſtroyed, in open court.

Penalty of inrolling, &c. any matter or thing not duly ſtampt, is 20 l.

XXI. And be it further enacted by the authority aforeſaid That if any regiſter, publick officer, clerk, or other perſon i any court, regiſtry, or office within any of the ſaid colonies o plantations, ſhall, at any time after the ſaid firſt day of *Novemb* one thouſand ſeven hundred and ſixty five, enter, regiſter, or in roll, any matter or thing hereby charged with a ſtamp duty, un leſs the ſame ſhall appear to be duly ſtamped; in every ſuc caſe ſuch regiſter, publick officer, clerk, or other perſon, ſha for every ſuch offence, forfeit the ſum of twenty pounds.

Counſellors, or others to whom it belongs, neglecting to file or record in due time any matter for which a duty is payable, &c. forfeit 50 l.

XXII. And be it further enacted by the authority aforeſai That from and after the ſaid firſt day of *November*, one tho ſand ſeven hundred and ſixty five, if any counſellor, clerk, o ficer, attorney, or other perſon, to whom it ſhall appertain, o who ſhall be employed or intruſted, in the ſaid colonies or plan tations, to enter or file any matter or thing in reſpect wherec any duty ſhall be payable by virtue of this act, ſhall neglect t enter, file, or record the ſame, as by law the ſame ought to b entered, filed, or recorded, within the ſpace of four mont after he ſhall have received any money for or in reſpect of th ſame, or ſhall have promiſed or undertaken ſo to do; or ſha neglect to enter, file, or record, any ſuch matter or thing, be fore any ſubſequent, further or other proceeding, matter, o thing, in the ſame ſuit, ſhall be had, entered, filed, or recorded that then every ſuch counſellor, clerk, officer, attorney, or oth perſon ſo neglecting or offending, in each of the caſes aforeſai ſhall forfeit the ſum of fifty pounds for every ſuch offence.

Penalty of writing, &c. any matter, for which a duty is payable, on paper, &c. whereon other matters, chargeable with a duty, were before written, &c. or fraudulently eraſing the names, or other thing therein, or taking off the ſtamp to uſe it for any other matter, is 50 l.

XXIII. And be it further enacted by the authority afore ſaid, That if any perſon or perſons, at any time after the ſai firſt day of *November*, one thouſand ſeven hundred and ſixty fiv ſhall write, ingroſs, or print, or cauſe to be written, ingroſſe or printed, in the ſaid colonies or plantations, or any other part his ſaid Majeſty's dominions, either the whole or any part of a matter or thing whatſoever in reſpect whereof any duty is pa able by this act, upon any part of any piece of vellum, parch ment, or paper, whereon there ſhall have been before writte any other matter or thing in reſpect whereof any duty was pa able by this act; or ſhall fraudulently eraſe, or cauſe to be era ed, the name or names of any perſon or perſons, or any ſuc date, or other thing, ingroſſed, written, or printed, in ſuc matter or thing as aforeſaid; or fraudulently cut, tear, or ge off, any mark or ſtamp from any piece of vellum, parchment, or paper, or any part thereof, with intent to uſe ſuch ſtamp or mark for any other matter or thing in reſpect whereof any duty ſhall be payable by virtue of this act; that then, and ſo often, and in every ſuch caſe, every perſon ſo offending ſhall, for every ſuch offence, forfeit the ſum of fifty pounds.

Part of all writings, &c.

XXIV. And be it further enacted by the authority aforeſaid, That every matter and thing, in reſpect whereof any duty ſhall be payable in purſuance of this act, ſhall be ingroſſed, written,

or

or printed, in ſuch manner, that ſome part thereof ſhall be either upon, or as near as conveniently may be, to the ſtamps or marks denoting the duty; upon pain that the perſon who ſhall ingroſs, write, or print, or cauſe to be ingroſſed, written, or printed, any ſuch matter or thing in any other manner, ſhall, for every ſuch offence, forfeit the ſum of five pounds.

to be upon, or as near to, the ſtamps as may be; on penalty of 5 l.

XXV. And be it further enacted by the authority aforeſaid, That every officer of each court, and every juſtice of the peace or other perſon within the ſaid colonies and plantations, who ſhall iſſue any writ or proceſs upon which a duty is by this act payable, ſhall, at the iſſuing thereof, ſet down upon ſuch writ or proceſs the day and year of his iſſuing the ſame, which ſhall be entered upon a remembrance, or in a book to be kept for that purpoſe, ſetting forth the abſtract of ſuch writ or proceſs; upon pain to forfeit the ſum of ten pounds for every ſuch offence.

The day and year of iſſuing any writ or proceſs, for which a duty is payable, is to be ſet down on the writ, and an entry made thereof, on penalty of 10 l.

XXVI. And, for the better collecting and ſecuring the duties hereby charged on pamphlets containing more than one ſheet of paper as aforeſaid, be it further enacted by the authority aforeſaid, That from and after the ſaid firſt day of *November*, one thouſand ſeven hundred and ſixty five, one printed copy of every pamphlet which ſhall be printed or publiſhed within any of the ſaid colonies or plantations, ſhall within the ſpace of fourteen days after the printing thereof, be brought to the chief diſtributor in the colony or plantation where ſuch pamphlet ſhall be printed, and the title thereof, with the number of the ſheets contained therein, and the duty hereby charged thereon, ſhall be regiſtered or entered in a book to be there kept for that purpoſe; which duty ſhall be thereupon paid to the proper officer or officers appointed to receive the ſame, or his or their deputy or clerk, who ſhall thereupon forthwith give a receipt for the ſame on ſuch printed copy, to denote the payment of the duty hereby charged on ſuch pamphlet; and if any ſuch pamphlet ſhall be printed or publiſhed, and the duty hereby charged thereon ſhall not be duly paid, and the title and number of ſheets ſhall not be regiſtered, and a receipt for ſuch duty given on one copy, where required ſo to be, within the time herein before for that purpoſe limited; that then the author, printer, and publiſher, and all other perſons concerned in or about the printing or publiſhing of ſuch pamphlet, ſhall, for every ſuch offence, forfeit the ſum of ten pounds, and ſhall loſe all property therein, and in every other copy thereof, ſo as any perſon may freely print and publiſh the ſame, paying the duty payable in reſpect thereof by virtue of this act, without being liable to any action, proſecution, or penalty for ſo doing.

A printed copy of every pamphlet to be brought within 14 days to the chief diſtributor, in order to be regiſtered, and the duty aſcertained and paid.

Receipt to be given for the ſame on the copy;

Pamphlet printed or publiſhed without duty paid as directed, the author, printer, and publiſher, &c. to forfeit 10 l. and their property in the copy.

XXVII. And it is hereby further enacted by the authority aforeſaid, That no perſon whatſoever ſhall ſell or expoſe to ſale any ſuch pamphlet, or any news paper, without the true reſpective name or names, and place or places of abode, of ſome known perſon or perſons by or for whom the ſame was really and truly printed or publiſhed, ſhall be written or printed thereon;

Penalty of ſelling any pamphlet or news paper not having the name and place of abode of the printer or publisher, 20 l. thereon; upon pain that every person offending therein shall, for every such offence, forfeit the sum of twenty pounds.

No stamps for pamphlets or news papers to be delivered, till security be given for paying the duties for advertisements thereon.

XXVIII. And be it further enacted by the authority aforesaid, That no officer appointed for distributing stamped vellum, parchment, or paper, in the said colonies or plantations, shall sell or deliver any stamped paper for printing any pamphlet, or any publick news, intelligence, or occurrences, to be contained in one sheet, or any lesser piece of paper, unless such person shall give security to the said officer, for the payment of the duties for the advertisements which shall be printed therein or thereupon.

The stamps upon such news papers and pamphlets as shall remain unsold, are to be cancelled; the person tendering the same, being examined on oath as to the truth thereof, &c.

Officer to allow a like number of stamps in lieu of those cancelled.

Commissioners to make orders for regulating the method and times for such cancelling and allowance.

XXIX. And whereas it may be uncertain how many printed copies of the said printed news papers or pamphlets, to be contained in one sheet or in a lesser piece of paper, may be sold; and to the intent the duties hereby granted thereupon may not be lessened by printing a less number than may be sold, out of a fear of a loss thereby in printing more such copies than will be sold; it is hereby provided, and be it further enacted by the authority aforesaid, That the proper officer or officers appointed for managing the said stamp duties, shall and may cancel, or cause to be cancelled, all the stamps upon the copies of any impression of any news paper or pamphlet contained in one sheet, or any lesser piece of paper, which shall really and truly remain unsold, and of which no profit or advantage has been made; and upon oath, or if by a quaker, upon solemn affirmation, made before a justice of the peace, or other proper magistrate, that all such copies, containing the stamps so tendered to be cancelled, are really and truly remaining unsold, and that none of the said copies have been fraudulently returned or rebought, or any profit or advantage made thereof; which oath or affirmation such magistrate is hereby authorized to administer, and to examine upon oath or affirmation into all circumstances relating to the selling or disposing of such printed copies, shall and may deliver, or cause to be delivered, the like number of other sheets, half sheets, or less pieces of paper, properly stamped with the same respective stamps, upon payment made for such paper, but no duty shall be taken for the stamps thereon; any thing herein contained to the contrary notwithstanding: and the said commissioners for managing the stamp duties for the time being are hereby impowered, from time to time, to make such rules and orders for regulating the methods, and limiting the times, for such cancelling and allowance as aforesaid, with respect to such news papers and pamphlets, as they shall, upon experience and consideration of the several circumstances, find necessary or convenient, for the effectual securing the duties thereon, and doing justice to the persons concerned in the printing and publishing thereof.

Stamps may be delivered by the officer for printing

XXX. Provided always, and be it further enacted by the authority aforesaid, That any officer or officers employed by the said commissioners for managing the stamp duties, shall and may deliver to any person, by or for whom any almanack or almanacks

nacks ſhall have been printed, paper marked or ſtamped according to the true intent and meaning hereof, for the printing ſuch almanack or almanacks, upon his or her giving ſufficient ſecurity to pay the amount of the duty hereby charged thereon, within the ſpace of three months after ſuch delivery; and that the ſaid officer or officers, upon bringing to him or them any number of the copies of ſuch almanacks, within the ſpace of three months from the ſaid delivery and requeſt to him or them in that behalf made, ſhall cancel all the ſtamps upon ſuch copies, and abate to every ſuch perſon ſo much of the money due upon ſuch ſecurity as ſuch cancelled ſtamps ſhall amount to.

almanacks, upon giving ſecurity for the duties.

And he is to allow for almanacks brought to be cancelled within a certain time.

XXXI. Provided always, That where any almanack ſhall contain more than one ſheet of paper, it ſhall be ſufficient to ſtamp only one of the ſheets or pieces of paper upon which ſuch almanack ſhall be printed, and to pay the duty accordingly.

Where almanacks contain more than one ſheet, one of the ſheets only may be ſtampt.

XXXII. And it is hereby further enacted by the authority aforeſaid, That from and after the ſaid firſt day of *November*, one thouſand ſeven hundred and ſixty five, in caſe any perſon or perſons, within any of the ſaid colonies or plantations, ſhall ſell, hawk, carry about, utter, or expoſe to ſale, any almanack, or calendar, or any news paper, or any book, pamphlet, or paper, deemed or conſtrued to be, or ſerving the purpoſe of, an almanack or news paper, within the intention and meaning of this act, not being ſtamped or marked as by this act is directed; every ſuch perſon, ſhall for every ſuch offence, forfeit the ſum of forty ſhillings.

Perſons ſelling or hawking almanacks, or news papers, not being duly ſtampt, forfeit 40 s.

XXXIII. And be it further enacted by the authority aforeſaid, That from and after the ſaid firſt day of *November*, one thouſand ſeven hundred and ſixty five, the full ſum or ſums of money, or other valuable conſideration received, or in any wiſe directly or indirectly given, paid, agreed, or contracted, for, with, or in relation to any clerk or apprentice, within any of the ſaid colonies or plantations, ſhall be truly inſerted, or written in words at length, in ſome indenture or other writing which ſhall contain the covenants, articles, contracts, or agreements, relating to the ſervice of ſuch clerk or apprentice; and ſhall bear date upon the day of the ſigning, ſealing, or other execution of the ſame, upon pain that every maſter or miſtreſs to or with whom, or to whoſe uſe, any ſum of money, or other valuable conſideration whatſoever, ſhall be given, paid, ſecured, or contracted, for or in reſpect of any ſuch clerk or apprentice, which ſhall not be truly and fully ſo inſerted and ſpecified in ſome ſuch indenture, or other writing, ſhall, for every ſuch offence, forfeit double the ſum, or double the amount of any other valuable conſideration ſo given, paid, agreed, ſecured, or contracted for; to be ſued for and recovered at any time, during the term ſpecified in the indenture or writing for the ſervice of ſuch clerk or apprentice, or within one year after the determination thereof; and that all ſuch indentures, or other writings, ſhall be brought, within the ſpace of three months, to the pro-

Sums given with clerks or apprentices to be inſerted in the indentures,

and bear date the day of execution,

on forfeiture of double the ſaid ſums.

Indentures to be brought to the proper

per

officer within three months, and the duty to be then paid, &c.

per officer or officers, appointed by the ſaid commiſſioners for collecting the ſaid duties within the reſpective colony or plantation; and the duty hereby charged for the ſums, or other valuable conſideration inſerted therein, ſhall be paid by the maſter or miſtreſs of ſuch clerk or apprentice to the ſaid officer or officers, who ſhall give receipts for ſuch duty on the back of ſuch indentures or other writings; and in caſe the duty ſhall not be paid within the time before limited, ſuch maſter or miſtreſs ſhall forfeit double the amount of ſuch duty.

on forfeiture of double the amount.

Indentures declared void, where the fee is not inſerted, and the duty duly paid.

XXXIV. And be it further enacted by the authority aforeſaid, That all indentures or writings within the ſaid colonies and plantations, relating to the ſervice of clerks or apprentices, wherein ſhall not be truly inſerted or written the full ſum or ſums of money, or other valuable conſideration, received, or in any wiſe directly or indirectly given, paid, agreed, ſecured, or contracted for, with, or in relation to any ſuch clerk or apprentice, and a receipt given for the ſame by the officer or officers aforeſaid, or whereupon the duties payable by this act ſhall not be duly paid or lawfully tendered, according to the tenor and true meaning of this act, within the time herein for that purpoſe limited, ſhall be void and not available in any court or place, or to any purpoſe whatſoever.

Where maſter, &c. neglect to pay the duties, apprentice in ſuch caſe, upon payment of double duties, &c. is intitled to recover the apprentice fee;

XXXV. And be it further enacted by the authority aforeſaid, That if any maſter or miſtreſs of any clerk or apprentice ſhall neglect to pay the ſaid duty, within the time herein before limited, and any ſuch clerk or apprentice ſhall in that caſe pay, or cauſe to be paid, to the amount of double the ſaid duty, either during the term of ſuch clerkſhip or apprenticeſhip, or within one year after the determination thereof, ſuch maſter or miſtreſs not having then paid the ſaid double duty although required by ſuch clerk or apprentice ſo to do; then, and in ſuch caſe, it ſhall and may be lawful to and for any ſuch clerk or apprentice, within three months after ſuch payment of the ſaid double duty, to demand of ſuch maſter or miſtreſs, or his or her executors or adminiſtrators, ſuch ſum or ſums of money, or valuable conſideration, as was or were paid to ſuch maſter or miſtreſs, for or in reſpect of ſuch clerkſhip or apprenticeſhip; and in caſe ſuch ſum or ſums of money, or valuable conſideration, ſhall not be paid within three months after ſuch demand thereof made, it ſhall and may be lawful to and for any ſuch clerk or apprentice, or any other perſon or perſons on his or her behalf, to ſue for and recover the ſame, in ſuch manner as any penalty hereby inflicted may be ſued for and recovered; and ſuch clerks or apprentices ſhall, immediately after payment of ſuch double duty, be and are hereby diſcharged from their clerkſhips or apprenticeſhips, and from all actions, penalties, forfeitures, and damages, for not ſerving the time for which they were reſpectively bound, contracted for, or agreed to ſerve, and ſhall have ſuch and the ſame benefit and advantage of the time they ſhall reſpectively have continued with and ſerved ſuch maſter or miſtreſs, as they would

and to be diſcharged.

would have been intitled to in caſe ſuch duty had been paid by ſuch maſter or miſtreſs, within the time herein before limited for that purpoſe.

XXXVI. And be it further enacted by the authority aforeſaid, That all printed indentures, or contracts for binding clerks or apprentices, after the ſaid firſt day of *November*, one thouſand ſeven hundred and ſixty five, within the ſaid colonies and plantations, ſhall have the following notice or memorandum printed under the ſame, or added thereto, *videlicet*, Printed indentures to have the following notice added thereto.

THE *indenture muſt bear date the day it is executed, and the money or other thing, given or contracted for with the clerk or apprentice, muſt be inſerted in words at length, and the duty paid, and a receipt given on the back of the indenture, by the diſtributor of ſtamps, or his ſubſtitute, within three months after the execution of ſuch indenture, under the penalties inflicted by law.* The notice.

And if any printer, ſtationer, or other perſon or perſons, within any of the ſaid colonies or plantations, or any other part of his Majeſty's dominions, ſhall ſell, or cauſe to be ſold, any ſuch indenture or contract, without ſuch notice or memorandum being printed under the ſame, or added thereto; then, and in every ſuch caſe, ſuch printer, ſtationer, or other perſon or perſons, ſhall, for every ſuch offence, forfeit the ſum of ten pounds. Penalty of ſelling any ſuch indenture, without ſuch notice added, is 10 l.

XXXVII. And, for the better ſecuring the ſaid duty on playing cards and dice; be it further enacted by the authority aforeſaid, That from and after the ſaid firſt day of *November*, one thouſand ſeven hundred and ſixty five, no playing cards or dice ſhall be ſold, expoſed to ſale, or uſed in play, within the ſaid colonies or plantations, unleſs the paper and thread incloſing, or which ſhall have incloſed, the ſame, ſhall be or ſhall have been reſpectively ſealed and ſtamped, or marked, and unleſs one of the cards of each pack or parcel of cards, ſo ſold, ſhall be alſo marked or ſtamped on the ſpotted or painted ſide thereof with ſuch mark or marks as ſhall have been provided in purſuance of this act, upon pain that every perſon who ſhall ſell, or expoſe to ſale, any ſuch cards or dice which ſhall not have been ſo reſpectively ſealed, marked, or ſtamped, as hereby is reſpectively required, ſhall forfeit for every pack or parcel of cards, and every one of ſuch dice ſo ſold or expoſed to ſale, the ſum of ten pounds. No unſtamped cards or dice to be ſold, or uſed, on penalty of 10 l.

XXXVIII. And it is hereby enacted by the authority aforeſaid, That if any perſon within the ſaid colonies or plantations, or any other part of his Majeſty's dominions, ſhall ſell or buy any cover or label which has before been made uſe of for denoting the ſaid duty upon cards, in order to be made uſe of for the incloſing any pack or parcel of cards; every perſon ſo offending ſhall, for every ſuch offence, forfeit twenty pounds. Penalty of buying or ſelling covers, &c. before made uſe of, denoting the duty, in order to incloſe other cards, is 20l.

XXXIX. Provided always, and be it enacted by the authority aforeſaid, That if either the buyer or ſeller of any ſuch cover or label ſhall inform againſt the other party concerned in buying or ſelling ſuch cover or label, the party ſo informing ſhall be admitted Buyer or ſeller informing, is indemnified againſt the penalty.

mitted to give evidence against the party informed against, and shall be indemnified against the said penalties.

Penalty of fraudulently inclosing cards in a stamp cover before made use of, is 20 l.

XL. And be it further enacted by the authority aforesaid, That if any person or persons shall fraudulently inclose any parcel or pack of playing cards in any outside paper so sealed and stamped as aforesaid, the same having been made use of for the purpose aforesaid; then, so often, and in every such case, every person so offending in any of the particulars before-mentioned, shall, for every such offence, forfeit the sum of twenty pounds.

Officers delivering out licences for retailing spirituous liquors or wine, are to transmit, within every two months, an account of the number so delivered, and the parties names,

on forfeiture of 50 l.

XLI. And be it further enacted by the authority aforesaid, That from and after the said first day of *November*, one thousand seven hundred and sixty five, every clerk, officer, and other person employed or concerned in granting, making out, or delivering licences for retailing spirituous liquors or wine within any of the said colonies or plantations, shall, and he is hereby required and directed, within two months after delivering any such licences, to transmit to the chief distributor of stamped vellum, parchment, and paper, a true and exact list or account of the number of licences so delivered, in which shall be inserted the names of the persons licensed, and the places where they respectively reside; and if any such clerk, officer, or other person shall refuse or neglect to transmit any such list or account to such distributor, or shall transmit a false or untrue one, then, and in every such case, such clerk, officer, or other person, shall, for every such offence, forfeit fifty pounds.

Such licences to be in force for one year only.

XLII. And be it further enacted by the authority aforesaid, That licences for selling or uttering by retail spirituous liquors or wine within any of the said colonies and plantations, shall be in force and serve for no longer than one year from the date of each licence respectively.

Where a person licenced shall die or remove, the licence shall be good for the unexpired term thereof.

XLIII. Provided nevertheless, and be it enacted by the authority aforesaid, That if any person licenced to sell spirituous liquors or wines, shall die or remove from the house or place wherein such spirituous liquors or wine shall, by virtue of such licence, be sold, it shall and may be lawful for the executors, administrators, or assigns of such person so dying or removing, who shall be possessed of such house or place, or for any occupier of such house or place, to sell spirituous liquors or wine therein during the residue of the term for which such licence shall have been granted, without any new licence to be had or obtained in that behalf; any thing to the contrary thereof in any wise notwithstanding.

Persons selling wine or spirits in a less quantity than one gallon, without taking out a licence, forfeit 20 l.

XLIV. And it is hereby enacted by the authority aforesaid, That if any person or persons shall sell or utter by retail, *that is to say*, in any less quantity than one gallon at any one time, any kind of wine, or any liquor called or reputed wine, or any kind of spirituous liquors, in the said colonies or plantations, without taking out such licence yearly and every year, he, she, or they so offending shall, for every such offence, forfeit the sum of twenty pounds.

XLV. And be it further enacted by the authority aforesaid,

That

That every perſon who ſhall retail ſpirituous liquors or wine in any priſon or houſe of correction, or any workhouſe appointed or to be appointed for the reception of poor perſons within any of the ſaid colonies or plantations, ſhall be deemed a retailer of ſpirituous liquors or wine within this act.

Perſons retailing ſpirituous liquors or wine in any priſon, &c. are deemed retailers.

XLVI. Provided always, and be it further enacted by the authority aforeſaid, That if at any time after the ſaid firſt day of *November*, one thouſand ſeven hundred and ſixty five, there ſhall not be any proviſion made for licenſing the retailers of wine or ſpirituous liquors, within any of the ſaid colonies or plantations; then, and in every ſuch caſe, and during ſuch time as no proviſion ſhall be made, ſuch licences ſhall and may be granted for the ſpace of one year, and renewed from time to time by the governor or commander in chief of every ſuch reſpective colony or plantation.

If no proviſion ſhall be made for licenſing retailers, licences may be granted and renewed by the reſpective governors.

XLVII. And it is hereby further enacted by the authority aforeſaid, That every perſon who ſhall at any one time buy of any chief diſtributor within any of the ſaid colonies or plantations, vellum, parchment, or paper, the duties whereof ſhall amount to five pounds ſterling money of *Great Britain*, or upwards, ſhall be allowed after the rate of four pounds *per centum*, upon the prompt payment of the ſaid duties to ſuch chief diſtributor.

Perſons buying at any one time, of the chief diſtributors, ſtamps to the amount of 5l. are to be allowed 4l. per cent. on prompt payment.

XLVIII. And be it further enacted by the authority aforeſaid, That all publick clerks or officers within the ſaid colonies or plantations, who ſhall from time to time have in their cuſtody any publick books, or other matters or things hereby charged with a ſtamp duty, ſhall, at any ſeaſonable time or times, permit any officer or officers thereunto authorized by the ſaid commiſſioners for managing the ſtamp duties, to inſpect and view all ſuch publick books, matters, and things, and to take thereout ſuch notes and memorandums as ſhall be neceſſary for the purpoſe of aſcertaining or ſecuring the ſaid duties, without fee or reward; upon pain that every ſuch clerk or other officer who ſhall refuſe or neglect ſo to do, upon reaſonable requeſt in that behalf made, ſhall, for every ſuch refuſal or neglect, forfeit the ſum of twenty pounds.

Commiſſioners officers to be allowed to inſpect, and take notes from all publick books in the publick offices where ſtamp duties are charged, in order to aſcertain the duties, on penalty of 20l.

XLIX. And be it further enacted by the authority aforeſaid, That the high treaſurer of *Great Britain*, or the commiſſioners of his Majeſty's treaſury, or any three or more of ſuch commiſſioners, for the time being, ſhall once in every year at leaſt, ſet the prices at which all ſorts of ſtamped vellum, parchment, and paper, ſhall be ſold by the ſaid commiſſioners for managing the ſtamp duties, and their officers; and that the ſaid commiſſioners for the ſaid duties ſhall cauſe ſuch prices to be marked upon every ſuch ſkin and piece of vellum and parchment, and ſheet and piece paper: and if any officer or diſtributor to be appointed by virtue of this act, ſhall ſell, or cauſe to be ſold, any vellum, parchment, or paper, for a greater or higher price or ſum, than the price or ſum ſo ſet or affixed thereon; every ſuch officer or diſ-

Treaſury to ſet annually the price of ſtamps; the prices ſo ſet to be marked thereon; officers ſelling them at a higher price, forfeit 20l.

diſtributor ſhall, for every ſuch offence, forfeit the ſum of twenty pounds.

Officers employed in raiſing or paying the reſpective duties, to exhibit an atteſted account thereof yearly, or oftner, before the governor, in order that the ſame be tranſmitted to the commiſſioners.

L. And be it alſo enacted by the authority aforeſaid, That the ſeveral officers who ſhall be reſpectively employed in the raiſing, receiving, collecting, or paying, the ſeveral duties hereby charged, within the ſaid colonies and plantations, ſhall every twelve months, or oftner, if thereunto required by the ſaid commiſſioners for managing the ſaid duties, exhibit his and their reſpective account and accounts of the ſaid ſeveral duties upon oath, or if a quaker upon affirmation, in the preſence of the governor, or commander in chief, or principal judge of the colony or plantation where ſuch officers ſhall be reſpectively reſident, in ſuch manner as the high treaſurer, or the commiſſioners of the treaſury, or any three or more of ſuch commiſſioners for the time being, ſhall, from time to time, direct and appoint, in order that the ſame may be immediately afterwards tranſmitted by the ſaid officer or officers to the commiſſioners for managing the ſaid duties, to be comptrolled and audited according to the uſual courſe and form of comptrolling and auditing the accounts of the ſtamp duties ariſing within this kingdom: and if any of the ſaid officers ſhall neglect or refuſe to exhibit any ſuch account, or to verify the ſame upon oath or affirmation, or to tranſmit any ſuch account ſo verified to the commiſſioners for managing the ſaid duties, in ſuch manner, and within ſuch time, as ſhall be ſo appointed or directed; or ſhall neglect or refuſe to pay, or cauſe to be paid, into the hands of the receiver general of the ſtamp duties in *Great Britain*, or to ſuch other perſon or perſons as the high treaſurer, or commiſſioners of the treaſury, or any three or more of ſuch commiſſioners for the time being, ſhall, from time to time, nominate or appoint, the monies reſpectively raiſed, levied, and received, by ſuch officers under the authority of this act, at ſuch times, and in ſuch manner, as they ſhall be reſpectively required by the ſaid high treaſurer, or commiſſioners of the treaſury; or if any ſuch officers ſhall divert, detain, or miſapply, all or any part of the ſaid monies ſo by them reſpectively raiſed, levied, and received, or ſhall knowingly return any perſon or perſons *inſuper* for any monies or other things duly anſwered, paid, or accounted for, by ſuch perſon or perſons, whereby he or they ſhall ſuſtain any damage or prejudice; in every ſuch caſe, every ſuch officer ſhall be liable to pay treble the value of all and every ſum and ſums of money ſo diverted or miſapplied; and ſhall alſo be liable to pay treble damages to the party grieved, by returning him *inſuper*.

Officer refuſing ſo to do, or not duly paying over the money in his hands; or diverting or miſapplying any part thereof: or returning any perſon *inſuper* for monies paid; forfeits treble the ſums diverted or miſapplied, and treble damages to the party grieved.

Receivers general of the duties to exhibit their accounts to the auditors of the impreſt, between 10 Oc-

LI. And be it further enacted by the authority aforeſaid, That the commiſſioners, receiver or receivers general, or other perſon or perſons, who ſhall be reſpectively employed in *Great Britain*, in the directing, receiving, or paying, the monies ariſing by the duties hereby granted, ſhall, and are hereby required, between the tenth day of *October* and the fifth day of *January* following, and ſo from year to year, yearly, at thoſe times, to to exhibit their reſpective accounts thereof to his Majeſty's auditors of the impreſt in *England* for the time being, or one of them, to be declared before the high treaſurer, or commiſſioners of the treaſury and chancellor of the exchequer for the time being, according to the courſe of the exchequer.

tob. and 5 Jan. yearly, to be declared before the treaſury and exchequer.

LII. And be it further enacted by the authority aforeſaid, That if the ſaid commiſſioners for managing the ſaid duties, or the ſaid receiver or receivers general, ſhall neglect or refuſe to pay into the exchequer all or any of the ſaid monies, in ſuch manner as they are required by this act to pay the ſame, or ſhall divert or miſapply any part thereof; then they, and every of them ſo offending, ſhall be liable to pay double the value of all and every ſum and ſums of money ſo diverted or miſapplied.

Commiſſioners or receivers general not duly paying the monies into the exchequer, or miſapplying any part thereof, liable to pay double the value of the ſums miſapplied.

LIII. And be it further enacted by the authority aforeſaid, That the comptroller or comptrollers for the time being of the duties hereby impoſed, ſhall keep perfect and diſtinct accounts in books fairly written of all the monies ariſing by the ſaid duties; and if any ſuch comptroller or comptrollers ſhall neglect his or their duty therein, then he or they, for every ſuch offence, ſhall forfeit the ſum of one hundred pounds.

Comptroller of the duties to keep an account of the monies ariſing thereby, on penalty of 100 l.

LIV. And be it further enacted by the authority aforeſaid, That all the monies which ſhall ariſe by the ſeveral rates and duties hereby granted (except the neceſſary charges of raiſing, collecting, recovering, anſwering, paying, and accounting for the ſame, and the neceſſary charges from time to time incurred in relation to this act, and the execution thereof) ſhall be paid into the receipt of his Majeſty's exchequer, and ſhall be entered ſeparate and apart from all other monies, and ſhall be there reſerved to be from time to time diſpoſed of by parliament, towards further defraying the neceſſary expences of defending, protecting, and ſecuring, the ſaid colonies and plantations.

Monies ariſing by the duties (charges thereon excepted) to be paid into the exchequer apart, and reſerved for the diſpoſition of parliament, &c.

LV. And whereas, it is proper that ſome proviſion ſhould be made for payment of the neceſſary expences which have been, and ſhall be incurred in relation to this act, and the execution thereof; and of the orders and rules to be eſtabliſhed under the authority of the ſame, before the ſaid duties ſhall take effect, or the monies ariſing thereby ſhall be ſufficient to diſcharge ſuch expences; be it therefore enacted by the authority aforeſaid, That his Majeſty may, and he is hereby impowered by any warrant or warrants under his royal ſign manual, at any time or times before the twentieth day of *April*, one thouſand ſeven hundred and ſixty ſix, to cauſe to be iſſued and paid out of any of the ſurpluſſes, exceſſes, overplus monies, and other revenues compoſing the fund commonly called *The ſinking fund* (except ſuch monies of the ſaid ſinking fund as are appropriated to any particular uſe or uſes, by any former act or acts of parliament in that behalf) ſuch ſum and ſums of money as ſhall be neceſſary to defray the ſaid expences; and the monies ſo iſſued, ſhall be reimburſed, by payment into the exchequer of the like ſum or

Charges attending the execution of this act before the duties take effect, to be paid out of the ſinking fund, by warrant from the King, at any time before 20 April, 1766; the ſaid monies to be repaid out of the duties. or ſums out of the firſt monies which ſhall ariſe by virtue of this act; which monies, upon the payment thereof into the exchequer, ſhall be carried to the account, and made part of the ſaid fund.

Three commiſſioners impowered to act. LVI. And it is hereby further enacted and declared, That all the powers and authorities by this act granted to the commiſſioners for managing the duties upon ſtamped vellum, parchment, and paper, ſhall and may be fully and effectually carried into execution by any three or more of the ſaid commiſſioners; any thing herein before contained to the contrary notwithſtanding.

Penalties and forfeitures incurred after 29 Sept. 1765, for offences againſt act 4 Geo. 3. LVII. And be it further enacted by the authority aforeſaid, That all forfeitures and penalties incurred after the twenty ninth day of *September*, one thouſand ſeven hundred and ſixty five, for offences committed againſt an act paſſed in the fourth year of the reign of his preſent Majeſty, intituled, *An act for granting certain duties in the* Britiſh *colonies and plantations in* America; *for continuing, amending, and making perpetual, an act paſſed in the ſixth year of the reign of his late majeſty King* George *the Second, intituled,* An act for the better ſecuring and encouraging the trade of his Majeſty's ſugar colonies in *America*; *for applying the produce of ſuch duties, and of the duties to ariſe by virtue of the ſaid act, towards defraying the expences of defending, protecting, and ſecuring, the ſaid colonies and plantations*; *for explaining an act made in the twenty fifth year of the reign of King* Charles *the Second, intituled,* An act for the encouragement of the *Greenland* and *Eaſtland* trades, and for the better ſecuring the plantation trade; *and for altering and diſallowing ſeveral drawbacks on exports from this kingdom, and more effectually preventing the clandeſtine conveyance of goods to and from the ſaid colonies and plantations, and improving and ſecuring the trade between the ſame and* Great Britain, and for offences committed againſt any other act or acts of parliament relating to the trade or revenues of the ſaid colonies or plantations; ſhall and may be proſecuted, ſued for, and recovered, in any court of record, or in any court of admiralty, in the reſpective colony or plantation where the offence ſhall be committed, or in any court of vice admiralty appointed or to be appointed, and which ſhall have juriſdiction within ſuch colony, plantation, or place, (which courts of admiralty or vice admiralty are hereby reſpectively authorized and required to proceed, hear, and determine the ſame) at the election of the informer or proſecutor.

where to be proſecuted and recovered.

The monies granted as duties and impoſitions, &c. to be conſidered and paid as ſterling money of Great Britain; at the rate of 5s. 6d. per oz. in ſilver. LVIII. And it is hereby further enacted and declared by the authority aforeſaid, That all ſums of money granted and impoſed by this act as rates or duties, and alſo all ſums of money impoſed as forfeitures or penalties, and all ſums of money required to be paid, and all other monies herein mentioned, ſhall be deemed and taken to be ſterling money of *Great Britain*, and ſhall be collected, recovered, and paid, to the amount of the value which ſuch nominal ſums bear in *Great Britain*; and that ſuch monies ſhall and may be received and taken, according to the pro-

proportion and value of five ſhillings and ſix pence the ounce in ſilver; and that all the forfeitures and penalties hereby inflicted, and which ſhall be incurred, in the ſaid colonies and plantations, ſhall and may be proſecuted, ſued for, and recovered, in any court of record, or in any court of admiralty, in the reſpective colony or plantation where the offence ſhall be committed, or in any court of vice admiralty appointed or to be appointed, and which ſhall have juriſdiction within ſuch colony, plantation, or place, (which courts of admiralty or vice admiralty are hereby reſpectively authorized and required to proceed, hear, and determine the ſame,) at the election of the informer or proſecutor; and that from and after the twenty ninth day of *September*, one thouſand ſeven hundred and ſixty five, in all caſes, where any ſuit or proſecution ſhall be commenced and determined for any penalty or forfeiture inflicted by this act, or by the ſaid act made in the fourth year of his preſent Majeſty's reign, or by any other act of parliament relating to the trade or revenues of the ſaid colonies or plantations, in any court of admiralty in the reſpective colony or plantation where the offence ſhall be committed, either party, who ſhall think himſelf aggrieved by ſuch determination, may appeal from ſuch determination to any court of vice admiralty appointed or to be appointed, and which ſhall have juriſdiction within ſuch colony, plantation, or place, (which court of vice admiralty is hereby authorized and required to proceed, hear, and determine ſuch appeal) any law, cuſtom, or uſage, to the contrary notwithſtanding; and the forfeitures and penalties hereby inflicted, which ſhall be incurred in any other part of his Majeſty's dominions, ſhall and may be proſecuted, ſued for, and recovered, with full coſts of ſuit, in any court of record within the kingdom, territory, or place, where the offence ſhall be committed, in ſuch and the ſame manner as any debt or damage, to the amount of ſuch forfeiture or penalty, can or may be ſued for and recovered.

Penalties and forfeitures in the colonies and plantations are recoverable in any of the courts of record where the offence is committed, &c.

but perſons aggrieved by the determinations of any of the ſaid courts, under this act, or the act of 4 Geo. 3. may appeal to a vice-admiralty court.

Penalties and forfeitures incurred in other parts, to be recovered with full coſts, in any court of record in the place.

LIX. And it is hereby further enacted, That all the forfeitures and penalties hereby inflicted ſhall be divided, paid, and applied, as follows; (that is to ſay) one third part of all ſuch forfeitures and penalties recovered in the ſaid colonies and plantations, ſhall be paid into the hands of one of the chief diſtributors of ſtamped vellum, parchment, and paper, reſiding in the colony or plantation wherein the offender ſhall be convicted, for the uſe of his Majeſty, his heirs, and ſucceſſors; one third part of the penalties and forfeitures, ſo recovered, to the governor or commander in chief of ſuch colony or plantation; and the other third part thereof, to the perſon who ſhall inform or ſue for the ſame; and that one moiety of all ſuch penalties and forfeitures recovered in any other part of his Majeſty's dominions, ſhall be to the uſe of his Majeſty, his heirs, and ſucceſſors, and the other moiety thereof, to the perſon who ſhall inform or ſue for the ſame.

Forfeitures, &c. in the colonies and plantations to be paid over, one third to the chief diſtributor, for the King's uſe, one third to the governor, and one third to the proſecutor.

In other parts, one moiety to the King, and the other to the proſecutor.

LX. And be it further enacted by the authority aforeſaid, That

Offences made felonies, to be tried in any of the courts of law where committed.

That all the offences which are by this act made felony, and shall be committed within any part of his Majesty's dominions, shall and may be heard, tried, and determined, before any court of law within the respective kingdom, territory, colony, or plantation, where the offence shall be committed, in such and the same manner as all other felonies can or may be heard, tried, and determined, in such court.

Governors to be sworn to the due execution of this act.

Penalty on not taking such oath,

or not discharging their duty, the same as is expressed in act 7 & 8 Will. 3.

Oath by whom to be administered.

LXI. And be it further enacted by the authority aforesaid, That all the present governors or commanders in chief of any *British* colony or plantation, shall, before the said first day of *November*, one thousand seven hundred and sixty five, and all who hereafter shall be made governors or commanders in chief of the said colonies or plantations, or any of them, before their entrance into their government, shall take a solemn oath to do their utmost, that all and every the clauses contained in this present act be punctually and *bona fide* observed, according to the true intent and meaning thereof, so far as appertains unto the said governors or commanders in chief respectively, under the like penalties, forfeitures, and disabilities, either for neglecting to take the said oath, or for wittingly neglecting to do their duty accordingly, as are mentioned and expressed in an act made in the seventh and eighth year of the reign of King *William* the Third, intituled, *An act for preventing frauds, and regulating abuses, in the plantation trade*; and the said oath hereby required to be taken, shall be administered by such person or persons as hath or have been, or shall be, appointed to administer the oath required to be taken by the said act made in the seventh and eighth year of the reign of King *William* the Third.

Records and other writings charged with the duties, to be ingrossed and written as usually.

LXII. And be it further enacted by the authority aforesaid, That all records, writs, pleadings, and other proceedings in all courts whatsoever, and all deeds, instruments, and writings whatsoever, hereby charged, shall be ingrossed and written in such manner as they have been usually accustomed to be ingrossed and written, or are now ingrossed and written within the said colonies and plantations.

General issue.

Treble costs.

LXIII. And it is hereby further enacted, That if any person or persons shall be sued or prosecuted, either in *Great Britain* or *America*, for any thing done in pursuance of this act, such person and persons shall and may plead the general issue, and give this act and the special matter in evidence; and if it shall appear so to have been done, the jury shall find for the defendant or defendants: and if the plaintiff or plaintiffs shall become nonsuited, or discontinue his or their action after the defendant or defendants shall have appeared, or if judgement shall be given upon any verdict or demurrer against the plaintiff or plaintiffs, the defendant or defendants shall recover treble costs, and have the like remedy for the same, as defendants have in other cases by law.

CAP.

CAP. XIII.

An act for impowering the commissioners for putting in execution the several acts passed for paving, cleansing, and lighting the squares, streets, and lanes, within the city and liberty of Westminster, *and parts adjacent, to collect certain tolls on* Sundays, *upon the several roads therein mentioned, and apply the same for the purposes of the said acts.*

WHEREAS *an act was made in the second year of his present Majesty's reign, intituled,* An act for paving, cleansing, and lighting, the squares, streets, and lanes, within the city and liberty of *Westminster*; the parishes of *Saint Giles in the Fields*, *Saint George the Martyr*, *Saint George Bloomsbury*, that part of the parish of *Saint Andrew's Holbourn* which lies in the county of *Middlesex*, the several liberties of the *Rolls* and *Savoy*, and that part of the duchy of *Lancaster* which lies in the county of *Middlesex*, and for preventing annoyances therein, and for other purposes therein mentioned: *and whereas an act was made in the third year of his present Majesty's reign, to explain, amend, and render more effectual, the said former act: and whereas an act was made the last session of parliament, to explain, amend, and render more effectual, the said two former acts: and whereas great progress has been made in executing and performing the several powers and authorities in the said acts contained; but for want of a sufficient fund the same cannot be completed:* wherefore, and to the end and intent that so useful an undertaking may be effectually carried into execution, may it please your Majesty, that it may be enacted; and be it enacted, *&c.* Preamble.

A street toll to be paid at the several turnpikes here mentioned, before any cattle or carriage shall be permitted to pass. The tolls. The said tolls to be taken above and exclusive of all other tolls. Tolls vested in commissioners. Tolls to be levied by distress and sale. Distress may be sold after 4 days. Commissioners may erect turnpikes, &c. Turnpikes, &c. vested in the commissioners. Tolls may be collected at the turnpikes already erected. Tolls to be paid but once a day. Commissioners may lease, &c. the tolls. Commissioners may appoint officers. Officers to account upon oath. Officers refusing to account, justices to inquire into the default, and commit the offender, until payment or composition be made. Commissioners to allow officers salaries. Penalty on forcibly passing through the gates, &c. or giving or receiving tickets, &c. to avoid payment of the tolls. Tolls may be assigned for money borrowed. Assignments to be entered in a book. Assignments may be transferred. Entries of all assignments to be made. All creditors deemed equal in degree. Commencement and continuance of the tolls. Charges of passing this act to be first paid. Persons aggrieved may appeal to the quarter session. Notice of appeal to be given. Recognizance to be entered into. Proceedings not to be quashed for want of form, nor removeable by Certiorari. Writings to be without stamps. Limitation of actions. General issue. Treble costs. Publick act.

CAP. XIV.

An act for the more effectual preservation fish in fish ponds and others waters; and conies in warrens; and for preventing the damage done to sea banks, within the county of Lincoln, *by the breeding conies therein.*

Preamble.

WHEREAS *the several laws in being for the preservation of the fish in rivers, ponds, pools, moats, stews, and other waters, are by experience found to be ineffectual to deter divers loose, idle, and disorderly persons, from stealing, taking away, or destroying, the fish therein bred and preserved*; may it therefore please your most excellent Majesty, that it may be enacted; and be it enacted by the King's most excellent majesty, by and with the advice and consent of the lords spiritual and temporal and commons, in this present parliament assembled, and by the authority of the same, That in case any person or persons from and after the first day of *June*, one thousand seven hundred and sixty five, shall enter into any park or paddock fenced in and inclosed, or into any garden, orchard, or yard, adjoining or belonging to any dwelling-house, in or through which park or paddock, garden, orchard, or yard, any river or stream of water shall run or be, or wherein shall be any river, stream, pond, pool, moat, stew, or other water, and by any ways, means, or device whatsoever, shall steal, take, kill, or destroy, any fish bred, kept, or preserved, in any such river or stream, pond, pool, moat, stew, or other water aforesaid, without the consent of the owner or owners thereof; or shall be aiding or assisting in the stealing, taking, killing, or destroying, any such fish as aforesaid; or shall receive or buy any such fish knowing the same to be so stolen or taken as aforesaid; and being thereof indicted within six calendar months next after such offence or offences shall have been committed, before any judge or justices of goal delivery for the county wherein such park or paddock, garden, orchard, or yard, shall be, and shall on such indictment be, by verdict, or his or their own confession or confessions, convicted of any such offence or offences as aforesaid; the person or persons so convicted shall be transported for seven years.

After 1 June, 1765, persons convicted, within 6 months after the offence, of stealing or destroying fish in fish ponds, &c. or aiding or assisting therein; or knowingly receiving or buying such fish; are to be transported for 7 years.

II. And, for the more easy and speedy apprehending and convicting of such person or persons as shall be guilty of any of the offences before-mentioned, be it further enacted by the authority aforesaid, That in case any person or persons shall, at any time after the said first day of *June*, commit or be guilty of any such offence or offences as are herein before mentioned, and shall surrender himself to any one of his Majesty's justices of the peace in and for the county where such offence or offences shall have been committed; or, being apprehended and taken, or in custody for such offence or offences, or on any other account, and shall voluntarily make a full confession thereof, and a true discovery, upon oath, of the person or persons who was or were his accomplice or accomplices in any of the said offences, so

Any offender making a discovery of, and convicting, his accomplices, is intitled to pardon.

ſo as ſuch accomplice or accomplices may be apprehended and taken, and ſhall, on trial of ſuch accomplice or accomplices, give ſuch evidence of ſuch offence or offences, as ſhall be ſufficient to convict ſuch accomplice or accomplices thereof; ſuch perſon making ſuch confeſſion and diſcovery, and giving ſuch evidence as aforeſaid, ſhall, by virtue of this act, be pardoned, acquitted, and diſcharged of and from the offence or offences ſo by him confeſſed as aforeſaid.

III. And be it further enacted by the authority aforeſaid, That in caſe any perſon or perſons ſhall, after the ſaid firſt day of *June*, take, kill, or deſtroy, or attempt to take, kill, or deſtroy, any fiſh, in any river or ſtream, pond, pool, or other water (not being in any park or paddock, or in any garden, orchard, or yard, adjoining or belonging to any dwelling houſe, but ſhall be in any other incloſed ground which ſhall be private property) every ſuch perſon, being lawfully convicted thereof by the oath of one or more credible witneſs or witneſſes, ſhall forfeit and pay, for every ſuch offence, the ſum of five pounds, to the owner or owners of the fiſhery of ſuch river or ſtream of water, or of ſuch pond, pool, moat, or other water: and it ſhall and may be lawful to and for any one or more of his Majeſty's juſtices of the peace of the county, diviſion, riding, or place, where ſuch laſt mentioned offence or offences ſhall be commited, upon complaint made to him or them, upon oath, againſt any perſon or perſons, for any ſuch laſt-mentioned offence or offences, to iſſue his or their warrant or warrants to bring the perſon or perſons ſo complained of, before him or them; and, if the perſon or perſons ſo complained of ſhall be convicted of any of the ſaid offences laſt-mentioned, before ſuch juſtice or juſtices, or any other of his Majeſty's juſtices of the ſame county, diviſion, riding or place aforeſaid, by the oath or oaths of one or more credible witneſs or witneſſes, which oath ſuch juſtice or juſtices are hereby authorized to adminiſter, or by his or their own confeſſion; then, and in ſuch caſe, the party ſo convicted ſhall, immediately after ſuch conviction, pay the ſaid penalty of five pounds, hereby before impoſed for the offence or offences aforeſaid, to ſuch juſtice or juſtices before whom he ſhall be ſo convicted, for the uſe of ſuch perſon or perſons as the ſame is hereby appointed to be forfeited and paid unto; and, in default thereof, ſhall be committed by ſuch juſtice or juſtices to the houſe of correction, for any time not exceeding ſix months, unleſs the money forfeited ſhall be ſooner paid.

Perſons convicted of taking or deſtroying, &c. fiſh in rivers or other waters,

forfeit to the owner of the fiſhery 5l.

On complaint of the offence, juſtice to iſſue his warrant for apprehending the offender;

and the penalty to be paid down upon conviction; otherwiſe the offender to be committed to the houſe of correction for 6 months;

IV. Provided nevertheleſs, That it ſhall and may be lawful to and for ſuch owner or owners of the fiſhery of ſuch river or ſtream of water, or of ſuch pond, pool, or other water, wherein any ſuch offence or offences laſt-mentioned ſhall be committed as aforeſaid, to ſue and proſecute for, and recover the ſaid ſum of five pounds, by action of debt, bill, plaint, or information, in any of his Majeſty's courts of record at *Weſtminſter*; and in ſuch action or ſuit, no eſſoin, wager of law, or more than one imparlance ſhall be allowed; provided that ſuch action or ſuit be brought, or commenced, within ſix calendar months next after ſuch offence or offences ſhall have been committed.

or an action may be brought for the penalty in any of the courts at Weſtminſter,

within 6 months after the offence.

V. Pro-

None liable to forfeit for taking fish in any river, &c. wherein they have a right.

V. Provided always, and be it further enacted by the authority aforesaid, That nothing in this act shall extend, or be construed to extend, to subject or make liable any person or persons to the penalties of this act, who shall fish, take, or kill, and carry away any fish, in any river or stream of water, pond, pool, or other water, wherein such person or persons shall have a just right or claim to take, kill, or carry away any such fish.

VI. And whereas there are many thousand acres of land in this kingdom altogether unfit for cultivation, and yet the same are capable of rendering great profit, by the breeding and maintaining conies, as well to the owners of such lands, as to a multitude of industrious manufacturers, who gain their livelihood by working up coney wool: and whereas a great part of the said land is already used as warrens, in the breeding and maintaining conies, but, because divers disorderly persons, neglecting their own lawful trades, have betaken themselves to the taking, killing, and stealing of conies, in the night-time, whereby the owners and occupiers of such warrens are greatly discouraged, and many such owners and occupiers have been induced to destroy such warrens, and others have been deterred from stocking other lands, to the great prejudice of the manufactures of this kingdom: and whereas the provisions already subsisting have, by experience, been found insufficient for the effectual preservation of of conies in warrens: for remedy whereof, be it further enacted,

Persons convicted of entering warrens, in the night-time, and taking or killing conies there,

or aiding or assisting therein,

may be punished by transportation, or by whipping, fine, or imprisonment.

That if any person or persons shall, from and after the first day of *June*, one thousand seven hundred and sixty five, wilfully and wrongfully, in the night-time, enter into any warren or grounds lawfully used or kept for the breeding or keeping of conies, although the same be not inclosed, and shall then and there wilfully and wrongfully take or kill, in the night-time, any coney or conies, against the will of the owner or occupier thereof, or shall be aiding and assisting therein, and shall be convicted of the same before any of his Majesty's justices of oyer and terminer, or general gaol delivery, for the county where such offence or offences shall be committed; every such person and persons so offending, and being thereof lawfully convicted in manner aforesaid, shall and may be transported for the space of seven years, or suffer such other lesser punishment by whipping, fine, or imprisonment, as the court, before whom such person or persons shall be tried, shall, in their discretion, award, and direct.

Persons convicted on this act, not liable to be convicted under any former act.

VII. Provided always, and be it enacted, That no person who shall be convicted of any offence against this act, shall be liable to be convicted for any such offence under any former act or acts, law or laws, now in force.

This act not to extend to the destroying

VIII. And whereas great mischief and damage has been, and still may be, occasioned by the increase of conies upon the sea and river banks in the county of *Lincoln*, or upon the land or ground within a certain distance from the said banks: for remedy thereof, be it enacted by the authority aforesaid, That nothing in this act contained shall extend, or be construed to extend

tend, to prevent any person or persons from killing and destroying, or from taking and carrying away, in the day-time, any conies that shall be found on any sea or river banks, erected, or to be erected, for the preservation of the adjoining lands from being overflowed by the sea or river waters, so far as the flux and reflux of the tide does or shall extend, or upon any land or ground within one furlong distance of such sea or river banks; but that it shall and may be lawful to and for any person or persons, to enter upon any such banks, land, or ground, as aforesaid, within the said county of *Lincoln*, and to kill, destroy, take, and carry away, in the day-time, to his or their own use, any conies so found upon any such banks, land, or ground, as aforesaid, within the said county, he or they doing as little damage as may be to the owner or tenant of such banks, land, or ground; any thing in this or any other act contained to the contrary notwithstanding.

conies, in the day-time, on the sea and river banks in the county of Lincoln, &c.

IX. Provided also, That no person or persons shall be obliged to make satisfaction for any damages that may be occasioned by such entry, unless such damages shall exceed the sum of one shilling.

No satisfaction to be made for damages occasioned by entry, unless they exceed 1s.

CAP. XV.

An act for enlarging the times limited for executing and performing several provisions, powers, and directions, in certain acts of this session of parliament.

Preamble.

WHEREAS *by certain acts of this present session of parliament; several provisions, powers, and authorities, therein contained, have been or may be required, directed, or authorized, to be executed on or before the day of the passing of such acts respectively, whereby several doubts and difficulties may arise with respect to the execution of the said acts, and the good purposes thereby intended may be defeated:* be it therefore enacted by the King's most excellent majesty, by and with the advice and consent of the lords spiritual and temporal, and commons, in this present parliament assembled, and by the authority of the same, That in case any act of parliament hath passed, or doth or shall pass, at any time whatsoever during this present session of parliament, whereby any provision, power, or authority, or any matter or thing, hath been, is, or shall be, directed, required, or authorized, to be executed, done, or performed, on or before any day which hath been, is, or shall be, the day of the passing, or which hath, is, or shall have elapsed before the passing of any such act respectively; in each and every such case, all such provisions, powers, authorities, matters, and things, as have been, are, or shall be, directed or required to be executed, done, or performed, on or before the days respectively limited in every such act, shall be, and are hereby directed and required to be executed, done, and performed, on or before the day fortnight next after the end of this present session of parliament, by the persons respectively who, in every such act respectively, have been, are, or shall be, directed or required to execute, do, or per-

Where it shall happen, that any provisions or powers, in any act of this session, shall be directed to be executed on or before the day on which such act shall pass, or which shall have elapsed before the passing such act; such provisions and powers may be executed on or before the day fortnight next after the end of this session.

perform the same, on or before the days therein limited: and all such provisions, powers, authorities, matters, and things, as have been, are, or shall be, authorized to be executed, done, or performed, on or before the respective days limited in every such act respectively, may be, and are hereby authorized to be, executed, done, and performed, on or before the day fortnight next after the end of this present session of parliament, by the persons respectively who have been, are, or shall be, authorized to execute, do, or perform the same: and all such provisions, powers, authorities, matters, and things, so executed, done, and performed, on or before the day fortnight next after the end of this present session of parliament, shall be as valid and effectual, and be deemed and taken, to all intents and purposes, as if the same had been executed, done, and performed, on or before the days limited in every such act respectively; any thing therein contained to the contrary notwithstanding.

CAP. XVI.

An act for altering the times of payment of certain annuities, established by two acts made in the thirty third year of the reign of his late Majesty, and in the second year of the reign of his present Majesty.

Preamble, reciting clauses in Act 33 Geo. 2. & act 2 Geo. 3.

WHEREAS *several annuities after the rate of four pounds* per centum, *for certain terms of years, and, after the expiration thereof, at three pounds* per centum, *redeemable by parliament, were established by an act made in the thirty third year of the reign of his late majesty King* George *the Second, intituled,* An act for granting to his Majesty several duties upon malt; and for raising the sum of eight millions, by way of annuities and a lottery, to be charged on the said duties; and to prevent the fraudulent obtaining of allowances in the guaging of corn making into malt; and for making forth duplicates of exchequer bills, tickets, certificates, receipts, annuity orders, and other orders, lost, burnt, or otherwise destroyed; *and several other annuities after the like rate of four pounds* per centum, *for a certain term of years, and, after the expiration thereof, in like manner, at three pounds* per centum, *were established by an act made in the second year of the reign of his present Majesty, intituled,* An act for raising by annuities, in manner therein mentioned, the sum of twelve millions, to be charged on the sinking fund; and for applying the surplus of certain duties on spirituous liquors, and also the monies arising from the duties on spirituous liquors, granted by an act of this session of parliament; *all which said annuities were, by the said act, made payable half-yearly on the fifth day of* July, *and the fifth day of* January, *in every year, and were, by the said last-mentioned act, consolidated, and made one joint stock of annuities for the principal sum of twenty millions two hundred and forty thousand pounds: and whereas it is expedient that the times appointed by the said acts, for the payment of the said annuities, should, with the consent of the proprietors thereof, be altered*; may it therefore please your

our Majesty, that it may be enacted, and be it enacted by the King's most excellent Majesty, by and with the advice and consent of the lords spiritual and temporal, and commons, in this present parliament assembled, and by the authority of the same, That from and after the payment of the said annuities for the half year which shall become due on the fifth day of *July*, one thousand seven hundred and sixty five, the subsequent payments thereof shall, with the consent of the proprietors, be made in manner following; that is to say, one quarterly payment of such annuities shall be made on the tenth day of *October*, one thousand seven hundred and sixty five; and from and after the said tenth day of *October*, such annuities shall be paid and payable half-yearly, on the fifth day of *April*, and the tenth day of *October*, in every year, until redemption thereof by parliament, in the manner authorized by the said acts.

Times of payment of the annuities granted by the recited acts to be changed, viz. After payment of the half year due on 5 July, 1765, the subsequent payments, with consent of the proprietors, are to be made, 1 quarter on 10 Oct. 1765, and from thence forwards half-yearly, on 5 April and 10 Oct. yearly.

II. And be it further enacted by the authority aforesaid, That such proprietors of the said annuities who shall not, on or before the first day of *June*, one thousand seven hundred and sixty five, signify their dissent to the said alteration of the times for the payment of the said annuities, in books to be opened at the bank of *England* for that purpose, shall be deemed and taken to assent thereto; any thing to the contrary thereof in any wise notwithstanding.

Proprietors not entering their dissent thereto by 1 June, 1765, deemed to assent.

III. Provided nevertheless, That all the provisions, powers, and directions, in the said acts, relative to the payment of the said annuities at the times therein mentioned, shall take effect, operate, and be executed, with respect to the payment of the said annuities on the days hereby appointed, as fully and effectually as if the same were herein repeated, re-enacted, and applied to the payments to be made by the authority of this act.

All other provisions, relative to the payment of the said annuities, to be in force.

CAP. XVII.

An act to confirm all leases already made by archbishops and bishops, and other ecclesiastical persons, of tythes and other incorporeal hereditaments, for one, two, or three life or lives, or twenty one years; and to enable them to grant such leases, and to bring actions of debt for recovery of rents reserved and in arrear on leases for life or lives.

WHEREAS *it may be doubtful whether, by the laws now in being, archbishops or bishops, master and fellows, or any other head and members of colleges or halls, deans and chapters, precentors, prebendaries, masters and guardians of hospitals, or any other person or persons having any spiritual or ecclesiastical promotions, heretofore had, or now have, any power to make or grant any lease or leases of tythes, or other incorporeal hereditaments only, which lie in grant and not in livery, for one, two, or three lives, or for any term or terms of years not exceeding twenty one years, although the ancient rent, or yearly sum is thereby mentioned to be reserved, and all other requi-*

Preamble.

ſites preſcribedby the acts of parliament now in being to that end, or any of them, were or are juſtly and truly obſerved and performed, by reaſon that there is generally no place wherein a diſtreſs can be had or taken for ſuch rent or yearly ſum; and it may be alſo doubtful whether, in caſes of ſuch leaſes for life or lives, there is any remedy in law for ſuch eccleſiaſtical or other perſons by action of debt or otherwiſe, for recovering the rent or yearly ſum due and arrear which is mentioned to be reſerved on ſuch leaſes for life or lives: therefore for obviating all doubts touching the ſame, and enabling the ſaid archbiſhops and biſhops, maſters and fellows, or other heads and members of colleges or halls, deans and chapters, precentors, prebendaries, maſters and guardians of hoſpitals, and other eccleſiaſtical perſons, to make valid leaſes of ſuch their incorporeal hereditaments, and to recover the rents or yearly ſum mentioned to be reſerved on any leaſes by them already granted, or to be granted, for one, two, or three lives, as aforeſaid; and alſo to make good and effectual all ſuch leaſes as have already been granted by them, or any of them: may it pleaſe your Majeſty, that it may be enacted; and be it enacted by the King's moſt excellent majeſty, by and with the advice and conſent of the lords ſpiritual and temporal, and commons, in this preſent parliament aſſembled, and by the authority of the ſame, That all leaſes for one, two, or three life or lives, or any term not exceeding twenty one years, already made and granted, or which ſhall at any time from and after the paſſing this act be made or granted, of any tythes, tolls, or other incorporeal hereditaments, ſolely, and without any lands or corporeal hereditaments, by any archbiſhop or biſhop, maſter and fellows, or other head and members of colleges or halls, deans and chapters, precentors, prebendaries, maſters and guardians of hoſpitals, and every other perſon and perſons who are enabled by the ſeveral ſtatutes now in being, or any of them, to make any leaſe or leaſes for one, two, or three life or lives, or any term or number of years not exceeding twenty one years, of any lands, tenements, or other corporeal hereditaments, ſhall be, and are hereby deemed and declared to be, as good and effectual in law againſt ſuch archbiſhop, biſhop, maſters and fellows, or other heads and members of colleges or halls, deans and chapters, precentors, prebendaries, maſters and guardians of hoſpitals, and other perſons ſo granting the ſame, and their ſucceſſors, and every of them, to all intents and purpoſes, as any leaſe or leaſes already made or to be made by any ſuch archbiſhop or biſhop, maſter and fellows, or other heads and members of colleges or halls, deans and chapters, precentors, prebendaries, maſters and guardians of hoſpitals, and other perſons having ſpiritual promotion, of any lands or other corporeal hereditaments now are, by virtue of the ſtatute of the thirty ſecond year of King *Henry* the Eighth, or any other ſtatute now in being; any law, cuſtom, or uſage, to the contrary thereof in any wiſe notwithſtanding.

Leaſes already made, or that ſhall be made, by eccleſiaſtical perſons, of tythes and other incorporeal hereditaments, for life or lives, or years, declared to be good in law, as thoſe granted by virtue of act 32 Hen. 8.

II. Provided always, That nothing herein contained ſhall extend, or be conſtrued to extend, to enable any maſter and fellows,

Maſters and fellows of

lows, or other head and members of colleges or halls, deans and chapters, precentors, prebendaries, masters and guardians of hospitals, or other ecclesiastical persons as aforesaid, to grant leases for any longer or other terms than, by the local statutes of their several foundations, they are now respectively enabled to do.

Colleges, &c. disabled from granting leases for any longer term than their statutes allow.

III. And be it further enacted and declared by the authority aforesaid, That in case the rent or rents, or yearly sum or sums, reserved or made payable in or by any lease or leases already made, or to be made, by any archbishop or bishop, master and fellows, or other head and members of colleges or halls, deans and chapters, precentors, prebendaries, masters and guardians of hospitals, and every other person or persons so enabled to make leases as aforesaid for one, two, or three life or lives, or years, in pursuance of the several acts of parliament already in being, or by this present act, or any part thereof, shall be behind or unpaid by the space of twenty eight days next or over after any of the days whereon the same, by such lease or leases, now are or hereafter shall or may be reserved and made payable; then, and so often, and from time to time, as it shall so happen; it shall and may be lawful for such archbishop or bishop, master and fellows, or other head and members of colleges or halls, deans and chapters, prebendaries, precentors, masters and guardians of hospitals, and other persons so making or granting, or having made or granted, such leases as aforesaid, or their executors, administrators, and successors respectively, to bring an action or actions of debt against any lessee or lessees, to whom any such lease or leases for life or lives, or years, now are or hereafter shall be made and granted, his, her or their heirs, executors, administrators, or assigns, for recovering the rent or rents which shall be then due and in arrear to any such archbishop or bishops, masters and fellows, or other heads and members of colleges or halls, deans, chapters, precentors, prebendaries, master and guardians of hospitals, and other person or persons before mentioned, his or their executors, administrators, or successors, in such and the same manner, and as fully and effectually to all intents and purposes, as any landlord or lessor, or other person or persons, could or might do for recovering of arrears of rent due on any lease or leases for life or lives, or years, by the laws now in being; any law, statute, usage, or custom, to the contrary notwithstanding.

Actions may be brought for recovery of rents reserved and in arrear on leases for life or lives.

IV. And it is hereby further enacted and declared by the authority aforesaid, That this act shall be deemed and taken to be a publick act; and shall be judicially taken notice of as such, in all courts of law and equity without specially pleading the same.

Publick act.

CAP. XVIII.

An act for continuing an act, made in the thirty first year of his late Majesty's reign, for encouraging the growth and cultivation of madder in that part of Great Britain *called* England, *by ascertaining the tythe thereof.*

Preamble.

WHEREAS *an act made in the thirty first year of his late majesty King* George *the Second, intituled,* An act to encourage the growth and cultivation of madder in that part of *Great Britain* called *England*, by ascertaining the tythe thereof, *was to continue in force from the first day of* August, *one thousand seven hundred and fifty eight, for the space of fourteen years, and from thence to the end of the then next session of parliament: and whereas the cultivation of madder, from the setting to its being fit for use, requires so long a time, and the buildings, mills, and other requisites necessary to be provided and maintained for manufacturing it, are so expensive, that many people may be unwilling to begin the culture of it during the subsisting term of the said act: and whereas the price of foreign madder is of late greatly raised, and the same does not come into the consumers hands so good as it may be manufactured here;* be it therefore enacted by the King's most excellent majesty, by and with the advice and consent of the lords spiritual and temporal, and commons, in this present parliament assembled, and by the authority of the same, That the said act shall be, and the same is hereby declared to be, further continued from the expiration thereof, for and during the further term of fourteen years, and to the end of the then next session of parliament.

The recited act continued for the further term of 14 years.

CAP. XIX.

An act for raising a certain sum of money by loans or exchequer bills, for the service of the year one thousand seven hundred and sixty five.

Most gracious Sovereign,

Preamble.

WE, your Majesty's most dutiful and loyal subjects, the commons of *Great Britain*, in parliament assembled, towards raising the necessary supplies which we have chearfully granted to your Majesty in this session of parliament, have resolved to give and grant unto your Majesty the sum herein after mentioned; and do therefore most humbly beseech your Majesty, that it may be enacted; and be it enacted by the King's most excellent majesty, by and with the advice and consent of the lords spiritual and temporal, and commons, in this present parliament assembled, and by the authority of the same, That it shall and may be lawful to and for the commissioners of his Majesty's treasury now or for the time being, or any three or more of them, or the high treasurer for the time being, at any time or times before the fifth day of *January*, one thousand seven hundred and sixty six, to cause or direct any loans to be taken or received at his Majesty's

Treasury impowered, at any time before 5 Jan. 1766, to direct the receiving loans, or issuing bills, at

ſty's exchequer, from any perſon or perſons, natives or foreigners, body or bodies politick or corporate, or any number of exchequer bills to be made out there, for any ſum or ſums of money not exceeding in loans and exchequer bills together, in the whole, the ſum of eight hundred thouſand pounds, in the ſame or like manner, form, and order, and according to the ſame or like rules and directions, as in and by an act of this preſent ſeſſion of parliament, intituled, *An act for continuing and granting to his Majeſty certain duties upon malt, mum, cyder, and perry, for the ſervice of the year one thouſand ſeven hundred and ſixty five*, are enacted and preſcribed, concerning the loans or exchequer bills to be taken or made in purſuance of the ſaid act.

the exchequer, for any ſum or ſums not exceeding in the whole 800,000l. in like manner as is preſcribed by malt act of this ſeſſion.

II. And be it further enacted by the authority aforeſaid, That all and every the clauſes, proviſoes, powers, privileges, advantages, penalties, forfeitures, and diſabilities, contained in the ſaid laſt mentioned act, relating to the loans or exchequer bills authorized to be made by the ſame act, except ſuch clauſes as do charge the ſame on the taxes granted by the ſame act, and (except ſuch clauſes as limit the rate of intereſt to be paid for the forbearance of money lent on the credit of the ſaid act, and alſo except as is herein after mentioned) ſhall be applied and extended to the loans and exchequer bills to be made in purſuance of this act, as fully and effectually, to all intents and purpoſes, as if the ſame loans or exchequer bills had been originally authorized by the ſaid laſt mentioned act, or as if the ſaid ſeveral clauſes or proviſoes had been particularly repeated and reenacted in the body of this act.

The clauſes, &c. in the ſaid act to extend to the loans and bills hereby authorized to be received and made out.

III. Provided always, and be it further enacted by the authority aforeſaid, That no exchequer bill or bills to be made out by virtue of this act, ſhall, after the ſame hath or have been iſſued at the exchequer, be afterwards at any time before the ſixth day of *April*, one thouſand ſeven hundred and ſixty ſix, received or taken, or paſs or be current to any receiver or collector in *Great Britain* of the cuſtoms, exciſe, or any revenue, ſupply, aid, or tax whatſoever, due or payable to his Majeſty, his heirs or ſucceſſors, or at the receipt of the exchequer, from any ſuch receiver or collector, or from any other perſon or perſons, bodies politick or corporate, otherwiſe, or on any other account, than for the diſcharge and cancelling of ſuch bills, in caſe the ſame ſhall be in due courſe or order of payment before the ſaid ſixth day of *April*; nor ſhall any ſuch receiver or collector exchange, at any time before the ſaid ſixth day of *April*, for any money of ſuch revenues, aids, taxes, or ſupplies, in his hands, any exchequer bill or bills, which ſhall have been iſſued as aforeſaid by virtue of this act; nor ſhall any action be maintained againſt any ſuch receiver or collector, for neglecting or refuſing to exchange any ſuch bill or bills for ready money before the ſaid ſixth day of *April*; any thing in the ſaid act made in this preſent ſeſſion of parliament, intituled, *An act for continuing and granting to his Majeſty certain duties upon malt, mum, cyder, and perry, for the*

Exchequer bills ſo iſſued, not to be received in payment of any of the publick taxes, before 6 April, 1766; unleſs the ſame ſhall be in courſe of payment before the ſaid day.

the service of the year one thousand seven hundred and sixty five, or this act, contained to the contrary notwithstanding.

The loans and bills, and interest, &c. attending, charged on the next aids, or on the sinking fund, if no sufficient aid shall be granted before 5 July, 1766.

IV. And be it further enacted by the authority aforesaid, That all such loans or exchequer bills, together with the interest, premium, rate, and charges, incident to or attending the same, shall be and are hereby charged and chargeable upon, and shall be repaid or borne by or out of, the first aids or supplies which shall be granted in the next session of parliament; and in case sufficient aids or supplies for that purpose shall not be granted before the fifth day of *July*, one thousand seven hundred and sixty six, then all the said loans or exchequer bills, with the interest, premium, rate, and charges, incident to or attending the same, shall be and are hereby charged and chargeable upon such monies as, at any time or times at or after the said fifth day of *July*, shall be or remain in the receipt of the exchequer, of the surplusses, excesses, overplus monies, and other revenues composing the fund commonly called *The sinking fund* (except such monies of the said sinking fund as are appropriated to any particular use or uses, by any act or acts of parliament in that behalf) and such monies of the said sinking fund shall and may be issued and applied, as soon as the same can be regularly stated and ascertained, for and towards paying off, cancelling, and discharging, such loans or exchequer bills, interest, premium, rate, or charges, until the whole of them shall be paid off, cancelled, and discharged, or money sufficient for that purpose be kept and reserved in the exchequer, to be payable on demand to the respective proprietors thereof.

Monies issued out of the sinking fund to be replaced out of the first supplies.

V. Provided always, and be it enacted by the authority aforesaid, That whatever monies shall be so issued out of the said surplusses, excesses, overplus monies, or other revenues composing the sinking fund, shall, from time to time, be replaced by and out of the first supplies to be then after granted in parliament; any thing herein contained to the contrary notwithstanding.

Bank of England authorized to advance monies upon the credit of loan hereby granted, notwithstanding act 5 & 6 W. & M.

VI. And be it declared and further enacted by the authority aforesaid, That it shall and may be lawful for the governor and company of the bank of *England*, to advance or lend to his Majesty in like manner, at the receipt of the exchequer, upon the credit of loan granted by this act, any sum or sums of money not exceeding, in the whole, the sum of eight hundred thousand pounds; any thing in an act made in the fifth and sixth years of the reign of King *William* and Queen *Mary*, intituled, *An act for granting to their Majesties several rates and duties upon tonnage of ships and vessels, and upon beer, ale, and other liquors, for securing certain recompences and advantages, in the said act mentioned, to such persons as shall voluntarily advance the sum of one million five hundred thousand pounds, towards carrying on the war against* France, to the contrary thereof in any wise notwithstanding.

CAP. XX.

An act for explaining and rendering more effectual two acts, one made in the twelfth year of the reign of Queen Anne, *intituled,* An act for providing a publick reward for such person or persons as shall discover the longitude at sea; *and the other in the twenty sixth year of the reign of King* George *the Second, intituled,* An act to render more effectual an act made in the twelfth year of the reign of her late majesty Queen *Anne*, intituled, *An act for providing a publick reward for such person or persons as shall discover the longitude at sea,* with regard to the making experiments of proposals made for discovering the longitude; and to enlarge the number of commissioners for putting in execution the said act.

WHEREAS *by two several acts made, the one in the twelfth year of the reign of her late majesty Queen* Anne, *intituled,* An act for providing a publick reward for such person or persons as shall discover the longitude at sea; *and the other in the twenty sixth year of the reign of his late majesty King* George *the Second, intituled,* An act to render more effectual an act made in the twelfth year of the reign of her late majesty Queen *Anne*, intituled, *An act for providing a publick reward for such person or persons as shall discover the longitude at sea,* with regard to the making experiments of proposals made for discovering the longitude; and to enlarge the number of commissioners for putting in execution the said act; *the commissioners named in, and constituted by the said acts, were impowered to receive proposals for discovering the said longitude, and make experiments of the same: and whereas by the said act of the twelfth of Queen* Anne, *it was enacted, That the first author or authors, discoverer or discoverers, of a proper method for finding the said longitude within certain distances, should be intitled to and receive certain rewards therein mentioned; that is to say, a reward or sum of ten thousand pounds, if it determines the said longitude to one degree of a great circle, or sixty geographical miles; fifteen thousand pounds, if it determines the same to two thirds of that distance; and twenty thousand pounds, if it determines the same to one half the same distance: and whereas in and by the said act it was further enacted, That if, upon trial, any proposal for discovering the said longitude should not prove to be of so great use as before mentioned, yet if the same, in the judgement of the said commissioners, or the major part of them, should be found of considerable use to the publick, then the said author or authors of such proposal should receive such less reward as the said commissioners, or the major part of them, should think reasonable: and whereas the said commissioners have, from time to time, in pursuance of the powers vested in them by the said act, received proposals from Mr.* John Harrison *for discovering the said longitude, by means of certain machines or time keepers* in-

Preamble, reciting clauses in act 12 Ann.

26 Geo. 2. &c.

invented by him, and have directed several sums of money to be paid to the said John Harrison *to enable him to finish his said machines or time keepers, or some of them, upon condition of his delivering the same up to and for the use of the publick: and whereas the said* John Harrison *did, by direction of the said commissioners, enter into articles with the commissioners of the navy, whereby he agreed, in consideration of the sums so advanced to him, to deliver up the three several machines or time keepers in the said articles mentioned: and whereas, upon trial of one other watch machine or time keeper in a voyage to* Jamaica, *the major part of the said commissioners did adjudge the same to be of considerable use to the publick, and did accordingly order the payment of the sum of two thousand five hundred pounds to the said* John Harrison, *which sum was to be deemed and taken as part of such of the rewards, in and by the said act allowed for discovering the said longitude, as he might become intitled to, and as such has been by him received; and the said watch or time keeper was to become the property of the publick: and whereas upon a further trial of the said last mentioned watch or time keeper, a ship has sailed, by the appointment of the commissioners for the discovery of the longitude, from* Portsmouth *in* Great Britain, *to* Bridgetown *in the island of* Barbadoes *in the* West Indies; *and whereas by means of the said watch or time keeper invented by Mr.* John Harrison, *the said ship did not lose it's longitude beyond ten geographical miles: and whereas the method for finding the longitude at sea, within half a degree of a great circle, or thirty geographical miles, by means of the said watch or time keeper invented by the said* John Harrison, *may be made generally practicable, and of general utility, if the principles upon which the said watch or time keeper is constructed are fully discovered and explained, and other watches or time keepers of the same kind can be made; but doubts may arise, whether, by the words of the said act of the twelfth of Queen* Anne, *the said commissioners can direct the payment of the said reward of twenty thousand pounds to the said* John Harrison, *upon a discovery of the principles of the said watch or time keeper, and upon other watches or time keepers of the same kind being made: and whereas great progress has been made towards discovering the longitude at sea by a set of lunar tables constructed by* Tobias Mayer *deceased, late professor at* Goetingen *in* Germany, *upon the principles of gravitation laid down by Sir* Isaac Newton; *in the construction of which tables he was considerably assisted from theorems furnished by professor* Euler *of the university of* Berlin: *and whereas the said tables are of considerable use to the publick, and may be further improved, and made of more general utility: and whereas the widow, or other representatives of the said professor* Mayer, *are, within the intention of the said act, deserving of a publick reward, upon her or their assigning the property of the said tables to the said commissioners for the use of the publick; and the said professor* Euler *is also deserving of an honorary and pecuniary acknowledgment for his useful and ingenious labours towards the discovery of the longitude: and whereas it is necessary that the powers of the said act of the twelfth year of Queen* Anne, *and also of the said act of the twenty sixth year of King* George *the Second, should be be explained and made effectual, as well for receiving the discovery and explanation of the principles upon which the said watch or time keeper is constructed, and for making trial of other watches or time keepers to be made in consequence thereof, and for paying the said reward to the said* John Harrison, *his executors, administrators, or assigns, as for giving proper rewards to the said professor* Euler, *and to the widow or representatives of the said professor* Mayer, *and to such person or persons as shall improve the said tables of the moon, and make the same of more general utility; and also to such person or persons as shall make other discoveries or improvements useful to navigation:* may it therefore please your Majesty, that it may be enacted; and be it enacted by the King's most excellent majesty, by and with the advice and consent of the lords spiritual and temporal, and commons, in this present parliament assembled, and by the authority of the same, That one moiety of the greatest reward which is directed in and by the said act, made in the twelfth year of the reign of Queen *Anne*, to be paid to the first author or authors, discoverer or discoverers, of a proper method for finding the said longitude at sea, shall be paid to the said *John Harrison* his executors, administrators, or assigns, when and so soon as the principles upon which his said watch or time keeper is constructed are fully discovered, and explained to the satisfaction of the said commissioners for the discovery of the longitude, or the major part of them; and when and so soon as the said *John Harrison* hath assigned to the said commissioners, for the use of the publick, the property of the three several time keepers which, in and by the said articles, he agreed to deliver up, and also the property of the said last mentioned watch or time keeper, deducting from and out of the said moiety, so to be paid to the said *John Harrison*, his executors, administrators, or assigns, the sum of two thousand five hundred pounds already advanced and paid to him; and that the other moiety of the said greatest reward mentioned in the said act shall, when and so soon as other time keepers of the same kind shall be made, and shall, upon trial, be found to be of a sufficient correctness to determine the said longitude within half a degree of a great circle, or thirty geographical miles, to the satisfaction of the said commissioners, or the major part of them, be paid to the said *John Harrison*, his executors, administrators, or assigns.

10,000 l. to be paid, as a present reward, to Mr. John Harrison, pursuant to the act of 12 ann. upon his discovering the principles of his time keeper, and assigning the property of 3 of those instruments, and the last mentioned watch, for the use of the publick; deducting the 2,500 l. already advanced him; and other 10,000 l. to be paid when the other time keepers are made, and proved to be of sufficient correctness.

II. Provided always, and be it enacted by the authority aforesaid, That the said Master *John Harrison* shall not be intitled, by virtue of any thing contained in this act, to the said reward, or any part thereof, unless the discovery and explanation of the principles upon which his said time keeper is constructed, shall be made within six months after the passing of this act.

Discovery of the principles on which the time keeper is constructed, to be made within 6 months.

III. And be it further enacted by the authority aforesaid, That a reward or sum of money, not exceeding three hundred pounds in the whole, shall be paid to the said professor *Euler*.

300 l. to be paid to professor Euler.

IV. And be it further enacted by the authority aforesaid, That a reward or sum of money, not exceeding three thousand pounds in the whole, shall be paid to the widow or other representatives

and 3000 l. to the widow of professor Mayer, upon assigning the property of the lateſt MS lunar tables conſtructed by him.

ſentatives of the ſaid profeſſor *Mayer* upon her or their aſſigning the property of the ſet of the lateſt manuſcript lunar tables, conſtructed by the ſaid *Tobias Mayer*, to the ſaid commiſſioners, to and for the uſe of the publick.

5,000 l. propoſed to any who ſhall improve the ſaid tables, or ſhall make any diſcovery or improvement uſeful to navigation.

V. And be it further enacted by the authority aforeſaid, That any reward or rewards, ſum or ſums of money not exceeding in the whole the ſum of five thouſand pounds, ſhall and may be paid to ſuch perſon or perſons, as ſhall improve the ſaid tables of the moon; or that ſhall make any diſcovery or diſcoveries, improvement or improvements, uſeful to navigation; which ſaid reward or rewards, ſum or ſums of money, ſhall and may be paid to ſuch perſon or perſons, and in ſuch proportion or proportions, as the ſaid commiſſioners ſhall, from time to time, think proper and direct.

Clauſes, &c. in the acts of 12 Annæ and 26, Geo. 2. continued in force, where not altered by this act.

VI. And be it further enacted by the authority aforeſaid, That all the clauſes, powers, authorities, matters, and things, contained in any or either of the ſaid two acts, made in the twelfth year of the reign of Queen *Anne*, and in the twenty ſixth year of the reign of King *George* the Second, not altered by this act, ſhall continue in full force, and extend, and be conſtrued to extend, to this act, as fully and amply as if again repeated and re-enacted in the body of this preſent act; and that all and every the reward or rewards, ſum or ſums of money, by this act granted and allowed, ſhall, from time to time, be certified under the hands and ſeals of the ſaid commiſſioners for the diſcovery of the longitude, to the commiſſioners of the navy for the time being; and the commiſſioners of the navy for the time being ſhall make out a bill or bills for the ſum or ſums contained in the ſaid certificate or certificates, payable by the treaſurer of the navy; and ſuch ſum or ſums of money the ſaid treaſurer of the navy is hereby required to pay immediately, to the perſon or perſons mentioned in the ſaid certificate or certificates, out of any money that ſhall be in his hands unapplied for the uſe of the navy, in ſuch and the ſame manner, and according to the ſame rules and directions as are preſcribed in and by the ſaid two recited acts, or either of them, with regard to any reward or rewards, ſum or ſums of money, allowed to be given and paid in and by the ſaid acts or either of them.

Rewards, by this act granted, to be certified by the commiſſioners for the longitude to the commiſſioners of the navy; who are to make out bills for the ſame, payable by the treaſurer of the navy, out of the unapplied money in his hands.

Where any reward exceeds 1,000 l. it is to be certified by the majority of the commiſſioners; and not exceeding, that ſum, may be certified by five.

VII. Provided always, That all and every ſuch reward or ſum of money that ſhall exceed the ſum of one thouſand pounds, ſhall be certified under the hands and ſeals of the ſaid commiſſioners, or the major part of them; but in caſe ſuch reward or ſum of money ſhall not exceed the ſum of one thouſand pounds, then, and in that caſe, it ſhall and may be certified under the hands and ſeals of the ſaid commiſſioners, or any five or more of them.

Commiſſioners for the longitude impowered to adminiſter oaths,

VIII. And be it further enacted by the authority aforeſaid, That it ſhall and may be lawful to and for the ſaid commiſſioners for the diſcovery of the longitude, or the major part of them, and they are hereby authorized and impowered for their better ſatisfaction, if they ſhall ſee occaſion, to adminiſter an oath

oath or oaths to ſuch perſon or perſons as they ſhall think proper, for the purpoſes of carrying this act into execution: which oath or oaths, it ſhall and may be lawful to and for any two or more of the ſaid commiſſioners to adminiſter accordingly.

for the purpoſes of this act.

IX. And whereas, ſince the paſſing of the ſaid act of the twelfth of Queen *Anne*, another profeſſorſhip for the purpoſe of aſtronomy has been eſtabliſhed in the univerſity of *Cambridge*; be it therefore enacted, That the *Lowndes's* profeſſor of aſtronomy in the univerſity of *Cambridge* for the time being ſhall be, and he is hereby added to, and joined with, the commiſſioners appointed by the ſaid act of the twelfth of Queen *Anne*, and by another act paſſed in the twenty ſixth year of King *George* the Second; and the ſaid profeſſor of aſtronomy is hereby appointed a commiſſioner, and ſhall and may act, to all intents and purpoſes, for putting in execution the ſaid acts and this preſent act, as fully and effectually as if he had been appointed a commiſſioner by the ſaid acts of the twelfth of Queen *Anne*, and of the twenty ſixth of King *George* the Second, or either of them.

Lowndes's profeſſor of aſtronomy in Cambridge made a joint commiſſioner for the longitude.

X. And whereas the publication of nautical almanacks conſtructed by proper perſons, under the direction of the ſaid commiſſioners, would greatly contribute to make the ſaid lunar tables more generally uſeful; be it further enacted by the authority aforeſaid, That it ſhall and may be lawful to and for the ſaid commiſſioners to cauſe ſuch nautical almanacks, or other uſeful tables, to be conſtructed, and to print, publiſh, and vend, or cauſe to be printed, publiſhed, and vended, any nautical almanack or almanacks, or other uſeful table or tables, which they, or the major part of them, ſhall, from time to time, judge neceſſary and uſeful, in order to facilitate the method of diſcovering the longitude at ſea; any law, ſtatute, excluſive privilege, private charter, or other cuſtom, to the contrary thereof notwithſtanding.

The conſtruction and publication of nautical almanacks, or other tables, recommended to the commiſſioners for the longitude.

XI. And be it enacted by the authority aforeſaid, That no perſon or perſons ſhall print, publiſh, or vend, or cauſe to be printed, publiſhed, or vended, any nautical almanack or almanacks, or other table or tables conſtructed under the direction of the ſaid commiſſioners, without being firſt licenſed by the ſaid commiſſioners, or the major part of them; and if any perſon or perſons not ſo licenſed, or not being authorized by the perſon or perſons ſo licenſed by the ſaid commiſſioners, ſhall print, publiſh, or vend, or cauſe to be printed, publiſhed, or vended, any ſuch nautical almanack or almanacks, or other table or tables, every ſuch perſon or perſons ſhall, for every copy of ſuch nautical almanack or table ſo printed, publiſhed, or vended, forfeit and pay the ſum of twenty pounds; to be recovered by action of debt, bill, plaint, or information, in any of his Majeſty's courts of record at *Weſtminſter*; and that one moiety of ſuch penalty and forfeiture ſhall be to his Majeſty, his heirs, and ſucceſſors, and the other moiety to him or them that ſhall proſecute, inform, or ſue for the ſame.

None to print, publiſh, or vend the ſame, but ſuch as ſhall be licenſed,

under penalty of 20 l. for every copy.

CAP.

CAP. XXI.

An act for appointing commissioners to put in execution an act of this session of parliament, intituled, An act for granting an aid to his Majesty by a land tax, to be raised in *Great Britain,* for the service of the year one thousand seven hundred and sixty five, *together with those named in two former acts for appointing commissioners of the land tax; and for indemnifying persons who have acted as commissioners of the land tax, by virtue of estates of or above a certain value, though the same were not rated or assessed at the value of one hundred pounds* per annum; *and for limiting a time within which suits and prosecutions shall be commenced, with respect to the qualifications of persons who shall act as commissioners of the land tax.*

CAP. XXII.

An act for the further encouragement of the British *white herring fishery.*

Preamble, reciting clauses in act 23 Geo. 2.

WHEREAS *by virtue of an act of parliament, made in the twenty third year of the reign of his late majesty King* George *the Second, intituled,* An act for the encouragement of the *British* white herring fishery, *his said late Majesty did, by letters patent under the great seal of* Great Britain, *incorporate sundry persons by the name of* The Society of the free *British* fishery, *for the purpose of carrying on and improving the* British *white herring fisheries: and by the said act the said society were impowered, by a voluntary subscription, to raise the sum of five hundred thousand pounds, to be their capital stock; and as an encouragement to such persons as should become subscribers thereto, the sum of three pounds by the year, for each hundred pounds which should be actually employed in the said fisheries, and proportionably for any greater or lesser sum, was directed to be paid to the proprietors of the said stock, for and during the space of fourteen years from the date of the said charter, by the receiver general of his Majesty's customs, by equal half yearly payments; provided the said society should employ the sum of one hundred thousand pounds at least in the said fisheries, within the space of eighteen months from the date of such subscription: and as a further encouragement to persons to engage in the said white herring fisheries, a bounty of thirty shillings* per *ton is, by the said act, given and made payable, in manner therein mentioned, to the owner or owners of all decked vessels from twenty to eighty tons burthen, which should be built, after the commencement of the said act, for the use of the said fisheries, whether by the said society or any other person or persons, in manner, and under the regulations, and upon such conditions, as in the said act are mentioned; which bounty was to be paid yearly, during the space of fourteen years from the commencement of the said act, and no longer: and*

whereas

whereas by another act, made in the twenty eighth year of the reign of his said late Majesty, the said allowance of three pounds per centum per annum, *and also the said bounty of thirty shillings* per *ton, granted by the said acts, for the respective terms therein mentioned, were continued for the further term of three years, to be computed immediately from and after the expiration of the said respective terms for which the same were granted as aforesaid: and whereas by another act, made in the thirtieth year of the reign of his said late Majesty, intituled,* An act for allowing a further bounty on all vessels employed in the white herring fishery, for giving liberty to alter the present form and size of the nets used in the said fishery, and for other purposes therein mentioned, *it is enacted, That the said bounty of thirty shillings* per *ton, by the said two several acts granted and continued for the respective terms of years therein respectively mentioned, should cease, determine, and be at an end; and that in lieu thereof, a bounty of fifty shillings* per *ton, on all vessels employed in the said fisheries, should be paid and payable for such term and terms of years, to the said society, and such other persons as would have been intitled to the said bounty of thirty shillings* per *ton, by virtue of or under the said several acts herein before recited, in case the said act had not been made; and that such bounty of fifty shillings* per *ton should be paid and payable at such times, and in such manner, and by such person and persons, and out of such monies, as the said bounty of thirty shillings* per *ton is by the said two several acts, or either of them, directed to be paid: and whereas the terms, for which the said allowance and bounty were respectively granted, will expire the twenty second day of* October, *one thousand seven hundred and sixty seven, and the term of the said charter will not expire until the twenty second day of* October, *one thousand seven hundred and seventy one: and whereas it is necessary, for the further encouragement of the* British *white herring fisheries, that the said allowance and bounty should be continued;* may it therefore please your Majesty, that it may be enacted; and be it enacted by the King's most excellent majesty, by and with the advice and consent of the lords spiritual and temporal, and commons, in this present parliament assembled, and by the authority of the same, That the said allowance of three pounds *per centum per annum* granted by the said several acts, and also the bounty of fifty shillings *per* ton granted by the said act of the thirtieth year of the reign of his said late Majesty, for the respective terms therein mentioned, shall be continued for the further term of four years, to be computed from and immediately after the expiration of the said respective terms for which the same were respectively granted as aforesaid; and shall be paid and payable, for the said further term of four years, to the said society, and to such other person or persons as are or may be respectively intitled to the said allowance, by virtue of or under the said several acts, in such manner, and by such person and persons, and out of such monies, as the same are now payable, by virtue of or under the said several acts, or any of them.

Act 28 Geo. 2.

& act 30 Geo. 2.

The allowance of 3 l. per cent. per annum, on the capital employed by the society, and the bounty of 50 s. per ton on the vessels employed in the fisheries, granted by the recited acts, continued for the further term of 4 years.

CAP.

CAP. XXIII.

An act for granting annuities, to be attended with a lottery, to satisfy and discharge certain navy, victualling, and transport bills; and for charging the payment of such annuities on the sinking fund.

Most gracious Sovereign,

Preamble. WE, *your Majesty's most dutiful and loyal subjects the commons of* Great Britain, *in parliament assembled, have taken into our serious consideration the present state of the debt of your Majesty's navy; and being desirous to make some provision towards satisfaction thereof, have resolved, that all persons interested in, or intitled unto, any bill or bills payable in the course of the navy or victualling offices, or for transports, which were made out on or before the thirtieth day of* June, *one thousand seven hundred and sixty four, who should, on or before the twenty sixth day of* March, *one thousand seven hundred and sixty five, carry the same, after having had the interest thereupon computed to the sixth day of* April *following, and marked upon the said bills at the navy or victualling office respectively, to the office of the treasurer of his Majesty's navy, should have in exchange for the same from such treasurer, or his paymaster or cashier, a certificate to the governor and company of the bank of* England, *for every intire sum of one or more hundred pounds of which such bill or bills, together with the interest so marked, should consist, until the several intire sums of one or more hundred pounds for which such certificates were to be made forth, should amount, together, to one million five hundred thousand pounds, and also one other certificate for the fractional part of one hundred pounds, being the remainder of such bill or bills; and the persons who should be possessed of such first-mentioned certificates, should, upon delivery thereof to the said governor and company, be intitled, in respect of the same, to certain annuities therein mentioned; but in case the several intire sums, for which certificates were to be so granted, should not amount to the sum of one million five hundred thousand pounds, all persons possessed of such certificates for fractional parts, or of navy, victualling, or transport bills, which were made out on or before the thirtieth day of* June, *one thousand seven hundred and sixty four, and did not amount, together with the interest thereupon computed to the sixth day of* April *following, to one hundred pounds, might, on or before the fifth day of* April, *one thousand seven hundred and sixty five, after having had the interest thereupon marked in such manner as was before-mentioned, bring the same to the office of the treasurer of his Majesty's navy, and should have in exchange for the same from such treasurer, or his paymaster or cashier, a certificate to the said governor and company for the sums contained in such certificates, and for the amount of the principal and interest of which such bills should consist; and upon delivery thereof, and payment of so much money to the said governor and company as should, with the sums so certified, amount to one hundred pounds, should be intitled to the annuities and advantages therein mentioned; and that in case the monies so certified,* to-

together with the sums paid and payable at the bank of England, *with the certificates for such fractional parts, and for such of the said bills as, together with the interest thereupon, did not amount to one hundred pounds, should not, on the said fifth day of* April, *make up the full sum of one million five hundred thousand pounds, the monies which should be so wanting to compleat the same, should be raised by contributions, to be received at the bank of in* England, *in intire sums of one or more hundred pounds, to be paid on or before the eighteenth day of* April, *one thousand seven hundred and sixty five; and that the contributors should be intitled, for the monies so by them advanced, to such annuities, benefits and advantages, as were to be allowed to the proprietors of the said certificates:* we your Majesty's faithful commons do therefore most humbly beseech your Majesty that it may be enacted, and be it enacted by the King's most excellent majesty, by and with the advice and consent of the lords spiritual and temporal, and commons in this present parliament assembled, and by the authority of the same, That all persons, and bodies politick or corporate, who have delivered, or shall deliver, to the governor and company of the bank of *England*, any certificate or certificates for the intire sum of one or more hundred pounds, so made out, on or before the said twenty sixth day of *March*, one thousand seven hundred and sixty five; or any certificate or certificates, so made out, after the said twenty sixth day of *March*, one thousand seven hundred and sixty five, and have paid to the said governor and company so much money as, with the sum contained in each of the said last-mentioned certificates, did amount to one hundred pounds; and also all persons, and bodies politick or corporate, who have so paid to the cashier or cashiers of the said governor and company, any sum or sums of money, by way of contribution, to complete the said sum of one million five hundred thousand pounds, shall, for the monies so respectively certified, paid, or contributed, be intitled to, and have in respect of the same, such annuities or advantages as are herein after appointed; that is to say, for two fifth parts of such monies, an annuity after the rate of three pounds *per centum per annum*, redeemable by parliament; for two other fifth parts of such monies, or a proportionable number of tickets of the value of ten pounds each, in a lottery to consist of sixty thousand tickets, and to be drawn in such manner as is herein after directed; the blanks, after the rate of six pounds each, together with the prizes in such lottery, to be attended with the like annuities after the rate of three pounds *per centum per annum*, redeemable by parliament; and for the remaining one fifth part of the said monies, a like annuity after the rate of three pounds *per centum per annum*, redeemable by parliament, with liberty to convert every share of such last-mentioned annuities, in right of one hundred pounds capital stock, into an annuity for life after the same rate, with the benefit of survivorship, in manner herein after authorized; all which said redeemable annuities shall be paid at the bank of *England*; and shall commence from the fifth day of *April*, one thousand seven hundred

Persons delivering to the bank certificates for the entire sum of one or more 100 l. made out on or before 26 March, 1765; or certificates for fractional sums made out after that time, and paying therewith so much as will make up the same 100 l. and persons who have advanced money to complete the sum of 1,500,000 l. are intitled to annuities after the rate of 3 l. per cent. per ann. for two fifth parts of such monies; and to a proportionable number of lottery tickets for the other two fifth parts, with other advantages. Annuities made redeemable, and to commence

hundred

from 5 April 1765; and to be paid at the bank half yearly, on 10 Octo. & 5 April. The first payment to be made on 10 Octo.

hundred and sixty five, and until redemption thereof by parliament (except as herein after directed, with respect to the said life annuities) be paid and payable to such respective persons, and bodies politick or corporate, his, her, or their executors, administrators, successors, or assigns, half-yearly, at two of the most usual days of payment in the year (that is to say) the tenth day of *October*, and the fifth day of *April*; the first payment thereof to become due on the tenth day of *October*, one thousand seven hundred and sixty five.

Such certificates for fractional sums, as shall not be redelivered, &c. to the treasurer of the navy, by 5 April, 1765, are to be paid off;

II. Provided always, and be it further enacted by the authority aforesaid, That if any of the certificates granted on or before the said twenty sixth day of *March*, one thousand seven hundred and sixty five, for such fractional parts of one hundred pounds, shall not have been redelivered, and subscribed, to the said treasurer of the navy on or before the fifth day of *April*, one thousand seven hundred and sixty five; in every such case, the said certificates shall be paid according to the course of the navy, in such order as the bills, in part of which such certificates shall have been granted, were payable; and such of the said certificates as were granted in part of bills bearing interest, shall, from the said fifth day of *April*, one thousand seven hundred and sixty five, carry interest after such rate as would have been payable in respect of the sums mentioned in the said bills; any thing herein contained to the contrary notwithstanding; and that all the said certificates which shall not have been so redelivered to the treasurer of his Majesty's navy, shall and may be assignable by indorsement thereupon made, until the same shall be paid in the course of the navy as aforesaid; and that none of the said assignments shall be charged with any stamp duties whatsoever.

and such as were granted in part of bills bearing interest, are to carry interest, after 5 April; and the same are made assignable by indorsement.

Treasurer of the navy to give an account to the cashier of the bank, of the certificates delivered out.

III. And be it further enacted by the authority aforesaid, That the treasurer of his Majesty's navy shall deliver to the chief cashier or cashiers of the said governor and company, such account or accounts of the certificates so delivered out, as the said cashier or cashiers shall think necessary for his or their information.

Annuities made a personal estate,

IV. And be it further enacted by the authority aforesaid, That all persons and corporations intitled to any of the said redeemable annuities, and their executors, administrators, successors, and assigns respectively, and all persons and corporations lawfully claiming under them, shall have good, sure, absolute, and indefeazible estates and interests in the same, according to the tenor and true meaning of this act; and shall be possessed thereof as of a personal estate, which shall not be descendable to heirs, nor liable to any foreign attachment by the custom of *London*, or otherwise; any law, custom, or usage to the contrary notwithstanding; and that none of the certificates granted in manner herein mentioned, or of the annuities hereby established, shall be subject to any taxes, charges, or impositions whatsoever.

and not descendable to heirs, &c.

and to be tax free.

Executors and trustees, &c. delivering up

V. And be it further enacted by the authority aforesaid, That every person who was possessed of any of the said bills as executor,

executor, adminiſtrator, or truſtee, or as guardian of any infant or infants, or as committee of any ideot, lunatick, or perſon of unſound mind, or as depoſitary or mortgagee, and hath delivered up ſuch bill or bills to the ſaid treaſurer of the navy as aforeſaid, ſhall be and is hereby indemnified for ſo doing; and ſhall, in reſpect of ſuch bill or bills, be intituled to the annuities and advantages hereby provided; but in caſe of executors or adminiſtrators, the annuities which they ſhall be ſo intitled to ſhall be aſſets in their hands, in like manner as ſuch bill or bills were or would have been if not ſo delivered up; and in caſe of guardians, truſtees, committees, depoſitaries or mortgagees, the annuities to which they ſhall be ſo intitled ſhall be ſubject and liable to the ſame truſts and equity of redemption reſpectively, as ſuch bills were or would have been if not ſo delivered up.

bills to the treaſurer of the navy, are indemnified for ſo doing; and are intitled to the annuities and advantages provided by the act. The annuities to be deemed aſſets in the hands of executors; and in truſtees hands, to be ſubject to the ſame truſts,

VI. And be it further enacted by the authority aforeſaid, That the ſaid governor and company of the bank of *England*, and their ſucceſſors, or ſuch perſon or perſons as they ſhall appoint for that purpoſe, ſhall, and he and they is and are hereby reſpectively authorized and required, to give credit, in a book or books to be prepared for that purpoſe, for the ſum contained in every ſuch certificate brought or to be brought to him or them, and for the ſums ſo paid and contributed as aforeſaid; and the reſpective perſons, bodies politick or corporate, to whoſe credit ſuch ſums ſhall be entered in the ſaid book or books, his, her, or their executors, adminiſtrators, ſucceſſors, or aſſigns, ſhall and may have power to aſſign and transfer all or any part of his, her, or their ſhare or proportion thereof, which ſhall be then attended with the ſaid redeemable annuities, to any other perſon or perſons, bodies politick or corporate whatſoever, in the books of the bank of *England*; and the ſaid governor and company for the time being ſhall alſo, on or before the twenty fourth day of *June*, one thouſand ſeven hundred and ſixty ſeven, tranſmit an atteſted duplicate fairly written on paper, of the ſaid book or books firſt herein before mentioned, into the office of the auditor of the receipt of his Majeſty's exchequer, there to remain for ever.

Credit to be given in books at the bank for the ſums in the certificates, and for the ſums paid in; which may be aſſigned.

Duplicate of the ſaid books to be tranſmitted to the receipt of the exchequer by 24 June, 1767.

VII. And be it further enacted by the authority aforeſaid, That the ſaid annuities payable at the bank of *England* ſhall, from the commencement thereof, be charged and chargeable upon, and payable out of, the monies which ſhall, from time to time, ariſe and be in the receipt of his Majeſty's exchequer, of or for the ſurpluſſes, exceſſes, or overplus monies, commonly called *The Sinking Fund*, after paying, or reſerving ſufficient to pay, all ſuch ſums of money as have been directed by any former act or acts of parliament to be paid out of the ſame.

Annuities charged on the ſinking fund.

VIII. And be it further enacted, That all the monies paid or contributed as aforeſaid at the bank of *England*, ſhall, by or on the behalf of the ſaid governor and company, be from time to time paid into the receipt of the exchequer, within the ſpace of ſeven days after notice in writing ſhall, on the behalf of the commiſſioners of the treaſury, or any three or more of them, or the

Monies contributed at the bank to be paid into the exchequer within 7 days after notice given;

and to be applied by the treasury towards discharging bills payable in the course of the navy or victualling offices, made out on or before 30 June, 1764.

the high treasurer for the time being, be delivered to the cashier or cashiers of the said governor and company for that purpose, and shall be accounted for in the exchequer, according to the due course thereof; and that all the monies so paid into the said receipt, shall and may be issued and applied by any three or more of the commissioners of the treasury, or the high treasurer for the time being, towards discharging bills payable in the course of the navy or victualling offices, or for transports, which were made out on or before the said thirtieth day of *June*, one thousand seven hundred and sixty four; and for the more easy and sure payment of the said annuities hereby directed to be paid at the bank of *England*.

Bank to employ a chief clerk and accountant general.

IX. And, for the more effectual execution of this act, be it further enacted by the authority aforesaid, That the said governor and company of the bank of *England*, and their successors, shall, from time to time, until the said annuities shall be redeemed according to this act, appoint or employ one or more sufficient person or persons within their office in the city of *London* to be their chief or first cashier or cashiers, and one other sufficient person within the same office to be their accountant general; and that so much of the monies, from time to time, and at any time, arising or being in the receipt of the exchequer of or for the surplusses, excesses, or overplus monies, commonly called *The Sinking Fund*, as shall be sufficient, from time to time, to answer the half-yearly payments of the said annuities, shall (after paying, or reserving sufficient to pay, all such sums of money as, before the passing of this act, shall have been directed by any other act or acts of parliament to be paid out of the said fund) by order of the commissioners of the treasury, or any three or more of them, or the high treasurer for the time being, without any further or other warrant to be sued for, had, or obtained, in that behalf, be issued and paid at the said receipt of exchequer to the said first or chief cashier or cashiers of the said governor and company of the bank of *England* and their successors for the time being, by way of imprest and upon account, for the payment of the said annuities; and that such cashier or cashiers to whom the said monies shall, from time to time, be issued, shall from time to time, without delay, apply and pay the same accordingly, and render his or their accounts thereof according to the due course of the exchequer.

Monies to be issued out of the sinking fund, from time to time to the said clerk for payment of the annuities; who is to apply the same accordingly, and render an account thereof.

Cashier to give security

X. Provided always, and be it further enacted by the authority aforesaid, That such cashier or cashiers shall give security to the good liking of any three or more of the commissioners of the treasury, or the high treasurer, for the time being, for duly answering and paying into the receipt of his Majesty's exchequer all monies which he or they hath or have received, or shall receive, in such manner as herein before mentioned, and for accounting duly for the same, and for performance of the trust reposed in him or them by this act.

Accountant general to inspect the receipts and

XI. And it is hereby also enacted, That the said accountant general for the time being shall, from time to time, inspect and examine all receipts and payments of the said cashier or cashiers, and

and the vouchers relating thereunto, in order to prevent any fraud, negligence, or delay.

payments, with the vouchers.

XII. And be it further enacted by the authority aforesaid, That all the monies to which any person or persons shall be intitled by virtue of this act, in respect of the first mentioned two fifth parts of the said one million five hundred thousand pounds, on which the said redeemable annuities, after the rate of three pounds *per centum per annum*, shall be attending, shall, from the fifth day of *April*, one thousand seven hundred and sixty five, be added to and made part of the joint stock of annuities transferrable at the bank of *England*, into which the several sums, reduced from four pounds to three pounds *per centum per annum*, were converted by two acts of parliament, made in the twenty fifth and twenty sixth years of his late Majesty's reign; subject, nevertheless, to redemption by parliament, in such manner and upon such notice as in the said act of the twenty fifth year of his said late Majesty's reign is directed, in respect of the several and respective sums, or any part thereof, for which the several and respective annuities therein mentioned, or any of them, are payable; and that all the monies to which any person or persons shall be intitled by virtue of this act, in respect of other two fifth parts of the said one million five hundred thousand pounds, to be determined by the drawing of the said lottery, on which the like redeemable annuities shall be attending, together with so much of the remaining one fifth part of the said one million five hundred thousand pounds, on which the like redeemable annuities shall be attending, as shall not be exchanged for annuities on lives with the benefit of survivorship, in manner authorized by this act, shall also be added to and made a part of such joint stock, from the fifth day of *April*, one thousand seven hundred and sixty six, and shall be subject to redemption in manner aforesaid; and that all and every person and persons, and corporations whatsoever, in proportion to the money to which he, she, or they, shall be intitled as aforesaid, shall have and be deemed to have a proportional interest and share in the said joint stock of annuities.

Annuities, in respect of the first mentioned two fifth parts of the 1,500,000 l. to be consolidated with the reduced annuities, of 25 & 26 Geo. 2.

Annuities depending on the lottery, with those that shall not be exchanged for annuities on lives, to be made a joint stock.

XIII. And be it further enacted by the authority aforesaid, That books shall be constantly kept by the said accountant general for the time being, wherein all assignments or transfers of any part or parts of the said annuities, payable at the bank of *England*, and of the principal sum in respect whereof they were established, shall be entered and registered; which entries shall be conceived in proper words for that purpose, and shall be signed by the parties making such assignments or transfers; or if any such party or parties be absent, by his, her, or their attornies, hereunto lawfully authorized by writing under his, her, or their hands and seals, to be attested by two or more credible witnesses; and that the person or persons, to whom such transfer shall be made, shall respectively underwrite his, her, or their acceptance thereof; and that no other method of assigning or transferring any part of the said annuities or principal sum shall be

Books to be kept at the accountant general's office for entering assignments and transfers.

Persons accepting such transfers to underwrite their acceptance.

be good and available in law, and that no ſtamp duties whatſoever ſhall be charged on the ſaid transfers, or any of them.

Annuities may be deviſed by will, but no payment to be made till entry is made of ſuch deviſe, &c.

XIV. Provided always, That all perſons poſſeſſed of any ſhare or intereſt in the ſaid annuities, payable at the bank of *England*, or any eſtate on intereſt therein, may deviſe the ſame by will; but that no payment ſhall be made upon any ſuch deviſe, until ſo much of the ſaid will as relates to ſuch eſtate, ſhare, or intereſt, be entered in the ſaid office; and that in default of ſuch transfer or deviſe, ſuch ſhare, eſtate, or intereſt, ſhall go to the executors, adminiſtrators, or ſucceſſors.

Bank to incur no diſability for what they ſhall do under this act.

XV. Provided always, and it is hereby further enacted by the authority aforeſaid, That the ſaid governor and company of the bank of *England*, or any member thereof, ſhall not incur any diſability for or by reaſon of his or their doing of any matter or thing in purſuance of this act.

No fee to be taken for certificates, annuities, or transfers,

on penalty of 20 l.

XVI. And be it further enacted, That no fee, reward, or gratuity, ſhall be demanded or taken of any of his Majeſty's ſubjects for receiving the ſaid certificates and monies, or for iſſuing the monies for payment of the ſaid annuities, or for any transfer to be made in purſuance of this act, or for any other matter or thing hereby required to be tranſacted or done at the bank of *England*, upon pain that every perſon ſo offending ſhall forfeit the ſum of twenty pounds to the party aggrieved, with full coſts of ſuit, to be recovered by action of debt, bill, plaint, or information, in any of his Majeſty's courts of record at *Weſtminſter*; wherein no eſſoin, protection, privilege, or wager of law, injunction, or order of reſtraint, or more than one imparlance, ſhall be granted or allowed.

Treaſury to reward the perſon employed in the execution of this act; and to defray incidental charges, out of the ſinking fund; with allowances for the chief clerk,

and accountant general, at the diſpoſal of governor and company of the bank.

XVII. Provided always, and be it enacted by the authority aforeſaid, That the commiſſioners of the treaſury, or any three or more of them, or the high treaſurer for the time being, ſhall have power, and he and they is and are hereby authorized to reward all ſuch perſons as ſhall be any ways employed in the execution of this act, for their ſervice, pains, and labour; and alſo to defray ſuch incidental charges as ſhall neceſſarily attend the ſame, out of the ſurpluſſes, exceſſes, or overplus monies, commonly called *The Sinking Fund*; and alſo to appoint ſuch allowances as they ſhall think proper, out of the ſaid ſurpluſſes, exceſſes, or overplus monies, for the ſervice, pains, and labour of the ſaid caſhier or caſhiers, in the receiving the ſaid certificates and monies, and payment of the ſaid annuities, and for executing the other truſts hereby in him or them repoſed; and alſo for the ſervice, pains, and labour of the ſaid accountant general for performing the truſt hereby repoſed in him; all which allowances to be made as aforeſaid in reſpect to the ſervice, pains, and labour, of any officer or officers of the ſaid governor and company, ſhall be for the uſe and benefit of the ſaid governor and company, and at their diſpoſal only.

Certificates to be granted at the bank to the proprietors of ſtock

XVIII. And be it further enacted by the authority aforeſaid, That every perſon and body politick or corporate, who ſhall become poſſeſſed of one hundred pounds or more capital ſtock in the redeemable annuities herein before granted, in reſpect of the

one

one fifth part of the ſums certified, paid, and contributed as aforeſaid, ſhall, upon application to the ſaid caſhier or caſhiers, or accomptant general, at any time on or before the fifth day of *April*, one thouſand ſeven hundred and ſixty ſix, be intitled to receive from ſuch caſhier or caſhiers, or accomptant, for every intire ſum of one hundred pounds, of which ſuch perſon or body politick or corporate ſhall be then poſſeſſed in ſuch ſtock a certificate under the hand or hands of ſuch caſhier or caſhiers, or accomptant, directed to the auditor of the receipt of his Majeſty's exchequer, and to be printed or written upon cheque paper, and cut out indentwiſe through ſome flouriſh or device to be contrived by the ſaid caſhier or caſhiers, or accomptant; which certificate ſhall contain the names and additions of ſuch reſpective proprietors; and the ſaid caſhier or caſhiers, or accomptant, is or are hereby required to grant a diſtinct certificate for every ſuch one hundred pounds, in manner as aforeſaid; which certificates may be aſſignable by indorſement thereon to be made, and witneſſed by two perſons, at any time before the firſt day of *May*, one thouſand ſeven hundred and ſixty ſix; for which aſſignment no ſtamp duty ſhall be paid: and in order to prevent the auditor of the ſaid receipt from being impoſed upon by any counterfeit or forged certificate, the ſaid caſhier or caſhiers, or accomptant, ſhall tranſmit to the ſaid auditor a counterpart of the cheques of all the ſaid certificates delivered out by them as aforeſaid; upon which counterparts ſhall be expreſſed the number of the certificate, and the names of the reſpective proprietors to whom ſuch certificates ſhall have been granted.

in the redeemable annuities, &c.

A diſtinct certificate to be granted for every 100 l. to be aſſignable by indorſement, and witneſſed before 1 May, 1766.

Counterpart of the cheques to be tranſmitted to the auditor of the exchequer.

XIX. And be it further enacted by the authority aforeſaid, That the ſaid reſpective proprietors, or their executors or adminiſtrators, ſhall, on or before the ſixth day of *May*, one thouſand ſeven hundred and ſixty ſix, deliver every ſuch certificate to the ſaid auditor of the receipt of the exchequer, to be exchanged for orders to be made out in the manner herein after appointed; and ſhall alſo at the ſame time, by writing on the back of every ſuch certificate, name, and in manner herein after mentioned, deſcribe the perſon for whoſe life he, ſhe, or they, ſhall deſire to have an annuity, with the benefit of ſurvivorſhip, as is herein after alſo mentioned; and in caſe any ſuch certificate ſhall not be delivered to the ſaid auditor, and ſuch nominee be appointed on or before the ſixth day of *May*, one thouſand ſeven hundred and ſixty ſix, then, and in ſuch caſe, every proprietor of ſuch certificate ſhall forfeit all right and title to any ſuch life annuity as aforeſaid; but upon redelivery of ſuch certificate to the ſaid caſhier or caſhiers, or accomptant, ſhall become intitled to ſtock in the ſaid redeemable annuities ſo conſolidated as aforeſaid, to the amount of the ſum ſo certified, in ſuch and the ſame manner as ſuch reſpective proprietor would have been intitled in caſe ſuch certificate had not been taken out; and the ſaid caſhier or caſhiers, or accomptant, is or are hereby required to cancel every ſuch certificate upon the redelivery thereof.

Certificates to be delivered up at the exchequer by 6 May, 1766, to be exchanged for orders; and the perſons for whoſe lives annuities are deſired, are to be then named; otherwiſe the right to ſuch life annuities are forfeited; but the right to a ſhare in the redeemable conſolidated annuities, ſhall remain, upon redelivery of the certificates to the bank.

XX. And be it further enacted by the authority aforeſaid, That

Annuities for lives to be

paid at the exchequer at the rate of 3l. per cent. with benefit of survivorship; to commence from 5 April, 1766, and to be paid half yearly, on 10 Oct. and 5 April. First payment to be made on 10 Oct. 1766. Annuities payable at the bank till 5 April, 1766, &c.

That the said proprietors, who shall deliver to the said auditors such certificates as aforesaid, and appoint their nominees on or before the said sixth day of *May*, one thousand seven hundred and sixty six, shall be intitled to have and receive, during the lives of such nominees respectively, an annuity, payable at the exchequer, at the rate of three pounds for every one hundred pounds, so certified to the said auditor, to be attended with the benefit of survivorship in manner hereafter-mentioned; which said annuities shall commence from the fifth day of *April*, one thousand seven hundred and sixty six, and be payable half yearly, during the lives of the respective nominees, on the tenth day of *October*, and the fifth day of *April*, in every year; the first payment thereof to become due on the tenth day of *October*, one thousand seven hundred and sixty six; and the annuities payable at the bank of *England*, in respect of the monies so converted into life annuities, shall be paid there to the said fifth day of *April*, one thousand seven hundred and sixty six; and all right and title to the same, and the principal sum in respect whereof such annuity shall have been payable, shall from thenceforth cease and determine.

A distinct order to be made out at the exchequer for a life annuity for every 100l. certified.

XX. And be it further enacted by the authority aforesaid, That the auditor of the said receipt of exchequer shall, as soon as conveniently may be after such certificate or certificates shall be delivered to him, cause a separate and distinct order to be made out in the exchequer for the payment of a life annuity for every one hundred pounds so certified; which orders shall be made out upon vellum or parchment, and shall contain the names, surnames, additions, and places of abode, of the respective proprietors or their assigns, and of their nominees, and the reputed ages and parents of such nominees, with other descriptions which shall best ascertain the person of such nominees, and also the annuity payable during the lives of such respective, nominees; and all such orders shall be signed by the commissioners of the treasury, or any three or more of them, or the high treasurer for the time being; and, after signing thereof, the same shall be firm, good, valid, and effectual, in law, according to the purpose and true meaning thereof, and of this act; and shall not be determinable by or upon the deaths or removals of any commissioner or commissioners of the treasury, or high treasurer, nor shall they or any of them have power to revoke, countermand, or make void, such orders so signed as aforesaid.

Orders to be numbered arithmetically, and the nominees to be formed into classes, of 1,500l. each.

XXI. And be it further enacted by the authority aforesaid, That the said orders shall be numbered in arithmetical progression, according to the course in which the said certificates shall be delivered to the said auditor; and the nominees, and the annuities payable upon their lives, shall be formed by the said auditor into classes, each class to consist of annuities to the amount of one thousand five hundred pounds at least, in manner following; that is to say, The annuities made payable in respect of the first five hundred orders shall form the first class; the annuities

nuities made payable in respect of the suceeding five hundred orders shall form the second class; and so in like method the annuities made payable by the remaining orders, shall, according to the numerical course of such orders, be formed into other classes, which shall be numbered in succession, until the several annuities, which shall make up several and distinct sums of one thousand five hundred pounds, shall be so classed and ranked; and if, over and above the said several and distinct sums of one thousand five hundred pounds, any annuities shall remain which shall not amount in the whole to one thousand five hundred pounds, such remaining annuities shall be distributed amongst, and added to, the several classes, in equal proportions as near as may be, so that the proportion of such annuities to be added to the first class, shall be according to the numerical course of the orders immediately succeeding the orders provided for in the last of the said classes, and so in like succession with respect to the proportions to be added to the second and other subsequent classes; and if any annuity or annuities shall remain which cannot be equally apportioned amongst all the said classes, in such case, if there shall be only an annuity payable in respect of one order, such annuity shall be added to the first class; or if there shall be more annuities than one, then such annuities shall, according to the numerical course of the orders for payment thereof, be added in equal proportions to such of the said classes as such proportions can extend to, beginning with the class number one, and proceeding to the next succeeding classes, until all the said annuities shall be ranked and classed.

Supernumerary fractional annuities to be distributed amongst the other classes.

XXII. Provided nevertheless, and be it further enacted by the authority aforesaid, That if any of the said proprietors, upon their delivering in to the said auditor any two or more of the said certificates, whereby one and the same nominee shall be appointed, shall signify their desire that the annuities to be paid in respect thereof may be placed in different classes, then, and in each and every such case, the said auditor may postpone the making out any order or orders upon the said certificates, until the same may be numbered in such manner as to be ranked, as far as may be, in different classes, according to the desire of the said proprietors.

Where the same person shall be a nominee in two or more certificates, the auditor, upon request, may postpone the making out orders till the annuities can be placed in different classes, according to desire.

XXIII. And be it further enacted by the authority aforesaid, That, from time to time, upon the death of each and every nominee in each respective class, the annuity or annuities which shall have been payable in such class, during the life of such nominee, shall be equally divided among the rest of the proprietors of the annuities in the same class, during the lives of their respective nominees; and when there shall be only one surviving nominee in any such class, the person or persons intitled to an annuity or annuities therein upon the life of such survivor, shall, during such life, have and receive the whole of the annuities contained in every such class respectively; and, from time to time, upon the decease of such survivor, the annuities payable in such respective class shall cease and determine; and in

Upon the death of every nominee, the annuities to be divided among the survivors in the same class, till the whole be determined.

Life annuities not amounting to 3,000 l. to be paid with like benefit of survivorship.

in case the life annuities do become payable in respect of the said certificates, shall not amount to the sum of three thousand pounds, then the said annuities shall be payable and paid with the like benefit of survivorship upon the whole of such annuities, in like manner as is before provided and directed with respect to the survivorships in such classes.

Books to be kept at the exchequer and pells for entering the names of the proprietors and their nominees, and their respective classes, &c.

XXIV. And it is hereby further enacted, That in the offices of the auditor of the receipt of the exchequer, and clerk of the pells severally, there shall be provided and kept one or more book or books, in which the names of all such proprietors and their nominees, during whose lives respectively the said annuities shall be payable, shall be fairly entered; and also a book or books, in which the several classes, and the names of the persons appointed nominees, and the said annuities, and the names of the proprietors of such annuities in each class, shall be also fairly entered; which books it shall be lawful for the respective proprietors, their executors, administrators, or assigns, from time to time to resort to, and to inspect without fee or reward.

Money sufficient for payment of the said annuities to be set apart out of the sinking fund.

XXV. And be it further enacted by the authority aforesaid, That from and out of the monies composing the said fund, commonly called *The Sinking Fund* (after paying, or reserving sufficient to pay, all such sums of money as, before the passing of this act, shall have been directed by any other act or acts of parliament to be paid out of the said fund) there shall and may be separated, set apart, and applied, from time to time, at the receipt of the exchequer, such sums of money as shall be necessary for payment of the said annuities upon lives, in manner as aforesaid.

Orders made assignable during the lives of the respective nominees;

XXVI. And be it further enacted by the authority aforesaid, That it shall and may be lawful for any such proprietor, or his or her executors, administrators, or assigns, at any time during the life of his or her nominee or nominees, by proper words of assignment to be indorsed on his, her, or their order or orders, to be witnessed by two persons, to assign or transfer his, her, or their right, title, interest, and benefit, of such order or orders, to any other person or persons; which being notified in the office of the auditor of the said receipt of the exchequer, the officers there shall cause an entry or memorial thereof to be made in the book of registry for such orders, without fee or charge; and after such entry made, such assignment shall intitle such assignee or assignees, his, her, or their executors, administrators, or assigns, to the benefit thereof, and payment thereon; and such assignee or assignees may, in like manner, assign again, and so *toties quoties*; and afterwards it shall not be in the power of such person or persons, who shall make such assignment, to make void, release, or discharge the same, or any monies thereby due, or any part thereof; and for which assignment no stamp duty shall be paid.

such assignments to be entered at the exchequer.

The nominee not appearing personally at the time of

XXVII. And, for preventing all frauds in receiving the said annuities, be it further enacted by the authority aforesaid, That every proprietor, his or her executors, administrators, assigns, or agents,

agents, upon demand of any half-yearly payment of his or her respective shares of the said annuities (unless the nominee appears in person at the said receipt) shall produce a certificate of the life of his, her, or their respective nominee, signed by the minister and churchwardens of the parish where such nominee shall be then living upon the day when the said half-yearly payments shall become due, if such nominee shall be then residing in that part of *Great Britain* called *England*, dominion of *Wales*, or town of *Berwick upon Tweed*; or otherwise, it shall and may be lawful to and for every such proprietor, his or her executors, administrators, or assigns, at his or her election, to make oath of the truth of his or their respective nominee's life upon the day when the said half-yearly payments shall become due, before one or more of the justices of the peace of the respective county, riding, city, town, or place, wherein such person, at the time of making of such oath, shall reside; and in like manner, every such proprietor, his or her executors, administrators, assigns, or agents, whose nominee shall reside in any town or place, being extraparochial, upon the day when any of the said half-yearly payments shall become due, shall make a like oath before any such justice or justices aforesaid of the life of such nominee on that day (which oaths the said justice or justices of the peace is or are hereby impowered to administer) and such justice or justices shall make a certificate thereof; for which oath and certificate no fee or reward shall be demanded or paid; and the said certificate shall be filed in the office of the auditor of the said receipt of the exchequer.

demanding the half-yearly payment of the annuity, a certificate of his life is to to be produced; or attested upon oath.

Certificate to be filed.

XXVIII. And be it further enacted by the authority aforesaid, That if any person shall be guilty of a false oath, or shall forge any certificate touching the premisses, and be thereof lawfully convicted, such person shall incur the pains and penalties inflicted upon persons committing wilful perjury and forgery.

Penalty of making a false oath, or forging a certificate.

XXIX. And be it further enacted by the authority aforesaid, That in case any nominee shall, at the time of such demand, be resident in that part of *Great Britain* called *Scotland*, or in the kingdom of *Ireland*, and any one or more of the barons of the exchequer there for the time being shall certify, that, upon proof to him or them made (which proof he and they is and are hereby authorized and required to take in a summary way) it doth seem probable to him or them, that the said nominee is living (which certificate is to be given on examination made without fee or charge) the said certificate, being filed as aforesaid, shall be a sufficient warrant for making the said half-yearly payment to the respective proprietors, their executors, administrators, or assigns; and in case any such nominee shall, at the time of such demand, be resident in any parts beyond the seas, the respective proprietors of all such orders, or their agents, shall produce certificates of the life of his, her, or their respective nominees under the hand of the *British* minister residing at the place where any such nominee shall be living upon the day when the half-yearly payment shall become due; which certificates

Certificates with respect to nominees resident in Scotland or Ireland,

or in parts beyond the seas, by whom to be granted.

shall

ſhall be given without fee or reward; and in caſe no *Britiſh* miniſter ſhall reſide at the place where any ſuch nominee ſhall live, then the ſaid proprietors of ſuch orders or ſuch agents ſhall produce a certificate of the life of his, her, or their reſpective nominees under the hand and ſeal of the chief magiſtrate of any city, town, or place, where any ſuch nominee ſhall be then living, upon the day when the ſaid half-yearly payment ſhall become due as aforeſaid: and ſuch proprietors, agent or agents, ſhall alſo annex to every ſuch certificate an affidavit to be made before one or more of the barons of the exchequer, that he or they do believe that ſuch certificate is true; which certificate and affidavit being filed as aforeſaid, ſhall be a ſufficient warrant for making the ſaid half-yearly payment to the reſpective proprietors, or their agent or agents: and if any perſon or perſons ſhall receive one or more half-yearly payment or payments upon his, her, or their annuity or annuities for any time beyond the death of his, her, or their nominee or nominees when the ſame ought to ceaſe, ſuch perſon or perſons knowing ſuch nominee or nominees, to be dead, ſhall forfeit treble the value of the monies ſo by him, her, or them received, and alſo the ſum of five hundred pounds; whereof one moiety ſhall go to his Majeſty, his heirs and ſucceſſors, and the other moiety to him or them who will ſue for the ſame, by action of debt, bill, ſuit, or information; in which no eſſoin, protection, privilege, wager of law, injunction, or more than one imparlance, ſhall be allowed.

Perſons knowingly receiving annuities beyond the deaths of their nominees, forfeit treble the ſum received, and 500 l. One moiety to the King, and the other to the proſecutor.

XXX. And be it further enacted by the authority aforeſaid, That every proprietor, his or her executors, adminiſtrators, or aſſigns, within one month next after notice of the death of his, her, or their reſpective nominee or nominees, ſhall certify ſuch death to the auditor of the ſaid receipt of exchequer for the time being; and ſhall alſo, within three months after ſuch notice, deliver or cauſe to be delivered up to the ſaid auditor, his, her, or their order or orders, by which he, ſhe, or they, was and were intitled, during the life of ſuch nominee, to any ſhare of the ſaid annuities, in caſe ſuch order or orders be in his, her, or their hands or power; and in default thereof, ſuch proprietor, his or their executors, adminiſtrators, and aſſigns, ſhall forfeit the ſum of ten pounds, to be recovered by action of debt as aforeſaid, and to be had and received for the uſe of any perſon who ſhall ſue for the ſame.

Deaths of nominees to be certified within one month, to the exchequer, and the order for the annuity to be delivered up within three months after; on penalty of 10 l. to go to the proſecutor.

XXXI. And be it further enacted by the authority aforeſaid, That the ſaid annuities ſhall be free from all taxes, charges, and impoſitions whatſoever, and ſhall be deemed a perſonal eſtate; and in all caſes, where the ſame do not depend on the proprietor's own life, ſhall go to his executors and adminiſtrators, and not be deſcendable to heirs.

Annuities made tax free, and to be deemed a perſonal eſtate, &c.

XXXII. And be it further enacted by the authority aforeſaid, That if any proprietor of any ſuch life annuity, who ſhall be intitled to receive any half-yearly payment thereof, ſhall at any time neglect to demand the ſame, until within twenty days before the expiration of one year from the time when ſuch payment ſhall have become due, he ſhall forfeit ſuch half-yearly

Such half year's payment as is neglected to be demanded until within 20 days be-

ly payment ſo neglected to be demanded; and the ſame ſhall be divided amongſt the proprietors of annuities in the ſame claſs, as if the nominee for the annuity, in reſpect whereof ſuch default ſhall be made, had been dead, and ſo, from time to time, upon every default.

fore the expiration of the year, is forfeited for the benefit of the other annuitants in the ſame claſs.

XXXIII. Provided neverthelеſs, That if ſuch proprietor ſhall afterwards make a demand in due time, in manner as aforeſaid, for any following half-yearly payment, ſuch proprietor ſhall, for the future, have his ſhare of the ſaid annuities, as if ſuch default had not been made.

Proprietor entitled to the following half year's dividend, duly demanding the ſame.

XXXIV. And, to the intent it may appear and be aſcertained upon every half-yearly payment, unto and amongſt what perſons, and in what proportions, the ſaid annuities are to be diſtributed; be it enacted, That in the ſaid office of auditor of the receipt, every half-year, within twenty days before the reſpective days of payment, there ſhall be made up an account of the ſaid nominees whoſe deaths are come to knowledge, and of the ſeveral proprietors who have made default in making demand as aforeſaid, that ſo the reſt of the proprietors may have the advantage thereof.

Account to be made up half-yearly of the deaths of nominees; and the defaults of thoſe not demanding their dividends.

XXXV. And whereas it may ſo happen that, in proceſs of time, ſeveral of the ſtanding o ders may be loſt, burnt, or deſtroyed, or may become defaced, obliterated, or incumbered with many aſſignments thereon, and it may be neceſſary that new orders ſhould be made forth in lieu thereof; be it therefore enacted by the authority aforeſaid, That in all or any the ſaid caſes, any three or more of the commiſſioners of the treaſury, or the high treaſurer for the time being, ſhall, and he or they is or are hereby impowered, from time to time, upon certificate under the hand of the lord chief baron, or any other of the barons of the coif of his Majeſty's court of exchequer, that he or they is or are ſatisfied, by proof upon oath before him or them made, that any ſuch order or orders have been loſt, burnt, or otherwiſe deſtroyed, to cauſe new orders to be made forth at the exchequer, to be ſigned by him or them, in lieu of ſuch orders ſo certified to be loſt, burnt, or deſtroyed; and the reſpective officers in the ſaid exchequer are hereby directed to pay the intereſt, which ſhall, from time to time, become due on ſuch new orders, as if the original order or orders had been produced; and all ſuch payments ſhall be allowed in their reſpective accounts; provided that the perſon or perſons, intitled to receive the intereſt due upon any ſuch order or orders, do give ſecurity to the King, to the good liking of the perſon appointed to pay the ſame, for paying into the exchequer, for the uſe of the publick, ſo much money as ſhall be paid thereupon, if the order or orders, ſo certified to be loſt, burnt, or otherwiſe deſtroyed, be thereafter produced; and the ſaid commiſſioners of the treaſury, or the high treaſurer for the time being, ſhall alſo have power to cauſe new ſtanding orders to be made forth for

New orders to be granted, in lieu of ſuch as ſhall be certified to be loſt, burnt, or deſtroyed; and the intereſt to be duly paid thereon; the party giving ſecurity.

New ſtanding orders may be made out in lieu of ſuch as ſhall be defaced.

and

Old orders to be cancelled;

and in lieu of ſuch orders as ſhall become defaced, obliterated, or otherwiſe incumbered as aforeſaid; which ſaid order or orders ſhall be at the ſame time delivered up and cancelled, and the new order or orders, to be made out in lieu thereof, ſhall be made payable, and delivered to the perſon or perſons who ſhall appear to be the proprietor or proprietors of the ſaid order or orders, ſo to be delivered up and cancelled, at the time of ſuch delivery as aforeſaid; and the auditor of the receipt as aforeſaid ſhall always take care, that ſuch entries or memorandums be made upon the ſaid new orders, as may denote their being made in lieu of ſuch defaced, obliterated, incumbered, or otherwiſe defective orders, cancelled, and as may ſecure the publick againſt any double payments, for or by reaſon of the making out or iſſuing ſuch new orders in manner aforeſaid.

and an entry made on the new orders, denoting their being in lieu of thoſe cancelled.

Penalty of forging any certificate, order, aſſignment, receipt, letter of attorney, &c., or proprietors names,

XXXVI. And be it enacted by the authority aforeſaid, That if any perſon or perſons whatſoever ſhall forge or counterfeit, or procure to be forged or counterfeited, or knowingly or wilfully act and aſſiſt in the forging or counterfeiting any certificate or certificates, given by ſuch caſhier or caſhiers, or any order or orders to be made forth in lieu thereof, in purſuance of this preſent act, or any aſſignment or aſſignments of ſuch order or orders, or of the annuities payable thereon, or of any receipt or diſcharge to the exchequer for the annuities due or to grow due on any ſuch order or orders, or of any letter of attorney, or other authority or inſtrument, to transfer, aſſign, alien, or convey any ſuch order or orders, or to receive the annuities due or to grow due thereon, or any part thereof; or ſhall forge or counterfeit, or procure to be forged or counterfeited, or knowingly or wilfully act or aſſiſt in the forging or counterfeiting the name or names of any of the proprietors of any ſuch order or orders, in or to any ſuch pretended aſſignment or aſſignments, receipt, letter of attorney, certificate, inſtrument, or authority; or ſhall falſely and deceitfully perſonate any true and real proprietor or proprietors of any of the ſaid orders, and thereby aſſign, or endeavour to aſſign, any of the ſaid orders; or receive, or endeavour to receive, the money of ſuch true and lawful proprietor, as if ſuch offender were the true and lawful owner thereof; then, and in every ſuch caſe, all and every ſuch perſon and perſons, being thereof lawfully convicted in due form of law, ſhall be adjudged guilty of felony, and ſhall ſuffer death as in caſes of felony, without benefit of clergy.

or of perſonating a proprietor, or falſly receiving or endeavouring to receive his money, is felony, without benefit of clergy.

Officer taking any fee for payment of the annuities, or entry of aſſignments, &c.

XXXVII. And be it further enacted, That no fee, reward, or gratuity whatſoever, ſhall be demanded or taken by any officer of the exchequer for paying the ſaid life annuities, or any of them; or for the entry of any aſſignment thereof, to be made in purſuance of this act, or for any thing hereby directed to be done at the exchequer, upon pain that any perſon offending by taking or demanding any ſuch fee, reward, or gratuity, ſhall, for every ſuch offence, forfeit the ſum of twenty pounds to the party aggrieved, with full coſts of ſuit; and in caſe the officers of the exchequer ſhall miſapply or divert any of the monies

to forfeit 20l. and miſapplying any of the

nies

nies to be paid into the exchequer upon this act, or ſhall pay or iſſue out of the ſame, otherwiſe than according to the intent of this act, or ſhall not keep ſuch books, regiſters, or make entries, and do and perform all other things which by this act they are directed and required to do and perform, every ſuch offender ſhall forfeit his place, and be for ever after incapable of any office or place of truſt whatſoever; and if the proprietor of any ſuch annuity ſhall any ways ſuffer thereby, he ſhall be intitled to treble damages againſt ſuch officer or officers, with full coſts of ſuit, to be recovered by action of debt, bill, plaint, or information, in any of his Majeſty's courts of record at *Weſtminſter*, wherein no eſſoin, protection, privilege, or wager of law, injunction, or order of reſtraint, or any more than one imparlance, ſhall be granted or allowed.

monies, or otherwiſe not doing his duty, to forfeit his place, and be incapacitated. Proprietor ſuffering thereby intitled to treble damages, and full coſts.

XXXVIII. Provided always, and be it enacted, That in caſe any officer of the exchequer ſhall make payment of any ſhare or ſhares of the ſaid annuities upon lives upon any ſuch certificate or certificates as aforeſaid, ſuch officer ſhall not incur any penalty, forfeiture, or diſability, though the ſaid certificate be forged or falſe, or the ſaid nominee be dead, unleſs the ſaid officer did know, at the time of ſuch payment, that the ſaid nominee was dead, or that the ſaid certificate was forged or falſe.

Officer not to incur any penalty or diſability for payment of annuities upon a falſe certificate, not knowing the ſame to be falſe.

XXXIX. And, for eſtabliſhing a proper method for drawing the ſaid lottery, be it further enacted by the authority aforeſaid, That ſuch perſons as the commiſſioners of his Majeſty's treaſury, or any three or more of them now being, or the high treaſurer, or any three or more of the commiſſioners of the treaſury for the time being, ſhall nominate or appoint, ſhall be managers and directors for preparing and delivering out tickets, and to overſee the drawing of lots, and to order, do, and perform, ſuch other matters and things as are hereafter in and by this act directed and appointed by ſuch managers and directors to be done and performed; and that ſuch managers or directors ſhall meet together, from time to time, at ſome publick office or place, for the execution of the powers and truſts in them repoſed by this act; and that the ſaid managers and directors, or ſo many of them as ſhall be preſent at any ſuch meeting, or the major part of them, ſhall cauſe books to be prepared, in which every leaf ſhall be divided or diſtinguiſhed into three columns; and upon the innermoſt of the ſaid three columns there ſhall be printed ſixty thouſand tickets, to be numbered one, two, three, and ſo onwards in an arithmetical progreſſion, where the common exceſs is to be one, until they riſe to and for the number of ſixty thouſand; and upon the middle column in every of the ſaid books ſhall be printed ſixty thouſand tickets of the ſame breadth and form, and numbered in like manner; and in the extreme column of the ſaid books there ſhall be printed a third rank or ſeries of tickets, of the ſame number with thoſe of the other two columns; which tickets ſhall ſeverally be of an oblong figure, and in the ſaid books ſhall be joined with oblique lines, flouriſhes, or devices, in ſuch manner as the ſaid managers and directors, or the major part of them, ſhall think moſt ſafe and con-

Managers and directors of the lottery to be appointed by the treaſury.

Method of the lottery books.

convenient; and that every ticket in the third or extreme column of the ſaid books ſhall have written or printed thereupon (beſides the number of ſuch ticket) words to this effect:

LOTTERY, Anno *one thouſand ſeven hundred and ſixty five.*

THIS *ticket will intitle the bearer thereof to ſix pounds, or to a better chance, in annuities, at the rate of three pounds* per centum, *eſtabliſhed by an act of parliament made in the fifth year of his Majeſty's reign, and transferrable at the bank of* England.

Managers to examine the books with the tickets, and deliver them after to the caſhiers of the bank, taking a receipt for the ſame.

XL. And it is hereby enacted, That the ſaid managers and directors, or ſo many of them as ſhall be preſent at ſuch meeting, or the major part of them then preſent, ſhall carefully examine all the ſaid books, with the tickets therein, and take care that the ſame be contrived, numbered, and made, according to the true intent and meaning of this act; and ſhall deliver, or cauſe to be delivered, the ſame books, and every or any of them, as they ſhall be examined, to the caſhier or caſhiers of the governor and company of the bank of *England*, taking from ſuch caſhier or caſhiers an acknowledgement in writing, under his or their hand or hands, importing his or their receipt of ſuch book or books and ſo many tickets therein as ſhall be delivered to him or them reſpectively; and all and every ſuch caſhier or caſhiers reſpectively is and are hereby directed and required, from time to time, to cut out of the ſaid book or books ſo to be put into his or their cuſtody, through the ſaid oblique lines, flouriſhes, or devices, indentwiſe, in the ſaid extreme columns, ſuch tickets as ſhall be neceſſary to be delivered to the ſeveral perſons intitled thereto as aforeſaid; which tickets the ſaid caſhier or caſhiers ſhall ſign with his or their own name or names; and he or they ſhall permit the reſpective perſon or perſons ſo intitled, if it be deſired, to write his or her name or mark on the correſponding ticket in the ſame book; and at the ſame time the ſaid caſhier or caſhiers ſhall deliver to ſuch perſon or perſons the ticket ſo cut off, which he, ſhe, or they, are to keep and uſe for the better aſcertaining and ſecuring the intereſt which he, ſhe, or they, his, her, or their executors, adminiſtrators, ſucceſſors, or aſſigns, ſhall or may have in the ſaid annuities.

Caſhiers to return the books with the remainder of the tickets.

XLI. And be it further enacted by the authority aforeſaid, That the ſaid caſhier or caſhiers, on or before the twenty ſixth day of *Auguſt*, one thouſand ſeven hundred and ſixty five, ſhall re-deliver to the ſaid managers and directors, at their ſaid office or place of meeting, all the ſaid books, and therein all the tickets which the ſaid caſhier or ſhall not have cut out of the ſame.

Tickets of the middle columns to be rolled up, and faſtened with ſilk;

XLII. And be it further enacted, That the ſaid managers and directors, or the major part of them, which ſhall be preſent at a meeting as aforeſaid, ſhall cauſe all the tickets of the middle columns in the books made out with three columns as aforeſaid, which ſhall be delivered back to them, by or from the ſaid caſhier or caſhiers as aforeſaid, to be carefully rolled up and made faſt with thread or ſilk; and the ſaid managers

managers or directors, or the major part of them as aforesaid, shall, in their presence, and in the presence of such contributors or adventurers as will be there, cause all the said tickets, which are to be so rolled up and made fast as aforesaid, to be cut off indentwise through the said oblique lines, flourishes, or devices, into a box to be prepared for that purpose, and to be marked with the letter (A) which is presently to be put up into another strong box, and to be locked with seven different locks and keys, to be kept by as many of the said managers, and sealed with their seals, or the seals of some of them, until the said tickets are to be drawn, as is herein after mentioned; and that the tickets in the first or innermost columns of the said books, shall remain still in the books for discovering any mistake or fraud (if any such should happen to be committed) contrary to the true meaning of this act.

and cut off indentwise into a box marked with the letter (A)

Box to be locked up and sealed.

XLIII. And be it further enacted by the authority aforesaid, That the said managers and directors, or the major part of them, which shall be present at any meeting as aforesaid, shall also prepare, or cause to be prepared, other books in which every leaf shall be divided or distinguished into two columns; and upon the innermost of those two columns there shall be printed sixty thousand tickets, and upon the outermost of the said two columns there shall be printed sixty thousand tickets, all which shall be of equal length and breadth, as near as may be; which two columns in the said books shall be joined with some flourish or device, through which the outermost tickets may be cut off indentwise: and that eleven thousand nine hundred and forty five tickets, part of those to be contained in the outer-most columns of the books last-mentioned, shall be, and be called the fortunate tickets, to which extraordinary benefits shall belong, as is herein after mentioned; and the said managers and directors, or the major part of them, or such of them as shall be present at a meeting as aforesaid, shall cause the said fortunate tickets to be written upon, or otherwise expressed, as well in figures as in words at length, in manner following; that is to say, upon two of them severally ten thousand pounds principal money; upon two of them severally five thousand pounds principal money; upon every one of four of them severally, two thousand pounds principal money; upon every one of ten of them severally, one thousand pounds principal money; upon every one of twenty of them severally, five hundred pounds principal money; upon every one of one hundred of them severally, one hundred pounds principal money; upon every one of two hundred and one of them severally, fifty pounds principal money; upon every one of eleven thousand six hundred and six of them severally, twenty pounds principal money: which principal sums, so to be written, or otherwise expressed upon the said fortunate tickets, together with five hundred pounds principal money, to be allowed to the owner of the first drawn ticket, and one thousand pounds principal money to the owner of the last drawn ticket, over and above the benefits

Books to be prepared with 2 columns, on each of which 60,000 tickets to be printed.

The number and value of the fortunate tickets.

500l. to the first drawn ticket, and 1000l. to the last drawn.

which may happen to belong to the two laſt mentioned tickets, and, together with the ſum of ſix pounds to be paid or allowed for and upon each blank or unfortunate ticket of the ſaid lottery, will amount in the whole to the principal ſum of ſix hundred thouſand pounds, to be converted into annuities by virtue of this act in reſpect of the ſaid lottery; and the ſaid managers and directors, or the major part of them, who ſhall be preſent at a meeting as aforeſaid, ſhall cauſe all the ſaid tickets, contained in the outermoſt columns of the ſaid laſt-mentioned books, to be, in the preſence of the ſaid managers and directors, or the major part of them, which ſhall be preſent at a meeting as aforeſaid, and in the preſence of ſuch contributors or adventurers as will then be there, to be carefully rolled up and faſtened with thread or ſilk, and carefully cut out indentwiſe through the ſaid flouriſh or device, into another box, to be prepared for this purpoſe, and to be marked with the letter (B), which box ſhall be put into another ſtrong box, and locked up with ſeven different locks and keys, to be kept by as many of the ſaid managers, and ſealed up with their ſeals, or the ſeals of ſome of them, until theſe tickets ſhall alſo be drawn in the manner and form herein after mentioned; and that the whole buſineſs of rolling up, and cutting off, and putting into the ſaid boxes the ſaid tickets, and locking up and ſealing the ſaid boxes, ſhall be performed by the ſaid managers and directors, or ſuch of them as aforeſaid, before the laſt ſix days immediately preceding the day by this act appointed for the drawing the ſaid lottery: and to the end every perſon concerned may be well aſſured that the counterpart of the ſame number with his or her ticket is put into the box marked with the letter (A) from whence the ſame may be drawn, and that other matters are done as hereby directed, ſome publick notification in print ſhall be given of the preciſe time or times of putting the ſaid tickets into the ſaid boxes, to the end that ſuch adventurers, as ſhall be minded to ſee the ſame done, may be preſent at the doing thereof.

Tickets of the outermoſt columns of the laſt mentioned book to be rolled up and tied, and cut out indentwiſe, into a box marked with the letter (B) Box to be locked up and ſealed.

Publick notice to be given of times of putting the tickets into the boxes.

XLIV. And be it further enacted by the authority aforeſaid, That on or before the eighteenth day of *November*, one thouſand ſeven hundred and ſixty five, the ſaid managers and directors ſhall cauſe the ſaid ſeveral boxes, with all the tickets therein, to be brought into the guildhall of the city of *London*, ſo that the ſame may be there, and placed on a table provided for that purpoſe, by nine of the clock in the forenoon of the ſame day, and ſhall then and there ſeverally attend this ſervice, and cauſe the two boxes containing the ſaid tickets, to be ſeverally taken out of the other two boxes, in which they ſhall have been locked up; and the tickets or lots in the reſpective innermoſt boxes being, in the preſence of the ſaid managers and directors, or ſuch of them as ſhall be then preſent, and of ſuch adventurers as will be there for the ſatisfaction of themſelves, well ſhaken and mingled in each box diſtinctly; ſome one indifferent and fit perſon, to be appointed and directed by the ſaid managers, or the major part of them, or ſuch of them as ſhall be then

Lottery to begin drawing on 18 Nov. 1765.

Method to be obſerved in drawing, &c.

present, ſhall take out and draw one ticket from the box where the ſaid numbered tickets ſhall be as aforeſaid put; and one other indifferent or fit perſon, to be appointed and directed in like manner, ſhall take out a ticket or lot from the box where the ſaid eleven thouſand nine hundred and forty five fortunate, and forty eight thouſand and fifty five blank tickets ſhall be promiſcuouſly put as aforeſaid; and immediately both the tickets ſo drawn ſhall be opened, and the number, as well of the fortunate as the blank ticket, ſhall be named aloud; and if the ticket taken or drawn from the box containing the fortunate and blank lots ſhall appear to be a blank, then the numbered ticket ſo drawn with the ſaid blank at the ſame time drawn, ſhall both be put upon one file; and if the ticket ſo drawn or taken from the box containing the fortunate and blank lots ſhall appear to be one of the fortunate tickets, then the principal ſum written upon ſuch fortunate ticket, whatſoever it be, ſhall be entered by a clerk, which the ſaid managers, or the major part of them as aforeſaid, ſhall employ and overſee for this purpoſe, into a book to be kept for entering the numbers coming up with the ſaid fortunate tickets, and the principal ſums whereunto they ſhall be intitled reſpectively, and two of the ſaid managers ſhall ſet their names as witneſſes to ſuch entries; and the ſaid fortunate and numbered tickets ſo drawn together, ſhall be put upon another file; and ſo the ſaid drawing of the tickets ſhall continue, by taking one ticket at a time out of each box, and with opening, naming aloud, and filing the ſame, and by entering the fortunate lots in ſuch method as is before mentioned, until the whole number of eleven thouſand nine hundred and forty five fortunate tickets, and one more for the laſt drawn as aforeſaid, ſhall be completely drawn; and as the ſame cannot be performed in one day's time, the ſaid managers and directors ſhall cauſe the boxes to be locked up and ſealed in manner as aforeſaid, and adjourn till the next day, and ſo from day to day, and every day (except *Sundays*, *Chriſtmas-day*, thankſgiving and faſt days) and then open the ſame, and proceed as above, till the ſaid whole number of eleven thouſand nine hundred and forty five fortunate tickets, and one more, ſhall be completely drawn as aforeſaid; and afterwards the ſaid numbered tickets ſo drawn, with the fortunate tickets drawn againſt the ſame, ſhall be and remain in a ſtrong box locked up as aforeſaid, and under the cuſtody of the ſaid managers, until they ſhall take them out to examine, adjuſt, and ſettle the property thereof.

After each day's drawing, the boxes to be locked up and ſealed.

XLV. And, to the end the fortunate may know, whether abſent or preſent, to what degree they have been ſo; be it enacted, That the ſaid managers ſhall, as ſoon as conveniently may be, after the ſaid drawing is over, cauſe to be printed and publiſhed the number of the tickets drawn againſt each fortunate ticket, and the principal ſum written on the ſame; and if any contention or diſpute ſhall ariſe in the adjuſting the property of the ſaid fortunate tickets, the major part of the ſaid managers agreeing therein, ſhall determine to whom it doth or ought to belong:

Numbers of the fortunate tickets, and the ſums, to be printed.

Diſputes relating thereto, to be adjuſted by the managers.

 and

Penalty of forging tickets or certificates.

and if any person or persons ſhall forge or counterfeit any ticket or tickets, certificate or certificates, to be made forth by this act, or alter any the number thereof, or utter, vend, barter, or diſpoſe of, or offer to diſpoſe of, any falſe, altered, forged, or counterfeit ticket or tickets, certificate or certificates, or ſhall bring any forged or counterfeit ticket or certificate, or any ticket or certificate the number whereof is altered (knowing the ſame to be ſuch) to the ſaid managers, or any of them, or to the caſhier or caſhiers, or accomptant general of the bank of *England* for the time being, or to any other perſon or perſons whatſoever with a fraudulent intention; then every ſuch perſon or perſons being thereof convicted in due form of law, ſhall be adjudged a felon, and ſhall ſuffer death as in caſes of felony, without benefit of clergy: and the ſaid managers and directors, or any two or more of them, are hereby authorized, required, and impowered, to cauſe any perſon or perſons bringing or uttering ſuch forged or counterfeit ticket or tickets, certificate or certificates, as aforeſaid, to be apprehended, and to commit him, her, or them, to his Majeſty's gaol of *Newgate*, or to the common gaol of the county or place where ſuch perſon or perſons ſhall be ſo apprehended, to be proceeded againſt for the ſaid felony according to law.

Felony.

Managers to be ſworn.

XLVI. Provided always, and it is hereby enacted by the authority aforeſaid, That every perſon that ſhall be appointed as aforeſaid to be a manager and director for putting this act in execution, before his acting in ſuch commiſſion, ſhall take the oath following; that is to ſay,

The oath.

I A. B. as a manager and director of the lottery to be drawn in purſuance of an act of parliament made in the fifth year of his Majeſty's reign, do ſwear, That I will faithfully execute the truſt repoſed in me, and that I will not uſe any indirect art or means, or permit or direct any perſon to uſe any indirect art or means, to obtain a prize or fortunate lot therein, for myſelf, or any other perſon whatſoever; and that I will do the utmoſt of my endeavour to prevent any undue or ſiniſter practice to be done by any perſon whatſoever; and that I will to the beſt of my judgement declare to whom any prize, lot, or ticket, of right does belong, according to the true intent and meaning of the ſaid act.

Which ſaid oath ſhall and may be adminiſtered by any two or more of the other managers and directors.

Caſhier, on receiving the reſidue of the ſums ſubſcribed,

to give receipts for the ſame,

XLVII. Provided always, That it ſhall and may be lawful to and for the ſaid caſhier or caſhiers, having giving ſecurity as aforeſaid, at any time or times, before ſuch caſhier or caſhiers ſhall have received any book or books from the ſaid managers, comprehending the ſaid ſixty thouſand tickets as aforeſaid, in three columns as aforeſaid, and he or they is or are hereby required to give a note, under his or their hand or hands, for the delivery of tickets to ſuch perſon or perſons as ſhall be intitled thereto; and ſhall be obliged thereby, and by this act, to give the

the bearer of every ſuch note ſuch number as ſhall be therein mentioned of tickets, of the extream column of the three columns book or books aforeſaid, as ſoon as he or they ſhall be enabled thereunto, by delivery of any ſuch book or books to him or them from the ſaid managers as aforeſaid; any thing herein contained to the contrary notwithſtanding. the bearers intitled to one lottery ticket for every 10l. ſubſcribed.

XLVIII. Provided alſo, and it is hereby enacted by the authority aforeſaid, That out of the monies compoſing the fund, commonly called *The ſinking fund*, it ſhall and may be lawful to and for any three or more of the commiſſioners of the treaſury, or the high treaſurer for the time being, to reward the ſaid managers and directors, and the clerks and officers to be employed by and under them, and any other officers and perſons that ſhall and may be any ways employed in this affair, for their labour and pains, and to diſcharge ſuch incident expences as ſhall neceſſarily attend the execution of this act, in ſuch manner as any three or more of the commiſſioners of the treaſury, or the high treaſurer for the time being, ſhall, from time to time, think fit and reaſonable in that behalf; any thing in this act contained to the contrary notwithſtanding.

Managers, &c. to be paid by the commiſſioners of the treaſury out of the lottery money.

XLIX. And be it further enacted by the authority aforeſaid, That no perſon or perſons ſhall ſell the chance or chances of any ticket or tickets in the ſaid lottery, or any ſhare or ſhares of any ticket or tickets in the ſaid lottery, for a day or part of a day, or for a longer time leſs than the whole time of drawing the lottery then to come; or ſhall receive any money whatſoever in conſideration of the repayment of any ſum or ſums of money, in caſe any ticket or tickets in the ſaid lottery ſhall prove fortunate; or ſhall lay any wager relating to the drawing of any ticket or tickets in the ſaid lottery, either as to the time of ſuch ticket or tickets being drawn, or whether ſuch ticket or tickets be drawn fortunate or unfortunate; and all and every perſon and perſons who ſhall offend in any of the ſaid matters, ſhall forfeit and pay treble the ſum and ſums of money which ſhall have been received by ſuch perſon and perſons, contrary to the true intent and meaning of this act; to be recovered by action of debt, bill, plaint, or information, in any of his Majeſty's courts of record at *Weſtminſter*; in which no eſſoin, protection, privilege, or wager of law, or more than one imparlance, ſhall be allowed; one moiety whereof to be for the uſe of his Majeſty, his heirs, or ſucceſſors, and the other moiety to be paid to the perſon or perſons who ſhall ſue for the ſame; and every ſuch ſale, wager, or contract, and every agreement relating thereto, ſhall be, and is hereby declared null and void.

Limitation of ſale of chances, &c.

Penalty.

L. And be it further enacted by the authority aforeſaid, That if any perſon or perſons ſhall keep any office or offices, or ſhall print or publiſh any ſcheme or propoſal, for receiving any ſum or ſums of money in conſideration of any intereſt to be granted for the ſame, in any ticket or tickets in the ſaid lottery, whereof ſuch perſon or perſons ſhall not then be actually poſſeſſed, or in conſideration of any ſum or ſums of money to be re-

Perſons ſelling ſhares in tickets of which they are not poſſeſſed.

paid in case any ticket, or number of tickets, in the said lottery, which shall not be in the actual possession of such person or persons, shall prove fortunate or unfortunate; all and every such person and persons shall forfeit and pay the sum of five hundred pounds; to be recovered by action of debt, bill, plaint, or information, in any of his Majesty's courts of record at *Westminster*; in which no essoin, protection, or wager of law, or more than one imparlance, shall be allowed; one moiety whereof to be for the use of his Majesty, his heirs and successors, and the other moiety to be paid to the person or persons who shall sue for the same; and also shall suffer three months imprisonment without bail or mainprize.

Offences committed in Ireland against acts for preventing unlawful lotteries, declared to be punishable, and may be sued for in Dublin.

LI. And be it further enacted by the authority aforesaid, That if any offence against this act, or any of the acts of parliament made in this kingdom for preventing private and unlawful lotteries, shall be committed in *Ireland*, the offender shall incur the like penalty and punishment to be inflicted in like manner as if the offence was committed in this kingdom; and that such penalties as, by this act, or any of the said acts, are directed to be recovered in any of his Majesty's courts of record at *Westminster*, shall, in case of offences committed against this act or any of the said acts in *Ireland*, be recovered in any of his Majesty's courts of record in *Dublin*.

After the drawing of the lottery, the tickets to be exchanged for certificates.

LII. And to the end that all and every the payments, as well upon the fortunate as upon the unfortunate tickets, may be more easily ascertained, settled, and adjusted, for the persons who shall become intitled thereunto; be it further enacted by the authority aforesaid, That as soon as conveniently may be after the drawing of the said lottery shall be completed and ended, all and every the said tickets to be given out as aforesaid, shall be exchanged for certificates to be signed by such of the said managers as shall be appointed for that purpose.

Managers to give notice of the time for taking in the tickets, and delivering out the certificates, &c.

LIII. And be it further enacted, That such of the said managers as any three or more of the commissioners of the treasury, or the high treasurer for the time being, shall appoint to take in the said tickets, and deliver out the said certificates for and in lieu thereof, shall give timely notice, by advertisement to be printed and published in manner as they shall think fit, of the days and times for taking in the said tickets, and delivering out the said certificates, for and in lieu of the same; and every person's certificate shall be numbered in course, according to their bringing their tickets to the managers so to be appointed for exchanging the same; to which purpose, such managers shall enter, or cause to be entered, into a book or books to be by them kept for that purpose, the name of every person who shall bring any ticket or tickets to be exchanged for such certificate or certificates, and the number or numbers of the ticket or tickets which shall be so brought by such person or persons, the value in principal money payable thereupon, and the day of the month, and the year of our Lord, when the same was so brought, which book and books shall lie open in the office to be appointed for taking in the

Books to be kept for entering persons names, and the number of their tickets, &c.

the ſaid tickets to be exchanged for ſuch certificates, for all perſons concerned to peruſe; all which certificates ſhall be ſigned by the managers ſo to be appointed, or the major part of them, and be directed to the accomptant general of the bank of *England* for the time being.

Certificates to be ſigned, &c.

LIV. And be it further enacted by the authority aforeſaid, That the ſaid accomptant general of the bank of *England* for the time being, to whom the ſaid certificates are to be directed as aforeſaid, ſhall, upon receiving and taking in the ſaid certificates, or any of them, give credit to the perſons named therein, in a book or books to be by him provided and kept, for the principal ſums contained in every ſuch certificate; and the perſons to whoſe credit ſuch principal ſums ſhall be entered in the ſaid book or books, his, her, or their executors, adminiſtrators, ſucceſſors, and aſſigns, ſhall and may have power to aſſign or transfer the ſame, or any part, ſhare, or proportion thereof, to any other perſon or perſons, bodies politick or corporate whatſoever, in books to be prepared and kept by the ſaid accomptant general; and the ſaid principal ſums ſo aſſigned or transferred ſhall carry the ſaid annuity of three pounds *per centum per annum*, and ſhall be taken and deemed to be ſtock transferrable by virtue of this act, until the redemption thereof in manner herein mentioned; and the ſaid accomptant general of the bank of *England* for the time being, is hereby authorized and directed to cancel and file the certificates, as they ſhall from time to time be received and taken in by him; and to give the perſons bringing in the ſame a note under under his hand, teſtifying the principal money for which they ſhall have credit in the ſaid book or books, by reaſon or means of the certificates ſo received, taken in, and cancelled as aforeſaid, and of the annuities attending the ſame.

Accomptant general to give credit for the principal ſums in the certificates.

Aſſignments may be made of the ſaid ſums, &c.

Certificates to be filed and cancelled, and notes to be given in lieu thereof.

LV. And be it further enacted by the authority aforeſaid, That if any perſon or perſons ſhall be ſued, moleſted, or proſecuted, for any thing done, by virtue or in purſuance of this act, ſuch perſon or perſons ſhall and may plead the general iſſue, and give this act, and the ſpecial matter in evidence, in his, her, or their defence or defences; and if afterwards a verdict ſhall paſs for the defendant or defendants, or the plaintiff or plaintiffs ſhall diſcontinue his, her, or their action or actions, or be nonſuited, or judgement ſhall be given againſt him, her, or them, upon demurrer or otherwiſe, then ſuch defendant or defendants ſhall have treble coſts awarded to him, her, or them, againſt any ſuch plaintiff or plaintiffs.

General iſſue.

Treble coſts.

CAP. XXIV.

An act to oblige agents for prize money to account for such sums of money as remain in their hands unclaimed, the property of any of his Majesty's land forces; and for the application thereof.

Preamble.

WHEREAS *several sums of prize money, the property of his Majesty's land forces, remain unclaimed, in the hands of the several agents, and no provision is made for the distribution of the same*; may it please your Majesty that it may be enacted, and be it enacted by the King's most excellent majesty, by and with the advice and consent of the lords spiritual and temporal, and commons, in this present parliament assembled, and by the authority of the same, That the colonels, for the time being, of the regiments which were employed in any service during the late war, where the captures became the property of his Majesty's land forces; the adjutant general of his Majesty's forces for the time being, the right honourable the lord viscount *Barrington* in the kingdom of *Ireland*, the honourable colonel *William Howe*, *Peter Burrel* esquire, colonel *John Burgoyne*, and colonel *Isaac Barré*, shall be, and they are hereby declared to be, commissioners for the examining, stating, and settling, all accounts of such prize money due to any of his Majesty's land forces, and so remaining unclaimed in the hands of any agent or agents.

Commissioners for examining and settling the accounts of prize money due to his Majesty's land forces.

Power given them to summon the agents, &c.

II. And, for the better enabling the said commissioners to examine, state, and settle, such accounts, be it further enacted by the authority aforesaid, That it shall and may be lawful to and for the said commissioners, or any three or more of them, by writing under their hands, to summon before them, at such time and place as in and by the said writing shall be expressed, any agent or agents, or other person concerned in the receipt of such prize money as aforesaid; and to order such respective agents to produce, upon oath, all books, accounts, and vouchers, necessary for the information of the said commissioners in the premisses: and if any agent, or other person, shall refuse to comply with such summons, or to produce such respective books, accounts, or vouchers, as aforesaid, and to give the commissioners such information, upon oath, as he is able, in the premisses; every such agent or such other person shall, for every such offence, forfeit and pay the sum of five hundred pounds; to be recovered and applied in manner herein after-mentioned.

to produce their books, accounts, and vouchers, on oath;

and to give information in the premisses; which they are to obey, on penalty of 500l.

Upon settling the accounts, the agents are to pay over the money to the commissioners, or their order;

III. And be it further enacted by the authority aforesaid, That when the said accounts of unclaimed prize money shall be adjusted and settled, the said agents, in whose hands the same shall appear to be, shall immediately pay over the said unclaimed prize money into the hands of the said commissioners, or such other person or persons as they, or any three or more of them, shall order and direct; who shall immediately, or as soon thereafter as conveniently may be, pay such part of the prize money

money, so remaining unclaimed in each company, to the respective persons who were captains of the several companies, to whom such prize money shall appertain, at the time of the surrender of the place at which such prize money was acquired; or, in case of the death of such captains, or any of them, then such prize money shall be paid to the widows, or heirs at law, of such captains respectively, whose respective receipts thereof shall be a discharge to the said commissioners for the same; and such captains, captains widows, or heirs at law, shall and are hereby required, upon demand thereof made by the several persons intitled to the respective shares of any prize money in their hands, their heirs, executors, or administrators, to pay over such share of the said prize money to such persons so intitled to the same: and if any dispute shall arise concerning the distribution of the said prize money, such dispute shall be determined by the commissioners, or any three or more of them; whose determination shall be final.

who are to repay the same to the captains of the several companies; or, in case of death, to the widows or heirs at law of such captains; who are to distribute the same among the respective persons intitled thereto. Commissioners to determine disputes arising thereupon;

IV. Provided always, and be it further enacted by the authority aforesaid, That the said commissioners shall, and they are hereby impowered, out of any money which shall come to their hands of such unclaimed prize money, in the first place, to satisfy and discharge all such expences as shall arise to any person or persons employed by them in settling the said accounts, and all other reasonable expences attending the execution of this act.

and to discharge out of the prize money the expences attending the execution of this act.

V. And be it further enacted by the authority aforesaid, That all penalties and forfeitures, incurred by this act, may be sued for and recovered in any of his Majesty's courts of record at *Westminster*, wherein no essoin, privilege, protection, or wager of law, nor more than one imparlance shall be allowed; and such penalties and forfeitures, when recovered, shall be applied, one moiety to the use of his Majesty, his heirs and successors, and the other moiety to the person or persons who shall inform or sue for the same.

Recovery of the penalties and forfeitures, and application thereof.

VI. And be it further enacted by the authority aforesaid, That no such claim of any prize money shall be admitted or allowed after the first day of *January*, one thousand seven hundred and sixty seven, or such further day as the said commissioners, or any three or more of them, shall appoint.

No claim of prize money to be admitted after 1 Jan. 1767.

CAP. XXV.

An act to alter certain rates of postage, and to amend, explain, and enlarge several provisions in an act made in the ninth year of the reign of Queen Anne, *and in other acts relating to the revenue of the post office.*

Most gracious Sovereign,

WHEREAS *the security and improvement of correspondence, throughout your Majesty's dominions, is a matter of great concernment, and highly necessary for the preservation and extension of trade and commerce: and whereas by an act made in the ninth year of*

Preamble.

of the reign of her late majesty Queen Anne, *several rates are settled for the port and conveyance of letters and packets passing to and from the several parts of the* British *dominions in* Europe *and* America: *and whereas by the increase of trade and commerce since the passing of the said act, and by the vast accession of territory gained by the late treaty of peace, several communications are opened, and new posts have been or may be established to and from the several parts of your Majesty's dominions in* America, *for which the rates of postage cannot, under the present law, be properly ascertained: and whereas the present rates of postage may in some parts be reduced, and the revenue nevertheless may hereafter be improved, by means of a more extensive circulation:* we your Majesty's most dutiful and loyal subjects, the commons of *Great Britain* in parliament assembled, do most humbly beseech your Majesty that it may be enacted; and be it enacted by the King's most excellent majesty, by and with the advice and consent of the lords spiritual and temporal, and commons, in this present parliament assembled, and by the authority of the same, That so much of the said act made in the ninth year of the reign of her said late majesty Queen *Anne*, intituled, *An act for establishing a general post office for all her Majesty's dominions, and for settling a weekly sum out of the revenues thereof for the service of the war, and other her Majesty's occasions*, as establishes certain rates or sums for the port or conveyance of letters and packets passing between *London* and the *British* dominions in *America*, and between any places within the said dominions, shall, from and after the tenth day of *October*, one thousand seven hundred and sixty five, be, and is hereby, repealed.

Repeal of so much of the act of 9 Annæ, as establishes the rates of postage of letters between London and the British dominions in America, and places within the said dominions:

II. And, to the end that more easy and equal rates of postage may be settled and established, and the benefit of posts be in time extended to every part of the *British* dominions in *America*, be it enacted by the authority aforesaid, That from and after the said tenth day of *October*, one thousand seven hundred and sixty five, it shall and may be lawful to and for his Majesty's post master general for the time being, and his deputy and deputies by him thereunto sufficiently authorized, to and for the use of his Majesty, his heirs, and successors, to demand, have, receive and take, for the port and conveyance of all and every the letters, packets, and other things, that shall be carried or conveyed to or from *London*, from or to any of the *British* dominions in *America*, and to or from any part of the said dominions, from or to any other part thereof, according to the several and respective rates and sums hereafter mentioned; the same being rated either by the letter, or by the ounce; that is to say,

and from and after 10 Oct. 1765, instead of the rates thereby established, those following are to take place.

For all letters and packets passing from *London* to any port within the *British* dominions in *America*, and from any such port unto *London*, for every single letter one shilling; for every double letter two shillings; for every treble letter three shillings; and for every ounce four shillings; and so in proportion for every packet of deeds, writs, or other things.

Rates of postage from London to any port within the British dominions in America, and from any such port to London;

For

For all letters and packets conveyed by sea from any port in the *British* dominions in *America* to any other port within the said dominions, for every single letter four pence; for every double letter eight pence; for every treble letter one shilling; and for every ounce one shilling and four pence; and so in proportion for every packet of deeds, writs, or other things.

and from any port in the said dominions to any other port therein, by sea.

For the inland conveyance of all letters and packets to or from any chief post office established, or to be established, within the *British* dominions in *America*, from or to any other part of the said dominions, not exceeding sixty *British* miles distant from such chief offices respectively; or from the office where such letters or packets, not passing through any such chief office, may be put in, for every single letter four pence; for every double letter eight pence; for every treble letter one shilling; and for every ounce one shilling and four pence; and, being upwards of sixty such miles, and not exceeding one hundred such miles, for every single letter six pence; for every double letter one shilling; for every treble letter one shilling and six pence; and for every ounce two shillings; and, being upwards of one hundred such miles, and not exceeding two hundred such miles, for every single letter eight pence; for every double letter one shilling and four pence; for every treble letter two shillings; and for every ounce two shillings and eight pence; and for every distance not exceeding one hundred such miles beyond such two hundred miles, and for every such further distance, for every single letter two pence; for every double letter four pence; for every treble letter six pence; and for every ounce eight pence; and so in proportion, according to the said several and respective rates and distances, for every packet of deeds, writs, or other things.

Rates of inland postage in America for any distance not exceeding 60 miles; for upward of 60 and not exceeding 100 miles; for upwards of 100 and not exceeding 200 miles; and for upwards of 200 and not exceeding 100 miles further, &c.

III. And whereas by certain clauses in the said act, made in the ninth year of the reign of her said late majesty Queen *Anne*, it is enacted, That all letters and packets that, by any master of any ship or vessel, or any of his company, or any passengers therein, should or might be brought to any port town, or which should arrive or touch at any port belonging to any port town within any her Majesty's dominions, or any the members thereof, or which should be on board any ship or vessel which should or did touch or stay at any such port town (other than such letters as in the said act are excepted) should, by such master, passenger, or other person or persons, be forthwith delivered unto the deputy or deputies of such post master general for the time being by him appointed for such place or port town, and to be, by such deputy or deputies, sent post unto the said general post office, to be delivered according to the several and respective directions of the same; upon pain of forfeiting the sum of five pounds of *British* money for every several offence against the tenor of the said act: and whereas the said provision, in the said above recited clause, hath been found ineffectual for the purposes intended; be it therefore further enacted by the au-

Recital of clauses in act 9 Annæ.

From and after 10 Oct. 1765, no vessel to be admitted to make entry, or break bulk, till the letters on board are delivered to the post office;

authority aforesaid, That from and after the tenth day of *October*, one thousand seven hundred and sixty five, no ship or vessel shall be permitted to break bulk, or to make any entry in any port in the *British* dominions, until all letters and packets brought by any master of any such ship or vessel, or by any of his company, or any passenger on board the same, to any port in the said dominions where posts are or hereafter may be established, and from whence such letters and packets can or may be dispatched by post, shall be delivered to the deputy or deputies, or agents, of the said post master general for the time being, to be by him or them forwarded, according to their respective directions, in the same course that other letters are sent from such respective ports; except such letters, commissions, and other matter and things, as are excepted in the said act made in the ninth year of the reign of her late majesty Queen *Anne*; and also, except all such letters and packets as shall or may be brought in any ship or vessel liable to the performance of quarentine; all which letters or packets last-mentioned shall be delivered, by the person or persons having possession thereof, to the person or persons appointed to superintend the quarentine, that all proper precautions may be by him or them taken before the delivery thereof; and when due care has been had therein, the said letters or packets shall be by him or them dispatched, in the usual and accustomed manner, by the post; and all masters, mariners, passengers, and other person or persons, neglecting or refusing to deliver the letters or packets brought by them as aforesaid, shall, for every such neglect or refusal respectively, forfeit the sum of twenty pounds; to be sued for and recovered by action of debt, bill, plaint, or information, in any court of record within the kingdom, colony, plantation, or place, where the offence shall be committed; and no essoin, privilege, protection, or wager of law, shall be admitted; one moiety of the said penalty to his Majesty, his heirs, and successors, and the other moiety thereof to such person or persons who shall or will inform against such offender or offenders, and sue for the said penalties and forfeitures; and for every recovery such person or persons, so informing and prosecuting for the said penalties and forfeitures, shall recover and have also taxed and paid their full costs of suit; any thing in the said act, made in the ninth year of the reign of her majesty Queen *Anne*, to the contrary thereof notwithstanding.

except in such cases where they are to be delivered to the superintendant of the quarentine;

to be dispatched by him to the post office.

Persons refusing to deliver up such letters, forfeit 20l.

One moiety to the King, the other to the prosecutor;

with full costs.

1 d. extra charged on all ship letters not brought by the packet boats.

IV. And be it further enacted by the authority aforesaid, That it shall and may be lawful to and for the said deputy or deputies to demand, have, receive, and take, for every such letter and packet so delivered from any ship or vessel, other than packet boats, to such deputy or deputies at the ports in his Majesty's dominions, as shall be directed to any place within the town belonging to such port, or within the limits of the delivery of letters and packets by such deputy and deputies, the rate or sum of one penny, over and above what may now be received for the same.

V. And

V. And be it further enacted by the authority aforesaid, That from and after the tenth day of *October*, one thousand seven hundred and sixty five, the rates now payable for the postage of letters and packets, sent or conveyed by the general post, not exceeding one post stage in *Great Britain* and *Ireland*, and not exceeding two post stages in that part of *Great Britain* called *England*, do cease and determine; and that from and after the said tenth day of *October*, one thousand seven hundred and sixty five, it shall and may be lawful to and for the said post master general, and his deputy and deputies by him thereunto sufficiently authorized, to and for the use of his Majesty, his heirs and successors, to demand, have, receive, and take, for the port and conveyance of all such letters and packets which he shall convey, carry, or send post, within the kingdom of *Great Britain* and *Ireland*, according to the several rates and sums hereafter-mentioned (the same being rated either by the letter or by the ounce) that is to say,

From and after 10 Oct. 1765, the present rates of postage by the general post, not exceeding 1 post stage in Great Britain and Ireland, and not exceeding 2 in England, are to cease, and the following rates are to take place;

For the port or conveyance of every single letter, so conveyed or carried by the post as aforesaid, not exceeding one whole post stage from the office where such letter may be put in, within the kingdoms aforesaid, the sum of one penny; for every double letter two pence; for every treble letter three pence; and for every ounce four pence; and so in proportion for every packet of deeds, writs, or other things.

viz. Rates for postage not exceeding one post stage;

And for the port and conveyance of every single letter, so conveyed or carried by the post as aforesaid; above one post stage, and not exceeding two post stages, from the office where such letter may be put in, within that part of *Great Britain* called *England*, the sum of two pence; for every double letter four pence; for every treble letter six pence; and for every ounce eight pence; and so in proportion for every packet of deeds, writs, or other things.

above 1 and not exceeding 2 post stages.

VI. Provided always, and be it further enacted by the authority aforesaid, That nothing herein before contained shall extend, or be construed to extend, to alter, or in any wise to affect, the rates or sums to be paid for letters or packets passing or repassing by the carriage called *The Penny Post*.

But these regulations are not to extend to The penny post.

VII. And whereas, for the more ready and extensive conveyance of letters and packets between that part of *Great Britain* called *England*, and *Ireland*, and for the conveniency of trade and commerce between the said kingdoms, it may be convenient and expedient to improve the communication for the conveyance of such letters and packets by the post through *Carlisle*, *Dumfries*, and *Port Patrick*, or some other convenient port in *Scotland*; and through *Donaghadee*, or some other convenient port in *Ireland*; be it further declared and enacted by the authority aforesaid, That it shall and may be lawful to and for the said post master general, and his deputy or deputies by him thereunto sufficiently authorized, to demand, have receive, and take, for the port and conveyance of all letters and packets, passing

Rates of postage between England and Ireland, thro Carlisle, Dumfreis, port

Patrick, and Donaghadee, or other convenient ports.

paſſing and repaſſing by the poſt between *England* and *Ireland*, through *Carliſle*, *Dumfries*, *Port Patrick*, and *Donaghadee*, or other convenient ports in *Scotland* and *Ireland*, the ſame rates or ſums for *Engliſh* poſtage, according to the number of miles or ſtages ſuch letters and packets are carried by the poſt in *England*, as alſo the ſame rates or ſums for *Scotch* poſtage, according to the number of miles or ſtages ſuch letters and packets are carried by the poſt in *Scotland*, and moreover the ſame rates or ſums for packet poſtage between *Port Patrick* and *Donaghadee*, or other convenient ports in *Scotland* and *Ireland*, as likewiſe the ſame rates or ſums for *Iriſh* poſtage, according to the number of miles or ſtages ſuch letters are carried by the poſt in *Ireland*, as are reſpectively ſettled, eſtabliſhed, and aſcertained, by the ſaid act made in the ninth year of the reign of her ſaid late majeſty Queen *Anne*, or by this preſent act.

Repeal of ſo much of the act 9 Anne, as directs the poſtage between Port Patrick and Donaghadee to be paid where the letters are delivered.

VIII. And be it further enacted by the authority aforeſaid, That ſo much of the ſaid act, made in the ninth year of the reign of her late majeſty Queen *Anne*, as directs, that the rates or ſums to be paid for the conveyance of letters, to be ſent by packet boats, between *Port Patrick* and *Donaghadee*, ſhall be paid at the place where ſuch letter or letters are delivered, in order to be ſent by ſuch packet boats, ſhall, from and after the ſaid tenth day of *October*, one thouſand ſeven hundred and ſixty five, be, and is hereby, repealed.

To prevent diſputes, poſt roads may be meaſured;

IX. And, to the end that all letters or packets may be charged with poſtage, according to the rated diſtance they are reſpectively carried by the poſt, and for preventing all diſputes touching the ſame, be it further enacted by the authority aforeſaid, That it ſhall and may be lawful to and for ſuch perſon and perſons as the poſt maſter general for the time being ſhall appoint, to meaſure, or cauſe to be meaſured, by the wheel, all the poſt roads which are now ſettled and eſtabliſhed, or which ſhall hereafter be ſettled and eſtabliſhed, in any part of the kingdoms of *Great Britain* and *Ireland*, and other the *Britiſh* dominions.

and a return to be made thereof upon oath; and entered in the three chief poſt offices in Great Britain and Ireland; and the chief offices in America. Fair ſurveys to be made out, and depoſited in the reſpective offices here mentioned,

X. Provided always, That ſuch perſon or perſons, who ſhall be ſo appointed as aforeſaid to meaſure the ſaid diſtances, and every of them, ſhall be ſworn to perform the ſame according to the beſt of their ſkill and judgement; which oath ſhall and may be adminiſtered by any juſtice of the peace, who is hereby authorized and required to adminiſter the ſame, and to make certificates thereof in writing, to be entered, without fee or charge, in the three chief poſt offices in *Great Britain* and *Ireland*; and the chief poſt offices eſtabliſhed, or to be eſtabliſhed, in *America*; and moreover, that ſuch perſon or perſons ſo to be appointed by ſuch poſt maſter as aforeſaid, ſhall, and they are hereby required to cauſe fair ſurveys or books to be made out; one of each whereof ſhall be left with his Majeſty's poſt maſter general in *London*, another of each to be left at the chief poſt office in *Edinburgh* with the poſt maſter general's deputy there, another of each to be left at the chief poſt office at *Dublin* with the

the post master general's deputy there, and another of each of such surveys or books shall be left at each of the chief post offices established, or to be established, in *America*, with the respective deputies of the post master general there, to remain in the said post offices; each of which said surveys or books shall be signed by the person or persons making the same, who shall and are hereby respectively required to make oath of the truth of such surveys; which oath or oaths shall and may be administered by any justice of the peace, who is hereby authorized and required to administer the same; and a certificate of his or their having sworn to the truth thereof shall be signed by the post master general for the time being, or by his deputy or deputies, in such chief post offices in *Great Britain* and *Ireland*, and in the *British* dominions in *America*; which books and surveys shall determine the distances on all the said post roads: and in case of any suspicion of error or wrong admeasurement, it shall and may be lawful for the said post master general to cause new surveys to be made; and the last surveys which shall be made, and shall be verified and attested as above directed, shall, in all courts of justice, be evidence of the distances on such post roads; and all rates granted by any former act or acts, or by this present act, for the port or conveyance of letters and packets, shall be paid and taken according to such surveys.

signed by the persons making the same, and attested upon oath, and certified by the post master general or his deputies.

On suspicion of error, new surveys may be made out,

according to which postage is to be charged.

XI. And be it further enacted by the authority aforesaid, That it shall and may be lawful to and for the post master general for the time being, and his deputy and deputies by him thereunto sufficiently authorized, to settle and establish an office, to be called *The Penny Post Office*, in any city or town, and the suburbs thereof, and places adjacent, within the kingdoms of *Great Britain* and *Ireland*, and the *British* dominions in *America*, where such post shall, by the post master general, be adjudged necessary and convenient; and to demand, have, receive, and take, the same rates and sums for the postage and conveyance of all letters and packets, conveyed by such penny post, as are or may be taken for the carriage of letters and packets, sent or conveyed by the carriage called *The Penny Post*, established and settled within the cities of *London* and *Westminster*, and borough of *Southwark*, and parts adjacent, according to the extent and meaning of the said act made in the ninth year of her said late majesty Queen *Anne*, and of an act made in the fourth year of his late majesty King *George* the Second, and of this present act.

Power given to settle Penny Post Offices where convenient.

XII. And be it further enacted by the authority aforesaid, That when such penny post office or offices shall be settled and established in such cities, towns, suburbs, or places adjacent, within the kingdoms of *Great Britain* and *Ireland*, and the *British* dominions in *America*, as aforesaid, no person or persons whatsoever shall make any collection of letters or packets in or near such city, town, suburbs, or places, where such penny post office or offices shall be established, without licence or leave of the post master general for the time being; upon pain of incurring

Where such offices are established, no person may collect the letters without being duly licensed.

ring

ring the forfeitures and penalties to be forfeited and paid by persons collecting, receiving, carrying, recarrying and delivering letters, contrary to the said act made in the ninth year of the reign of her said late majesty Queen *Anne*, to be recovered in manner as by the said act is directed, and with full costs of suit.

Letters, &c. brought by the inland or foreign post to the London office, and directed beyond the department of the general post, but within the delivery of the penny post, may be sent by the penny post, and charged accordingly.

XIII. And be it further enacted and declared by the authority aforesaid, That all letters and packets whatsoever, which shall or may be brought, by the inland or foreign post, to the general post office in *London*, directed to any person or persons at any place or places beyond the delivery of the inland or foreign departments of the general post office respectively, and within the delivery of the said office called *The Penny Post Office*, shall be conveyed and delivered by the said penny post office; and that it shall and may be lawful for any messenger or person, carrying or transmitting such letters or packets, to demand and take for the carriage and delivery of the same, one penny, and no more, over and above the rates of postage which shall have become due, for the port or conveyance of such letters or packets to the general post office.

From and after 5 July, 1765, no packet exceeding 4 oz. (except those sent by the general post, &c.) may be sent by the penny post.

XIV. And whereas the weight of letters and packets, sent or conveyed by the carriage called *The Penny Post*, hath not yet been ascertained by any law or statute: and whereas many heavy and bulky packets and parcels are now sent and conveyed by such carriage, which, by their bulk and weight, greatly retard the speedy delivery thereof; be it thereof enacted by the authority aforesaid, That from and after the fifth day of *July*, one thousand seven hundred and sixty five, no letter, packet, or parcel whatsoever, shall be forwarded, sent, or conveyed, by any carriage called *The Penny Post* already established, or hereafter to be established, if the weight of such letter, packet, or parcel, shall exceed the weight of four ounces, other than such letters or packets as have first come by the post to the general post office, or shall be passing by the said carriage called *The Penny Post*, into the said general post office.

From 5 July, 1765, the same rates of postage are to take place between London and Hamburgh, as between London and Germany.

XV. And whereas by the said act, made in the ninth year of the reign of her said late majesty Queen *Anne*, certain rates are established for all letters passing from *London* through the *Spanish Netherlands*, or the *United Provinces*, to *Hamburgh* (post-paid to *Antwerp* or *Amsterdam*) and from *Hamburgh* through the *Spanish Netherlands*, or the *United Provinces*, unto *London*; be it enacted, That so much of the said act, made in the ninth year of the reign of her said late majesty Queen *Anne*, as establishes the rates last above mentioned, shall, from and after the fifth day of *July*, one thousand seven hundred and sixty five, be, and the same is hereby repealed; and the said rates shall from thenceforth cease and determine: and from and after the said fifth day of *July*, it shall and may be lawful to and for the said post master general, and his deputy or deputies by him thereunto sufficiently authorized, to and for the use of his Majesty, his heirs, and successors, to demand, have, receive, and take, for the port and conveyance of all letters and packets, sent or conveyed by the

the post from *London* to *Hamburgh*, or from *Hamburgh* to *London*, the same rates or sums of money which, by the said act made in the said ninth year of the reign of her said late majesty Queen *Anne*, are settled, and appointed to be taken for all letters and packets passing by the post from *London* to all other parts of *Germany*.

XVI. And be it further enacted by the authority aforesaid, That it shall and may be lawful to and for the said post master general, and his deputy and deputies, if such post master general shall deem it necessary and expedient, to cause the rates or sums for the postage of all letters and packets which are to be sent by the post out of the kingdom of *Great Britain*, to be paid upon their being put into any post office within the said kingdom.

The postage of letters to be sent out of Great Britain, may, if deemed necessary, be demanded upon their being put into the office.

XVII. And be it further enacted by the authority aforesaid, That if any deputy, clerk, agent, letter carrier, or other officer whatsoever, appointed, or to be hereafter appointed and employed in the business of the post office, shall, from and after the tenth day of *October*, one thousand seven hundred and sixty five, secrete, embezzle, or destroy, any letter, packet, bag, or mail of letters, which he, she, or they, shall and may be respectively entrusted with, or which shall have come to his, her, or their hands or possession, by virtue of their respective employments in the said post office, containing any bank note, bank post bill, bill of exchange, exchequer bill, *South Sea* or *East India* bond, dividend warrant of the bank, *South Sea*, *East India*, or any other company, society, or corporation, navy or victualling bill, seaman's ticket, state lottery ticket, goldsmith's note for the payment of money, or other bond or warrant, bill, or promissory note for the payment of money, or *American* provincial bill of credit; or shall steal and take, out of any letter or packet that shall come to his, her, or their hands or possession, by virtue of their respective employments, any such bank note, bank post bill, bill of exchange, exchequer bill, *South Sea* or *East India* bond, dividend warrant of the bank, *South Sea*, *East India*, or any other company, society, or corporation, navy or victualling bill, seaman's ticket, state lottery ticket, goldsmith's note for the payment of money, or other bond or warrant, or promissory note for the payment of money, or *American* provincial bill of credit, with intent to secrete, embezzle, or destroy the same; every such offender or offenders, being thereof convicted in due form of law, shall be deemed guilty of felony, and shall suffer death as a felon.

Penalty of any officer of the post office secreting or embezzling any letter with any bank bill or note, &c. therein, or taking out any such note or bill; is felony.

XVIII. And be it further enacted by the authority aforesaid, That from and after the said tenth day of *October*, one thousand seven hundred and sixty five, if any person or persons whatsoever shall rob any of his Majesty's mails of any letter or letters, packet or packets, bag or mail of letters, although such robbery shall not appear, or be proved, to be a taking from the person, or upon the King's highway, or to be a robbery committed in any dwelling-house, or any coach-house, stable, barn, or any outhouse belonging to a dwelling-house, and although it

Penalty of robbing mails.

is felony. should not appear that any person or persons were put in fear by such robbery, yet such offender or offenders, being thereof convicted as aforesaid, shall nevertheless respectively be deemed guilty of felony, and shall suffer death as a felon.]

Penalty of any officer, &c. imbezzling or misapplying the postage money received by him, or destroying any letter or packet, or advancing the rates, and not accounting for the same, is felony.

XIX. And be it further enacted by the authority aforesaid, That if any deputy, clerk, agent, letter carrier, or other servant, appointed, authorized, and intrusted, to take in letters or packets, and receive the postage thereof, shall, after the said tenth day of *October*, imbezzle, or apply to his, her, or their own use, any money or monies by him, her, or them, received with such letters or packets, for the postage thereof; or shall burn or otherwise destroy any letter or letters, packet or packets, by him, her, or them, so taken in or received; or who, by virtue of their respective offices, shall advance the rates upon letters or packets sent by the post, and shall not duly account for the money by him, her, or them, received for such advanced postage; every such offender or offenders, being thereof convicted as aforesaid, shall be deemed guilty of felony.

Post boy quitting or deserting the mail, or suffering any person (except the guard) to ride on the horse or carriage, or loitering on the road, &c. to be committed to hard labour;

XX. And be it further enacted by the authority aforesaid, That if any post boy or rider, having taken any of his Majesty's mails, or bags of letters or packets, under his care, in order to convey the same to the next post town or stage, shall, after the said tenth day of *October*, quit or desert the same before his arrival at such post town or stage, or shall suffer any other person or persons (the person or persons employed to guard such mail or bags of letters and packets only excepted) to ride on the horse or carriage along with the said mails or bags of letters and packets; or shall loiter on the road, and wilfully mispend his time, so as to retard the arrival of the said mails or bags of letters at the next post town or stage; or shall not, in all possible cases, convey such mails or bags of letters after the rate of six *English* miles an hour at the least; every such offender, for every such offence, being thereof convicted, either by voluntary confession of the party, or by the oath or oaths of one or more credible witness or witnesses, before any one or more justice or justices of the peace (which oath and oaths the said justice or justices is and are hereby respectively impowered and required to administer) shall be sent to the house of correction, and confined to hard labour for any time not exceeding one month, nor less than fourteen days.

and unlawfully collecting, conveying, or delivering, letters or packets, he forfeits 10s. for every letter, &c.

XXI. And be it further enacted by the authority aforesaid, That from and after the said tenth day of *October*, if any post boy or post boys, rider or riders, shall, by himself or themselves, or in combination with others, unlawfully collect or receive letters or packets, or convey, or cause letters and packets to be unlawfully conveyed, and shall thereof be convicted, either by the voluntary confession of the party, or by the oath of one or more credible witness or witnesses, before any one or more justice or justices of the peace (which oath and oaths the said justice and justices is and are hereby respectively impowered and required to administer) every such offender or offenders shall, for every letter or packet so by him or them unlawfully collected, con-

conveyed, or delivered, forfeit the sum of ten shillings, to be paid to the informer; and if the same shall not be forthwith paid upon conviction, it shall and may be lawful for such justice and justices to commit such offender or offenders to the house of correction, there to remain at hard labour for any space not exceeding two months, nor less than one month.

and if not paid forthwith, he is to be committed to hard labour.

XXII. And be it further enacted by the authority aforesaid, That all and every the clauses, provisoes, powers, privileges, advantages, disabilities, penalties, forfeitures, and methods for the recovery of the same matters and things, contained in the said act made in the ninth year of the reign of her said late majesty Queen *Anne*, or in any other act or acts whatsoever, touching the general post office, or the carriage called *The Penny Post Office*, and not herein and hereby expresly altered or repealed, shall be applied and extended, and shall be construed to apply and extend, to this present act, as fully and effectually, to all intents and purposes, as if the same had been particularly repeated and re-enacted in the body of this present act.

Clauses, &c. in the act of 9 Annæ, or in any other act touching the general or penny post office, not hereby altered, or repealed, extended to this act.

XXIII. And be it further enacted and declared, That all rates or sums of money established or appointed by this act, and also all sums of money imposed as forfeitures or penalties, and all sums of money required to be paid, and all other monies herein mentioned, shall be deemed and taken to be sterling money of *Great Britain*, and shall be collected, taken, recovered, and paid, to the amount of the value which such nominal sums bear in *Great Britain*.

Rates, and pecuniary penalties, to be deemed sterling money.

XXIV. And be it further enacted by the authority aforesaid, That all the monies arising by the rates aforesaid, except the monies which shall be necessary to defray such expences as shall be incurred in the collection and management of the same, and all other expences attending the said office, and the due execution of the acts relating thereto, shall be appropriated and applied to such and the same uses, to which the present rates of postage are respectively now by law appropriated and made applicable.

Monies arising by this act, to be applied as the present rates of postage.

XXV. Provided always, and be it further enacted by the authority aforesaid, That all charges, out-goings, and disbursements, necessary for the receipt and management of the said rates, and the rates granted by former acts, and all other expences attending the said office, and the due execution of the several acts relating thereto, be allowed and paid, in like manner as the same have heretofore been allowed, authorized, and paid, at any time since the commencement of the rates granted by the said act made in the ninth year of the reign of Queen *Anne*; any thing in this act, or in an act passed in the first year of his Majesty's reign, intituled, *An act for the support of his Majesty's houshold, and of the honour and dignity of the crown of* Great Britain, *to the contrary notwithstanding.*

All necessary charges, &c. in the receipt and management of rates, to be allowed as usual.

XXVI. And whereas by an act made in the fourth year of the reign of his present Majesty, intituled, *An act for preventing frauds and abuses, in relation to the sending and receiving of letters and*

Clause in act 4 Geo. 3.

and packets free from the duty of postage, it is enacted, That from and after the first day of *May*, one thousand seven hundred and sixty four, so long as the revenue arising in the general letter office or post office, or office of post master general, shall continue to be made part of the aggregate fund, no letters or packets sent by the post, to or from any place whatsoever, shall be exempted from paying the duty of postage, except such letters and packets as are therein particularly excepted: and whereas the privilege of sending and receiving letters and packets, free from the duty of postage, is not by the said act extended to the pay master general of his Majesty's forces for the time being, or to the clerk of the parliaments, or to the clerk of the house of commons of *Great Britain*, for the time being, who, by virtue of their respective offices and employments, necessarily send and receive many letters relating to the publick concerns of these kingdoms; be it therefore enacted by the authority aforesaid, That from and after the passing of this act, the said pay master general of his Majesty's forces for the time being, shall and may send and receive letters, free from the duty of postage, in the same manner, and under such restrictions, as other officers mentioned in the said act are thereby permitted, in respect of their offices, to send and receive; and that the said clerk of the parliaments, and clerk of the house of commons of *Great Britain*, for the time being, shall and may respectively, from and after the passing of this act, send and receive letters, free from the duty of postage, in the same manner, and under such restrictions, as any member of either of the two houses of parliament of *Great Britain* now send and receive the same, in pursuance of the said act.

Pay master general,

Clerk of the parliaments, and clerk of the house of commons, impowered to send and receive letters free of postage.

Limitation of actions.

XXVII. And be it further enacted by the authority aforesaid, That if any action or suit shall be commenced against any person or persons for any thing done in pursuance of this act, the same shall be commenced within six months after the fact committed, and not afterwards; and the defendant or defendants in such action or suit shall and may plead the general issue, and give this act, and the special matter, in evidence; and that the same was done in pursuance, and by the authority of this act: and if it shall appear so to be done, or that such action or suit shall be commenced after the time before limited for bringing the same, that then the jury shall find for the defendant or defendants; and upon a verdict for the defendant, or if the plaintiff or plaintiffs shall be nonsuited, or discontinue his, her, or their action or suit, after the defendant or defendants shall have appeared; or if, upon demurrer, judgment shall be given against the plaintiff or plaintiffs, the defendant or defendants shall and may recover treble costs, and have the like remedy for the same, as any defendant or defendants hath or have in any other cases by law.

General issue.

Treble costs.

CAP.

CAP. XXVI.

An act for carrying into execution a contract made, pursuant to the act of parliament of the twelfth of his late majesty King George *the First, between the commissioners of his Majesty's treasury and the duke and dutchess of* Atholl, *the proprietors of the* Isle of Man, *and their trustees, for the purchase of the said island and its dependencies, under certain exceptions therein particularly mentioned.*

"WHEREAS his late majesty King *Henry* the Fourth, by his letters patent under the great seal of *England*, bearing date at *Westminster* the sixth day of *April*, in the seventh year of his reign, did grant to Sir *John de Stanley* knight, the island, castle, pele, and lordship, of *Man*, and all the islands and lordships to the said island of *Man* appertaining, which did not exceed the value of four hundred pounds by the year; to have and to hold to the said *John* and his heirs and assigns, all the islands, castle, pele, and lordship aforesaid, together with the royalties, regalities, franchises, liberties, sea ports, and all things to port reasonably and duly belonging, homages, fealties, wards, marriages, reliefs, escheats, forfeitures, waifs, estrays, courts baron, views of frankpledge, leets, hundreds, wapentakes, wreck of the sea, mines of lead and iron, fairs, markets, free customs, meadows, pastures, woods, parks, chaces, lawns, warrens, assarts, purprestures, chiminages, piscaries, mills, moors, marshes, turbarys, waters, pools, fish ponds, ways, passages, and commons, and other commodities, emoluments, and appurtenances whatsoever, to the said islands, castle, pele, and lordship, in any wise appertaining or belonging, together with the patronage of the bishoprick of the said island of *Man*, and also knights fees, advowsons, and patronages of abbies, priories, hospitals, churches, vicarages, chapels, chaunteries, and other ecclesiastical benefices whatsoever, to the said islands, castle, pele, and lordship, likewise belonging, of the said King and his heirs for ever, by liege homage, and the service of rendering to the said King two falcons once only; that is to say, immediately after the same homage done, and of rendering to his heirs, Kings of *England*, two falcons on the days of their coronations, instead of all other services, customs, and demands, as freely, fully, and entirely, as Sir *William le Scrope*, deceased, in the said letters patent named, or any other lord of the said island, was ever, in former times, in the best and freest manner accustomed to have and hold those islands, castle, pele, and lordship, with the appurtenances, together with all other the premisses therein and herein before mentioned, the said liege homage, and rent of falcons, only excepted: and whereas the monastry and priory of *Rushing* and *Douglas*, and the *Fryers Minors*, commonly called *The Grey Fryers of Brymaken*, otherwise *Bymaken*, with their appurtenances, in the said island of *Man*, Preamble.

 were,

were, on or about the general diſſolution of the leſſer religious houſes, by force and virtue of an act for that purpoſe made in the twenty ſeventh year of the reign of his late majeſty King *Henry* the Eighth, diſſolved, and veſted in his ſaid Majeſty, his heirs and ſucceſſors: and whereas by an act of parliament made in the thirty third year of the reign of his ſaid late King *Henry* the Eighth, for diſſevering the biſhoprick of *Cheſter*, and of the *Iſle of Man*, from the juriſdiction of *Canterbury* to the juriſdiction of *York*, it was enacted, That the biſhoprick and dioceſe of *Man*, in the *Iſle* of *Man*, ſhould be annexed, adjoined, and united, to the province and metropolitical juriſdiction of *York*, in all points, and to all purpoſes and effects, as the biſhoprick of *Cheſter* was annexed, adjoined, and united, to the ſame: and whereas on the death of *Ferdinando* earl of *Derby*, couſin and heir male of the body of the ſaid Sir *John de Stanley*, which happened in or about the thirty ſixth year of the reign of her late majeſty Queen *Elizabeth*, a controverſy aroſe concerning the inheritance of the ſaid iſlands, caſtle, pele, and lordſhip, with the appurtenances, between the daughters and coheirs of the ſaid *Ferdinando* earl of *Derby* on the one part, and *William* earl of *Derby* his ſurviving brother on the other part; which controverſy was, by her ſaid Majeſty's command, referred to the lord keeper of the great ſeal, and others of her Majeſty's privy council, together with the chief juſtices of the courts of *Queen's Bench* and *Common Pleas*, and the chief baron of the court of *Exchequer*; and till the ſaid controverſy, and certain other doubts which aroſe on the ſaid letters patent, ſhould be determined, the ſaid iſland, caſtle, pele, and lordſhip, of *Man*, with the appurtenances, and all other the premiſſes in the ſaid letters patent mentioned, were taken into the hands of her ſaid Majeſty, in right of the crown of *England*: and whereas his late majeſty King *James* the Firſt, by his letters patent under the great ſeal of *England*, bearing date at *Weſtminſter* the ſeventeenth day of *March*, in the third year of his reign, did, in conſideration of a fine of one hundred and one pounds, fifteen ſhillings, and eleven pence, paid into the receipt of his ſaid Majeſty's exchequer by Sir *Thomas Leighe* knight, and *Thomas Spencer* eſquire, and for other conſiderations, demiſe, leaſe, and to farm-lett, to the ſaid Sir *Thomas Leighe* knight, and *Thomas Spencer*, all thoſe houſes, ſcites, circuits, and precincts, formerly the monaſtry and priory of *Ruſhing* and *Douglas*, and the *Fryers Minors*, commonly called the *Grey Fryers* of *Brymaken*, otherwiſe *Bymaken*, with all their appurtenances in his iſland of *Man*, and all thoſe his rectories and churches of *Kirkecriſt* in *Shelding* and *Kirklovan*, with their appurtenances in his ſaid iſland of *Man*, formerly belonging to the monaſtry of *Ruſhing* aforeſaid, and being parcel of the poſſeſſions thereof, thentofore uſually lett at the annual rent of one hundred and one pounds, fifteen ſhillings, and eleven pence; except, and always reſerved to his Majeſty, his heirs, and ſucceſſors, all and all manner of woods, underwoods, wardſhips, marriages, mines, and quarries, belonging to the premiſſes; to be be had and holden to the said Sir *Thomas Leighe*, and *Thomas Spencer*, their executors and assigns, for the term of forty years from the making the said letters patent, under the said annual rent of one hundred and one pounds, fifteen shillings, and eleven pence, and the several other payments issuing out of the premisses, therein particularly mentioned, amounting, in the whole, to the sum of twenty one pounds, seventeen shillings: and whereas his said late majesty King *James* the First, by certain other letters patent under the great seal of *England*, bearing date at *Westminster* the fourteenth day of *August*, in the fifth year of his reign, at the petition of *William* earl of *Derby* cousin and heir male of the body of the said Sir *John de Stanley* deceased, *Henry* earl of *Huntingdon* and *Elizabeth* his wife, *Graye Bridges* lord *Chandoys* and *Anne* his wife, and Sir *John Egerton* knight, son and heir male apparent of *Thomas* lord *Eilesmere* then chancellor of *England* and *Frances* his wife (which *Anne*, *Frances*, and *Elizabeth*, were the cousins and heirs of the said Sir *John de Stanley*) did grant to *Henry* earl of *Northampton*, and *Robert* earl of *Salisbury*, the said island, castle, pele, and lordship of *Man*, and all the islands and lordships to the same appertaining, and all and singular the royal regalities, franchises, liberties, and all other the rights, profits, and commodities thereunto belonging, in the same letters patent particularly mentioned and contained (except all those houses, scites, circuits, and precincts, formerly the monastry and priory of *Rushinge* and *Douglas*, and the fryers minors commonly called the *Grey Fryers* of *Brymaken*; otherwise *Bymaken*, and the rectories and churches of *Kirkecriste* in *Shelding* and *Kirklovan*, formerly to the said monastry of *Rushing* belonging and appertaining, and parcel of the possessions of the same, with their rights, members, and appurtenances, therein more particularly described) to be had and holden to the said *Henry* earl of *Northampton*, and *Robert* earl of *Salisbury*, their heirs and assigns, of the said King, his heirs and successors for ever, by the liege homage, and by the service of rendring two falcons in manner and form aforesaid; which said island, castle, pele, and lordship of *Man* aforesaid, and all the islands and lordships thereunto belonging, and other the premisses before mentioned (except as before excepted) were granted, or mentioned to be granted, by the late King *Henry* the Fourth, to the said Sir *John de Stanley*, by letters patent, bearing date at *Westminster* the sixth day of *April*, in the seventh year of his reign; and the said King did also grant to the said *Henry* earl of *Northampton*, and *Robert* earl of *Salisbury*, all and all manner of issues, revenues, and profits, of the said island, castle, pele, and lordship of *Man*, and all and singular the premisses (except as before excepted) which had not been paid to the late Queen, or to his then present Majesty, without any account to be rendered to his Majesty for the same: and whereas by indenture inrolled of record, and made, or mentioned to be made, the eighteenth day of *June*, in the said seventh year of the reign of his said late majesty King *James* the

First, between the said King of the one part, and the said *Robert* earl of *Salisbury* lord treasurer of *England*, *Henry* earl of *Northampton* keeper of the King's privy seal, *William* earl of *Derby*, *Henry* earl of *Huntingdon* and *Elizabeth* his wife, *Graye Bridges* lord *Chandoys* and *Anne* his wife, and *John Egerton* knight and *Frances* his wife, of the other part, but not executed or acknowledged of record by the said *William* earl of *Derby*, the said *Robert* earl of *Salisbury*, *Henry* earl of *Northampton*, *William* earl of *Derby*, *Henry* earl of *Huntingdon* and *Elizabeth* wife, *Graye Bridges* lord *Chandoys* and *Anne* his wife, *John Egerton* knight and *Frances* his wife, did give, grant, bargain, sell, surrender, and confirm, or were mentioned to give, grant, bargain, sell, surrender, and confirm, to the said King, his heirs and successors for ever, the said island, castle, pele, and lordship of *Man*, and all the islands and lordships to the same appertaining, and all and singular the royal regalities, franchises, liberties, and all other the rights, profits, and commodities, thereunto belonging, in the same letters patent, and also in the letters patent herein last before recited, particularly mentioned and contained, and all their right, title, state, use, possession, interest, claim, and demand whatsoever, in the said island, castle, pele, lordship, and premisses, or in any part thereof, to be had and holden to and for the use of the said King, his heirs, and successors, for ever: and whereas his said late majesty King *James* the First, by certain other letters patent under the great seal of *England*, bearing date at *Westminster* the twenty eighth day of *June*, in the seventh year of his reign, did demise, grant, and to farm-lett, to the said *Robert* earl of *Salisbury*, and *Thomas* earl of *Suffolk*, the said island, castle, pele, and lordship of *Man*, with all their rights, members, and appurtenances, and all his islands, lordships, castles, monasteries, abbies, priories, farms, messuages, lands, tenements, and hereditaments whatsoever, to the said island of *Man* appertaining or belonging, or situate, lying, or being, in or within the same, with all and singular their rights, members, and appurtenances, and all and singular the royal regalities, franchises, liberties, sea ports, and all things to port reasonably and duly appertaining; lands thentofore overflowed by, and then gained from, the sea, and reduced to dry soil; lands then overflowed by the sea, and which thereafter should be gained and reduced to dry soil; homages, fealties, knights fees, wards, marriages, reliefs, escheats, forfeitures, waifs, goods and chattels of felons, fugitives, persons outlawed, attainted, condemned, and put in exigent; estrays, deodands, villeins, and naifs, with their issue; estovers, and commons of estovers; courts leet, views of frankpledge, courts baron, courts of admiralty, courts of portmote, leets, hundreds, wapentakes, and the perquisites and profits of courts, views of frankpledge, courts baron, courts of admiralty, courts of portmote, and leets, and all that to courts leet, views of frankpledge, courts baron, and courts of portmote belonged, or thereafter could or ought to belong, wrecks of the sea, mines of lead and iron, quarries, fairs, fair days, markets, tolls, and issues of fairs, free customs, rights, jurisdictions, franchises, privileges, manors,

vills,

vills, towns, caſtles, granges, meſſuages, houſes, edifices, mills, barns, ſtables, dove-houſes, orchards, fruiteries, gardens, tofts, cottages, curtilages, lands, tenements, meadows, feedings, paſtures, demeſne lands, glebe lands, leaſows, waſtes, heaths, moors, marſhes, ways, void grounds, paths, eaſements, woods, under-woods, wood lands and trees, and the ſoil and ground of the ſaid woods, underwoods, and trees, tithes of corn, grain, and hay, wool, flax, hemp, lambs, and all other tithes whatſoever, as well great as ſmall, rectories, advowſons, donations, and rights of patronage, of all and ſingular hoſpitals, churches, vicarages, chapels, and all other eccleſiaſtical benefices whatſoever, oblations, obventions, fruits, profits, waters, water-courſes, ſtreams, aqueducts, ſuits, ſokes, multures, and alſo all and ſingular foreſts, parks, chaſes, lawns, warrens, aſſarts, purpreſtures, chiminages, piſcaries, fiſhings, rents, penſions, portions, frankfolds, turbaries, pools, fiſh-ponds, ways, paſſages, commons, rents, reverſions, and ſervices, rents charge, rents ſeck, rents of aſſize, and rents and ſervices of tenants, as well free as cuſtomary, works of tenants, annual farm rents, fee farms, annuities, heriots, fines, amerciaments, tolls, duties, anchorages, groundages, profits, commodities, advantages, emoluments, hereditaments, and appurtenances whatſoever, as well ſpiritual as temporal, ſituate, lying, or being, coming, growing, renewing, or ariſing, within the ſaid iſland, caſtle, pele, and lordſhip of *Man*, or within the ſea to the ſame iſland contiguous and adjoining, or within any other iſlands, lordſhips, peles, caſtles, farms, or lands, to the ſaid iſland of *Man* appertaining, or to the ſame or any of them appurtenant, incident, appendant, or belonging, or at any time heretofore had, known, taken, occupied, uſed, demiſed, let, or reputed to be members, parts, or parcels of the ſame, and the patronage of the biſhoprick of the ſaid iſland of *Man*, and the patronage of the biſhoprick of *Sodor*, and the patronage of the biſhoprick of *Soder and Man*, and the temporalties of the ſaid biſhopricks, whenſoever they ſhould happen to be vacant, and the reverſion and reverſions, remainder and remainders, of all and ſingular the ſaid iſlands, caſtles, peles, lordſhips, patronages of biſhopricks, rectories, foreſts, chaſes, parks, farms, granges, meſſuages, lands, tenements, and hereditaments whatſoever, and of the reſt of the premiſſes therein before demiſed, and every parcel thereof, dependant and expectant on any gift, demiſe, or grant, for term of life or lives, or years, or in fee tail or otherwiſe, of the premiſſes, or any part thereof, however made, or being of record, or not of record, and the rents and profits thereupon reſerved, or in any manner incident to the ſame, or any part thereof (except the ſaid houſes, ſcites, circuits, and precincts, formerly the monaſtery and priory of *Ruſhing* and *Douglas*, and the fryers minors of *Brymaken*, otherwiſe *Bymaken*, and the rectories and churches of *Kirkecriſt* in *Sheldon* and *Kirkelovan*, with their and every of their rights, members, and appurtenances, therein particularly deſcribed) to be had and holden, to the ſaid *Robert* earl of *Saliſbury*, and *Thomas* earl of *Suffolk*, their executors

tors and assigns, from the feast of Saint *Michael the archangel* then last past, for the term of twenty one years from thence next following, at and under the yearly rent of twenty shillings of lawful money of *England*: and whereas his said late majesty King *James* the First, by certain other letters patent under the great seal of *England*, bearing date at *Westminster* the seventh day of *July*, in the seventh year of his reign, reciting the said letters patent herein last before recited, did give and grant unto the said *William* earl of *Derby* and *Elizabeth* his wife, and *James Stanley* lord *Stanley* his son and heir apparent, all the said island, castle, pele, and lordship of *Man*, and all the islands and lordships to the same belonging, and all and singular the royal regalities, franchises, liberties, and all and singular other the premisses in the said therein and herein recited letters patent demised and granted, with all their rights, members, and appurtenances (except the said houses, scites, circuits, and precincts, and other the premisses in the said therein recited letters patent excepted) and farther, that the said *William* earl of *Derby* and *Elizabeth* his wife, and *James Stanley* lord *Stanley*, and the heirs and assigns of the said *James*, should have, hold, and enjoy, within the said island, castle, pele, and lordship of *Man*, and other the premisses, such and the like courts leet, profits of courts leet, views of frank pledge, courts of portmote, courts of admiralty, and every thing to all and every the said courts belonging, law days, assize and assay of bread, wine, and beer, waifs, estrays, goods and chattels of felons, fugitives, felons of themselves, clerks convict or attainted, traitors, or of those who being indicted of treason, murder, or felony, refuse to answer to the same according to the law and custom of *England*, or stand obstinately mute, or refuse to stand to the judgement thereupon to be given, or of persons otherwise convicted or condemned, deodands, knights fees, wards, marriages, reliefs, escheats, heriots, forests, chases, free warrens, parks, liberties of parks, wrecks of the sea, anchorage and groundage, and all other rights royal, regalities, jurisdictions, franchises, liberties, customs, privileges, profits, commodities, advantages, emoluments, and hereditaments whatsoever, as well spiritual as temporal, as fully, freely, and intirely, and in as ample manner and form, as Sir *William Le Scrope* knight, *Henry Percye* earl of *Northumberland*, Sir *John Stanley* knight, or any of them, or any other person or persons thentofore had, held, used, or enjoyed the same, within the said island, castle, pele, and lordship, farms, messuages, lands, and hereditaments, and other the premisses therein before granted, or any part or parcel thereof, by reason or pretence of any charter, gift, grant, confirmation, or letters patent, from any Kings or Queens of *England*, or of any act or acts of parliament, or of any lawful prescription, usage, or custom, or of any other right or title whatsoever, and as fully, freely, and in as ample manner and form, as his said Majesty, or any of the former Kings or Queens of *England*, had and enjoyed, or ought to have had, used, and enjoyed, the said island, castle, pele, and lordship of *Man*,

farms,

farms, messuages, lands, tenements, and hereditaments, and all and singular other the premisses therein before granted, or any part or parcel thereof, to be had and holden, to and to the use of the said *William* earl of *Derby* and *Elizabeth* his wife, for and during the natural life and lives of them and the survivor of them, and after their deceases, to and to the use of the said *James Stanley* lord *Stanley*, and his heirs for ever, of his said Majesty, his heirs and successors, for ever, by liege homage, and by the service of rendering to the said King two falcons once only; that is to say, immediately after the said homage done, and of rendering to his said Majesty's heirs, Kings of *England*, two falcons on the days of their coronations, in lieu of all other services, customs, and demands; and the said King did moreover give and grant to the said *William* earl of *Derby* and *Elizabeth* his wife, and *James Stanley* lord *Stanley*, his heirs and assigns, all and all manner of rents, arrearages of rent, issues, revenues, and yearly profits of the said island, castle, pele, and lordship of *Man*, and other the premisses (except as before excepted) heretofore due, and not paid to his late dear sister *Elizabeth* late Queen of *England*, or to himself, or to any of his progenitors, to be by them received, without any account for the same: and whereas his said late majesty King *James* the First, by certain other letters patent under the great seal of *England*, bearing date at *Westminster* the second day of *May* in the eighth year of his reign, did give and grant to the said *William* earl of *Derby* and *Elizabeth* his wife, and the heirs of the said *William*, all those houses, scites, circuits, and precincts, formerly the monastry and priory of *Rushing* and *Douglas*, and the fryers minors commonly called *The Grey Fryers of Brymaken*, otherwise *Bymaken*, with all their appurtenances in the *Island of Man*, and all those his rectories and churches of *Kirkecrist* in *Shelding* and *Kirklovan* with their appurtenances in the said *Island of Man*, formerly belonging to the monastry of *Rushing* aforesaid, and being parcel of the possessions thereof, by a particular thereof extending to the clear annual rent or value of one hundred and one pounds, fifteen shillings, and eleven pence, over and above certain other payments in the said letters patent mentioned issuing thereout, and amounting in the whole to twenty one pounds, seventeen shillings, and all and singular his monasteries, abbies, granges, lands, tithes, tenements, and hereditaments whatsoever, with all and singular their rights, members, aud appurtenances, in the said *Island of Man*, and all messuages, mills, houses, edifices, buildings, barns, stables, dovehouses, orchards, fruiteries, gardens, lands, tenements, tofts, cottages, pools, fishponds, meadows, feedings, pastures, heaths, moors, marshes, ways, void grounds, roads, paths, easements, woods, underwoods, coppice woods, woodlands, trees, fruits, profits, commodities, streams, banks, rivulets, watercourses, aqueducts, piscaries, fishings, rents, avenues, and services, tithes of corn in sheaf, corn in blade, grain, and hay, and all other tithes whatsoever as well great as small, oblations, obventions, hawkings, huntings,

frank-

frankfolds, turbaries, ſuits, ſokes, multures, warrens, mines, quarries, rents and ſervices as well of free as of cuſtomary tenants, rent charges, rents ſeck, and rents and ſervices reſerved upon any demiſes, or grants of the premiſſes, or any parcel thereof, works of tenants, annual farm rents, fee farms, cuſtoms, annuities, knights fees, wards, marriages, eſcheats, reliefs, aids, heriots, fines, amerciaments, courts leets, views of frankpledge, perquiſites and profits of courts and leets, and all that to courts leet or view of frankpledge belonged, or thereafter could or ought to belong, waifs, goods and chattels of petty traitors, felons, fugitives, perſons outlawed, attainted, condemned, and put in exigent, and of thoſe who being indicted of any petty treaſon, murder, or felony, ſhall ſtand obſtinately mute, or will not anſwer directly and juſtify themſelves according to the law and cuſtom of *England*, and of all perſons convicted or attainted, eſtrays, deodands, villeins and naifs with their iſſue, eſtovers and commons of eſtovers, fairs, markets, ſtallages, tolls, duties, impoſts, rights, juriſdictions, franchiſes, liberties, cuſtoms, privileges, profits, commodities, advantages, emoluments, and hereditaments, with all and ſingular their rights, members, and appurtenances, within the ſaid *Iſland of Man*, to the ſaid monaſteries and priories of *Ruſhing* and *Dowglaſs*, and the fryers minors of *Brymaken*, otherwiſe *Bymaken*, and rectories and churches of *Kirkecriſt* in *Shelding*, and *Kirklovan*, and other the premiſſes therein before given and granted, or to any parcel thereof, belonging, appertaining, incident, or appendant, and the reverſion and reverſions of the ſame expectant on any grant or demiſe for term of life or lives, or years, or otherwiſe, whether the ſame be of record or not of record, and all woods, underwoods, coppice woods, and trees whatſoever, growing and being in and upon the premiſſes, or any part thereof, and the land, ground, and ſoil of the ſame, and all rents and annual profits reſerved upon any demiſe or grant of the premiſſes, or any part thereof; and alſo that the ſaid *William* earl of *Derby* and *Elizabeth* his wife, and the heirs of the ſaid *William*, ſhould have, hold, and enjoy, all ſuch and the like courts leets, views of frankpledge, law days, aſſiſe and aſſay of bread, wine, and beer, waifs, eſtrays, chattels of felons, fugitives, and perſons put in exigent, deodands, knights fees, wards, marriages, reliefs, eſcheats, heriots, free warrens, hawkings, huntings, and all other rights, juriſdictions, franchiſes, liberties, cuſtoms, privileges, profits, commodities, advantages, emoluments, and hereditaments whatſoever, and as fully, freely, and intirely, as any abbot or prior of the ſaid former monaſtery and priory of *Ruſhing* and *Dowglas*, and the fryers minors of *Brymaken*, otherwiſe *Bymaken*, or any other perſon or perſons heretofore having, poſſeſſing, or being ſeiſed of the ſaid monaſtery, priory, fryers minors, rectories, churches, and other the premiſſes, ever had, held, uſed, or enjoyed, or ought to have had, held, uſed or enjoyed, the ſame, or any part thereof, by reaſon or pretence of any charter, gift, grant, or confirmation, by his ſaid Majeſty, or any of his anceſtors Kings or Queens of *England*, or of any act or acts of par-

liament,

liament, or of any lawful prescription, usage, or custom, or otherwise howsoever by any lawful means, right, or title, and as fully, freely, and intirely, as his said Majesty, or any of his said ancestors, ever had and enjoyed, or ought to have had and enjoyed, the same, and in as ample manner and form as the same came, or ought to have come, to the hands of his said Majesty, or any of his said ancestors, by reason or pretence of the dissolution or surrender of any of the said monasteries or priories, or by reason or pretence of any act or acts of parliament, escheats, exchanges, attainders, or forfeitures, or by any other lawful means, right, or title whatsoever; to be had, holden, and enjoyed, to and to the use of the said *William* earl of *Derby* and *Elizabeth* his wife, and the heirs of the said *William*, for ever, of his said Majesty, his heirs and successors, as of the manor of east *Greenwich* in *Kent*, by fealty only, in free and common soccage, and not in chief, or by knight service, at and under the yearly rent of one hundred and one pounds, fifteen shillings, and eleven pence, of lawful money of *England*, to be paid at the receipt of his Majesty's exchequer at *Westminster*, at the feast of Saint *Michael the Archangel*, and the annunciation of the blessed Virgin *Mary*, by equal portions, in lieu of all other rents, services, exactions, and demands whatsoever, and it was agreed, that the said *William* earl of *Derby* and *Elizabeth* his wife, and the heirs of the said *William*, should yearly and every year pay, or cause to be paid, the several sums therein mentioned, due and issuing out of the premisses, and amounting in the whole to the sum of twenty pounds, seventeen shillings, yearly; and thereof should acquit, discharge, and save harmless, his said Majesty, his heirs, and successors: and whereas by an act of parliament made in the eighth year of the reign of his said late majesty King *James* the First, intituled, *An act for the assuring and establishing of the* Isle of Man, *in order to continue the said island, castle, pele, and lordship of* Man, *with their rights, members, and appurtenances, in the name and blood of the said* William *earl of* Derby, it was enacted, that the said *William* earl of *Derby* and *Elizabeth* his wife, for and during their lives, and the longer liver of them, and after their deaths the said *James* lord *Stanley*, and the heirs male of his body lawfully begotten, and after his death without such issue, *Robert Stanley* second son of the said earl, and the heirs males of his body lawfully begotten, and after his death without such issue, the heirs males of the body of the said *William* earl of *Derby* lawfully begotten, and for default of such issue, the right heirs of the said *James* lord *Stanley*, should and might for ever thereafter have, hold, and quietly enjoy, freely and clearly, against his said Majesty, his heirs and successors (by the tenures, rents, and services, therein after mentioned to be reserved) against *Thomas* lord *Ellesmere* lord chancellor of *England* and *Alice* countess of *Derby* his wife, late the wife of *Ferdinando* earl of *Derby* deceased, and against *Henry* earl of *Huntingdon* and *Elizabeth* his wife, *Gray* lord *Chandoys* and *Anne* his wife, Sir *John Egerton* knight son and heir apparent of the

the ſaid *Thomas* lord *Elleſmere* and *Frances* his wife, and the heirs of the ſaid *Elizabeth*, *Anne*, and *Frances*, who were the only daughters and ſole heirs of the ſaid *Ferdinando* late earl of *Derby*, and to whom and their huſbands the ſaid *William* earl of *Derby* had paid divers ſums of money for their claim, right, and title, to the ſaid iſle, caſtle, pele, and lordſhip of *Man*, as appeared by their deed, bearing date the fourteenth day of *February* in the ſixth year of his ſaid Majeſty's reign, whereby they had agreed to give their conſents for the paſſing of an act of parliament, for the giving and extinguiſhing of ſuch their right, title, and intereſt, and againſt the heirs of the ſaid *Ferdinando* late earl of *Derby*, and againſt *Thomas Ireland* eſquire, his executors, adminiſtrators, and aſſigns, all the ſaid iſle, caſtle, pele, and lordſhip of *Man*, with the rights, members, and appurtenances, and all the then or late monaſtery and priory of *Ruſhing* and *Douglas*, and the fryers minors commonly called *The grey fryers of Brymaken*, otherwiſe *Bymaken*, with their rights, members, and appurtenances, and the rectories and churches of *Kirkecriſte* in *Shelding* and *Kirkelovan*, with their appurtenances, and the patronage of the biſhoprick and biſhopricks aforeſaid, and all other the hereditaments whatſoever granted by his ſaid Majeſty by his ſaid ſeveral letters patent, the one bearing date the ſeventh day of *July* in the ſeventh year of his ſaid Majeſty's reign, and the other bearing date the ſecond day of *May* in the eighth year of his ſaid Majeſty's reign, which laſt mentioned letters patent were made and granted during the then ſeſſion of parliament: and it was further enacted, That neither the ſaid lord *Stanley*, nor the ſaid *Robert Stanley*, nor any of the heirs males of their bodies reſpectively nor any of the heirs males of the body of the ſaid *William* earl of *Derby*, ſhould have any power to alien, ſell, or convey, the ſaid iſle, caſtle, pele, and lordſhip of *Man*, and other the premiſſes, or any part of them, from his or their iſſue, or other perſons appointed by the ſaid act to enjoy the ſame, but that the ſame ſhould remain and continue as by the ſaid act is appointed; and that all gifts, grants, alienations, bargains, ſales, conveyances, aſſurances, and acts done or to be done to the contrary (except as therein is excepted) ſhould be utterly void, and of none effect: and it was further enacted, That neither the ſaid act, nor any thing therein contained, ſhould extend or be conſtrued to avoid, fruſtrate, abridge, impair, diminiſh, or prejudice, the ſtate, intereſt and term of years of Sir *Thomas Leigh* knight, and *Thomas Spencer* eſquire, their executors, adminiſtrators, and aſſigns, of the meſſuage, lands, tenements, tithes, profits, hereditaments, and other things in the ſaid iſle of *Man*, granted by the ſaid letters patent, bearing date the ſeventeenth day of *March* in the third year of his ſaid Majeſty's reign, for the term of forty years; and that they and every of them ſhould and might peaceably and quietly, during the ſaid term, have, hold, occupy and enjoy, the ſame, upon ſuch yearly rents, reſervations, covenants, proviſoes, and agreements, as were mentioned and expreſſed in the ſaid letters patent; ſaving to the archbiſhop of *York* and his ſuc-

successors, all metropolitical jurisdiction in all points, and to all purposes of the bishopricks and diocese of *Man* in the said isle of *Man*, as is given, united, limited, and appointed, to the province and archbishoprick of *York*, by the said act of parliament made in the three and thirtieth year of the reign of the said King *Henry* the Eighth: and whereas his late majesty King *Charles* the Second by his letters patent, bearing date at *Westminster*, the twelfth day of *February* in the nineteenth year of his reign, did give and grant unto *Charles* earl of *Derby* (son and heir of the said *James* lord *Stanley* afterwards earl of *Derby* deceased) all and all manner of mines royal of gold or silver, or holding gold or silver to such a proportion as, according to the laws of *England*, doth make the same a mine royal, situate, lying, and being, in the isle of *Man*, whether the same be opened or not opened; to be had and holded unto the said *Charles* earl of *Derby*, and to the heirs males of his body lawfully begotten, at and under the yearly rent and payment therein contained and expressed; which said grant, upon the failure of heirs male of the body of the said *Charles* earl of *Derby* by the death of *James* late earl of *Derby*, which happened on or about the first day of *February*, in the year of our Lord one thousand seven hundred and thirty five, expired, and the right of the said mines royal revested in his then majesty King *George* the Second, his heirs and successors: and whereas in and by one other act of parliament, made in the twelfth year of the reign of his late majesty King *George* the First, intituled, *An act for the improvement of his Majesty's revenues of customs, excise, and inland duties*, after laying several restrictions upon the fraudulent trade then carried on between *Great Britain* and the said *Isle of Man*, it was (for the better enabling his Majesty to prevent the said frauds and abuses) enacted, That it should and might be lawful to and for the commissioners of his Majesty's treasury then or for the time being, or any three or more of them, or the lord high treasurer for the time being, on the behalf of his Majesty, his heirs and successors, and also to and for the right honourable *James* earl of *Derby*, his tenants, or assigns, the right honourable *John* lord *Ashburnham* for and on behalf of his daughter *Henrietta Bridget Ashburnham* an infant, *Bryan Fairfax* esquire, trustee for the said infant, or the survivor of them, and all or any other person or persons claiming or to claim by, from, or under, the said earl, or any of his ancestors, to treat, contract, and agree for the absolute purchase or sale, release or surrender to or for the use of his Majesty, his heirs and successors, of all or any estate, right, title, or interest, which he the said earl, his tenants, the said *Henrietta Bridget Ashburnham*, or such other person or persons then had or claimed, or could or might have or claim, in or to the said island or lordship of *Man*, or in or to all or any regalities, powers, honours, superiorities, jurisdictions, rights, privileges, duties, customs, revenues, profits, or other advantages whatsoever, in, over, or about the said island of *Man*, or its dependencies, for such sum or sums of money, or upon ſuch other terms or conditions, as they ſhould think fitting; and that upon the executing of ſuch contracts or agreements by or on the behalf of the ſaid earl, his tenants, the ſaid *Henrietta Bridget Aſhburnham*, or ſuch other perſon or perſons claiming or to claim under him, or any of his anceſtors as aforeſaid, or upon executing ſuch other conveyances, aſſignments, releaſes, or ſurrenders, as in ſuch contract or contracts ſhould be agreed on for that purpoſe, it ſhould and might be lawful to and for the ſaid commiſſioners of the treaſury then or for the time being, or any three or more of them, or the lord high treaſurer for the time being, and they were thereby impowered, by and out of any monies ariſen or to ariſe to his Majeſty, his heirs, or ſucceſſors, of or for any cuſtoms, ſubſidies, impoſitions, or other duties, upon the importation or exportation of any goods or merchandizes whatſoever, already granted or payable, or thereafter to be granted or payable to his Majeſty, his heirs or ſucceſſors, in *Great Britain*, *Wales*, or *Berwick upon Tweed*, to order and direct the payment of ſuch ſum or ſums of money, from time to time, as ſhould be ſo contracted or agreed on for ſuch purchaſe or purchaſes, to ſuch perſon or perſons as, according to the terms of ſuch contracts or agreements, ſhould be intitled to have and receive the ſame: and whereas the moſt noble *James* late duke of *Atholl*, as right heir of the ſaid *James* lord *Stanley*, on failure of heirs male of the body of the ſaid *William* earl of *Derby* by the death of the ſaid *James* late earl of *Derby*, became ſeiſed to him and his heirs of the ſaid iſland, caſtle, pele, and lordſhip of *Man*, and all other the premiſſes aforeſaid, except the mines royal ſo reveſted in the crown as aforeſaid; and by a certain indenture or deed of feoffment, with livery of ſeiſin thereon indorſed, bearing date the fourteenth day of *November* in the year of our Lord one thouſand ſeven hundred and thirty ſeven, and made, or mentioned to be made, between the ſaid late duke of *Atholl* of the one part, the right honourable *John* late earl of *Dunmore*, and the right honourable *William* now lord *Mansfield*, by the name and deſcription of the honourable *William Murray* of *Lincoln's Inn London* eſquire, and *John Murray* of the city of *Edinburgh* eſquire (ſince deceaſed) of the other part, the ſaid *James* duke of *Atholl* did grant, bargain, ſell, alien, enfeoff, and confirm unto the ſaid *John* earl of *Dunmore*, and *William* now lord *Mansfield*, and *John Murray*, all the ſaid iſland, caſtle, pele, and lordſhip of *Man*, and all other the premiſſes therein and herein more particularly mentioned and deſcribed, except as before excepted; to be had and holden to the ſaid *John* earl of *Dunmore*, *William* now lord *Mansfield*, and *John Murray*, their heirs and aſſigns for ever, upon the truſts, and to and for the intents and purpoſes, therein mentioned and declared, of and concerning the ſame; in which ſaid indenture or deed of feoffment a power was reſerved to the ſaid *James* duke of *Atholl*, by any deed or deeds, or by his laſt will and teſtament, executed and atteſted as is therein mentioned, to revoke and make void all and every or any of the ſaid truſts, directions, declarations, and agree-

agreements, and to declare, limit, or appoint, any farther, other, or different trusts, uses, or directions thereof, or of so much thereof as should be so revoked and made void, with or without power of revocation, as to the said duke should seem proper: and whereas by indenture bearing date the fourth day of *May*, one thousand seven hundred and forty eight, and expressed to be made between the same parties as are parties to the last recited indenture, the said *James* duke of *Atholl*, in pursuance of the powers in him vested, did revoke and make void all and every the said trusts, directions, declarations, and agreements, contained in the said recited indenture or deed of feoffment of the fourteenth day of *November*, one thousand seven hundred and thirty seven, of and concerning the said island, castle, pele and lordship of *Man*, and all other the premisses; and did direct, limit, and appoint, that the said *John* earl of *Dunmore*, *William* now lord *Mansfied*, and *John Murray*, and their heirs and assigns, should stand seised of the premisses upon such other trusts, and to and for such intents and purposes, as therein are mentioned and declared of and concerning the same; in which said indenture was also reserved to the said duke of *Atholl*, a like power of revocation, with authority to declare, limit, or appoint, any farther, other, or different trusts or directions of the same, or any part thereof, with or without power of revocation, as to him should seem proper: and whereas by one other indenture or deed of feoffment, with livery of seisin thereon indorsed, bearing date the sixth day of *April*, in the year of our Lord one thousand seven hundred and fifty six, and made, or mentioned to be made, between the said *James* duke of *Atholl* of the first part; the said *William* now lord *Mansfield*, by the name and description of the honourable *William Murray* of *Lincoln's Inn* in the county of *Middlesex* esquire his Majesty's attorney general, of the second part, and the most noble *Archibald* late duke of *Argyle*, the right honourable *David* lord viscount *Stormont*, and *John Sharpe* of *Lincoln's Inn* in the county of *Middlesex* esquire, since deceased, of the third part; reciting (amongst other recitals therein contained) that proposals had, from time to time, been made to the said *James* duke of *Atholl* on the part of the King's majesty that then was, in order to purchase of the said duke of *Atholl* the said isle and territories of *Man*, and other the hereditaments and premisses therein mentioned; and that the said duke, though reluctant to alien so honourable a principality from his family, had always been ready to submit to his Majesty's will and pleasure therein, who had never proposed to purchase but upon paying a full and adequate consideration for the same; but that it was uncertain whether any such sale would be made of the said isle, hereditaments and premisses, in the life-time of the said duke of *Atholl*; and that therefore he the said duke was minded and desirous that the same should be settled, assured and conveyed, upon such trusts, and to and for such intents and purposes, as therein and herein after are expressed; the said *James* duke of *Atholl*, in pursuance of the powers reserved to him by the ſaid laſt-mentioned indenture, and of all other powers to him given in that behalf, did revoke and make void all and every the truſts, declarations and agreements, in the ſaid indenture contained concerning the ſaid iſle, caſtle, pele, lordſhip and territories of *Man*, and all other the premiſſes as aforeſaid; and further the ſaid *James* duke of *Atholl*, and alſo the ſaid *William* now lord *Mansfield*, by the direction and appointment of the ſaid duke, did grant, bargain, ſell, alien, infeoff and confirm, unto the ſaid *Archibald* duke of *Argyle*, *David* lord viſcount of *Stormont*, and *John Sharpe* eſquire, the ſaid iſle, caſtle, pele, lordſhip and territories of *Man*, with the rights, royalties, members, dependencies, juriſdictions and appurtenances thereof, or thereunto belonging, and all and ſingular other the hereditaments and premiſſes aforeſaid, to be had and holden unto the ſaid *Archibald* duke of *Argyle*, *David* lord viſcount of *Stormont*, and *John Sharpe*, their heirs and aſſigns for ever, of our ſovereign lord the King, his heirs and ſucceſſors, by the rents, tenures, ſuits and ſervices, by which the ſaid *James* duke of *Atholl*, and *William* now lord *Mansfield*, or either of them, then held the ſame; upon truſt (among other things) after the deceaſe of the ſaid *James* duke of *Atholl*, that they the ſaid *Archibald* duke of *Argyle*, *David* lord viſcount of *Stormont* and *John Sharpe*, and the ſurvivors of them, their nominees and aſſigns, ſhould, at any time thereafter, with the conſent and approbation of the perſon or perſons who, after the death of the ſaid *James* duke of *Atholl*, ſhould, by virtue of the truſts therein expreſſed, be, from time to time, intitled to the actual receipt of the rents, revenues and profits, of the ſaid iſle and premiſſes (ſuch perſon and perſons being then of the age of twenty one years), ſell and convey, or releaſe and ſurrender the ſaid iſle, caſtle, pele, lordſhip and territories of *Man*, and other the truſted premiſſes (whereof no appointment ſhould have been made by the ſaid *John* duke of *Atholl* in his life-time, purſuant to a power to him therein reſerved and mentioned unto the King's majeſty, his heirs or ſucceſſors, for ſuch price in ready money as they could reaſonably get, and ſhould judge to be a proper equivalent and adequate conſideration for the ſame; and ſhould, with ſuch conſent and approbation as aforeſaid, lay out and inveſt the money to ariſe by the ſale and diſpoſition thereof, in the purchaſe of lands of inheritance in that part of *Great Britain* called *Scotland*; and after ſuch purchaſe or purchaſes made, ſhould convey, ſettle and entail the lands ſo to be purchaſed, with all the proper prohibitive, irritant and reſolutive clauſes, ſo as the ſame might be effectually limited and unalienably intailed, as far as the rules of the law of *Scotland* would permit, to, upon and for, ſuch perſons, uſes, intents and purpoſes, as are therein declared concerning the ſame; that is to ſay, to the heirs male of the body of the ſaid *James* duke of *Atholl*, remainder to the heirs female of the body of the ſaid *James* duke of *Atholl* (the eldeſt heir female always ſucceeding without diviſion, and excluding heirs portioners) remainder to the moſt noble *John* now duke of *Atholl*, by by the name and description of *John Murray* of *Strowan* in *Scotland* esquire, nephew of the said *James* duke of *Atholl*, and husband of the right honourable the lady *Charlotte Murray*, the only daughter then living of the said *James* duke of *Atholl* (now dutchess of *Atholl* and baroness *Strange*) and the heirs male of his body, with like remainders to *James* and *George Murray* esquires, brothers of the said *John* now duke of *Atholl*, successively, and the heirs male of their respective bodies, with divers other remainders over in tail male, remainder to the heirs and assigns of the said *James* duke of *Atholl* whatsoever, with power to the trustees (with the consent of the person or persons who would have been intitled to the receipt of the rents and profits of the premisses, in case there had been no sale) to place out the money arising by such sale on real securities in *Scotland*, or in any other part of *Great Britain*, or in the purchase of stocks in the publick companies, or in the publick funds, or upon government securities, and to call in and place out the same again upon new or other securities of the like nature, the yearly interest and dividends whereof should be paid to such person or persons as, for the time being, would be intitled to be in the actual receipt of the rents and profits of the lands thereby directed to be purchased in *Scotland*, in case the same had been so purchased, settled and entailed as aforesaid; and with power also to the surviving trustees, in case of the death of any of them, to re-enfeoff other trustees to the same uses; and likewise with power to the said *James* duke of *Atholl*, by deed or will to be by him executed, and attested as therein mentioned, to revoke or alter all or any the uses and trusts therein expressed, of or concerning the premisses, or any part thereof, and to limit and appoint any new and further uses and directions thereof, as to him should seem meet: and whereas by a certain other indenture or deed of feoffment, with livery and seisin thereon endorsed, bearing date on or about the twenty first day of *November*, which was in the year of our Lord one thousand seven hundred and sixty one, and made, or mentioned to be made, between the said *James* duke of *Atholl* of the first part, the said *David* lord viscount *Stormont* of the second part, the said *John* now duke of *Atholl* of the third part, *John Wood* esquire governor and commander in chief of the said isle of *Man* of the fourth part, Sir *Charles Frederick* knight of the most honourable order of the *Bath*, and *Edmund Hoskins* of *Lincoln's Inn* in the county of *Middlesex* esquire, of the fifth part, and the right honourable *George* earl of *Aberdeen* of the sixth part, reciting, that the said *Archibald* duke of *Argyle* and *John Sharpe*, were both dead, and that several proposals had been made to the said *James* duke of *Atholl* for the purchase of the several rectories, impropriations, and tythes, within the said isle, part of the trusted premisses; and that to facilitate the sale thereof, he was determined to revoke all the trusts of the said rectories, impropriations and tythes, declared by the said last recited indenture or deed of feoffment; and further reciting, that the said *David* lord viscount *Stormont*

 had,

had, with the privity and approbation of the ſaid *James* duke of *Atholl*, nominated the ſaid Sir *Charles Frederick* and *Edmund Hoskins*, to ſupply the place of the ſaid *Archibald* duke of *Argyle* and *John Sharpe*, in the execution of ſuch of the truſts in the ſaid laſt recited indenture as were not revoked, or intended ſo to be by the ſaid indenture, he the ſaid *James* duke of *Atholl* did revoke, determine and make void, all the truſts before declared concerning the ſaid rectories, impropriations and tythes; and the ſaid *James* duke of *Atholl*, and the ſaid *David* lord viſcount *Stormont* by his direction and appointment, did grant and enfeoff the ſame to the ſaid *John* now duke of *Atholl*, upon the truſts therein mentioned: and as concerning the ſaid iſle, lordſhip and territory of *Man*, and all other the premiſſes (other than the ſaid rectories, impropriations and tythes) the ſaid *James* duke of *Atholl*, and the ſaid *David* lord viſcount *Stormont* by his direction and appointment, did grant and enfeoff the ſame to the ſaid *John Wood*, his heirs and aſſigns, to the intent that he and they ſhould re-enfeoff the ſame to the ſaid *David* lord viſcount *Stormont*, Sir *Charles Frederick* and *Edmund Hoskins*, their heirs and aſſigns, upon the truſts, and for the intents and purpoſes, and under the limitations in the ſaid laſt recited indenture or deed of feoffment, of the ſixth day of *April* one thouſand ſeven hundred and fifty ſix, declared concerning the ſame; in which ſaid indenture was alſo contained a further power of revocation: and whereas the ſaid *John Wood* did, by a certain deed poll by him duly executed, bearing date the eighth day of *July* one thouſand ſeven hundred and ſixty two, re-enfeoff accordingly the ſaid iſle, caſtle, pele and lordſhip, and other the premiſſes laſt mentioned, unto the ſaid *David* lord viſcount *Stormont*, Sir *Charles Frederick* and *Edmund Hoskins*, and their heirs: and whereas the ſaid *James* duke of *Atholl* departed this life on or about the eighth day of *January* in the year one thouſand ſeven hundred and ſixty four, without revoking or altering the ſaid laſt recited indenture of feoffment, leaving the ſaid *Charlotte* (wife of the ſaid *John* now duke of *Atholl*) now dutcheſs of *Atholl* and baroneſs *Strange*, his daughter and only child; and thereupon they the ſaid now duke and ducheſs of *Atholl* became intitled to the ſaid iſle, caſtle, pele and territories of *Man*, and other the hereditaments and premiſſes (the ſaid rectories, impropriations and tythes excepted) under and by virtue of the ſaid recited indentures of feoffment, and according to the eſtate and intereſt thereby limited to them reſpectively therein: and whereas a treaty having been ſet on foot between the right honourable the commiſſioners of his Majeſty's treaſury and the ſaid *John* duke of *Atholl* and *Charlotte* dutcheſs of *Atholl* and baroneſs *Strange* his wife, for the ſale of their eſtate and intereſt in the ſaid iſland and premiſſes, or ſuch part thereof as ſhould be found expedient to veſt in his Majeſty for the publick ſervice, they the ſaid duke and dutcheſs did, in their letter bearing date the twenty ſeventh day of *February* one thouſand ſeven hundred and ſixty five, and addreſſed to their lordſhips, incloſe an abſtract of the clear revenue of the

Iſle

Isle of Man for ten years, from the year one thousand seven hunpred and fifty four, to the year one thousand seven hundred and sixty three, both inclusive (a copy whereof is contained in the schedule annexed to this act) and did declare that they were ready, if it should be deemed necessary for the publick service, to part with all their rights held under the several grants of the *Isle of Man*; but apprehended, that the reservation of their landed revenue, together with the patronage of the bishoprick, and other ecclesiastical benefices in the island, could not interfere with the interest of the publick; and presumed, there could be no objection to their preserving the honourable distinction and service which their ancestors had so long enjoyed, and by which they held their rights in this island, of presenting the two falcons at the coronation; and notwithstanding the difficulty of proposing a proper compensation (which might expose them to the imputation of making an unreasonable demand on the one hand, and of not doing sufficient justice to their family on the other) yet, as the circumstances of the case had made it necessary, they did therefore hope, that neither his Majesty, nor the parliament, would think the clear sum of seventy thousand pounds too great a price to be paid them, in full compensation for the absolute surrender of the isle, castle and pele of *Man*, and all rights, jurisdictions and interests, in or over the said island, and all its dependencies, holden under the several grants thereof, or under any other title whatsoever, reserving only their landed property, with all their rights in and over the soil as lords of the manor, with all courts baron, rents, services and other incidents to such courts belonging, their wastes, commons and other lands, inland waters, fisheries and mills, and all mines, minerals and quarries, according to their present rights therein, felons goods, deodands, waifs, estrays and wrecks at sea, together with the patronage of the bishoprick, and of the other ecclesiastical benefices in the said island, to which they were then intitled, to be holden of the crown by the honourable service above-mentioned: and whereas by a certain contract or agreement in writing, bearing date the seventh day of *March*, in the year of our Lord one thousand seven hundred and sixty five, and duly executed under the hands and seals of four of the commissioners of his Majesty's treasury of the one part, and the said duke and dutchess of *Atholl*, Sir *Charles Frederick* and *Edmund Hoskins* of the other part, the said commissioners of the treasury contracted and agreed with the said duke and dutchess of *Atholl*, and the said Sir *Charles Frederick* and *Edmund Hoskins* their trustees, for the absolute purchase of the said island of *Man*, with its dependencies, except as therein is excepted, for the said price or sum of seventy thousand pounds of lawful money of *Great Britain*, to be paid in the manner, and at the time, therein mentioned: and whereas the said *David* lord viscount *Stormont* is now resident at *Vienna*, in the character of his Majesty's embassador extraordinary at that court; and whereas the said contract and agreement cannot be effectually established and carried into execution, without the authority of parliament:" be it enacted by the King's most excellent majesty, by and with the advice and consent of the lords spiritual and temporal, and commons in this present parliament assembled, and by the authority of the same, That from and immediately after the payment into the bank of *England* by his Majesty, his heirs or successors, in the names of the said *John* duke of *Atholl*, and *Charlotte* duchess of *Atholl* his wife baroness *Strange*, Sir *Charles Frederick* and *Edmund Hoskins*, or the survivors or survivor of them, of the sum of seventy thousand pounds of lawful money of *Great Britain*, free and clear of all taxes, impositions, fees, rewards and other deductions whatsoever, on or before the first day of *June* in the year of our Lord one thousand seven hundred and sixty five (to be by them the said *John* duke of *Atholl*, and *Charlotte* his wife baroness *Strange*, Sir *Charles Frederick* and *Edmund Hoskins*; or the survivors or survivor of them, and the executors and administrators of such survivor, paid, applied, and disposed of, for the uses, intents and purposes, expressed and contained in the said indenture or deed of feoffment, bearing date the sixth day of *April*, one thousand seven hundred and fifty six) the said island, castle, pele and lordship of *Man*, and all the islands and lordships to the said island of *Man* appertaining, together with the royalties, regalities, franchises, liberties, and sea ports, to the same belonging, and all other the hereditaments and premisses comprized, mentioned and granted, in the said letters patent, bearing date respectively the sixth day of *April* in the seventh year of the reign of King *Henry* the Fourth, the twenty eighth day of *June* in the seventh year of the reign of King *James* the First, and the second day of *May*, in the eighth year of the reign of the same King *James* the First, and the said statute or act of parliament made in the said eighth year of the reign of the said King *James* the First, and every or any of them (except as herein after is excepted) shall be, and they are hereby, unalienably vested in his Majesty, his heirs and successors, freed and discharged, and absolutely acquitted, exempted and indemnified, of, from and against all estates, uses, trusts, intails, reversions, remainders, limitations, charges, incumbrances, titles, claims and demands whatsoever, from, by or under the said letters patent and act of parliament, and every or any of them, or from, by or under any other means, right or title whatsoever, as fully, freely and intirely, as if the said letters patent and act of parliament, and the estates, interests, hereditaments and premisses therein, or in any of them comprized, mentioned and granted, were herein again transcribed and repeated.

Upon payment by his Majesty into the bank of 70,000l. on or before 1 June, 1765, in the names of the duke and duchess of Atholl, Sir Cha. Frederic and Edm. Hoskins, the isle of Man, and the islands, &c. thereunto appertaining, &c. to vest unalienably in the crown.

II. And be it further enacted by the authority aforesaid, That the receipt or receipts of the proper clerk or cashier, clerks or cashiers of the governor and company of the bank of *England*, under his or their hand or hands respectively, testifying the payment of the said sum of seventy thousand pounds, or any part thereof, by the said commissioners of the treasury, or such person or persons as they, or any three of them, shall order

Cashier's receipt, testifying the payment of the said sum,

der and direct to pay the same, into the said bank of *England*, in the names of the said duke and duchess of *Atholl*, Sir *Charles Frederick* and *Edmund Hoskins*, or the survivors or survivor of them, shall be a sufficient discharge to his Majesty, his heirs and successors, of and for the said sum of seventy thousand pounds, or so much thereof as such receipt or receipts shall be given for; and that his Majesty, his heirs and successors, upon and after such receipt or receipts given as aforesaid, shall be absolutely acquitted and discharged of and from the said monies, notwithstanding any subsequent loss, non-application or misapplication of the same, or any part thereof.

to be a sufficient discharge to his Majesty.

III. Provided always, That the lands which shall be purchased with the said sum of seventy thousand pounds, or any part thereof, pursuant to the trusts, intents and purposes, expressed and contained in the said indenture or deed of feoffment, bearing date the sixth day of *April* one thousand seven hundred and fifty six, and till such purchase shall be made, the said sum of seventy thousand pounds, or such part thereof as shall not be so invested in the purchase of lands as aforesaid, shall be and continue subject to such and the same estates, interests, rights, titles, claims and demands, and no other, as any person or persons, bodies politick or corporate, had and enjoyed at the time of the passing of this act, of, in, to or out of the said island, castle, pele and lordship of *Man*, or any other the hereditaments and premisses hereby vested in his Majesty, or could or ought to have had or enjoyed, in case this act had never been made.

The said sum, or the lands which shall be purchased therewith, pursuant to the trusts expressed in the deed of feoffment of 6 April, 1756, are to be subject to the same estates, &c. as the said island.

IV. Provided also, and it is hereby further declared and enacted by the authority aforesaid, That nothing in this act contained shall extend, or be construed to extend, to vest in his Majesty, his heirs or successors, the patronage of the bishoprick of the said island of *Man*, or of the bishoprick of *Soder*, or of the bishoprick of *Soder* and *Man*, or the temporalties of the said bishoprick or bishopricks, whenever it or they shall become vacant; or the right of advowson, patronage, presentation, collation, donation, nomination or free disposition, of or to any archdeaconries, canonries, prebends, colleges, hospitals, churches, chapels, rectories, vicarages or other ecclesiastical benefices or promotions whatsoever, within the said island, lordship and territory of *Man*, or the dependencies thereof, or any hundreds, wapentakes, manors, towns, vills, churches, monasteries, abbies, priories, or the scites, circuits or precincts thereof, farms, messuages, houses, granges, tofts, cottages, curtilages, barns, stables, mills, dove-houses, orchards, fruiteries, gardens, lands, demesne lands, glebe lands, meadows, leasows, feedings, pastures, woodlands, woods, underwoods, coppices, trees or the soil or ground thereof, wastes, void grounds, roads, paths, heaths, furzes, moors, marshes, mines of lead or iron or other base metals, collieries, quarries, inland waters, pools, fish ponds, watercourses, streams, rivulets, aqueducts, rents, arrearages of rent, rent services, rent charges, rents seck, rents reserved, annual farm rents, fee farm rents, rents of assize, annuities, herriots,

Reservation of patronage, and other rights not vested in the crown;

riots, services or works of tenants either free or customary, rectories, tythes or impropriations of tythes either great or small, predial, personal or mixed, portions of tythes, pensions, oblations, obventions, commons, frankfolds, estovers, commons of estovers, turbaries, ways, passages, easements, forests, parks, liberties of parks, chases, lawns, warrens, assarts, purprestures, chiminages, hawkings, huntings, piscaries, fishings, fairs, fair days, markets, stallages, tolls, multures, waifs, estrays, deodands, wrecks of the sea, assize or assay of bread, wine or beer, fealties, reliefs, escheats, forfeitures, goods and chattels of traitors, felons, clerks convict, fugitives, persons convicted, attainted, condemned, outlawed, put in exigent or standing mute, suits of tenants, courts baron, profits or perquisites of courts baron, fines, amerciaments or any thing to courts baron appertaining, or any profits, commodities, advantages, emoluments or appurtenances, spiritual or temporal, to the said reserved and excepted premisses, or any of them, belonging, incident, appendant or in any wise appertaining, or any interest therein in possession, remainder or reversion within the said island of *Man*, or any of the islands and dependencies to the same belonging; but that the same, and every part thereof, shall stand and be fully and clearly excepted and reserved out of this act, and all and every the provisions herein contained; and shall be, remain and continue, vested in such and the same person and persons, for such and the same estate or estates, and to and for such and the sames uses, intents and purposes, as if this act had never been made; and shall be holden of his Majesty, his heirs and successors, by the said honorary service of rendering to his Majesty's heirs and successors, Kings and Queens of *England*, two falcons on the days of their respective coronations; and at and under the said yearly rent of one hundred and one pounds, fifteen shillings and eleven pence, to be paid at the receipt of his Majesty's exchequer at *Westminster*, in manner and form aforesaid.

but to be held by usual honorary service; and yearly rent of 101l. 15s. 11d.

Publick act.

V. And be it further enacted by the authority aforesaid, That this act shall be deemed, adjudged and taken to be a publick act; and shall be judicially taken notice of as such, by all judges, justices, and all other persons whatsoever.

THE

L E

ct.

ABSTRAC Tom the Year 1754 to the Year

Years.	Land Revenue c Amount.		venue Abbey alties.	The Income of Lands in the Hands of the Lord of the *Isle*, including the Rent of *Calf Isle*.			Total.		
1754	£. 1,376	9	5	101	6	6 ¼	7,905	17	7
1755	1,380	13	5	98	2	2	6,967	18	2
1756	1,405	16	5	97	18	8	6,785	4	5
1757	1,424	19	5	102	15	11	7,270		10
1758	1,395	16	5	99	6	8	7,170	6	5
1759	1,396	7	5	107	19	1	10,091	12	4
1760	1,439	17	5	135	4	2	9,606	18	5
1761	1,376	0	5	106	8	9	11,596	10	1
1762	1,375	6	5	107	8	9	8,486	9	3
1763	1,409	17	5	107	8	9	9,204	8	9
	£. 13,981	4	0	1,063	19	5 ¼	85,085	6	6

The wh*anks*, £. 7 *Manks* makes £. (
*Briti*72,930 5 7 which, at a Me
dium

CAP. XXVII.

An act to provide for the administration of the government, in case the crown should descend to any of the children of his Majesty, being under the age of eighteen years; and for the care and guardianship of their persons.

Most gracious Sovereign,

WHEREAS *your Majesty, from a tender concern for your faithful subjects, and anxious desire to provide for every possible event which may affect their future happiness or security, hath been graciously pleased to communicate from the throne to both houses of parliament, that your Majesty's late indisposition (which filled the breasts of all your subjects with the most alarming apprehensions) had led your Majesty to consider the situation in which your kingdoms and your family might be left, if it should please God to put a period to your Majesty's life, whilst your successor is of tender years; and that the high importance of this subject to the publick safety, good order and tranquility, the paternal affection which your Majesty bears to your children and to all your people, and your earnest desire that every precaution should be taken which may tend to preserve the constitution of* Great Britain *undisturbed, and the dignity and lustre of its crown unimpaired, had determined your Majesty to lay this weighty business before your parliament; to whose most serious deliberation your Majesty was pleased to recommend the making such provisions as would be necessary, in case any of your children should succeed to the throne before they should respectively attain the age of eighteen years; and to this end, your Majesty was also pleased to propose to their consideration, whether under the present circumstances, it would not be expedient to vest in your Majesty the power of appointing, from time to time, by instruments in writing under your sign manual, either the Queen or any other person of your royal family, usually residing in* Great Britain, *to be the guardian of the person of such successor, and the regent of these kingdoms, until such successor shall attain the age of eighteen years; subject to the like restrictions and regulations as are specified and contained in an act passed upon a similar occasion, in the twenty fourth year of the reign of his late Majesty your royal grandfather; and that the regent so appointed should be assisted by a council of regency, to be established by authority of parliament: and whereas in return for this paternal goodness, expressed in so early and provident a care for an event so truly deplorable, and being filled with the most cordial sense of duty and gratitude to your Majesty, for the tender concern and regard which your Majesty has always, and now more especially, demonstrated for the happiness of your people, and the lasting security of their religion, laws and liberties, we have taken this important business into our most serious consideration; and being justly alarmed at the unhappy situation in which these kingdoms and your Majesty's royal family would be left, in case it should please Almighty God to put a period to your Majesty's inestimable life (for the long and glorious continuance of which we offer up our daily and most fer-* Preamble.

fervent prayers to heaven) before your royal successor shall be of sufficient years to support the weight of government; and being likewise thoroughly convinced of the wisdom and expediency of what your Majesty has thought fit to propose upon this weighty occasion, are fully and zealously determined to contribute every thing in our power to the firm and lasting establishment of the protestant succession, as settled by the laws of the land, in your Majesty's royal family, the auspicious encrease of which we consider as the bulwark of our civil and religious liberties, and the pledge of perpetual security to the laws and constitution of Great Britain: we therefore your Majesty's most dutiful and loyal subjects, the lords spiritual and temporal, and commons in parliament assembled, do most humbly beseech your Majesty that it may be enacted, and be it enacted by the King's most excellent majesty, by and with the advice and consent of the lords spiritual and temporal, and commons, in this present parliament assembled, and by the authority of the same,

Power vested in his Majesty of appointing, from time to time, by three instruments under his sign manual, a guardian to his successor, in case the crown shall descend to any of his children being under the age of eighteen years.

That whensoever and as often as the imperial crown of this realm shall descend to his royal highness *George Augustus Frederick* prince of *Wales*, the eldest son of his present Majesty (whom *God* long preserve) or to any other of the children of his present Majesty, now born or hereafter to be born, if at the respective times of such descent, his said royal highness *George Augustus Frederick* prince of *Wales*, or such other of the said children succeeding to the crown as aforesaid, shall be under the age of eighteen years, such person (subject to the restrictions herein after-mentioned) as his present Majesty, by three instruments under his royal sign manual, revocable, from time to time, at his will and pleasure (to be sealed and deposited in such manner and with such persons as herein after-mentioned) shall nominate and appoint, shall be the guardian, and have the care, tuition and education of the person of his said royal highness *George Augustus Frederick* prince of *Wales*, or such other successor as aforesaid, until his said royal highness or such other successor shall have attained his or her respective age of eighteen years; and

Such guardian to have the care of and management of the tuition of the person of such minor,

that such guardian shall, till his said royal highness, or such other successor, shall have attained such respective age, have the disposition, ordering, and management, of all matters and things relating to the said care, tuition, and education; and that such person so nominated and appointed as aforesaid, shall, during such time as his said royal highness *George Augustus Frederick* prince of *Wales*, or such other successor as aforesaid, shall respectively be under the said age of eighteen years, and no longer, have full power and authority, in the name of his said royal highness, or such other successor, and in his or her stead,

and to execute the office of regent of the kingdom;

and under the stile and title of *Regent of the kingdom*, to exercise and administer, according to the laws and constitution of *Great Britain*, the regal power and government of this realm, and of all the dominions, countries, and territories, to the crown of *Great Britain* belonging; and shall use, execute, and perform, all prerogatives, authorities, and acts of government, and administration of government, which belong to the King or Queen of this realm

realm to use, execute, and perform, according to the laws thereof; but in such manner, and subject to such conditions, restrictions, limitations, and regulations, as are herein after for that purpose specified, mentioned, and contained.

II. Provided always, and be it further enacted by the authority aforesaid, That no person shall be capable of being so nominated and appointed to be guardian and regent as aforesaid, other than and except her present Majesty our most gracious Queen *Charlotte* his Majesty's royal consort, or her royal highness *Augusta* princess dowager of *Wales*, or other than and except some one person of his Majesty's royal family, descended from the late King his Majesty's royal grandfather, whose usual residence, at the time of passing this act, shall have been, and from thenceforth, until such nomination and appointment, shall continue to be, in *Great Britain*.

and to be either the Queen, or princess dowager of Wales, or one of the descendants of the late King, usually residing in Great Britain.

III. Provided nevertheless, That it shall and may be lawful for his Majesty to nominate and appoint, in and by such instruments as aforesaid, any number of persons, under the restrictions aforesaid, (as to his royal wisdom shall seem meet) severally to succeed each other in the guardianship and regency aforesaid, by way of substitution, in case the person or persons first nominated and appointed shall happen to die, during such time as his said royal highness, or such other successor as aforesaid, shall respectively be under the age of eighteen years; but so as that no more than one person shall at any one time be intitled to such guardianship and regency as aforesaid.

A number in succession, by way of substitution, in case of death, may be nominated to succeed in the guardianship and regency; but no more than one person may act as such at one time.

IV. Provided always, and be it enacted by the authority aforesaid, That no person so nominated and appointed to be guardian and regent as aforesaid, shall be capable of succeeding to, or holding such office of guardian and regent, unless the usual residence of such person, from the time of such nomination and appointment, to the time of his or her succeeding to such office of guardian and regent, shall continue to be in *Great Britain*; and in case any person shall become so disqualified by non-residence as aforesaid, or in case any person so nominated and appointed as aforesaid, who shall have succeeded to, and shall be in the actual exercise of, the said office of guardian and regent, shall not afterwards continue to be resident in *Great Britain*; or in case any person so nominated and appointed to be guardian and regent as aforesaid, shall at any time marry a papist; then, and in every such case, such nomination and appointment of the said person shall cease and determine in the same manner as if such person were naturally dead.

And any such persons are disqualified to act as guardians and regents by non-residence, or by marrying a papist.

V. And be it further enacted by the authority aforesaid, That the said three instruments of nomination and appointment being sealed up under three several covers with any seal which his Majesty shall think fit to make use of for that purpose, shall each be sealed also with the several seals of the archbishop of *Canterbury* for the time being, of the lord chancellor or lord keeper or the first commissioner named in any commission then sub-

Instruments of nomination to be sealed with the King's seal; and the seals of the archbishop of Canterbury, lord chancellor, and president of the council; and to be severally deposited with them: subsisting for the custody of the great seal of *Great Britain* for the time being, and of the president of the council for the time being; and one of the said instruments shall be lodged and deposited in the hands of the said archbishop for the time being, another in the hands of the said lord chancellor or lord keeper or first commissioner for the custody of the great seal for the time being, and the third in the hands of the said president of the council for the time being:

But upon the revocation or alteration of such instruments by the King; or death of any of the depositaries, they are to be delivered up; and if his Majesty shall be willing to revoke or alter his nomination or appointment made as aforesaid, and shall by three writings, under his hand and seal, require the said instruments so deposited as aforesaid, to be delivered up to some person or persons thereby authorized to receive the same, then, and in such case, the persons with whom the said instruments shall be deposited as aforesaid, and every of them, and in case of the deaths of any of them, their executors and administrators respectively, and every other person in whose custody any of the said instruments shall happen to be, shall deliver up the same accordingly;

as likewise, in case of removal of any of the said officers of state; and in case the said archbishop of *Canterbury*, or the said lord chancellor, lord keeper, or first commissioner for the custody of the great seal, or the said president of the council, shall die, or be removed from their said offices, before the re-delivery of such instruments as aforesaid, the persons so removed, and the executors and administrators of the person so dying, and every person in whose custody such instrument shall happen to be, shall deliver the same with all convenient speed to the successor or successors of the person so dying or being removed:

and on the demise of the King, during such minority, the privy council is to assemble, and the said instruments to be there produced and read. and after the demise of his Majesty, whensoever and as often as such successor or successors respectively shall be under the age of eighteen years, the said three persons, their executors or administrators, and all other persons in whose custody the said instruments shall then be, shall immediately bring the same before the privy council then existing, which it is hereby enacted shall be forthwith, on such demise, assembled; and such instruments shall be there opened and read, and presently afterwards inrolled in the high court of chancery.

Person guilty of opening any of the said instruments, without his Majesty's order, or refusing to deliver up the same to the privy council, incurs the penalties of premunire. VI. And be it further enacted by the authority aforesaid, That if any of the said persons with whom the said instruments shall be so deposited, or any of their executors or administrators, or any other person having the custody thereof, shall open any of the said instruments in the life of his present Majesty, without his Majesty's order; or shall wilfully neglect or refuse to produce and deliver the same to the privy council; every person so offending, neglecting, or refusing, shall incur the pains and penalties of premunire inflicted by the statute of premunire made in the sixteenth year of the reign of King *Richard* the Second.

One of the instruments being produced, deemed effectual to give authority to VII. And be it further enacted by the authority aforesaid, That if all the said three instruments shall not be produced before the said privy council as aforesaid; then any one or two of the said instruments so produced, shall be effectual to give such autho-

authority as aforesaid to the person and persons successively therein respectively named.

VIII. And be it further enacted by the authority aforesaid, That all acts of regal power, prerogative, government, or administration of government, of what nature or kind soever, which shall be done or executed by any King or Queen so succeeding as aforesaid, under his or her respective age of eighteen years, during the regency established by this act, otherwise than by and with the consent and authority of the said regent, in the manner, and according to the directions of this act set forth and prescribed; shall be absolutely null and void to all intents and purposes.

IX. And be it further enacted by the authority aforesaid, That in order to assist the said regent in the administration of the government, there shall be, during the time that such successor or successors respectively shall be under the age of eighteen years, a council to be called *The Council of Regency*, which shall consist of their royal highnesses his Majesty's brothers *Edward Augustus* duke of *York* and *Albany*, *William Henry* duke of *Gloucester* and *Edinburgh*, prince *Henry Frederick*, and prince *Frederick William*, and his royal highness his Majesty's uncle *William Augustus* duke of *Cumberland* (the said prince *Henry Frederick* and prince *Frederick William* to be members of the said council of regency when they shall respectively attain the age of twenty one years, and not sooner) and also of the persons and officers following; that is to say, the archbishop of *Canterbury* for the time being; the lord chancellor or lord keeper, or the first commissioner named in any commission then subsisting for the custody of the great seal of *Great Britain* for the time being; the lord treasurer of *Great Britain*, or the first commissioner named in any commission then subsisting for executing that office for the time being; the lord president of the council for the time being; the lord privy seal for the time being; the lord high admiral of *Great Britain*, or the first commissioner named in any commission then subsisting for executing that office for the time being; the two principal secretaries of state for the time being; and the lord chief justice of the court of *King's* or *Queen's Bench* for the time being: and if it shall happen that all or any of their said royal highnesses *Edward Augustus* duke of *York* and *Albany*, *William Henry* duke of *Gloucester* and *Edinburgh*, prince *Henry Frederick*, prince *Frederick William*, and *William Augustus* duke of *Cumberland*, shall depart this life during the reign of his present Majesty; or if any of them shall be nominated and appointed by his Majesty, to be the said regent of the kingdom immediately on the demise of his Majesty, while such successor shall be under the age of eighteen years; then, and in any of such cases, it shall and may be lawful to and for his Majesty, by three instruments under his royal sign manual, revocable at his will and pleasure, from time to time, to nominate and appoint some one person, being a natural born subject of this realm, to be a member of the said council of regency, in the room or place of each and every of their said royal highnesses so dying, or being constituted

[Margin notes:]

the person nominated regent.

All acts of regal power, done otherwise than by consent and authority of the regent, declared void.

Council of regency established to assist the regent.

But if any of the King's brothers, or his uncle, shall die, during his Majesty's reign, or shall be nominated regent on his demise; his Majesty, by 3 instruments under his sign manual, sealed and deposited as aforesaid, and revocable at pleasure, may appoint some other person to be of the council;

ſtituted immediate regent as aforeſaid; which ſaid three laſt mentioned inſtruments ſhall be ſealed up and depoſited in the ſame manner, and with the ſame perſons, as is herein before directed with reſpect to the three firſt mentioned inſtruments which ſhall contain his Majeſty's nomination and appointment of the regent aforeſaid; and the perſon and perſons with whom the ſaid three laſt mentioned inſtruments ſhall be depoſited, their executors and adminiſtrators, ſhall reſpectively keep, diſpoſe of, and produce the ſame unopened, in ſuch and the ſame manner, to ſuch and the ſame perſons, at ſuch and the ſame times and places, and under ſuch and the ſame penalties, as are herein before ſpecified, directed, and enacted, with reſpect to the ſaid three firſt mentioned inſtruments, which ſhall contain his Majeſty's nomination and appointment of the regent aforeſaid.

and ſuch inſtruments of nomination are to be produced unopened to the privy council.

The council is to meet as the regent ſhall direct; and five (where it is not otherwiſe ſpecially provided) may act.

X. And be it further enacted by the authority aforeſaid, That the ſaid council of regency ſhall, from time to time, meet and ſit as the ſaid regent for the time being ſhall be pleaſed to direct; and that any five of the ſaid council, but not any leſs number, being ſo aſſembled, ſhall be ſufficient to act as ſuch council of regency; and all acts to be done by a major part of the council ſo aſſembled, ſhall be deemed to be acts of the council of regency, excepting in ſuch particular caſes, wherein it is otherwiſe provided by this act.

An oath of office is to be taken by the regent;

XI. And be it further enacted by the authority aforeſaid, That the ſaid regent for the time being, before he or ſhe ſhall act or enter upon the ſaid office of regent, or within one calendar month after, ſhall take the following oath of office; that is to ſay,

I A. B. *do ſolemnly promiſe and ſwear, That I will truly and faithfully execute the office of regent of the kingdom of* Great Britain, *according to an act of parliament made in the fifth year of the reign of his majeſty King* George *the Third, intituled,* An act to provide for the adminiſtration of the government, in caſe the crown ſhould deſcend to any of the children of his Majeſty, being under the age of eighteen years, and for the care and guardianſhip of their perſons; *and that I will adminiſter the government of this realm, and of all the dominions thereunto belonging, according to the laws, cuſtoms, and ſtatutes thereof; and will in all things, to the utmoſt of my power and ability, conſult and maintain the ſafety, honour, and dignity, of his or her* (as the caſe ſhall require) *Majeſty, and the welfare of his or her* (as the caſe ſhall require) *people.*

So help me God.

and by each member of the council,

and each of the members of the ſaid council of regency, and their ſucceſſors, ſhall, before they ſhall reſpectively act in or enter upon their reſpective offices as members of the ſaid council, take the following oath of office; that is to ſay,

I A. B. *do ſolemnly promiſe and ſwear, That I will truly and faithfully ſerve his or her* (as the caſe ſhall require) *Majeſty in the*

office

office of one of the council of regency, established by an act of parliament made in the fifth year of the reign of his majesty King George *the Third, intituled,* An act to provide for the administration of the government, in case the crown should descend to any of the children of his Majesty, being under the age of eighteen years, and for the care and guardianship of their persons; *and that I will duly and faithfully execute the said office, according to the true intent and meaning of the said act; and that in all matters and things, which shall be moved, debated, and considered, in the council of regency, I will truly and faithfully declare my mind and opinion, according to my heart and conscience, and the best of my judgement; and will support, maintain, and defend the person, honour, crown, and dignity, of his or her* (as the case shall require) *Majesty, to the utmost of my power.*

So help me God.

to be administered by the privy council, and entered in the council books.

Each of which oaths shall be taken before the privy council then in being, who are hereby required and impowered to administer the same, and to enter the same in the council books.

The regent and council are to qualify themselves as for offices and places of trust.

XII. And be it further enacted by the authority aforesaid, That the said regent for the time being, and every person who shall be of the council of regency, by virtue of this act, and of the powers hereby given, shall be deemed and taken to be persons having and executing offices or places of trust within *England*, and take and subscribe such oaths, make and subscribe such declaration, and do all such acts as are required by the laws and statutes of this kingdom, to qualify persons to hold and continue in offices and places of trust, within such times, and in such manner, and under such pains, penalties, forfeitures, and disabilities, as in and by the said laws and statutes are required.

The regent taking and subscribing the oaths and declaration before the privy council; and receiving the sacrament in one of the royal chapels.

XIII. Provided nevertheless, and be it enacted by the authority aforesaid, That it shall be lawful for the said regent for the time being, to take and subscribe the said oaths, and make and subscribe such declaration, in and before the privy council, and the certificate of his or her having received the sacrament of the Lord's supper in any of the royal chapels, signed by the person administering the same, shall be registered in the said privy council; and such taking and subscribing the said oaths, and making and subscribing the said declaration, and taking the said sacrament, shall be to all intents and purposes as effectual, as if the same had been taken, made, and subscribed, in the manner now required by law, for the qualification of persons to hold and continue in offices and places of trust.

Upon his Majesty's demise, during the minority of his successor, the privy to council is meet, and cause such successor to be proclaim-

XIV. And be it further enacted by the authority aforesaid, That whensoever his present Majesty (whom God long preserve) shall happen to demise, leaving such successor as aforesaid under the age of eighteen years, the privy council for the kingdom of *Great Britain* in being at the time of such demise shall, with all convenient speed, assemble, and cause such next successor, intitled to the crown of *Great Britain*, by virtue of an act of the twelfth year of the reign of King *William* the Third (intituled, *An*

ed, pursuant to act 12 W. 3.

An act for the further limitation of the crown, and better securing the rights and liberties of the subject) to be openly and solemnly proclaimed in the usual manner in *Great Britain* and *Ireland*; and that all and every member and members of the said privy council, wilfully neglecting or refusing to cause such proclamations to made, shall be guilty of high treason, and suffer upon conviction thereof pains of death, and all other losses and forfeitures, as in cases of high treason.

upon pain of incurring the penalties of high treason.

The consent of the majority of five or more of the council is necessary to make good all creations, pardons, gifts, grants, dispositions, instructions, orders, or authorities.

XV. Provided always, and be it enacted by the authority aforesaid, That in the creation of all peerages of *Great Britain* or *Ireland*, in the pardoning of all crimes of high treason, and in the gift, grant, and disposition, of all archbishopricks and bishopricks in *England* or *Ireland*, and of the offices of lord chancellor, or lord keeper, or commissioners for the custody of the great seal of *Great Britain* or *Ireland*, of lord treasurer or treasurers of the exchequer, or commissioners for executing the office of treasurer of the exchequer, of lord president of the council, lord privy seal, lord high admiral, or commissioners for executing the office of lord high admiral, the principal secretaries of state, master of the rolls in *Great Britain* and *Ireland*, and of all the judges of the courts of *King's* or *Queen's Bench* and *Common Pleas*, and barons of the courts of *Exchequer* in *England* and *Ireland*; and of the judges of the court of *Session*, court of *Justiciary*, and barons of the court of *Exchequer* in *Scotland*, and in the giving instructions, orders, and authorities, for the making any treaties with any foreign powers; the consent of the said council of regency, or the major part of any five or more of them so assembled as aforesaid, shall be necessary to make the said creations, pardons, gifts, grants, dispositions, instructions, orders, or authorities, good and effectual.

The regent disabled to make war or peace; to ratify treaties; or to prorogue, adjourn, or dissolve the parliament, without the consent of the majority of the council.

XVI. Provided also, and be it enacted by the authority aforesaid, That it shall not be lawful for the said regent for the time being, to make war or peace; to ratify any treaty with any foreign power; or to prorogue, adjourn, or dissolve, any parliament, without the consent of the major part of the whole council of regency then in being, and in *Great Britain*, in case there shall then be an unequal number in *Great Britain*; and if the number then in *Great Britain*, shall be an equal number then, without the consent of one half part of the said council; and that the said regent for the time being, either with or without the consent of the said council of regency, shall not give, or have power to give, the royal assent to any bill or bills in parliament, for repealing, changing, or in any respect varying from the order and course of succession to the crown of this realm, as the same stands now established in the illustrious house of *Hanover*, by the said act of the twelfth year of the reign of King *William* the Third, (intituled, *An act for the further limitation of the crown, and better securing the rights and liberties of the subject*) or to any act for repealing or altering the act made in the thirteenth year of the reign of King *Charles* the Second (intituled, *An act for the uniformity of publick prayers, and administration of sacraments, and other rites*

Nor may the regent give the royal assent to any act for altering the succession to the crown, as established by act 12 W. 3.

rites and ceremonies; and for establishing the form of making, ordaining, and consecrating, bishops, priests, and deacons, in the church of England) or one act of the fifth year of the reign of Queen *Anne*, made in *Scotland* (intituled, *An act for securing the protestant religion and presbyterian church government.*)

or for repealing or altering the act of 13 Car. 2. or of 5 Annæ.

XVII. Provided also, and be it further enacted by the authority aforesaid, That the archbishop of *Canterbury*, or any other person appointed by this act to be of the said council of regency, in virtue or by reason of his dignity or office, shall continue no longer of the said council than he shall continue in such his said dignity or office, and his successor in such dignity or office shall become one of the said council; and that the lord chancellor or lord keeper, or first commissioner for the custody of the great seal for the time being, the lord treasurer or first commissioner of the treasury for the time being, the lord president of the council for the time being, the lord privy seal for the time being, the lord high admiral or first commissioner of the admiralty for the time being, and the two principal secretaries of state for the time being, so appointed to be of the said council of regency by this act, shall continue in their said respective offices, after such descent of the crown to any of the children of his Majesty, during the time that such King or Queen shall respectively remain under the age of eighteen years, as well after as before the expiration of six months from the time of such descent, unless removed by the said regent for the time being, with the consent of a major part of the whole council of regency then in being, and in *Great Britain*, in case there shall then be an unequal number in *Great Britain*; and if the number then in *Great Britain* shall be an equal number, then with the consent of one half part of the said council; or upon the address of both houses of parliament, in which latter case the said regent for the time being alone may remove any of the said officers against whom such address shall be presented.

Members who are appointed of the council, in virtue of their dignity or office, are to be no longer of the council, than they continue in such dignity or office.

Great officers of state appointed of the council, are to continue in their offices, in case of the descent of the crown during such minority, for six months after; unless removed by consent of the majority of the council; or upon address of both houses of parliament.

XVIII. Provided nevertheless, That the archbishop of *Canterbury* for the time being, and the lord chief justice of the court of *King's* or *Queen's Bench* for the time being, notwithstanding their remaining in such dignity and office respectively, may be removed from being of the council of regency by the said regent for the time being, with the consent of the major part of the council of regency then in being, and in *Great Britain*, in case there shall then be an unequal number in *Great Britain*; and if the number then in *Great Britain* shall be an equal number, then with the consent of one half part of the said council; or upon the address of both houses of parliament; and that any other of the members of the said council not so appointed in virtue or by reason of their dignities or offices, may be removed likewise by the said regent for the time being, with the like consent; or upon the address of both houses of parliament; and within two calendar months after such descent of the crown as aforesaid, in case any vacancy or vacancies of any of the said offices shall happen then to be, and within the space of two calendar months after

Archbishop of Canterbury, & lord chief justice of the King's Bench, may be removed, in like manner, from the council; as also any other members who are not constituted such in virtue of their dignities or offices.

vacancies in the council,

after every vacancy which ſhall happen by means of ſuch removal, or by the death or reſignation of any member of the ſaid council of regency, or by any ſuch member's ſucceeding to the office of regent, or by the death of either of their ſaid royal highneſſes prince *Henry Frederick*, and prince *Frederick William*, under the age of twenty one years, the ſaid regent for the time being ſhall and is required, with the conſent of the council of regency, or the major part of thoſe preſent, not being leſs than five, to fill up ſuch vacancy by the appointment of a new officer, where the vacancy happens by the death, removal or reſignation, of one of the members of the ſaid council ſo appointed in virtue or by reaſon of his dignity or office; or by the appointment of a new member of the ſaid council, being a natural-born ſubject of this realm, where the vacancy happens by the death or removal, or reſignation of any member, not being one of the officers named in this act, or by any ſuch member's ſucceeding to the office of regent, or by the death of either of their ſaid royal highneſſes prince *Henry Frederick*, and prince *Frederick William*, under the age of twenty one years, or by the reſignation or removal of the archbiſhop of *Canterbury*, or of the lord chief juſtice of the *King's* or *Queen's Bench*, from being of the ſaid council of regency.

by removal, death, or reſignation, or by ſucceeding to the office of regent, or by death of the King's younger brothers, being under age, are to be filled up within two months, by the regent and council.

XIX. Provided always, and be it enacted by the authority aforeſaid, That nothing herein contained ſhall take away or prejudice the rights, authorities, powers, and juriſdictions, of the privy council; but the ſaid regent for the time being ſhall have full power to ſummon and hold, or to cauſe the ſame to be ſummoned and holden, in the uſual manner; and any of the members of the ſaid council of regency may be and continue of the privy council alſo.

Rights of the privy council reſerved; and the regent impowered to ſummon and hold the ſame as uſual; and members of the regency may be alſo of the privy council.

XX. And be it further enacted by the authority aforeſaid, That whenſoever, and as often as, the crown ſhall deſcend to ſuch ſucceſſor as aforeſaid, being under the age of eighteen years, in caſe a parliament ſhall be then in being, which ſhall have met and ſat, ſuch parliament ſhall continue for three years, from the time of ſuch deſcent, unleſs ſuch ſucceſſor, to whom the crown ſhall deſcend as aforeſaid, ſhall ſooner attain his or her age of eighteen years; or ſuch parliament ſhall be ſooner diſſolved by the ſaid regent for the time being with the conſent of a major part of the council of regency, then in being, and in *Great Britain*, in caſe there ſhall then be an unequal number in *Great Britain*, and if the number then in *Great Britain* ſhall be an equal number, then with the conſent of one half part of the ſaid council; and in caſe at the time of ſuch deſcent, there ſhall be no parliament in being, which ſhall have met and ſat, then the laſt preceding parliament ſhall immediately convene and ſit at *Weſtminſter*, and be a parliament to continue for three years as aforeſaid, to all intents and purpoſes, as if the ſame had never been diſſolved; unleſs ſuch ſucceſſor ſhall ſooner attain his or her age of eighteen years, or ſuch parliament ſhall be ſooner diſ-

Upon deſcent of the crown to a minor, the parliament then in being is to continue for three years; unleſs ſuch ſucceſſor ſhall be ſooner of age; or ſuch parliament be diſſolved by the regent with conſent of the council; but if there ſhall be no parliament then in being, which ſhall

diſſolved by the ſaid regent for the time being, with ſuch conſent as laſt mentioned.

have met, and ſat, the preceding parliament is to convene, and ſit for three years; except as before excepted.

XXI. And be it further enacted by the authority aforeſaid, That his royal highneſs *George Auguſtus Frederick* prince of *Wales*, in caſe the crown ſhall deſcend or come to him before his age of eighteen; or any other of the children of his Majeſty, to whom the ſame ſhall deſcend before his or her age of eighteen years; ſhall not, during ſuch regency, be married to any perſon whatſoever, without the conſent of the ſaid regent for the time being, and of a major part of the ſaid council of regency then in being, and in *Great Britain*, in caſe there ſhall then be an unequal number in *Great Britain*, and if the number then in *Great Britain* ſhall be an equal number, then without the conſent of one half part of the ſaid council; and every marriage ſo had without ſuch conſent, ſhall be null and void to all intents and purpoſes; and every perſon who ſhall be acting, aiding, abetting, or concerned in obtaining, procuring, or bringing about, any ſuch marriage, and the perſon who ſhall be ſo married to ſuch King or Queen, under the age of eighteen years, ſhall be guilty of high treaſon, and ſuffer and forfeit as in caſes of high treaſon.

Succeſſor to the crown, being a minor, is not to be married during ſuch minority, without conſent of the regent and council; on pain of the marriage being void, and the perſons concerned therein incurring the penalty of high treaſon.

XXII. And be it further enacted by the authority aforeſaid, That in all caſes where the members of the council of regency ſhall be equally divided in their voices, the ſaid regent for the time being ſhall and may decide and determine the queſtion or matter concerning which they ſhall be ſo equally divided, if ſuch regent ſhall be pleaſed to give his or her own opinion thereupon.

In caſes of an equality of voices in the council, the regent is to decide.

XXIII. And be it further enacted by the authority aforeſaid, That in all caſes where the conſent of a major or one half part of the ſaid council of regency then in being, and in *Great Britain*, is by this act made neceſſary to the validity of any act, matter, or thing, ſuch conſent ſhall be ſigned by the reſpective members giving ſuch conſent in the council books; and that a clerk or clerks of the council of regency ſhall be appointed by the ſaid regent for the time being; and ſuch clerk or clerks ſhall provide books for entering the acts of ſuch council, and ſhall enter the ſame duly and faithfully, and ſhall keep the ſaid books, and ſhall be anſwerable for the ſame; and ſuch clerk or clerks, before he or they enter upon the execution of their ſaid office, ſhall take an oath before ſuch council, for the due execution of ſuch office or place reſpectively.

Where the conſent of a majority, or one half part of the council is made neceſſary to the validity of any act, the members conſenting thereto are to ſign the ſame in the council books.

Clerk of the council to be appointed by the regent; and take an oath of office.

XXIV. And be it further enacted by the authority aforeſaid, That all commiſſions, letters patent, orders, matters, and things, to be made, paſſed, had, or done, by the ſaid regent for the time being, either with or without the conſent of the ſaid council of regency, in order unlawfully to ſet aſide, change, or vary the order and method of government, and adminiſtration of government ſettled by this act, during the time that ſuch ſucceſ-

All commiſſions, &c. to ſet aſide, or change, the orders of government ſettled by this act, during the minority of the successor, are declared void; and the persons concerned therein incur the penalties of premunire.

for or successors respectively shall be under the age of eighteen years, shall be absolutely null and void to all intents and purposes; and every person advising, concurring, promoting, or assisting therein, shall incur the pains and penalties of *Premunire* inflicted by the said statute of *Premunire*.

CAP. XXVIII.

An act to impower the high court of Chancery *to lay out, upon government securities, a sum of money therein mentioned, out of the common and general cash in the bank of* England *belonging to the suitors of the said court; and to apply the interest arising therefrom, towards augmenting the income of the masters of the said court.*

Preamble.

WHEREAS *by an act of parliament, passed in the twelfth year of the reign of his late majesty King* George *the First intituled,* An act for relief of the suitors of the high court of *Chancery, it was, amongst other things enacted, That all the money and cash then deposited in the* Bank, *or that should at any time thereafter be paid into or deposited in the bank, on the account of the suitors of the court of* Chancery, *or any of them, or by order of the said court, should be accounted and taken to be one common and general cash, and should be promiscuously issued and issuable when and as the court of* Chancery *should direct, for the answering, paying, and clearing, the debts and demands of any of the suitors of the said court: and whereas, from many years experience, it hath been found, that there always hath been, and there now is, a very large sum of money, belonging to the suitors of the court of* Chancery, *which lies dead and unemployed in the bank: and whereas the offices of the masters in the court of* Chancery *are very ancient, and are offices of great trust and consequence to the suitors of the said court; and the profits belonging thereto are not adequate to the attendance, trouble, and importance, of the said offices:* wherefore, in order to make a further provision for the said offices, be it enacted by the King's most excellent majesty, by and with the advice and consent of the lords spiritual and temporal, and commons, in this present parliament assembled, and by the authority of the same, That out of the cash that now lies, or shall hereafter lie, dead and unemployed in the bank of *England*, belonging to the suitors of the court of *Chancery*, a sum not exceeding eighty thousand pounds shall and may, by virtue of any order or orders of the said court, to be made for that purpose, from time to time, be placed out in one entire sum, or in parcels, on such government or parliamentary securities, as in and by such order or orders shall be directed; to the intent that the interest and annual produce, arising from the money so to be placed out as aforesaid, may be applied for the purposes herein after mentioned; and that the said court of *Chancery* may, by order or orders of the said court, from time to time change the security or securities on which the said monies shall be so placed out as the said court shall think expedient.

The high court of chancery impowered to order the placing out occasionally, upon government securities, 80,000 l. out of the general cash in the bank belonging to the suitors of the court; and to change the securities as shall be expedient; the interest to be received

II. And be it further enacted, That the interest and annual pro-

produce arising from the said securities shall, from time to time, be received by the governor and company of the bank of *England*, and placed to the credit of an account to be raised in the books kept there for the suitors of the said court, of interest arising from money placed out in pursuance of this act; and that out of such interest and annual produce there shall be paid, by half-yearly payments, by the governor and company of the bank of *England*, by virtue of an order or orders of the court of *Chancery* to be made for that purpose, the annual sum of two hundred pounds to each and every of the eleven of the masters in ordinary of the said court of *Chancery*, free from parliamentary taxes; which said annual sums shall commence from the fifth day of *January*, in the year of our Lord one thousand seven hundred and sixty five; and that the residue of the interest and annual produce arising from the said securities, shall be accounted for, and taken, as part of the common and general cash of and belonging to the suitors of the said court of *Chancery*; and shall be issued and applied pursuant and according to the directions of the before recited act of parliament.

and accounted for by the bank; and 200l. *per annum* to be paid thereout half-yearly, by an order of court of Chancery, to each of the eleven masters of the court; to commence from 5 Jan. 1765; the surplus money to go to, and be accounted as part of, the general cash of the suitors.

III. Provided always, and be it further enacted and declared, That if, at any time hereafter, the whole, or any part of the said sum of eighty thousand pounds, shall be wanted, to answer any of the demands of the suitors of the said court of *Chancery*, then, and in such case, the said court may and shall direct the same, or any part thereof, to be called in, or the securities on which the same shall be placed to be disposed of, in order that the suitors of the said court may, at all times, be paid their respective demands, out of the common and general cash belonging to such suitors.

If the whole, or part of the sum so placed out to interest, shall be wanted, the court may call in the same, &c. that the suitors demands may be paid.

CAP. XXIX.

An act for repealing the duties now payable upon raw silk imported, and for granting other duties in lieu thereof; for allowing a drawback on the exportation of raw or thrown silk to Ireland, *and for prohibiting the exportation of raw silk from* Ireland.

WHEREAS *the throwing of silk has, till of late, been carried on to a very considerable extent in this kingdom, and has employed many thousands of poor persons of both sexes, and all ages: and whereas the lessening the duties now payable upon the importation of raw silk, would be an encouragement to the said business of throwing of silk in this kingdom:* therefore we your Majesty's most dutiful and loyal subjects, the commons of *Great Britain*, in parliament assembled, being desirous of encouraging the manufactures carried on in this kingdom, do humbly beseech your Majesty that it may be enacted, and be it enacted by the King's most excellent Majesty, by and with the advice and consent of the lords spiritual and temporal, in this present parliament assembled, and by the authority of the same, That from and after the twenty

Preamble.

From and after 24 June,

1765, the duties now payable on raw ſilk imported to ceaſe;

twenty fourth day of *June*, one thouſand ſeven hundred and ſixty five, the ſeveral rates, duties, ſubſidies, and impoſitions, payable upon the importation of raw ſilk into *Great Britain*, ſhall ceaſe, determine, and be no longer paid.

and the following duties to take place in lieu thereof;

II. And be it further enacted by the authority aforeſaid, That from and after the ſaid twenty fourth day of *June*, one thouſand ſeven hundred and ſixty five, the following duties ſhall be paid to his Majeſty, his heirs, and ſucceſſors, in lieu of the ſaid former duties; that is to ſay,

Viz. on raw ſilk, 24 oz. to the pound, 1 s. 3 d. per *lib.*

For every pound weight of raw ſilk imported into *Great Britain*, each pound containing twenty four ounces, the ſum of one ſhilling and three pence.

On thrown ſilk, 16 oz. to the pound, 6d. *per lib.* additional to all other duties.

And for every pound weight of thrown ſilk imported into *Great Britain*, each pound containing ſixteen ounces, the ſum of ſix pence; over and above all other rates and duties by any act or acts of parliament impoſed thereupon.

The ſaid duties to be collected and applied, as the duties upon Italian raw ſilk, &c.

III. And be it further enacted by the authority aforeſaid, That the ſeveral duties by this act granted, ſhall be raiſed, levied, collected, paid, and applied, in ſuch manner, and for the ſame purpoſes, as the duties hitherto payable upon *Italian* raw ſilk have been raiſed, levied, collected, paid, and applied; and all proviſions of or in every act, law, or ſtatute, now in force, for raiſing, levying, collecting, and paying, the duties by this act repealed, ſhall be in full force, and ſhall be put in execution, for raiſing, levying, collecting, and paying, the duties by this act granted, as fully and effectually, to all intents and purpoſes, as if the ſame had been particularly repeated and re-enacted in this act.

A drawback of 1 s. *per lib.* allowed on exportation of raw ſilk to *Ireland*;

IV. Provided always, and be it further enacted by the authority aforeſaid, That from and after the ſaid twenty fourth day of *June*, one thouſand ſeven hundred and ſixty five, upon the exportation to *Ireland* of any of the ſaid commodities, within the time allowed by law, for which the duties chargeable by this act ſhall have been firſt paid or ſecured, there ſhall be allowed a drawback of one ſhilling, and no more, upon every pound weight, containing twenty four ounces of ſuch raw ſilk, ſo exported; and of the whole of the ſaid additional duty on ſuch thrown ſilk ſo exported; which reſpective drawbacks ſhall be made or allowed according to ſuch rules and methods, as drawbacks are allowed by any law now in force relating to the cuſtoms.

and the whole of the additional duty on thrown ſilk.

No raw ſilk to be exported from Ireland, on penalty of forfeiture thereof, with the veſſel, and furniture, &c.

V. Provided alſo, and be it further enacted by the authority aforeſaid, That from and after the ſaid twenty fourth day of *June*, one thouſand ſeven hundred and ſixty five, no raw ſilk ſhall be exported from *Ireland*, upon pain that the ſame, together with the ſhip, boat, or veſſel, upon which any ſuch raw ſilk ſhall be exported, ſhipped, or laden to be exported, and all her guns, tackle, apparel, and furniture, ſhall be forfeited, and ſhall and may be ſeized by any officer of the cuſtoms or revenue in in *Ireland*; one moiety of all which forfeitures ſhall be to his Majeſty, his heirs and ſucceſſors, and the other moiety to him or them that ſhall ſue for the ſame; to be recovered in ſuch and the like manner as any forfeiture, incurred by any laws of the revenue, may be ſued for and recovered, in the kingdom of *Ireland*; and that the maſter and mariners of any ſuch ſhip, boat, or veſſel, wherein any ſuch offence ſhall be committed, knowing ſuch offence, and wittingly and willingly aiding and aſſiſting therein, and being thereof duly convicted, ſhall be impriſoned for the ſpace of three months without bail or mainprize.

and the maſter and crew aſſiſting, to be committed.

CAP. XXX.

An act for more effectually ſupplying the export trade of this kingdom to Africa, *with ſuch coarſe printed callicoes, and other goods of the product or manufacture of the* Eaſt Indies, *or other places beyond the* Cape of Good Hope, *as are prohibited to be worn and uſed in* Great Britain; *for encouraging the importation of bugles into this kingdom; for the better ſupply of the export trade thereof; and for diſcontinuing the bounty payable in* Great Britain, *and all bounties and allowances in* Ireland, *upon the exportation of corn, grain, malt, meal, and flour, from thence to the* Iſle of Man.

Preamble.

WHEREAS *the exporting to* Africa *coarſe printed callicoes, and other goods of the product or manufacture of the* Eaſt Indies, *or other places beyond the* Cape of Good Hope, *which are prohibited to be worn and uſed in* Great Britain, *and alſo certain* Eaſt India *goods called* Cowries *and* Arangoes, *is very beneficial to the trade of this kingdom: and whereas it may happen, that the quantity of ſuch goods imported from the* Eaſt Indies *by the united company of merchants of* England *trading thither, may not always be ſufficient to anſwer that purpoſe, and to keep the price of ſuch goods in this kingdom at a reaſonable rate:* be it therefore enacted by the King's moſt excellent majeſty, by and with the advice and conſent of the lords ſpiritual and temporal, and commons in this preſent parliament aſſembled, and by the authority of the ſame, That from and after the firſt day of *June*, one thouſand ſeven hundred and ſixty five, in every ſuch caſe, it ſhall and may be lawful for the ſaid united company of merchants of *England* trading to the *Eaſt Indies*, and their ſucceſſors, to import into *Great Britain*, in *Britiſh* ſhips navigated according to law, from any part of *Europe* not within his Majeſty's dominions, ſuch quantities of the ſaid goods, being the product or manufacture of the *Eaſt Indies*, as they ſhall think neceſſary for the *African* trade, ſubject to the ſame duties, and to the ſame rules, regulations, and reſtrictions, in all reſpects, as are preſcribed and practiſed with reſpect to ſuch goods imported by them from the *Eaſt Indies*; ſo as notice be firſt given to the commiſſioners of his

Eaſt India company allowed to import from abroad ſuch coarſe printed callicoes, and other goods of the growth or manufacture of the Eaſt Indies, &c. as ſhall be fit for the African trade;

upon payment of the uſual duties;

and giving notice to the treasury.

his Majesty's treasury, or the lord high treasurer for the time being, of the quantities and species of goods so intended to be imported, with the name of the ship and master in which the same are to be laden; and taking a licence under the hands of the said commissioners of the treasury, or any three or more of them, or the said high treasurer for the time being, for the lading and importing thereof as aforesaid, which licence they are hereby authorized and impowered to grant to the said company, without any fee or reward, or any other charge; any law, custom, or usage to the contrary notwithstanding.

and obtaining a licence from them.

If they shall not furnish the market with a sufficient supply of such goods at reasonable prices,

II. Provided always, and be it further by enacted the authority aforesaid, That if the said united company of merchants of *England* trading to the *East Indies* shall at any time neglect or refuse to keep this market supplied with a sufficient quantity of such goods at reasonable prices, to answer the *African* trade, it shall and may be lawful to and for the said commissioners of the treasury, or any three or more of them, or the said high treasurer for the time being, if he or they shall think proper, to grant licences to any other person or persons, body or bodies politick or corporate, to import such goods into any port of *Great Britain*, from any parts of *Europe* not within his Majesty's dominions, in such and the like manner, and under such restrictions and limitations, as are herein before prescribed and directed, with respect to such goods to be imported by the said united company of merchants of *England*, trading to the *East Indies*; and that the goods, so imported by virtue of such last mentioned licences, shall be liable to the payment of one half of the old subsidy granted by the act of tonnage and poundage, passed in the twelfth year of the reign of King *Charles* the Second, which shall be paid down in ready money, and shall not be afterwards drawn back or repaid upon the exportation of the same goods; and such goods shall, upon landing, be immediately lodged and secured in such warehouse belonging to his Majesty, his heirs and successors, as the commissioners of his Majesty's customs, or any three or more of them for the time being, shall direct and appoint; and shall not be delivered out of such warehouse, otherwise than on condition to be exported to *Africa* only, under the like security, regulations, and restrictions, penalties, and forfeitures, as *East India* goods prohibited to be worn or used in *Great Britain*, are liable to by law.

the treasury may grant licences to other Persons,

they paying one half of the old subsidy on importation;

and lodging the goods in the King's warehouses; but to have no drawback;

and to give security on exportation.

Unrated goods, imported by virtue of the last-mentioned licences,

III. Provided also, That in case such of the aforesaid goods as are not rated in either of the book of rates, made in the twelfth year of the reign of King *Charles* the Second, or in the eleventh year of the reign of King *George* the First, or in any other act, of parliament, shall be imported, by virtue of the last mentioned licence, by any person or persons, body or bodies politick or corporate, except the said united company of merchants of *England* trading to the *East Indies*, the price and value of such unrated goods shall be ascertained by the oath or affirmation of the importer, by the like rules, regulations, and restrictions, as are prescribed by an act passed in the eleventh year of the reign of King

to pay duty according to the price and value, as ascertained upon oath;

King *George* the First, intituled, *An act for rating such unrated goods and merchandizes as are usually imported into this kingdom and pay duty* ad valorem, *upon the oath of the importer; and for ascertaining the value of all goods and merchandizes not inserted in the former or present book of rates; and for repealing certain duties upon drugs and rags; and for continuing the duty upon apples; and for ascertaining the method of admeasuring pictures imported*; and the half of the old subsidy shall be paid for such goods, according to such price and value; any law, custom, or usage, to the contrary notwithstanding. pursuant to act 11 Geo. 1.

IV. And, in order to promote and encourage the importation of bugles into this kingdom, to be exported from hence to foreign parts, and to ease the merchants and dealers therein from the difficulty of paying or securing the full duties for such goods when imported for that purpose; be it further enacted by the authority aforesaid, That no duty or customs whatsoever shall be paid, or secured to be paid, for any bugles which shall be imported into this kingdom, from and after the first day of *June*, one thousand seven hundred and sixty five; other than one half of the old subsidy granted by the act of tonnage and poundage passed in the twelfth year of the reign of King *Charles* the Second, which shall be paid down in ready money, and shall not be afterwards drawn back or repaid upon the exportation of the same goods; provided such bugles shall, upon landing, be immediately lodged and secured in such warehouse belonging to his Majesty, his heirs, and successors, as the commissioners of his Majesty's customs, or any three or more of them for the time being, shall direct and appoint; and shall not be delivered out of such warehouse but upon the following conditions; that is to say, if such bugles, or any part thereof, shall be delivered for exportation to foreign parts, the same shall be subject to the like security, regulations, and restrictions, as *East India* goods, prohibited to be worn or used in *Great Britain*, are now liable to by law; but if such bugles, or any part thereof, shall be taken out in order to be used in this kingdom, the person or persons so taking out the same, shall first pay up the remainder of the duties which would have been due and payable upon the importation of such goods into this kingdom; and they shall, in all other respects, be liable to the same restrictions and regulations, as they would have been subject and liable to if this act had not been made.

After 1 June, 1765, bugles may be imported upon paying one half of the old subsidy, without any drawback upon exportation; lodging the same in the King's warehouse, and giving security on exportation; but if for Home consumption, the full duty is then to be paid.

V. Provided always, and it is hereby further enacted, That if such bugles shall not be either exported, or the full duties paid for the same, within five years from the importation thereof, but shall then continue and be still remaining in the said warehouses; in such case it shall and may be lawful for the said commissioners of the customs for the time being, or any three or more of them, to cause the said bugles, so remaining, to be publickly sold by auction, or inch of candle, to the best bidder; and the money arising by such sale to be applied, first, in discharge of the said duties and the expences of such sale; and the overplus, if

If they shall not be exported, or the full duties paid within 5 years; the commissioners of the customs may put up the same to publick sale, and deduct the duties and charges,

if any, to be paid to the importer or proprietor of ſuch bugles, or other perſons authorized to receive the ſame.

Bugles imported before 1 June, 1765, for which duties were paid

being duly warehouſed, are to be allowed the drawback on exportation, &c.

VI. And be it further enacted by the authority aforeſaid, That all and every perſon and perſons having in his or their cuſtody, any bugles, imported before the ſaid firſt day of *June*, one thouſand ſeven hundred and ſixty five, for which the duties have been paid or ſecured according to law, who ſhall, on or before the ſaid firſt day of *June*, bring and depoſit, or cauſe to be brought and depoſited, ſuch bugles, in ſuch warehouſe as ſhall be approved of by the commiſſioners aforeſaid for that purpoſe, ſhall thereupon be repaid and allowed, by the collector or other proper officer of the cuſtoms at the port where ſuch bugles were imported, all the duties which ſuch bugles would be intitled to draw back upon the exportation thereof, in the ſame manner and form as if ſuch bugles were actually exported: and the ſame ſhall be liable to the ſame rules and regulations as they would be liable to, by this act, if they had been warehouſed upon their firſt importation.

Bugles imported after the ſaid 1 June, not being warehouſed,

are to pay full duties, ſubject to the uſual diſcounts.

VII. Provided always, and it is hereby further enacted by the authority aforeſaid, That from and after the ſaid firſt day of *June*, every perſon importing any bugles into *Great Britain*, which ſhall not be warehouſed in the manner herein before directed, ſhall pay down in ready money all the ſeveral duties due for the ſame, ſubject to the uſual diſcounts; any law, cuſtom, or uſage, to the contrary notwithſtanding.

Commiſſioners of the cuſtoms impowered to grant licences at any time before 5 July, next, for importation from the iſle of Man, of rum, brandy, iron, gunpowder, and Eaſt India goods, &c. proper for the African trade, which were imported there before 1 March 1765; due notice being firſt given them of the quantities and ſpecies, &c. and oath made of the time of importation.

VIII. And be it further enacted by the authority aforeſaid, That it ſhall and may be lawful for the commiſſioners of the cuſtoms in that part of *Great Britain* called *England*, or any three or more of them, at any time before the fifth day of *July*, next, but no longer, to grant licence without fee or reward, in ſuch caſes as they ſhall think proper, to any perſon or perſons, to import into any port in *England* from the iſle of *Man*, in *Britiſh* ſhips navigated according to law, any quantity of rum, brandy, iron, gunpowder, cowries, arangoes, and ſuch coarſe printed calicoes, of the product and manufacture of the *Eaſt Indies*, as are fit and neceſſary for the *African* trade, which were imported into the ſaid iſle of *Man* before the firſt day of *March* one thouſand ſeven hundred and ſixty five; ſo as notice be firſt given to the ſaid commiſſioners of the quantities, ſpecies, and package of ſuch goods, ſo intended to be imported, together with the marks and numbers thereof, with the name of the ſhip and maſter in which the ſame are intended to be laden, and the port into which they are intended to be brought; and proof be made by oath of the proprietor (or if the proprietor be a *Quaker*, by his affirmation) and by the oath of one other credible perſon, of the time when the goods, for which ſuch licence is deſired, were imported into the ſaid iſle of *Man*.

Such goods to pay only

IX. And be it further enacted, That the goods ſo imported, by virtue of ſuch licence, ſhall not be liable to the payment of any

any customs or duties whatsoever, other than one half of the old subsidy granted by the act of tonnage and poundage, passed in the twelfth year of the reign of *Charles* the Second, which shall be paid down in ready money, and shall not be afterwards drawn back or repaid upon the exportation of the same goods; and that all such goods, except gunpowder, shall, upon landing, be immediately lodged and secured in such warehouses belonging to his Majesty, his heirs, and successors, as the said commissioners of the customs shall direct and appoint; and that all gunpowder, so imported, shall be immediately lodged and secured in such warehouse or magazine as shall be provided at the expence of the proprietor of such gunpowder, and approved of by the said commissioners, under the joint locks of the King and the said proprietor; and upon entry of any of the goods aforesaid, the licence granted for importing the same shall be delivered up by the master, or other person taking charge of the vessel, to the collector or other principal officer of the customs at the port of importation, to be by such officer transmitted to the said commissioners of the customs to be cancelled: and the said goods shall not be delivered out of such warehouse or magazine in which they shall be secured as aforesaid, otherwise than on condition to be exported to *Africa* only, under the like securities, regulations, and restrictions, penalties and forfeitures, as *East India* goods prohibited to be worn or used in *Great Britain* are liable to by law; any law, custom, or usage to the contrary notwithstanding.

one half of the old subsidy

and to be warehoused upon landing

and the gunpowder secured.

Upon entry of the goods, the licence to be delivered up,

and transmitted to the commissioners.

Conditions of exportation.

X. Provided always, That the said one half of the old subsidy for such of the goods aforesaid, as are unrated in either of the books of rates made in the twelfth year of the reign of King *Charles* the Second, or in the eleventh year of the reign of King *George* the First, or in any other act of parliament, shall be paid according to the price and value of such goods, to be ascertained by the oath or affirmation of the importer, by the like rules, regulations, and prescriptions, as are prescribed and practised by law for other unrated goods imported into this kingdom.

Unrated goods to pay according to the price and value.

XI. And whereas it is proper, that the bounty payable in *Great Britain*, and all bounties and allowances payable in *Ireland*, upon the exportation of corn, grain, malt, meal, and flour, exported to the isle of *Man*, should be discontinued; be it therefore enacted by the authority aforesaid, That from and after the first day of *June*, one thousand seven hundred and sixty five, no bounty shall be allowed or paid for any sort of corn, grain, malt, meal, or flour, which shall be entered for exportation from *Great Britain* to the isle of *Man*; and that no bounty or allowance shall be allowed or paid for any sort of corn, grain, malt, meal, or flour, which shall be entered for exportation from *Ireland* to the said isle; and that the said isle of *Man* shall be added to and included in the bond, which is now by law required to to be given upon the exportation of such corn, grain, malt, meal, or flour, to parts beyond the seas.

From and after 1 June, 1765. the bounty upon exportation of corn, &c. to the isle of Man is to be discontinued.

and the isle of Man is to be included in the bonds to be given on exportation of corn, &c. to parts beyond the seas

XII. Provided always, and be it enacted, That nothing herein

Rights of the East India company reserved.

in contained, ſhall be conſtrued to prejudice ſuch right and privileges as are given to the united company of merchants of *England* trading to the *Eaſt Indies*, by the charter granted by his late majeſty King *William* the third, in the tenth year of his reign, otherwiſe than is herein before contained.

Limitation of actions.

General iſſue.

Treble coſts.

XIII. And be it further enacted by the authority aforeſaid, That if any action or ſuit ſhall be commenced againſt any perſon or perſons for any thing done in purſuance of this act, the defendant or defendants, in ſuch action or ſuit, may plead the general iſſue, and give this act and the ſpecial matter in evidence, at any trial to be had thereupon; and that the ſame was done in purſuance, and by the authority of this act; and if it ſhall appear ſo to have been done, the jury ſhall find for the defendant or defendants; and if the plaintiff ſhall be nonſuited, or diſcontinue his action after the defendant or defendants ſhall have appeared, or if judgement ſhall be given upon any verdict or demurrer againſt the plaintiff, the defendant or defendants ſhall recover treble coſts; and have the like remedy for the ſame, as defendants have in other caſes by law.

CAP. XXXI.

An act to diſcontinue, for a limited time, the duties upon wheat and wheat flour imported; and alſo the bounty payable on the exportation of wheat and wheat flour.

Preamble.

Duties diſcontinued upon ſuch wheat and wheat flour as ſhall be imported before 24 Auguſt, 1765;

and the ſame allowed to be carried coaſtwiſe.

WHEREAS the diſcontinuing of the duties, for a limited time, upon wheat and wheat flour imported into this kingdom, may be of advantage to his Majeſty's ſubjects, be it therefore enacted by the King's moſt excellent majeſty, by and with the advice and conſent of the lords ſpiritual and temporal, and commons, in this preſent parliament aſſembled, and by the authority of the ſame, That from and after the paſſing this act, no ſubſidy, cuſtom, rate, duty, or other impoſition whatſoever ſhall be demanded, collected, received, or taken, upon any wheat or wheat flour, which ſhall be imported into this kingdom at any time or times before the twenty fourth day of *Auguſt*, one thouſand ſeven hundred and ſixty five; but that all ſuch wheat and wheat flour ſhall and may be imported, brought in and landed, duty free; and may alſo be carried coaſtwiſe, under ſuch regulations as corn of the growth of this kingdom is now allowed to be carried coaſtwiſe, at all times before the ſaid twenty fourth day of *Auguſt*; any former law, ſtatute, act or acts of parliament, to the contrary in any wiſe notwithſtanding.

Due entry to be made of ſuch importation,

on penalty of paying the duties.

II. Provided always, and be it further enacted by the authority aforeſaid, That a due entry ſhall be made, in ſuch manner and form as were uſed and practiſed before the making of this act, of all wheat and wheat flour which ſhall be imported, or brought into this kingdom, before the ſaid twenty fourth day of *Auguſt*, at the cuſtom-houſe belonging to the port into which the ſame ſhall be imported or brought in; or otherwiſe in default of making ſuch entry, ſuch wheat and wheat flour ſhall be liable and ſubject to ſuch and the ſame duties, as were payable upon on the importation thereof before the making of this act; any thing in this act contained to the contrary notwithstanding.

III. And be it further enacted by the authority aforesaid, That if any action or suit shall be commenced against any person or persons, for any thing done in pursuance of this act, in that part of *Great Britain* called *England*, the defendant or defendants in any such action or suit may plead the general issue, and give this act, and the special matter, in evidence, at any trial to be had thereupon, and that the same was done in pursuance and by the authority of this act; and if it shall appear so to have been done, the jury shall find for the defendant or defendants: and if the plaintiff shall be nonsuited, or discontinue his action after the defendant or defendants shall have appeared; or if judgement shall be given upon any verdict or demurrer against the plaintiff; the defendant or defendants shall and may recover treble costs, and have the like remedy for the same, as any defendant or defendants hath or have in other cases by law; and if such action or suit be commenced or prosecuted in that part of *Great Britain* called *Scotland*, the court, before whom such action or suit shall be brought, shall allow the defender to plead this act on his defence; and if the pursuer shall not insist on his action, or if judgement shall be given against such pursuer, the defender shall and may recover the full and real expences he may have been put to by any such action or suit.

Limitation of actions.

General issue.

Treble costs.

IV. And be it further enacted by the authority aforesaid, That from and after the passing of this act, no bounty shall be allowed or payable, upon the exportation of wheat or wheat flour from *Great Britain*, until and after the twenty fourth day of *August* next.

Bounty discontinued for a time upon all wheat or wheat flour which shall be exported from Great Britain.

CAP. XXXII.

An act to enable his Majesty, with the advice of his privy council, to prohibit the exportation of wheat, wheaten meal, flour, bread, biscuit, and starch, during the next recess of parliament, at such time, and in such manner, as the necessity of the time may require, and he, in his wisdom shall think convenient and needful.

WHEREAS the prices of wheat, wheaten meal, flour, bread, biscuit, and starch, are at present very high, and may become higher, to the great prejudice of his Majesty's subjects, if not timely prevented; may it therefore please your majesty that it may be enacted, and be it enacted by the King's most excellent majesty, by and with the advice and consent of the lords spiritual and temporal, and commons, in this present parliament assembled and by the authority of the same, That it shall and may be lawful for his Majesty, during the next recess of parliament, by and with the advice of his privy council, from time to time, as often as the price of wheat shall be at six shillings *per* bushel, or upwards, at the market at bear key, to prohibit

Preamble.

His Majesty enabled, during the next recess of parliament, with *the advice of his privy council, to prohibit by proclamation, the exportation of wheat, &c. from Great Britain or Ireland, when the price thereof at Bear Key, ſhall be at 6s. per buſhel; and if any ſhall be exported contrary thereto the ſame is forfeited; with 20s. per buſhel for ſuch wheat, &c. and 12d. per lib. for ſuch bread, &c. together with the veſſel, &c. to be recovered in the ſeveral courts within England.*

hibit the exportation from *Great Britain* or *Ireland*, any ſort of wheat, wheaten meal, flour, bread, biſcuit, or ſtarch, as his Majeſty, in his great wiſdom, ſhall think convenient and needful, and as the neceſſity of the times may require, and in ſuch manner as his Majeſty ſhall think fit to direct; any thing in any act or acts of parliament to the contrary notwithſtanding; and that all the ſaid commodities that ſhall be exported, ſhipped, or carried out, within any of the times appointed by his Majeſty, by and with the advice of his privy council, by his royal proclamation for prohibiting the exportation thereof during the next receſs of parliament, ſhall be forfeited; and that every offender or offenders therein ſhall forfeit the ſum of twenty ſhillings for every buſhel of wheat, wheaten meal, or flour, and twelve pence of lawful money of *Great Britain* for every pound weight of bread, biſcuit, or ſtarch, and ſo in proportion for any greater or leſs quantity, which ſhall be ſo exported, ſhipped, or put on board to be exported; and alſo the ſhip, boat, or veſſel, upon which any of the ſaid commodities ſhall be exported, ſhipt, or laden to be exported, and all her guns, tackle, apparel, and furniture, ſhall be forfeited; and one moiety of all the ſaid penalties and forfeitures ſhall be to the King's majeſty, his heirs and ſucceſſors, and the other moiety to him or them that will ſue for the ſame: and for offences that ſhall be committed in that part of *Great Britain* called *England*, ſuch penalties and forfeitures ſhall be recovered by action of debt, bill, plaint, or information, in any of his Majeſty's courts of record at *Weſtminſter*, or before the juſtices of aſſize, or at the great ſeſſions in *Wales*, or by information at any general quarter ſeſſions of the peace for the county, city, riding, diviſion, or place, where the offence ſhall be committed; and in ſuch ſuit no eſſoin, protection, privilege, or wager of law, ſhall be allowed; and for offences which ſhall

Scotland.

be committed in that part of *Great Britain* called *Scotland*, by action, or ſummary bill or information, in the courts of ſeſſion or *exchequer* in *Scotland*: and for offences which ſhall be com-

and Ireland.

mitted in *Ireland*, in his Majeſty's courts of record in *Dublin*, or at the general quarter ſeſſions of the peace for the county, city, or place, where the offence ſhall be committed: and that

and the maſter and crew to be committed.

the maſter, and mariners of any ſuch ſhip, boat, or veſſel, wherein any ſuch offence ſhall be committed, knowing ſuch offence, and wittingly and willingly aiding and aſſiſting thereunto and being thereof duly convicted in any ſuch courts as aforeſaid, ſhall be impriſoned for the ſpace of three calendar months without bail or mainprize.

Any officer of the cuſtoms, or other perſon authorized by the treaſury, may make ſuch ſeizure, &c.

II. And be it further enacted by the authority aforeſaid, That it ſhall and may be lawful to and for any perſon or perſons, being an officer or officers of the cuſtoms, or being lawfully authorized in this behalf by the lord high treaſurer of *Great Britain*, or the commiſſioners of the treaſury for the time being, or any three or more of them, to take or ſeize all ſuch of the ſaid commodities not allowed to be exported by this act, or by his Majeſty's royal proclamation, or ſuch order of council in pur-

pursuance of this act, as he or they shall happen to find, know or discover to be laid on board any ship, or other vessel or boat at sea, or in any port, or in any navigable river or water, to the intent or purpose to be exported, transported or conveyed out of *Great Britain* or *Ireland*, contrary to the true intent of this act; and also the ship, vessel or boat, in which the same shall be found; and to bring the said goods to the King's warehouse or warehouses, belonging to the custom-house next to the place where such seizures shall be made, or to some other safe place (where there are no such warehouses) in order to be proceeded against according to law; and in case of recovery, to be divided according to the directions of this act.

III. Provided always, That this act, or any thing herein contained, shall not extend to prohibit the exportation, or carrying out, of such or so much of the said commodities as shall be necessary to be carried in any ship or ships, or other vessel or vessels, in their respective voyages, for the sustenance, diet and support of the commanders, masters, mariners, passengers or others, in the same ships or vessels only; or for the victualling or providing any of his Majesty's ships of war, or other ships or vessels in his Majesty's service; or for his Majesty's forces, forts or garrisons; any thing herein contained to the contrary notwithstanding.

Provisions necessary for a ship's voyage; or for victualing the King's ships, forces or garrisons, excepted;

IV. Provided also, That this act, or any thing herein contained, shall not extend to prohibit any person or persons to ship or put on board any of the commodities aforesaid, to be carried coastwise; that is to say, from any port, creek or member of the kingdoms of *Great Britain* or *Ireland*, to any other port, creek or member of the same respectively, having such or the like coast coquet or sufferance for that purpose, and such or the like sufficient security being first given for the landing and discharging the same in some other port, member or creek of the said kingdoms, and returning a certificate in six months, as is required by law in cases where goods, which are liable to pay duties on exportation, are carried coastwise from one port of *Great Britain* to another, and not otherwise.

and such also as shall be carried coastwise, having a sufferance, and security being given for the due landing thereof, and returning a certificate within six months;

V. Provided always, That this act, or any thing herein contained, shall not extend to any of the said commodities which shall be exported, or shipped to be exported, out of or from *Great Britain* to *Ireland*, or from *Ireland* to *Great Britain*, or from *Great Britain* or *Ireland* to *Gibraltar*, or unto any of his Majesty's islands or colonies in *America*, that have usually been supplied with any of the said commodities from *Great Britain* or *Ireland*, for the sustentation of the inhabitants of the said islands, colonies or dominions, or for the benefit of the *British* fishery in those parts only; so as the exporter do, before the shipping or laying on board the same, declare the island, colony or dominion, islands, colonies or dominions, for which the said commodities are respectively designed; and do become bound, with some other sufficient security, in treble the value thereof, to the commissioners or chief officer or officers of his Majesty's

and except such as shall be exported to and from Great Britain and Ireland reciprocally, or to Gibraltar, the British plantations in America, or for the British fisheries; the exporter declaring the place for which the

jesty's customs belonging to the port or place where the same shall be shipped or put on board (who hath or have hereby power to take such security in his Majesty's name, and to his Majesty's use) that such commodities shall not be landed or sold in any parts whatsoever, other than the kingdoms, islands or colonies, for which the same shall be so declared; and that a certificate under the hand and seal of the collector, comptroller or other chief officer of the customs, or, if no such, of the naval officer, or some other principal officer of the port where the same shall be landed, shall, within the respective times herein after for that purpose mentioned (the danger of the seas excepted) be returned to the officers who took the said bonds, that the said commodities have been landed at the port or place for which the same shall be so declared; and for the taking of such security, and giving such certificates (which the respective officers aforesaid are hereby on demand required to give) no fee or reward shall be demanded or received; and if any officer shall make any false certificate of any such commodities being so landed, such officer shall forfeit the sum of two hundred pounds, and lose his employment, and be incapable of serving his Majesty, his heirs or successors, in any office relating to the customs: and if any person shall counterfeit, rase or falsify, any such certificate, or knowingly publish any such counterfeit, rased, or false certificate, he shall forfeit the sum of two hundred pounds; and such certificate shall be void, and of no effect: which said penalties, for offences committed in *Great Britain* or *Ireland*, shall be recovered in the same courts, and in the same manner, as the other penalties inflicted by this act are recoverable; and for offences committed in the colonies or plantations in *America*, or other the dominions belonging to the crown of *Great Britain* in *Europe*, shall be recovered in the high court of *Admiralty*, or in any other chief court of civil or criminal jurisdiction in such respective colonies, plantations or dominions; and shall be divided into moieties between his Majesty and the informer: and the said bond or bonds, if not prosecuted within three years, shall be void.

same are intended, and giving security, and returning a certificate in due time.

Officer granting a false certificate, forfeits 200l. and is also incapacitated; and persons forging or falsifying a certificate; or knowingly publishing such, forfeit 200l.

VI. Provided, That nothing herein contained shall extend to prohibit the united company of merchants of *England* trading to the *East Indies*, from exporting any of the said commodities to any of their forts, factories or settlements, for the support of the persons residing there; so as the like security be given, for the exporting thereof, as is required by this act to be given by persons carrying any of the said commodities to the *British* colonies in *America*.

Provisions sent by the East India company to their settlements abroad, are also excepted, upon giving security, &

VII. Provided also, That this act, or any thing herein contained, shall not extend to any wheat to be transported out of or from the port of *Southampton* only, unto the islands of *Jersey* and *Guernsey*, or either of them, for the only use of the inhabitants of those islands; so as the exporter, before the lading of such wheat, or laying the same on board, do become bound, with other sufficient security (which the customer or comptroller of

and such as are exported from Southampton to Jersey and Guerinsey, for the use of the inhabitants, giving security,

of the ſame port hath hereby power to take in his Majeſty's name, and to his Majeſty's uſe, and for which ſecurity no fee or reward ſhall be given or taken) that ſuch wheat ſhall be landed in the ſaid iſlands of *Jerſey* and *Guernſey*, or one of them (the dangers of the ſeas only excepted) for the uſe of the inhabitants there, and ſhall not be landed or ſold in any other parts whatſoever; and to return the like certificates of the landing the ſame there, as is herein before required on the exportation of the ſaid commodities to the *Britiſh* colonies in *America*, and within the time for that purpoſe herein after mentioned; and ſo as the quantity of wheat, which, at any time or times after the paſſing of this act, and before the firſt day of *October*, ſhall be ſhipped at the ſaid port for *Jerſey* and *Guernſey*, or either of them, as aforeſaid, doth not exceed in the whole five thouſand quarters; any thing herein contained to the contrary notwithſtanding.

and returning a certificate; and ſo as the quantity do not exceed 5000 quarters.

VIII. And be it further enacted by the authority aforeſaid, That the commiſſioners of the cuſtoms for the time being ſhall, and they are hereby required to give a full and true account, in writing, to both houſes of parliament, at the beginning of the next ſeſſion thereof, of all wheat, wheaten meal, flour, bread, biſcuit, and ſtarch, that ſhall, before that time, be exported to any place whatſoever, by virtue or in purſuance of any of the liberties or powers hereby given or granted for that purpoſe.

Return to be made by the commiſſioners of the cuſtoms to both houſes of parliament of the quantities exported.

IX. And be it further enacted by the authority aforeſaid, That all certificates of the landing and diſcharging of the ſaid commodities to be exported, other than coaſtwiſe, ſhall be returned within the reſpective times following; that is to ſay, where the bonds are taken in reſpect of any of the ſaid commodities to be exported from *Great Britain* or *Ireland*, to any of the ſaid colonies or plantations in *America*, within eighteen calendar months after the date of the ſaid bonds; and where to *Gibraltar*, within twelve calendar months after the date of ſuch bonds; and where to the iſlands of *Guernſey* or *Jerſey*, within ſix calendar months after the date of ſuch bonds; and where from *Great Britain* to *Ireland*, or from *Ireland* to *Great Britain*, within ſix calendar months after the date of ſuch bonds reſpectively.

Limitation of the times for returning certificates from America, Gibraltar, Guernſey & Jerſey, and to and from Great Britain and Ireland reſpectively.

CAP. XXXIII.

An act to amend and render more effectual, in his Majeſty's dominions in America, *an act paſſed in this preſent ſeſſion of parliament, intituled,* An act for puniſhing mutiny and deſertion, and for the better payment of the army and their quarters.

Preamble.

WHEREAS *in and by an act made in the preſent ſeſſion of parliament, intituled,* An act for puniſhing mutiny and deſertion, and for the better payment of the army and their quarters; *ſeveral regulations are made and enacted for the better government of the army, and their obſerving ſtrict diſcipline, and for providing quarters for the army, and carriages on marches and other*

other necessary occasions, and inflicting penalties on offenders against the same act, and for many other good purposes therein mentioned; but the same may not be sufficient for the forces that may be employed in his Majesty's dominions in America: *and whereas, during the continuance of the said act, there may be occasion for marching and quartering of regiments and companies of his Majesty's forces in several parts of his Majesty's dominions in* America: *and whereas the publick houses and barracks, in his Majesty's dominions in* America, *may not be sufficient to supply quarters for such forces: and whereas it is expedient and necessary that carriages and other conveniencies, upon the march of troops in his Majesty's dominions in* America, *should be supplied for that purpose:* be it enacted by the King's most excellent majesty, by and with the advice and consent of the lords spiritual and temporal, and commons, in this present parliament assembled, and by the authority of the same, That for and during the continuance of this act, and no longer, it shall and may be lawful to and for the constables, tithingmen, magistrates, and other civil officers of villages, towns, townships, cities, districts, and other places, within his Majesty's dominions in *America*, and in their default or absence, for any one justice of the peace inhabiting in or near any such village, township, city, district or place, and for no others; and such constables, tythingmen, magistrates, and other civil officers as aforesaid, are hereby required to quarter and billet the officers and soldiers, in his Majesty's service, in the barracks provided by the colonies; and if there shall not be sufficient room in the said barracks for the officers and soldiers, then and in such case only, to quarter and billet the residue of such officers and soldiers, for whom there shall not be room in such barracks, in inns, livery stables, ale-houses, victualling-houses, and the houses of sellers of wine by retail to be drank in their own houses or places thereunto belonging, and all houses of persons selling of rum, brandy, strong water, cyder or metheglin, by retail, to be drank in houses; and in case there shall not be sufficient room for the officers and soldiers in such barracks, inns, victualling and other publick alehouses, that in such and no other case, and upon no other account, it shall and may be lawful for the governor and council of each respective province in his Majesty's dominions in *America*, to authorize and appoint, and they are hereby directed and impowered to authorize and appoint, such proper person or persons as they shall think fit, to take, hire and make fit, and, in default of the said governor and council appointing and authorizing such person or persons, or in default of such person or persons so appointed neglecting or refusing to do their duty, in that case it shall and may be lawful for any two or more of his Majesty's justices of the peace in or near the said villages, towns, townships, cities, districts, and other places, and they are hereby required to take, hire, and make fit for the reception of his Majesty's forces, such and so many uninhabited houses, outhouses, barns, or other buildings, as shall be necessary, to quarter therein the residue of such officers

Constables, &c. to quarter officers and men in the barracks provided for them;

and if there shall not be sufficient room there, to billet the residue in inns, ale-houses, &c.

and if these shall be also insufficient, then in hired uninhabited houses to be provided and furnished for the purpose.

ficers and ſoldiers for whom there ſhould not be room in ſuch barracks and publick houſes as aforeſaid, and to put and quarter the reſidue of ſuch officers and ſoldiers therein.

II. And it is hereby declared and enacted, That there ſhall be no more billets at any time ordered, than there are effective ſoldiers preſent to be quartered therein: and in order that this ſervice may be effectually provided for, the commander in chief in *America*, or other officer under whoſe orders any regiment or company ſhall march, ſhall, from time to time, give, or cauſe to be given, as early notice as conveniently may be, in writing, ſigned by ſuch commander or officer of their march, ſpecifying their numbers and time of marching as near as may be, to the reſpective governors of each province through which they are to march; in order that proper perſons may be appointed and authorized, in purſuance of this act, to take up and hire, if it ſhall be neceſſary, uninhabited houſes, outhouſes, barns, or other buildings, for the reception of ſuch ſoldiers as the barracks and publick houſes ſhall not be ſufficient to contain or receive.

No more billets to be ordered than there are effective men.

Commander in chief to give early notice to the reſpective governors, of the marching of the troops and their numbers, that quarters may be provided accordingly.

III. And be it further enacted by the authority aforeſaid, That if any military officer ſhall take upon himſelf to quarter ſoldiers, in any of his Majeſty's dominions in *America*, otherwiſe than is limitted and allowed by this act; or ſhall uſe or offer any menace or compulſion to or upon any juſtice of the peace, conſtable, tithingman, magiſtrate, or other civil officer before mentioned, in his Majeſty's dominions in *America*, tending to deter and diſcourage any of them from performing any part of the duty hereby required or appointed; ſuch military officer, for every ſuch offence, being thereof convicted before any two or more of his Majeſty's juſtices of the peace living within or near ſuch villages, towns, townſhips, cities, diſtricts or other places, by the oaths of two or more credible witneſſes, ſhall be deemed and taken to be *ipſo facto* caſhiered, and ſhall be utterly diſabled to have or hold any military employment in his Majeſty's ſervice, upon a certificate thereof being tranſmitted to the commander in chief in *America*; unleſs the ſaid conviction ſhall be reverſed upon an appeal brought, within ſix months, in the proper court for hearing appeals againſt convicting by juſtices of the peace: and in caſe any perſon ſhall find himſelf aggrieved, in that ſuch conſtable, tythingman, magiſtrate, or other civil officer, ſhall have quartered or billeted in or upon his houſe a greater number of ſoldiers than he ought to bear in proportion to his neighbours, and ſhall complain thereof to one or more juſtice or juſtices of the peace of the village, town, townſhip, city, diſtrict, or other place, where ſuch ſoldiers are quartered, ſuch juſtice or juſtices has or have hereby power to relieve ſuch perſon, by ordering ſuch and ſo many of the ſoldiers to be removed, and quartered upon ſuch other perſon or perſons, as they ſhall ſee cauſe; and ſuch other perſon or perſons ſhall be obliged to receive ſuch ſoldiers accordingly.

Military officers taking on themſelves to quarter ſoldiers; or uſing any menace to a civil officer, to deter them from their duty; to be caſhiered;

unleſs the conviction be reverſed upon appeal.

Perſons aggrieved by being quartered on, may complain to the juſtices, and be relieved.

IV. Provided alſo, and be it further enacted, That no juſtice or juſtices of the peace, having or executing any military office or com-

No juſtice having any military office to be con-

commiſſion in his Majeſty's regular forces in *America*, may, during the continuance of this act, directly or indirectly, act or be concerned in the quartering, billeting or appointing any quarters, for any ſoldier or ſoldiers, according to the diſpoſition made for quartering of any ſoldier or ſoldiers by virtue of this act (except where there ſhall be no other juſtice or juſtices of the peace) but that all warrants, acts, matters, or things, executed or appointed by ſuch juſtice or juſtices of the peace for or concerning the ſame, ſhall be void; any thing in this act contained to the contrary notwithſtanding.

cerned in billeting ſoldiers.

except where there ſhall be no other juſtice.

Officers and ſoldiers quartered in inns, or alehouſes, are to be furniſhed with proviſions, at a certain rate.

V. Provided nevertheleſs, and it is hereby enacted, That the officers and ſoldiers ſo quartered and billeted as aforeſaid (except ſuch as ſhall be quartered in the barracks, and hired uninhabited houſes, or other buildings as aforeſaid) ſhall be received and furniſhed with diet, and ſmall beer, cyder, or rum mixed with water, by the owners of the inns, livery ſtables, alehouſes, victualling-houſes, and other houſes in which they are allowed to be quartered and billeted by this act; paying and allowing for the ſame the ſeveral rates herein after mentioned to be payable, out of the ſubſiſtence-money, for diet and ſmall beer, cyder, or rum mixed with water.

What innholders, &c. may allow men quartered on them inſtead of meat.

VI. Provided always, That in caſe any innholder, or other perſon, on whom any non-commiſſion officers or private men ſhall be quartered by virtue of this act, in any of his Majeſty's dominions in *America* (except on a march, or employed in recruiting, and likewiſe except the recruits by them raiſed, for the ſpace of ſeven days at moſt, for ſuch non-commiſſion officers and ſoldiers who are recruiting, and recruits by them raiſed) ſhall be deſirous to furniſh ſuch non-commiſſion officers or ſoldiers with candles, vinegar, and ſalt, and with ſmall beer or cyder, not exceeding five pints, or half a pint of rum mixed with a quart of water, for each man *per diem*, *gratis*, and allow to ſuch non-commiſſion officers or ſoldiers the uſe of fire, and the neceſſary untenſils for dreſſing and eating their meat, and ſhall give notice of ſuch his deſire to the commanding officer, and ſhall furniſh and allow the ſame accordingly; then, and in ſuch caſe, the non-commiſſion officers and ſoldiers ſo quartered ſhall provide their own victuals; and the officer to whom it belongs to receive, or that actually does receive, the pay and ſubſiſtence of ſuch non-commiſſion officers and ſoldiers, ſhall pay the ſeveral ſums herein after-mentioned to be payable, out of the ſubſiſtence-money, for diet and ſmall beer, to the non-commiſſion officers and ſoldiers aforeſaid, and not to the innholder or other perſon on whom ſuch non-commiſſion officers and ſoldiers are quartered; any thing herein contained to the contrary notwithſtanding.

What officers and ſoldiers quartered in barracks, or hired houſes, are to be fur-

VII. And whereas there are ſeveral barracks in ſeveral places in his Majeſty's ſaid dominions in *America*, or ſome of them, provided by the colonies, for the lodging and covering of ſoldiers in lieu of quarters, for the eaſe and conveniency as well of the inhabitants of and in ſuch colonies, as of the ſoldiers; it it is hereby further enacted, That all such officers and soldiers, so put and placed in such barracks, or in hired uninhabited houses, out-houses, barns, or other buildings, shall, from time to time, be furnished and supplied there by the persons to be authorized or appointed for that purpose by the governor and council of each respective province, or upon neglect or refusal of such governor and council in any province, then by two or more justices of the peace residing in or near such place, with fire, candles, vinegar, and salt, bedding, utensils for dressing their victuals, and small beer or cyder, not exceeding five pints, or half a pint of rum mixed with a quart of water, to each man, without paying any thing for the same.

nished with at the provincial expence.

VIII. And that the several persons who shall so take, hire, and fit up as aforesaid, such uninhabited houses, out-houses, barns, or other buildings, for the reception of the officers and soldiers, and who shall so furnish the same, and also the said barracks, with fire, candles, vinegar, and salt, bedding, utensils for dressing victuals, and small beer, cyder, or rum, as aforesaid, may be reimbursed and paid all such charges and expences they shall be put to therein, be it enacted by the authority aforesaid, That the respective provinces shall pay unto such person or persons all such sum or sums of money so by them paid, laid out, or expended, for the taking, hiring, and fitting up, such uninhabited houses, out-houses, barns, or other buildings, and for furnishing the officers and soldiers therein, and in the barracks, with fire, candles, vinegar, and salt, bedding, utensils for dressing victuals, and small beer, cyder, or rum, as aforesaid; and such sum or sums are hereby required to be raised, in such manner as the publick charges for the provinces respectively are raised.

How the expences incurred thereby are to be reimbursed.

IX. Provided always, and be it enacted by the authority aforesaid, That if any officer, within his Majesty's said dominions of *America*, shall take, or cause to be taken, or knowingly suffer to be taken, any money, of any person, for excusing the quartering of officers or soldiers, or any of them, in any house allowed by this act; every such officer shall be cashiered, and be incapable of serving in any military employment whatsoever.

Penalty on taking money to excuse any person from being quartered on.

X. And whereas some doubts may arise, whether commanding officers of any regiment or company, within his Majesty's said dominions in *America*, may exchange any men quartered in any village, town, township, city, district, or place, in his Majesty's said dominions in *America*, with another man quartered in the same place, for the benefit of the service; be it declared and enacted by the authority aforesaid, That such exchange as above mentioned may be made by such commanding officers respectively, provided the number of men do not exceed the number at that time billeted on such house or houses; and the constables, tythingmen, magistrates, and other chief officers of the villages, towns, townships, cities, districts, or other places where any regiment or company shall be quartered, are hereby required to billet such men so exchanged accordingly.

Commanding officers may exchange men in their quarters.

Penalty on conſtables, &c. delaying to quarter or billet officers or ſoldiers, after due notice;

XI. And be it further enacted by the authority aforeſaid, That if any conſtable, tythingman, magiſtrate, or other chief officer or perſon whatſoever, who, by virtue or colour of this act, ſhall quarter or billet, or be employed in quartering or billeting, any officers or ſoldiers, within his Majeſty's ſaid dominions in *America*, ſhall neglect or refuſe, for the ſpace of two hours, to quarter or billet ſuch officers or ſoldiers, when thereunto required, in ſuch manner as is by this act directed, provided ſufficient notice be given before the arrival of ſuch forces; or ſhall receive, demand, contract, or agree for, any ſum or ſums of money, or any reward whatſoever, for or on account of excuſing, or in order to excuſe, any perſon or perſons whatſoever from quartering, or receiving into his, her, or their houſe or houſes, any ſuch officer or ſoldier; or in caſe any victualler, or any other perſon, within his Majeſty's dominions in *America*, liable by this act to have any officer or ſoldier billeted or quartered on him or her, ſhall refuſe to receive or victual any ſuch officer or ſoldier ſo quartered or billeted upon him or her as aforeſaid; or in caſe any perſon or perſons ſhall refuſe to furniſh or allow, according to the directions of this act, the ſeveral things herein before directed to be furniſhed or allowed to officers and ſoldiers, ſo quartered or billeted on him or her, or in the barracks, and hired uninhabited houſes, out-houſes, barns or other buildings, as aforeſaid, at the rate herein after mentioned; and ſhall be thereof convicted before one of the magiſtrates of any one of the ſupreme chief or principal common law courts of the colony where ſuch offence ſhall be committed, either by his own confeſſion, or by the oath of one or more credible witneſs or witneſſes (which oath ſuch magiſtrate of ſuch court is hereby impowered to adminiſter) every ſuch conſtable, tythingman, magiſtrate, or other chief officer or perſon ſo offending ſhall forfeit, for every ſuch offence, the ſum of five pounds ſterling, or any ſum of money not exceeding five pounds, nor leſs than forty ſhillings, as the ſaid magiſtrate (before whom the matter ſhall be heard) ſhall in his diſcretion think fit; to be levied by diſtreſs and ſale of the goods of the perſon offending, by warrant under the hand and ſeal of ſuch magiſtrate before whom ſuch offender ſhall be convicted, to be directed to a conſtable or other officer within the village, town, townſhip, city, diſtrict, or other place, where the offender ſhall dwell; and ſhall direct the ſaid ſum of five pounds, or ſuch other ſum as ſhall be ordered to be levied in purſuance of this act as aforeſaid, when levied, to be paid into the treaſury of the province or colony where the offence ſhall be committed, to be applied towards the general charges of the ſaid province or colony.

or receiving money to excuſe any perſon from being quartered on; and on perſons refuſing to receive the officers and ſoldiers billeted on them, or to furniſh them with neceſſaries as the act directs;

is any ſum not exceeding 5l. nor leſs than 40s.

to be paid to the treaſurer of the colony.

XII. And, that the quarters both of officers and ſoldiers, in his Majeſty's ſaid dominions in *America*, may hereafter be duly paid and ſatisfied, be it enacted by the authority aforeſaid, That from and after the twenty fourth day of *March*, in the year one thouſand ſeven hundred and ſixty five, every officer to whom it belongs to receive, or that does actually receive, the pay of

Officers to give notice to inn keepers, &c. of ſub-

ſub-

ſubſiſtence-money either for a whole regiment, or particular companies, or otherwiſe, ſhall immediately, upon each receipt of every particular ſum which ſhall from time to time be paid, returned, or come to his or their hands, on account of pay or ſubſiſtence, give publick notice thereof to all perſons keeping inns, or other places where officers or ſoldiers are quartered by virtue of this act: and ſhall alſo appoint the ſaid innkeepers and others to repair to their quarters, at ſuch times as they ſhall appoint for the diſtribution and payment of the ſaid pay or ſubſiſtence money to the ſaid officers or ſoldiers, which ſhall be within four days at fartheſt after receipt of the ſame as aforeſaid, and the ſaid inn-keepers and others ſhall then and there acquaint ſuch officer or officers with the accounts or debts (if any ſhall be) between them and the officers and ſoldiers ſo quartered in their reſpective houſes; which account the ſaid officer or officers are hereby required to accept of, and immediately pay the ſame, before any part of the ſaid pay or ſubſiſtence be diſtributed either to the officers or ſoldiers; provided the accounts exceed not for a commiſſion officer of foot, being under the degree of a captain, for ſuch officers diet and ſmall beer *per diem*, one ſhilling; and if ſuch officer ſhall have a horſe or horſes, for each horſe or horſes, for their hay and ſtraw *per diem*, ſix pence, nor for one foot ſoldier's diet and ſmall beer, cyder, or rum mixed as aforeſaid, *per diem*, four pence: and if any officer or officers as aforeſaid ſhall not give notice as aforeſaid, and not immediately, upon producing ſuch account ſtated, ſatisfy, content, and pay the ſame, upon complaint and oath made thereof by any two witneſſes, before two of his Majeſty's juſtices for the village, town, townſhip, city, diſtrict, or other place where ſuch quarters were (which oath ſuch juſtices are hereby authorized and required to adminiſter) the paymaſter or paymaſters of his Majeſty's guards and garriſons, upon certificate of the ſaid juſtices before whom ſuch oath was made, of the ſum due upon ſuch accounts, and the perſons to whom the ſame is owing, are hereby required and authorized to pay and ſatisfy the ſaid ſums out of the arrears due to the ſaid officer or officers; upon penalty that ſuch paymaſter or paymaſters ſhall forfeit their reſpective place or places of paymaſter, and be diſcharged from holding the ſame for the future; and in caſe there ſhall be no arrears due to the ſaid officer or officers, then the ſaid paymaſter or paymaſter are hereby authorized and required to deduct the ſums, he or they ſhall pay purſuant to the certificates of the ſaid juſtices, out of the next pay or ſubſiſtence money of the regiment to which ſuch officer or officers ſhall belong: and ſuch officer or officers ſhall, for every ſuch offence, or for neglecting to give notice of the receipt of ſuch pay or ſubſiſtence money as aforeſaid, be deemed and taken, and is hereby declared, to be *ipſo facto* caſhiered.

ſiſtence money in their hands;

and their accounts to be paid off according to the rates of ſubſiſtence here eſtabliſhed.

Officers not giving ſuch notice,

the accounts to be diſcharged out of their arrears of pay;

if no arrears are due, then out of the ſubſiſtence-money of the regiment.

and the officer to be caſhiered.

XIII. And, where it ſhall happen that the ſubſiſtence-money due to any officer or ſoldier, within his Majeſty's ſaid dominions in *America*, ſhall, by occaſion of any accident, not be

 paid

paid to ſuch officer or ſoldier, or ſuch officer or ſoldier ſhall neglect to pay the ſame, ſo that quarters cannot be or are not paid as this act directs; and where any forces ſhall be upon their march, in his Majeſty's ſaid dominions in *America*, ſo that no ſubſiſtence can be remitted to them to make payment as this act directs: or they ſhall neglect to pay the ſame; in every ſuch caſe, it is hereby further enacted, That every ſuch officer ſhall before his or their departure out of his or their quarters, where ſuch regiment, troop, or company ſhall remain for any time whatſoever, make up the accounts with every perſon with whom ſuch regiment or company ſhall have quartered, and ſign a certificate thereof, and give the ſaid certificate, ſo by him ſigned, to the party to whom ſuch money is due, with the name of ſuch regiment or company to which he or they ſhall belong, to the end the ſaid certificate may be forthwith tranſmitted to the paymaſter of his Majeſty's guards and garriſons, who is hereby required immediately to make payment thereof to the perſon or perſons to whom ſuch money ſhall be due, to the end the ſame may be applied to ſuch regiment or company reſpectively; under pain as before in this act directed for nonpayment of quarters.

On nonpayment of quarters, for want of money, the officer to make up the accounts and give certificates for the ſums due.

XIV. And, for the better preventing abuſes in quartering or billeting the ſoldiers in his Majeſty's dominions in *America*, in purſuance of this act, be it further enacted by the authority aforeſaid, That it ſhall and may be lawful to and for any one or more juſtices of the peace, or other officer, within their reſpective villages, towns, townſhips, cities, diſtricts, or other places, in his Majeſty's ſaid dominions in *America*, by warrant or order under his or their hand and ſeal, or hands and ſeals, at any time or times during the continuance of this act, to require and command any conſtable, tithingman, magiſtrate, or other chief officer, who ſhall quarter or billet any ſoldiers in purſuance of this act, to give an account in writing unto the ſaid juſtice or juſtices, or other officer requiring the ſame, of the number of officers and ſoldiers who ſhall be quartered or billeted by them, and alſo the names of the houſe-keepers or perſons upon whom, and the barracks and hired uninhabited houſes, or other buildings as aforeſaid, in which and where every ſuch officer or ſoldier ſhall be quartered or billeted, together with an account of the ſtreet or place where every ſuch houſe-keeper or perſon dwells, and where every ſuch barrack or hired uninhabited houſe or building is or are, and of the ſigns (if any) which belong to their houſes; to the end that it may appear to the ſaid juſtice or juſtices, or other officer, where ſuch officers or ſoldiers are quartered or billeted, and that he or they may thereby be the better enabled to prevent or puniſh all abuſes in the quartering or billeting them.

Juſtices may demand an account of quartering of the officers and ſoldiers in order to prevent and remedy abuſes in quartering.

XV. And be it further enacted by the authority aforeſaid, That for the better and more regular proviſion of carriages for his Majeſty's forces in their marches, or for their arms, cloaths, or accoutrements, in his Majeſty's ſaid dominions in *America*, all juſtices

Juſtices in purſuance of orders received, are to iſſue orders to

justices of the peace within their several villages, towns, townships, cities, districts, and places, being duly required thereunto by an order from his Majesty, or the general of his forces, or of the general commanding, or the commanding officer there shall, as often as such order is brought and shewn unto one or more of them, by the quarter-master, adjutant, or other officer of the regiment, detachment, or company, so ordered to march, issue out his or their warrants to the constables, tythingmen, magistrates, or other officers of the villages, towns, townships, cities, districts, and other places, from, through, near, or to which such regiment, detachment, or company, shall be ordered to march, requiring them to make such provision for carriages, with able men to drive the same, as shall be mentioned in the said warrant: allowing them reasonable time to do the same, that the neighbouring parts may not always bear the burthen: and in case sufficient carriages cannot be provided within any such village, town, township, city, district, or other place, then the next justice or justices of the peace of the village, town, township, city, district, or other place, shall, upon such order as aforesaid being brought or shewn to one or more of them, by any of the officers as aforesaid, issue his or their warrants to the constables, tythingmen, magistrates, or other officers, of such next village, town, township, city, district, or other place, for the purposes aforesaid, to make up such deficiency; and such constable, tythingman, magistrate, or other officer, shall order or appoint such person or persons, having carriages, within their respective villages, towns, townships, cities, districts, or other places, as they shall think proper, to provide and furnish such carriages and men, according to the warrant aforesaid; who are hereby required to provide and furnish the same accordingly.

constables to provide carriages for the troops on their march.

XVI. And be it further enacted, That the pay or hire for a *New York* waggon, carrying twelve hundred pounds gross weight, shall be seven pence sterling for each mile; and for every other carriage in that and every other colony in his Majesty's said dominions in *America*, in the same proportion; and at or after the same rate or price for what weight every such other carriage shall carry; and that the first day's pay or hire for every such carriage, shall be paid down by such officer to such constable, tythingman, magistrate, or other civil officer, who shall get or procure such carriages, for the use of the owner or owners thereof; and the pay or hire for every such carriage after the first day, shall be paid every day, from day to day, by such officer as aforesaid, into the hands of the driver or drivers of such carriages respectively, until such carriages shall be discharged from such service, for the use of the owner and owners thereof.

rates of carriages.

XVII. Provided always, and be it further enacted, That no such waggon, cart, or carriage, imprest by authority of this act, shall be liable or obliged, by virtue of this act, to carry above twelve hundred weight; any thing herein contained to the contrary notwithstanding.

Carriages not obliged to carry above 12 cwt.

XVIII. Provided also, That no such waggon, cart, or carriage,

nor to travel above 1 day's March, unleſs other carriages cannot be procured.

riage, ſhall be obliged to travel more than one day's march, if, within that time, they ſhall arrive at any other place where other carriages may be procured; but, in caſe other ſufficient carriages cannot be procured, then ſuch carriages ſhall be obliged to continue in the ſervice till they ſhall arrive at ſuch village, town, townſhip, city, diſtrict, or other place, where proper and ſufficient carriages, for the ſervice of the forces, may be procured.

Penalty on conſtables, &c. neglecting to provide or furniſh carriages.

XIX. And be it further enacted by the authority aforeſaid, That if any conſtable, tithingman, magiſtrate, or other civil officer, within his Majeſty's dominions in *America*, ſhall wilfully neglect or refuſe to execute ſuch warrants of the juſtices of the peace, as ſhall be directed unto them for providing carriages as aforeſaid; or if any perſon or perſons appointed by ſuch conſtable, tythingman, magiſtrate, or other civil officer, to provide or furniſh any carriage and man, ſhall refuſe or neglect to provide the ſame; or any other perſon or perſons whatſoever ſhall wilfully do any act or thing whereby the execution of the ſaid warrants ſhall be delayed, hindered, or fruſtrated; every ſuch conſtable, tythingman, magiſtrate, civil officer, or other perſon ſo offending, ſhall, for every ſuch offence, forfeit any ſum not exceeding forty ſhillings ſterling, nor leſs than twenty ſhillings, to be paid into the treaſury of the province where any ſuch offence ſhall be committed; to be applied towards the aforeſaid contingent charges of the province: and all and every ſuch offence or offences, and all and every other offence or offences, in this act mentioned, and not otherwiſe provided, ſhall and may be inquired of, heard, and fully determined, by two of his Majeſty's juſtices of the peace dwelling in or near the village, town, townſhip, city, diſtrict, or place, where ſuch offence ſhall be committed; who have hereby power to cauſe the ſaid penalty to be levied by diſtreſs and ſale of the offenders goods and chattels, rendering the overplus (if any) to the owner.

Colony to repay the extra expences of carriages.

XX. And whereas the allowance hereby provided, for the payment of the carriages that may be neceſſary in the marching of troops, may not be a ſufficient compenſation for the ſame, and to ſatisfy the conſtables, tithingmen, magiſtrates, and other civil officers, their charges and expences therein; for remedy whereof, be it further enacted by the authority aforeſaid, That the conſtables, tithingmen, magiſtrates, and civil officers, procuring ſuch carriages, ſhall pay a reaſonable expence or price for every carriage ſo procured; and that every ſuch conſtable, tithingman, magiſtrate, civil officer, or other perſon, ſhall be repaid what he or they ſhall ſo expend, together with his or their own charges and expences attending the ſame, by the province or colony where the ſame ſhall ariſe.

Where carriages ſhall be neceſſarily provided for long marches

XXI. Provided always, and be it further enacted by the authority aforeſaid, That where it ſhall be neceſſary to take waggons or other carriages for long marches, beyond the ſettlements, an appraiſement ſhall be made of the value of ſuch horſes and carriages, at the time of the taking them up to be employed in

ſuch

ſuch marches beyond the ſettlements, by two indifferent perſons, the one to be choſen by the commanding officer of ſuch forces, and the other by the owner of ſuch cattle or carriages; a certificate of which appraiſement ſhall be given to the owner or owners of ſuch cattle or carriages reſpectively: and in caſe any of the cattle or carriages, ſo taken up for ſuch ſervice, ſhall in the execution thereof, be loſt or deſtroyed; that then, and in every ſuch caſe, upon producing the ſaid certificate and proper vouchers upon oath of ſuch loſs or deſtruction, to the paymaſter general of his Majeſty's guards and garriſons, the ſaid paymaſter ſhall, and he is hereby required to pay to the reſpective owners of ſuch cattle or carriages, the ſums ſpecified, in ſuch certificates and vouchers, to be the value of ſuch cattle or carriages ſo loſt or deſtroyed.

beyond the ſettlements, the horſes and carriages are to be fairly appraiſed; and if loſt or deſtroyed to be paid for according to certificate.

XXII. And whereas ſeveral ſoldiers, being duly inliſted in his Majeſty's ſervice, do often deſert ſuch ſervice; for remedy whereof, be it further enacted by the authority aforeſaid, That it ſhall and may be lawful to and for the conſtable, tithingman, magiſtrate, or other civil officer, of the village, town, townſhip, city, diſtrict, or place, within the ſaid dominions in *America*, where any perſon, who may be reaſonably ſuſpected to be ſuch a deſerter, ſhall be found, to apprehend, or cauſe him to be apprehended; and to cauſe ſuch perſon to be brought before any juſtice of the peace or other chief magiſtrate living in or near ſuch village, town, townſhip, city, diſtrict or place, who hath hereby power to examine ſuch ſuſpected perſon; and if by his confeſſion, or the teſtimony of one or more witneſs or witneſſes upon oath, or the knowledge of ſuch juſtice of the peace, or other magiſtrate, it ſhall appear, or be found, that ſuch ſuſpected perſon is a liſted ſoldier, and ought to be with the regiment or company to which he belongs, ſuch juſtice of the peace or other magiſtrate ſhall forthwith cauſe him to be conveyed to the gaol of the village, town, townſhip, city, diſtrict, county, or place where he ſhall be found, or to the houſe of correction or other publick priſon in ſuch village, town, townſhip, city, diſtrict, county, or place, where ſuch deſerter ſhall be apprehended, and tranſmit an account thereof to the commander in chief of his Majeſty's forces in the ſaid dominions in *America*, or to the commanding officer of the forces poſted neareſt to ſuch juſtice or juſtices, or other magiſtrate or magiſtrates, for the time being, to the end that ſuch perſon may be proceeded againſt according to law: and the gaoler or keeper of ſuch gaol, houſe of correction, or priſon, ſhall receive the full ſubſiſtence of ſuch deſerter or deſerters during the time that he or they ſhall continue in his cuſtody for the maintenance of ſuch deſerter or deſerters: but ſhall not be intitled to any fee or reward on account of the impriſonment of ſuch deſerter or deſerters; any law, uſage, or cuſtom to the contrary notwithſtanding.

Deſerters may be apprehended, and committed; Gaoler to receive his ſubſiſtence-money in the interim.

XXIII. Provided always, That if any perſon ſhall harbour, conceal, or aſſiſt, any deſerter from his Majeſty's ſervice within his Majeſty's ſaid dominions in *America*, knowing him to be ſuch,

Penalty on perſons harbouring deſerters;

such, the person so offending, shall forfeit for every such offence, the sum of five pounds; or if any person shall knowingly detain, buy or exchange, or otherwise receive, any arms, clothes, caps, or other furniture belonging to the King, from any soldier or deserter, or any other person, upon any account or pretence whatsoever, within his Majesty's dominions in *America*, or cause the colour of such clothes to be changed; the person so offending shall forfeit, for every such offence, the sum of five pounds; and upon conviction upon the oath of one or more credible witness or witnesses, before any of his Majesty's justices of the peace, the said respective penalties of five pounds, and five pounds, shall be levied by warrant under the hands of the said justice or justices of the peace, by distress and sale of the goods and chattels of the offenders; one moiety of the said first-mentioned penalty of five pounds to be paid to the informer, by whose means such deserter shall be apprehended; and one moiety of the said last mentioned penalty of five pounds to be paid to the informer; and the residue of the said respective penalties to be paid to the officer to whom any such deserter or soldier did belong: and in case any such offenders, who shall be convicted as aforesaid, of harbouring or assisting any such deserter or deserters; or having knowingly received any arms, clothes, caps, or other furniture belonging to the King; or having caused the colour of such clothes to be changed, contrary to the intent of this act, shall not have sufficient goods and chattels, whereon distress may be made, to the value of the penalties recovered against him for such offence, or shall not pay such penalties within four days after such conviction; then, and in such case, such justice of the peace shall and may, by warrant under his hand and seal, commit such offender to the common gaol, there to remain, without bail or mainprize, for the space of three months, or cause such offender to be publickly whipt, at the discretion of such justice.

or buying soldiers arms or clothes, &c.

Penalty on officer breaking open a house to search for deserters without warrant.

XXIV. And be it further enacted, That no commission officer shall break open any house, within his Majesty's dominions in *America*, to search for deserters, without warrant from a justice of the peace, and in the day-time; and that every commission officer who shall, in the night, or without warrant from one or more of his Majesty's justices of the peace (which said warrants the said justice or justices are hereby impowered to grant) forcibly enter into, or break open, the dwelling-house, or out-houses of any person whatsoever under pretence of searching for deserters, shall, upon due proof thereof, forfeit the sum of twenty pounds.

XXV. And whereas several crimes and offences have been and may be, committed by several persons, not being soldiers, at several forts or garrisons, and several other places within his Majesty's dominions in *America*, which are not within the limits or jurisdiction of any civil government there hitherto established; and which crimes and offences are not properly cognizable or triable and punishable, by a court-martial, but by the civil magistrate;

magiſtrate; by means whereof ſeveral great crimes and offences may go unpuniſhed, to the great ſcandal of government; for remedy whereof, be it further enacted by the authority aforeſaid, That from and after the twenty fourth day of *March*, one thouſand ſeven hundred and ſixty five, and for ſo long afterwards as this act ſhall continue in force, if any perſon or perſons, not being a ſoldier or ſoldiers, do or ſhall commit any crime or crimes, or offence or offences, in any of the ſaid forts, garriſons or places, within his Majeſty's dominions in *America*, which are not within the limits or juriſdiction of any civil government hitherto eſtabliſhed, it ſhall and may be lawful for any perſon or perſons to apprehend ſuch offender or offenders, and to carry, him, her, or them, before the commanding officer for the time being of his Majeſty's forces there; and ſuch offender being charged upon oath in writing, before the ſaid commanding officer, and which oath the ſaid commanding officer is hereby impowered to adminiſter, that then, and in every ſuch caſe, the ſaid commanding officer ſhall receive and take into his cuſtody, and ſafely keep, every ſuch offender, and ſhall convey and deliver, or cauſe to be conveyed and delivered, with all convenient ſpeed, every ſuch offender to the civil magiſtrate of the next adjoining province, together with the cauſe of his or her detainer, to be committed and dealt with by ſuch civil magiſtrates or magiſtrate according to law; and every ſuch civil magiſtrate is hereby commanded and required to commit every ſuch offender, that he or ſhe may be dealt with according to law; and in every ſuch caſe, it ſhall and may be lawful to proſecute and try every ſuch offender in the court of ſuch province or colony, where crimes and offences of the like nature are uſually tried, and where the ſame would be properly tried in caſe ſuch crime or offence had been committed within the juriſdiction of ſuch court, and ſuch crime ſhall and may be alledged to be committed within the juriſdiction of ſuch court; and ſuch court ſhall and may proceed therein to trial, judgement, and execution, in the ſame manner as if ſuch crime or offence had been really committed within the juriſdiction of ſuch court; any law, uſage, cuſtom, matter, or thing, whatſoever to the contrary notwithſtanding.

Perſons not being ſoldiers committing any offences in any fort or garriſon, &c. not within the juriſdiction of any civil government, may be apprehended; and being charged on oath with the offence, may be committed to ſafe cuſtody, till delivered over to the civil magiſtrate.

XXVI. And be it further enacted by the authority aforeſaid, That every bill, plaint, action, or ſuit, againſt any perſon or perſons, for any act, matter, or thing, to be acted or done in purſuance of this act, or the ſaid other in part recited act, in any of his Majeſty's dominions in *America*, ſhall be brought and proſecuted in and before ſome principal court of record in the colony where ſuch matter or thing ſhall be done or committed; and in caſe the ſame ſhall not be done or commited within the juriſdiction of any ſuch court, then in the court of the colony next to the place where the ſame ſhall be done and committed, and in no other court whatſoever.

Suits in what courts to be proſecuted.

XXVII. And be it further enacted by the authority aforeſaid, That where any troops or parties upon command have oc-

How the troops are to pay in passing ferries.

occasion in their march, in any of his Majesty's dominions in *America*, to pass regular ferries, it shall and may be lawful for the commanding officer either to pass over with his party as passengers, or to hire the ferry-boat entire to himself and his party, debarring others for that time in his option; and in case he shall chuse to take passage for himself and party as passengers he shall only pay for himself and for each person, officer or soldier, under his command, half of the ordinary rate payable by single persons at any such ferry; and in case he shall hire the ferry-boat for himself and party, he shall pay half of the ordinary rate for such boat or boats; and in such places where there are no regular ferries, but that all passengers hire boats at the rate they can agree for, officers with or without parties are to agree for boats at the rates that other persons do in the like cases.

Pecuniary penalties to be paid at the rate of 4s. 8d. Sterling, the Spanish milled dollar.

XXVIII. And be it further enacted by the authority aforesaid, That all sum and sums of money mentioned in this act, and all penalties and forfeitures whatsoever to be incurred or forfeited for any offence, cause, matter, or thing whatsoever, to be done, committed, or omitted to be done in his Majesty's colonies and dominions in *America*, contrary to the true intent and meaning of this act, shall be, and shall be paid and forfeited in lawful money of the colony or place where the same shall be forfeited or become due, at the rate of four shillings and eight pence sterling money for a *Spanish* milled dollar, and not otherwise.

Limitation of actions.

XXIX. And be it further enacted by the authority aforesaid, That if any action, bill, plaint, or suit, shall be brought or commenced against any person or persons for any act, matter, or thing, done or acted in pursuance of this act, that it shall and may be lawful to and for all and every person or persons so sued to plead thereto the general issue that he or they are not guilty, and to give the special matter in evidence to the jury who shall try the cause; and if the verdict therein shall pass for the defendant or defendants, or the plaintiff or plaintiffs therein shall become nonsuit, or suffer a discontinuance, or by any other means judgement therein shall be given for the defendants or defendant therein; that in every such case the justice or justices, or other judge or judges of the court in which such action shall be brought, shall by force and virtue of this act allow unto such defendant or defendants his or their treble costs, which he or they shall have sustained, or be put to, by reason of the defence of such suit, for which cost such defendant and defendants shall have the like remedy as in other cases where costs are by the law given to defendants.

General issue.

Treble costs.

This act to be in force from 24 March, 1765. to 24 March, 1767.

XXX. And be it further enacted by the authority aforesaid, That this act and every thing herein contained, shall continue and be in force in all his Majesty's dominions in *America*, from the twenty fourth day of *March*, in the year one thousand seven hundred and sixty five, until the twenty fourth day of *March* in the year of our Lord one thousand seven hundred and sixty seven.

CAP.

CAP. XXXIV.

An act for applying the money granted in this session of parliament, for defraying the charge of the pay and clothing of the militia of that part of Great Britain *called* England *for one year, beginning the twenty fifth day of* March, *one thousand seven hundred and sixty five; and for punishing militia men for neglecting their duty.*

Preamble.

WHEREAS the sum of eighty thousand pounds has been granted to his Majesty, for defraying the charge of pay and cloathing for the militia, for one year, from the twenty fifth day of *March*, one thousand seven hundred and sixty five: in order therefore that the charge of pay and cloathing for such militia may be duly and properly defrayed and satisfied; be it enacted by the King's most excellent majesty, by and with the advice and consent of the lords spiritual and temporal and commons in this present parliament assembled, and by the authority of the same, That in every county, riding, or place, within that part of *Great Britain* called *England*, where the militia is or shall be raised, the receiver or receivers general of the land tax of such county, riding, or place respectively, shall issue and pay the whole sums required, in the manner and for the several uses, herein after mentioned; that is to say, for the pay of the said militia for four calendar months in advance, at the rate of six shillings a day for each adjutant, where an adjutant is appointed; and at the rate of one shilling for each serjeant, with the addition of two shillings and six pence a week for each serjeant major, where a serjeant major is appointed; and at the rate of six pence a day for each drummer, with the addition of six pence a day for each drum major, where a drum major is appointed; and also at the rate of six pence a month for each private man and drummer, for defraying the contingent expences of each regiment, battalion, or independant company of militia, one penny whereof shall be applied to defraying the hospital expences of each regiment, battalion, or independant company, during the time of the mens being from home, on account of their annual exercise; and also for half a year's salary for the clerk of each regiment or battalion of militia belonging to such county, riding, or place, at the rate of fifty pounds a year; and also for the respective allowances to the clerk of the general meetings, and clerks of the several subdivision meetings, at the rates following; that is to say, To the clerk of the general meetings, at the rate of five pounds five shillings for each meeting; and to the several clerks of the subdivision meetings, at the rate of one pound one shilling for each meeting; and also for the cloathing of the militia for such county, riding, or place, after the rate of three pounds ten shillings for each serjeant, and two pounds for each drummer, with the addition of one pound for each serjeant major, and each drum major; and with respect to the private militia men, where the militia hath been embodied, or having not been embodied, hath not been cloathed within

Where the militia is or shall be raised, the receiver general of the county is to issue 4 months pay in advance, according to the establishment of pay here set down;

with half a year's salary to the regimental and battalion clerks;

and the allowances to the clerks of the general and subdivision meetings;

and pay for cloathing of the militia.

three years, at the rate of one pound ten ſhillings for each private man.

The above ſums are not to be paid, if pay has not before been iſſued, till the ld. lieut. or deputies ſhall have certified to the treaſury and receivers general the inrolment of 3 fifths of the men and officers.

II. Provided nevertheleſs, That in any county or place, where pay has not been yet iſſued for the militia, no pay ſhall be iſſued until his Majeſty's lieutenant, or, in his abſence, any three deputy lieutenants, of any ſuch county, riding, or place, ſhall have certified to the commiſſioners of his Majeſty's treaſury, and to the receiver general of the land tax, That three fifths of the number of private militia men of ſuch county, riding, or place, have been inrolled, and that three fifths of the proportion of their commiſſion officers have accepted their commiſſions, and entered their qualifications as by law required.

The money is to be paid by the receiver-general to the clerk of the regiment or battalion (except the allowances to the clerks of the meetings) upon producing the warrant of his appointment; and for independant companies, to the reſpective captains, or to their order; according to the eſtabliſhment laid down in the militia act of 2 Geo. 3.

III. And be it enacted, That all ſuch ſums of money aforeſaid, except ſuch as ſhall be due to the ſeveral clerks of the meetings aforeſaid, ſhall, where the militia has never been embodied, be paid by the ſaid receiver or receivers-general of the land tax, into the hands of the clerk or clerks of the regiments or battalions of militia belonging to ſuch county, riding, or place, upon his or their producing his or their warrant or warrants of appointment to ſuch office, under the hand and ſeal of his Majeſty's lieutenant for ſuch reſpective county, riding, or place; and where the militia has been embodied, into the hands of the clerk or clerks of the regiments or battalions, upon his or their producing his or their warrant or warrants of appointment to ſuch office, under the hand and ſeal of the colonel, or, where there is no colonel, of the commanding officer of each regiment or battalion reſpectively, notwithſtanding ſuch militia ſhall have been diſembodied; and where the militia ſhall be formed into an independant company, or independant companies, ſuch ſums as aforeſaid ſhall be paid by the ſaid receiver or receivers-general of the land tax, into the hands of the reſpective captain of each independant company of militia, or to ſuch perſon as ſuch reſpective captain ſhall authorize to receive the ſame, according to the number of perſons hereby intitled to receive pay and cloathing, of which ſuch regiment or regiments, battalion or battalions, independant company or independant companies, ſhall have been appointed to conſiſt, according to the eſtabliſhment laid down in an act paſſed in the ſecond year of the reign of his preſent Majeſty, intituled, *An act to explain, amend, and reduce into one act of parliament, the ſeveral laws now in being, relating to the raiſing and training the militia within that part of* Great Britain *called* England; and ſuch receiver or receivers-general of the land tax ſhall alſo, within fourteen days after the expiration of the third calendar month from the time of the ſaid firſt payment, make a ſecond payment for four calendar months in advance; and ſhall alſo, within fourteen days after the expiration of the third calendar month from the time of the ſaid ſecond payment, make a third payment for four calendar months in advance, for the pay and contingent expences of the militia, and for the allowances to the regimental or battalion clerk or clerks aforeſaid, in the proportions herein before mentioned; and the receipts of ſuch clerk or clerks, and of ſuch captain

A ſecond payment is alſo to be made within 3 months after the firſt; and a third within three months after the ſecond.

Receipts of the perſons to whom the money ſhall be ſo

captain of an independant company or captains of independant companies, or of ſuch perſon or perſons as ſuch captain or captains ſhall ſo authorize to receive ſuch money as aforeſaid, ſhall be a ſufficient diſcharge to ſuch receiver or receivers-general of the land tax for the ſeveral ſums of money ſo by him or them paid.

paid, diſcharge the receivers general.

IV. And be it enacted, That the clerk of each regiment or battalion of militia ſhall forthwith, after the receipt of ſuch ſums of money as aforeſaid, pay, or cauſe to be paid, one calendar month's pay in advance to the adjutant of ſuch regiment or battalion reſpectively; and to the captain or commanding officer of each company belonging to ſuch regiment or battalion, two months pay in advance for the ſerjeants, drummers, and the contingent expences of his reſpective company; out of which ſaid contingent money each captain ſhall pay to the commanding officer of each regiment or battalion one penny a month for each private man and drummer, for the defraying the expences of the hoſpital; and alſo to the commanding officer of the company to which the ſerjeant-major and drum-major ſhall belong, two months pay in advance for ſuch ſerjeant and drum-major; and ſo from time to time ſo long as any money on that account ſhall remain in his hands: which pay every ſuch captain or commanding officer is hereby required to diſtribute to each perſon belonging to his company, by this act intitled to receive the ſame, as it ſhall become due; and ſhall, once in every year, give in to the clerk of the regiment or battalion to which ſuch company ſhall belong, or, if captain of an independant company, to the receiver-general, an account of the ſeveral payments he ſhall have made in purſuance of this act, according to the following form:

The regimental and battalion clerks are to pay in advance one month's pay to the adjutant; and 2 months pay to each captain, for the ſerjeants, drummers, and contingent expences of the ſaid company; captain to pay for each man 1 d. *per* month out of the contingent money, towards charges of the hoſpital; and for the ſerjeant major and drum-major; to be paid to the commanding officer of the company to which they belong; captains to diſtribute the pay accordingly; and account for the ſame yearly to the clerk or receiver general, if an independant company, according to the following form;

County of Dr.			*Per Contra* Cr.		
To caſh received of Mr. regimental or battalion clerk, or receiver general, *as the caſe ſhall be*, for two months pay in advance			Paid ſerjeant for days pay from the of to the of following —— ——		
			Ditto as ſerjeant-major (if one in the company)		
			Paid ſerjeant for days pay from the of to the of following —— ——		
			Paid drummer days at ſix pence from the of to the of following ——		
			Ditto as drum-major (if one in the company)		
			Paid drummer days from the of to the of following		
			Two months contingencies for men and two drummers, at ſix pence per month each		

And ſhall pay back to the ſaid clerk, or to the receiver-general, as the caſe ſhall be, the ſurplus (if any) of the money by him from time to time received, and then remaining in his hands (except the money by this act allowed for contingent expences) which ſhall once in every year be accounted for by the captain of each company reſpectively, in manner aforeſaid, and the balance thereof ſhall be by him paid into the hands of the clerk of the regiment or battalion to which ſuch company ſhall belong, to be applied to the general uſe of the ſaid regiment or battalion, as the field officers and captains thereof, or the greater part of them, ſhall direct; and the captain of each independant company is hereby required to diſtribute to each perſon belonging to his company intitled thereto, ſuch money as he ſhall receive by virtue of this act; and the ſaid money allowed for the contingent expences of each independant company of militia, ſhall be reſpectively applied to the particular uſe of ſuch independant company, by the captain thereof.

and pay back the ſurplus monies in his hands, except the contingent expences, which is to be accounted for, and applied to the general uſe of the regiment, &c. Captains of independant companies to diſtribute the pay to their men, and apply the money allowed for contingent expences.

V. And be it enacted, That the ſaid regimental or battalion clerk may and ſhall retain to his own uſe, out of the money ſo by him received, ſuch further ſums as ſhall complete the allowance herein before made for his ſalary; and ſuch regimental or battalion clerk ſhall pay to ſuch perſon or perſons as ſhall produce an order from the commanding officer of ſuch regiment or battalion, ſuch ſums of money as ſhall be due and owing for or on account of the cloathing of the ſaid regiments or battalions, not exceeding the rates herein before-mentioned.

Clerk to retain money in his hands for his own ſalary; and diſcharge the cloathing bills.

VI. And be it further enacted, That whenever his Majeſty's lieutenant, or any three or more deputy lieutenants, of any county, riding, or place, ſhall have fixed the days of exerciſe for the militia, he or they ſhall, as ſoon as may be, certify the ſame to the receiver-general of ſuch county, riding or place, ſpecifying the number of men, and the number of days ſuch men are to be abſent from home on account of ſuch exerciſe; and ſuch receiver-general is hereby required, within fourteen days after the receipt of ſuch certificate, to iſſue and pay to the clerk of the ſeveral regiments or battalions, at the rate of ſeven ſhillings and ſix pence *per* day for the captain of each company, and at the rate of three ſhillings and ſix pence *per* day for each lieutenant, and of three ſhillings *per* day for each enſign; and alſo at the rate of one ſhilling *per* day for each private militia man, with the addition of ſix pence *per* day for each corporal of the militia, ſo to be called out to exerciſe, for the number of days ſuch officers and men ſhall be abſent from home on account of ſuch exerciſe; and in ſuch counties where there ſhall be independant companies only, the receiver-general of each ſuch reſpective county ſhall iſſue and pay to the captains of the independant companies, at the rate of ſeven ſhillings and ſix pence *per* day for each captain, three ſhillings and ſix pence *per* day for each lieutenant, and three ſhillings *per* day for each enſign; and alſo at the rate of one ſhilling *per* day for each private militia man, with the addition of ſix pence *per* day for each corporal

When the ld. lieuts. or deputies ſhall have fixed the days of exerciſe, they are to certify the ſame to the receiver general, ſpecifying the number of men, and days they ſhall be abſent from home. Receiver-general to iſſue thereupon pay for officers and men to the regimental clerk, &c. Where there ſhall be independant companies only, the receiver-general is to iſſue pay to the captains, according to

poral of the militia, so to be called out to exercise, for the number of days such officers and men shall be absent from home on account of such exercise; and the said regimental or battalion clerks are hereby required forthwith to pay the proportion of pay belonging to each captain of the said regiments or battalions, the proportion of pay belonging to each captain, and likewise the pay belonging to their respective companies.

the rate here set down.

Regimental clerk to pay over the money to the respective captains.

VII. And be it further enacted, That the captain of each company shall make up an account of all monies received and paid by him on account of such exercise, according to the following form:

Captains to make up their account according to the following form;

County of	Dr.			Per Contra	Cr.		
To cash received of the regimental or battalion clerk, or receiver general, *as the case shall be*, for days pay of men				Paid militia men days			
				Paid additional pay to corporals days			

Which acount shall be signed by the said captain, and countersigned by the commanding officer; and such captain shall, within ten days after the time of such exercise, deliver such account, and pay the balance, if there be any due, to the regimental or battalion clerk; or, if captain of an independant company, to the receiver-general: and such accounts shall be allowed as sufficient vouchers in the passing of the accounts of such receiver general, at the receipt of his Majesty's exchequer.

to be signed by them, and countersigned by the commanding officer, and delivered with the balance to the clerk, or receiver general.

Accounts allowed sufficient vouchers.

VIII. Provided always, and be it enacted, That where any regiment, battalion, or independant company of militia, is or shall be embodied, and called out into actual service, and thereby the officers and private militia men are or shall be intitled to the same pay, as the officers and private men in his Majesty's other regiments of foot receive, all pay from the receiver or receivers general of the land tax for the county, riding, or place, to which such regiment, battalion, or independant company of militia shall belong, whether to the adjutants, serjeants, private militia men, or others; and all money allowed as aforesaid for the contingent expences of such regiment, battalion, or independant company of militia; and also the allowance to the clerk of such regiment or battalion, shall, during such time of actual service, and until such regiment, battalion, or independant company, shall be disembodied and returned home by order of their commanding officers, cease and not be paid.

During the time the troops are embodied, and called out into actual service, and receive pay as the King's other forces, all pay and allowances from the receivers general is to cease.

IX. And be it enacted, That the said receiver or receivers of the land tax shall pay to the clerk of the general meetings his allowance, at the rate of five pounds five shillings for each meeting, upon his producing an order or orders for that purpose from his Majesty's lieutenant, or from three deputy lieutenants assembled at some general meeting or meetings; and shall also pay to each and every the clerks of the subdivision meetings their several allowances, at the rate of one pound one shilling

Receivers general to pay the allowances to clerks of the general meetings, and to the clerks of the subdivision meetings, upon producing orders from the lieutenant or dep. lieutenants. Orders to discharge receivers general. for each meeting, upon his or their producing an order or orders from one or more deputy lieutenant, or deputy lieutenants assembled in the several subdivision meetings; which said order or orders shall be to the said receiver or receivers general of the land tax, a sufficient discharge for the payment of such allowances, and be allowed in his and their account.

Regimental and battalion clerks to give security for paying and accounting for the monies received by them; the bonds to be lodged with the receivers general, and put in suit by them on non-performance of the condition; and they are intitled thereupon to full costs and charges, and 5 l. *per cent.* of the money recovered; the residue to be accounted for to the auditor.

X. Provided always, and be it enacted, That the clerk of each regiment or battalion of militia, shall give security to the receiver or receivers general of the land tax of the county, riding, or place, to which such regiment or battalion shall belong, by a bond to his Majesty in the penalty of one half of the sum required for the whole year's charge of the regiment or battalion of militia to which such clerk shall belong, for duly answering and paying such sums as he shall, from time to time, have received, and for duly accounting for the same, and for performance of the trust hereby in him reposed; which said bond shall be lodged in the hands of the receiver or receivers general of the land tax for the respective county, riding, or place, who, in case the said regimental or battalion clerk shall not duly perform the conditions comprized in the said bond, shall, and is hereby required forthwith to put the said bond in suit in the name of his Majesty, his heirs, and successors; the full costs and charges of which suit, in case judgement shall be given against such regimental or battalion clerk, shall be paid by him to the said receiver or receivers general of the land tax, who shall likewise be intitled to, and receive to his or their own use, at the rate of five pounds *per centum* out of all such monies as shall be by him or them recovered thereon; and shall account for the residue thereof with the proper auditor of his Majesty's revenue; the said receiver or receivers general of the land tax charging himself or themselves, therewith, upon the next account of the land tax to be by him or them passed.

The regimental and battalion clerks, and captains of independant companies, are to deliver in accounts of their receipts and disbursements, and pay over the balance to the receivers general; who are to transmit the accounts into the auditor's office.

XI. And be it enacted, That the clerk of every regiment or battalion of militia, and the captain of every independant company of militia, in every county, riding, and place within that part of *Great Britain* aforesaid, shall, between the twenty fifth day of *March* and the twenty fourth day of *June*, one thousand seven hundred and sixty five, deliver to the receiver or receivers general of the land tax for the county, riding, or place, to which such regiment, battalion, or independant company shall belong, a fair account in writing, of all monies by him received and disbursed for the service of the preceding year, in pursuance of this act, with proper vouchers for the same; and shall pay back to the said receiver or receivers general of the land tax, any surplus of such monies that shall then be in his hands; which said accounts signed by such regimental or battalion clerk, or by such captain of an independant company respectively, shall be transmitted by the said receiver or receivers general of the land tax, into the office of the proper auditor of his Majesty's revenue.

Recovery of penalties, &c.

XII. Provided always, and be it enacted, That all penalties, all costs and charges of suit, and all sums of money for which any perſon or perſons is or are by this act made anſwerable, may, and ſhall be recovered in any of his Majeſty's courts of record at *Weſtminſter*, by action of debt, bill, plaint, or information, wherein no eſſoin, wager at law, or protection, or more than one imparlance, ſhall be allowed.

No fee payable for any warrant or ſum of money iſſued in purſuance of this act.

XIII. Provided always, and be it enacted, That no fee or gratuity whatſoever, ſhall be given or paid for or upon account of any warrant or ſum of money which ſhall be iſſued in relation to, or in purſuance of, this act.

Officers on half-pay ſerving in the militia, may receive the ſubſiſtence-money payable to lieutenants or enſigns, they taking the following oath before a juſtice.

XIV. Provided always, and be it enacted, That any perſon being on half-pay, and ſerving in the militia, ſhall and may, and he is hereby impowered to receive and take the ſubſiſtence-money, by this act directed to be paid to captains, lieutenants, or enſigns; and the receiving and taking ſuch ſubſiſtence-money by any ſuch captain, lieutenant, or enſign, ſhall not be deemed a receiving or taking pay, ſo as in any manner to prevent ſuch perſon on half-pay receiving his half-pay; and ſuch perſon ſhall take the following oath before ſome juſtice of the peace, who is hereby impowered to adminiſter the ſame;

The oath.

I A. B. *do ſwear, That I had not, between the* *any place or employment of profit civil or military under his Majeſty, beſides my allowance of half-pay as a reduced* *in* *late regiment of* *ſave and except my ſubſiſtence as a lieutenant or enſign*, as the caſe may be, *for ſerving in the militia of the county of*

And the taking the ſaid oath ſhall be ſufficient to intitle ſuch perſon to receive his half-pay, without taking any other oath; any law, uſage, or cuſtom, to the contrary thereof notwithſtanding.

Act 2. Geo. 3.

XV. And whereas great difficulties occur in recovering one of the penalties inflicted by an act paſſed in the ſecond year of his preſent Majeſty's reign, intitled, *An act to explain, amend, and reduce into one act of parliament, the ſeveral laws now in being, relating to the raiſing and training the militia within that part of* Great Britain *called* England; which penalty is to enforce an attendance on the annual exerciſe, by puniſhing ſuch militia men (not labouring under any infirmity incapacitating them) as ſhall not appear at the times and places of exerciſe appointed as by the ſaid act is directed, which difficulties, if not timely removed, may prove detrimental to the ſervice; be it therefore enacted by the authority aforeſaid, That if any militia man (not labouring under any infirmity incapacitating him,) ſhall not appear at the time and place of exerciſe appointed as aforeſaid, and at which he ought to appear in purſuance of the ſaid act, every ſuch militia man may, for every ſuch offence, be apprehended, without any previous ſummons, by warrant from any one juſtice of the peace of the ſame county, riding, or place, or of any other county, riding, or place, within which ſuch offender ſhall be found, upon oath made before ſuch juſtice of the peace, that

Militia man (not being incapacitated) neglecting to appear at the appointed time and place of exerciſe may be apprehended;

ſuch militia man did not appear at the time and place appointed as aforeſaid for exerciſe; and upon producing alſo to the ſame juſtice a certificate, ſigned by the clerk of the proper ſubdiviſion meeting of the county wherein ſuch militia man was inrolled, that it appears to him, the ſaid clerk, by the roll in his cuſtody, that the ſaid defaulter is, or, at the time of ſuch offence committed, was a militia man for the county wherein he ought to have appeared as aforeſaid, mentioning in ſuch certificate the date of his inrollment; and alſo upon proof made upon oath before the ſaid juſtice of peace, of the hand writing of the ſaid clerk (both which oaths before-mentioned the ſaid juſtice is hereby impowered to adminiſter;) and if any militia man ſo apprehended as aforeſaid, ſhall not prove to the ſatisfaction of the juſtice of peace, before whom he ſhall be brought on ſuch warrant, that he the ſaid militia man did, at the time appointed for ſuch appearance, labour under ſome infirmity incapacitating him, or that he had then changed his place of abode, and removed upon ſuch notice and certificate as in the ſaid act is for that purpoſe directed, into the ſubdiviſion wherein he ſhall be dwelling at the time of his being ſo apprehended; or that he, at the time of ſuch default of appearance, was inrolled alſo to ſerve in the militia of ſome other county, riding, or place, and hath thereby forfeited, and upon conviction thereof actually paid the penalty of ten pounds inflicted for that offence by an act paſſed in the fourth year of his preſent Majeſty's reign, to explain and amend the above mentioned act, he the ſaid defaulter (not making ſatisfactory proof as aforeſaid of one or other of the ſaid three cauſes of excuſe) ſhall ſtand immediately convicted of his ſaid offence by the juſtice of peace before whom he ſhall be ſo brought (whether ſuch juſtice be of the ſame county, riding, or place for which ſuch militia man is or was inrolled to ſerve, or of any other county, riding, or place) and the ſaid juſtice of the peace ſhall then require and demand of ſuch offender the immediate payment of the ſaid penalty; and upon refuſal or neglect to make ſuch immediate payment into the hands of the ſaid juſtice, or of ſuch perſon as he ſhall then direct, for the uſe of the regiment or battalion of militia wherein ſuch defaulter is or was inrolled, to ſerve as part of the common ſtock of ſuch regiment or battalion, the juſtice of peace before whom ſuch militia man ſhall be ſo convicted ſhall, by warrant, commit him to the common gaol of the county, riding, or place, where he ſhall be ſo convicted, there to remain without bail or mainprize for the ſpace of ſix months, or until he ſhall have paid the ſaid penalty of twenty pounds.

Oath being made before a juſtice of ſuch default. and that he was inrolled, &c. and alſo proof made of the hand writing of the clerk; and if he ſhall not make ſatisfactory proof of one or other of the three cauſes of excuſe here allowed.

he ſhall forfeit 20 l.

and if not paid forthwith, he ſhall be committed for 6 months.

XVI. And to obviate any difficulties which may otherwiſe ariſe in carrying into execution a clauſe in the ſaid act paſſed in the fourth year of his preſent Majeſty's reign, whereby the like penalty and puniſhment are inflicted on militia men who, after having joined their corps, ſhall deſert during the time of annual exerciſe, and ſhall not be taken till after the time thereof is expired, as are, by the above mentioned act of the ſecond year of the

Juſtice may proceed againſt deſerters in like

the ſaid reign, inflicted on militia men neglecting to appear; be it enacted by the authority aforeſaid, That one juſtice of the peace in any county, riding, or place, wherein ſuch deſerter ſhall be found, may proceed againſt ſuch deſerter in the ſame manner, and execute the like powers in that caſe, as are herein before given in the caſe of militia men not appearing at the time and place appointed for annual exerciſe.

manner, as againſt militia men neglecting to appear at the appointed time and place of annual exerciſe.

CAP. XXXV.

An act for granting to his Majeſty certain duties on the exportation of coals; and of ſeveral East India *goods; and upon policies of aſſurance for retaining, upon the exportation of white callicoes and muſlins, a further part of the duties paid on the importation thereof; and for obviating a doubt with reſpect to ſtamp duties impoſed upon deeds by two former acts.*

Moſt gracious Sovereign,

WHEREAS *by an act made in this ſeſſion of parliament, certain annuities are granted in reſpect of ſeveral navy, victualling and tranſport bills, and charged upon the fund commonly called* The Sinking Fund: *we your Majeſty's moſt dutiful and loyal ſubjects, the commons of* Great Britain *in parliament aſſembled, towards making good the payment of the ſaid annuities ſo charged on the ſaid fund, have reſolved to give and grant unto your Majeſty the ſeveral rates, duties, and ſums of money, herein after mentioned*; and do moſt humbly beſeech your Majeſty, that it may be enacted; and be it enacted by the King's moſt excellent majeſty, by and with the advice and conſent of the lords ſpiritual and temporal, and commons, in this preſent parliament aſſembled, and by the authority of the ſame, That from and after the firſt day of *June*, one thouſand ſeven hundred and ſixty five, there ſhall be raiſed, levied, collected, and paid, unto his Majeſty, his heirs, and ſucceſſors, for every chaldron of coals, *Newcaſtle* meaſure, which ſhall be ſhipped for exportation to any part beyond the ſeas, except to *Ireland*, the iſle of *Man*, or the *Britiſh* dominions in *America*, an additional duty of four ſhillings, and after that rate for any greater or leſs quantity, over and above the preſent duties now payable for the ſame; which ſaid additional duty hereby granted, ſhall be raiſed, levied, collected, and paid, in the ſame manner, and under ſuch reſtrictions, penalties, and forfeitures, and by ſuch rules, ways, and methods, as the former duties payable to his Majeſty, upon the exportation of coals, are raiſed, levied, collected, and paid, as fully and to all intents and purpoſes as if the ſeveral clauſes, powers, directions, penalties, and forfeitures, relating thereto, were particularly repeated and again enacted in the body of this preſent act.

Preamble.

From and after 1 June, 1765, the following additional duties are to take place; viz. 4 s. *per* chaldron on all coals ſhipped for exportation to parts beyond ſeas, except to Ireland, the iſle of Man, and Britiſh dominions in America;

II. And it is hereby further enacted by the authority aforeſaid, That from and after the ſaid firſt day of *June*, there ſhall be raiſed, levied, collected, and paid, unto his Majeſty, his heirs, and

5 l. per cent. *ad valorem* on all wrought ſilks and

stuffs from Persia, China, and India; and on printed callicoes.

and successors, for and upon all wrought silks, bengals, and stuffs mixed with silk or herba, of the manufacture of *Persia*, *China*, or *East India*, and upon all callicoes, printed, dyed, painted, or stained there, which shall be shipped for exportation from *Great Britain* to any part beyond the seas, except to *Africa* or the *British* dominions in *America*, a subsidy of poundage of twelve pence for every twenty shillings, of the true and real value of such goods, according to the gross price at which they were sold at the sales of the united company of merchants of *England* trading to the *East Indies*, if the said goods were sold at the company's sales, or according to the gross price at which they were sold at the custom-house sales, in case the said goods were after condemnation sold there; which subsidy hereby granted shall be paid without any allowance or deduction whatsoever; and shall be raised, levied, collected, and recovered, in the same manner, and by such ways and means, and under such penalties and forfeitures, and with such allowances for goods lost or taken at sea, as the subsidy of poundage for any goods and merchandizes exported from this kingdom, may be raised, levied, collected, and recovered, by any act of parliament now in force, as fully to all intents and purposes as if the several clauses, powers, directions, penalties, and forfeitures, relating thereto, were particularly repeated and again enacted in the body of this present act.

to be paid without any deduction, &c.

Additional clause to be inserted in the bond to be given on exportation of the said goods:

III. And it is hereby further enacted by the authority aforesaid, That from and after the said first day of *June*, upon the entry of any wrought silks, bengals, and stuffs mixed with silk or herba, of the manufacture of *Persia*, *China*, or *East India*, or callicoes, painted, dyed, printed, or stained there, for exportation to *Africa*, or the *British* dominions in *America*, the bond which is now by law required to be given for the due exportation of such goods, shall be with further condition, that the same shall be there landed accordingly, and not in any other part or place beyond the seas; and to produce a certificate within eighteen months under the hands and seals of the collector, or other principal officer of the customs, resident at the port or place in the *British* dominions in *America*, for such of the said goods as shall be entered for and landed there, testifying the landing thereof; and for such of the said goods as shall be entered for *Africa*, the bonds so as aforesaid entered into, shall not be delivered up or discharged, until proof is made by the oath of the master, mate, purser, or other person having the charge of the ship or vessel, during the voyage in which the said goods were exported, that the said goods and every part thereof, were fairly landed or disposed of, in or on some part of the coast of *Africa*, and that no part of the said goods had been relanded in any part of *Great Britain*, or the islands of *Guernsey*, *Jersey*, *Alderney*, *Sark*, or *Man*, or either of them, or any other part or place beyond the seas, except some part of *Africa*; and by the oath of the merchant exporter (if living) that, to the best of his, her, or their knowledge and belief, such goods had been disposed of at the place or places mentioned in the oath made by the master, mate, purser,

and a certificate to be returned of the due landing thereof; if in America, within 18 months.

Bond given on goods entered for Africa, not to be discharged, till oath be made by the master of the due landing and disposal thereof, thereof with-

purser, or other person, having the charge of the ship or vessel, during the voyage; which proof shall be made within eighteen months from the date of each respective bond, before the collector and comptroller, or other principal officer of the customs, at the port for the time being where such bonds shall be entered into, who are hereby respectively impowered to administer the same; and in case no such proofs shall be made as aforesaid, within the time herein before mentioned, it shall and may be lawful for the respective commissioners of the customs in *Great Britain*, to cause such bonds to be put in suit, unless they shall find sufficient cause to forbear the same; any law, custom, or usage, to the contrary in any wise notwithstanding.

out being relanded, &c. and be confirmed by the exporter's oath.

Proof to be made within 18 months; otherwise the bond to be put in suit.

IV. And be it further enacted by the authority aforesaid, That from and after the said first day of *June*, there shall be raised, levied, collected, and paid, unto his Majesty, his heirs, and successors, for every skin or piece of vellum or parchment, or sheet or piece of paper, upon which shall be ingrossed, written, or printed, any policy of assurance to be made or entered into within the cities of *London* or *Westminster*, or elsewhere within the limits of the weekly bills of mortality, over and above all other duties, an additional stamp duty of two pence; and for every skin or piece of vellum or parchment, or sheet or piece of paper, upon which shall be ingrossed, written, or printed, any policy of assurance to be made or entered into within all other parts of *Great Britain*, over and above all other duties, an additional stamp duty of two shillings and six pence.

After 1 June, 1765, an additional duty of 2 d. to take place on all policies and assurances within the weekly bills;

and of 2 s. 6d. within all other parts of Great Britain.

V. And be it further enacted by the authority aforesaid, That all powers, regulations, provisions, articles, clauses, penalties, forfeitures, distribution of penalties and forfeitures, and all other matters and things prescribed, inflicted, and appointed, by any former act or acts of parliament, relating to the duties on vellum, parchment, and paper (not hereby altered) shall be in full force and effect, with relation to the additional stamp duties hereby imposed; and shall be applied and put in execution, for the managing, raising, levying, collecting, securing, receiving, and paying thereof, and accounting for the same, as fully to all intents and purposes, as if such powers, regulations, provisions, articles, clauses, penalties, forfeitures, distribution of penalties and forfeitures, and other matters and things, were herein repeated, re-enacted, and applied to the said stamp duties hereby granted.

Clauses and provisions, &c. in other acts, relating to the duties on vellum, parchment, and paper, extended to the additional duties here laid.

VI. And be it further enacted by the authority aforesaid, That if any person or persons shall counterfeit or forge, or procure to be counterfeited or forged, any seal, stamp, or mark, to resemble any seal, stamp, or mark, directed or allotted to be used by this act for the purpose of denoting the duties by this or any other act of parliament granted on policies of assurance; or shall counterfeit or resemble the impression of the same, thereby to evade the payment of any of the said duties; or shall utter, vend, or sell, any vellum, parchment, or paper, liable to any such stamp duties, with such counterfeit

The counterfeiting or forging any of the stamps or seals.

or vending counterfeit stamps.

stamp,

stamp, mark, or impression thereon (knowing the same to be counterfeit) or shall privately or fraudulently use any seal, stamp, or mark, allowed to be used by this act, relating to the said stamp duties, with intent to defraud his Majesty, his heirs and successors, of any of the said duties; every such person so offending, and being thereof lawfully convicted, shall be adjudged a felon, and shall suffer death as in cases of felony, without benefit of clergy.

or fraudulently using the legal ones, is felony, without benefit of clergy.

10 per cent. of the duties payable on the importation of white callicoes, and muslins, besides the one half of the old subsidy, is to be retained on the exportation thereof to parts beyond seas, except to Africa, and the British American plantations.

VII. And it is hereby further enacted by the authority aforesaid, That from and after the said first day of *June*, there shall be retained out of the duties which shall have been paid upon the importation of white callicoes or muslin, for such of the said goods as shall be exported from this kingdom without having been printed, stained, painted, or died therein, to any parts or places beyond the seas (except to *Africa*, or the *British* colonies and plantations in *America*) besides the one half of the rate or duty commonly called *The Old Subsidy*, which now remains, and is not drawn back for the same, the further sum of two pounds for every one hundred pounds of the true and real value of such goods, according to the gross price at which they were sold at the sale of the united company of merchants trading to the *East Indies*; which sum of two pounds shall be retained, without any abatement or deduction, out of the net duties granted on such goods respectively by two several acts of parliament, the one made in the eleventh and twelfth year of the reign of King *William* the Third, intituled, *An act for laying further duties upon wrought silks, muslins, and some other commodities of the* East Indies; *and for enlarging the time for purchasing certain reversionary annuities therein mentioned*; and the other made in the third and fourth year of the reign of Queen *Anne*, intituled, *An act for continuing duties upon low wines; and upon coffee, tea, chocolate, spices, and pictures; and upon hawkers, pedlars, and petty chapmen, and upon muslins; and for granting new duties upon several of the said commodities; and also upon callicoes, china ware, and drugs*; any law, usage, or custom, to the contrary notwithstanding.

Act 11 & 12 W. 3.

& 3 & 4 Anne.

Addition to the oath to be made on exportation of white callicoes and muslins.

VIII. And it is hereby further enacted by the authority aforesaid, That from and after the said first day of *June*, if any white callicoes or muslin shall be entered for exportation, from this kingdom to any part of *Africa*, in every case where the exporter is required by any law now in force to swear that such goods are not landed or intended to be landed in *Great Britain*, *Ireland*, the *Isle of Man*, or any *British* colonies or plantations in *America*, there shall also be added to and included in the oath upon the debenture for such goods, "*or any other place whatsoever in* "*parts beyond the seas (except* Africa):" and if any such white callicoes or muslins so entered for *Africa*, shall nevertheless be carried to, and landed at, any other place or country in parts beyond the seas, the exporter of such goods, and the master or person having the charge of the ship or vessel on board which the same were loaden and exported, shall forfeit double the amount

Landing the said goods, &c. otherwise than where entered for; is forfeiture of double the amount of the drawback,

mount of the drawback paid or to be paid for the ſame, and alſo treble the value of the ſaid goods.

and treble value of the goods.

IX. And be it further enacted by the authority aforeſaid, That the monies ariſing by the ſeveral and reſpective additional duties by this act granted, and alſo from ſuch part of the duties as are hereby directed to be retained, and not drawn back on the exportation of callicoes and muſlins (the neceſſary charges of management, and of raiſing, collecting, receiving, paying, and accounting for the ſaid monies, excepted) ſhall, from time to time, be paid reſpectively into the receipt of his Majeſty's exchequer at *Weſtminſter*, diſtinctly and apart from all other branches of the publick revenue, and ſhall be carried to and made part of the fund commonly called *The ſinking fund*, towards making good the annuities payable in reſpect of the ſaid navy, victualling, and tranſport bills, charged upon the ſaid fund by an act of this ſeſſion of parliament.

These duties, &c. to be paid into the exchequer apart from all other branches of the publick revenue, and to be carried into the ſinking fund.

X. And whereas ſome doubts have ariſen, whether vellum, parchment, and paper, containing policies of aſſurance and charter parties, are ſubject to the ſtamp duties granted in reſpect of deeds, by two acts of parliament made in the twelfth year of the reign of her late majeſty Queen *Anne*, and the thirtieth year of the reign of his late majeſty King *George* the Second; it is hereby declared and enacted by the authority aforeſaid, That the ſtamp duty of ſix pence impoſed by an act made in the twelfth year of the reign of her ſaid late majeſty Queen *Anne*; and alſo the ſtamp duty of one ſhilling impoſed by an act made in the thirtieth year of the reign of his ſaid late majeſty King *George* the Second, on every ſkin or piece of vellum or parchment, or ſheet or piece of paper, upon which ſhall be ingroſſed, written, or printed, in *Great Britain*, any indenture, leaſe, bond, or other deed, not thereby reſpectively otherwiſe charged, ſhall be deemed and taken to extend to, and are hereby extended to charge every ſkin or piece of vellum or parchment, or ſheet or piece of paper, upon which ſhall be ingroſſed, written, or printed, any policy of aſſurance, or any charter party, made or entered into with *Great Britain*, after the ſaid firſt day of *June*.

Policies of aſſurance and charter parties ſubject to the 6d. duty impoſed by act 12 Annæ, and to the 1s. duty impoſed by act 30 Geo. 2.

XI. And be it further enacted by the authority aforeſaid, That every deed, inſtrument, note, memorandum, letter, or other minument or writing, between the captain or maſter, or owner of any ſhip or veſſel, and any merchant, trader, or other perſon, in reſpect to the freight or conveyance of any money, goods, wares, merchandize, or effects, laden or to be laden on board of any ſuch ſhip or veſſel, ſhall be deemed and adjudged to be a charter party.

What ſhall be deemed a charter party.

XII. And it is hereby enacted by the authority aforeſaid, That if any perſon or perſons ſhall at any time be ſued or proſecuted for any thing by him or them done or executed in purſuance of this act, or of any matter or thing in this act contained, ſuch perſon or perſons ſhall and may plead the general iſſue, and give this act and the ſpecial matter in evidence; and if it ſhall appear ſo to have been done, the jury ſhall find for the de-

General iſſue.

defendant or defendants: and if the plaintiff or plaintiffs shall become nonsuited, or discontinue his or their action, after the defendant or defendants shall have appeared; or if judgement shall be given, upon any verdict or demurrer, against the plaintiff or plaintiffs, the defendant or defendants shall recover treble costs, and have the like remedy for the same, as defendants have in other cases by law.

Treble costs.

CAP. XXXVI.

An act to explain, amend, and enforce, the several laws now in being relating to the raising and training the militia within that part of Great Britain *called* England.

Preamble, reciting clause in act 2 Geo. 3.

WHEREAS *by an act of parliament made in the second year of his present Majesty's reign, intituled,* An act to explain, amend, and reduce into one act of parliament, the several laws now in being relating to the raising and training the militia within that part of *Great Britain* called *England*, *it is enacted, That in all counties and places where the militia had not been raised by virtue or in pursuance of the former acts for that purpose, or by virtue or in pursuance of the said act, the sum of five pounds should be annually paid, for and in lieu of every private militia man therein mentioned to be raised within the same; and that his Majesty's lieutenant of every such county and place, or any three or more deputy lieutenants, at the expiration of every year in which the militia for such county and place shall not be raised, shall, from year to year, certify the same in writing under his or their hands; and also the whole amount of the several sums of five pounds* per *man, to be raised in such county not raising the militia as aforesaid, to the justices of the peace, at their general or quarter sessions next held, after the full end and accomplishment of the said year, for such respective county or place: and whereas doubts have arisen, whether such lieutenants are compellable to make such certificates according to the intent and meaning of the said act, and also at what time each respective year ends or is accomplished*; for remedy whereof, be it enacted by the King's most excellent majesty, by and with the advice and consent of the lords spiritual and temporal, and commons in parliament assembled, and by the authority of the same, That from and after the passing of this act, every year, with respect to the certificate herein after directed to be made by his Majesty's lieutenants, or the deputy lieutenants, of each respective county, riding, or place, not raising the militia, shall be deemed and taken to end and be accomplished on the second *Tuesday* in *May* in each respective year; and his Majesty's lieutenants of every county, riding, and place wherein the militia shall not have been raised, or shall not continue to be raised pursuant to, and by virtue of, the several acts of parliament for raising and training the militia of this kingdom, shall, and they, and each and every of them, is and are hereby required to certify in writing under his and their hand and hands, yearly and every year, to the justices of the peace of each respective county, riding and place,

The year, with respect to certificates to be made by lieuts. and dep. lieuts. of counties, the militia whereof has not been duly raised, is to end on the 2d Tuesday in May in every year; and the certificates to be

place, at their general or quarter ſeſſions which ſhall be next holden after the ſecond *Tueſday* in *May* in each year, that the militia has not been raiſed for ſuch county or place for the preceding year; and alſo the whole amount of the ſeveral ſums of five pounds *per* man to be raiſed on ſuch county, riding or place, as aforeſaid.

made to the quarter ſeſſions next after; together with the amount of the ſums to be raiſed.

II. And whereas it may happen that ſome of his Majeſty's lieutenants may be in parts beyond the ſeas, and thereby be incapable of certiſying in the manner directed by the ſaid recited act and this act; be it therefore further enacted by the authority aforeſaid, That in caſe any of his Majeſty's lieutenants ſhall be in parts beyond the ſeas, ſuch lieutenants, and each and every of them, is and are hereby required, by writing under their reſpective hands and ſeals, to appoint three or more deputy lieutenants to certify as aforeſaid; and ſuch deputy lieutenants, or ſome one or more of them, for each reſpective county, riding, and place, is and are hereby required to certify the ſame accordingly, to the juſtices of the peace aſſembled at their general or quarter ſeſſions as aforeſaid.

Where the lieut. of any county ſhall be beyond ſeas, he is to appoint three or more dep. lieuts. who are to certify accordingly.

III. And whereas in ſome counties there may happen to be no lieutenants, by means whereof the ſeveral laws now in being, for raiſing and training the militia, cannot be carried into execution; for remedy whereof, be it further enacted by the authority aforeſaid, That in ſuch counties, ridings, or places, as may happen to have no lieutenant, three or more of the deputy lieutenants in ſuch county, riding, or place, to be nominated and appointed by his Majeſty's ſign manual, are hereby authorized and impowered to proceed and do every act and acts that are neceſſary for the carrying into execution the ſeveral powers of the ſaid acts of the ſecond and fourth years of his preſent Majeſty's reign, and of this act.

In counties, &c. where there ſhall be no lieut. three or more d. lieuts. appointed under the royal ſign manual, are to carry the recited acts into execution.

IV. And be it further enacted by the authority aforeſaid, That in caſe any of his Majeſty's lieutenants ſhall be in parts beyond the ſeas, and no deputy lieutenants ſhall be appointed to certify as aforeſaid for any county, riding, or place, the clerk of the peace for ſuch county, riding, or place, ſhall, and he is hereby required to certify as aforeſaid to the juſtices of the peace at their general quarter ſeſſions aſſembled; and the ſaid juſtices of the peace are hereby required to proceed on ſuch certificate of the clerk of the peace, in the ſame manner as if ſuch certificate had been made by his Majeſty's lieutenant in manner aforeſaid.

Where the lieut. ſhall be beyond ſeas, and no d. lieuts. appointed, the clerk of the peace is to certify.

V. And whereas by an act made in the fourth year of the reign of his preſent Majeſty, intituled, *An act to explain and amend an act paſſed in the ſecond year of the reign of his preſent Majeſty, intituled,* An act to explain, amend, and reduce into one act of parliament, the ſeveral laws now in being, relating to raiſing and training the militia within that part of *Great Britain* called *England*; it is enacted, That in all caſes where the militia had not been raiſed, or ſhould not at any time thereafter continue to be raiſed, for any county or riding, within which any city, town,

Clauſe in act 4 Geo. 3.

town, or place, should not be rated to the rate called *The county rate*, the payment of the said sum of five pounds *per* man, upon the number of private militia men directed to be raised within every county or riding, should be divided and apportioned between each respective county and riding, and each such respective city, town, and place, within the same, and should be paid in the manner directed by the said act: and whereas doubts have arisen about the method of enforcing the payment of such sum and sums of money, as is and are in and by the said act of the fourth year of his present Majesty directed to be paid by such cities, towns, and places, as are not rated to the said rate called *The county rate*; for remedy whereof, be it further enacted by the authority aforesaid, That if any sum or sums of money, which ought to be paid by any such city, town, or place, not rated to the county rate as aforesaid, shall not be paid to the treasurer of the respective county, riding, or place, before the tenth day of *September*, in every year, according to the true intent and meaning of the said act of the fourth year of his present Majesty's reign, and of this act, the justices of the peace for such county, riding, or place, shall, and they are hereby required, at the next *Michaelmas* quarter sessions, to issue out an order to the overseers of the poor of each respective parish or place, within each city, town, or place, not rated to the county rate as aforesaid, requiring such overseers to certify and return to the said justices at their next *Christmas* quarter sessions, the several *Quota's* that each parish or place (within such city, town, or place, not paying to the county rate as aforesaid) pays to the land tax for that year; and such overseers of the poor are hereby required to make such certificate and return accordingly; and upon such certificate and return being made, the said justices so assembled at their *Christmas* quarter sessions, are hereby authorized and required (by their bench warrant, directed to any constable or tythingman, within such respective parishes and places) to cause the same to be levied by distress and sale of the goods and chattels of any churchwarden or churchwardens, or any overseer or overseers of the poor of each and every parish or place within such city, town, or place, not paying to the county rate as aforesaid, rendering the overplus (if any) to the owners of such goods and chattels, after such sum and sums of money, together with the reasonable charges attending such distress and sale, shall be fully paid and satisfied; and such churchwardens and overseers of the poor shall be reimbursed the sum and sums of money so levied on them respectively, by the same ways and means as overseers of the poor are reimbursed the money by them expended for the relief of the poor by any laws now in being.

Where the sums payable by virtue of the recited act, by any city or place, not rated to the county rate, shall not be paid by 10 Sept. yearly, to the treasurer of the county, the justices at their quarter sessions are to issue an order to the parish overseers to certify to the Xtmas quarter session their respective Quota's to the land tax; and according thereto, a bench warrant is to be issued, for levying the sum on the churchwardens and overseers,

who are to be reimbursed the same in like manner as the poor rates.

VI. And whereas it frequently happens, that persons inrolled to serve in the militia, inlist themselves to serve in his Majesty's other forces, before the time of their service in the militia is expired, to the great prejudice of both services; and it is found by experience, that the provisions in the said act of the second year of his present Majesty's reign have been ineffectual for preventing this practice; for remedy whereof, be it further enacted, by the authority aforesaid, That from and after the passing of this act, if any person who is sworn and inrolled to serve in the militia, shall presume to inlist in his Majesty's other forces, contrary to the true intent and meaning of the said act, and of this act, the overseer of the poor of the parish or place for which such man serves, shall, as soon as it comes to his knowledge, acquaint the adjutant of the regiment to which such militia man belongs, with such inlisting; and such adjutant shall forthwith apply to one of his Majesty's justices of the peace; and it shall and may be lawful for such justice of the peace for the county, riding, or place, for which any person so inlisted was inrolled to serve in the militia as aforesaid, to issue his warrant to apprehend such militia man; and such adjutant is hereby impowered to send any serjeant or serjeants, drummer or drummers, belonging to such militia, to search for and apprehend, by virtue of such warrant, any militia man so inlisted as aforesaid; and it shall and may be lawful for any of his Majesty's justices of the peace for any county, riding, or place, where any such militia man shall or may be found, to indorse such warrant (upon application made to him for that purpose) and to cause such militia man to be apprehended and brought before him, or some other justice of the peace for the county, riding, or place, where such militia man shall be apprehended: and if it shall appear upon oath (which oath such justice is hereby impowered to administer) to the justice before whom such person shall be brought, that such person was inrolled to serve in the militia at the time of his inlisting to serve in his Majesty's other forces as aforesaid, and did not acquaint the officer inlisting him therewith, such justice is hereby required, by warrant under his hand and seal, to commit the person so offending to the house of correction of and belonging to the county, riding, or place, where such militia man shall be so apprehended, there to be kept to hard labour for any time not exceeding three months; and such inlisting shall be, and the same is hereby declared to be, null and void; unless the officer with whom such person shall have so inlisted shall, within the space of twenty days, pay to the overseer or overseers of the poor of the parish or place for which such militia man served, the sum of five pounds; which said sum of five pounds shall be applied in the same manner as the money directed to be paid for militia men so inlisting as aforesaid is, by the said act of the second year of his present Majesty's reign, directed to be applied.

Where any person inrolled in the militia shall inlist in his Majesty's other forces, the overseer of the parish is to acquaint the adjutant therewith; who is to apply to a justice for a warrant, and send in pursuit of the offender; and the warrant may be backed by any other justice:

and if it appear that the officer inlisting was not acquainted with such inrollment, the offender is to be committed to hard labour for 3 months,

and the inlisting is void; unless the officer pay 5l. to the overseer, within 20 days, to be applied as by act 2 Geo. 3. is directed.

CAP. XXXVII.

An act for laying certain duties upon Gum Senega *and* Gum Arabic *imported into or exported from* Great Britain, *and for confining the exportation of* Gum Senega *from* Africa *to* Great Britain *only.*

WE, your Majesty's most dutiful and loyal subjects, the commons of *Great Britain* in parliament assembled, towards

Preamble.

wards raising, in such manner as may be least burthensome to your Majesty's subjects, the necessary supplies for defraying the publick expences, have resolved to give and grant unto your Majesty the several rates and duties herein after-mentioned, and do most humbly beseech your Majesty that it may be enacted, and be it enacted by the King's most excellent majesty, by and with the advice and consent of the lords spiritual and temporal, and commons, in this present parliament assembled, and by the authority of the same, That from and after the twenty fourth day of *June*, one thousand seven hundred and sixty five, there shall be raised, collected and paid, unto his Majesty, his heirs and successors, the several rates and duties following; that is to say,

From and after 24 June, 1765, the additional duties following to take place; viz.

For every hundred weight avoirdupois of *Gum Senega* or *Gum Arabic*, which shall be imported into *Great Britain*, the sum of six pence, over and above all other duties imposed by any former act of parliament.

And for every hundred weight avoirdupois of *Gum Senega* or *Gum Arabic*, which shall be exported from *Great Britain* to any parts beyond the seas, the sum of one pound ten shillings, over and above all other duties imposed thereon by any former act of parliament; and after those rates for any greater or less quantity of such goods.

On every Cwt. of Gum Senega and Gum Arabic imported, 6d. and for every Cwt. thereof exported from Great Britain, 1l. 10s.

II. And be it further enacted by the authority aforesaid, That the said duties hereby charged upon *Gum Senega* or *Gum Arabic* imported into *Great Britain*, shall be paid down in ready money without any discount or allowance; and shall not be afterwards drawn back or repaid upon the exportation of the same goods; and shall be raised, levied, collected, and paid, in the same manner and form, and by such rules, ways, and means, and under such penalties and forfeitures, as are prescribed or appointed for raising, levying, collecting and paying, the duty of customs upon goods imported into this kingdom, by any act or acts of parliament now in force; and that the aforesaid duty hereby charged upon *Gum Senega* or *Gum Arabic* exported from *Great Britain*, shall be paid down without any allowance or deduction whatsoever, and shall be raised, levied, collected and recovered, in the same manner, and by such ways and means, and under such penalties and forfeitures, and with such allowances for goods lost at sea, as the subsidy of poundage for any goods and merchandizes exported from *Great Britain* may be raised, levied, collected and recovered, by any act of parliament now in force, as fully to all intents and purposes as if the several clauses, powers, directions, penalties and forfeitures respectively relating thereto, were particularly repeated and again enacted in the body of this present act.

Duties to be paid down, without discount; and without drawback;

III. And be it further enacted by the authority aforesaid, That the money arising by the several rates and duties herein before granted (except the necessary charges of raising, collecting

and to be paid into the exchequer di-ing, recovering and paying the ſame) ſhall, from time to time, be paid into the receipt of his Majeſty's exchequer, diſtinctly and apart from all other branches of the publick revenue; and after ſatisfying the charges laid thereupon by any act of this ſeſſion of parliament, ſhall be there reſerved, to be from time to time diſpoſed of by parliament. ſtinct from all other branches of the publick revenue.

IV. And whereas it may be for the benefit and encouragement of the manufactures of this kingdom, to confine the exportation of *Gum Senega* from *Africa* to *Great Britain* only; be it therefore enacted by the authority aforeſaid, That from and after the twenty fourth day of *June*, one thouſand ſeven hundred and ſixty five, no *Gum Senega* ſhall be exported from any port or place upon the coaſt of *Africa*, unto any other place unleſs to *Great Britain* only, under the like ſecurities, penalties, and forfeitures, as are particularly mentioned in an act of parliament made in the twelfth year of the reign of King *Charles* the Second, intituled, *An act for the encouraging and increaſing of ſhipping and navigation*; and alſo in an act of parliament made in the twenty ſecond year of his ſaid majeſty King *Charles* the Second, intituled, *An act to prevent the planting of tobacco in* England, *and regulating the plantation trade*, or either of them, with reſpect to the goods in thoſe acts particularly enumerated; and all the proviſions, powers, and clauſes, in the ſaid recited acts, or in any other act of parliament now in force, for reſtraining the importation of any of the goods therein enumerated to *Great Britain*, or ſome of his Majeſty's plantations, ſhall be applied, practiſed, and put in execution, for reſtraining and ſecuring the importation of *Gum Senega* into *Great Britain*, according to the true intent and meaning of this act, as fully as if the ſeveral proviſions, powers, and clauſes relating thereto, were particularly repeated and again enacted in this preſent act; any law, cuſtom, or uſage, to the contrary notwithſtanding.

Exportation of Gum Senega from Africa confined to Great Britain only, under like ſecurities and penalties as are mentioned in act 12 Car. 2. & act 22 Car. 2.

CAP. XXXVIII.

An act to continue part of an act made in the thirtieth year of the reign of his late majeſty King George *the Second, intituled*, An act to render more effectual the ſeveral laws now in being, for the amendment and preſervation of the publick highways and turnpike roads of this kingdom; *and for making further proviſions for the preſervation of the ſaid roads.*

WHEREAS *by an act made in the thirtieth year of the reign of his late majeſty King* George *the Second, intituled*, An act to render more effectual the ſeveral laws nows in being, for the amendment and preſervation of the publick highways and turnpike roads of this kingdom, *it was amongſt other things enacted, That during the time of ſeven years, to be computed from the twenty fourth day of* June, *one thouſand ſeven hundred and fifty eight, the truſtees appointed or to be appointed by virtue or under the authority of any act of parliament made, or to be made, for making, repairing,*

Preamble, reciting clauſes in act 30 Geo. 2.

or amending turnpike roads, or such person or persons as are or shall be authorized by them, shall and may, and they are hereby required to demand and take for every waggon, wain, cart, or carriage having the fellies of the wheels thereof of less breadth or gage than nine inches from side to side at the least, at the bottom or sole thereof, or for the horses or beasts of draughts drawing the same, one half more than the tolls or duties which are or shall be payable for the same respectively by any act or acts of parliament made, or to be made, for making, amending, or repairing turnpike roads; except carts or carriages drawn by one horse or two oxen, or by two horses or four oxen, having the fellies of the wheels thereof of the breadth or gage of six inches, at the bottom from side to side: and it is by the said act recited, That there are in several acts of parliament made for making, amending and repairing turnpike roads, exemptions allowed from payment of tolls in particular cases in the said acts respectively mentioned, and liberties allowed in particular cases to pay lesser tolls than are charged upon other waggons, carts or carriages, passing through turnpike gates or bars; and that it would tend to the advantage and preservation of turnpike roads, to confine such exemptions, liberties, privileges and advantages, to carriages with wheels of the breadth or gage of nine inches; it is therefore enacted, That during the time aforesaid, no persons shall, by virtue of any of the said acts of parliament, have, claim or take, the benefit or advantage of any exemption from tolls, or part of tolls, or to pay lesser toll for or in respect of any waggon, wain, cart or other carriage, or horses drawing the same, than other carriages of the like nature ought to pay, unless such waggon, wain, cart or carriage, have fellies of the wheels thereof of the breadth or gage of nine inches, except as before excepted: and it is thereby also enacted, That during the time aforesaid, it shall not be lawful for any waggon or wain, having the fellies of the wheels thereof of the breadth or gage of nine inches as aforesaid, to pass upon any turnpike road, or through any turnpike gate or bar, unless the same be drawn by horses, or beasts of draught, in pairs; provided, that where there is an odd horse, or beast of draught, belonging to such waggon or wain, it should be lawful for such odd horse or beast of draught, to draw such waggon or wain, together with the other horses, or beast of draught, drawing in pairs; and provided, that such horses, or beasts of draught, do not in the whole exceed the number of horses, or beasts of draught, allowed by law; and that it should not be lawful for any waggon or wain, having the fellies of the wheels thereof of less breadth or gage than nine inches, to pass upon any turnpike road, or through any turnpike gate or bar, if the same be drawn by horses or beasts of draught, in pairs, and not by oxen: and it is thereby likewise enacted, That any person driving, or causing to be driven, on any turnpike road, any common stage waggon thereby prohibited, shall be punished for the same by indictment or information, and shall at the election of the prosecutor or informer, for every such offence, be subject and liable to the like penalties and forfeitures as the owners of waggons and carriages, having the fellies of the wheels of less breadth or gage than nine inches from side to side, are made subject and liable to, by an act made in the

twenty

twenty sixth year of the reign of his late majesty King George *the Second, intituled,* An act for the amendment and preservation of the publick highways and turnpike roads of this kingdom, and for the more effectual execution of the laws relating thereto; *to be paid and applied to such uses and purposes, and to be levied and recovered, as is thereby directed; and that no composition shall be made for or in respect of any waggon, wain, cart or carriage, or horses or beasts of draught drawing the same, unless such waggons, wains, carts and carriages, have the fellies of the wheels thereof of the breadth or gage of nine inches; except as before excepted: and whereas it will tend to the advantage and preservation of turnpike roads, that so much of the said act as is herein before recited should be further continued;* be it therefore enacted by the King's most excellent majesty, by and with the advice and consent of the lords spiritual and temporal, and commons, in this present parliament assembled, and by the authority of the same, That so much of the said act as is herein before recited, shall (except only where the same is hereby altered or varied) be further continued from the said twenty fourth day of *June*, one thousand seven hundred and sixty five, for and during the time or term of seven years.

& act 26 Geo. 2.

So much of the said act here recited as is not otherwise altered by this act, is continued for the further term of 7 years.

II. Provided always, That nothing herein contained shall extend, or be construed to extend, to continue a clause in the said act, which enacts, That during the continuance of the said act, the trustees appointed or to be appointed by virtue or under the authority of any act of parliament, made or to be made, for making, repairing, or amending, turnpike roads, and such person and persons as shall be authorized by them, shall and may, and they are hereby required to permit and suffer all waggons, wains, carts, and carriages, having the fellies of the wheels thereof of the breadth or gage of nine inches from side to side, at the bottom or sole thereof, and drawn according to law, to pass through any turnpike gate or gates, bar or bars, within one hundred miles from *London*, upon paying only so much tolls or duties as shall not exceed one half of the full toll or duty payable for such waggons, wains, carts and carriages respectively, or for the horses or beasts of draught, drawing the same, by virtue of any act or acts of parliament made, or to be made, for making, repairing, or amending, turnpike roads; but the said clause, and every matter and thing therein contained, shall, from and after the said twenty fourth day of *June*, one thousand seven hundred and sixty five, cease and determine; except the wheels of such waggons and wains shall be fixed thereto in the manner hereafter described and directed.

Clause in the recited act, granting particular exemptions from paying full tolls to broad wheel carriages, repealed;

except the wheels shall be fixt in manner herein described.

III. And be it further enacted by the authority aforesaid, That from and after the said twenty fourth day of *June*, the trustees appointed or to be appointed by any act of parliament, passed or to be passed, for the making, repairing, or amending, any turnpike road, or any person authorized and appointed by them, shall, during the time aforesaid, permit and suffer all waggons and wains, having the axle-trees thereof of such different

How the wheels are to be fixed in order to intitle carriages to the exemption from full tolls.

ferent lengths, that the diſtance from wheel to wheel, of one pair of the ſaid wheels, be not more than four feet two inches, to be meaſured at the ground; and that the diſtance from wheel to wheel, of the other pair thereof, be ſuch, that the fore and hind wheels of ſuch waggons and wains ſhall roll a ſurface of at leaſt ſixteen inches wide, on each ſide of the ſaid waggons or wains; and having the fellies of the wheels thereof of the breadth of nine inches from ſide to ſide, at the bottom or ſole thereof; to paſs upon any turnpike road, and through any toll gate or bar, upon paying only ſo much of the tolls and duties as ſhall not exceed one half of the full toll or duty payable, or by this act intended to be paid, for all waggons or wains having the fellies of the wheels of the breadth or gage of nine inches from ſide to ſide, or for the horſes or beaſts of draught, drawing the ſame, and not rolling a ſurface of ſixteen inches, in the manner herein before ſet forth.

Surveyor permitting any obſtruction to remain on the roads,

IV. And be it further enacted, That if any ſurveyor or ſurveyors, or other perſon or perſons, having the care of any turnpike road, ſhall, during the time aforeſaid, ſuffer to be or remain, for the ſpace of forty eight hours, in any part thereof, within twelve feet on either ſide of the middle of ſuch road, any poſt or poſts, heap or heaps of ſtone, rubbiſh or earth, ſet up or raiſed in or above the ſurface of the ſaid road, by which the paſſage thereof ſhall or may be obſtructed, impeded, confined or ſtraitened, ſuch ſurveyor or other perſon ſhall forfeit and pay to the informer the ſum of forty ſhillings; to be recovered before one juſtice of the peace, whether ſuch juſtice be or be not a truſtee of ſuch road; and ſhall be levied by diſtreſs and ſale of the goods and chattels of ſuch perſon or perſons, by warrant under the hand and ſeal of ſuch juſtice, which warrant ſuch juſtice is hereby impowered to grant: and if any perſon or perſons ſhall think him, her or themſelves, aggrieved by the determination of ſuch juſtice, he, ſhe or they may appeal to the general quarter ſeſſions of the peace, who ſhall finally determine the matter, and allow ſuch coſts, not exceeding forty ſhillings, to either party, as ſuch ſeſſions ſhall think fit; in which caſe no *Certiorari* ſhall lie or be brought.

forfeits 40s.

Appeal may be made to the quarter ſeſſions.

Where truſtees ſhall neglect to meet on the day appointed for their firſt, or any adjourned meeting; or for want of adjournment; two truſtees, or the clerk, may appoint a meeting, giving due notice.

V. And whereas the truſtees appointed or to be appointed, by any act or acts of parliament made or to be made, for making, amending or repairing, any particular highways or roads, may have neglected, or may hereafter neglect, to meet on the day appointed, or to be appointed, by any ſuch act or acts reſpectively, for their firſt meeting; or to meet on the day appointed or to be appointed by adjournment for their meeting, or for want of a proper adjournment; by which means, or ſome, or one of them, the intent of the ſaid act or acts may be fruſtrated; be it therefore enacted by the authority aforeſaid, That in all or either of the ſaid caſes, it ſhall be lawful for any two or more of the truſtees appointed or to be appointed by the ſaid acts reſpectively, or their clerk or clerks, to cauſe notice in writing to be affixed on all the turnpikes that ſhall be then erected on the ſaid rorespective roads; or, if no turnpikes shall be then erected, to cause the like notice to be affixed, in the most conspicuous place, in one of the principal towns or places nearest to which the roads directed to be repaired do lie, at least ten days before the intended meeting, appointing such trustees to meet at such place where the preceding meeting was appointed to have been held, or at the place directed for the first meeting of such trustees, if no preceding meeting shall have been held; and the said trustees when met, in pursuance of such notice, shall and may, and they are hereby required to proceed to carry such act or acts into execution in the same, and as full and ample a manner, to all intents and purposes, as they might or could have done if no such neglect had happened.

Clause in act 26 Geo. 2.

VI. And whereas by an act of parliament made in the twenty sixth year of the reign of his late majesty King *George* the Second, intituled, *An act for the amendment and preservation of the publick highways and turnpike roads of this kingdom, and for the more effectual execution of the laws relating thereto*; it is, amongst other things enacted, That it shall and may be lawful for any waggon, or other four wheel carriage, having the fellies of the wheels thereof of the breadth or gage of nine inches, to travel, pass or be driven, upon any turnpike road, with any number of horses, or beasts of draught, not exceeding eight; and for every cart, or other two wheel carriage, having the fellies of the wheels thereof of the breadth or gage aforesaid, with any number of horses, or beasts of draught, not exceeding five; without being subject or liable to be weighed at any crane, machine or engine: and whereas great damage hath been done to the turnpike roads in many parts of this kingdom, by the excessive weights which have been carried by such waggons and carts; be it therefore enacted by the authority aforesaid, That so much of the said recited act of the twenty sixth year of his said late Majesty, as exempts such waggons, carts and carriages, from being weighed at any crane, machine or engine, shall be, and the same, is hereby repealed; and that it shall and may be lawful to and for all trustees appointed, or who shall hereafter be appointed, by any act or acts of parliament for the repair of any highway or highways within that part of *Great Britain* called *England*, or for any five of them, at any or as many gate or gates, bar or bars, which they have erected or shall erect for the receiving of any toll or tolls, or at any other convenient place upon the said roads, during the time aforesaid, to order or cause to be built or erected, if they think fit, any crane, machine, or engine, which they shall judge proper for the weighing of waggons, carts, or other carriages, for the conveying of any goods or merchandize; and by writing signed by them, or any five of them, to order all and every or any waggons, carts or carriages (although the fellies of the wheels of such waggons, carts, or carriages, shall be of the breadth or gage of nine inches) which shall pass through any such gate or bar, or which shall pass any such crane, machine or engine, to be weighed, together with the

So much of the recited act, as exempts broad wheel carriages from being subject to be weighed, is repealed;

and the trustees are impowered to erect weighing engines,

and order all such carriages as well as others, to be weighed thereat; (except those with regulated wheels)

the lading thereof (except such waggons and wains as aforesaid, the fore and hind wheels of which shall roll a surface of at least sixteen inches wide, on each side of such waggons and wains); and for them, or any five or more of them, or for any person or persons impowered by them, or any five or more of them, to receive and take, over and above the toll already granted, or hereafter to be granted, the sum of twenty shillings a hundred weight, for every hundred weight which every such waggon, together with the loading thereof, shall weigh, over and above the weight of six ton; and also the sum of twenty shillings a hundred weight, for every hundred weight which every such cart or other carriage, together with the loading thereof, shall weigh, over and above the weight of three ton; and that the money arising from such additional duties of twenty shillings a hundred weight, shall be applied to the repair of such highway or highways, where such gate or gates, bar or bars, are or shall be placed; any thing contained in the said recited act to the contrary thereof notwithstanding.

and take (over and above the tolls) 20s. per Cwt. for all waggons weighing above 6 ton;

& 20s. per Cwt. for all carts above 3 ton;

to be applied to the repair of the said roads.

Act 14 Geo. 2.

VII. Provided always, That nothing in an act, intituled, *An act for the preservation of the publick roads, in that part of* Great Britain *called* England, passed in the fourteenth year of his late majesty King *George* the Second; nor in an act, intituled, *An act to explain and amend an act passed in the fourteenth year of his Majesty's reign, intituled,* An act for the preservation of the publick roads, in that part of *Great Britain* called *England*; and so much of an act passed in the third year of the reign of King *William* and Queen *Mary*, intituled, *An act for the better repairing and amending the highways, and for settling the rates of the carriage of goods*; as relates to the settling of the rates of the carriage of goods, passed in the twenty first year of his said late Majesty, nor in this act, shall be understood to compel the trustees of any turnpike road to erect any crane, machine, or engine, for the weighing carts, waggons, or other carriages, having wheels of the breadth of nine inches, or to weigh the same.

3 Will. & Mary.

Trustees not obliged to erect engines in pursuance of the said acts, for weighing broad wheel carriages.

VIII. And whereas inconveniencies have arisen for making hedges or other fences, and from ploughing or breaking up the soil of lands or grounds, near the middle or centre of turnpike roads; for remedy thereof, be it further enacted by the authority aforesaid, That after the passing of this act, no person shall make, or cause to be made, any hedge, or other fence, on any turnpike road not inclosed on both sides, within the distance of thirty feet, or plough or break up the soil of any land or ground within the distance of fifteen feet, from the middle or centre of any turnpike road made or to be made within this kingdom: and if any person shall hereafter make, or cause to be made, any hedge or fence contrary hereto, within the distance of thirty feet from the middle or centre of any turnpike road, it shall be lawful for the trustees for the care of such road, or any five or more of them, to cause such hedge or fence to be taken down at the expence of the person or persons to whom the same shall belong; and

Where hedges or fences shall be made within 30 feet of the centre of turnpike roads not inclosed on both sides; or ground ploughed within 15 feet of the same; the hedges are to be taken down at the expence of the owner;

and in case such person shall neglect or refuse to pay such expence to the said trustees, or such person or persons as they, or any five or more of them, shall appoint to receive the same, it shall and may be lawful for any one or more justice or justices of the peace for the county or place where the offence shall be committed, by warrant under his or their hand and seal, or hands and seals (which warrant such justice or justices is and are hereby authorized and impowered) to levy the same by distress and sale of the offenders goods and chattels, rendering the overplus to the owner on demand: and if any person shall hereafter plough or break up the soil of any land or ground within the distance of fifteen feet from the middle or centre of any turnpike road, such person shall forfeit the sum of forty shillings; and it shall and may be lawful for any one or more justice or justices of the peace of the county or place where such offence shall be committed, upon complaint to him or them made upon oath (which oath such justice or justices is and are hereby authorized and required to administer) to levy the same by distress and sale of the offender's goods and chattels, rendering the overplus to the owner, on demand.

and the person ploughing within the prohibited distance, forfeits 40s.

IX. And be it further enacted, That if any person or persons shall think him, her, or themselves aggrieved, by the determination of such justice of the peace, he, she, or they, may appeal to the general quarter session of the peace, who shall finally determine the matter of such appeal, and allow such costs, not exceeding forty shillings, to either party, as such session shall think fit; in which case no *Certiorari* shall lie or be brought.

Persons aggrieved may appeal to the quarter sessions.

X. And whereas the trustees of several turnpike roads are not sufficiently impowered to punish nuisances in the several roads under their care; be it therefore further enacted by the authority aforesaid, That the said trustees of the several roads respectively, or any five or more of them, may, and they are hereby required, if they shall think fit, to direct prosecutions by indictment against the offender or offenders for any nuisance done, committed, or continued, in, to, or upon, any of the turnpike roads under their care respectively, at the expence of the revenues belonging to such turnpike roads respectively.

Trustees may prosecute for nuisances committed on the roads.

XI. And be it enacted by the authority aforesaid, That if any action or suit shall be commenced against any person or persons for any thing done or acted in pursuance of this act; then, and in every such case, such action or suit shall be commenced or prosecuted within six calendar months next after the fact committed, and not afterwards; and the same, and every such action or suit, shall be brought in the county, riding, or place, where the person, against whom such action or suit shall be commenced, doth ordinarily inhabit and reside, or in the county or riding where the fact was committed, and not elsewhere; and the defendant or defendants, in every such action or suit, shall and may plead the general issue, and give this act and the special matter in evidence, at any trial to be had thereupon; and that the same was done in pursuance and by the authority of this

Limitation of actions.

General issue.

present act: and if the same shall appear so to have been; or if any such action or suit shall be brought after the time herein before limited for bringing the same, or be brought or laid in any other county, riding, or place, than as afore-mentioned, then the jury shall find for the defendant or defendants; or if the plaintiff or plaintiffs shall become nonsuited, or discontinue his, her, or their action, after the defendant or defendants shall have appeared; or if, upon demurrer, judgement shall be given against the plaintiff or plaintiffs, the defendant or defendants shall and may recover treble costs, and have the like remedy for recovery thereof, as any defendant or defendants hath or have in any other cases by law.

Treble costs.

CAP. XXXIX.

An act for more effectually preventing the mischiefs arising to the revenue and commerce of Great Britain *and* Ireland, *from the illicit and clandestine trade to and from the* Isle of Man.

Preamble, reciting clause in act 7 Geo. 1.

WHEREAS *by an act of parliament made in the seventh year of the reign of King* George *the First, intituled,* An act for the further preventing his Majesty's subjects from trading to the *East Indies* under foreign commissions; and for encouraging and further securing the lawful trade thereto; and for further regulating the pilots of *Dover, Deal,* and the *Isle of Thanet*; *it is, amongst other things enacted, That no commodity of the growth, product or manufacture of the* East Indies, *or other places beyond the* Cape of Good Hope, *shall be imported or carried into the islands of* Jersey, Guernsey, Alderney, Sarke *or* Man, *or other places in the said act mentioned, but such only as shall be* bona fide, *and without fraud, loaden and shipt in* Great Britain, *in ships navigated according to law, under the penalty of forfeiting all such goods, or the value thereof, together with the ship or vessel in which they shall be imported, with all her guns, tackle, furniture, ammunition, and apparel, to be seized and prosecuted as in the said act is directed: and whereas great quantities of tea and other goods of the product or manufacture of the* East Indies, *and other places beyond the* Cape of Good Hope, *are imported from foreign parts and landed in the* Isle of Man, *contrary to the said in part recited act of parliament; which goods, as well as great quantities of brandy and other foreign liquors, are brought from the said* Isle of Man, *and clandestinely run ashore in this kingdom, to the great prejudice of the trade and revenues thereof:* to prevent which practices for the future, and to render the said act, as well as several other acts of parliament relative to the trade and revenues of this kingdom, more effectual; may it please your Majesty that it may be enacted, and be it enacted by the King's most excellent majesty, by and with the advice and consent of the lords spiritual and temporal, and commons in this present parliament assembled, and by the authority of the same, That from and after the first day of *June*, one thousand seven hundred and sixty five, all

Power given to the officers of the customs

all and every officer and officers of his Majeſty's cuſtoms and excise, ſhall have the ſame powers and authorities for viſiting and ſearching of ſhips and veſſels in any bay, harbour, river, creek, or other place, in, of, or belonging to, the ſaid *Iſle of Man*, as are by any act of parliament provided for ſuch officers viſiting and ſearching ſhips or veſſels within the ports or on the coaſts of *Great Britain*; and to ſeize and ſecure, either on the land or water, in the manner directed or allowed by the ſeveral acts of parliament in force in *Great Britain*, any goods which have been brought or imported into the ſaid *Iſle of Man*, contrary to this or to any other act of parliament, or which ſhall be landed there, without payment of any duties which may be due and payable to his Majeſty, his heirs and ſucceſſors.

and exciſe, to viſit and ſearch ſhips in the iſle of Man,

and to ſeize contraband goods.

II. And it is hereby further enacted by the authority aforeſaid, That from and after the firſt day of *June*, one thouſand ſeven hundred and ſixty five, no wrought ſilks, bengalls, and ſtuffs mixt with ſilk or herba, of the manufacture of *Perſia*, *China*, or *Eaſt India*, nor callicoes painted, dyed, printed, or ſtained there, nor any cambricks or *French* lawns, ſhall be exported from *Great Britain* to the *Iſle of Man*; and if any ſuch goods ſhall be ſhipt or laden, or ſhall be concealed in the ſame package with any other goods which are entered for, or are intended to be laden on board any ſhip or veſſel bound from *Great Britain* to the ſaid *Iſle of Man*, ſuch goods ſhall be forfeited, as well as the goods contained in the ſame package therewith, whether the ſame ſhall be ſhipt or laden, or not; and ſhall and may be ſeized and proſecuted by any officer of his Majeſty's cuſtoms.

Prohibited goods imported thither from Great Britain,

may be ſeized; and are forfeited, together with the package.

III. And it is further enacted, That the *Iſle of Man* ſhall be added to, and included in, the bond which is now by law required to be given, that ſuch goods ſhall be duly exported, and not relanded again in any part of *Great Britain*.

Iſle of Man to be included in the bond to be given on exportation of ſuch goods from Great Britain.

IV. And it is hereby further enacted by the authority aforeſaid, That from and after the firſt day of *July*, one thouſand ſeven hundred and ſixty five, no foreign brandy, arrack, rum, ſtrong waters, or ſpirits whatſoever, ſhall be imported or carried into the *Iſle of Man*, but ſuch only as ſhall be *bona fide*, and without fraud, laden and ſhipt in *Great Britain*, and carried thither directly from thence, upon the forfeiture of ſuch goods, or the value thereof, together with the ſhip or veſſel in which they ſhall be imported or carried, with all her guns, furniture, ammunition, tackle, and apparel, to be ſeized and proſecuted as is hereafter directed.

No foreign brandy or ſpirits to be imported into the ſaid iſle, but from Great Britain directly; on forfeiture of the goods and veſſel.

V. And it is hereby further enacted by the authority aforeſaid, That from and after the twenty ninth day of *September*, one thouſand ſeven hundred and ſixty five, no rum, or other ſpirits, ſhall be ſhipped or laden on board any ſhip or veſſel in any *Britiſh* colony or plantation in *America*, but on condition that the ſame ſhall not be carried to, or landed in, the *Iſle of Man*, under the like ſecurities, penalties, and forfeitures, as are preſcribed and mentioned in two acts of parliament made in the twelfth and twenty fifth years of the reign of King *Charles* the Second,

Spirits ſhipped in America to be conditioned not to be landed in the iſle of Man; under the penalties of acts 12 & 25 Car. 2.

Second, the former intituled, *An act for the encouraging and increasing of shipping and navigation*, and the latter intituled, *An act for the encouragement of the* Greenland *and* Eastland *trades, and for the better securing the plantation trade*, or either of them, with respect to the goods in those acts particularly enumerated; any law, custom, or usage, to the contrary notwithstanding.

No foreign spirits to be exported from the said island, carried coastwise in casks under 60 gallons; or wines to be imported, or exported, or carried coastwise in casks under 25 gallons, and in ships not less than 100 tons; on forfeiture of the ship and goods.

VI. And it is hereby further enacted by the authority aforesaid, That from and after the first day of *June*, one thousand seven hundred and sixty five, no foreign brandy, arrack, rum, strong waters, or spirits whatsoever, shall be exported from the *Isle of Man*, or carried coastwise from one part of the said isle to another, in any ship or vessel of less burthen than one hundred tons; nor in any vessel or cask under sixty gallons (except only for the use of the seamen then belonging to, and on board such ship, or vessel, not exceeding two gallons for each seaman, nor shall any wine be imported into, or exported from, the said island, or carried coastwise from one part of the said island to another, in any vessel or cask that shall contain less than twenty five gallons, nor in any ship or vessel of less burthen than one hundred tons, upon forfeiture of all such goods, together with the ship, or vessel, and all her tackle, furniture, and apparel, to be seized and prosecuted as herein after is directed.

Vessels found hovering on the coast, &c. with prohibited goods on board,

are liable to forfeiture, together with the goods.

VII. And be it further enacted by the authority aforesaid, That from and after the first day of *July*, one thousand seven hundred and sixty five, where any ship or vessel whatsoever, having on board any goods, which by this or any other act of parliament passed in *Great Britain*, are made liable to forfeiture for being brought or imported into, or exported from, or carried coastwise in the *Isle of Man*; or where any ship or vessel arriving from *Great Britain*, having on board any goods prohibited to be exported from thence into the *Isle of Man*, shall be found in any bay, harbour, river, or creek, of or belonging to the said *Isle of Man*, or at anchor; or hovering within three leagues of the shores thereof; or shall be discovered so to have been (unless in case of unavoidable necessity and distress of weather, of which necessity and distress, the master, purser, or person, having or taking the charge or command of such ship or vessel, shall, immediately after the arrival of such ship or vessel into any bay, harbour, river, or creek, of or belonging to the said *Isle of Man*, give notice and make proof of before the collector or other chief officer of the customs resident at the nearest port in the said island) all such goods, together with the ship or vessel in which the same shall be found, with all her guns, tackle, furniture, ammunition, and apparel, shall be deemed and taken to be forfeited within the intent and meaning of this and such other acts whether bulk shall then have been broken or not, and shall and may be seized by any officer or officers of the customs or excise.

No spirits to be imported into Great Britain from

VIII. And be it further enacted by the authority aforesaid, That from and after the first day of *June*, one thousand seven hundred and sixty five, no brandy, rum, strong waters, or spirits, of any kind whatsoever, shall be brought or imported from the

the *Isle of Man* into *Great Britain*; or *Ireland*, upon any pretence whatsoever; and where any ship or vessel coming or arriving from the said *Isle of Man*, and having on board any such brandy, rum, strong waters, or spirits (except only for the use of the seamen then belonging to and on board such ship or vessel, not exceeding two gallons for each seaman) or any other goods or commodities which are prohibited to be imported from thence into *Great Britain* or *Ireland*, shall be found at anchor, or hovering within the limits of any of the ports of *Great Britain* or *Ireland*, or within three leagues of the shores thereof, or shall be discovered so to have been, and not proceeding on her voyage, wind and weather permitting, unless in case of unavoidable necessity and distress of weather; (of which necessity and distress, the master, purser, or other person, having or taking the charge or command of such ship or vessel, shall give notice to, and make proof of, before the collector or other chief officer of the customs of such port as aforesaid, immediately after the arrival of such ship or vessel into the said port) all such goods, together with the ship or vessel in which the same shall be so brought or imported, or on board which such goods shall be found as aforesaid, with all her guns, tackle, furniture, ammunition, and apparel, shall be forfeited (whether bulk shall then have been broken or not) and the same shall and may be seized and sued for by any officer or officers of the customs or excise.

the Isle of Man. Vessels coming from thence, with spirits or prohibited goods on board, found hovering on the coast, are liable to be forfeited, together with the goods.

IX. And it is hereby further declared and enacted by the authority aforesaid, That all seizures made in pursuance of the powers given by this act, shall and may be brought to any port in *Great Britain* or *Ireland*, or into any port in the *Isle of Man*, and shall and may be prosecuted in any of his Majesty's courts of record at *Westminster* or *Dublin*, or in the court of *Exchequer* in *Scotland*, or in any courts to be holden in his Majesty's name, or by virtue of his authority, in the said *Isle of Man*, at the election of the informer or prosecutor, and after condemnation, disposed of and divided in the same manner, and by the same rules, regulations and restrictions, as are prescribed and practised in respect to seizures made in *Great Britain*: and all the powers, provisions, articles, and clauses, in any act of parliament contained for the indemnity, ease, benefit, or relief, of officers of the customs or excise, making seizures in *Great Britain* or *Ireland* respectively, shall be observed, applied, practised, and put in execution, as well with respect to any seizure or prosecution made or carried on in pursuance of this act, as with respect to any action, suit, or prosecution, that may be brought or commenced against any officer or officers of the customs or excise, for any thing done in pursuance thereof, as fully and effectually to all intents and purposes as if the same were particularly and at large re-enacted in the body of this present act.

Seizures where to be secured and prosecuted.

X. And it is hereby further enacted by the authority aforesaid, That from and after the first day of *June*, one thousand seven hundred and sixty five, if any ship or vessel liable to seizure, either for importing any goods into, or exporting any goods for the

Licenced goods found on board vessels liable to seizure,

the ſaid *Iſle of Man*, or for having any goods on board, contrary to this act, ſhall, at the time of ſeizure, be laden with any goods which are not liable to forfeiture, it ſhall and may be lawful for the officer ſeizing ſuch ſhip or veſſel, to bring ſuch laſt mentioned goods, with the veſſel in which the ſame ſhall be laden as aforeſaid, to *Great Britain* or *Ireland*, or into any of the ports of the ſaid *Iſle of Man*, and to ſecure ſuch goods in his Majeſty's warehouſes until ſuch time as the owner or proprietor of ſuch goods, or the maſter of the veſſel, or ſome other perſon duly authorized by letter of attorney from ſuch owner or proprietor, atteſted by a notary publick in the uſual form, ſhall apply for the ſame to the reſpective commiſſioners of the cuſtoms or exciſe at *London* or *Edinburgh*, or to the commiſſioners of the revenue at *Dublin*, or to the collector or other principal officer of the cuſtoms or exciſe by whom the goods ſhall be ſecured; and ſuch goods ſhall be thereupon delivered to the perſon ſo applying; to be diſpoſed of as by law he may, upon giving a receipt for the ſame; and the officer ſeizing ſuch ſhip or veſſel, or any perſon acting in his aid or aſſiſtance, or in ſecuring ſuch goods, ſhall not be liable to any action, ſuit, or proſecution, on account of the ſtoppage or detention of ſuch goods.

are to be lodged in the King's warehouſes, till claimed; and the officer is indemnified.

XI. Provided always, and it is hereby further enacted, That in caſe no application ſhall be made for ſuch goods as aforeſaid, within the ſpace of twenty days after the ſame ſhall be ſecured, in his Majeſty's warehouſe, the ſaid reſpective commiſſioners of the cuſtoms or exciſe in this kingdom, or the commiſſioners of the revenue in *Ireland*, ſhall, with all convenient ſpeed, cauſe the name or deſcription of the veſſel on board which ſuch goods were laden, with the names of the maſter or commander thereof, and of the officer by whom ſhe was ſeized, and the port to which ſhe was brought, to be publiſhed for three ſeveral weeks ſucceſſively in the *London Gazette*, if ſuch goods ſhall be ſecured in any port of *England*, and in any publick news paper printed at *Edinburgh*, if the goods ſhall be ſecured in *Scotland*, and in the *Dublin Gazette*, if the ſaid goods, ſhall be ſecured in any port within the kingdom of *Ireland*; and if it ſhall appear to the ſaid reſpective commiſſioners, by any papers on board the veſſel, to whom the ſaid goods are conſigned, the ſaid reſpective commiſſioners ſhall cauſe the like notice to be tranſmitted to ſuch conſignee, by the common poſt; and in caſe the ſaid goods ſhall be brought to the ſaid *Iſle of Man*, and ſecured there, the collector, or other principal officer of the cuſtoms or exciſe, by whom the ſame ſhall be ſecured, ſhall cauſe the like notice to be affixed to the caſtle in *Caſtle Town*, and to the publick market-houſe in the town of *Douglas*; and if no application ſhall be made as aforeſaid, for ſuch goods, within the ſpace of ſix months after ſuch notice has been given, publiſhed and tranſmitted, in the manner before directed, it ſhall and may be lawful for the ſaid reſpective commiſſioners of the cuſtoms and exciſe in *Great Britain*, and the commiſſioners of the revenue in *Ireland*, and the collector or other principal officer of the cuſtoms or exciſe by whom the ſaid goods are

If no claim be made within 20 days, the goods are to be advertized; and notice ſent to the conſignee, if known; and if not claimed within 6 months,

are secured in *The Isle of Man*, to cause the said goods to be publickly sold by auction or inch of candle to the best advantage, and to apply the produce thereof, first, to or towards the charges of warehouse room, and other charges that shall arise thereon; next, to the customs and duties that shall or may be due and payable for such goods; and the overplus (if any) to the proprietor or other person authorized to receive the same.

they are to be publickly sold, and the duties and charges to be paid thereout.

XII. Provided always, That in case the said goods, or any part thereof, shall be perishable in their nature, it shall and may be lawful for the said respective commissioners and officers aforesaid, to cause the same to be forthwith sold, and the produce disposed of and applied in the manner herein before directed.

Where the goods shall be perishable, they may be sold forthwith.

XIII. And it is hereby further enacted by the authority aforesaid, That from and after the first day of *June*, one thousand seven hundred and sixty five, for every ship or vessel that shall set sail out of or from *Great Britain* or *Ireland*, for any part of *Africa*, or any of his Majesty's dominions out of this realm, sufficient bond shall be given, with one surety besides the master, to the collector or other principal officer of the customs of the port or place from whence the said ship or vessel shall depart, to the value of one thousand pounds, if the said ship or vessel shall be of less burthen than one hundred tons, and of the sum of two thousand pounds, if the ship shall be of greater burthen, with condition that such ship or vessel shall not, during the course of the voyage, take on board any stores, goods, or merchandizes whatsoever, at the *Isle of Man*, nor out of or from any ship, vessel, or boat, at sea or elsewhere, any stores, goods, or merchandizes, which shall have been brought from thence; which bond shall continue in force for one year, from and after the completion of the voyage; and in case no fraud shall appear within that time, it shall and may be lawful for the respective commissioners of his Majesty's customs in *Great Britain*, or the commissioners of the revenue in *Ireland*, or any three or more of them, to direct the said bond to be delivered up.

Vessels sailing from Great Britain or Ireland, for Africa, &c. to give bond and surety,

conditioned not to take in any goods or stores at the Isle of Man, nor out of any vessel from thence.

XIV. And it is hereby further enacted by the authority aforesaid, That from and after the first day of *June*, one thousand seven hundred and sixty five, all officers acting in the execution of this act shall be subject to the same penalties, forfeitures, and disabilities, for any corruptions, frauds, connivances, concealments, or collusive agreements, in breach of their duty, as they would be liable to if such offences were committed in *Great Britain*; and that every person who shall give or offer to give any bribe to such officer or officers; or shall make any collusive agreement with him or them; or who shall any wise obstruct, molest, or assault, maim or wound, any such officer or officers, or any other person acting in their aid and assistance, in the due execution of their duty; or who shall be assisting or otherwise concerned either in the unshipping, landing, or receiving, any goods subject to the payment of duties, without paying the same, or any goods prohibited to be imported into the said *Isle of Man*, or in shipping or loading outwards any goods prohibited to be

Penalty on officers guilty of any corruption, fraud, or collusion, in the execution of their duty;

and on persons offering bribes,

or obstructing or assaulting them;

or assisting in running of goods, &c.

exported

exported from thence, shall, in each and every such case, be subject to the like pains, penalties, and forfeitures, as are provided by any act of parliament for the like offences in *Great Britain*; and every such offence and offences shall and may be enquired of, examined, tried, and determined, in any county within this kingdom or *Ireland*, in such manner and form, and by the same rules, regulations, and restrictions, as if the same offence had been therein committed; or in any courts to be holden in his Majesty's name, or by virtue of his authority, in the said *Isle of Man*, according to the usual course of proceedings in such courts, at the election of the respective commissioners of the customs or excise in *Great Britain*, or the commissioners of the revenue in *Ireland*, under whose directions any suit, indictment, or prosecution, shall be commenced and carried on; and in case any suit, indictment, or prosecution, shall be commenced in pursuance of this act, in any of the courts in *Great Britain* or *Ireland*, the like process shall and may issue thereupon as would have issued if the said offence had been therein committed, and shall and may be directed to such person or persons as usually and ordinarily execute process issuing out of the courts of justice in the said *Isle of Man*; and the same shall and may be executed by such person or persons in any part of the said *Isle of Man*, or on board any ship, vessel, or boat, being in any bay, harbour, river, or creek, of or belonging to the said *Isle of Man*, or within three leagues of the shores thereof; and the offender or offenders shall give the like bail and security for his and their appearance, and to answer the forfeiture and penalties incurred for such offence or offences, in the same manner and according to the usual course of proceeding upon such process in *Great Britain* or *Ireland* respectively; and every person residing or being in the said *Isle of Man*, who shall be there served with any process of *Subpœna*, issuing out of any of his Majesty's courts of record at *Westminster*, *Edinburgh*, or *Dublin*, requiring such person to appear in the said courts respectively, either to answer any information, indictment, bill, or complaint, therein exhibited, or to give evidence upon the trial of any cause therein depending, shall be compelled to appear or attend as required by the said *Subpœna*, under the same pains, penalties, and forfeitures, as such person would incur and be liable to for refusing or neglecting to appear or attend, if he or they had been served with such process in *Great Britain* or *Ireland* respectively; which pains, penalties, and forfeitures, the said respective courts are hereby authorized and impowered to inflict accordingly; any law, custom, or usage, to the contrary notwithstanding.

courts for trying and punishing offenders.

Penalty of insuring the fraudulent conveyance of goods to or from the said island.

XV. And it is hereby further enacted by the authority aforesaid, That all and every person and persons who, from and after the said first day of *June*, one thousand seven hundred and sixty five, shall by way of insurance, or otherwise, undertake or agree that any goods or commodities shall be carried to, or landed in, the *Isle of Man*, or brought from thence or landed in *Great Britain* or *Ireland*, contrary to the true intent and meaning

ing of this or any other act of parliament made in *Great Britain* or *Ireland*, or who shall pay, or agree to pay, any sum or sums of money for the insuring, conveying, or delivering, of such goods, shall, for each and every such offence, forfeit the sum of five hundred pounds; one moiety of which forfeiture shall be to the use of his Majesty, his heirs, and successors, and the other moiety to such officer or officers of the customs or excise as shall prosecute for the same; to be sued for and recovered in like manner and form as any other forfeitures and penalties are by this act recoverable.

XVI. And be it further enacted by the authority aforesaid, That in case the insurer, conveyer, or manager, of or in such fraud, shall, within the space of six months after such transaction or agreement, first discover the same to the commissioners of the customs or excise in *England* or *Scotland*, or to the commissioners of the revenue in *Ireland*, he shall not only keep the insurance money or premium given him, and be discharged of the penalties to which he is liable by reason of such offence, but shall have, to his own use, one moiety of the forfeiture which shall be recovered from the party making such insurance or agreement; and in case the party or parties insured shall, within the like space of six months, first make discovery thereof, in the manner before mentioned, he or they so discovering shall recover back such insurance money or premium as he or they hath or have paid upon such insurance or agreement, and shall have, to his and their own use, one moiety of the forfeiture which shall be recovered from such insurer, conveyer, or manager, as aforesaid, and shall be clearly acquitted and discharged of the penalty hereby imposed upon him or them.

Insurer, conveyer, or manager of such fraud, discovering the same, is intitled to the insurance money, and a moiety of the forfeiture.

Party insured discovering is intitled to recover the insurance money, and a moiety of the forfeiture.

CAP. XL.

An act for granting to his Majesty a certain sum of money out of the sinking fund; for applying certain monies therein mentioned for the service of the year one thousand seven hundred and sixty five; for further appropriating the supplies granted in this session of parliament; for allowing to the receivers general of the duties on offices and employments in Scotland *a reward for their trouble; and for allowing further time to such persons as have omitted to make and file affidavits of the execution of indentures of clerks to attornies and solicitors.*

Most gracious Sovereign,

WE your Majesty's most dutiful and loyal subjects, the commons of *Great Britain* in parliament assembled, towards raising the necessary supplies which we have chearfully granted to your Majesty in this session of parliament, have resolved to give and grant to your Majesty the sum herein after mentioned: and do therefore most humbly beseech your Majesty that it may be enacted, and be it enacted by the King's most

Preamble.

most excellent majesty, by and with the advice and consent of the lords spiritual and temporal, and commons, in this present parliament assembled, and by the authority of the same, That by or out of such monies as shall, from time to time, be and remain in the receipt of the exchequer, of the surplusses, excesses, overplus monies, and other revenues composing the fund commonly called *The Sinking Fund* after paying or reserving sufficient to pay all such sums of money as have been directed by any former act or acts of parliament to be paid out of the same, there shall and may be issued, and applied, for and towards making good the supply granted to his Majesty for the service of the year one thousand seven hundred and sixty five, a sum not exceeding two million and one hundred thousand pounds, and the commissioners of his Majesty's treasury, or any three or more of them now being, or the high treasurer, or any three or more of the commissioners of the treasury for the time being, are hereby authorized and impowered to issue and apply the same accordingly.

2,100,000l. granted out of the sinking fund, for the service of the current year

to be issued by the treasury accordingly.

II. And it is hereby enacted by the authority aforesaid, That in case the said commissioners of his Majesty's treasury, or any three or more of them now being, or the high treasurer, or any three or more of the commissioners of the treasury for the time being, shall think it adviseable to raise the said sum of two million and one hundred thousand pounds, or any part thereof, by loans or exchequer bills, in manner herein after mentioned, that it shall and may be lawful to and for any person or persons, natives or foreigners, bodies politick or corporate, to advance or lend to his Majesty, at the receipt of his Majesty's exchequer, any sum or sums of money not exceeding the said sum of two million and one hundred thousand pounds, upon the credit of the said surplusses, excesses, and overplus monies, or other revenues composing the sinking fund, and to have and receive interest for the forbearance of the money lent, so as such loans be allowed to be made by the said commissioners of the treasury, or any three or more of them now being, or the high treasurer, or any three or more of the commissioners of the treasury for the time being, who are hereby authorized to issue their warrants for that purpose as fast as such loans shall be wanted for the publick service; and moreover that no money to be lent upon the security of this act shall be rated or assessed to any tax or assessment whatsoever.

Treasury impowered to raise the said sum, or any part thereof, by loans or exchequer bills, on the credit of the sinking fund.

III. And be it further enacted, That all and every person or persons who shall lend any money upon the credit of this act as aforesaid, and pay the same into the receipt of the exchequer, shall immediately have a tally of loan struck for the same, and an order for his, her, or their repayment, bearing the same date with his, her, or their tally, in or upon which order shall be also contained a warrant for payment of interest for the forbearance thereof, and to be paid every three months, until the repayment of the principal; and all such orders for repayment of money so to be lent shall be registred in course according

and to strike tallies of loan with orders for repayment of the money so advanced;

the interest thereof to be paid quarterly.

ing to the dates reſpectively; and that all and every perſon and perſons ſhall be paid in courſe, according as their orders ſhall ſtand regiſtred in the ſaid regiſter books, ſo as the perſon or perſons, natives or foreigners, his, her, or their executors, adminiſtrators, or aſſigns, who ſhall have his, her, or their order or orders firſt entered in the ſaid books of regiſter, ſhall be taken and accounted to be the firſt perſon or perſons to be paid out of the ſaid ſurpluſſes, exceſſes, or other revenues, and he, ſhe, or they, who ſhall have his, her, or their order or orders next entered, ſhall be taken and accounted to be the ſecond perſon to be paid, and ſo ſucceſſively and in courſe; and that the monies to come in, of, or for the ſaid ſurpluſſes, exceſſes, and overplus monies, or other revenues compoſing the ſinking fund, as aforeſaid, ſhall be in the ſame order liable to the ſatisfaction of the ſaid reſpective perſons, and body or bodies politick or corporate, their executors, adminiſtrators, ſucceſſors, or aſſigns reſpectively, without any undue preference of one before another, and not otherwiſe, and ſhall not be diverted or divertible to any other uſe, intent, or purpoſe whatſoever (other than ſuch uſes and purpoſes as are appointed by any other act or acts of parliament in that behalf as aforeſaid;) and that no fee, reward, or gratuity directly or indirectly ſhall be demanded or taken of any of his Majeſty's ſubjects for providing or making of any ſuch books or regiſters, or any entries, views, or ſearches in or for payment of money lent, or the intereſt thereof as aforeſaid, by any of his Majeſty's officer or officers, their clerks, or deputies, on pain of payment of treble damages to the party grieved by the party offending, with full coſts of ſuit; or if the officer himſelf take or demand any ſuch fee or reward, then to loſe his place alſo; and if any undue preference of one before another ſhall be made either in point of regiſtry or payment, contrary to the true meaning of this act, by any ſuch officer or officers, then the party offending ſhall be liable by action of debt, or on the caſe, to pay the value of the debt with full coſts of ſuit to the party grieved, and ſhall be forejudged of his place or office; and if any ſuch preference be unduly made by any his deputy or clerk, without direction or privity of his maſter, then ſuch deputy or clerk only ſhall be liable to ſuch action, debt, damages, and coſts, and ſhall be for ever after incapable of his office or place; and in caſe the auditor of the receipt ſhall not direct the ſaid orders of loan, or the clerk of the pells record, or the teller make payment upon ſuch orders, according to each perſon's due place and order as before directed, then he or they ſhall be adjudged to forfeit, and the reſpective deputies and clerks therein offending, to be liable to ſuch action, debt, damages, and coſts, in ſuch manner as aforeſaid; all which ſaid penalties, forfeitures, damages, and coſts, to be incurred by any the officers of the exchequer, or any their deputies or clerks, ſhall and may be recovered by action of debt, bill, plaint, or information, in any of his Majeſty's courts of record at *Weſtminſter*; wherein no eſſoin, pro-

Orders to be regiſter'd, in courſe.

No undue preference to be given in payment.

nor fee to be taken;

on forfeiture of treble damages, with full coſts.

Penalty of undue preference in point of regiſtry or payment;

to be recovered in any of the courts of record at Weſtminſter.

image
not
available

of new exchequer bills, for any sum or sums of money not exceeding in the whole the said sum of two million and one hundred thousand pounds, together with such loans aforesaid, in the same or like manner, form, or order, and according to the same or like rules and directions, as in and by a certain act of this present session of parliament, intituled, *An act for continuing and granting to his Majesty, certain duties upon malt, mum, cyder, and perry, for the service of the year one thousand seven hundred and sixty five*, are enacted and prescribed concerning the exchequer bills to be made in pursuance of the said act.

VIII. And be it further enacted by the authority aforesaid, That all and every the clauses, provisoes, powers, privileges, advantages, penalties, forfeitures, and disabilities, contained in the said last-mentioned act relating to the loans or exchequer bills authorized to be made by the same act (except such clauses as do charge the same on the taxes granted by the same act, and except such clauses as limit the rate of interest to be paid for the forbearance of money lent on the credit of the said act) shall be applied and extended to the exchequer bills to be paid in pursuance of this act, as fully and effectually to all intents and purposes as if the said exchequer bills had been originally authorized by the said last mentioned act, or as if the said several clauses or provisoes had been particularly repeated and re-enacted in the body of this present act.

All advantages and penalties in the malt act of this session, relating to loans or exchequer bills thereby authorized to be made forth, extended to this act.

IX. And be it enacted by the authority aforesaid, That all the exchequer bills, which shall be made in pursuance of this act, and the interest, premium, rate, and charges incident to, or attending the same, shall be and are hereby charged and chargeable upon, and shall be repaid and borne by and out of, the growing produce of the said surplusses, excesses, and overplus monies, or other revenues composing the sinking fund (except such monies of the said sinking fund as are appropriated to any particular use or uses by any former or other act or acts of parliament in that behalf) and such monies of the said sinking fund shall and may be issued and applied as soon as the same can be regularly stated and ascertained, for and towards the paying off, cancelling, and discharging such exchequer bills, interest, premium, rate, or charges, until the whole of them shall be paid off, cancelled, and discharged, or money sufficient for that purpose be kept and reserved in the exchequer, to be payable on demand to the respective proprietors thereof.

The said exchequer bills, interest, and charges, are to be paid out of the sinking fund.

X. And be it declared and further enacted by the authority aforesaid, That it shall and may be lawful for the governor and company of the bank of *England* to advance or lend to his Majesty in like manner at the receipt of the exchequer, upon the credit of loan granted by this act, any sum or sums of money, not exceeding in the whole the sum of two million and one hundred thousand pounds; any thing in an act made in the fifth and sixth years of the reign of King *William* and Queen *Mary*, intituled, *An act for granting to their Majesties several rates and duties upon tonnage of ships and vessels, and upon beer, ale, and other liquors;*

Bank authorized to lend the said sum,

notwithstanding act 5 & 6 W. & M.

XIII. And be it further enacted by the authority aforesaid, That a sum not exceeding sixty thousand pounds of the monies arisen or to arise out of such of the duties granted or continued by an act made in the last session of parliament, as were thereby directed to be reserved in the exchequer to be disposed of by parliament, towards defraying the necessary expences of defending, protecting, and securing, the *British* colonies and plantations in *America*, be issued and applied towards maintaining his Majesty's forces and garrisons in the plantations, and for provisions for the forces in *North America*, *Nova Scotia*, *Newfoundland*, and the ceded islands, for the year one thousand seven hundred and sixty five; and the commissioners of his Majesty's treasury now or for the time being, or any three or more of them, or the high treasurer for the time being, is or are hereby authorized and impowered to issue and apply the same accordingly.

60,000 l. out of the monies granted the last session, and reserved for the disposition of parliament, to be applied towards maintaining the forces and garrisons in America.

XIV. Provided always, and it is hereby enacted by the authority aforesaid, That all the monies coming into the exchequer either by loans or exchequer bills, upon one act of this session of parliament, intituled, *An act for continuing and granting to his Majesty certain duties upon malt, mum, cyder, and perry, for the service of the year one thousand seven hundred and sixty five*; and so much money, if any such be, of the duties thereby granted, as shall arise or remain after all the loans or exchequer bills made or to be made on the same act, and all the interest, premium, rate and charges thereon, and the charges thereby allowable for raising the said duties, shall be satisfied, or money sufficient shall be reserved in the exchequer to satisfy and discharge the same; and also all the monies coming into the exchequer, either by loans or exchequer bills, upon one other act of this session of parliament, intituled, *An act for granting an aid to his Majesty by a land tax, to be raised in* Great Britain, *for the service of the year one thousand seven hundred and sixty five*; and so much money, if any such be, of the tax thereby granted as shall arise or remain after all the loans or exchequer bills made or to be made on the same act, and all the interest, premium, rate and charges thereon, and the charges allowable thereby for raising the said land tax, shall be satisfied, or money sufficient shall be reserved in the exchequer to satisfy and discharge the same; and also the sum of eight hundred thousand pounds granted by one other act of this session of parliament, intituled, *An act for raising a certain sum of money by loans or exchequer bills, for the service of the year one thousand seven hundred and sixty five*; and also the said sum of one hundred thirty five thousand two hundred thirteen pounds, five shillings, and one farthing, remaining in the receipt of the exchequer, on the tenth day of *October*, one thousand seven hundred and sixty four, for the disposition of parliament, of the monies which had then arisen of the surplusses, excesses, or overplus monies, and other revenues of the fund, commonly called *The Sinking Fund*; and also the said sum not exceeding three hundred and eight thousand pounds, of the monies

Appropriation of the supplies.

The monies arising by the malt tax, land tax, loans, &c. and other sums remaining in the exchequer, &c.

monies agreed to be paid by a convention between his Majesty and the *French* King, concluded and signed at *London* the twenty seventh day of *February*, one thousand seven hundred and sixty five, for the maintenance of the late *French* prisoners of war; and also the said sum of eighty thousand pounds remaining in the receipt of the exchequer, which was granted to his Majesty in the last session of parliament, upon account, for defraying the charge of the pay and cloathing of the militia for one year, beginning the twenty fifth day of *March*, one thousand seven hundred and sixty four; and also the said sum not exceeding twelve thousand pounds, out of the monies which shall arise of the produce of the duties laid by an act made in this session of parliament upon the importation and exportation of *Gum Senega* and *Gum Arabic*; and also the further sum of two million and one hundred thousand pounds by this act granted, out of such monies as shall or may arise of the surplusses, excesses, or overplus monies, and other revenues, composing the fund commonly called *The Sinking Fund*, shall be further appropriated, and are hereby appropriated, and shall be issued and applied for and towards the several uses and purposes herein after expressed, together with the residue of the monies arising from the sale of *French* prizes taken before the declaration of war, which his Majesty has declared in a most gracious speech to his parliament in the last session, that he has directed for the ease of his subjects, to be applied to the public service.

Duties on gum senega and gum arabic, and 2,100,000 l. granted out of the sinking fund; together with the residue of the money arising by the sale of French prizes.

XV. And it is hereby also enacted by the authority aforesaid, That out of all or any the aids or supplies provided as aforesaid, there shall and may be issued and applied any sum or sums of money, not exceeding one million four hundred thirty nine thousand seven hundred thirty four pounds, eleven shillings, and three pence, for or towards the naval services herein after particularly expressed (that is to say) for or towards victuals, wages, wear and tear of the navy, and the victualling thereof, performed and to be performed; and for or towards sea services in the office of ordnance, performed and to be performed; and for or towards defraying the ordinary of his Majesty's navy, and for half pay to sea and marine officers; and for or towards maintaining four thousand two hundred and eighty seven marines; and for or towards the buildings, rebuildings, and repairs, of his Majesty's ships, for the year one thousand seven hundred and sixty five.

Viz. out of the aids in general, 1,439,734 l. 11 s. 3 d. towards naval services herein specified.

XVI. And it is hereby also enacted by the authority aforesaid, That out of all or any the aids or supplies aforesaid, there shall and may be issued and applied any sum or sums of money, not exceeding five thousand pounds, upon account, to be applied by the commissioners or governors of the royal hospital for seamen at *Greenwich*, for the support and relief of seamen, worn out and become decrepit in the service of their country, who shall not be provided for within the said hospital.

5,000 l. towards the support of Greenwich hospital.

XVII. And it is hereby also enacted by the authority aforesaid, That out of all or any the aids or supplies aforesaid, there shall and may be issued and applied any sum or sums of money, not exceeding one thousand two hundred thirty one pounds, seventeen

1,231 l. 17 s. 6 d. bounty to certain chaplains who

ſeventeen ſhillings, and ſix pence, for paying a bounty, for the year one thouſand ſeven hundred and ſixty five, of two ſhillings and ſix pence *per* day to fifteen chaplains; and of two ſhillings *per* day to fifteen more chaplains, who have ſerved longeſt on board his Majeſty's ſhips of war, provided it appears by the books of the ſaid ſhips, that they have been actually borne and muſtered thereon for the ſpace of four years during the late war with *France* and *Spain*, and provided likewiſe, that ſuch chaplains do not enjoy the benefit of ſome eccleſiaſtical living or preferment from the crown or otherwiſe, of the preſent annual value of fifty pounds. ſerved in the navy the laſt war.

XVIII. And it is hereby alſo enacted by the authority aforeſaid, That out of all or any the aids or ſupplies aforeſaid, there ſhall and may be iſſued and applied any ſum or ſums of money, not exceeding one hundred ſeventy four thouſand ſix hundred ſeventy three pounds, fifteen ſhillings, and ten pence, for the charge of the office of ordnance for land ſervice, for the year one thouſand ſeven hundred and ſixty five. 174,673 l. 15 s. 10 d. for charge of the office of ordnance, for the year 1765.

XIX. And it is hereby alſo enacted by the authority aforeſaid, That out of all or any the aids or ſupplies aforeſaid, there ſhall and may be iſſued and applied any ſum or ſums of money, not exceeding fifty five thouſand five hundred nineteen pounds, ten ſhillings, and ſeven pence, for defraying the expence of ſervices performed by the office of ordnance for land ſervice, and not provided for by parliament, in one thouſand ſeven hundred and ſixty four. 55,519 l. 10 s. 7 d. to the ſaid office, for ſervices performed in 1764, not provided for.

XX. And it is hereby alſo enacted by the authority aforeſaid, That out of all or any the aids or ſupplies aforeſaid, there ſhall and may be iſſued and applied any ſum or ſums of money, not exceeding two million one thouſand ſix hundred two pounds, ten ſhillings, ſix pence, and one eighty eighth part of a penny, for and towards maintaining his Majeſty's land forces, and other ſervices herein after more particularly expreſſed; that is to ſay, any ſum or ſums of money, not exceeding ſix hundred eight thouſand one hundred thirty pounds, ten ſhillings, and ſeven pence, for defraying the charge of ſeventeen thouſand four hundred and twenty one effective men, commiſſioned and non-commiſſioned officers included; and including two thouſand ſix hundred and twenty eight invalids, for guards, garriſons, and other his Majeſty's land forces in *Great Britain*, *Guernſey*, and *Jerſey*, for the year one thouſand ſeven hundred and ſixty five; and any ſum or ſums of money, not exceeding three hundred twenty ſeven thouſand five hundred and two pounds, three ſhillings, and eleven pence halfpenny, for further maintaining his Majeſty's forces and garriſons in the plantations, including thoſe in garriſon at *Minorca* and *Gibraltar*; and for proviſions for the forces in *North America*, *Nova Scotia*, *Newfoundland*, *Gibraltar*, and the ceded iſlands, for the year one thouſand ſeven hundred and ſixty five; and any ſum or ſums of money, not exceeding ſix thouſand three hundred forty ſix pounds, three ſhillings, and five pence, for defraying the charge of the difference of pay be- 2,001,602 l. 10 s. 6 d. towards the land forces and other ſervices in general; of which 608,130 l. 10 s. 7 d. for guards and garriſons in Great Britain, Guernſey, and Jerſey; 327,502 l. 3 s. 11 d. 2 q. for guards and Garriſons in the plantations. Minorca, and Gibraltar; and proviſions for the forces abroad; 6,346 l. 3 s. 5 d. to make good difference of pay between the British and Irish establishments of 5 regiments of foot at Gibraltar, Minorca, and ceded islands; 11,291 l. 8 s. 6 d. 2 q. for general and general staff officers; 80,000 l. towards pay and cloathing of the militia; 135,606 l. 12 s. 6 d. to the reduced officers of the land forces, and marines; 2,361 l. 14 s. 2 d. to the officers and gentlemen of horse guards, &c. reduced; 1,664 l. to the pensions of officers widows; 109,107 l. 18 s. 4 d. to the out-pensioners of Chelsea hospital; 10,343 l. 16 s. 9 d. subsidy to the duke of Brunswick; 50,000 l. succour to the landgrave of Hesse Cassel; 404,496 l. 7 s. 6 d. extraordinary expences of the land forces, and other services, incurred in 1764, not provided for 248,259 l. 17 s 4 d. 1 q. to-

tween the *British* and *Irish* establishments of five regiments of foot serving at *Gibraltar*, *Minorca*, and the ceded islands, for the year one thousand seven hundred and sixty five; and any sum or sums of money, not exceeding eleven thousand two hundred ninety one pounds, eight shillings, and six pence halfpenny, for the pay of the general and general staff officers in *Great Britain*, for the year one thousand seven hundred and sixty five; and any sum or sums of money, not exceeding eighty thousand pounds upon account, for defraying the charge of the pay and cloathing of the militia for one year, beginning the twenty fifth day of *March*, one thousand seven hundred and sixty five; and any sum or sums of money, not exceeding one hundred thirty five thousand six hundred six pounds, twelve shillings, and six pence, upon account of the reduced officers of his Majesty's land forces and marines, for the year one thousand seven hundred and sixty five; and any sum or sums of money, not exceeding two thousand three hundred sixty one pounds, fourteen shillings, and two pence, for defraying the charge for allowances to the several officers and private gentlemen of the two troops of horse guards, and regiment of horse reduced, and to the superannuated gentlemen of the four troops of horse guards, for the year one thousand seven hundred and sixty five; and any sum or sums of money, not exceeding one thousand six hundred sixty four pounds, for the paying of pensions to the widows of such reduced officers of his Majesty's land forces and marines as died upon the establishment of halfpay in *Great Britain*, and who were married to them before the twenty fifth day of *December*, one thousand seven hundred and sixteen, for the year one thousand seven hundred and sixty five; and any sum or sums of money, not exceeding one hundred nine thousand one hundred seven pounds, eighteen shillings, and four pence, upon account, towards defraying the charge of outpensioners of *Chelsea* hospital, for the year one thousand seven hundred and sixty five; and any sum or sums of money, not exceeding ten thousand three hundred forty three pounds, sixteen shillings, nine pence, and seven eleventh parts of a penny, to enable his Majesty to defray the charge of the subsidies due to the duke of *Brunswick*, pursuant to treaties, for the year one thousand seven hundred and sixty five; and any sum or sums of money, not exceeding fifty thousand pounds, on account, towards assisting his Majesty to grant a reasonable succour in money to the landgrave of *Hesse Cassel*, pursuant to treaty; and any sum or sums of money, not exceeding four hundred four thousand four hundred ninety six pounds, seven shillings, and six pence, for defraying the extraordinary expences of his Majesty's land forces, and other services incurred between the twenty fourth day of *December*, one thousand seven hundred and sixty three, and the twenty fifth day of *December*, one thousand seven hundred and sixty four, and not provided for by parliament; and any sum or sums of money, not exceeding two hundred forty eight thousand two hundred fifty nine pounds, seventeen shillings, and four pence farthing, upon account, to-

wards

ging such unsatisfied claims and demands, l during the late war in *Germany*, as appear orts of the commissioners appointed by his ing and stating such claims and demands; ; of money, not exceeding six thousand four . pounds, seventeen shillings, four pence, of a penny, for defraying the charge of three ies of foot to be raised for his Majesty's ser- *Africa*, and for provisions for the same from of *December*, one thousand seven hundred e twenty fourth day of *December*, one thou- and sixty five, both days inclusive, being xty five days.

wards the unsatisfied claims in Germany;

6,491 l. 17 s. 4d. charge of 3 independant companies in Africa;

ereby also enacted by the authority aforesaid, ny the aids or supplies aforesaid, there shall nd applied the sum of eight hundred thou- ying off and discharging the exchequer bills of an act passed in the last session of parlia- *act for raising a certain sum of money by loans d for applying certain monies remaining in the vice of the year one thousand seven hundred and plication of certain savings of public monies, and he sale of military stores; and for further ap- s granted in this session of parliament; and for have omitted to insert in indentures, or other agreed to be paid with clerks, apprentices, and* charged upon the first aids to be granted in nent.

800,000 l. towards paying off exchequer bills issued pursuant to an act of the last session;

hereby also enacted by the authority afore- l or any the aids or supplies aforesaid, there ued and applied any sum or sums of money, housand nine hundred eleven pounds, four- leven pence, upon account, for maintaining civil establishment of his Majesty's colony of year one thousand seven hundred and sixty r sums of money, not exceeding seven thou- account of sundry expences, for the ser- , in the years one thousand seven hun- e thousand seven hundred and fifty one, n hundred and fifty two, one thousand sixty two, and one thousand seven hundred . not provided for by parliament; and any ney, not exceeding three thousand nine hun- pounds, upon account, for defraying the l establishment of his Majesty's colony of ncidental expences attending the same, from ay of *June*, one thousand seven hundred and wenty fourth of *June*, one thousand seven ive; and any sum or sums of money, not ex- nd and two hundred pounds, upon account, arges of the civil establishment of his Ma- *st Florida*, and other incidental expences at-

4,911 l. 14s. 11d. for defraying the civil establishment of Nova Scotia;

7,000 l. for sundry expences incurred there in former years, not provided for;

3,966 l. for the civil establishment of Georgia;

5,200 l. for the civil establishment of East Florida;

tending

tending the ſame, from the twenty fourth of *June*, one thouſand ſeven hundred and ſixty four, to the twenty fourth of *June*, one thouſand ſeven hundred and ſixty five; and any ſum or ſums of money, not exceeding five thouſand and two hundred pounds, upon account, for defraying the charges of the civil eſtabliſhment of his Majeſty's colony of *Weſt Florida*, and other incidental expences attending the ſame, from the twenty fourth of *June*, one thouſand ſeven hundred and ſixty four, to the twenty fourth of *June*, one thouſand ſeven hundred and ſixty five; and any ſum or ſums of money, not exceeding one thouſand ſix hundred one pounds and fourteen ſhillings, upon account, for defraying the expence attending general ſurveys of his Majeſty's dominions in *North America*, for the year one thouſand ſeven hundred and ſixty five.

5,200 l. for the civil eſtabliſhment of Weſt Florida; 1,601 l. 14 s. towards expence of general ſurveys in America;

5000 l. towards building a Lazaret. 38,000 l. to the Foundling Hoſpital.

XXIII. And it is hereby alſo enacted by the authority aforeſaid, That out of all or any the aids or ſupplies aforeſaid, there ſhall and may be iſſued and applied any ſum or ſums of money, not exceeding five thouſand pounds, towards building a lazaret; and any ſum or ſums of money, not exceeding thirty eight thouſand pounds, upon account, towards enabling the governors and guardians of the hoſpital for the maintenance and education of expoſed and deſerted young children, to maintain and educate, or to place out as apprentices ſuch children as were received into the ſaid hoſpital on or before the twenty fifth day of *March*, one thouſand ſeven hundred and ſixty, from the thirty firſt day of *December*, one thouſand ſeven hundred and ſixty four incluſive, to the thirty firſt day of *December*, one thouſand ſeven hundred and ſixty five incluſive, and that the ſaid ſum be iſſued and paid for the uſe of the ſaid hoſpital without fee or reward, or any deduction whatſoever.

13,000 l. for maintaining the Britiſh forts and ſettlements in Africa; 7,000 l. for a block houſe at Cape Appolonia; 5,500 l. for defraying charges of a civil eſtabliſhment upon the coaſt of Africa;

XXIV. And it is hereby alſo enacted by the authority aforeſaid, That out of all or any the aids or ſupplies aforeſaid, there ſhall and may be iſſued and applied any ſum or ſums of money, not exceeding thirteen thouſand pounds, to be employed in maintaining and ſupporting the *Britiſh* forts and ſettlements upon the coaſt of *Africa*, and putting the ſaid forts into better repair; and any ſum or ſums of money, not exceeding ſeven thouſand pounds, for building a block houſe at or near *Cape Appolonia*, on the coaſt of *Africa*; and any ſum or ſums of money, not exceeding five thouſand and five hundred pounds, upon account, for defraying the charges of a civil eſtabliſhment upon that part of the coaſt of *Africa*, ſituate between the port of *Sallee* in *South Barbary* and *Cape Rouge*, for the year one thouſand ſeven hundred and ſixty five.

2,400 l. to make good to his Majeſty the like ſum iſſued in purſuance of addreſſes of the houſe of commons;

XXV. And it is hereby alſo further enacted by the authority aforeſaid, That out of all or any the aids or ſupplies aforeſaid, there ſhall and may be iſſued and applied the ſum of two thouſand and four hundred pounds, to make good to his Majeſty the like ſum which has been iſſued by his Majeſty's orders in purſuance of the addreſſes of the houſe of commons; and any ſum or ſums of money, not exceeding ten thouſand pounds, to enable his Majeſty to give a proper compenſation to the government

ment of the island of *Barbadoes*, for the assistance given by them to his Majesty's forces under the command of major general *Monckton*, in the expedition against the island of *Martinico*; and any sum or sums of money, not exceeding seven thousand pounds, to be paid into the chamber of the city of *London*, towards the finishing and compleating the works for improving, widening, and enlarging the passage over and through *London Bridge*, without account, other than as is directed for the monies raised by an act made in the twenty ninth year of his late Majesty's reign, intituled, *An act to improve, widen, and enlarge, the passage over and through* London Bridge.

10,000 l. compensation to the government of the island of Barbadoes.

7,000 l. towards repairing London Bridge;

XXVI. And it is hereby also enacted by the authority aforesaid, That out of all or any the aids or supplies aforesaid, there shall and may be issued and applied any sum or sums of money, not exceeding forty eight thousand one hundred seventy six pounds, one shilling, and eleven pence halfpenny, to replace to the sinking fund the like sum paid out of the same, to make good the deficiency on the fifth day of *July*, one thousand seven hundred and sixty four, of the several rates and duties upon offices and pensions, and upon houses, and upon windows or lights, which were made a fund by an act of the thirty first year of the reign of his late Majesty for paying annuities at the bank of *England*, in respect of five millions borrowed towards the supply granted for the service of the year one thousand seven hundred and fifty eight; and any sum or sums of money, not exceeding forty nine thousand seven hundred forty two pounds, one shilling, and two pence halfpenny, to replace to the sinking fund the like sum paid out of the same, to make good the deficiency on the tenth day of *October*, one thousand seven hundred and sixty four, of the several additional duties upon wines imported into this kingdom; and certain duties upon all cyder and perry which were made a fund by an act of the third year of the reign of his present Majesty, for paying annuities in respect of three million five hundred thousand pounds, borrowed towards the supply granted for the service of the year one thousand seven hundred and sixty three; and any sum or sums of money, not exceeding one hundred thirty nine thousand three hundred forty two pounds, two shillings, and four pence, to replace to the sinking fund the like sum issued thereout, for paying annuities after the rate of four pounds *per centum* for the year, ended the twenty ninth day of *September*, one thousand seven hundred and sixty four, which were granted in respect of certain navy, victualling, and transport bills, and ordnance debentures, delivered in and cancelled pursuant to an act of the third year of the reign of his present Majesty; and any sum or sums of money, not exceeding two hundred forty nine thousand six hundred sixty pounds, four shillings, and ten pence, to make good the deficiency of the grants for the service of the year one thousand seven hundred and sixty four.

48,176 l. 1 s. 11 d. 2 q. to replace to the sinking fund the deficiency of the duties on offices and pensions: and windows:

49,742 l. 1 s. 2 d. 2 q. to replace to the sinking fund, the deficiency of the additional duties upon wines imported: and upon cyder and perry:

139,342 l. 2 s. 4 d. to replace to the sinking fund the annuities granted in respect of navy and victualling bills, &c. cancelled:

249,660 l. 4 s. 10 d. to make good the deficiency of the grants for the last year.

XXVII. And it is hereby further enacted by the authority aforesaid, That the said aids and supplies provided as aforesaid, shall

These aids to be applied to no other uses.

ſhall not be iſſued or applied to any uſe, intent, or purpoſe whatſoever, other than the uſes and purpoſes before mentioned, or for the ſeveral deficiencies, or other payments directed to be ſatisfied thereout by any act or acts or any particular clauſe or clauſes for that purpoſe contained in any other act or acts of this preſent ſeſſion of parliament.

Rules to be obſerved in the application of the half-pay.

XXVIII. And, as to the ſaid ſum of one hundred thirty thouſand ſix hundred ſix pounds, twelve ſhillings, and ſix pence by this act appropriated on account of half-pay as aforeſaid, it is hereby enacted and declared by the authority aforeſaid, That the rules herein after preſcribed, ſhall be duly obſerved in the application of the ſaid half-pay; that is to ſay, That no perſon ſhall have or receive any part of the ſame, who was a minor, and under the age of ſixteen years, at the time when the regiment, troop, or company, in which he ſerved, was reduced; that no perſon ſhall have or receive any part of the ſame, except ſuch perſon who did actual ſervice in ſome regiment, troop, or company; that no perſon having any other place or employment of profit civil or military, under his Majeſty, ſhall have or receive any part of the ſaid half-pay; that no chaplain of any garriſon or regiment, who has any eccleſiaſtical benefice in *Great Britain* or *Ireland*, ſhall have or receive any part of the ſaid half-pay; that no perſon ſhall have or receive any part of the ſame, who has reſigned his commiſſion, and has had no commiſſion ſince; that no part of the ſame ſhall be allowed to any perſon by virtue of any warrant or appointment, except to ſuch perſons, as would have been otherwiſe intitled to the ſame as reduced officers; and that no part of the ſame ſhall be allowed to any of the officers of the five regiments of dragoons, and eight regiments of foot, lately diſbanded in *Ireland*, except to ſuch as were lately taken off the eſtabliſhment of half-pay in *Great Britain*.

Recital of clauſes in act 4 Geo. 3.

XXIX. And whereas by an act of parliament made in the fourth year of his preſent Majeſty's reign, intituled, *An act for raiſing a certain ſum of money by loans or exchequer bills; and for applying certain monies remaining in the exchequer, for the ſervice of the year one thouſand ſeven hundred and ſixty four; and for application of certain ſavings of publick monies, and of monies ariſen by the ſale of military ſtores; and for further appropriating the ſupplies granted in this ſeſſion of parliament; and for relief of perſons who have omitted to inſert in indentures, or other writings, the full ſum agreed to be paid with clerks, apprentices, and other ſervants*; the ſeveral ſupplies which had been granted to his preſent Majeſty, as is therein mentioned, were appropriated to the ſeveral uſes and purpoſes therein expreſſed; amongſt which, any ſum or ſums of money, not exceeding thirty thouſand one hundred and eighty eight pounds, and eighteen ſhillings, was appropriated to be paid to the reduced officers of his Majeſty's land forces and marines, for the year one thouſand ſeven hundred and ſixty four, and any ſum or ſums of money, not exceeding one hundred and twenty five thouſand four hundred and fifty five pounds,

pounds, and thirteen shillings, was appropriated to be paid to the reduced officers of his Majesty's land forces reduced and disbanded in the year one thousand seven hundred and sixty three, and such as were to be reduced and disbanded for the year one thousand seven hundred and sixty four; subject nevertheless to such rules to be observed in the application of the said half-pay, as in and by the aforesaid act were prescribed in that behalf: now it is hereby provided, enacted, and declared, by the authority aforesaid, That so much of the said sums of thirty thousand one hundred and eighty eight pounds, and eighteen shillings; and one hundred and twenty five thousand four hundred and fifty five pounds, and thirteen shillings, as are or shall be more than sufficient to satisfy the said reduced officers, according to the rules prescribed by the said act to be observed in the application thereof, or any part of such overplus, shall and may be disposed of to such officers who are maimed or have lost their limbs in the late wars, or such others, as by reason of their long service, or otherwise, his Majesty shall judge to be proper objects of charity, or to the widows or children of such officers, according to such warrant or warrants, under his Majesty's royal sign manual, as shall be signed in that behalf; any thing in this act, or the said former act to the contrary notwithstanding.

Rules to be observed in the application of the surplus of the several sums of 30,188 l. 18 s. and 125,455 l. 13 s. appropriated in 1764 to the payment of reduced officers.

XXX. And whereas by an act made in the thirty first year of the reign of his late majesty King *George* the Second, certain duties were laid upon offices and employments; and the monies thereby arising in that part of *Great Britain* called *Scotland*, were directed to be paid at *Edinburgh*, to such person or persons as the commissioners of the treasury, or the high treasurer of *Great Britain* for the time being, should constitute and appoint to be receiver general, or receivers thereof, for his Majesty's use; but no provision hath been made, or authority given, for allowing any compensation, or granting any reward, to such receiver or receivers, for his or their trouble in the receiving the said monies, and in the paying and accounting for the same; be it therefore enacted by the authority aforesaid, That it shall and may be lawful to and for such receiver or receivers, to retain out of the monies which have been and shall be paid into his or their hands in pursuance of the said act, such sum, as a compensation or reward for his or their trouble, as his Majesty, his heirs, and successors, shall appoint, not exceeding three pence in the pound.

Receiver of the duties on offices and employments in Scotland, allowed to retain 3 d. in the pound of the monies received by him.

XXXI. And whereas some persons have omitted to cause affidavits to be made, and afterwards to be filed in the proper office, of the actual execution of several contracts, in writing, entered into by them to serve as clerks to attornies or sollicitors, within the time in which the same ought to have been done, and many infants and others may thereby incur certain disabilities; for preventing whereof, and relieving such persons, be it likewise enacted by the authority aforesaid, That every person who hath neglected or omitted to cause any such affidavit or affidavits as aforesaid to be made and filed, and who, on or before the

Further time allowed, to 10 Oct. 1765, to make and file affidavits of clerkship, &c. omitted to be done in due time.

the tenth day of *October*, one thousand seven hundred and sixty five, shall cause one or more affidavit or affidavits to be made, and afterwards to be filed, in such manner as the same ought to have been made and filed in due time, shall be and is hereby indemnified, freed, and discharged, from and against all penalties, forfeitures, incapacities, and disabilities, in or by any act or acts of parliament mentioned and incurred, or to be incurred, for or by reason of any such neglect or omission, in not causing such affidavit or affidavits to be made and filed in such manner as the same ought to have been; and every such affidavit and affidavits so to be made, and which shall be duly filed on or before the said tenth day of *October* as aforesaid, shall be as effectual, to all intents and purposes, as if the same had been made and filed within the respective times the same ought, by the laws now in being for that purpose, to have been so made and filed.

CAP. XLI.

An act for the relief of insolvent debtors.

Preamble.

WHEREAS many persons by losses and other misfortunes, are rendered incapable of paying their whole debts; and though they are willing to make the utmost satisfaction they can, and many of them are able to serve his Majesty by sea and land, yet are detained in prison by their creditors, or have been forced to go into foreign parts out of this realm: and whereas such unhappy debtors have always been deemed the proper objects of publick compassion; and by several acts of parliament, have been discharged on the conditions in such acts mentioned; for the relief therefore of insolvent prisoners and fugitives who shall comply with the terms contained in this act to be respectively observed by them, and faithfully discover, upon oath, and deliver up and assign, all their effects and estates whatsoever for the benefit of their creditors; and to prevent, as far as possible, the many frauds and abuses which, in a great measure, have obstructed the good ends of such acts; be it enacted by the King's most excellent Majesty, by and with the advice and consent of the lords spiritual and temporal, and commons, in this present parliament assembled and by the authority of the same, That from and after the passing of this act, all and every gaoler, or keeper of any prison, in any county, riding, division, city, town, place, or liberty, within this kingdom, shall, is, and are hereby required to make a true, exact, and perfect list, alphabetically, of the name or names of all and every person or persons who, upon the first day of *January*, one thousand seven hundred and sixty five, was or were, or at any time since have been, and at the time of making out every such list shall be, really an actual prisoner or prisoners, in the custody of any gaoler or gaolers, or keeper of any prison respectively, upon any process whatsoever for or by reason of any debt, damage, costs, sum or sums of money, contempt, or otherwise, and an account of the time when

Alphabetical lists to be made out of prisoners in custody for debt on 1 Jan. 1765, or since then;

when ſuch priſoner or priſoners was or were reſpectively charged in cuſtody, or received in priſon, together with the name or names of the perſon or perſons at whoſe ſuit or proſecution ſuch priſoner or priſoners is or are detained; and ſhall deliver the ſame to the juſtices of the peace at their firſt or ſecond general or general quarter ſeſſions of the peace, to be held after the ſeventeenth day of *June*, one thouſand ſeven hundred and ſixty five, or at ſome adjournment thereof, for ſuch county, riding, diviſion, city, town, place, or liberty reſpectively.

with the time when charged, and at whoſe ſuit; the ſame to be delivered in to the quarter ſeſſions.

II. And be it further enacted, That the warden of his Majeſty's priſon of the *Fleet*, and marſhal of the *King's Bench* priſon, ſhall ſeverally, on the delivering in of any ſuch liſt of priſoners in their reſpective cuſtody, take an oath in the open court of ſuch general or general quarter ſeſſion of the peace, or at ſome adjournment thereof, to the effect following; (that is to ſay)

The warden of the Fleet, and marſhal of the King's Bench priſon, to take the following oath on delivering in their liſts.

I A. B. *upon my corporal oath, in the preſence of Almighty God, do ſolemnly ſwear, profeſs and declare, That all and every perſon and perſons, whoſe name or names is or are inſerted and contained in the firſt part of the liſt by me now delivered in and ſubſcribed, was and were to the beſt of my knowledge and belief, upon the firſt day of* January, *one thouſand ſeven hundred and ſixty five, really and truly priſoners, in actual cuſtody, in the priſon or gaol of* [inſert the name of the priſon] *at the ſuit or ſuits of the ſeveral perſon or perſons therein reſpectively mentioned; and alſo that all and every perſon and perſons, whoſe name or names is or are inſerted or contained in the ſecond part of the ſaid liſt now by me delivered in and ſubſcribed as aforeſaid, have, ſince the ſaid firſt day of* January, *one thouſand ſeven hundred and ſixty five, been committed or ſurrendered to the ſaid gaol or priſon of* [inſert the name of the gaol or priſon] *at the ſuit or ſuits of the ſeveral perſon or perſons therein reſpectively mentioned; except ſuch perſon or perſons who is or are in ſuch liſt particularly mentioned and deſcribed to have died, been diſcharged, or removed to ſome other priſon, by proceſs of law, ſince the ſaid firſt day of* January, *one thouſand ſeven hundred and ſixty five; and alſo except ſuch perſon or perſons who is or are in ſuch liſt particularly mentioned and deſcribed to have been permitted to have gone out of the ſaid priſon, by day rules of the court of* [Common Pleas or King's Bench, as the caſe ſhall be] *ſince the ſaid firſt day of* January, *one thouſand ſeven hundred and ſixty five, to tranſact their affairs: and alſo except ſuch perſon or perſons who is or are therein alſo particularly mentioned and deſcribed to have, upon the ſaid firſt day of* January, *one thouſand ſeven hundred and ſixty five, or ſince, been in the rules of the ſaid priſon* [of the *Fleet* or *King's Bench*, as the caſe ſhall be] *by leave of the* [warden or marſhall of the ſaid priſon, as the caſe ſhall be] *and have to the beſt of my knowledge and belief, really and truly, ever ſince continued and remained in actual cuſtody in the ſaid priſon* of the [*Fleet*, or *King's Bench*, as the caſe ſhall be] *or the liberties thereof, at the ſuit or ſuits of the ſeveral perſons in the ſaid liſt reſpectively mentioned* [and if any priſoners have, ſince the ſaid firſt day of *January*, one thouſand ſeven hundred and ſixty five, eſcaped out of either of the said prisons, then insert, *except* [insert the name or names of the prisoner or prisoners who have escaped] *who, without my knowledge, privity, or consent, hath or have escaped out of the said prison of* *and that the said list is a true, exact, perfect, and just list of all such persons who were really and truly prisoners in actual custody in the said gaol or prison of* *on the said first day of* January, *one thousand seven hundred and sixty five, and who, since the said first day of* January, *one thousand seven hundred and sixty five, have been committed to, and really have been, and now is or are, prisoner or prisoners in actual custody in the said gaol or prison of* *or the liberties thereof; and that none of such prisoners, to my knowledge, or with my privity, have voluntarily, or with design, or in expectation to take any benefit from or under any act of parliament to be made for relief of insolvent debtors, surrendered themselves, or been committed to the said prison, or got their names entered as prisoners in the books of the said prison; or since the same first day of* January, *one thousand seven hundred and sixty five, to my knowledge, or with my privity, have resided out of the said prison of* *or the rules thereof* [but if any have so done, add *except* naming such by name]

Other gaolers to take the following oath on delivering in their lists.

And that every other gaoler and keeper of any other prison or prisons in any county, city, town, riding, division, place, or liberty, shall severally, on the delivering in of any such list respectively, take an oath in the open court of the general or general quarter session of the county, city, town, division, liberty, or place, for which he or she shall deliver in any such list, and swear to the effect following; (that is to say)

I A. B. *upon my corporal oath, in the presence of Almighty God, do solemnly swear, profess, and declare, That all and every person and persons, whose name or names are inserted and contained in the first part of the list by me now delivered in and subscribed, was and were, to the best of my knowledge and belief, upon the first day of* January, *one thousand seven hundred and sixty five, really and truly prisoners in actual custody, in the prison or gaol of* *at the suit or suits of the several persons therein respectively mentioned; and also that all and every person and persons, whose name or names is or are inserted or contained in the second part of the said list now by me delivered in and subscribed as aforesaid, have, since the said first day of* January, *one thousand seven hundred and sixty five, been committed or surrendered to the said gaol or prison of* (if any such prisoner or prisoners hath or have, since the said first day of *January*, one thousand seven hundred and sixty five, been committed or surrendered to such gaol or prison) *at the suit or suits of the several person or persons therein respectively mentioned; except* [if any exception is necessary] *such persons as are therein particularly mentioned and described to have died, been discharged, or removed to some other prison by process of law, or to have escaped out of such prison, without my privity, knowledge, or consent, since the said first day of* January, *one thousand seven hundred and sixty five, and that all*

all and every of them, whose name and names is and are contained in the first part of the said list (except as before excepted) to the best of my knowledge and belief, have really and truly continued and remained in actual custody, in the said gaol or prison of ever since the said first day of January, *one thousand seven hundred and sixty five; and that the said list is a true, exact, perfect, and just list, of all such persons as were really and truly prisoners in actual custody, in the gaol or prison of on the said first day of* January, *one thousand seven hundred and sixty five, and who, since the said first day of* January, *one thousand seven hundred and sixty five, have been really and truly committed, or surrendered to the said gaol or prison of* (except as before excepted) *to the best of my knowledge and belief; and that none of such prisoners, to my knowledge, or with my privity, have voluntarily, or with design, or in expectation to take any benefit, from or under any act of parliament to be made for relief of insolvent debtors, surrendered, or been committed to the said prison of or got his, her, or their name or names entered as prisoner or prisoners in the books of the said prison, or, since their commitment, have, to my knowledge, or with my privity, resided out of the said prison of* [if any have so done, then add *except* inserting their names]

Which said respective oaths the said justices at the first or second general or quarter session aforesaid, or at some adjournment thereof, within their respective jurisdictions, are hereby impowered and required to administer in open court; and the words of the said oath herein before directed to be taken by the said warden and marshal respectively, shall be entered or written at the end or bottom of the list which shall be delivered in by them respectively, and shall be subscribed and sworn to by them respectively in open court; and the words of the oath to be taken by every other gaoler or keeper respectively, shall be entered or written at the end or bottom of the list which shall be delivered by them respectively, and shall be subscribed, and sworn to by them respectively in open court: and every such list which shall be so delivered in, subscribed, and sworn to, in pursuance of this act, shall be kept by the clerk of the peace of every such county, riding, division, city, town, place, or liberty respectively, in which any such list as aforesaid shall be sworn to, for the better satisfaction of the said justices, and information of all or any prisoner or prisoners therein named; and so as the same may, from time to time, be seen and examined by any creditor or creditors of such prisoner or prisoners, without fee or reward.

The oaths to be administered by the justices in court.

and entered and subscribed at the bottom of each list.

List to be kept by the clerk of the peace.

III. And be it further enacted by the authority aforesaid, That all and every gaoler and gaolers, and keeper of any gaol or prison, is and are hereby required, ten days at least before the first or second general or quarter session of the peace shall be held after the said seventeenth day of *June*, one thousand seven hundred and sixty five, for the county, riding, division, city, town, place, or liberty, in which any such gaol or prison shall be, or to which the same belong, to fix up, in some conspicu-

Copies of the lists to be delivered in to be fix'd up in the prisons, and on the gates thereof.

ous place or places in every ſuch priſon, and at the moſt frequented and uſual gate, door, or entrance into every ſuch priſon, three or more true copies of the liſt or liſts propoſed or intended to be delivered in by any ſuch gaoler or keeper, at the ſaid general or quarter ſeſſion, or at ſome adjournment thereof.

Perſons inſerted in the liſts being priſoners, without a fraudulent intention, on 1 Jan. 1765.

IV. And be it further enacted, That all and every perſon and perſons whoſe name or names ſhall be inſerted in any ſuch liſt to be delivered in as aforeſaid, who, upon the firſt day of *January*, one thouſand ſeven hundred and ſixty five, were really and truly priſoners in the actual cuſtody of any gaoler or gaolers, or keeper of any priſon reſpectively of this kingdom, and did not come into or get his, her, or their names entered in the book of any gaol or priſon as a priſoner or priſoners there, with a view or deſign to take the benefit of ſome act for relief of inſolvent debtors, and who ſhall take the oath herein after-mentioned, and ſhall perform on his or her part what is required to be done by him or her by this act, ſhall be for ever releaſed and diſcharged from his or her impriſonment, in ſuch manner as hereafter is provided.

conforming to the regulations of this act, ſhall be diſcharged.

Priſoners in cuſtody at the time of paſſing this act, who were arreſted for debt on or before 1 Jan. 1765, and held to bail, and rendered themſelves, on or before 12 Feb. 1765, on conforming to the regulations of this act, ſhall be diſcharged.

V. Provided always, and be it enacted by the authority aforeſaid, That any priſoner or priſoners who ſhall be in actual cuſtody at the time of paſſing this act, and was or were, on or before the firſt day of *January*, one thouſand ſeven hundred and ſixty five, arreſted for any ſum or ſums of money by virtue of any writ or proceſs iſſuing out of any court of record, and held to bail thereon, and did, on or before the twelfth day of *February*, one thouſand ſeven hundred and ſixty five, render him, her, or themſelves, or was or were ſurrendered in diſcharge of his, her, or their bail, and thereupon committed to priſon, and has or have continued therein until the paſſing of this act, by virtue of ſuch commitment; every ſuch priſoner or priſoners ſhall, upon due proof of the premiſſes upon oath, be diſcharged from ſuch debt or demand, in like manner as if ſuch priſoner or priſoners had been actually in priſon upon the ſaid firſt day of *January*, one thouſand ſeven hundred and ſixty five, and continued therein as aforeſaid; ſubject nevertheleſs to the ſame reſtrictions and proviſions, and a compliance with the like terms, conditions, and qualifications, herein before impoſed upon priſoners actually in cuſtody upon the ſaid firſt day of *January*, one thouſand ſeven hundred and ſixty five; and alſo ſubject to the ſame terms and proviſions relating to the eſtate and effects of every ſuch priſoner as aforeſaid.

Juſtices upon the petition of the priſoner, and his delivering a ſchedule of his eſtate.

VI. And be it further enacted, That it ſhall be lawful for any juſtice or juſtices of any county, riding, diviſion, city, town, place, or liberty, within this kingdom, upon the petition of any ſuch priſoner or priſoners to any juſtice or juſtices of the peace within his or their reſpective juriſdictions, upon every ſuch priſoner or priſoners ſo petitioning, and, at the time of his or her ſo petitioning, leaving with the juſtice or juſtices of the peace, who ſhall be ſo petitioned, a true copy of the ſchedule, containing his or her intended diſcovery of his or her real and perſonal eſtate;

eſtate; to be ſworn to at the firſt or ſecond general or quarter ſeſſion next enſuing after every ſuch petition, or ſome adjournment thereof, by warrant under his hand and ſeal, or their hands and ſeals, to require the ſheriff or ſheriffs, gaoler or gaolers, or keeper of any ſuch priſon within the juriſdiction of any ſuch juſtice or juſtices, to bring before the juſtices at the firſt or ſecond next general or general quarter ſeſſion of the peace, or any adjournment thereof, to be held, as the caſe ſhall happen to be, next after the expiration of ten days from the date of ſuch warrant, for ſuch reſpective county, riding, diviſion, city, town, place, or liberty, the body of any perſon being in the ſaid priſon as aforeſaid, with the warrant or warrants of his or her detainer, together with a copy or copies of the cauſe or cauſes which he, ſhe, or they, is or are charged with in any ſuch gaol or priſon as aforeſaid, at the time aforeſaid; which warrant of every ſuch juſtice or juſtices every ſuch ſheriff and ſheriffs, gaoler or keeper, is and are hereby commanded to obey.

are to iſſue their warrant for bringing the priſoner to the quarter ſeſſions, &c.

with the warrant of detainer and copy of the writ, &c.

Gaoler, &c. to obey ſuch warrant.

VII. And be it alſo enacted, That the copy of every ſchedule which ſhall be left with any ſuch juſtice or juſtices, ſhall, within ten days after the ſame ſhall be ſo left, be tranſmitted by the juſtice or juſtices, with whom the ſame ſhall be ſo left, to the clerk of the peace for the county, riding, diviſion, city, town, place, or liberty, in which the ſame ſhall have been ſo left, there to remain and be inſpected, from time to time, as occaſion ſhall require, by any creditor of any ſuch priſoner who ſhall deſire to inſpect the ſame.

Schedule of the priſoner's eſtate to be tranſmitted to the clerk of the peace, for the inſpection of the creditors.

VIII. And be it further enacted, that all and every priſoner and priſoners, who ſhall intend to petition to be diſcharged under this act, as aforeſaid, ſhall firſt cauſe publick notice to be inſerted in three ſeveral *London Gazettes* previous to ſuch general or quarter ſeſſion, or the adjournment thereof, at which the ſaid priſoner or priſoners ſhall apply to be diſcharged from any goal in *London*, or within the weekly bills of mortality; and if ſuch priſoner ſhall be in cuſtody in any gaol out of *London*, or the weekly bills of mortality, then alſo in ſome news paper which ſhall be publiſhed in or near the county, riding, diviſion, city, town, liberty, or place, in the goal whereof he or ſhe ſhall be ſo in cuſtody; containing the name, trade, and occupation, and two laſt places of abode, if ſo many, of every ſuch priſoner and priſoners, and the priſon wherein he, ſhe, or they, is or are confined, and of his, her, or their intention to take the benefit of this act, and mentioning ſuch notice in each gazette or news paper, to be the firſt, ſecond, or third notice, according to the time of publiſhing each of ſuch notices; and for the inſerting of each of which ſaid ſeveral notices in the ſaid gazette, or in any other news paper, there ſhall be paid, each time, by every ſuch priſoner, two pence, and no more: the firſt of which ſaid notices ſhall be ſo inſerted in the ſaid gazette, or in the ſaid other news paper, as the caſe may require, thirty days at leaſt, and the laſt of the ſaid notices ten days at leaſt, before any ſuch firſt or ſecond general or quarter ſeſſion, or adjournment thereof, ſhall

Priſoners intending to petition for their diſcharge, are to give previous notice thereof thrice in the gazette and other news papers;

contents of the notice.

2d. each time and no more to be paid for inſerting ſuch notices.

Firſt notice to be inſerted 30 days, and the laſt 10 days,

before the quarter sessions, &c.

shall be held as as aforesaid; so that as well all the creditors who have not charged the said prisoner or prisoners in custody, as those creditors who have charged such prisoner or prisoners in execution, or on mesne process, or otherwise, may have sufficient notice thereof.

Prisoner being brought into court, due publication of the notices required being proved, &c.

IX. And be it further enacted, That every such prisoner as aforesaid, who in pursuance of any such warrant as aforesaid, shall be brought to any general or general quarter session, or any adjournment thereof, shall, in case it shall be proved upon oath or by producing the said three gazettes and news papers before mentioned to the said justices at any such session, or the adjournment thereof, that such notices were so inserted in the *London Gazette*, and other news papers, where required, in manner as herein before is directed; and that the person or persons so petitioning, was or were actually a prisoner or prisoners on the said first day of *January*, one thousand seven hundred and sixty five, or since, in the gaol or prison in which his, her, or their name or names is or are specified in the list of prisoners there delivered in at any such first or second session, or any adjournment thereof as aforesaid, in pursuance of this act, shall, in open court at the said general or quarter session, or any adjournment thereof, subscribe and deliver in a true schedule or account of all his or her real estate, either in possession, reversion, remainder, or expectancy; and also of the whole of his or her personal estate which he or she, or any person or persons in trust for him or her, or for his or her use, benefit, or advantage, is or are seized of, interested in, or intitled to, with the names of his or her several debtors, and where they respectively live, or may be met with; and the several sums of money from them respectively owing, and how the same respectively became due, and are secured; and if by mortgage, specialty, contract, note, or other writing, then the name and names and places of abode of the several witnesses who can prove such debts or contracts (if there be any such) and shall also make oath and swear to the effect following; (that is to say)

is to deliver in a schedule of his estate, debts, and creditors

Prisoner's oath on delivering in the said schedule.

I A. B. *upon my corporal oath, in the presence of Almighty God, do solemnly swear, protest, and declare, That on the first day of* January, *one thousand seven hundred and sixty five, I was a prisoner, or else*, as the case may be, *that since the first day of* January, *one thousand seven hundred and sixty five, I have surrendered, or have been committed to the prison of*   *in discharge of my bail, or for want of bail*, as the case shall be; *and that I was actually arrested before the said first day of* January, *one thousand seven hundred and sixty five, in the action or suit, actions or suits, in which I surrendered, or was committed, as aforesaid, to the said gaol or prison of*   *and that I have, ever since my said surrender or commitment, continued a prisoner within the prison of*   *in the actual custody of the gaoler or keeper of the said prison of*   *or within the liberties thereof, at the suit of*   *and without any*

any fraud or collusion whatsoever; and that the schedule now delivered by me and subscribed, doth contain to the best of my knowledge, remembrance, and belief, a full, just, true, and perfect account and discovery of all the goods, effects, and estates, real and personal, either in possession, reversion, remainder, or expectancy, which I, or any person in trust for me, or for my benefit or advantage, am seised or possessed of, interested in, or intitled to; and of all debts as are to me owing, or to any person or persons in trust for me; and of all the securities and contracts whereby any money now is, or will or may hereafter become payable, or any benefit or advantage may accrue to me, or to my use, or to any person or persons in trust for me; and the names and places of abode of the several persons from whom such debts are due and owing; and of the witnesses that can prove such debts or contracts, if any such there be; *and that neither I, nor any other person or persons in trust for me, or for my use, have any lands, money, stock, or any estate, real or personal, in possession, reversion, or remainder, or expectancy, other than what are in the said schedule contained; except wearing apparel, and bedding for myself and family, working tools, and necessary implements for my occupation and calling, and these in the whole not exceeding the value of ten pounds; and that I have not, nor any body for me hath, directly or indirectly, sold, lessened, or otherwise conveyed, disposed of in trust, or concealed, all or any part of my lands, money, goods, chattels, stock, debts, securities, contracts, or estate, real or personal, whereby to secure the same, or to receive or expect any profit or advantage thereof, or with intent to defraud or deceive any creditor or creditors, to whom I am or was indebted in any wise howsoever.*

So help me *GOD.*

And the said schedule and oath shall be by every such prisoner subscribed in the presence of the justices in open session of the peace as hereby is directed, and shall be kept by, and remain with the clerk of the peace for the county, city, liberty, division, town, or place, where the same shall be subscribed and taken, for the better information of all the creditors of such prisoner who shall desire, or may have occasion, to resort thereto; and every such creditor shall be at liberty at seasonable times in the day-time, to peruse and examine over the same.

Schedule and oath to be subscribed in the court; and lodged with the clerk of the peace, for the examination of the creditors.

X. And be it further enacted, That the justices within their respective jurisdictions, at any such general or general quarter session, or adjournment thereof, at the request of any creditor or creditors of any such prisoner, are hereby authorized to cause the deputy warden and marshal of the *Fleet* and *King's Bench* prison, and any other under officer, tipstaff and turnkey of any gaol or prison, and any other person to come before them, and to examine them respectively on oath, touching any of the matters contained in any of the oaths prescribed by this act to be taken, and the truth thereof; and if the oath which shall have been taken in open court by any such prisoner or prisoners shall not be disproved by good testimony of any credible person or

Court, if required by the creditor, may administer an oath to the gaoler, or any other person, touching any of the matters prescribed to be sworn to.

The prisoner's oath not being disproved, the court is to discharge him;

upon paying a fee of 1s. to the gaoler.

Gaoler indemnified for the escape.

persons on oath, and such justices, or the major part of them, present at any such general or quarter session, shall be satisfied with the truth of the oath taken by any such respective prisoner, then such justices shall, in such session, or some adjournment thereof, command the said sheriff or sheriffs, gaoler or gaolers, or keeper of such prison or prisons, forthwith to set at liberty such prisoner or prisoners, without having or taking any fee or reward, other than one shilling for his or their attendance with such prisoner or prisoners at such general or quarter session, or any adjournments thereof, in order for his, her, or their discharge, and which every such sheriff or sheriffs, gaoler or gaolers, keeper or keepers of such prison or prisons, is and are hereby authorized to receive and take for every such order: and every such order shall be a sufficient discharge to the sheriff or sheriffs, gaoler or gaolers, or keeper of such prison or prisons, and shall indemnify him or them against any escape or escapes, or action or actions whatsoever for escape, which shall or may be brought, commenced, or prosecuted against him or them.

Estate and effects of the prisoner, upon his discharge, to vest in the clerk of the peace,

who is to make over the same to the assignees named by the court.

for which he is to be paid 2s. and no more.

Assignees impowered to sue,

XI. And be it further enacted by the authority aforesaid, That all the estate, right, title, interest, and trust, of such prisoner, of, in, and unto, all the real estate, as well freehold and copy as customaryhold, and to all the personal estate, debts, and effects, of every such prisoner, shall, immediately after the discharge of any such prisoner, be, and the same is hereby vested in the clerk of the peace of and for the county, riding, city, town corporate, division, liberty, or place, where any such prisoner shall be respectively discharged; and every such clerk of the peace is hereby directed and required to make an assignment and conveyance of every such prisoner's estate and effects, vested in such clerk of the peace as aforesaid, to such creditor or creditors of the said prisoner as the justices at any general or general quarter session of the peace, or at any adjournment thereof, which shall be held by them within their respective jurisdictions, shall order or direct (which assignment and conveyance shall be good and effectual in law to all intents and purposes whatsoever, without being wrote on parchment or paper stamped) and to vest the estates thereby assigned and conveyed, in the party or parties to whom the same shall be so assigned and conveyed, his, her, and their heirs, executors, administrators, and assigns, according to the estate and interest the prisoner had therein; and for the preparing, ingrossing, and executing, of which assignment and conveyance, no clerk of the peace shall take any greater fee than two shillings; and every such assignment and conveyance shall be in trust for the benefit of the creditor or creditors of every such prisoner to whom the same shall be made, and the rest of the creditors of such prisoner, in respect or in proportion to their respective debts: and every person and persons to whom any such assignment and conveyance as aforesaid shall be made, is and are hereby fully impowered to sue, from time to time, as there may be occasion, in his, her, or their own name or names, for the recovery and attaining

ing any estate or effects of any such prisoner, and also to execute any trust or power vested in, or created for, the use or benefit of any such prisoner; but in trust, for the benefit of him or themselves, and the rest of the creditors of every such prisoner; and to give discharge and discharges to any debtor or debtors to any such prisoner as shall be requisite: and every such assignee and assignees shall, with all convenient speed after his or their accepting any such assignment or conveyance, use his and their best endeavours to receive and get in the estate and effects of every such prisoner; and shall, with all convenient speed, make sale, or disposition of sale, of all the estates of such prisoner vested in such assignee or assignees; and if any such prisoner shall be interested in, or intitled to, any real estate, either in possession, reversion, or expectancy, the same, within the space of two months after every such assignment and conveyance, shall be sold by publick auction in such manner, and at such place, as the major part of the creditors of any such prisoner who shall assemble together on any notice in writing published in the *London Gazette*, or in some daily paper, if the prisoner before his going to gaol resided in *London*, or in the weekly bills of mortality, and if elsewhere, then in some news paper which shall be published in or near the county, riding, division, city, town, liberty or place, in which such prisoner dwelt before he or she was committed to gaol, thirty days before any such sale shall be made, shall, under his hand, or their hands, agree on: and every such assignee and assignees, at the end of three months at farthest from the time of his accepting any such assignment or conveyance as aforesaid, shall make a just and fair dividend of all such prisoner's estates and effects which shall have been then got amongst his or her creditors, in proportion and in regard to each creditor's respective debts; but before any such dividend shall be made, such assignee or assignees shall make up an account of such prisoner's estate and make oath in writing before one or more justice or justices of the peace of the county, riding, division, town, liberty, or place, in which any such prisoner shall have been discharged, that every such account contains a just and fair account of the estate and effects of every such prisoner got in by or for such assignee or assignees, and of all payments made in respect thereof, and that all payments in every such account charged, were truly and *bona fide* made and paid; and notice of the making of every such dividend shall be published in like manner as a meeting of creditors is herein before directed to be published, thirty days at least before the same shall be made: and no creditor shall be allowed to receive any share of such dividend, until he shall have made out the justness and identity of his respective debt by oath, or due proof in writing, before some such justice or justices; and if any creditor of such prisoner shall be dissatisfied with the reality or fairness of any debt claimed by any other creditor, then the same, at the request of any such creditor or creditors so dissatisfied, shall be examined into by the justices of the county, riding, division, city, liberty,

and execute any trust or power in the prisoner's behalf; and give discharges. They are to get in, with all speed, the estate and effects of the prisoner, and make sale, within 2 months, of prisoner's real estate, in manner agreed upon at a meeting of the creditors summoned for that purpose;

and make a dividend within 3 months;

first making up their accounts, and verifying the same upon oath.

30 days notice to be given of making any dividends, and none to receive any share thereof but such as shall prove their debts. Debts entered, to be examined into and determined by the court.

ty, or place, in which ſuch priſoner ſhall have been diſcharged, at their next general or general quarter ſeſſion, and what they ſhall there determine in the premiſſes, ſhall be concluſive to all parties: and if, after payment of all ſuch priſoner's creditors, there ſhall any of his eſtate and effects remain after payment of all reaſonable charges, the ſame ſhall be paid to ſuch priſoner, his executors or adminiſtrators.

Surplus of the priſoner's eſtate, after ſatisfying all claims thereon, to go to the priſoner.

XII. Provided further, and be it alſo enacted, That no ſuit in equity ſhall be commenced by any aſſignee or aſſignees of any ſuch priſoner's eſtate and effects, without the conſent of the majo part, in value, of the creditors of ſuch priſoner, who ſhal meet together purſuant to a notice to be given in the *Londo Gazette* for that purpoſe.

No ſuit in equity to be commenced, but by conſent of the majority in value of the creditors.

XIII. And be it further enacted by the authority aforeſaid That the clerk of the peace of every reſpective county, city, an county town, and county, riding, diviſion, cinque port, liber ty, and place, with whom any ſchedule of the eſtates of an inſolvent debtor or debtors, fugitive or fugitives, ſhall be lef and his ſucceſſors, clerks of the peace as aforeſaid, ſhall, o the reaſonable requeſt of any creditor or creditors of ſuch inſo vent debtor or debtors, fugitive or fugitives, or his or their at torney, produce and ſhew to ſuch creditor or creditors, or h or their attorney, in the day-time, the ſchedule of the eſtates any ſuch inſolvent debtor or debtors, fugitive or fugitives, whic ſhall be left with any ſuch clerk of the peace, or his predeceſſ in that office; the perſon ſo requiring to ſee and peruſe any ſuc ſchedule, paying or tendering to the clerk of the peace, in who cuſtody any ſuch ſchedule ſhall be, or his deputy, the ſum one ſhilling, for his trouble in ſearching for, and looking ou ſuch ſchedule, and attending whilſt the ſame ſhall be peruſ by the party or parties requiring to have the ſame looked ou and to peruſe the ſame; and that a true copy of every ſuch ſch dule, ſigned by the clerk of the peace in whoſe cuſtody the ſan ſhall be, or his deputy, purporting, the ſame to be a true co of ſuch ſchedule, without being wrote on ſtamp paper, and f which copy no more ſhall be paid than ſix pence by the ſhe each ſheet to contain ninety words, and ſo in proportion for leſſer number of words in any ſheet, ſhall, at all times, be a mitted in all courts whatſoever as legal evidence of the ſam and if any clerk of the peace, or his deputy, ſhall, on reaſo able requeſt as aforeſaid, neglect or refuſe to produce to any ſu creditor or creditors as aforeſaid, or his or their attorney, a ſuch ſchedule as aforeſaid, and to permit the ſame to be inſpe ed as aforeſaid, in the day-time, on ſuch payment or tender aforeſaid, being made to him; or ſhall aſk or take more than ter the rate of ſix pence by the ſheet, each ſheet to contain nin ty words, and ſo in proportion for leſs than ninety words i ſheet; or ſhall refuſe to make and deliver a copy of any ſu ſchedule, on being requeſted as aforeſaid ſo to make the ſam and having the money tendered to him for payment of ſu copy, after the rate aforeſaid; ſhall, for every ſuch offence, f

Clerk of the peace to exhibit to the creditor, or his attorney, upon payment of 1s. the ſchedule of the priſoner's eſtate and effects:

atteſted copy thereof to be granted;

which ſhall be evidence in all courts.

Clerk of the peace refuſing to produce ſuch ſchedule, or to deliver a copy thereof, or taking exorbitant fees for the ſame,

feit and pay the ſum of ten pounds, which ſhall and may be ſued for and recovered in any of his Majeſty's courts of record at *Weſtminſter*, by action of debt, together with treble coſts of ſuit, in the name of any perſon who will proſecute for the ſame: and one moiety of which money forfeited, ſhall, when recovered, go to the party who proſecutes for the ſame, and the other moiety thereof to the poor of the pariſh in which the offence ſhall be committed.

forfeits 10l. and treble coſts; one moiety to the proſecutor, and the other to the poor of the pariſh.

XIV. Provided always, and be it enacted, That before ſuch time as any aſſignee or aſſignees, as aforeſaid, ſhall enter on, or take any profit from, any copyhold or cuſtomary eſtate as aforeſaid, he or they ſhall agree and compound with the lord or lords of the manor or manors of whom the ſame ſhall be holden, for the payment of ſuch fine or income as, upon any ſurrender and admiſſion thereto, hath heretofore been moſt uſually accuſtomed to be paid; and that upon every ſuch agreement or compoſition, the ſaid lord or lords for the time being, at the next court, or ſome ſubſequent court, which ſhall be holden for the ſaid manor or manors, after ſuch agreement made, ſhall admit ſuch aſſignee or aſſignees tenant to ſuch copyhold or cuſtomary premiſſes, according to the cuſtom of the ſaid manor or manors of which the ſame ſhall be holden, for and during ſuch eſtate and intereſt as the priſoner had therein at the time of his or her being diſcharged as aforeſaid, reſerving the rents, duties, heriots, cuſtoms, and ſervices, payable and to be rendered in reſpect of the ſaid copyhold and cuſtomary premiſſes.

Aſſignees of copyhold and cuſtomary eſtates to compound with the lord of the manor, and to be admitted tenants thereupon.

XV. Provided alſo, That nothing herein contained ſhall extend to prejudice or affect any eſtate, or intereſt, or right whatſoever, of any other perſon or perſons, other than the ſaid priſoner or fugitive, which may be expectant upon, or ſubject unto, the eſtate or intereſt of the ſaid priſoner or fugitive hereby veſted in the ſaid clerk of the peace; but that the eſtate, intereſt, and right whatſoever, of every other perſon and perſons, ſhall remain, continue, and be ſaved to them, in the ſame manner as if this act had not been made.

The priſoner's, &c. right and intereſt only to be affected by this act.

XVI. Provided further, and be it enacted by the authority aforeſaid, That where any rent, not exceeding two years rent, ſhall be due to any perſon or perſons from ſuch priſoner or priſoners, at the time of his or their reſpective diſcharges, in reſpect to any meſſuages, lands, or tenements, then in leaſe to ſuch priſoner or priſoners reſpectively, for life or lives, for years, at will, or otherwiſe, no goods or chattels then lying or being in or upon the reſpective tenements, liable to be diſtrained, ſhall be aſſigned by the clerk of the peace in manner aforeſaid, but ſhall, by ſuch clerk of the peace, be transferred to ſuch landlord or landlords, or ſome perſon or perſons intruſted for him or them reſpectively, towards ſatisfaction of the rent then due, not exceeding two years rent, as aforeſaid, unleſs the perſon or perſons to whom ſuch aſſignment and conveyance ſhall be made by ſuch clerk of the peace, ſhall, by writing under his hand, or their reſpective hands, before ſuch aſſignment ſhall be made, agree

Effects on the premiſſes, where rent is due, are to be transferred to the landlord, and not made over to the aſſignees; unleſs they ſhall agree to ſatisfy the landlord,

agree to pay or satisfy to such landlord or landlords the rent to him or them respectively due, not exceeding two years rent as aforesaid; to the intent that such landlord or landlords may be satisfied the rent or rents to him or them respectively due, before any division of the estate or effects of such prisoner or prisoners shall be made among his other creditors, in like manner as he or they might be satisfied the rent to him or them respectively due, before the removal of such goods and chattels, by virtue of an execution, by force of the statute made in the eighth year of her late Majesty's reign, intituled, *An act for the better security of rents, and to prevent frauds committed by tenants*; any thing herein before contained to the contrary thereof notwithstanding.

Act 8 Annæ.

All mortgages, statutes, recognizances, and judgements, are to take place, preferable to claims of an inferior nature.

XVII. Provided also, and be it enacted by the authority aforesaid, That nothing in this act shall extend, or be construed to hinder or prevent, any mortgage or mortgages upon the estate of such prisoner or prisoners, or any part thereof, to take place upon the lands, tenements, or hereditaments, comprised in such mortgage or mortgages respectively; nor to prevent any statute staple, statute merchant, recognizance, or judgement, acknowledged by, or obtained against, any such prisoner or prisoners, to take place upon the lands, tenements, or real estate of such prisoner or prisoners; and also where any inquisition shall have been taken upon any such statute or recognizance, or any writ of execution shall have been taken out and delivered to the sheriff or proper officer, upon any such judgement before such discharge shall be given in open session to any such person as aforesaid, the personal estate of every such prisoner respectively shall be subject thereto, in the first place, for so much as shall remain really due upon such mortgage, statute, recognizance, or judgement respectively, in like manner as such mortgagees and creditors, by statute, recognizance, or judgement, would have been preferred to other creditors of an inferior nature, against the real or personal estate of such prisoner and prisoners respectively, if this act had not been made; any thing herein before contained to the contrary thereof in any wise notwithstanding.

XVIII. And whereas many persons who may be intitled to, and claim the benefit of, this act, are seised and possessed of lands, tenements, and hereditaments, to hold to such prisoners for the term of their natural lives, with power of granting leases, and taking fines, reserving small rents on such estates, for one, two, or three lives, in possession or reversion, or for some number of years determinable upon lives; which said powers ought to be executed for the benefit of the creditors of such prisoners; be it therefore enacted by the authority aforesaid, That in every such case, all and every the powers of leasing such lands, tenements, and hereditaments, which are or shall be vested in any such prisoner or prisoners as aforesaid, shall be, and are hereby vested in the assignee or assignees of the real and personal estate of such prisoner, by virtue of this act,

Power in the prisoner of leasing lands, &c. to vest in the assignees.

act, to be by ſuch aſſignee or aſſignees executed for the benefit of all and every the creditors of ſuch priſoners as aforeſaid.

XIX. And whereas in ſome gaols or priſons in this kingdom, the office of gaoler or keeper is held in fee for life, or otherwiſe, by perſons who never act as gaolers or keepers themſelves, or know any thing of the priſoners therein, but depute or employ ſome perſon or perſons under them as gaolers or keepers of ſuch gaols or priſons; be it therefore enacted, That in every ſuch caſe, the perſon who ſhall have been actually employed and acted as deputed gaoler or keeper of any ſuch gaol or priſon, at the time of the delivering in the liſts, hereby directed to be delivered in, of priſoners in any ſuch gaol or priſon, at any general or quarter ſeſſion of the peace, or ſome adjournment thereof, and not the principal gaoler or keeper (unleſs where ſuch principal gaoler or keeper ſhall act as gaoler or keeper himſelf) ſhall take the oath herein before appointed to be taken by the gaoler or keeper of every ſuch gaol or priſon.

The acting gaoler at the time of delivering the liſts, only liable to be ſworn.

XX. And be it further enacted by the authority aforeſaid, That the juſtices at any general or quarter ſeſſion of the peace, or adjournment thereof, to which any priſoner ſhall be brought in purſuance of this act, ſhall, if required by any creditor or creditors of any ſuch priſoner or priſoners who ſhall oppoſe his or her diſcharge, adminiſter and give to the gaoler, or the perſon who acts as gaoler or keeper of any ſuch priſon, at the time of bringing up any ſuch priſoner in order to be diſcharged under this act, an oath to the following effect (that is to ſay)

Court, if required by a creditor, oppoſing the priſoner's diſcharge, is to adminiſter the following oath to the gaoler.

The oath.

I A. B. *do ſwear, That* *was really and truly a priſoner in my cuſtody, in the priſon of* *to the beſt of my knowledge and belief, at or upon* *and that the copy or copies of the cauſe or cauſes of his or her commitment or detainer, now by me brought with the body of the ſaid* *and produced to this court, is or are a true copy or copies of the cauſe or cauſes of ſuch detainer or commitment, without any fraud or deceit by me, or any other perſon whatſoever, to the beſt of my knowledge and belief.*

So help me *GOD.*

And if any perſon who was gaoler or keeper, or deputed gaoler or keeper, of any ſuch gaol or priſon on the ſaid firſt day of *January*, one thouſand ſeven hundred and ſixty five, or ſince, ſhall not happen to be the gaoler or keeper, or deputed gaoler or keeper, of any ſuch gaol or priſon, at the time any ſuch liſt as aforeſaid is hereby required to be delivered in, then the juſtices at any ſuch ſeſſion, or at any adjournment thereof, may, and are hereby required to adminiſter and give the reſpective perſon or perſons who ſhall be gaoler or keeper, or deputed gaoler or keeper, of any ſuch gaol or priſon, and deliver in any ſuch liſt as aforeſaid at any ſuch general or quarter ſeſſion, or any adjournment thereof, an oath, touching the commitments or books of com-

If ſuch perſon ſhall not have been the gaoler on 1 Jan. 1765, &c. then the following oath is to be adminiſtered to him.

commitment of any ſuch priſon, to the effect following (that is to ſay)

The oath.

I A. B. *do ſwear, That I have examined the commitments, or books kept of or concerning the commitment, of priſoners to the priſon of* *in the* (county, riding, diviſion, city, town, place, or liberty of as the caſe ſhall be) *and that I do verily believe that the ſaid commitments, or books of commitment, are really true, and not fictitious, nor calculated for this purpoſe; and by them it doth appear that,* *was on the* *day of* *really and truly a priſoner in the actual cuſtody of* *the then gaoler or keeper, or deputed gaoler or keeper, of the ſaid priſon, without fraud or deceit, by me, or any other perſon or perſons to my knowledge.*

So help me *GOD.*

Court, if required by a creditor, may ſummon the perſon who acted as gaoler on 1 Jan. 1765, or ſince,

XXI. And, in order to diſcover any fraudulent entries or commitments of priſoners in any gaol books, be it further enacted by the authority aforeſaid, That the juſtices at any general or quarter ſeſſion of the peace, or any adjournment thereof, are hereby authorized, at the requeſt of any creditor or creditors of any priſoner, to convene before them, at ſome certain time to be appointed by them, any perſon or perſons who was or were gaoler or keeper, or reputed gaoler or keeper, of any gaol or priſon within their reſpective juriſdictions, on the ſaid firſt day of *January* one thouſand ſeven hundred and ſixty five, or at any time ſince, and to examine every ſuch gaoler or keeper, or deputed gaoler or keeper, on oath, touching the commitment and continuance in cuſtody of any ſuch priſoner, as the juſtices, at any ſuch general or quarter ſeſſion, or adjournment thereof, ſhall think fit: and if any ſheriff, gaoler, or keeper, or reputed gaoler or keeper, ſhall neglect or refuſe to bring before ſuch juſtices at any ſeſſion of the peace, or adjournment thereof, any priſoner as ſhall be directed and required by warrant of any juſtice or juſtices as aforeſaid, or to attend, or being ſummoned for that purpoſe; or if any gaoler or keeper attending, ſhall refuſe to make anſwer and diſcovery in the premiſſes, as ſhall be reaſonably required at ſuch general or quarter ſeſſion, or any adjournment thereof; he, ſhe, or they, ſo offending in the premiſſes, ſhall for every ſuch offence, forfeit and pay the ſum of one hundred pounds, to be recovered by and in the name, and for the uſe, of the party injured, by action of debt, to be brought in his or her name, in any of his Majeſty's courts of record at *Weſtminſter*, together with treble coſts of ſuit.

and examine him touching the commitment and continuance in cuſtody of the priſoner. Gaoler diſobeying the warrant, or order of the court, &c. forfeits 100l. with treble coſts.

XXII. And whereas great number of workmen, ſkilful in the ſeveral trades and manufactures of this kingdom, and alſo many able ſeamen and mariners, finding themſelves unable to ſatisfy the whole of their reſpective debts, and dreading the miſeries,

ſeries of a gaol, have choſe to leave their employments and native country, and have entered themſelves in foreign ſervice: and whereas their continuance abroad muſt be of great prejudice to the trade of this kingdom; in order therefore to induce and enable ſuch perſons to return, be it enacted by the authority aforeſaid, That all and every debtor and debtors, who was or were actually beyond the ſeas in foreign parts on the ſaid firſt day of *January*, one thouſand ſeven hundred and ſixty five, and did not go into ſuch foreign parts with the view or intent to gain or have the benefit of an inſolvent debtor's act, who ſhall return and ſurrender himſelf or themſelves unto the gaoler or gaolers, keeper or keepers, of the priſons of the *King's Bench*, *Marſhalſea*, or *Fleet*, or to the gaoler or keeper, or deputed gaoler or keeper, of the priſon or priſons of ſuch county, city, town, riding, diviſion, liberty, or place, where ſuch debtor or debtors laſt dwelt for the ſpace of ſix months (which ſaid gaoler or gaolers, keeper or keepers, is and are hereby required and impowered to receive and detain ſuch debtor or debtors ſurrendering as aforeſaid, in order to their diſcharge as herein after mentioned) ſhall, from and immediately after ſuch ſurrender as aforeſaid, be deemed a priſoner or priſoners within, and be to all intents and purpoſes intitled to, the benefit of this act; and ſhall, upon due proof of the ſaid premiſſes, by the oath of ſuch debtor or debtors (not diſproved by any credible witneſs) be diſcharged in the ſame manner as if he, ſhe, or they, had been actually in priſon on the ſaid firſt day of *January*, one thouſand ſeven hundred and ſixty five, and continued therein as aforeſaid; ſubject nevertheleſs to the ſame reſtrictions and proviſions, and a compliance with the like terms, conditions, and qualifications, herein before impoſed upon the ſaid priſoners actually in cuſtody upon the ſaid firſt day of *January*, one thouſand ſeven hundred and ſixty five, and alſo ſubject to the terms and proviſions relating to the eſtate and effects of ſuch priſoner as aforeſaid; excepting only ſuch particulars thereof, as require the name of a priſoner to be inſerted in the gaoler's or keeper's liſt as aforeſaid, or relate to the oaths of ſuch gaoler or keeper herein before appointed to be taken, which particulars cannot poſſibly be applied to the caſe of perſons ſurrendering themſelves as aforeſaid; and alſo except the ſaid oath herein before appointed to be taken by priſoners in cuſtody upon the ſaid firſt day of *January*, one thouſand ſeven hundred and ſixty five, inſtead whereof, the ſaid perſon or perſons ſo ſurrendering ſhall take an oath in open court at ſome general or quarter ſeſſion of the peace, or ſome adjournment thereof, of the county, city, town, riding, diviſion, place, or liberty, in the priſon of which any ſuch fugitive or debtor, ſhall be held after the ſurrender of any ſuch fugitive or debtor, to the effect following; which the ſaid juſtices authorized to put this act in execution, are hereby required and impowered to adminiſter, in ſuch manner as the oaths herein before-mentioned are to be adminiſtered.

Debtors who were beyond the ſeas on 1 Jan. 1765, ſurrendering themſelves, may take the benefit of this act,

upon the ſame terms as other priſoners;

excepting ſuch particulars wherein the caſes of both differ.

I *A. B.*

or quarter session of the peace, or adjournment thereof, shall order; and who are hereby impowered to cause the same to be levied by distress and sale of the goods of any such clerk of the peace, or his deputy, so offending.

Prisoner convicted of perjury to suffer as a felon.

XXVI. And be it further enacted by the authority aforesaid, That if any prisoner as aforesaid, or any other person or persons, who shall take the benefit of this act, shall forswear or perjure himself, herself, or themselves, in any oath to be taken under this act, and shall be lawfully convicted thereof, he, she, or they, so offending, shall be adjudged a felon, and suffer as such, without benefit of clergy.

Persons discharged by this act, not liable to arrest for debts, &c. contracted before 1 Jan. 1765.

XXVII. And be it further enacted by the authority aforesaid, That no person to be discharged by this act shall, at any time hereafter, be imprisoned by reason of any judgement or decree obtained for payment of money only, or for any debt, damages, contempts, costs, sum or sums of money, contracted, incurred, occasioned, owing, or growing due, before the said first day of *January*, one thousand seven hundred and sixty five; but that upon every arrest upon every judgement or such decree, or for such debts, damages, contempts costs, sum and sums of money, it shall and may be lawful for any judge of the court where the process issued, upon shewing the copy of the order of such prisoners discharge or discharges, to release and discharge out of custody such prisoner or prisoners as aforesaid; and every such judge is hereby impowered so to do on such prisoners causing a common appearance to be entered for him in every such action and suit.

Justices, sheriffs, and gaolers, may plead this act to any action of escape, or suit brought against them and recover treble costs.

XXVIII. And be it further enacted by the authority aforesaid, That if any action of escape, or any suit or action, be brought against any justice or justices of the peace, sheriff, gaoler, or keeper of any prison, for performing their office, in pursuance of this act, they may plead the general issue, and give this act in evidence; and if the plaintiff be nonsuited, or discontinue his action, or verdict pass against him, or judgement upon demurrer, the defendant shall have treble costs.

Persons discharged may plead generally, &c. to all actions or judgements brought against them before 1 Jan. 1765, &c.

XXIX. And be it further enacted by the authority aforesaid, That if any *scire facias*, or action of debt, or upon judgement, shall be brought against any prisoner, his or her heirs, executors, or administrators, upon any judgement obtained against any such prisoner, or on any statute or recognizance acknowledged by him or her, before the said first day of *January*, one thousand seven hundred and sixty five, with respect to prisoners in actual custody, or with respect to debtors beyond the seas, as aforesaid, upon the said first day of *January*, one thousand seven hundred and sixty five, it shall be lawful for any such prisoner, his or her heirs, executors, or administrators, to plead generally that such prisoner was actually a prisoner in such prison at such a person's suit, or was or were beyond the seas in foreign parts on the said first day of *January*, one thousand seven hundred and sixty five, and was or were duly discharged according to this act, at the general or quarter session, or adjournment

ment thereof, held at such time and place for such county, riding, division, liberty, city, town, or place, (as his, her, or their case is) without pleading any matter specially; and in case any other suit or action shall be commenced against him, her, or them, for any other debt, sum or sums of money, due before the said first day of *January*, one thousand seven hundred and sixty five, to plead in discharge of his or her person from execution (over and above such matters as aforesaid) that such debt or sum of money (as the case shall happen) was contracted or due before the said first day of *January*, one thousand seven hundred and sixty five, without pleading any other matter specially; whereto the plaintiffs shall or may reply generally, and deny the matters pleaded as aforesaid, or reply any other matter or thing which may shew the said defendant not to be intitled to the benefit of this act, or not duly discharged according to it, in the same manner as the plaintiff might have replied, in case the defendant had pleaded this act, and his discharge by virtue of this act, specially; and if the plaintiff be nonsuited, discontinue his action, or verdict pass against him, or judgement on demurrer, the defendant to have treble costs.

Bankrupts not obtaining their certificates in due time, excluded from the benefit of this act.

XXX. Provided always, and be it enacted by the authority aforesaid, That no person against whom a commission of bankrupt hath been awarded and issued out, and who hath not already obtained his certificate and discharge of his debts, in pursuance of and in such manner as is directed by some or one of the acts of parliament now in force relating to or concerning bankrupts, or shall not obtain such certificate and discharge before such time as he shall be brought before the justices of the peace at their general or quarter session, or some adjournment thereof, held as aforesaid, in order to be discharged in pursuance of this act, shall have or receive any benefit or advantage of or under this act, nor be deemed to be within the meaning thereof.

Attornies embezzling, &c. clients money or effects, excluded the benefit of this act.

XXXI. Provided also, That nothing in this act contained shall extend, or be construed to extend, to release or discharge any attorney at law, or solicitor, or any other person or persons acting, or pretending to act, as such, with regard to any debt with which he or they shall stand charged, for any money, or other effects, recovered and received by him or them, for the use of any person or persons, bodies corporate or politick, and by any attorney, solicitor, or other person or persons acting as such, embezzled, concealed, or converted to his or their own use; any thing herein contained to the contrary thereof in any wise notwithstanding.

Gaoler to permit the speaking in private to prisoners, whose names are inserted in the list, or Gazette, &c.

XXXII. And be it further enacted by the authority aforesaid, That every gaoler or keeper of any prison shall and is hereby required to suffer, in the day-time, any person or persons desiring the same, to see and speak, in the lodge, or some convenient room of the said prison, with any prisoner or prisoners, whose names are inserted in the afore-mentioned list or lists, or *London Gazette*, or other news paper, or any of them, or any persons rendering themſelves purſuant to this act; and alſo ſee, in the true and genuine books of the ſaid priſon, the entries made of the name or names of ſuch priſoner or priſoners, together with the name or names of the perſon or perſons at whoſe ſuit or ſuits he, ſhe, or they are detained: and if any ſuch gaoler or keeper ſhall neglect or refuſe to comply with what is here above required, every ſuch gaoler or keeper, who ſhall ſo offend in the premiſſes, ſhall forfeit and pay to the perſon ſo refuſed and aggrieved, the ſum of forty pounds; to be recovered, with coſts of ſuit, by action of debt, bill, plaint, or information, in any of the courts of *Weſtminſter*, wherein no eſſoin, protection, wager of law, or more than one imparlance, ſhall be allowed, by and in the name or names of the perſon or perſons ſo refuſed and aggrieved.

and the examining the original books of entries, &c. on penalty of 40l. with coſts of ſuit.

XXXIII. Provided always, and be it enacted, That notwithſtanding the perſon of any priſoner or priſoners, fugitive or fugitives, ſhall be diſcharged under this act, the future eſtates and effects of every ſuch priſoner and fugitive ſhall remain and be liable to his, her, and their reſpective creditors as before the making of this act, (his, her, or their neceſſary wearing apparel, and bedding for his, her, or their families, and working tools and implements neceſſary for his, her, or their trade or occupation, not exceeding the value of ten pounds in the whole, only excepted) and any creditor or creditors of any ſuch priſoner or priſoners, fugitive or fugitives, may, at any time hereafter, ſue out execution, extents, or other proceſs, on any judgement at the time of ſuch diſcharge recovered, or ſtatute ſtaple, or recognizance acknowledged by, or ſentence or decree obtained againſt any ſuch priſoner or fugitive, but not againſt his, her, or their perſon, or his, her, or their reſpective wearing apparel, bedding, working tools, and implements, as aforeſaid.

Priſoners future eſtate and effects, notwithſtanding his perſonal diſcharge, liable to creditors; wearing apparel, bedding, and working tools, &c. not exceeding 10l. value, excepted.

XXXIV. And be it alſo enacted, That any creditor or creditors of any priſoner or priſoners, fugitive or fugitives, who ſhall be diſcharged under this act, may, at any time after any ſuch diſcharge, commence and proſecute any action or ſuit againſt any ſuch priſoner or fugitive, his, her, or their reſpective heirs, executors, or adminiſtrators, for the recovery of any ſum or ſums of money which ſhall be due from any ſuch priſoner or priſoners fugitive or fugitives, at the time of his or her ſaid diſcharge, but ſhall not hold the perſon of any ſuch priſoner or fugitive to special bail; nor ſhall take the perſon, neceſſary wearing apparel, bedding, tools, or implements, as aforeſaid, of any ſuch priſoner or fugitive in execution, or any judgement, ſentence, or decree, which ſhall hereafter be recovered or obtained againſt any ſuch priſoner or fugitive: and in any action or ſuit, which ſhall be hereafter commenced againſt any ſuch priſoner or fugitive, his or her heirs, executors, or adminiſtrators, no benefit or advantage ſhall be had or taken, for that the cauſe of action did not accrue within three years next before the commencing of any ſuch action or ſuit; nor ſhall any ſtatute of limitation be pleadable, or be allowed to be pleaded in bar of or in any ſuch actio[n]

Creditor may ſue for the recovery of debt due at the time of the priſoner's diſcharge, but not hold the priſoner to ſpecial bail, nor take his perſon, wearing apparel, bedding, or tools, in judgement, and no advantage is to be taken of the cauſe of action not accruing within 3 years, nor of the

action or suit, which shall be hereafter commenced by any such creditor or creditors, against any such prisoner or prisoners, unless such cause of action or suit did not accrue within three years next before any such prisoner or fugitive shall be discharged under this act; and in any such case, the same may be pleaded by any such prisoner his or her heirs, executors, or administrators.

statute of limitation.

Exception.

XXXV. Provided always, and be it likewise enacted, That by the discharge of any prisoner or fugitive by force of this act, no other person or persons who was or were partner or partners in trade with any such prisoner or fugitive, at the time of his or her discharge under this act, or then stood bound, engaged with or liable to, the payment of any debt with any such prisoner or fugitive, or engaged in any contract together with any such prisoner or fugitive, shall be discharged from any such debt or demand; but every such other person and persons shall severally stand and be chargeable with, and liable to pay, such debt and debts, and to perform such contracts, in like manner as if any such prisoner or fugitive had never been discharged from the same.

Discharge of prisoner no acquittal to the copartner or sureties.

XXXVI. And be it further enacted, That if any gaoler or keeper, or reputed gaoler or keeper, of any prison or prisons, shall make, or cause to be made, any false entries in any book or books belonging to any prison or gaol under his care, or of which he is or was gaoler, or shall prepare or keep, or cause to be prepared or kept, any false book or books, in order for any false or untrue entry or entries to be made therein; or shall insert in any list to be delivered in as aforesaid, the name or names of any person or persons who was not a prisoner or prisoners in actual custody in any such gaol or prison upon the said first day of *January*, one thousand seven hundred and sixty five, or shall not have ever since remained in such actual custody; except as the oath of any such gaoler or keeper, or deputed gaoler or keeper, shall be excepted; every such gaoler or keeper, or deputed gaoler or keeper, shall over and above the penalties which he shall be liable to for every such fraud, forfeit and pay the sum of five hundred pounds, to be recovered, with treble costs of suit, by and in the name, and for the use, of any person or persons who shall be prejudiced by any entry, or such false entries; which penalties shall and may be recovered by action of debt, bill, plaint, or information, in any of his Majesty's courts of record at *Westminster*, wherein no essoin, protection, or wager of law, or more than one impalance, shall be allowed.

Gaoler making false entries in the prison book or lists, forfeits 500l. with treble costs,

over and above all other penalties for such fraud.

XXXVII. And be it further enacted, That if any prisoner, being thereunto required by any creditor, shall refuse to discover and declare the trade or occupation and habitation or last place of abode, of the person or persons at whose suit he or she is detained or charged in custody; or being called for and desired, by any creditor or creditors, to come to the lodge of the prison in which such prisoner shall be confined, without some reasonable cause being made appear to the contrary; every such prisoner, upon

Prisoner refusing to declare the abode, &c. of the person at whose suit he is detained, or to come to the creditor in the lodge is excluded the benefit of this act.

upon proof being made thereof before the juſtices at any general or quarter ſeſſion of the peace, or any adjournment thereof, to be held as aforeſaid, ſhall not have or receive any benefit or diſcharge by or under this act; any thing herein contained to the contrary thereof in any wiſe notwithſtanding.

Juſtices for com' York and Lincoln to meet at the county gaols, &c. for diſcharge of priſoners.

XXXVIII. And whereas there is but one common or county goal for each of the reſpective counties of *York* and *Linc'n*, which ſaid counties are each of them divided into ſeveral ridings or diviſions, all which have ſeveral commiſſions of the peace; and if the goaler of thoſe gaols be obliged to carry the debtors, priſoners therein, to the quarter ſeſſion of each riding or diviſion, the ſame will be a very great charge, not only to ſuch gaolers, but alſo to the priſoners in thoſe large counties; be it therefore enacted by the authority aforeſaid, That it ſhall and may be lawful for two or more juſtices of the peace for each of the ridings and diviſions in the reſpective counties, at the common or county gaol thereof reſpectively, or at ſome convenient place near thereto, and they are hereby required to aſſemble and meet, and to hold ſeſſion there, by adjournment from their reſpective quarter ſeſſion, from time to time, for the diſcharge of the reſpective priſoners therein, according to the powers, limitations, and directions of this act.

Thoſe who are priſoners for their fees, or other demands of the gaoler or officer to be diſcharged.

XXXIX. And be it further enacted by the authority aforeſaid, That all debtors, and others, who were in priſon on or before the ſaid firſt day of *January*, one thouſand ſeven hundred and ſixty five, or ſince, in any of the gaols of this kingdom, and now remain there for not paying their fees, rents, or any other demands, due, or claimed as due, to the keeper or gaoler of ſuch priſon reſpectively, or to any other officer of any ſuch priſon, and upon no other account, ſhall be diſcharged therefrom, he, ſhe, or they, taking the oath by this act required to be taken by priſoners.

Debtors to the crown, and priſoners who owe above 1000 l. to one perſon, unleſs the creditors conſent, are excluded the benefit of this act.

XL. Provided always, That this act ſhall not extend to diſcharge any perſon out of priſon, ſeeking his or her diſcharge under this act, with reſpect to any debt with which he or ſhe ſhall ſtand charged at the ſuit of the crown, or ſhall be indebted to any body politick or corporate, or to any one perſon, in a ſum exceeding the ſum of one thouſand pounds, beſides intereſt and coſts, unleſs ſuch body politick or corporate, or creditor ſhall conſent thereto; and if any ſuch body politick or corporate, creditor or creditors, to whom a ſum exceeding one thouſand pounds ſhall be owing, ſhall oppoſe the diſcharge of ſuch priſoner, and ſhall inſiſt that ſuch priſoner be continued in gaol,

Creditor oppoſing priſoner's diſcharge, to allow him 3 s. 6 d. per week.

that then, and in ſuch caſe, ſuch body politick or corporate, creditor or creditors, oppoſing the ſaid priſoner's diſcharge as aforeſaid, ſhall, at his, her, or their proper coſts and charges, allow and pay in the whole ſuch a weekly maintenance to the ſaid priſoner, not exceeding three ſhillings and ſix pence *per* week, in ſuch manner as the ſaid juſtices in their general or quarter ſeſſion, or ſome adjournment thereof, ſhall order; and upon

On nonpayment, priſon-

nonpayment of the ſame for the ſpace of ſix weeks, the ſaid

ſoner, upon application to the ſaid juſtices in their general or quarter ſeſſion held as aforeſaid, ſhall be diſcharged purſuant to the intent and meaning of this act. er to be diſcharged.

XLI. Provided alſo that every perſon and perſons intitled, or to be intitled, to the benefit of this act, ſhall obtain their reſpective diſcharges on or before the firſt day of *Auguſt*, one thouſand ſeven hundred and ſixty ſeven, or ſhall be excluded from all benefit of this act. Diſcharges to be obtained by 1 Auguſt, 1767.

XLII. And whereas it may happen, that ſeveral perſons who may claim and be intitled to the benefit of this act, are ſeiſed of an eſtate tail, in ſome freehold or copyhold lands, tenements, or hereditaments; which entail, with the remainders thereupon expectant, they have by law power to defeat and bar, either by levying a fine or fines, ſuffering a common recovery or common recoveries, or by ſurrender or ſurrenders thereof, whereby ſuch perſon or perſons ſaid freehold or copyhold lands, tenements, or hereditaments, would be liable to the payment of their debts, and be delivered up, according to the terms of this act, for the benefit of their creditors; be it therefore enacted by the authority aforeſaid, That, in every ſuch caſe, ſuch perſon or perſons ſo ſeiſed as aforeſaid, and who ſhall be intitled to, and claim the benefit of this act, ſhall, to all intents and purpoſes whatſoever in law, be deemed and taken, and is and are hereby declared, to be ſeiſed of ſuch lands, tenements, and hereditaments, in fee; provided the ſame ſhall be delivered up to the creditor or creditors of every ſuch priſoner, in the ſame manner as if ſuch perſon or perſons had actually levied a fine, ſuffered a common recovery or recoveries, or made a ſurrender or ſurrenders thereof, and thereby had become ſeiſed in fee; any law, or conſtruction of law, to the contrary thereof in any wiſe notwithſtanding. Perſons ſeiſed of an eſtate tail, claiming the benefit of this act, are to deliver up the ſame to the creditors.

XLIII. And whereas many priſoners who may be intitled to, and claim the benefit of this act, have been great dealers, or otherwiſe engaged in large tranſactions, whereby they may be intitled to ſundry and great debts, and demands of various and intricate natures, and they may be intitled to equities of redemption of eſtates, ſubject and liable to mortgages, judgements, or other incumbrances, or to reverſions, remainders, or other contingent eſtates in lands, tenements, or hereditaments, or to other truſts or intereſts in eſtates, both real and perſonal, which may not be ſufficiently deſcribed or diſcovered in the ſchedule or inventory before directed to be delivered in, upon oath, by the priſoner to be diſcharged as aforeſaid, or which may want his aid or aſſiſtance to adjuſt, make out, recover, or manage, for the benefit of the creditors; be it therefore enacted by the authority aforeſaid, That it ſhall and may be lawful to and for the reſpective aſſignees of the eſtate and effects of ſuch priſoner or priſoners who ſhall obtain his, her, or their diſcharge, in purſuance of this act, or any other perſon or perſons duly authorized by them for that purpoſe, from time to time, to apply to any two or more of the juſtices of the peace for Aſſignees may apply for further examination of priſoner, touching the diſcovery of his effects, &c. and juſtices may ſend for and examine the priſoner accordingly.

for the county, riding, division, city, town, place, or liberty, where such prisoner or prisoners shall be then residing, thereby desiring, that such prisoner or prisoners may be further examined as to any matters or things relating to his, her, or their estate or effects; whereupon such justices shall send for, or call before them, such prisoner or prisoners by such warrant, summons, ways or means, as they shall think fit; and upon such prisoner's appearing, shall examine him, her, or them, as well upon oath as otherwise, as to such matters and things as such assignee shall desire, relating to the estate or effects of such prisoner or prisoners; and if any prisoner or prisoners (on payment or tender of payment of such reasonable charges as such justices shall judge sufficient) shall neglect or refuse to come and appear, not having a lawful excuse, to be made known to such justices, and by them allowed, or, being come before them, shall refuse to be sworn, or to answer to all such questions as by such justices shall be put to him, her, or them, relating to the discovery of his, her, or their estate or effects so vested, or intended to be vested, in such clerk of the peace, or in such assignees, as aforesaid, that then it shall and may be lawful to and for such justices, by warrant under their hands and seals, to apprehend such prisoner or prisoners so offending as aforesaid, and him, her, or them, to commit to the county gaol, there to remain without bail or mainprize, until such time as he, she, or they, shall submit him, her, or themselves, to such justices, and answer upon oath to all such lawful questions as shall by such justices be put to him, her, or them, for the purposes aforesaid.

Prisoner refusing to appear, or to answer upon oath, may be committed.

XLIV. And be it further enacted by the authority aforesaid, That all and every such person and persons who shall, within twelve months after the discharge of such prisoner or prisoners, voluntarily come in and make a discovery of any part of such debtor or debtors real or personal estate as shall not be comprized in such schedule as aforesaid, before any justices aforesaid, shall be allowed after the rate of twenty pounds *per centum*, out of the neat produce of such debtor or debtors estate, which will be recovered on such discovery, and which shall be paid such person or persons so discovering the same, by the assignee or assignees of such prisoner's estate and effects.

20l. *per cent.* allowed on discovering within 12 months, any part of the prisoner's estate not returned in the schedule.

XLV. Provided always, and be it enacted, That notwithstanding the discharge of any prisoner or prisoners by virtue of this act, if it shall hereafter appear the same was obtained fraudulently, or that any part of the oath taken by any such prisoner was not true; then, and in every such case, every such discharge shall be void and of none effect.

Discharge obtained fraudulently, void.

XLVI. And, for the better discovery of the estate and effects of any prisoner who shall be discharged by virtue of this act, be it enacted by the authority aforesaid, That any person or persons who shall have accepted of any trust or trusts, and shall wilfully conceal or protect any estate, real or personal, of any such prisoner from his creditors, and shall not, within thirty days after

Persons concealing any estate or effects of the prisoner, forfeit 100l. and double value, after any assignee or assignees shall, in pursuance of this act, be chose of any such prisoner's estate, discover and disclose to such assignee or assignees such trust and estate in writing, and deliver up or make over the same to such assignee or assignees, he, she, or they, so offending, shall, for every such offence, forfeit the sum of one hundred pounds, and also double the value of the estate, either real or personal, so concealed, to and for the use of the creditors of any such prisoner; to be recovered by action of debt, in any of his Majesty's courts of record at *Westminster*, in the name or names of the assignee or assignees of such prisoner's estate, together with treble costs of suit.

with treble costs of suit.

XLVII. And be it further enacted by the authority aforesaid, That it shall be lawful at all times hereafter, for any assignee or assignees of the estate or effects of any prisoner or prisoners, who shall be chose in pursuance of this act, by and with the consent of the major part in value of such prisoner or prisoners creditors, who shall be present at a meeting to be had on twenty one days publick notice being previously given for the purpose hereafter mentioned in the *London Gazette*, if the prisoner was in custody in *London*, or within the weekly bills of mortality, and if not, then also in some news paper which shall be published in the county, city, or place, in or near which any such person shall have been in gaol, to make composition with any person or persons, debtors or accountants to such prisoner or prisoners, where the same shall appear necessary or reasonable; and to take such reasonable part of any such debt as can, upon such composition, be gotten, in full discharge of such debts and accounts; and also to submit any difference or dispute between such assignee or assignees, and any person or persons, for or on account, or by reason or means of any matter, cause, or thing, relating to such prisoner or prisoners estate or effects, or to any debt or debts due, or claimed to be due, to or from such prisoner or prisoners, to the final end and determination of arbitrators to be chosen by the said assignee or assignees, and the major part in value of such creditors, and the party or parties with whom they shall have no difference, and to perform the award of such arbitrators, or of any umpire to be chosen by them; or otherwise to settle and agree the matters in difference and dispute between them, in such manner as the said assignee or assignees, with such consent as aforesaid, shall think fit, and can agree, and the same shall be binding to all the creditors of such prisoner or prisoners; and every such assignee or assignees is and are hereby indemnified for what they shall fairly do in the premisses in pursuance of this act.

Assignees with consent of the majority in value of the creditors, may compound for debts due to the prisoner's estate;

and may submit any dispute relating thereto to arbitration;

or otherwise may settle and agree the same as they shall think fit.

XLVIII. And, to the intent and purpose that the estate and effects of such prisoner or prisoners as shall be discharged by virtue of this act, may be truly and faithfully applied for the benefit of his, her, or their real creditors, be it enacted by the authority aforesaid, That it shall and may be lawful to and for the respective courts at *Westminster*, and the courts of great session in *Wales*, and the principality of *Chester*, and the counties palatine

Assignees may be petitioned against, for insufficiency, fraud, mismanagement, or other misbehaviour;

of *Lancaster* and *Durham*, respectively, from whence any process issued upon which any such prisoner or prisoners was or were committed, or where the process issued out of any other court, to and for the judges of the court of *King's Bench*, *Common Pleas*, and *Exchequer*, or of great sessions aforesaid, within their respective jurisdictions, or any one of them, from time to time, upon the petition of any such prisoner, or the creditor or creditors of such prisoner or prisoners, complaining of any insufficiency, fraud, mismanagement, or other misbehaviour of any assignee or assignees of the estate or effects of any such prisoner or prisoners, to summon all parties concerned, and upon hearing the parties concerned therein, to make and give such orders and directions therein, either for the removal or displacing such assignee or assignees, and the appointing any new assignee or assignees in the place or stead of such assignee or assignees so to be removed or displaced, or for the prudent, just, or equitable management or distribution of the estate and effects of any such prisoner for the benefit of the respective creditors, as the said courts or judges respectively shall think fit; and in case of the removal or displacing of any assignee or assignees, and the appointing of any new assignee or assignees, the estate or effects of such prisoner or prisoners shall, from thenceforth, be divested out of the assignee or assignees so removed or displaced, and be vested in, and delivered over to, such new assignee or assignees, in the same manner, and for the same intents and purposes, as the same were before vested in the assignee or assignees first chose as aforesaid; any thing in this act contained to the contrary notwithstanding.

the court thereupon is to summon the parties, and make such orders therein as they shall think fit.

Where mutual credit has been given, the balance to be stated and allowed.

XLIX. Provided always, and be it enacted by the authority aforesaid, That in all cases where mutual credit hath been given between any prisoner or prisoners who shall be discharged in pursuance of this act, and any other person or persons, or body politick or corporate, before the delivery of such schedule or inventory of the estate and effects of such prisoner or prisoners, upon oath, as aforesaid, the respective assignee and assignees of such prisoner or prisoners is and are hereby authorized and required, on his and their parts, to state and allow an account between them and the other party or parties concerned; and nothing more shall be deemed to be vested in such clerk of the peace, or such assignee or assignees under such clerk of the peace, as the estate or effects of such prisoner or prisoners, than what shall appear to be justly due to him, her, or them respectively, as and for the balance of such account when truly stated.

Those who are prisoners upon process out of courts of conscience to have the benefit of this act.

L. And whereas great numbers of poor people have been, and are now, imprisoned for debt upon processes issuing out of courts of conscience; it is hereby enacted and declared, That all such prisoners shall be intitled to have the benefit of this act, and be discharged under the same, provided he, she, or they, conform to the directions herein before prescribed, touching other prisoners who shall be discharged by virtue of this act.

Quakers affirmation to

LI. And be it further enacted by the authority aforesaid, That in all cases wherein by this act an oath is required, the solemn

lemn affirmation of any person being a *Quaker*, shall and may be accepted and taken in lieu thereof; and every person making such affirmation, who shall be convicted of wilful and false affirming, shall incur and suffer such and the same penalties as are inflicted and imposed by this act upon persons convicted of wilful and corrupt perjury. be taken in lieu of an oath.

LII. Provided always, and be it further enacted by the authority aforesaid, That no person who took the benefit of an act passed in the first year of the reign of his present majesty King *George* the Third, intituled, *An act for relief of insolvent debtors*, shall have or receive any benefit or advantage of or under this act, nor be deemed to be within the intent and meaning thereof, so as to be discharged under the same; any thing herein before contained to the contrary notwithstanding. Persons who took the benefit of the act of 1 Geo. 3. excluded.

LIII. Provided also, and it is hereby enacted, That nothing in this act contained shall extend to that part of *Great Britain*, called *Scotland*. This act not to extend to Scotland.

CAP. XLII.

An act for redeeming one fourth part of the joint stock of annuities established by an act made in the third year of his present Majesty's reign, in respect of several navy, victualling, and transport bills, and ordnance debentures.

Most gracious Sovereign,

WHEREAS *by an act of parliament made in the third year of your Majesty's reign, intituled,* An act for granting annuities to satisfy certain navy, victualling, and transport bills, and ordnance debentures; and for charging the payment of such annuities on the sinking fund; and making good the same to the said fund, in manner therein mentioned; *it was provided and directed, That all and every person and persons, bodies politick and corporate, who should, within the time therein limited, deliver in certain navy, victualling, and transport bills, and ordnance debentures, to be cancelled in manner thereby directed, should, for the principal sum or sums contained therein, and also for the interest marked upon such of the said bills as bore an interest, be respectively intitled to, and have an annuity after the rate of four pounds* per centum per annum, *to commence from the twenty fifth day of* March, *one thousand seven hundred and sixty three, and to be payable half yearly, at the bank of* England, *to such person or persons, bodies politick or corporate, or such as he, she, or they, should appoint his, her, or their executors, administrators, successors, or assigns, until redemption thereof by parliament, in manner therein mentioned: and that all such monies should be deemed to be one capital or joint stock, on which the said annuities should be attending: and whereas the several principal monies contained in the bills and debentures delivered in and cancelled, together with such interest as aforesaid, which were converted into a capital or joint stock in pursuance of the said act, amount to the sum of three millions four hundred eighty three thousand five hundred fifty three pounds, one shilling, and ten pence:* and whereas your Majesty's most dutiful Preamble, reciting clauses in act 3 Geo. 3.

dutiful and loyal subjects, the commons of *Great Britain* in parliament assembled, have resolved, that one fourth part of the said capital stock be redeemed and paid off on the twenty fifth day of *December*, one thousand seven hundred and sixty five; and several publick notices have been given of the said resolution by the speaker of the house of commons, pursuant to the order of that house; and therefore your faithful commons do most humbly beseech your Majesty that it may be enacted; and be it enacted by the King's most excellent majesty, by and with the advice and consent of the lords spiritual and temporal, and commons, in this present parliament assembled, and by the authority of the same, That such notices as aforesaid shall be, and be deemed, adjudged, and taken to be, good and sufficient notice or notices, within the true intent and meaning of the said act, for the redemption of one fourth part of the said capital or joint stock, and of the annuities attending on such part; and the same shall be redeemable and redeemed accordingly.

Notices given of the intention of parliament to redeem one fourth part of the joint stock of annuities established by the recited act, deemed good and sufficient.

II. And be it further enacted by the authority aforesaid, That on or before the twenty fifth day of *December*, one thousand seven hundred and sixty five, there shall and may be issued and paid to the governor and company of the bank of *England*, the sum of eight hundred and seventy thousand eight hundred eighty eight pounds, five shillings, and five pence half-penny, out of all or any the aids or supplies granted in this session of parliament (except any particular aid or supply which hath been or shall be, in the same session, specially and intirely appropriated to any one particular use or purpose) which sum shall be applied, by the said governor and company in payment of the like sum of eight hundred and seventy thousand eight hundred eighty eight pounds, five shillings, and five pence half-penny, for the redemption and full satisfaction of one fourth part of the said capital or joint stock.

and 870,888 l. 5 s. 5 d. 2 q. out of the supplies granted for the service of the current year, to be paid, for that purpose, into the bank:

III. And be it further enacted by the authority aforesaid, That on or before the said twenty fifth day of *December*, one thousand seven hundred and sixty five, there shall and may, by order of the commissioners of the treasury, or any three or more of them, or the high treasurer for the time being, without any further or other warrant to be sued for, had, or obtained, in that behalf, be issued and paid at the receipt of his Majesty's exchequer to the governor and company of the bank of *England*, by way of imprest and upon account, out of the surplusses, excesses, or overplus monies, commonly called *The Sinking Fund* (upon which the said annuities were charged by the said act made in the third year of his present Majesty's reign) such sum of money as shall be necessary for the discharge of the annuities attending such one fourth part of the said joint stock, from the twenty ninth day of *September* one thousand seven hundred and sixty five, to the twenty fifth day of *December* following, inclusive; which sum shall be applied, by the said governor and company, in discharge of such annuities accordingly, at the same time that the respective principal monies, composing such one

and to be issued accordingly at the exchequer, upon an order from the treasury, out of the monies of the sinking fund:

one fourth part, shall be paid and satisfied; and that all such annuities, in respect of such one fourth part, shall cease and be extinguished from the twenty fifth day of *December*, one thousand seven hundred and sixty five.

and to be applied by the bank, in discharge of the said annuities.

IV. And be it further enacted by the authority aforesaid, That the sums of money which shall be issued and applied, by virtue of this act, out of the said surplusses, excesses, or overplus monies, for payment of the said annuities, shall be made good and replaced by and out of the supplies to be granted in the next session of parliament.

The sums so issued to be replaced out of the next supplies.

V. Provided always, and be it further enacted by the authority aforesaid, That if all or any part of the principal monies, composing such part of the said capital or joint stock hereby intended to be redeemed, shall be paid and satisfied at the bank of *England*, before the twenty fifth day of *December* one thousand seven hundred and sixty five, the said governor and company shall, notwithstanding the same, pay, and they are hereby impowered to pay, in respect of the principal monies so discharged, the full sums which the annuities attending the same would have amounted to, on the twenty fifth day of *December* one thousand seven hundred and sixty five; any thing herein or in any other act contained to the contrary notwithstanding.

The said annuities to be paid up in full to 25 Dec. 1765.

VI. Provided also, and be it further enacted by the authority aforesaid, That the said governor and company, or any member thereof, shall not incur any disability for or by reason of his or their doing any matter or thing in pursuance of this act.

Bank not to incur any disability by reason of this act.

VII. And be it further enacted by the authority aforesaid, That if any person or persons shall at any time or times be sued, molested, or prosecuted, for any thing by him or them done or executed in pursuance of this act, or of any matter or thing therein contained, such person or persons shall and may plead the general issue, and give the special matter in evidence for his and their defence; and if a verdict shall pass for the defendant or defendants, or the plaintiff or plaintiffs shall discontinue his or their action, or be nonsuited, or judgement shall be given against him or them, upon demurrer or otherwise, then such defendant or defendants shall have treble costs to him or them awarded against such plaintiff or plaintiffs.

General issue.

Treble costs.

CAP. XLIII.

An act for the better securing, and further improvement, of the revenues of customs, excise, inland and salt duties; and for encouraging the linen manufacture of the Isle of Man; *and for allowing the importation of several goods the produce and manufacture of the said island, under certain restrictions and regulations.*

Most gracious Sovereign,

YOUR *Majesty having been most graciously pleased, at the opening of this session of parliament, to recommend from the throne to*

Preamble.

to your faithful commons the continuance of that attention which hath hitherto been ſhewn to the improvement of the publick revenue, we have thought it our duty to apply ourſelves with the utmoſt zeal and aſſiduity to carry into execution every proper meaſure for the attainment of that end; and though we have already prepared ſeveral bills for that purpoſe, which have received your royal approbation, we are deſirous to eſtabliſh ſtill further regulations, which, by a more exact and equal collection of the publick revenue, and without laying any new burthens on your people, may tend to the accompliſhment of ſo great and ſalutary a deſign: and whereas by an act paſſed in the fourteenth year of the reign of his late majeſty King Charles *the Second* (*intituled,*

Act 14 Car. 2. An act for preventing frauds, and regulating abuſes, in his Majeſty's cuſtoms) *it is, amongſt other things, enacted, That the perſon or perſons which were or ſhould be appointed for managing the cuſtoms, and officers of his Majeſty's cuſtoms, and their deputies, ſhould be thereby authorized and enabled to go and enter aboard any ſhip or veſſel, as well ſhips of war as merchant ſhips, from thence to bring on ſhore all goods prohibited or uncuſtomed, except jewels, if they be outwards bound; and if they be ſhips or veſſels inwards bound, from thence to bring on ſhore into his Majeſty's ſtorehouſe, all ſmall parcels of fine goods, or other goods, which ſhould be found in cabins, cheſts, trunks, or other ſmall package, or in any private or ſecret place in or out of the hold of the ſhip or veſſel, which might occaſion a juſt ſuſpicion that they were intended fraudulently to be conveyed away; and all other ſorts of goods whatſoever, for which the duties of tonnage and poundage were not paid or compounded for within twenty days after the firſt entry of the ſhip, to be put and remain in the ſtorehouſe aforeſaid, until his Majeſty's duties thereupon be paid; unleſs the ſaid perſon or perſons which were or ſhould be appointed by his Majeſty for managing the cuſtoms, and officers of the cuſtoms, ſhould ſee juſt cauſe to allow a longer time, as in and by the ſaid recited act more at large appears: and whereas in the cheſts, trunks, bales, caſks, and other package, which contained goods ſo ſent and carried to his Majeſty's ſtorehouſe by the officers of the cuſtoms in purſuance of the ſaid act, and likewiſe in packages which are brought on ſhore by virtue of a ſpecial ſufferance or order from the commiſſioners or principal officers of the cuſtoms, to be examined before entry and payment of duties, at the requeſt and application of the owners thereof; and alſo in and amongſt ſuch goods themſelves, there are often found concealed and encloſed lace and other fine goods and merchandizes, which lie in little compaſs, and of which no entries are often intended to be made, or duties paid for, by the owners or proprietors thereof, or their agents, unleſs and until the ſame are diſcovered by the officers of his Majeſty's cuſtoms; by which fraudulent concealments the revenue thereof is greatly defrauded:* may it therefore pleaſe your Majeſty, that it may be enacted; and be it enacted by the King's moſt excellent majeſty, by and with the advice and conſent of the lords ſpiritual and temporal, and commons, in this preſent parliament aſſembled, and by the authority of the ſame, That from and after the firſt day of *June*, one thouſand ſeven hundred and ſixty five, all goods, wares, and merchandizes whatſoever, which ſhall be found en-

Unentered goods found concealed in any package, or merchandize ſent to the King's ſtorehouſes,

enclosed and concealed as aforesaid, in any chest, trunk, bale, cask, or other package, or in or amongst any of the goods, wares, or merchandizes contained therein, at any time after the same shall have been carried or sent to his Majesty's storehouse by any officer or officers of his Majesty's customs in pursuance of the said act, and which shall not have been, within the space of twenty days after the first entry of the ship in which they were imported, duly entered, and his Majesty's customs, and other duties, for them, paid or secured; or which shall be found concealed as aforesaid in any chest, trunk, bale, cask, or other package, or inclosed in or amongst any of the goods therein contained, which shall be brought on shore by special sufferance, or order from the commissioners or principal officers of the customs, at the request and application of the proprietor, or his agent, and shall not be particularly specified and described in such application, the same shall, in every such case, be forfeited and lost, and shall and may be seized and prosecuted by any officer or officers of his Majesty's customs; one moiety of which forfeitures shall be to the use of his Majesty, his heirs, and successors, and the other moiety shall be to the use of such person and persons as shall seize, inform, or sue for the same, after deducting the charges of condemnation and sale from the gross produce thereof; and such seizures and forfeitures shall and may be prosecuted, tried, and determined, in any of his Majesty's courts of record at *Westminster*, or in the court of *Exchequer* at *Edinburgh* respectively; wherein no essoin, protection, wager of law, or more than one imparlance, shall be allowed.

or in any package, or goods brought on shore by special sufferance, or order, and not specified therein,

are liable to seizure and forfeiture.

II. And whereas it does frequently happen, that goods and merchandizes imported, paying duty *ad valorem*, do, upon view and examination by the proper officers of the customs, appear not to have been valued, by the oath or affirmation of the importer, according to the true value and price thereof; and notwithstanding demand is made in writing by the customer or collector and comptroller of the port where such goods are entered, for delivery of the same into his Majesty's warehouse at the port of importation, for the use and benefit of the crown, agreeable to the directions of an act of parliament made in the eleventh year of the reign of his late majesty King *George* the First, (intituled, *An act for rating such unrated goods and merchandizes as are usually imported into this kingdom, and pay duty* ad valorem, *upon the oath of the importer; and for ascertaintng the value of all goods and merchandizes not inserted in the former or present book of rates; and for repealing certain duties upon drugs and rags; and for continuing the duties upon apples; and for ascertaining the method of admeasuring pictures imported*) yet the importers or proprietors of such goods or merchandizes do sometimes neglect or refuse to deliver the same, or to cause the same to be delivered, into his Majesty's warehouse; by which means the said recited act is rendered ineffectual to answer the purposes thereby intended; the officers of the customs not being thereby impowered to carry such goods or merchandizes to his Majesty's warehouse, although

Act 11 Geo. 1.

though the importers or proprietors thereof ſhall neglect or refuſe ſo to do; now, to remedy this inconvenience for the future, and for an encouragement to the officers of the cuſtoms to be diligent in the execution of their duty, be it enacted, That from and after the firſt day of *June*, one thouſand ſeven hundred and ſixty five, upon the importation of any goods or merchandizes, paying duty *ad valorem*, where, upon view and examination thereof by the proper officers of the cuſtoms, it ſhall appear to them that ſuch goods and merchandizes are not valued, by the oath or affirmation of the importer or proprietor, according to the true price or value thereof, according to the true intent and meaning of the ſaid recited act, or any other act or acts of parliament, it ſhall and may be lawful for the ſaid officers of the cuſtoms to take and detain ſuch goods and merchandizes, and to cauſe the ſame to be carried and conveyed into his Majeſty's warehouſe, at the port of importation, for the uſe and benefit of the crown; and the collector of the cuſtoms for ſuch port, with the privity of the comptroller, ſhall, out of any money in his hands, ariſing by cuſtoms, or other duties belonging to the crown, pay to the importer or proprietor of ſuch goods and merchandizes, upon demand, the value of ſuch goods and merchandizes ſo ſworn to or affirmed, together with an addition of ten pounds *per centum* thereon; and alſo the cuſtoms and other duties which ſhall have been paid for ſuch goods and merchandizes, taking a receipt for the ſame from ſuch importer or proprietor, in full ſatisfaction for the ſaid goods and merchandizes, as if they had been regularly ſold; and it ſhall and may be lawful to and for the commiſſioners of the cuſtoms for the time being (whether the value of the goods ſworn to, or affirmed, together with the ten pounds *per centum* thereon, and the duties which ſhall have been paid for ſuch goods, be demanded or not, or whether the receipt herein directed to be taken be given or not) to cauſe the ſaid goods to be fairly and publickly ſold, as ſoon as may be, for the beſt advantage; and out of the produce thereof, the money, herein before directed to be paid or advanced for ſuch goods, ſhall be paid to ſuch collector, to be by him replaced to ſuch funds from whence he borrowed the ſame, provided the ſame ſhall have been by him ſo paid or advanced; but if it has not, then the ſame ſhall remain in the hands of the ſaid collector, until the importer or proprietor ſhall demand the ſame, and give a receipt (which is herein before directed to be taken for the ſame;) and after deducting from the overplus (if any) the charges ariſing by the warehouſing and ſale of ſuch goods and merchandizes, the ſaid commiſſioners of the cuſtoms ſhall and may order the ſeveral and reſpective officers of the cuſtoms, concerned in the view and examination of ſuch goods and merchandizes, to be paid, as an encouragement for the faithful diſcharge of their duty thereon, one moiety of the remainder of ſuch overplus (if any) and the other moiety thereof ſhall be paid into his Majeſty's exchequer towards the ſinking fund; any thing in the herein

Where any goods or merchandize paying duty ad valorem, appear to be under rated by the importer or proprietor; the officer may carry them to the King's warehouſes, for the uſe of the crown; and the collector of the port is thereupon to pay the proprietor, &c. the value ſworn to, with the addition of 10l. per cent. and the duties paid; the goods to be afterwards ſold publickly, and the money advanced to be replaced; and after all charges deducted, one moiety of the ſurplus to go to the officers concerned, and the other moiety to the ſinking fund.

in before recited act contained, or any other law, custom, or usage, to the contrary notwithstanding.

III. And whereas by an act passed in the twelfth year of the reign of his late majesty King *George* the First, (intituled, *An act for the improvement of his Majesty's revenues of customs, excise, and inland duties*) the commissioners of his Majesty's customs are impowered to cause such wines as any merchant, or other person, shall refuse to pay or secure the duties for, as being damaged, corrupt, or unmerchantable, to be publickly sold, in order to be distilled into brandy, or to be made into vinegar, taking sufficient security to his Majesty's use, that such wines be not made use of for any other purpose whatsoever: and whereas it hath been found by experience, that the security by that act directed hath not been sufficient to answer the intent thereof, unless some proper ingredient, such as salt or vinegar, has been put into such wine before it has been delivered out of his Majesty's warehouse; and a doubt having lately arisen, whether the officers of his Majesty's customs are legally authorized to put any salt or vinegar into such wine without the consent of the proprietor or purchaser thereof: to obviate which doubt for the future, and more effectually to prevent such wines from being fraudulently used in this kingdom; be it further enacted by the authority aforesaid, That from and after the first day of *June*, one thousand seven hundred and sixty five, before the delivery of any refused wines, which shall be sold in pursuance of the direction of the said recited act, it shall and may be lawful for the commissioners, or other principal officers of his Majesty's customs, to cause so much salt or vinegar to be put therein, as they shall judge sufficient and proper to prevent the said wines from being made use of for any other purpose whatsoever, than being distilled into brandy, or made into vinegar, besides taking the security in the manner directed by the said recited act.

Clause in act 12 Geo. 1.

A sufficient quantity of salt or vinegar to be put into all damaged refused wines, sold in pursuance of the recited act, before delivery thereof out of the King's warehouses.

IV. And whereas by an act of parliament made in the twelfth year of the reign of his late majesty King *George* the First, intituled, *An act for the improvement of his Majesty's revenues of customs, excise, and inland duties*, it is enacted, That all tobacco stalks, or stems stript from the leaf, shall be prohibited to be imported; and, on seizure and condemnation thereof, the commissioners of his Majesty's customs shall and may cause the same to be publickly burnt, and shall and may allow the officer, for his encouragement in making the seizure, one penny for every pound weight of such stalks or stems, so seized and condemned, clear of all charges of condemnation: and forasmuch as no forfeitures are inflicted by the said recited act of the vessels or boats, or the horses and other cattle or carriages made use of in the landing or removing of the aforesaid goods, nor any penalties upon the persons who are concerned or assisting in the unshipping thereof, or to whose hands they shall come after the unshipping thereof, by reason whereof the aforesaid act made in the twelfth year of the reign of his late majesty King *George* the First, has hitherto proved insufficient for preventing the impor-

Clause in act 12 Geo. 1.

portation of the ſaid goods, to the great detriment of the revenue and fair traders: for remedy whereof, be it enacted by the authority aforeſaid, That if any tobacco ſtalks or ſtems ſtript from the leaf, ſhall at any time after the firſt day of *June*, one thouſand ſeven hundred and ſixty five, be imported into any part of *Great Britain*, then not only the ſaid goods ſhall be forfeited and loſt, and on ſeizure and condemnation thereof be publickly burnt, and the officer allowed one penny *per* pound weight for his encouragement in making the ſeizure, agreeable to the form and effect of the before recited act of parliament paſſed in the twelfth year of the reign of his ſaid late majeſty King *George* the Firſt; but alſo all and every perſon and perſons who ſhall be aſſiſting or otherwiſe concerned in the unſhipping the ſaid goods, or to whoſe hands the ſame ſhall knowingly come after the unſhipping thereof, ſhall forfeit treble the value thereof, together with the veſſels and boats made uſe of in the landing, removing, carriage, or conveyance of the ſaid goods, and alſo the bags, caſks, or other veſſels or things in which the ſaid goods are packed or contained, and the horſes, cattle, carts, and other carriages made uſe of in the loading, carrying, landing, or removing, the ſaid goods; one moiety of all which forfeitures and penalties ſhall be to the uſe of his Majeſty, his heirs and ſucceſſors, and the other moiety to ſuch officer or officers of his Majeſty's cuſtoms, as ſhall ſeize, inform, or ſue for the ſame, to be recovered by bill, plaint, or information, in any of his Majeſty's courts of record at *Weſtminſter*, or in the court of exchequer at *Edinburgh* reſpectively, wherein no eſſoin, protection or wager of law, ſhall be allowed.

Tobacco ſtalks or ſtems ſtript from the leaf, are not only liable to forfeiture on importation, &c. in purſuance of the recited act, but the perſons aſſiſting in unſhipping the ſame, or into whoſe hands the ſame ſhall afterwards knowingly come, forfeit treble the value; and the veſſels, boats, carriages, and cattle, employed therein, are forfeited alſo.

V. And be it further enacted by the authority aforeſaid, That a *Capias* in the firſt proceſs ſhall and may iſſue upon any bill, plaint, or information, commenced, filed, or proſecuted, againſt any perſon or perſons, for, upon, or by reaſon of any the offences before-mentioned, which *Capias* ſhall ſpecify the ſum of the penalty ſued for; and ſuch offender or offenders ſhall be obliged to give ſufficient bail or ſecurity by natural born ſubjects, or denizens, to the perſon or perſons to whom ſuch *Capias* ſhall be directed, to appear in the court out of which ſuch *Capias* ſhall iſſue, at the day of the return of ſuch writ, to anſwer ſuch ſuit or proſecution; and ſhall likewiſe at the time of ſuch appearing, give ſufficient bail or ſecurity by ſuch perſons as aforeſaid, in the ſaid court, to anſwer and pay all the forfeitures and penalties incurred for ſuch offence and offences, in caſe he, ſhe, or they, ſhall be convicted thereof, or to yield his, her, or their, body or bodies to priſon.

Capias to iſſue upon information againſt the party, and bail to be given thereupon for appearance; and at the return of the writ, ſecurity to be given to pay the penalties in caſe of conviction.

VI. Provided always, and it is hereby further enacted by the authority aforeſaid, That all veſſels and boats, and all horſes and other cattle, and carriages whatſoever, which from and after the ſaid firſt day of *June*, one thouſand ſeven hundred and ſixty five, ſhall be ſeized as forfeited by virtue of this act; or for removing any tobacco, tobacco ſtalks, or ſnuffs, contrary to an act paſſed in the twenty fourth year of the reign of his late majeſty

Veſſels, cattle, and carriages, forfeited by this act, or by 24 Geo. 2. for frauds relating to the fraudulent removing of tobacco,

jesty King *George* the Second (intituled, *An act for the more effectual securing the duties upon tobacco*) shall and may be prosecuted, adjudged, tried, and determined, by and before two or more of his Majesty's justices of the peace, residing near to the place where such seizure shall be made, in such manner and form, and by such rules, as are directed and prescribed in an act passed in the eighth year of the reign of his late majesty King *George* the First (intituled, *An act to prevent the clandestine running of goods, and the danger of infection thereby; and to prevent ships breaking their quarentine; and to subject copper ore of the production of the* British *plantations, to such regulations as other enumerated commodities of the like production are subject*) with respect to vessels, horses and carriages, which are forfeited by that act of parliament, for the removing, carriage or conveyance of the goods therein mentioned.

to be prosecuted as is prescribed in act 8 Geo. 1. with respect to forfeitures therein mentioned.

VII. And whereas there are several species of linen now manufactured in *Russia* imported into this kingdom, which are not rated either in the book of rates referred to by the act of tonnage and poundage made in the twelfth year of the reign of King *Charles* the Second, or in the additional book of rates referred to by the act of the eleventh year of the reign of his late majesty King *George* the First, or by any other act or acts of parliament, the duties upon which goods are now payable according to the value sworn to or affirmed, by the importers, which, by experience, has been found to be very unequal, from the various values fixed by the importers on the same species of goods, some persons greatly undervaluing the same, to the detriment of the revenue, and the discouragement of the fair traders: now for remedy thereof, and to put the trade upon a more equal foot, be it enacted by the authority aforesaid, That from and after the first day of *June*, one thousand seven hundred and sixty five, the duties now payable upon the importation of unrated linen cloth, of the manufacture of *Russia*, shall cease, determine, and be no longer paid or payable; and that all the provisions and clauses contained in any former act or acts of parliament, so far as the same relate to the ascertaining the value of such unrated linens, according to the oaths or affirmations of the importers, shall be, and are hereby repealed and made void.

The duties now payable on unrated Russia linens imported, to cease;

VIII. And it is hereby further enacted by the authority aforesaid, That in lieu of the said duties repealed by this act, from and after the first day of *June*, one thousand seven hundred and sixty five, all linen cloth or diaper of *Russia*, not otherwise rated, which shall be imported into any port or place within *Great Britain*, shall, upon the importation thereof, be rated to pay the old subsidy granted by the act of tonnage and poundage, made in the twelfth year of the reign of King *Charles* the Second, according to the several rates and values hereafter mentioned; that is to say,

and the old subsidy, granted by act 12 Car. 2. to be paid in lieu thereof,

according to the rates hereafter mentioned.

All linen cloth and diaper of *Russia*, not otherwise rated, exceeding thirty one inches and one half of an inch in breadth,

The rates.

and not exceeding forty five inches in breadth, for every one hundred and twenty *Engliſh* ells, ſix pounds.

And all linen cloth and diaper of *Ruſſia*, not otherwiſe rated, exceeding forty five inches in breadth, for every one hundred and twenty *Engliſh* ells, ten pounds; and in that porportion for any greater or leſs quantity of any of the ſaid goods.

Where any of the ſaid goods are liable to any additional ſubſidy or duty, the ſame is to be paid according to the above rates.

IX. And be it further enacted by the authority aforeſaid, That in all caſes where any of the ſaid goods are by law ſubject or liable to the payment of the further ſubſidy, the one third ſubſidy, the additional impoſt on any other ſubſidy or duty whatſoever, according to the reſpective value ſet thereon for the old ſubſidy, or in proportion thereto, the ſame ſhall, from and after the ſaid firſt day of *June*, one thouſand ſeven hundred and ſixty five, be paid proportionably according to the particular rates and values herein before ſet thereon for the old ſubſidy aforeſaid, and not according to the oath or affirmation of the importer, or any other rate or value whatſoever; any thing in the reſpective acts which granted the ſaid duties, or any other act to the contrary notwithſtanding.

These duties to be levied, paid, and applied, as mentioned in the ſeveral acts granting or continuing the ſame.

X. And be it further enacted by the authority aforeſaid, That the ſeveral ſubſidies, impoſitions and duties, upon the ſaid ſeveral ſorts of goods, ſhall be raiſed, levied, collected, paid, and applied, in ſuch manner and form, and by ſuch ways and means, and under ſuch penalties and forfeitures, and with ſuch diſcounts, allowances, and drawbacks, as are mentioned and expreſſed in the ſeveral acts of parliament, which granted, or continued, and appropriated, the ſame reſpectively; and all powers, penalties, proviſions, articles, and clauſes therein contained, (except in ſuch caſes where any alteration is made by this act) ſhall continue in full force and effect, during the continuance of the ſaid reſpective ſubſidies, impoſitions, and other duties; and ſhall be applied, practiſed and executed, for the raiſing, levying, collecting, anſwering, paying and appropriating the ſaid reſpective ſubſidies, impoſitions, and other duties, according to the true intent and meaning of this preſent act, as fully and effectually to all intents and purpoſes, as if the ſaid clauſes, matters and things, had been repeated and enacted in the body of this preſent act; any law, or other uſage, or cuſtom, to the contrary notwithſtanding.

XI. And whereas it may contribute to prevent any illicit trade being carried on by the inhabitants of the *Iſle of Man*, to the prejudice of the trade and revenues of his Majeſty's dominions, if the ſaid inhabitants are encouraged in the honeſt and lawful occupation of cultivating and improving the lands of the ſaid iſland, and of manufacturing the produce thereof, by allowing them to import the ſame into *Great Britain*, without payment of duties, under certain limitations and reſtrictions; for which purpoſe be it enacted by the authority aforeſaid, That from and after the firſt day of *July*, one thouſand ſeven hundred and ſixty five, the inhabitants of the ſaid *Iſle of Man*, ſhall and may im-

Beſtials, and other goods, the growth and manufac-

import directly from thence into any lawful port of *Great Britain*, bestials, or any goods, wares, and merchandizes, of the growth, produce, and manufacture of the said *Isle of Man*, except such as by any act of this session of parliament are prohibited to be imported into this kingdom; and also (except woollen manufactures, beer and ale) without paying any customs, subsidies or duties, for or in respect thereof (except such excise or other duty as is now, or shall hereafter for the time being, be due and payable for the like goods, wares and merchandizes, of the growth, produce, and manufacture of *Great Britain*) provided the master, or other person having the charge of the ship or vessel, so importing the same, shall bring with him a certificate or certificates from the governor, lieutenant governor, commander in chief, or chief magistrates for the time being, that oath has been made before him or them in the presence of the officer of the customs for the port or place where such bestials or goods shall be put on board, that the same are the growth, produce, or manufacture of the said *Isle of Man*; which certificate or certificates shall also be attested by the said officer of the customs, and shall express the number and tale of such bestials, with the marks and weight of the species of goods in each bale or parcel mentioned in the bill or bills of lading, with the name or names, place or places of abode of the exporter or exporters from the *Isle of Man*, and the name or names, place or places of abode, of such person or persons as shall have sworn the bestials or goods therein mentioned to be of the growth, produce and manufacture of the said *Isle of Man*, and where and to whom consigned in *Great Britain*; and the master or person taking charge of the ship or vessel importing the same, shall also make oath before the collector or principal officer of the customs of the port or place of importation in *Great Britain*, That the said bestials, bales and parcels, and the goods therein contained, are the same that were taken on board by virtue of the said certificate or certificates so to be produced; on failure whereof, or of any of the requisites herein before mentioned, the bestials, goods, wares or merchandizes, shall be liable to the same duties, penalties and forfeitures, as they would have been liable to by law, if this act had not been made.

(ture of the Isle of Man, except such as are prohibited by any act of this session, (woollen goods, beer, and ale, also excepted) may be imported from thence, on payment of the same duties as are payable on like goods of the produce and manufacture of Great Britain; and under the restrictions and regulations here mentioned.)

XII. Provided always, and it is hereby declared and enacted by the authority aforesaid, That nothing in this act contained shall extend, or be construed to extend, to give liberty to any person to import into *Great Britain*, from the said *Isle of Man*, any goods or commodities of the growth or product of any foreign nation or country, which may be in part or fully manufactured in the said island, except linen manufactures made there of hemp or flax, not being the produce of the said island.

(But no goods of the growth of any foreign nation manufactured in the said island may be imported, except those of hemp and flax.)

XIII. And it is hereby further enacted by the authority aforesaid, That from and after the first day of *July*, one thousand seven hundred and sixty five, the like bounties which are now allowed upon *British* and *Irish* linens exported from *Great Britain*, by virtue of an act made in the twenty ninth year of the reign

(Bounties payable upon exportation of British and Irish linens, by act 29 Geo. 2.)

reign of his late majesty King *George* the Second, intituled, *An act for granting a bounty upon certain species of* British *and* Irish *linens exported; and taking off the duties on the importation of foreign raw linen yarns made of flax*; shall be allowed and paid upon the like species of linen made in the *Isle of Man*, imported into *Great Britain*, in the manner herein before-mentioned, which shall be re-exported from *Great Britain*, under the same limitations, restrictions, penalties and forfeitures, in all respects, as are expressed and mentioned in the said recited act of parliament, with respect to the bounties thereby granted, as fully to all intents and purposes as if the several clauses, powers and directions relating thereto, were again repeated and enacted in this present act.

to be allowed on the like species made in the Isle of Man, and re-exported from Great Britain.

XIV. *And whereas by a clause in an act of parliament passed in the tenth year of the reign of her majesty Queen* Anne, *intituled*, An act for laying several duties upon all soap and paper made in *Great Britain*, or imported into the same; and upon chequered and striped linens imported; and upon certain silks, callicoes, linens and stuffs, printed, painted or stained; and upon several kinds of stampt vellum, parchment and paper; and upon certain printed papers, pamphlets and advertisements, for raising the sum of eighteen hundred thousand pounds by way of a lottery towards her Majesty's supply; and for licensing an additional number of hackney chairs; and for charging certain stocks of cards and dice; and for better securing her Majesty's duties to arise in the office for the stamp duties by licences for marriages and otherwise; and for relief of persons who have not claimed their lottery tickets in due time, or have lost exchequer bills, or lottery tickets; and for borrowing money upon stock (part of the capital of the *South Sea* company) for the use of the publick; *reciting, that it might frequently happen that stale or rotten soap, and also the cuttings of good soap (for which the duties by the said act should first have been duly paid or charged) might be put again into the copper or pan to be refreshed or made new; and the soap newly made from the same, or from a mixture of the same with other ingredients, would be chargeable with a new duty by the said act, it was therefore thereby provided and enacted, That in case such stale or rotten soap or cuttings, be put into the copper or pan, in the presence of an officer for the said duties, to be refreshed or made new as aforesaid; such officer should, from time to time, make an allowance of the duty of the stale or rotten soap, or cuttings so put in, and certify every such allowance upon his report to be returned to the head officer; any thing therein contained to the contrary notwithstanding: and whereas by an act made in the eleventh year of the reign of his majesty King* George *the First, intitled*, An act for more effectual preventing frauds and abuses in the public revenues; for preventing frauds in the salt duties, and for giving relief for salt used in the curing of salmon and codfish, in the year one thousand seven hundred and nineteen, exported from that part of *Great Britain* called *Scotland*; for enabling the insurance companies to plead the general issue in actions

Clauses in act 10 Annæ, and 11 Geo. 1.

tions brought against them; and for securing the stamp duties upon policies of insurance; *reciting the before mentioned clause, and that under colour and pretence of making such allowances pursuant to the aforesaid clause, and by combinations and confederacies between fraudulent makers of soap and corrupted officers of and for the said duties, who by bribes had been prevailed upon in such their reports of the making of soap, sometimes to certify great quantities of stale or rotten soap, or of cuttings of soap put into such makings of soap, when in fact and in truth no such stale or rotten soap, or cuttings of soap, had really and in fact been put into such makings of soap, and at other times when small quantities of stale or rotten soap, or of cuttings of soap, have been put into such makings of soap, such officers had been by the means aforesaid prevailed upon to certify in such his and their report and reports, quantities of such stale or rotten soap, or cuttings of soap, much greater and far exceeding the quantity or quantities which at such time and times, really and in fact had been, and were put into such respective makings of soap, whereby his Majesty had been greatly defrauded of and in his duties on soap: for preventing whereof for the future, it was enacted, That if any stale or rotten soap, or any cuttings of soap, in order to the refreshing thereof, should from and after the twenty fourth day of* June, *one thousand seven hundred and twenty five, be put into any making or makings of soap, unless of the intention and designing so to be put such stale or rotten soap, or cuttings of soap, there should be, or should have been given, to the officer of the division or place where such putting in was intended to be, such notice in writing as therein after was mentioned (that is to say) if such putting in was to be within the limits of the weekly bills of mortality, then, and in such case, by the space of twelve hours next before the respective time and times of such putting in such stale or rotten soap, or cuttings of soap; but if in any other place or places out of the limits of the said weekly bills, then and in such case, by the space of twenty four hours next before the respective time and times of such putting in such stale or rotten soap, or cuttings of soap, that in every such case and cases whatsoever, where such putting in should be, or should have been without such notice, the officer should not certify such putting in, or any allowance for or in respect thereof, nor should the maker or makers of soap, in any such case or cases, have, or be intitled to have, any allowance or allowances whatsoever, for or in respect of such putting in such stale or rotten soap, or of such cuttings of soap: and it was further enacted, That if from and after the said twenty fourth day of* June, *one thousand seven hundred and twenty five, any officer or officers of excise, or for the said duties on soap, should falsly pretend, that he or they hath or have had due notice in writing of such putting in of such stale or rotten soap, or of such cuttings of soap, in any case and cases where and in which he or they really and in fact should not have had such due notice in writing, and should make such allowance and allowances as aforesaid, and should falsly certify the same; every such officer and officers for every pound weight of such stale or rotten soap, or cuttings of soap, so falsly allowed, or certified as aforesaid, should forfeit and lose the sum of ten shillings; and every such maker or makers of soap, who ſhould demand, claim, have or take, any benefit or advantage for or in reſpect of any ſuch allowance ſo falſly made or certified by ſuch officer or officers, in every ſuch caſe and caſes, ſhould forfeit and loſe the ſum of ten ſhillings for every pound weight of ſuch ſtale or rotten ſoap, or cuttings of ſoap, as ſhould be claimed, demanded, had or taken, by ſuch maker or makers of ſoap, for and in reſpect of ſuch allowance ſo falſly made or certified for by ſuch officer or officers: and whereas, notwithſtanding the ſeveral before mentioned proviſions, great frauds have been carried on by divers makers of hard ſoap, under pretence of returning ſtale or rotten ſoap, or cuttings of ſoap, to the great detriment of the revenue, and the fair traders*; be it enacted by the authority aforeſaid, That from and after the fifth day of *July*, one thouſand ſeven hundred and ſixty five, the ſeveral before-recited proviſions, ſo far only as relates to hard ſoap, and the makers thereof, and no otherwiſe, ſhall be, and the ſame are hereby repealed; and in lieu of the before mentioned allowance hereby repealed, all and every the officers of exciſe, or for the duties on ſoap, ſhall, and they are hereby required, in charging the duties upon hard ſoap, to allow to the reſpective makers of hard ſoap, in their returns or reports of the ſeveral quantities of hard ſoap made by ſuch reſpective makers of hard ſoap, one pound in every ten pounds of hard ſoap, which ſuch officer or officers ſhall charge upon the reſpective makers thereof; which ſaid allowance of one pound in every ten pounds of hard ſoap, is hereby declared to be in full compenſation for all waſte, loſſes, or damages whatſoever.

The ſeveral before recited proviſions, ſo far as the ſame relate to hard ſoap, and the makers thereof, are repealed; and the makers are to be allowed 1 lib. in 10 lib. as a compenſation in lieu of all waſte, and other loſſes.

XV. And whereas great frauds have been committed by divers makers of hard ſoap, by removing and ſecreting large quantities of ſoap in the abſence of the officers from the copper, pan, or other utenſil wherein the ſame is made, before the ſame is put into the frame; for remedy thereof, be it enacted by the authority aforeſaid, That all and every perſon and perſons who, after the fifth day of *July*, one thouſand ſeven hundred and ſixty five, ſhall make any hard ſoap, ſhall, at his, her, or their own expence, find, provide, and affix ſufficient wooden covers (to be approved of in writing by and under the hands of the reſpective ſurveyors or ſuperviſors of exciſe of the diviſion or diſtrict in which every ſuch reſpective maker of hard ſoap ſhall reſide) to every copper, pan, or other utenſil wherein he ſhall boil or make any hard ſoap; which ſaid coppers, pans, or other utenſils, with the covers thereto affixed, and alſo the pipe or pipes that conveys or convey the waſte or ſalt lees from the copper, pan, or other utenſil, ſhall, and they are hereby required to be ſecurely locked and ſealed down by the officer of exciſe who ſurveys ſuch trader, as ſoon as the fire is damped or drawn from under the copper, pan, or other utenſil, whenever any ſoap, or any thing of a ſoapy quality, ſhall be left therein; which ſaid locks and keys to the ſame, and all other neceſſary faſtenings for ſecuring the coppers, pans, or other utenſils, and alſo the pipes, ſhall be provided by the reſpective ſurveyors or ſuperviſors of exciſe of the diviſion or diſtrict in which ſuch reſpective

Makers of hard ſoap to provide proper covers to their coppers, pans, and other utenſils; which the officer is to lock and ſeal down, when the fire is damped:

Superviſor to provide the locks, keys, pipes, and other faſtenings thereto,

ſpective makers of hard ſoap ſhall reſide, at the expence of ſuch reſpective makers; and whenever any ſuch maker of hard ſoap ſhall be deſirous of lighting a fire under ſuch copper, pan, or other utenſil ſo locked and ſealed down, and ſhall have given to the officer of exciſe of the diviſion or diſtrict twelve hours notice, if ſuch maker of hard ſoap ſhall reſide within the limits and juriſdicton of the head office of exciſe in *London*; or if ſuch maker of hard ſoap ſhall reſide in any other part of *Great Britain*, twenty four hours notice of ſuch his, her, or their intention, the officer of exciſe ſhall attend to unlock and open the copper, pan, or other utenſil, and the pipe or pipes ſo ſecured: and if any maker or makers of hard ſoap ſhall, after the ſaid fifth day of *July*, one thouſand ſeven hundred and ſixty five, preſume to make any hard ſoap before he, ſhe, or they ſhall have found, provided, and affixed ſufficient wooden covers, to be approved of as aforeſaid, to every copper, pan, or other utenſil wherein he, ſhe, or they ſhall boil or make any hard ſoap, according to the directions of this act; or ſhall refuſe to pay for the locks and keys, and other faſtenings to be provided in purſuance of the direction of this act; or if by any act, device, or contrivance whatſoever, any ſuch maker of hard ſoap ſhall open any copper, pan, or utenſil, or any pipe or pipes, after the ſame ſhall have been locked down and ſecured as aforeſaid, before the ſame ſhall have been unlocked and opened by the officer of exciſe, or ſhall wilfully break or damage any ſuch lock or ſeal, or other faſtening, every ſuch maker or makers of hard ſoap, offending in any of the ſaid caſes, ſhall, for every ſuch offence reſpectively forfeit and loſe the ſum of twenty pounds.

at the expence of ſuch makers; and makers are to give proper notice of lighting a fire under ſuch coppers, &c. and the officer to attend accordingly. Maker not providing ſuch covers, or refuſing to pay for the locks, faſtenings, &c. or opening any copper before the ſame is duly unlocked, &c. forfeits 20l.

XVI. And whereas very great frauds have been committed by ſeveral makers of hard ſoap, in lighting their fires under their coppers, pans, or other utenſils, under a pretence of cleanſing their coppers, or for the preparing of materials for the making of ſoap, without giving any notice thereof to the proper officer of exciſe; for remedy thereof, be it further enacted by the authority aforeſaid, That from and after the ſaid fifth day of *July*, one thouſand ſeven hundred and ſixty five, no maker or makers of hard ſoap do preſume, on any pretence, to light a fire under any copper, pan, or other utenſil uſed in the boiling of ſoap, or for cleanſing his, her, or their foul goods, or in the preparing any materials for the making of ſoap, without firſt giving in writing, to the proper officer of exciſe within the limits and juriſdiction of the head office of exciſe in *London*, twelve hours notice at leaſt, and to the proper officer or officers in other parts of *Great Britain*, twenty four hours notice at leaſt, of his, her, or their intention to light ſuch fire, on pain to forfeit, for every ſuch offence, the ſum of twenty pounds.

Maker to give due notice to the proper officer, of his intention of lighting fires, whether for making ſoap, or cleanſing his foul goods, &c. under penalty of 20l.

XVII. And it is hereby further enacted by the authority aforeſaid, That from and after the fifth day of *July*, one thouſand ſeven hundred and ſixty five, all and every maker and makers of hard ſoap ſhall make uſe of regular ſquare or oblong frames only, for the cleanſing or putting his, her, or their ſoap (whether perfect or not perfect) into, when taken out of the copper

Maker to provide proper frames for putting his ſoap in when taken out of the copper;

or other utensil where the same was boiled or prepared; and that the bottom, sides and ends, of every such frame, shall respectively be of the thickness of two inches at the least; and every such frame shall not exceed forty five inches in length, nor fifteen inches in breadth; of which frames all and every maker and makers of hard soap is and are hereby required to give notice in writing at the office for the duties on soap next to the place where such soap shall be made, before he, she, or they, do presume to use the same; all which said frames shall be marked and numbered by, or by the direction of, the respective surveyors or supervisors of excise who survey the respective makers of hard soap to whom such frames belong, at the expence of such respective makers: and that if any maker or makers of hard soap shall make use of any other sort of frame, or any other kind of vessel, for the purposes aforesaid; or if the bottom, or ends, or sides, of any of the said frames shall not be of the thickness before mentioned; or if any of the said frames shall exceed forty five inches in length, or fifteen inches in the breadth thereof; or if any such maker or makers of hard soap shall use any such frame, without giving such notice thereof as aforesaid, or before the same shall have been marked and numbered as aforesaid; he, she, or they shall, for every such offence respectively, forfeit and pay the sum of twenty pounds.

and to give notice thereof to the proper officer before using the same; and the frames to be marked and numbered by the supervisor, before using,

on penalty of 20 l.

XVIII. And it is hereby further enacted by the authority aforesaid, That no hard soap (whether perfectly made or not) after the same shall have been cleansed or put into the frame or frames, shall, on any pretence whatsoever, be returned or put again into the copper or other utensil for boiling or re-working; and if any such hard soap shall be so returned or put again into the copper or other utensil, the same shall be again charged with the duties on soap.

Hard soap once put into the frames, not to be returned again into the copper, without being charged afresh with the duties.

XIX. And whereas great frauds have been committed by private and clandestine makers of soap and starch, who, when discovered, do assume to themselves, and are called by other than their true names, and to avoid being prosecuted for the same, do withdraw and abscond themselves, that they may not personally have notice of any prosecution for the same, or be served with any process or summons to answer the same: for remedy whereof, be it enacted by the authority aforesaid, That from and after the said first day of *June*, one thousand seven hundred and sixty five, the leaving a summons at the place or places where any such discovery as aforesaid shall be made, directed to the person or persons by his, her, or their right or assumed name or names, who shall be prosecuted for making or having made use of any boiling-house, working-house, warehouse, store-house, shop, room or other place, for the making or keeping of soap, or for the boiling or keeping any oil, tallow, pot ash, lime, or other materials proper to be made into soap; or for using or having made use of any copper, kettle, furnace, fatt, cistern, trough or other vessel, for the boiling or making of soap, without first giving notice thereof in writing at the office

What shall be deemed legal and effectual notice and summons to private and clandestine makers of soap or starch, liable to prosecution for using unentered workshops, &c. and using assumed names, or absconding.

office for the ſaid duties on ſoap next to the place where ſuch ſoap ſhall be made, according to the directions of the ſtatute in in that caſe made and provided; or making or having made uſe of any work-houſe, ſtore-houſe, room, or other place, for the making and drying, or keeping of ſtarch, or for the converting or keeping any flour, meal, or other materials proper to be made into ſtarch; or for uſing or having made uſe of any fatt, trough, box, ſtove, utenſil, or other veſſel, for the making of ſtarch; without firſt giving notice thereof in writing at the office for the duties on ſtarch next to the place where ſuch ſtarch ſhall be made, according to the directions of the ſtatutes in that caſe made and provided, ſhall be deemed to be, and is hereby declared to be, as legal and effectual a notice or ſummons, to all intents and purpoſes, as if ſuch notice or ſummons was perſonally given or delivered to or into the hands of the party or parties for whom the ſame ſhall be deſigned; and as if ſuch notice or ſummons was directed to the party or parties to and for whom the ſame ſhall be deſigned, by his, her, or their proper name or names.

XX. And be it further enacted by the authority aforeſaid, That from and after the firſt day of *June*, one thouſand ſeven hundred and ſixty five, in caſe any officer or officers for the duties upon ſoap and candles, or either of them, ſhall have cauſe to ſuſpect that ſoap or candles is or are privately making in any place or places whatſoever; or that any ſoap or candles is or are lodged or concealed in any place or places whatſoever, with an intent to defraud his Majeſty of his duty; then, and in every ſuch caſe, upon oath made by ſuch officer or officers before the commiſſioners for the duties upon ſoap or candles for the time being reſpectively, or any one or more of them, or before one or more juſtice or juſtices of the peace, reſiding near the place where ſuch officer or officers ſhall ſuſpect the ſame to be privately making, or to be lodged, or concealed, ſetting forth the ground of his or their ſuſpicion, it ſhall and may be lawful to and for the ſaid commiſſioner or commiſſioners, juſtice or juſtices of the peace reſpectively, before whom ſuch oath ſhall be made, if he or they ſhall judge it reaſonable, by ſpecial warrant under his or their reſpective hands and ſeals, to authorize and impower ſuch officer or officers, by day or by night, (but if in the night, then in the preſence of a conſtable, or other lawful officer of the peace) to enter into all and every ſuch place or places, where he or they ſhall ſo ſuſpect that any ſoap or candles is or are ſo privately making, lodged, or concealed, and to ſeize and carry away all ſuch ſoap or candles, as he or they ſhall there find ſo privately making, together with all the materials of what kind ſoever that ſhall be then ready or preparing for the making either of ſoap or candles; and likewiſe all ſuch ſoap or candles as they ſhall find ſo lodged or concealed in any place or places whatſoever, as forfeited, together with all and every the boxes or other packages wherein ſuch ſoap or candles ſhall be contained; and the perſon or perſons that ſhall be found ſo privately

Where officer ſhall ſuſpect ſoap or candles are privately making, or lie concealed, and ſhall ſet forth the ground of his ſuſpicion upon oath;

a ſpecial warrant may be granted him to enter ſuch places,

and ſeize ſuch goods, with all the materials,

and all ſuch ſoap and candles as ſhall be found concealed there;

and where the duties ſhall not appear to have been paid, the parties forfeit 100l.

vately making either ſoap or candles, or the perſon or perſons in whoſe poſſeſſion any ſoap or candles ſhall be ſo found, unleſs, he, ſhe, or they, do make it appear that the duty has been paid for the ſame, ſhall reſpectively forfeit and pay the ſum of one hundred pounds.

Recital of clauſes in act 9 Annæ,

XXI. And whereas by an act paſſed in the ninth year of the reign of her late majeſty Queen *Anne*, intituled, *An act for laying certain duties upon hides and ſkins, tanned, tawed, or dreſſed, and upon vellum and parchment, for the term of thirty two years, for proſecuting the war, and other her Majeſty's moſt neceſſary occaſions*; it was (amongſt other things) enacted, That if any tanner, tawer, or dreſſer, of hides or ſkins, or any maker of vellum or parchment, chargeable by the ſaid act, ſhould remove or convey, or cauſe or procure to be removed or conveyed, from his, her, or their yard or drying place, any of the ſaid hides and ſkins, or pieces of hides and ſkins, or any ſuch vellum or parchment, before the ſaid duties ſhall be fully charged by weight or tale, or *ad valorem*, as the ſaid act in the reſpective caſes doth require; and before the ſame hides or ſkins, or pieces of hides and ſkins, and ſuch vellum and parchment reſpectively, ſhould be marked to denote the charging the duty as the ſaid act directs; that then, and in ſuch caſe, all and every ſuch tanner, tawer, dreſſer, and maker, ſhould, for every ſuch offence, forfeit and loſe the ſum of fifty pounds; one moiety thereof to the Queen, and the other moiety thereof to him or them that ſhould inform or ſue for the ſame: and moreover, that all the hides and ſkins, and pieces of hides and skins, vellum and parchment, which ſhould be ſold or removed contrary to the ſaid act, ſhould be forfeited, and ſhould and might be ſeized by any of her Majeſty's officers, for her Majeſty's uſe: and whereas by one other act paſſed in the fifth year of the reign of his late majeſty King *George* the Firſt, intituled, *An act for continuing the duties on malt, mum, cyder, and perry, for the ſervice of the year one thouſand ſeven hundred and nineteen; and for enlarging the time for entering at the exchequer ſuch aſſignments of reverſionary annuities as are therein mentioned; and for the better ſecuring the duties on hides and ſkins, vellum and parchment*; it was enacted, for the better aſcertaining the ſaid duties, and for preventing the carrying on of frauds between the officers for the ſaid duties, and the traders and dealers in the manufactures and goods charged with the ſaid duties; and to the intent that hides and ſkins, and pieces of hides and ſkins, and vellum and parchment, after they have been weighed and taken an account of by the officers for the ſaid duties, may again be weighed and taken an account of by the ſupervisors and ſurveyors of the ſaid duties; That from and after the tenth day of *January*, one thouſand ſeven hundred and eighteen, all tanners, tawers, and dreſſers of hides and ſkins, and pieces of hides and ſkins, vellum and parchment, ſhould, from time to time, keep all ſuch hides and ſkins, and pieces of hides and ſkins, vellum and parchment, which have not been duly ſtamped by the officers for the ſaid duties, ſeparate and apart from all other hides and ſkins, and

and 5 Geo. 1.

pieces

pieces of hides and ſkins, vellum and parchment, which have been duly ſtamped by the officers for the ſaid duties; and ſhould alſo, from time to time, keep all ſuch hides and ſkins, and pieces of hides and ſkins, and vellum and parchment, as from time to time ſhould have been laſt ſtamped by the officers for the ſaid duties, ſeparate and apart from all other hides and ſkins, and pieces of hides and ſkins, vellum and parchment, which at any time or times before ſhould have been ſtamped by the officers for the ſaid duties, during the reſpective times therein after mentioned (that is to ſay) within the limits of the weekly bills of mortality, by the ſpace of twenty four hours next after ſuch ſtamping thereof by the ſaid officers, and in other places out of the limits of the ſaid weekly bills, by the ſpace of two days next after ſuch ſtamping thereof, unleſs the ſame ſhould reſpectively ſooner have been weighed and taken an account of by the reſpective ſurveyors or ſupervifors for the ſaid duties, on pain to forfeit, for every offence therein, the ſum of ten pounds: and whereas, for want of an expreſs proviſion, that no tanner, tawer, or dreſſer of hides and ſkins, and pieces of hides and and ſkins, ſhall remove or convey, or cauſe to be removed or conveyed, from his, her, or their yard or drying place, any of the ſaid hides and ſkins, or pieces of hides or ſkins, after the ſame have been weighed and ſtamped by the officers for the ſaid duties, before the ſame have been again weighed and taken an account of by the reſpective ſurveyors or ſupervifors for the ſaid duties, it is notorious, that many ſuch tanners, tawers, and dreſſers of hides and ſkins, and pieces of hides and skins, have, through various pretences, frequently removed and conveyed their hides and ſkins, and pieces of hides and ſkins, from their yards and drying places, and immediately after the ſame have been weighed and marked by the officer for the ſaid duties, whereby the reſpective ſurveyors and ſupervifors for the ſaid duties have been prevented from re-weighing and taking an account thereof, ſo that great frauds have been committed between the ſaid traders and the inferior officers of exciſe, contrary to the true intent and meaning of the ſaid laſt recited clauſe, and to the great detriment of the revenue and fair trader: now, in order to prevent ſuch frauds, and abuſes agreeable to the intent of the ſaid laſt recited clauſe; it is hereby enacted and declared by the authority aforeſaid, That no tanner, tawer, or dreſſer of hides or ſkins, or pieces of hides or ſkins, chargeable with the reſpective duties by law payable for the ſame, ſhall at any time or times, from and after the fifth day of *July*, one thouſand ſeven hundred and ſixty five, remove or convey, or cauſe, procure, or ſuffer, to be removed or conveyed, from his, her, or their yard or drying place, or from his, her, or their entered ſtore-rooms, any hides or ſkins, or pieces of hides or ſkins, before the expiration of twenty four hours next after the ſtamping thereof by the officers for the ſaid duties, unleſs the ſame ſhall ſooner have been weighed by the reſpective ſupervifors or ſurveyors for the ſaid duties; to the end that the ſaid reſpective ſupervifors and ſurveyors may have an opportunity

Tanners, &c. not to remove the hides or skins, &c. from the drying places or ſtore-rooms for 24 hours after the ſtamping thereof by the officer for the duties, on penalty of 20 l. unleſs they ſhall have been ſooner weighed by the ſupervifor

and any additional weight which ſhall be then found, is to be charged with the duty.

tunity to re-weigh the ſame after the ſaid officers: and if upon the re-weighing any ſuch hides or ſkins, or pieces of hides or ſkins, any additional weight ſhall be found, ſuch hides or ſkins, or pieces of hides or ſkins, ſhall be liable to, and chargeable with, the reſpective rates and duties by law payable for ſuch hides or ſkins, according to ſuch laſt mentioned weight: and if any ſuch tanner, tawer, or dreſſer of hides or ſkins, or pieces of hides or ſkins, ſhall remove, or cauſe or ſuffer to be removed, any ſuch hides or ſkins, or pieces of hides or ſkins, from any of his, her, or their yards or drying places, or entered ſtore-rooms, contrary to the true intent and meaning of this act; he, ſhe, or they, ſhall, for every ſuch offence, forfeit and loſe the ſum of twenty pounds.

Tanners to provide proper ſcales and weights in their drying places,

XXII. And, to the end the ſaid reſpective ſurveyors and ſupervisors may not be unneceſſarily delayed in the execution of their duty, it is hereby enacted by the authority aforeſaid, That from and after the ſaid fifth day of *July*, one thouſand ſeven hundred and ſixty five, all and every ſuch tanners, tawers, and dreſſers of hides and ſkins, ſhall, at their reſpective yards or drying places, be obliged to provide and keep, at their own coſts and charges, ſufficient and juſt ſcales and weights for the re-weighing ſuch hides and ſkins, and pieces of hides and ſkins; and to bring the ſame to the ſcales, and to aſſiſt the ſaid reſpective ſurveyors and ſupervisors in the re-weighing ſuch hides and ſkins, and in examining, from time to time, the depending ſtock of every ſuch tanner, tawer, or dreſſer of hides and skins, and pieces of hides and skins, and if any ſuch tanner, tawer or dreſſer of hides and skins, or pieces of hides and skins, ſhall refuſe or neglect to provide and keep, at their reſpective yards or drying places, ſufficient and juſt ſcales and weights for the re-weighing ſuch hides and skins, and pieces of hides and skins, or to bring the ſame to the ſcales, or to aſſiſt the ſaid reſpective ſurveyors and ſupervisors in the re-weighing ſuch hides and skins, or pieces of hides and skins, or in the examining from time to time, their reſpective depending ſtocks as this act directs; every ſuch tanner, tawer, and dreſſer of hides and skins, or pieces of hides and skins, ſo refuſing or neglecting, ſhall, in each and every ſuch caſe, forfeit and loſe the ſum of fifty pounds.

and to bring the skins to the ſcales, and aſſiſt the ſupervisor in re-weighing the ſame, and in examining their depending ſtocks, on penalty of 50l.

Recital of clauſes in act 5 Annæ,

XXIII. And whereas by an act of parliament made and paſſed in the fifth year of the reign of her late majeſty Queen *Anne*, intituled, *An act for an union of the two kingdoms of* England *and* Scotland; it is, by the eighteenth article of the ſaid act of union, declared and enacted, That the laws concerning regulation of trade, cuſtoms, and ſuch exciſes to which *Scotland* is, by virtue of this treaty, made liable, be the ſame in *Scotland*, from and after the union, as in *England*; and by the ſeventh article of the ſaid act of union, it is alſo declared and enacted, That all parts of the united kingdom be, for ever, from and after the union, liable to the ſame exciſes upon all exciſeable liquors; excepting only that the thirty four gallons *Engliſh* barrel of beer or ale, amounting to twelve gallons *Scots* preſent meaſure, ſold in *Scotland* at nine ſhillings and ſix pence ſterling, excluding all duties,

duties, and retailed, including duties, at two pence the *Scotch* pint, or eighth part of the *Scots* gallon, be not after the union liable, on account of the present excise upon exciseable liquors in *England*, to any higher imposition than two shillings sterling upon the aforesaid thirty four gallons *English* barrel, being twelve gallons the present *Scots* measure; yet nevertheless doubts have been raised whether the brewers of that particular species of beer or ale mentioned and described in the said seventh article of the said treaty of union, and commonly called and known by the name of *Two Penny Beer* or *Ale*, are within the description and meaning of an act of parliament made and passed in the seventh and eighth years of the reign of King *William* the Third, intituled, *An act for laying several duties upon low wines or spirits of the first extraction; and for preventing the frauds and abuses of brewers, distillers, and other persons chargeable with the duties of excise*; and by reason of such doubts, great frauds and abuses have been, and are, daily committed and made by the brewers of such beer or ale, which is generally called *Two Penny Beer* or *Ale*, by their refusing to permit or suffer the gauger or gaugers, officer or officers, to stay and continue in their brew-houses, store-houses, or other places, in the same manner as all other brewers are obliged and accustomed to permit and suffer them, to see such guiles or brewings brewed off, cleansed, and carried out without mixture, and by their fraudulently carrying a great part of their beer or worts away from the sight and view of such gauger or gaugers, officer or officers, before the same have been charged with any duty, and which is evidently discovered to be the practice of such brewers, from the constant great disparities which have been, and still are, from time to time, found by the gauger or gaugers, officer or officers, on their surveys, between the cheque gauges of their beer or worts taken in the coppers, and the real gauges of the same beer or worts when cast out of the coppers and thrown into the backs or coolers, and from whence the duty is charged, whereby his Majesty's revenue has been lessened and diminished more than one half to what the same was formerly: now, for removing and putting an end to such doubts, and for the more effectual preventing the frauds aforesaid, and other frauds practised to the detriment of the revenue; be it declared and enacted by the authority aforesaid, That it is the true intent and meaning of the said act, and articles of union, that the said act made and passed in the seventh and eight years of the reign of his late majesty King *William* the Third, herein before mentioned, and every clause, matter, and thing, therein contained (except such part thereof as was repealed by an act passed in the eighth and ninth years of the reign of his said majesty King *William* the Third) doth now, and always did, by virtue of the said act, and articles of union, extend to that part of the united kingdom of *Great Britain*, called *Scotland*, and to all and every the brewers, inn-keepers, and victuallers therein, of what kind, quality, or denomination soever they shall brew or make their beer or ale; and that if hereafter any

and act of 7 & 8 W. 3.

The recited act of 7 & 8 W. 3. declared, in it's original intention and meaning, to extend to Scotland,

and to the brewers, inn-keepers, and victuallers therein, brewing their own beer or ale;

Officers accordingly to be admitted into such houses to gauge the worts,

any common brewer, inn-keeper, or victualler, in that part of *Great Britain* called *Scotland*, whether such common brewer, inn-keeper, or victualler, shall brew or make party guiles of strong and small beer, or party guiles of strong two penny beer or ale, and small beer, or whether such common brewer, inn-keeper, or victualler, shall brew or make intire guile or guiles of one sort of beer or ale only, of what kind or quality the same shall be, shall, upon due request or demand made by the gauger or gaugers, or other officer or officers, in the day-time, or, in the night, in the presence of a constable or other lawful officer of the peace, refuse to permit such gauger or gaugers, or other officer or officers, to enter and come into his house, brewhouse, storehouse, or other places belonging to or used by such brewer, inn-keeper, or victualler, or being lawfully entered, shall refuse such gauger or gaugers, or other officer or officers, to stay and continue in his brewhouse or place of brewing whilst his guile is brewing, and quietly gauge and take an account of all and every the wort and worts as they are brewed off and let into his backs, tuns, or other vessels, and to see their strong and small, or other beer or ale of what kind or quality soever, cleansed and carried out without mixture, and to gauge and take an account of the goods in the mash tun, or of the quantity of malt from which such wort or worts are drawn or made, or during such part of such brewing or operation as such gauger or gaugers, officer or officers, shall think fitting and convenient to stay and continue; such brewer, innkeeper, or victualler, for every such offence, shall forfeit and lose the sum of twenty pounds; and the informer or prosecutor shall not be obliged to prove that such brewer, innkeeper, or victualler, did carry or deliver out any part of such guile of beer or ale before he paid and cleared the duties for the same; any thing in the former acts of excise, or any other act or statute to the contrary notwithstanding.

and to continue there till they have done their duty;

on penalty of 20 l.

Act 8 & 9 W. 3.

XXIV. And whereas doubts have arisen upon the construction of an act of parliament made and passed in the eighth and ninth years of the reign of King *William* the Third, intituled, *An act for repealing a clause in a former act relating to party guiles, and for the better preventing frauds and abuses of brewers and others chargeable with the duties of excise*, whether such common brewers of the beer or ale aforesaid, commonly called or known by the name of *Two Penny Beer* or *Ale*, are by the said act obliged to declare to the gauger or gaugers, the quantity and quality of such beer or ale so brewed or made by them, in the same manner as common brewers of party guiles now do by virtue of the said act: now to obviate those doubts, be it enacted and declared by the authority aforesaid, That it is the true intent and meaning of the said act and articles of union, that the said act of the eighth and ninth years of the reign of King *William* the Third do, by virtue of the said act and articles, extend to all and every part of the united kingdom, and to all and every common brewer within the same: and that all and every common brewer,

The recited act of 8 & 9 W. 3. declared in it's original intention and meaning, to extend to Scotland, and to all common brewers within the same.

Common brewer to de-

brewer, whether of the beer or ale aforesaid, commonly called and known by the name of *Two Penny*, or of what kind or quality soever he shall make his worts, beer, or ale, shall declare (on demand made by the gauger or gaugers) the quantity and quality of the beer, ale, or worts, made and brewed by him or them on each respective guile or brewing, before any part of such guile is cleansed or removed out of his tuns, or other vessels or utensils: and in case any such brewer, or his respective servants, brewing or making such guile of beer or ale, shall refuse to make such declaration as aforesaid, such gauger or gaugers shall charge and return the whole of such guile to be strong, and such brewers shall pay the duties thereof accordingly; and shall also forfeit and lose, for every barrel of beer or ale contained in such guile, the sum of twenty shillings: and in case any common brewer, or his respective servant or servants, after such declaration made as aforesaid, shall make any increase of strong beer or strong ale, or two penny beer or ale, so declared by any ways or means whatsoever; or shall mix his beer or ale of one guile or brewing with any beer or ale of any other guile or brewing, or with small beer or returned drink, or with water, or by any other ways or means whatsoever; or in case such gauger or gaugers shall find any beer, ale, or worts, of the same guile laid off, over and above the quantity so declared as aforesaid; such brewers shall forfeit and lose for every barrel so increased or mixed, laid off, or found over and above the quantity so declared as aforesaid, the sum of five pounds; and the servant or servants of such brewer, or other person or persons, and every of them, who was or were any ways concerned, or aiding, or assisting, in making any such encrease or mixture after the said declaration, or in laying off any such beer or ale, or worts, of such guile, before such declaration made as aforesaid, shall forfeit and lose for every barrel so encreased, mixed, or laid off, the sum of twenty shillings; and in default of payment thereof, shall suffer three months imprisonment; unless it shall appear, that such encrease or mixture was made by adding to, or mixing with the same, any beer or ale that was left in his or her brewhouse of a former guile of his or her brewing; and unless it shall also appear, that such encrease or mixture was added or made in the sight and view of the proper gauger or officer.

clare to the officer the quantity and quality of the worts, before the guile is removed out of the tuns;

otherwise the whole is to be charged strong, and the duty to be paid accordingly; with 20 s. *per* barrel *extra*.

If, after declaration, any fraudulent increase or mixture shall be made in such beer;

or any of the guile shall be laid off: brewer to forfeit 5 l. *per* barrel,

and the persons assisting in such frauds to forfeit moreover 20s. *per* barrel: and on non-payment to be committed for 3 months.

XXV. And whereas by an act of parliament made and passed in the eighth and ninth years of his majesty King *William* the Third, intituled, *An act for repealing a clause in a former act relating to party guiles, and for the better preventing frauds and abuses of brewers and others chargeable with the duties of excise*; it is, amongst other things, enacted, That if any common brewer shall, at any time after the tenth day of *April*, which was in the year of our Lord one thousand six hundred and ninety seven, without notice first given at the next office, erect or set up any tun, batch, float, cooler, or copper, or shall alter or enlarge any tun, batch, float, cooler, or copper, already erected or set up, or shall have or keep any private or concealed tun, batch, float, cooler,

Recital of clause in act 8 & 9 W. 3.

cooler, or copper, other than ſuch as are openly diſcovered and known to be commonly uſed in his brewhouſe, or place of brewing; every ſuch brewer ſhall forfeit and loſe for every tun, batch, float, cooler, and copper, ſo erected, ſet up, altered, or enlarged, kept private or concealed, without ſuch notice given as aforeſaid, the ſum of two hundred pounds: and whereas it very frequently happens that brewers do alter the ſituation and poſition of ſuch of their utenſils in their own favour, and in prejudice to the revenue, without giving any ſuch notice, whereby it is very difficult, and ſometimes impoſſible for the gauger or officer to aſcertain the true dips, and the quantity of the liquor contained therein, and thereby the good intent of the ſaid act is greatly defeated and rendered ineffectual: for remedy whereof, be it therefore enacted by the authority aforeſaid, That if any common brewer ſhall, from and after the ſaid fifth day of *July*, one thouſand ſeven hundred and ſixty five, alter the ſituation or poſition of any tun, batch, float, cooler, or copper, after the ſame hath been ſet up and fixed, without firſt giving notice thereof in writing to the officer of the diviſion or place appointed to ſurvey, gauge, and take an account of his beer, ale, or worts; or ſhall place any boards, ſtone, wood, or any other materials, at, in, or upon, the dipping place or places, of any ſuch tun, batch, float, cooler, or copper, or ſhall by any other ways or means prevent or hinder ſuch gauger or officer from taking true dips and gauges of ſuch beer, ale, or worts, every ſuch brewer ſhall, for every ſuch offence, forfeit and loſe the ſum of twenty pounds.

Common brewer altering the ſituation or poſition of his brewing utenſils, without giving notice to the proper officer,

or placing any thing in the dipping place, &c. to prevent the taking the true gauge,

forfeits 20 l.

Recital of clauſe in act 18 Geo. 2.

XXVI. And whereas by a clauſe in an act of parliament paſſed in the eighteenth year of the reign of his late majeſty King *George* the Second, intituled, *An act for repealing the preſent inland duty of four ſhillings* per *pound weight upon all tea ſold in* Great Britain, *and for granting to his Majeſty certain other inland duties in lieu thereof*; *and for the better ſecuring the duty upon tea, and other duties of exciſe*; *and for purſuing offenders out of one county into another*; reciting, That whereas by the laws then in force concerning the duties of exciſe, and other duties under the management of the commiſſioners of exciſe, in that part of *Great Britain* called *England*, all forfeitures and offences made and committed within the immediate limits of the chief office in *London*, were to be heard, adjudged, and determined, by the chief commiſſioners and governors of exciſe; and all ſuch forfeitures and offences made and committed within all or any other the counties, cities, towns, or places, in *England*, were to be heard and determined, by any two or more of the juſtices of the peace, reſiding near to the place where ſuch forfeitures ſhould be made, or offence committed; and reciting alſo, that many perſons chargeable with duties of exciſe, or other duties under the management of the ſaid commiſſioners, or incurring penalties by offences againſt the ſaid laws, did frequently avoid proſecutions for the ſame, by removing out of the juriſdiction wherein ſuch duties were charged, or offence committed, to the great prejudice of the revenue, and discouragement of the fair traders: for remedy whereof, it was by the said act enacted, That from and after the twenty fourth day of *June*, one thousand seven hundred and forty five, it should and might be lawful for the said commissioners and justices respectively within whose jurisdiction any person charged with any of the said duties, or who should have committed any offence against the said laws, or any of them, or against the said act, should be found, to summon, hear, adjudge, and determine, and issue any process or warrant, in the same manner as such commissioners might then do, in case of such offences as were committed within their respective jurisdictions; and in case the said commissioners or justices should, upon any judgement given by them respectively, issue a warrant or warrants of distress, and the person or persons authorized to execute such warrant, or any of them, should make a return thereto, that no sufficient distress could be found, then it should and might be lawful for the said commissioners and justices respectively, within whose jurisdiction the party should at any time be found against whom such warrant should have been issued, upon producing to them such warrant and return thereof, to commit such offender to the next county gaol, till satisfaction should be made: and whereas, since the passing of the said clause, divers other rates and duties of excise, and other rates and duties, have by virtue of several acts parliament been put under the management of the respective commissioners of excise in *England* and *Scotland*; and it is proper that the provisions in the last recited clause should be extended to all and every law and laws concerning the duties of excise, or other duties under the management of the respective commissioners of excise in *England* and *Scotland*; be it therefore declared and enacted by the authority aforesaid, That all and every the powers, authorities, provisions, and directions, enacted by the said last recited clause, shall and may, from and after the fifth day of *July*, one thousand seven hundred and sixty five, be used, practised, applied, and put in execution, against all and every person or persons who shall commit any offence or offences against any act or acts of parliament concerning the duties of excise, or any other duties under the management of the respective commissioners of excise in *England* and *Scotland* for the time being, in as full and effectual manner, as if the said powers, authorities, provisions, and directions, had been enacted in the body of each respective act; any law, statute, or usage, to the contrary in any wise notwithstanding.

Powers and provisions enacted by the last recited clause, to be put in execution against all persons committing offences against any acts concerning the duties of excise.

XXVII. And whereas the laws already made to prevent the clandestine importing and landing of foreign brandy, rum, strong waters, or other spirits, in small vessels, which hover upon the coasts of this kingdom, have been found insufficient for that purpose; be it further enacted by the authority aforesaid, That from and after the fifth day of *July*, one thousand seven hundred and sixty five, if any foreign brandy, arrack, rum, strong waters, or spirits of any kind whatsoever, shall be imported

Where foreign spirits shall be brought into any part of Great Britain, in vessels of 100 tons burthen, or under,

ported or brought from any part of *Europ*
the first day of *December*, one thousand sev
five, shall be imported or brought from any
or *America*, into *Great Britain*, or into any p
or creek thereof, in any ship, vessel, or bo
one hundred tons, or under (except only f
men then belonging to and on board such
not exceeding two gallons for every such
ship, vessel or boat, with all her tackle, fu
and also all such brandy, arrack, rum, str
or the value thereof, shall be forfeited an
may be seized, prosecuted, condemned an
same manner as other forfeited goods and
exceeding fifty tons burthen, are directed t
ed, condemned and disposed of, by an act
year of the reign of his present Majesty,
the further improvement of his Majesty's re
for the encouragement of officers making seizu
vention of the clandestine running of goods int
jesty's dominions.

such spirits are liable to forfeiture, together with the vessel, &c. and may be seized, and sold, as forfeited goods, and vessels under 50 tons burthen, may by act 3 Geo. 3.

XXVIII. And it is hereby further ena
aforesaid, That from and after the fifth da
sand seven hundred and sixty five, no fore
neva, and that from and after the first d
thousand seven hundred and sixty five, no r
or brought into *Great Britain*, in any vess
not contain sixty gallons at the least (exce
of the seamen then belonging to and on b
in which the same shall be imported, not e
for each seaman) on forfeiture thereof, to
and divided, in the manner herein before r

No geneva or rum may be imported in less than 60 gallon casks,

on forfeiture thereof;

XXIX. Provided always, That in case
pear to the satisfaction of the commissioner
stoms in *England* or *Scotland* respectively,
the produce or manufacture of any of his
in *America*, shall be imported directly f
casks, without fraud or concealment, eith
master in the voyage, or for the private
traders so importing the same, or designed
by way of merchandize; that then, and
shall and may be lawful for the said respe
they think proper, to admit such rum to a
duties thereof to be accepted instead of t
before mentioned; any law, custom, or u
notwithstanding.

except British made rum from the plantations imported directly from thence and designed for private use,

which may be admitted to entry, and to pay the duties.

XXX. And whereas great quantities c
other spirits, are clandestinely run on shore i
small vessels which are cleared outwards fr
pretence of being destined with such goo
to prevent which practices for the future,
authority aforesaid, That from and after t

one thousand seven hundred and sixty five, if any brandy, rum, strong waters, or spirits of any kind whatsoever, shall be entered or shipped for exportation from the kingdom of *Ireland*, to any port or place not within the same kingdom, in any ship or vessel whatsoever, under the burthen of one hundred tons, except only for the use of the seamen then belonging to and on board such ship or vessel, not exceeding two gallons for each such seaman; every such ship or vessel, with all her tackle, furniture and apparel, and also all such brandy, rum, strong waters or spirits, shall be forfeited, and shall and may be seized by any officer or officers of the revenue in *Ireland*, and prosecuted, tried, determined and disposed of, in such and the like manner as any forfeiture incurred by the laws now in force in the said kingdom of *Ireland*, against the running or intending to run goods into that kingdom, may, by any act or acts of parliament now in force in that kingdom, be prosecuted, tried, determined, and disposed of.

Where spirits of any kind shall be shipped or entered for exportation from Ireland, in vessels under 100 tons burthen; such vessel, and spirits, may be seized, and are declared to be forfeited.

XXXI. And whereas tobacco, rum, and other goods, are shipped for exportation to the islands of *Faro* or *Ferro*, being part of the dominions of the king of *Denmark*, with no other intent than fraudulently to reland the same on the coasts of *Great Britain* or *Ireland*; which practices, if not prevented, will greatly diminish his Majesty's revenues of customs, and be very prejudicial to the fair traders: for remedy whereof, be it further enacted by the authority aforesaid, That no drawback or bounty shall be allowed for any goods whatsoever, which, from and after the fifth day of *July*, one thousand seven hundred and sixty five next, shall be exported from *Great Britain* or *Ireland*, to the said islands of *Faro* or *Ferro*; nor shall any cocket or clearance be granted for the exporting to the said islands any goods which are prohibited to be worn or used either in *Great Britain* or *Ireland*; any law, custom, or usage, to the contrary notwithstanding.

No drawback or bounty to be allowed for any goods exported from Great Britain or Ireland to the islands of Faro; nor cocket granted for exporting prohibited goods thither.

XXXII. And be it further enacted by the authority aforesaid, That if any merchant or other person shall enter any goods for exportation to foreign parts, other than to the said islands of *Faro* or *Ferro*, in order to obtain the drawback or bounty for the same; or if any goods which are prohibited to be worn or used in *Great Britain* or *Ireland*, shall be entered for exportation to foreign parts, other than to the said islands of *Faro* or *Ferro*; and such goods shall nevertheless be carried to the said islands, and landed there contrary to the true intent and meaning of this act; that then, and in every such case, the drawback or bounty paid or to be paid for the same, shall be forfeited; and the exporter of such goods, and the master of the ship or vessel on board which the same were loaden and exported, and every person concerned or assisting in the exportation or landing of the said goods, whether any drawback or bounty has been or is to be paid for the same or not, shall forfeit treble the value of the goods; and the ship or vessel on board which such goods were loaden and exported, with all her tackle, furniture and apparel, shall

Penalty of entering goods for exportation to foreign parts, other than the islands of Faro, in order to obtain the drawback or bounty; and also prohibited goods so enter'd; and afterwards landing the same at Faro, is forfeiture of the bounty, and treble value of the goods, together with the vessel.

ſhall alſo be forfeited, and ſhall and may be ſeized and proſecuted by any officer of the cuſtoms or exciſe in *Great Britain* or *Ireland*; and the ſeveral penalties and forfeitures herein beforementioned, ſhall and may be ſued for and recovered in ſuch and the like manner as any forfeiture incurred by any law of the revenue may be ſued for and recovered in the kingdoms of *Great Britain* or *Ireland* reſpectively; one moiety of which penalties and forfeitures (after deducting the charges of proſecution) ſhall be to the uſe of his Majeſty, his heirs and ſucceſſors; and the other moiety to ſuch officer of the cuſtoms or exciſe as ſhall ſue or proſecute for the ſame.

The iſlands of Faro to be included in the oath upon debentures for goods exported.

XXXIII. And be it further enacted by the authority aforeſaid, That from and after the ſaid fifth day of *July*, one thouſand ſeven hundred and ſixty five, the ſaid iſlands of *Faro* or *Ferro*, ſhall be added to, and included in the oath upon all debentures for goods exported, whereon the exporter is to ſwear, that ſuch goods are not landed or intended to be landed in *Great Britain* or *Ireland*.

No coffee to be imported in leſs packages than 112 lb. neat coffee,

on penalty of forfeiture.

XXXIV. And, for preventing the frauds frequently uſed in importing coffee in ſmall quantities, whereby the ſame is more eaſily conveyed away without payment of any duties for the ſame; be it hereby enacted by the authority aforeſaid, That from and after the fifth day of *July*, one thouſand ſeven hundred and ſixty five, no coffee ſhall be brought or imported from any part of *Europe*; or from and after the firſt day of *December*, one thouſand ſeven hundred and ſixty five, ſhall be brought or imported from any part of *Aſia*, *Africa*, or *America*, into *Great Britain*, or into any port, harbour, haven or creek thereof, in any ſhip or veſſel from any place or places whatſoever beyond the ſeas, otherwiſe than in caſk, cheſt, caſe, bag or other package, each caſk, cheſt, caſe, bag, or other package whereof, ſhall contain one hundred and twelve pounds of neat coffee at the leaſt, to be ſtowed openly in the hold of ſuch ſhip or veſſel importing the ſame; on pain to forfeit all the coffee ſo brought or imported contrary to this act, with the package containing the ſame, which ſhall and may be ſeized by any officer of the cuſtoms or exciſe.

Recital of clauſe in act 10 Geo. 1.

XXXV. *And whereas by an act of parliament paſſed in the tenth year of the reign of his majeſty King* George *the Firſt, intituled,* An act for repealing certain duties therein mentioned, payable upon coffee, tea, cocoa nuts, chocolate and cocoa paſte imported; and for granting certain inland duties in lieu thereof; and for prohibiting the importation of chocolate ready made, and cocoa paſte; and for better aſcertaining the duties payable upon coffee, tea, and cocoa nuts imported; and for granting relief to *Robert Dalziell*, late earl of *Carnwath*; *it was, amongſt other things, provided and enacted, That from and after the twenty fourth day of* June, *one thouſand ſeven hundred and twenty four, all coffee, tea, and cocoa nuts, imported into the kingdom of* Great Britain *from any foreign parts, upon the entry thereof at the cuſtom-houſe, and paying or ſecuring the ſeveral ſubſidies and additional impoſts which ſhould then remain due thereon, ſhould be forthwith carried or put ut into such warehouse or warehouses as should be for that purpose rovided, at the charge of the respective importer or importers of such offee, tea and cocoa nuts, and shall be approved of by the commission-rs of his Majesty's customs, or the major part of them, for the time eing: and whereas several persons have refused or neglected, for a ong time after the importation of such coffee, tea, and cocoa nuts, to nake due entry thereof, and to pay or secure the several subsidies and dditional imposts due thereon, and have insisted to keep the same on oard, by which means the revenue of excise hath been unnecessarily ut to a very considerable expence, by keeping tidesmen on board the hips; and great opportunities are also obtained for embezling or run-ing on shore all or part of the said coffee, tea and cocoa nuts, with-ut payment of any duties for the same, notwithstanding the utmost are and vigilance of the officers of excise to prevent the same;* for emedy whereof, be it hereby enacted by the authority afore-aid, That from and after the fifth day of *July*, one thousand se-ven hundred and sixty five, the importer or importers of any cof-ee, tea, or cocoa nuts, imported into *Great Britain*, within thir-y days next after the master or purser, for that voyage, of the hip or vessel wherein the said coffee, tea, or cocoa nuts, shall e imported or brought into the kingdom of *Great Britain*, shall ave, or ought to have, made a just and true entry or report, pon oath, of the burthen, contents, and lading of such ship r vessel, in pursuance of the directions of the statute made in he thirteenth and fourteenth years of the reign of King *Charles* he Second, intituled, *An act for preventing frauds and regulating ibuses in his Majesty's customs*, shall make due entry thereof, with an officer of the excise, to be appointed by the respective com-missioners of excise in *England* and *Scotland* for that purpose, and land the same, to be put in the warehouses as aforesaid, on pain to forfeit, for every neglect or refusal to make such entry, or to land the same according to the directions of this act, all such coffee, tea and cocoa nuts, with the package wherein the same shall be contained on board such ship or vessel, belonging to such importer or importers of the same so neglecting or refusing; which shall and may be seized by any officer or officers of the excise.

Importer of coffee, tea, or cocoa nuts, is to enter the same within 30 days after report made at the custom house of the ship's arrival, &c.

pursuant to act 13 & 14 Car. 2.

and is to duly land the same, to be put in the King's warehouses,

on forfeiture thereof;

XXXVI. Provided always, and it is hereby enacted and de-clared by the authority aforesaid, That the last-mentioned pro-vision shall not extend, or be construed to extend, to any cof-fee or tea imported, or to be imported, by the *East India* com-pany.

but this is not to extend to any tea or coffee imported by the East India company.

XXXVII. *And whereas in cases where any person or persons is or are at liberty to export to foreign parts any wares or merchandizes, subject to the duties under the management of the commissioners of ex-cise, such person or persons is or are required, by the laws now in be-ing, to make proof upon oath or by affirmation, that the duty of such wares or merchandizes hath been paid or secured, according to the several acts by which such duty is respectively laid upon such wares or merchandizes; which oath or affirmation the collector, who received the said duty, is thereby required and impowered to administer; and also*

alſo to give to ſuch perſon or perſons gratis *a certificate or certificates, expreſſing the kinds and weights of ſuch wares or merchandizes, and the duties paid for the ſame: and whereas it frequently happens, that ſuch collectors are abſent from home, in the execution of other parts of their duty, when ſuch perſons, ſo intending to export ſuch wares or merchandizes, do apply, in order to make ſuch proof upon oath or by affirmation, and to receive ſuch certificate, by which means ſuch perſons are prevented from or greatly delayed in the exportation of ſuch wares or merchandizes*; be it therefore enacted by the authority aforeſaid, That from and after the ſaid fifth day of *July*, one thouſand ſeven hundred and ſixty five, it ſhall and may be lawful for ſuch perſon or perſons, as ſhall be appointed by the commiſſioners of exciſe in *England* and *Scotland* reſpectively for the time being, or the major part of them reſpectively, within their ſeveral diſtricts, to adminiſter ſuch oath or affirmation, in the abſence of the reſpective collectors, to the perſons ſo applying for the ſame, in order to export ſuch wares and merchandizes as aforeſaid; and to give *gratis* to ſuch perſon ſuch certificate or certificates, ſo required by the ſeveral acts by which ſuch duty is reſpectively laid upon ſuch wares or merchandizes, in ſuch manner as the collectors of exciſe are now by law required and impowered to do.

Perſons ſpecially appointed by the commiſſioners of exciſe, may, in the abſence of the collector, adminiſter the oath required to be taken on the exportation of goods liable to the duties of exciſe, and grant proper certificates.

XXXVIII. *And whereas it is expedient that the like proviſions which are made by law to prevent the clandeſtine landing of tea, and foreign ſpirituous liquors, from veſſels hovering upon the coaſt of* Great Britain, *ſhould be extended to coffee, and ſuch goods as are liable to forfeiture upon being imported into this kingdom*; be it therefore enacted by the authority aforeſaid, That from and after the fifth day of *July*, one thouſand ſeven hundred and ſixty five, when any ſhip or veſſel whatſoever coming or arriving from foreign parts, and having on board twenty pounds weight of coffee, or any goods whatſoever which are liable to forfeiture by any act of parliament now in force, upon being imported into *Great Britain*, ſhall be found at anchor, or hovering within the limits of any of the ports of this kingdom, or within two leagues of the ſhore, or ſhall be diſcovered to have been within the limits of any port, and not proceeding on her voyage, wind and weather permitting, unleſs in caſe of unavoidable neceſſity and diſtreſs of weather, of which neceſſity and diſtreſs the maſter, purſer, or other perſon having or taking the charge or command of ſuch ſhip or veſſel, ſhall give notice to, and make proof of, before the collector or other chief officer of the cuſtoms of ſuch port as aforeſaid, immediately after the arrival of ſuch ſhip or veſſel into the ſaid port; all ſuch goods, together with the cheſts, boxes, caſks, and other package whatſoever, containing the ſame goods, or the value thereof, ſhall be forfeited and loſt, whether bulk ſhall then have been broken or not; and the ſhip or veſſel, on board which ſuch goods ſhall be ſo found, with all her tackle, furniture and apparel, ſhall alſo be forfeited and loſt, provided ſuch ſhip or veſſel doth not exceed the burthen of fifty tons; and the ſame ſhall and may be ſeized, proſecuted, condemned,

Veſſels not exceeding 50 tons burthen, arriving from foreign parts, found hovering on the coaſt, having 20lb. of coffee, or other goods on board liable to forfeiture,

may be ſeized; and the veſſels and goods are confiſcated,

ed, and disposed of, in the same manner as other forfeited goods and ships or vessels not exceeding fifty tons burthen, are directed to be seized, prosecuted, condemned, and disposed of, by an act made in the third year of the reign of his present Majesty, intituled, *An act for the further improvement of his Majesty's revenue of customs; and for the encouragement of officers making seizures; and for the prevention of the clandestine running of goods from any part of his Majesty's dominions.*

and are to be disposed of as directed by Act 3 Geo. 3.

XXXIX. And in order to prevent any collusive agreements between the officers of his Majesty's customs or excise making seizures, and the owners or other persons concerned in the importing or landing any goods liable to forfeiture; it is further enacted by the authority aforesaid, That, from and after the fifth day of *July*, one thousand seven hundred and sixty five, if any officer of the customs or excise, or other person authorized to make seizures, shall seize any goods as forfeited by this act; or any tea, foreign brandy, arrack, rum, strong waters, or spirits, as forfeited, by an act made in the ninth year of the reign of his late majesty King *George* the Second, intituled, *An act for indemnifying persons who have been guilty of offences against the laws made for securing the revenues of customs and excise, and for enforcing those laws for the future*; on board any ship or vessel whatsoever, and shall not seize and prosecute the ship or vessel on board which such goods shall have been brought, found, or seized; or if any such officer or officers shall seize any goods, wares, or merchandizes whatsoever, which shall have been unshipped, landed, removed, or carried, contrary to law, and shall not also seize and prosecute the boat, vessel, cart, horse, or other cattle or carriage, made use of in the removing, carrying, or conveying of such goods; and shall not discover to the commissioners of his Majesty's customs or excise, the persons concerned in unshipping, or receiving such goods, so that they may be prosecuted for the penalties incurred by law for such offences; such officer and officers shall, in each and every such case, in lieu and instead of the moiety or share which he or they is or are now intitled to by law upon the condemnation of such goods, be intitled to no more than one third part of the net produce arising by the sale of such goods; and the remaining two thirds shall be to the use of his Majesty, his heirs and successors; any law, custom, or usage, to the contrary notwithstanding.

Where officers shall make seizures pursuant to this act, or act 9 Geo. 2. on board any vessel, and not seize and prosecute the ship.

or shall make seizures on shore, and not seize and prosecute the cattle and carriage, &c. employed in running the same,

and discover the persons concerned therein;

they are to receive, instead of a moiety, but one third of the produce arising by the sale; the rest to go to the crown

XL. And whereas great frauds have been carried on by the makers and proprietors of salt, in collusion with the officers appointed for the duties on salt; which frauds have been greatly prejudicial, not only to the revenue, but to the fair trader: and whereas provision has not hitherto been made for subjecting such of the said officers as are guilty of these evil practices to any penalty, other than the penalty of the bond given by them for the faithful discharge of their trust, which penalty is not sufficient to prevent such frauds; be it therefore enacted by the authority aforesaid, That from and after the fifth day of *July*, one thouſand ſeven hundred and ſixty five, if any officer for the duties on ſalt ſhall deliver, or cauſe or ſuffer to be delivered, or be conſenting or privy to the delivering, removing, or conveying, *Britiſh* white ſalt, refined ſalt, rock ſalt, or ſalt rock, from any ſalt work, crib, ſtore-houſe, or other place, made uſe of for making, refining, or keeping, of any ſuch ſalt, or from any ſalt pit or pits, or to the landing any foreign ſalt out of any ſhip or veſſel, importing the ſame from parts beyond the ſeas, before the ſame be fairly, duly, and truly, entered and charged in the book or books enjoined to be kept for that purpoſe, whereby the maker, refiner, or owner of ſuch *Britiſh* white ſalt, refined ſalt, rock ſalt, or ſalt rock, or the merchant or importer of ſuch foreign ſalt, ſhall become chargeable with and liable to the full payment of the duties due and payable thereon to his Majeſty, his heirs, and ſucceſſors; ſuch officer or officers, for the duties on ſalt, ſo offending as aforeſaid, ſhall, in every ſuch caſe, forfeit and loſe, over and above the penalty of the bond he entered into, either by himſelf or ſureties, for the due performance of the truſt repoſed in him, double the value of ſuch ſalt, and alſo ten ſhillings *per* buſhel, and after that rate for any greater or leſſer quantity.

Officers for the ſalt duties being guilty of any fraud or colluſion in the execution of their office, forfeit over and above the penalty of the bonds given by them double the value of the ſalt, and alſo 10s per buſhel.

XLI. And whereas in all caſes where ſalt is ſhipped on board boats, barges, or other veſſels, in order to be carried down rivers or coaſtwiſe for the purpoſes of the fiſhery, or to be reſhipped for exportation, or otherwiſe, great care ſhould be taken for the preventing frauds that may be committed by clandeſtinely landing part of the ſaid ſalt in ſuch voyage: be it therefore enacted by the authority aforeſaid, That from and after the fifth day of *July*, one thouſand ſeven hundred and ſixty five, all ſuch ſalt, which ſhall be landed without the preſence of an officer for the duties on ſalt, ſhall be forfeited and loſt, and alſo ten ſhillings *per* buſhel, to be recovered of the owner of ſuch boat, barge, or other veſſel; and all veſſels, boats, barges, trows, or lighters, out of which any ſuch ſalt ſhall be taken or put on ſhore, together with their tackle and apparel, ſhall alſo be forfeited and loſt; and every perſon that ſhall take any ſuch ſalt out of any ſuch ſhip or veſſel of any kind, or carry the ſame on ſhore or convey the ſame from the ſhore when landed, or be aiding or aſſiſting therein, ſhall forfeit the ſum of twenty pounds for every ſuch offence.

Salt ſhipped for the fiſheries, &c, not to be landed but in preſence of an officer, on forfeiture thereof, and 10s per buſhel, with the veſſel, and 20l. by every perſon concerned therein.

XLII. And be it enacted by the authority aforeſaid, That from and after the fifth day of *July*, one thouſand ſeven hundred and ſixty five, it ſhall and may be lawful to and for the officer and officers of the ſaid duties on ſalt, at every place where he or they ſhall meet with any perſon or perſons carrying or conveying ſalt by day or by night, by land or by water, to demand a ſight of the permit or certificate which was granted by the collector or officer for the duties on ſalt, or ſome or one of them, for the carrying or conveying the ſaid ſalt; and if, upon producing ſuch permit or certificate, the ſaid officer or officers ſhall have reaſon to believe, or ſhall ſuſpect, that there is more

Where perſons ſhall be found carrying ſalt, officer may demand a ſight of the permits,

ſalt

ſalt than is expreſſed in ſuch permit or certificate, that then, and in every ſuch caſe, the ſaid officer or officers ſhall and may, at his own expence, re-weigh the ſaid quantity of ſalt; and if the ſalt, on the re-weighing the ſame, ſhall be found to be more in weight than what is contained in the ſaid permit or certificate that then the ſurpluſage that ſhall exceed the quantity contained in the ſaid permit or certificate ſhall be forfeited and loſt, and the perſon or perſons concerned in ſo carrying or conveying the ſame, ſhall alſo ſeverally be liable to the ſame penalties and forfeitures as any perſon or perſons is or are liable to by this and any other act or acts of parliament relating to the duties on ſalt for removing, conveying, or carrying, any ſalt or rock ſalt from any ſalt work or ſalt works, pit or pits, place or places, thereunto belonging, without due entry of the ſame, or payment of the duties, or giving ſecurity for ſuch duties, or without warrant, ticket, or licence, for conveying, carrying, or removing the ſame.

and re weigh ſuch ſalt, if he thinks it exceeds the quantity for which the permit is granted; the ſurplus ſalt is forfeited, and the perſons are liable to the penalties.

XLIII. And whereas it is neceſſary that the penalty inflicted by an act made in the firſt year of the reign of Queen *Anne*, upon perſons obſtructing the officers, for the ſaid duties, in the execution of their offices, or of the powers given by the ſaid act or any law relating to the ſaid duties then in force, ſhould be extended to perſons guilty of the like offences againſt this or any other act relating to the ſaid duties; be it further enacted, That if any perſon or perſons ſhall obſtruct or hinder any officer or officers, for the ſaid duties, in the execution of his or their offices, or of the powers given them by this act, or any other law relating to the ſaid duties, or ſhall beat or abuſe the ſaid officers, or any of them, in the execution of his or their offices; ſuch perſon and perſons ſhall, for every ſuch offence, forfeit and loſe the ſum of twenty pounds.

Perſons obſtructing, &c. officers in the execution of their duty, forfeit 20l.

XLIV. And be it declared and enacted by the authority aforeſaid, That from and after the fifth day of *July*, one thouſand ſeven hundred and ſixty five, if any ſalt, as well *Britiſh* as foreign rock ſalt, or ſalt refined from rock ſalt, or red herrings or white herrings, or any other ſort of fiſh, be ſeized for nonpayment of duties, or any other cauſe of forfeiture, by any of the laws relating to the duties on ſalt or fiſh now in force, and any diſpute ſhall ariſe whether the ſaid ſalt or herrings, or other kind of fiſh, had been duly entered, and the duties for the ſame duly paid, or ſecured to be paid; or that ſuch ſalt or herrings, or other kind of fiſh, had been legally condemned; or that the ſalt had been duly entered and locked up for the fiſhery, according to law; or that the quantity of ſalt uſed in the curing of fiſh as ſet forth in the curer's account, was truly uſed, then, and in ſuch caſes, the proof thereof ſhall lie on the owner or claimer of ſuch ſalt or herrings, or the curer of fiſh, and not on the officer who ſhall ſeize or ſtop ſuch ſalt, herrings, or other kind of fiſh; any thing in this or any other act of parliament to the contrary notwithſtanding.

Where ſalt or fiſh ſhall be ſeized for non-payment of duties, &c. and any diſpute ſhall ariſe thereupon, the *Onus probandi* is to lie on the owner.

XLV. And be it further enacted by the authority aforeſaid, That

Where salt or fish is made liable to forfeiture the package carriages and cattle employed therein, are forfeited also

That from and after the fifth day of *July*, one thousand seven hundred and sixty five, in all cases whatsoever where salt or fish of any kind shall be liable to seizure, by virtue of this or any former act of parliament, that the bags, sacks, casks, or other package, and also the carriages, horses, and other cattle, made use of in carrying and conveying the same, be also forfeited and lost; and that it be lawful for the officers of the salt duties, and the officers of the customs, to seize the same.

How all fines penalties, and forfeitures, for which no other provision is made, are to be sued for, recovered, or mitigated,

XLVI. And be it further enacted by the authority aforesaid, That all fines, penalties, and forfeitures, inflicted by this act, and for which no other directions are before particularly given, shall be sued for, recovered, levied, or mitigated, in manner following; that is to say, for all offences committed against any of the provisions herein before contained, with respect to the duties under the management of the commissioners of the customs, by such ways, means, and methods, as any fine, penalty, or forfeiture, is or may be sued for, recovered, levied, or mitigated, by any law or laws relating to the said duties; and for all offences committed against any of the provisions herein before contained, with respect to the duties under the management of the commissioners of excise, by such ways, means, and methods, as any fine, penalty, or forfeiture, is or may be sued for, recovered, levied or mitigated, by any law or laws of excise; and for all offences committed against any of the provisions herein before contained, with respect to the said duties on salt, by such ways, means, and methods, as any fine, penalty, or forfeiture, is or may be sued for, recovered, levied, or mitigated, by any law or laws relating to such duties; or that all or any of the said respective fines, penalties, and forfeitures, may be sued for and recovered by action of debt, bill, plaint, or information, in any of his Majesty's courts of record at *Westminster*, or in the court of exchequer in *Scotland* respectively; and that in all cases where it is not otherwise directed by this act, one moiety of every such fine, penalty, or forfeiture shall be to his Majesty, his heirs, or successors, and the other moiety to him or them who shall discover, inform, or sue for the same.

and applied.

XLVII. And be it further enacted by the authority aforesaid, That if any action or suit shall be commenced against any person or persons for any thing by him or them done or executed in pursuance of this act, or of any other act of parliament relating to his Majesty's revenues of customs, excise, or salt duties, the defendant or defendants in such action or suit shall and may plead the general issue, and give the said act and the special matter in evidence, at any trial to he had thereupon, and that the same was done in pursuance and by the authority of such act: and if afterwards a verdict shall pass for the defendant or defendants, or the plaintiff or plaintiffs shall become nonsuited, or discontinue his, her, or their action or prosecution, or judgement shall be given against him, her, or them, upon demurrer, or otherwise, then such defendant or defendants shall have treble costs awarded to him or them against such plaintiff or plaintiffs.

General issue.

Treble costs.

CAP.

CAP. XLIV.

An act for repealing the act made in the last session of parliament, intituled, An act for vesting the fort of *Senegal,* and its dependencies, in the company of merchants trading to *Africa*; *and to vest as well the said fort and its dependencies, as all other the* British *forts and settlements upon the coast of* Africa, *lying between the port of* Sallee *and* Cape Rouge, *together with all the property, estate and effects of the company of merchants trading to* Africa, *in or upon the said forts, settlements, and their dependencies, in his Majesty; and for securing, extending, and improving the trade to* Africa.

Preamble, reciting clauses in acts 23 and 25 Geo. 2.

WHEREAS *by two acts of parliament, the one made in the twenty third year of the reign of his late majesty King* George *the Second, intituled,* An act for extending and improving the trade to *Africa*; *and the other made in the twenty fifth year of the reign of his said late Majesty, intituled,* An act for the application of a sum of money therein mentioned, granted to his Majesty, for making compensation and satisfaction to the royal *African* company of *England,* for their charter, lands, forts, castles, slaves, military stores, and all other their effects whatsoever; and to vest the land, forts, castles, slaves, and military stores, and all other their effects, in the company of merchants trading to *Africa*; and for other purposes in the act mentioned; *all and every the* British *forts, lands, castles, settlements, and factories, on the coast of* Africa, *beginning at port* Sallee, *and extending from thence to the* Cape of Good Hope *inclusive, which had been granted to the royal* African *company of* England, *by their charter bearing date the twenty seventh day of* September, *in the twenty fourth year of the reign of King* Charles *the Second; or which had been after that time erected or purchased by the said company; and all other the regions, countries, dominions, territories, continents, coasts, ports, bays, rivers, and places, lying and being within the aforesaid limits, and the islands near adjoining to those coasts, and comprehended within the limits described by the said charter, and which at the time of passing the said last mentioned act were, or at any time theretofore had been, in the possession of, or claimed by, the said royal* African *company; together with the cannon and other military stores, canoemen, castle slaves, at and belonging to the said forts, castles, settlements, and factories, particularly mentioned and set forth in the first schedule to the said last mentioned act annexed; and also all contracts and agreements made by or for or on the behalf of the said royal* African *company, with any of the kings, princes, or natives, of any of the countries or places of the said coasts; and all other the property, estate, and effects whatsoever, of the said royal* African *company (except as in the said last mentioned act is excepted) were fully and absolutely vested in the corporation called and known by the name of* The company of merchants trading to *Africa, and their successors, to the intent and purpose that the said forts, settlements, and premisses, should be employed at all times thereafter only for the protection, encouragement and defence of the said trade: and whereas by another act made in the last session of parliament, intituled,* An act for vesting the fort of *Senegal*, and its dependencies, in the company of merchants trading to *Africa*; *the fort of* Senegal, *and its dependencies, were also vested in the said company of merchants, to be employed in the same manner, and under the same regulations, and subject to the same provisions, as the other forts and settlements on the coast of* Africa *were vested in the said company, and subject to, by virtue of the before-mentioned act made in the twenty third year of his late Majesty's reign:* and forasmuch as the good purposes proposed by the several before-recited acts of securing, improving, and extending, for the benefit of all his Majesty's subjects, the trade to and from *Africa* might be more effectually and compleatly provided for, if the said fort of *Senegal* and its dependencies, together with such other of the *British* forts and settlements upon the coast of *Africa* as lie to the northward of the cape commonly called *Cape Rouge*, were vested in his Majesty, his heirs and successors; be it therefore enacted by the King's most excellent Majesty by and with the advice and consent of the lords spiritual and temporal, and commons, in this present parliament assembled, and by the authority of the same, That the said act made in the last session of parliament, intituled, *An act for vesting the fort of* Senegal, *and its dependencies, in the company of merchants trading to* Africa, shall, except so much thereof as authorizes the committee of the company of merchants trading to *Africa*, to deduct annually out of the monies they shall receive, a further sum, not exceeding four hundred pounds, for the purposes in the said act mentioned, from and after the twenty fourth day of *June*, one thousand seven hundred and sixty five, be, and it is hereby repealed.

and act 4 Geo. 3.

Repeal of the act of 4 Geo. 3. except as to the annual deduction of 400l. by the committee of the African company.

African company divested of all the forts, territories, and factories, on the African coast, from the port of Sallee to Cape Rouge, &c.

II. And be it further enacted by the authority aforesaid, That from and after the said twenty fourth day of *June*, the said company of merchants trading to *Africa* shall be, and they are hereby absolutely divested of all and every the forts, lands, castles, settlements, and factories on the coast of *Africa*, beginning at the port of *Sallee* in *South Barbary*, and extending from thence to *Cape Rouge* inclusive, and all other the regions, countries, dominions, territories, continents, coasts, ports, bays, rivers, and places, lying and being within the aforesaid limits, and the islands near adjoining to those coasts, and comprehended within the said limits, and all other the property, estate and effects whatsoever, which by virtue of the said acts severally made in the twenty third and twenty fifth years of the reign of his late Majesty, or either of them, are now vested in the said company of merchants trading to *Africa*; and that from and after the said twenty fourth day of *June*, as well the said fort of *Senegal* and its

its dependencies, as all other the forts, lands, castles, settlements, and factories, on the coast of *Africa*, beginning at the port of *Sallee* in *South Barbary*, and extending from thence to *Cape Rouge* inclusive; and all other the property, estate, and effects whatsoever, possessed by the said company of merchants within the limits aforesaid, or claimed by them in respect to such their possessions within the said limits, be, and they are hereby, fully and absolutely vested in his Majesty, his heirs and successors.

and the same together with all other the property and effects the company possessed within the said limits, are vested in the crown.

III. And be it further enacted by the authority aforesaid, That all the powers, privileges, and authorities whatsoever, granted to the said company of merchants by either of the said acts made in the twenty third and twenty fifth years of his late Majesty's reign, so far as the same concern any of the territories, forts, settlements, or other the premisses lying within the limits aforesaid, and hereby vested in his Majesty, his heirs and successors, shall from and after the said twenty fourth day of *June* cease and determine.

Revocation of the powers and privileges granted to the African company;

IV. Provided always, and be it enacted by the authority aforesaid, That the trade to and from *Africa* shall continue free, and open to all his Majesty's subjects; and that it shall be lawful for all his Majesty's subjects, without preference or distinction, to trade and traffic to and from any of the ports or places hereby vested in his Majesty, his heirs, and successors, without any restraint whatsoever, other than and except the due observance of all such orders or regulations as shall, by and under the authority of his Majesty, his heirs, and successors, be established for the immediate defence of the forts, settlements, and factories, hereby vested in them, or for the better government of his Majesty's subjects residing or coming within the limits aforesaid; and that the forts, warehouses, and buildings, hereby vested in his Majesty, his heirs, and successors, shall continue to be free and open to all his Majesty's subjects, in the same manner and for the same purposes, as they have hitherto been under the authority of the said former acts.

and the trade to Africa declared open to all his Majesty's subjects;

together with the forts and warehouses, &c. hereby vested in the crown.

V. And be it further enacted by the authority aforesaid, That That it shall not be lawful for any of the officers or servants, employed by the committee of the said company on the coast of *Africa*, to export negroes from *Africa* upon their own account; and that if any such officer or servant shall be found to be directly or indirectly interested in such exportation of negroes from *Africa*, he shall be dismissed from the service of the said committee.

Committee's officers or servants not to export negroes on their own account, on penalty of dismission.

VI. And whereas, by the said act made in the twenty third year of his late Majesty's reign, it is enacted, That the committee of the said company of merchants shall give an account upon oath, of all the money received by them, and of the application thereof; but no provision is thereby made with respect to the accounts to be given by their officers and servants of the disposal or application of the goods and stores purchased, from time to time, by the said committee, and by them sent to the coast

coaſt of *Africa*, to be there uſed and applied as by the ſaid act is directed; be it therefore enacted by the authority aforeſaid, That every officer or other perſon, employed by the ſaid committee on the coaſt of *Africa*, to whom any part of ſuch goods or ſtores ſo purchaſed, and ſent out as aforeſaid, ſhall be conſigned and delivered, ſhall be required to tranſmit to the ſaid committee, once at leaſt in every year, an account of the diſpoſal and application of all ſuch goods and ſtores within the preceding year; having firſt made oath to the truth of ſuch account, before ſuch perſon as ſhall be authorized by his Majeſty, his heirs or ſucceſſors, to adminiſter the ſame; and that no ſuch officer or other perſon as aforeſaid, ſhall be deemed to be diſcharged, in reſpect of any ſuch goods and ſtores conſigned or delivered to him as aforeſaid, in any other manner than by an account given, upon oath, of the diſpoſal and application thereof; and if any ſuch officer or other perſon ſhall neglect to tranſmit to the ſaid committee ſuch account as is hereby required, the ſaid committee are hereby required and enjoined forthwith to ſuſpend him from the enjoyment of his ſalary; and in caſe, upon enquiry, they ſhall find ſuch neglect to have been wilful, they are hereby required and enjoined to diſmiſs him from their ſervice.

Committee's officers and ſervants to tranſmit an atteſted account once a year of the application and diſpoſal of the ſtores conſigned to them within the preceding year,

on penalty of ſuſpenſion of their ſalary.

VII. Provided nevertheleſs, and be it enacted by the authority aforeſaid, That it ſhall and may be lawful for his Majeſty, his heirs, and ſucceſſors, by and with the advice of his or their privy council, to make unto *George Glas*, and his aſſociates or aſſigns, a grant, by letters patent under the great ſeal, for any term not exceeding twenty one years, of the ſole right and privilege of carrying on trade and traffick to a certain port alledged to be diſcovered by him on the coaſt of *Africa*, called *Regeala* or *Gueder*, ſituate in *South Barbary*, between *Sallee* and *Cape Blanco*, and alſo to ſuch diſtrict of land adjoining thereto, as he ſhall have procured to be ceded, together with the ſaid port, to his Majeſty, upon ſuch terms, conditions, and reſervations, to be inſerted in the ſaid grant, as his Majeſty, his heirs, and ſucceſſors reſpectively, ſhall judge expedient; ſubject, however, to be redeemed at any time upon the payment of ſuch compenſation as the parliament ſhall think proper; any thing in the before recited act of the twenty third year of his late Majeſty's reign, or in this preſent act, contained to the contrary thereof in any wiſe notwithſtanding.

His Majeſty impowered to grant an excluſive right for 21 years, to Geo. Glas, of trading to port Regeala, &c.

ſubject however to redemption, by a parliamentary compenſation.

CAP. XLV.

An act for more effectually ſecuring and encouraging the trade of his Majeſty's American *dominions; for repealing the inland duty on coffee, impoſed by an act made in the thirty ſecond year of his late majeſty King* George *the Second; and for granting an inland duty on all coffee imported (except coffee of the growth of the* Britiſh *dominions in* America*); for altering the bounties and drawbacks upon ſugars*

ſugars exported; for repealing part of an act made in the twenty third year of his ſaid late Majeſty, whereby bar iron made in the ſaid dominions was prohibited to be exported from Great Britain, *or carried coaſtwiſe; and for regulating the fees of the officers of the cuſtoms in the ſaid dominions.*

Preamble.

WHEREAS *the improving and ſecuring the trade and commerce of the* Britiſh *colonies and plantations in* America *is highly beneficial, not only to the ſaid colonies and plantations but to* Great Britain: *and whereas it may on this account be proper to encourage the importation of deals, planks, boards and timber, from the ſaid colonies and plantations, whereby his Majeſty's royal navy, as well as ſhips employed in the merchants ſervice, may be furniſhed with ſuch materials at more reaſonable rates than at preſent; and great ſums of money at preſent expended among foreign nations, for the purchaſe of ſuch materials, may be ſaved:* may it therefore pleaſe your moſt excellent Majeſty, that it may be enacted, and be it enacted by the King's moſt excellent majeſty, by and with the advice and conſent of the lords ſpiritual and temporal, and commons, in this preſent parliament aſſembled, and by the authority of the ſame, That from and after the firſt day of *January*, one thouſand ſeven hundred and ſixty ſix, every perſon or perſons who ſhall, within the time appointed by this act, import, or cauſe to be imported, into this kingdom, directly from any of his Majeſty's dominions in *North America*, in any ſhip or ſhips that may lawfully trade thither, manned as by law is required, any good, ſound and merchantable deals, planks, boards and timber, of the following dimenſions, ſhall have and enjoy as a reward or premium for ſuch importation, the following ſums; that is to ſay,

Bounties granted on the importation of deals, planks, boards and timber, from North America;

For every hundred, containing ſix ſcore of ſuch deals, planks, and boards, not leſs than ten feet long, ten inches broad, and one inch and one quarter of an inch thick, ſo imported, from the firſt day of *January*, one thouſand ſeven hundred and ſixty ſix, to the firſt day of *January*, one thouſand ſeven hundred and ſixty nine, the ſum of twenty ſhillings; and in the like proportion for any greater length, and for any greater thickneſs, not exceeding four inches.

the premiums on the ſeveral ſpecies and dimenſions of ſuch goods.

For every load, containing fifty cubic feet of ſuch ſquared timber of all kinds, not leſs than ten inches ſquare, ſo imported, from the ſaid firſt day of *January*, one thouſand ſeven hundred and ſixty ſix, to the ſaid firſt day of *January*, one thouſand ſeven hundred and ſixty nine, the ſum of twelve ſhillings.

For every hundred of ſuch deals, planks and boards as above deſcribed, fifteen ſhillings; and for every load of ſuch timber, eight ſhillings; which ſhall be ſo imported, from and after the ſaid firſt day of *January*, one thouſand ſeven hundred and ſixty nine,

nine, to the first day of *January*, one thousand seven hundred and seventy two.

And for every hundred of such deals, planks and boards, ten shillings; and for every load of such timber, five shillings; which shall be imported, from and after the said first day of *January*, one thousand seven hundred and seventy two, to the first day of *January*, one thousand seven hundred and seventy five.

The bounty to be paid by the collector, or receiver general of the customs;

To be paid, upon demand, to the importer of such deals, planks, boards and timber, by the collector of the port where the same shall be imported, out of the customs, or any duties payable upon wood imported: and in case the collector of the port where the same shall be imported, shall not have money sufficient in his hands, he is hereby required to certify the same to the commissioners of the customs, who shall cause the same to be paid by the receiver general of his Majesty's customs; the bounty for the said goods imported into *England*, to be paid by the receiver general of the customs in *England*; and for such as shall be imported into *Scotland*, to be paid by the receiver general there.

A certificate being first produced, attested on oath, of such goods being of the growth and produce of the said colonies;

II. And in order to intitle the importer of such goods to the premium granted by this act, and to prevent frauds by importing foreign deals, planks, boards and timber; be it further enacted by the authority aforesaid, That all and every person or persons, importing any such deals, planks, boards and timber, into *Great Britain*, shall produce to the chief officer or officers of the customs, at the port of importation, a certificate or certificates, under the hand and seal of the governor, lieutenant governor, collector of his Majesty's customs, and naval officer, or any two of them, residing and being within any of his Majesty's dominions in *North America*, that, before the departure of such ship or vessel, ships or vessels, the person or persons, merchant, trader or factor, loading the same, had made oath before them, that the said goods so shipped on board (expressing in the said certificate the number, quantity and species, of each sort respectively) were truly and *bona fide* of the growth and produce of his Majesty's said dominions; which oath the said governor, lieutenant governor and collector of his Majesty's customs, and naval officer, or any two of them, are hereby authorized to administer; as likewise, upon oath to be made, in any port of *Great Britain*, by the master or masters of such ship or vessel, ships or vessels, importing such goods, that the same were truly laden on board such ship or vessel, ships or vessels, within some of his Majesty's dominions in *North America*; and that he or they know or believe, that the said goods were the produce of the said dominions.

and oath also being made at the port of arrival of their being duly laden on board in North America.

Officer, before granting a certificate for the bounty, may examine

III. And, that the officers of the customs may be the better able to discover any frauds intended for receiving the aforesaid premiums; be it further enacted by the authority aforesaid, That it shall and may be lawful for the said officers, and they are hereby required, before they make out any such certificate, to

examine

examine the ſaid goods by ſhifting the ſame, or by ſuch other means as they ſhall think proper, to find out and diſcover, whe- ther the ſame are good, ſound and merchantable.

IV. Provided always, That in caſe any doubt or diſpute ſhall ariſe between the ſaid ſurveyors or officers of the cuſtoms, and he owners or importers of ſuch of the aforeſaid goods as are mported into the port of *London*, as to the quality or condition of the ſame, it ſhall and may be lawful for the commiſſioners of is Majeſty's cuſtoms, if they ſhall think proper, to call two or nore merchants, or others well ſkilled in the commodity, who hall declare, upon oath, if required, their opinion, as to the uality and condition of the ſame: and according to the beſt of heir judgement, determine whether the ſaid goods are entitled o the premiums hereby granted, or not: and if any doubt or iſpute ſhall ariſe, as to the quality or condition of any of the foreſaid goods imported into any of the outports in *England*, roper and true deſcriptions of the quality and condition there- f, atteſted by two merchants, or others well ſkilled in the com- nodity, at the port or place where the ſame ſhall be imported; hich atteſtation ſhall be upon oath, before any one or more of is Majeſty's juſtices of the peace, who is or are hereby autho- zed to adminiſter the ſame; ſhall be ſent to the commiſſioners f the cuſtoms in *London*; and if imported into the outports in *cotland*, to the commiſſioners of the cuſtoms at *Edinburgh*, in ich manner as the reſpective commiſſioners ſhall direct, in or- er that, upon conſideration thereof by the reſpective commiſ- oners at *London* or *Edinburgh* reſpectively, it may be determin- d whether the ſame are intitled to the premiums hereby grant- l, or not.

Where there ſhall be any doubt as to the quality or condition of the goods; merchants may be called in to give their opinion, upon oath.

V. And be it further enacted by the authority aforeſaid, hat no fee, gratuity or reward ſhall be demanded, taken or ceived by any officer of his Majeſty's cuſtoms, for examining, ewing or delivering ſuch goods, with reſpect to the premium reward allowed by this act, or for the ſigning any of the cer- icates, in order to the receiving ſuch premium or reward, or r paying the ſame; and any ſuch officer demanding or taking ch fee or reward ſhall, for ſuch offence, forfeit his office, and for ever after incapable of executing any office or employ- ent under his Majeſty, his heirs and ſucceſſors.

Officer to take no fee for examining the goods, or granting a certificate, on penalty of diſability.

VI. And be it further enacted by the authority aforeſaid, hat if any ſuch deals, boards, planks or timber of the growth the *Britiſh* dominions in *North America*, ſhall, after the ſt day of *January*, one thouſand ſeven hundred and ſixty ſix, exported from *Great Britain*, that then, and in every ſuch ſe, the perſon or perſons ſo exporting the ſame ſhall, before entry thereof, pay unto the collector of the cuſtoms at the rt where the ſame ſhall be exported, or to the chief officer of cuſtoms there, the full ſum which is by this act allowed as a emium on all ſuch goods reſpectively as he intends to export.

The premium to be repaid on exportation of the ſaid goods;

VII. Provided always, That the ſaid collector or chief officer the cuſtoms, upon receiving of ſuch premium from the ex- porter

and the collector to charge him-

ſelf therewith accordingly; and to be brought to account.

porter of ſuch goods as aforeſaid, ſhall and do charge himſelf with the money ſo received; and the commiſſioners of his Majeſty's cuſtoms are to take particular care that the ſame be duly brought to the account of his Majeſty by ſuch collector or chief officer as aforeſaid.

If the goods ſhall be fraudulently exported without re-paying the premium, they are liable to forfeiture and double value.

VIII. And be it further enacted by the authority aforeſaid, That if any perſon or perſons, their agents or aſſigns, ſhall be found fraudulently to export ſuch goods, without paying ſuch premium to the collector or chief officer of the cuſtoms in manner as aforeſaid, ſuch perſon or perſons ſhall forfeit and loſe all ſuch goods and double the value thereof; one moiety whereof ſhall be to the uſe of his Majeſty, his heirs and ſucceſſors, and the other moiety to ſuch officer of the cuſtoms as ſhall ſeize or ſue for the ſame; to be proſecuted in any of his Majeſty's courts of record at *Weſtminſter*, or in the court of exchequer in *Scotland* reſpectively, wherein no eſſoin, protection or wager of law, or more than one imparlance, ſhall be allowed.

In caſe of doubt, with reſpect to the growth or product of ſuch goods Onus Probandi to lie on the owner.

IX. Provided always, That if any doubt or diſpute ſhall ariſe, whether any of the goods, or any part thereof, ſo to be exported, are of the growth or product of his Majeſty's dominions in *North America*, or of foreign growth or product, the *Onus Probandi* ſhall lie on the owner or claimer thereof, and not on the proſecutor; any law, cuſtom or uſage, to the contrary notwithſtanding.

Penalty of clandeſtinely importing, &c. like goods of foreign growth, and demanding the premium, is forfeiture of the veſſel, and 100l.

X. And be it further enacted by the authority aforeſaid, That if the maſter or owner of any ſhip or veſſel ſhall clandeſtinely import or receive in ſuch ſhip or veſſel, to be imported into *Great Britain*, any deals, boards, planks or timber, knowing the ſame to be foreign growth or product, and ſhall demand and receive for any ſuch foreign deals, boards, planks or timber, the reward or premium hereby granted, ſuch maſter or owner ſhall forfeit the ſum of one hundred pounds; and the ſhip or veſſel in which ſuch foreign deals, boards, planks or timber, ſhall be fraudulently imported, with all her guns, tackle, apparel and furniture, ſhall be alſo forfeited; and the ſame ſhall and may be ſeized, ſued for, proſecuted and divided, as herein before mentioned.

Recital of clauſe in act 32 Geo. 2.

XI. *And whereas by an act of parliament made in the thirty ſecond year of the reign of his late majeſty King* George *the Second, intituled,* An act for granting to his Majeſty a ſubſidy of poundage upon certain goods and merchandizes to be imported into this kingdom; and an additional inland duty on coffee and chocolate; and for raiſing the ſum of ſix millions ſix hundred thouſand pounds, by way of annuities and a lottery, to be charged on the ſaid ſubſidy and additional inland duty; *it was enacted and declared, That from and after the fifth day of* April, *one thouſand ſeven hundred and fifty nine, there ſhould be charged, levied, raiſed and paid, unto and for the uſe of his Majeſty, his heirs and ſucceſſors, for and upon all coffee to be ſold in* Great Britain, *wholeſale or retail, an additional inland duty, to be paid by the reſpective ſellers of ſuch coffee; (that is to ſay) for and upon all coffee to be ſold in* Great Britain, *an additional duty of one ſhilling* per *pound weight avoirdupois; and in that proportion for a greater or leſſer quantity, over and above the then preſent inland duty, and over and above all cuſtoms and duties then payable upon the importation thereof: and whereas it may tend to encourage the growth of coffee in the* Britiſh *dominions in* America, *and the importation thereof into this kingdom, if the ſaid additional duty granted by the ſaid laſt recited act was diſcontinued*; be it therefore enacted by the authority aforeſaid, That from and after the fifth day of *July*, one thouſand ſeven hundred and ſixty five, the ſaid additional duty of one ſhilling *per* pound weight avoirdupois, for and upon all coffee to be ſold in *Great Britain*, granted by the ſaid laſt recited act, ſhall ceaſe, and be no longer paid or payable: and that in lieu thereof, from and after the ſaid fifth day of *July*, one thouſand ſeven hundred and ſixty five, there ſhall be charged, levied, collected and paid, unto and for the uſe of his Majeſty, his heirs and ſucceſſors, for and upon all coffee, not being of the growth and product of the *Britiſh* plantations in *America*, to be ſold in *Great Britain* by wholeſale or retail, an additional inland duty, to be paid by the ſellers of ſuch coffee; (that is to ſay) for and upon all coffee, not being of the growth and product of the *Britiſh* plantations in *America*, to be ſold in *Great Britain*, an additional inland duty of ſix pence *per* pound weight avoirdupois; and in that proportion for a greater or leſſer quantity, over and above the inland duty of two ſhillings *per* pound paid on coffee, granted by an act made in the tenth year of the reign of his majeſty King *George* the Firſt, intituled, *An act for repealing certain duties therein mentioned payable upon coffee, tea, cocoa nuts, chocolate, and cocoa paſte imported; and for granting certain inland duties in lieu thereof; and for prohibiting the importation of chocolate ready made, and cocoa paſte; and for better aſcertaining the duties payable upon coffee, tea and cocoa nuts imported; and for granting relief to* Robert Dalzell, *late earl of* Carnwath, and over and above all cuſtoms and duties payable upon the importation thereof.

From and after 5 July, 1765, the additional inland duty of 1s. per lb. laid upon all coffee ſold in Great Britain, by the recited act, is to ceaſe; and 6d. per lb. to be paid in lieu thereof, for all coffee not of the growth of the Britiſh plantations in America, over and above the duties payable by act 10 Geo. 1.

XII. And be it further enacted by the authority aforeſaid, That the ſaid additional inland duty hereby granted to his Majeſty, ſhall be raiſed, levied, collected and paid, in the ſame manner, and under ſuch management, and under ſuch penalties, and forfeitures, and with ſuch power for recovering the ſame, and by ſuch rules, ways and methods as the former inland duties payable to his Majeſty upon coffee are raiſed, levied, collected and paid, as fully, to all intents and purpoſes, as if the ſeveral clauſes, powers, directions, penalties, and forfeitures relating thereto, were particularly repeated and again enacted in the body of this preſent act, and ſhall be paid into the exchequer in like manner, and appropriated to the ſame uſes to which the ſaid duty of one ſhilling *per* pound weight was made applicable.

The ſaid duty to be raiſed, &c. as former inland duty.

XIII. Provided always, and it is hereby further enacted, That nothing herein before contained ſhall extend, or be conſtrued to extend, to take off the additional duty of one ſhilling *per* pound upon coffee granted by the ſaid recited act of the thirty

The additional duty of 1s. per lb. laid by the recited act of 31 Geo. 2.

is not to be taken of ſuch coffee, as is or ſhall be lodged in the King's warehouſes before 5 July 1765, &c.

ty ſecond year of the reign of his late majeſty King *George* the Second, with reſpect to ſuch coffee which now is, or ſhall on or before the fifth day of *July*, one thouſand ſeven hundred and ſixty five, be lodged or ſecured in any warehouſe or warehouſes in purſuance of the directions of any former act or acts of parliament in that behalf made; nor ſhall the ſaid additional duty hereby granted be charged upon ſuch coffee ſo lodged or ſecured in any ſuch warehouſe or warehouſes.

Act 9 & 10 Will. 3.

XIV. *And whereas by an act of parliament made in the ninth and tenth year of the reign of King* William *the Third, intituled,* An act for granting to his Majeſty a further ſubſidy of tonnage and poundage, towards raiſing the yearly ſum of ſeven hundred thouſand pounds, for the ſervice of his Majeſty's houſhold, and other uſes therein mentioned, during his Majeſty's life; *and by ſeveral ſubſequent acts of parliament whichare now in force, ſeveral bounties or drawbacks, amounting in the whole to twelve ſhillings per hundred weight, are allowed upon the exportation of ſugar refined in this kingdom:* now to prevent any frauds that may be practiſed to the great prejudice of the revenue of the cuſtoms by the exportation of ſugars not completely refined, and ſugars made from ſcum, and other traſh and refuſe of ſugar houſes, under the denomination of refined ſugar, in order to obtain the bounties or drawbacks herein before-mentioned; be it enacted by the authority aforeſaid, That from and after the firſt day of *June*, one thouſand ſeven hundred and ſixty five, the ſeveral bounties or drawbacks allowed by the ſaid acts upon refined ſugars, ſhall ceaſe, determine and be no longer paid; and in lieu and inſtead thereof, a bounty of fourteen ſhillings and ſix pence *per* hundred weight ſhall be allowed and paid upon refined ſugar exported from *Great Britain* in the loaf compleat and whole, being net, that is to ſay, of one uniform whiteneſs throughout, and which hath gone through the operation of two or more clays ſince it was laſt in the pan, and hath been properly and thoroughly dried in the ſtove, according to the preſent practice of refining; any law, cuſtom or uſage, to the contrary notwithſtanding.

Drawbacks granted by former acts on exportation of refined ſugars, to ceaſe; and 14s. 6d. per Cwt. on loaf ſugar properly refined and dried, to be paid in lieu thereof.

Lump ſugars, duly refined, intitled to like drawback.

XV. Provided nevertheleſs, That if any of the ſaid refined ſugars, being either in ſmall or great loaves, commonly called *Lumps*, ſhall have gone through the operation of three clays, at the leaſt, ſince they were laſt in the pan, and ſhall be net, and ſhall have been thoroughly dried in the ſtove in the manner herein before directed, though ſuch loaves be exported without the ſmall ends or tips, they ſhall be eſteemed compleat and whole within the true intent and meaning of this act, and the exporter of the ſame ſhall receive the drawback or bounty accordingly.

In lieu of the former drawbacks on baſtards, ground ſugar, and candy,

XVI. And be it further enacted by the authority aforeſaid, That from and after the ſaid firſt day of *June*, one thouſand ſeven hundred and ſixty five, in lieu of all bounties and drawbacks which may have been allowed or paid, heretofore, on all refined ſugar called *Baſtards*, and *Ground Sugar*, and on refined ſugar called *Candy*, there ſhall be allowed and paid on the expor-

at *Britain* of all refined sugar called *Bastard*, or powdered refined sugar, and of all refined pieces (the said sugar having been twice clay- ied in the stove) and on all candy properly ctured, and free from dirt and scum, a boun- six shillings and four pence *per* hundred 'e; which said several bounties or drawbacks s and six pence, and six shillings and four e granted, shall be paid and allowed out of on which the former drawbacks or bounties ere payable.

a drawback is allowed of 6s. 4d. per. c. wt. on all such as shall be duly refined.

hereby further enacted by the authority a- e proper officers of the customs shall, upon on, either before or after shipping, find any h shall be entered for exportation, in order es or drawbacks thereon, to be less in quan- n the exporter's indorsement, or entered un- iination; or if such sugars shall not be re- ı the manner before directed; or if such roperly refined and manufactured, and free , all such sugar or candy shall be forfeited, e seized by any officer or officers of the cu- ed according to law.

Sugars fraudulently entered for exportation, in order to obtain the bounty,

may be seized, and are forfeited.

t further enacted by the authority aforesaid, wback or bounty is paid for any of the su- ı before mentioned, or any debenture made e refiner or refiners, not being the exporter sugar or candy, shall make oath before the oper officer of the customs, that he or they candy, expressing the quantity, and the time n or persons intending to export the same; s have respectively gone through the opera- expressed, and have been properly and ı the stoves, or that such candy has been manufactured according to the true intent act; and, as he or they verily believe, such produced from *Muscovado* sugar imported plantations in *America*; and that the several on were duly paid at the time of importing xporter or exporters of such sugars or candy, ı that such sugars or candy, being the sugars such bounty or drawback is then claimed, ars or candy, or part thereof, which were aid by such refiner or refiners; and before such debenture or debentures shall be paid, orters shall also make oath that the said su- een duly exported, his Majesty's searcher al- pping thereof, and all other requisites duly to the book of rates; and whenever the f such sugar or candy shall be the exporter , he or they shall then make oath, as well

Before the debenture is made out, refiner to make oath of the sale of such sugars to the exporter,

and of the quantity and quality thereof,

and that the same was produced from Muscovado sugar of the British plantations; and the duties paid.

Exporter also to make oath of the identity of such sugars, and of the due exportation thereof.

Refiner, being the exporter, to make like oath.

 of

of the due exportation of the ſame, as of the ſeveral particulars herein before directed to be ſworn to by him or them (excepting what relates to the ſale of the ſaid ſugars or candy) according to the true intent and meaning of this act.

Clauſe in act 4 Geo. 3.

XIX. And whereas by an act made in the laſt ſeſſion of parliament, intituled, *An act for granting for a limited time, a liberty to carry rice from his Majeſty's provinces of* South Carolina *and* Georgia, *directly to any part of* America *to the ſouthward of the ſaid provinces, ſubject to the like duty as is now paid, on the exportation of rice, from the ſaid colonies to places in* Europe *ſituate to the ſouthward of* Cape Finiſterre, which was to be in force for five years, from the twenty fourth day of *June*, one thouſand ſeven hundred and ſixty four, and from thence to the end of the next ſeſſion of parliament, liberty is granted to any of his Majeſty's ſubjects in any ſhip or veſſel built in *Great Britain*, or in his Majeſty's colonies in *America*, or belonging to any of his Majeſtys ſubjects, and navigated according to law, that ſhall clear outwards in any port of the ſaid provinces of *South Carolina* or *Georgia*, to ſhip or load rice in the ſaid provinces, and to carry the ſame directly to any part of *America* ſouthward of *South Carolina* or *Georgia*, without carrying the ſame to any other of his Majeſty's plantations in *America*, or to *Great Britain*; under certain limitations, reſtrictions, and penalties, therein contained; and whereas the granting the like liberty to export rice, in the ſame manner, from his Majeſty's colony of *North Carolina*, to any place in *America* ſouthward of *South Carolina* or *Georgia*, may be of great benefit to the ſaid colony of *North Carolina*; be it therefore further enacted by the authority aforeſaid, That from and after the fifth day of *July*, one thouſand ſeven hundred and ſixty five, it ſhall and may be lawful, during the continuance of the ſaid recited act, for any of his Majeſty's ſubjects, in any ſhip or veſſel built in *Great Britain*, or in his Majeſty's colonies in *America*, or belonging to any of his Majeſty's ſubjects, and navigated according to law, that ſhall clear outwards in any part of the ſaid province of *North Carolina*, to ſhip or load rice in the ſaid province, and to carry the ſame directly to any parts of *America* ſouthward of *South Carolina* and *Georgia*, without carrying the ſame to any other of his Majeſty's plantations in *America*, or to *Great Britain*, under the like entries, ſecurities, reſtrictions, regulations, limitations, duties, penalties, and forfeitures, as are particularly directed, appointed, limited, or enacted, with reſpect to rice carried from *South Carolina* and *Georgia*, to any part of *America* to the ſouthward of *South Carolina* or *Georgia*, in the ſaid in part recited act of the laſt ſeſſion of parliament, as fully and effectually, to all intents and purpoſes, as if the ſeveral clauſes, powers, directions, penalties, and forfeitures, relating thereto, were particularly repeated and again enacted in the body of this preſent act.

Liberty given to export rice from North Carolina, in the ſame manner as rice may be exported, under the recited act, from South Carolina and Georgia.

XX. And be it further enacted by the authority aforeſaid, That all duties which ſhall ariſe in reſpect of rice ſo carried from *North Carolina*, and the duties which, from and after the ſaid fifth

Duties payable upon the

fifth day of *July*, one thouſand ſeven hundred and ſixty five, ſhall ariſe in reſpect of rice carried from *South Carolina* and *Georgia*, in purſuance of the ſaid laſt recited act, be paid into the receipt of his Majeſty's exchequer, and there reſerved, to be, from time to time, diſpoſed of by parliament towards further defraying the neceſſary expences of defending, protecting, and ſecuring, the *Britiſh* colonies and plantations in *America*.

exportation of rice from the ſaid colonies to be paid into the exchequer, and reſerved for the diſpoſition of parliament.

XXI. And whereas, by ſeveral laws now in force, rice of the growth or produce of his Majeſty's colonies or plantations in *America* is, upon importation into, and being landed in *Great Britain*, ſubject and liable to various duties, all which (except the half of the old ſubſidy) are drawn back upon exportation: and whereas ſuch rice is frequently imported into the ports of *Plymouth*, *Exeter*, *Poole*, *Southampton*, *Chicheſter*, *Sandwich*, and *Glaſgow*, and the members thereunto belonging, for no other purpoſe but to be directly exported into foreign parts; and the obliging the importers to pay down the full duties in ſuch caſes, hath laid them under difficulties, and may be prejudicial to the trade of this kingdom; to remedy which for the future, and in order to give all fitting encouragement to this trade, be it enacted by the authority aforeſaid, That from and after the firſt day of *June*, one thouſand ſeven hundred and ſixty five, where any ſhip or veſſel ſhall arrive at any of the ports or places before-mentioned, from any of the *Britiſh* plantations in *America*, with rice of the growth and production of ſuch *Britiſh* plantation, and the importer of ſuch rice ſhall give notice to the collector and comptroller of the reſpective ports or places before-mentioned, wherein ſuch ſhips ſhall arrive, of his intention to export the whole cargo of ſuch rice immediately, in the ſame ſhip, to foreign parts, and the maſter of ſuch ſhip ſhall ſo report his cargo accordingly; that then, and in ſuch caſe, it ſhall and may be lawful for the importer to pay down, in ready money, one half of the old ſubſidy, granted by the act of tonnage and poundage, paſſed in the twelfth year of the reign of King *Charles* the Second, and no more; which ſhall not afterwards be drawn back or repaid on exportation of the ſame goods; and the importer of ſuch rice ſhall and may give bond, with one or more ſufficient ſecurities, to his Majeſty, his heirs, and ſucceſſors, in double value of the rice ſo imported, for the payment of the remaining duties within ſixty days from the date of ſuch bond, for all ſuch rice as ſhall be landed out of any ſhip ſo entered and reported; which bond ſhall and may be vacated and diſcharged upon payment of the ſaid remaining duties within the time before limited and appointed, or upon the ſaid rice being duly reſhipped and exported; any law, cuſtom, or uſage, to the contrary notwithſtanding.

Where veſſels ſhall arrive with rice from the Britiſh plantations, in America, at any of the above ports, and the whole cargo is to be immediately re-exported, the importer may pay down but one half of the old ſubſidy, and give bond for the remaining duties on ſuch as ſhall be landed.

XXII. And whereas by an act made in the laſt ſeſſion of parliament, intituled, *An act for granting certain duties in the* Britiſh *colonies and plantations in* America; *for continuing, amending, and making perpetual, an act paſſed in the ſixth year of the reign of his late majeſty King* George *the Second* (*intituled,* An act for the better

Clauſe in act 4 Geo. 3.

 ſecuring

ſecuring and encouraging the trade of his Majeſty's ſugar colonies in *America*;) *for applying the produce of ſuch duties, and of the duties to ariſe by virtue of the ſaid act, towards defraying the expences of defending, protecting, and ſecuring, the ſaid colonies and plantations; for explaining an act made in the twenty fifth year of the reign of King* Charles *the Second, (intituled,* An act for the encouragement of the *Greenland* and *Eaſtland* trades, and for the better ſecuring the plantation trade); *and for altering and diſallowing ſeveral drawbacks on exports from this kingdom, and more effectually preventing the clandeſtine conveyance of goods to and from the ſaid colonies and plantations, and improving and ſecuring the trade between the ſame and* Great Britain; it is, amongſt other things enacted, that from and after the twenty ninth day of *September*, one thouſand ſeven hundred and ſixty four, no iron, nor any ſort of wood, commonly called *Lumber*, as ſpecified in an act paſſed in the eighth year of the reign of King *George* the Firſt, intituled, *An act for giving further encouragement for the importation of naval ſtores, and for other purpoſes therein mentioned*, of the growth, production, or manufacture, of any *Britiſh* colony or plantation in *America*, ſhall be there laden on board any ſhip or veſſel to be carried from thence, until ſufficient bond ſhall be given, with one ſurety beſides the maſter of the veſſel, to the collector or other principal officer of the cuſtoms at the loading port, in a penalty of double the value of the goods, with condition, that the ſaid goods ſhall not be landed in any part of *Europe*, except *Great Britain*, and to bring certificates in diſcharge thereof within the reſpective times, and in the manner directed by the ſaid act: and whereas it may be expedient to extend the importation of ſuch iron to *Ireland*, and alſo to extend the importation of ſuch wood, commonly called *Lumber*, to *Ireland*, and to the *Madeiras* and the weſtern iſlands called the *Azores*, and any part of *Europe* to the ſouthward of *Cape Finiſterre*; be it therefore enacted by the authority aforeſaid, That from and after the fifth day of *July* one thouſand ſeven hundred and ſixty five, any iron, being the production or manufacture of any *Britiſh* colony or plantation in *America*, ſhall and may be there laden on board any ſhip or veſſel to be carried from thence to *Ireland*; and alſo that any wood commonly called *Lumber*, as ſpecified in the ſaid act of the eighth year of the reign of his late majeſty King *George* the Firſt, of the growth or production of any *Britiſh* colony or plantation in *America*, ſhall and may, in like manner, be there laden on board any ſhip or veſſel to be carried from thence to *Ireland*, or to the *Madeiras*, or the weſtern iſles called *The Azores*, or to any part of *Europe* to the ſouthward of *Cape Finiſterre*, upon ſufficient bond being given in the penalty and in the manner directed by the ſaid act made in the laſt ſeſſion of parliament, with condition, that the ſaid goods ſhall be there landed accordingly, and not in any other part of *Europe*, except *Great Britain*; and that certificates under the hands and ſeals of the collector or other principal officer of the cuſtoms reſident at the port or place where ſuch goods ſhall be landed in *Ireland*, teſtifying the landing thereof, ſhall be produced to the col-

[Margin: Act 8 Geo. 1.]

[Margin: Importation of Britiſh American iron extended to Ireland; and of lumber, to Ireland, the Madeiras, Azores, or to any part of Europe ſouth of Cape Finiſterre, upon giving bond.]

collector or other principal officer where bond shall have been given, within eighteen months from the date of such bond; and that for such of the said goods as shall be entered for, and landed at, the *Madeiras*, or the western isles called *The Azores*, or any part of *Europe* to the southward of *Cape Finisterre*, the like certificate shall be produced within the same time to the officers before mentioned, under the common seal of the chief magistrate, or under the hand and seal of the *British* consul, or hands and seals of two known *British* merchants residing where such goods shall be landed; and upon the producing of such certificate or proof upon oath being made by two credible persons, that the said goods were taken by enemies, or perished in the seas, the said bond shall be discharged; any thing in the said recited act to the contrary notwithstanding.

XXIII. And whereas by an act made in the twenty third year of the reign of his late majesty King *George* the Second, intituled, *An act to encourage the importation of pig and bar iron from his Majesty's colonies in* America, *and to prevent the erection of any mill, or other engine, for slitting or rolling of iron, or any plateing forge to work with a tilt hammer, or any furnace for making steel in any of the said colonies*; it is, amongst other things, enacted, That no bar iron made in his Majesty's colonies in *America*, which should be imported from thence into the port of *London* free of duty, as by the said recited act was permitted, should be afterwards exported or carried coastwise to be landed at any other port or place of *Great Britain*, except for the use of his Majesty's dock yards, under the penalties and forfeitures in the said recited act mentioned: and whereas by another act made in the thirtieth year of the reign of his said late majesty King *George* the Second, intituled, *An act to extend the liberty granted by an act of the twenty third year of the reign of his present Majesty, of importing bar iron from his Majesty's colonies in* America *into the port of* London, *to the rest of the ports of* Great Britain, *and for repealing certain clauses in the said act*; such bar iron may now be imported from the said *British* colonies in *America* into all the ports in *Great Britain* free of duty; and it will be to the advantage of the said colonies, as well as to the trade of this kingdom, if such bar iron was allowed to be exported from *Great Britain*, or carried coastwise therein; be it therefore enacted by the authority aforesaid, That from and after the first day of *June*, one thousand seven hundred and sixty five, the said clause in the before recited act of the twenty third year of his late Majesty, prohibiting the exportation of such bar iron, or carrying the same coastwise in *Great Britain*, shall be, and the same is hereby declared to be, repealed.

Clause in act 23 Geo. 2.

and in act 30 Geo. 2.

Repeal of clause in the recited act of 23 Geo. 2. prohibiting the exportation of iron, or carrying the same coastwise.

XXIV. And whereas the masters of several ships or vessels sailing from the *British American* colonies or plantations, have cleared out from thence in ballast, without taking any goods on board there, purposely to evade giving bond, as directed by the before recited act made in the last session of parliament, with condition, that in case any molasses or syrups, being the pro-

duce

duce of any of the plantations not under the dominion of his Majeſty, his heirs, or ſucceſſors, ſhall be laden on board ſuch ſhip or veſſel, the ſame ſhall (the danger of the ſeas and enemies excepted) be brought, without fraud or wilful diminution, by the ſaid ſhip or veſſel, to ſome of his Majeſty's colonies or plantations in *America*, or to ſome port in *Great Britain*; and the ſaid act may, by ſuch practices, be rendered ineffectual to anſwer the purpoſes thereby intended; for remedy whereof, be it further enacted by the authority aforeſaid, That from and after the tenth day of *October*, one thouſand ſeven hundred and ſixty five, the ſaid bond, with the condition in the ſaid recited act mentioned, ſhall be given for every ſhip or veſſel that ſhall ſet ſail from any *Britiſh* colony or plantation in *America*, whether any goods ſhall be there laden on board any ſuch ſhip or veſſel, or not; and if any ſhip or veſſel, not having taken any goods on board as aforeſaid, ſhall ſet ſail, or proceed from any *Britiſh* colony or plantation in *America*, before ſuch bond ſhall be given, ſuch ſhip or veſſel, with her furniture, ſhall be forfeited, and ſhall and may be ſeized and proſecuted in the manner directed by the ſaid recited act of parliament; any thing therein contained to the contrary notwithſtanding.

Veſſels ſailing from the Britiſh American plantations are to give bond, whether any goods ſhall be laded on board, or not;

on penalty of being forfeited.

XXV. And whereas in and by the ſaid recited act made in the laſt ſeſſion of parliament, it is, amongſt other things enacted, That a ſufferance and cocket ſhall be taken from the officers of the cuſtoms for all goods, wares, and merchandizes, of any kind whatſoever, which ſhall be laden on board any ſhip or veſſel in any *Britiſh* colony or plantation in *America*, to be carried from thence to any other colony or plantation, as in the ſaid act is expreſſed: and whereas the requiring ſuch ſufferances and cockets for goods of the growth or produce of the ſaid colonies, which are not liable to any duty by any act of parliament made in *Great Britain*, nor prohibited to be carried from the ſaid colonies, may lay an unneceſſary reſtraint upon the trade and correſpondence of his Majeſty's *American* ſubjects, when ſuch goods are carried merely for the uſe and ſuſtenance of the ſaid colonies, in boats or ſmall veſſels without decks which do not go to open ſea; for the eaſe therefore of his Majeſty's *American* ſubjects in this particular, be it enacted, That from and after the fifth day of *July*, one thouſand ſeven hundred and ſixty five, the ſaid recited act ſhall not extend, nor be conſtrued to extend, to require any perſon to take out any ſufferance or cocket for any goods of the growth, product, or manufacture, of the *Britiſh* colonies or plantations in *America*, which are not, by any act of parliament made in *Great Britain* liable to any duty either upon the importation into, or the exportation from, the ſaid colonies or plantations, nor are prohibited to be exported from thence, which ſhall be laden in any boat, flat, ſhallop, or other veſſel without a deck, not exceeding twenty tons burthen, and ſhall be carried within any river, lake, or other inland waters, within the ſaid colonies or plantations, and ſhall not be carried

Boats or ſmall veſſels without decks, carrying goods of the product or manufacture of the ſaid colonies, not liable to duties, nor prohibited to be exported, are not obliged to take out a cocket.

carried out to sea farther than one league from the shore; any thing in the said recited act to the contrary notwithstanding.

XXVI. And whereas by the said last recited act, made in the last session of parliament, one moiety of all seizures which shall be made at sea by the commanders or officers of his Majesty's ships or vessels of war, duly authorized to make seizures, and of the penalties and forfeitures recovered thereon, in any of his Majesty's colonies or plantations in *America*, first deducting the charges of prosecutions from the gross produce thereof, is to be paid to him or them who shall seize, inform, or sue for the same; subject to such distribution as his Majesty, his heirs, and successors, shall think fit to order and direct, by any order or orders of council, or by proclamation or proclamations, to be made for that purpose, as in and by the said recited act may more fully appear: now to obviate any doubts that have arisen, or may arise, concerning the construction of the words *seizures made at sea*; it is hereby further enacted and declared by the authority aforesaid, That the said words, *seizures made at sea*, in the said recited act of parliament, shall extend, and be construed to extend, to all seizures made by the commanders or officers of his Majesty's ships or vessels of war, duly authorized for that purpose, any where at sea, or in or upon any river, and which shall not be actually made on shore within any *British* colony or plantation in *America*.

Construction of the words *Seizures made at Sea*, in the recited act of 4 Geo. 3.

XXVII. And, in order to prevent any disputes concerning what fees the officers of his Majesty's customs in the *British* colonies or plantations in *America* may be intitled to, for making entries, or other business done by them in the execution of their employments; be it further enacted by the authority aforesaid, That until such time as the same shall be otherwise settled by authority of parliament, it shall and may be lawful for all and every collector, and other officer of his Majesty's customs, in any *British* colony or plantation in *America*, appointed by any deputation or commission from the commissioners of his Majesty's customs in *England*, to demand and receive such fees as they and their predecessors were intitled to demand and receive, on and before the twenty ninth day of *September*, one thousand seven hundred and sixty four; provided the fees so taken are not contrary to the express direction of any act of parliament made in *Great Britain*; and in all and every port or place in any *British* island in the *West Indies*, where no fees have been received as aforesaid by any officer of the customs, such officer shall, from and after the said fifth day of *July*, one thousand seven hundred and sixty five, be intitled to the same fees as have been received as aforesaid by the like officers, in the nearest port in the said island, before the said twenty ninth day of *September*, one thousand seven hundred and sixty four; and if no fees have been received as aforesaid by any officer in any port in the said island, such officer shall, from and after the said fifth day of *July*, one thousand seven hundred and sixty five, be intitled to such fees as have been received by the like officers in the

Regulations with respect to fees payable to the officers of his Majesty's customs in the British American plantations, until the same shall be otherwise settled by parliament;

viz. in the islands;

the iſland of *Barbadoes*, before the ſaid twenty ninth day of *September*, one thouſand ſeven hundred and ſixty four; and in all and every port or place on the continent of *America*, within his Majeſty's dominions, where no fees have been received as aforeſaid by any officer of the cuſtoms, ſuch officers ſhall, from and after the ſaid fifth day of *July*, one thouſand ſeven hundred and ſixty five, be intitled to the ſame fees as have been received as aforeſaid by the like officers, in the neareſt port in the ſaid colony or plantation, on or before the ſaid twenty ninth day of *September*, one thouſand ſeven hundred and ſixty four; and if no fees have been received as aforeſaid by any officer in any port in ſuch colony or plantation, ſuch officers ſhall, from and after the fifth day of *July*, one thouſand ſeven hundred and ſixty five, be intitled to ſuch fees as have been received by the like officers in the neareſt port within any *Britiſh* colony or plantation on or before the ſaid twenty ninth day of *September*, one thouſand ſeven hundred and ſixty four; and if no fees have been received by any comptroller of his Majeſty's cuſtoms for any port or place within any colony or plantation, or if the fees received by ſuch comptroller before the ſaid twenty ninth day of *September*, one thouſand ſeven hundred and ſixty four, have not been equal to one third part of the fees received as aforeſaid by the collector of his Majeſty's cuſtoms within the ſame port or place; it ſhall, from and after the ſaid fifth day of *July*, one thouſand ſeven hundred and ſixty five, in every ſuch caſe, be lawful for ſuch comptroller of his Majeſty's cuſtoms, to demand and receive for his fees, for any entry or other buſineſs done by him in the execution of his employment, from any merchant or other perſon, a ſum equal to one third part of the fees received as aforeſaid by ſuch collector for the like buſineſs; and every ſuch officer ſhall have and be entitled to the ſame remedy for recovery of ſuch fees, as is or has been heretofore allowed to any collector or other officer; any law, bye-law, or other act of aſſembly made in the ſaid plantations, to the contrary notwithſtanding; and if any collector, comptroller, or other officer of his Majeſty's cuſtoms in *America*, appointed as aforeſaid, ſhall exact, require, or receive, any other or greater fees than ſuch as are herein before allowed to be taken, he ſhall, for the firſt offence, forfeit the ſum of fifty pounds; one moiety of which penalty ſhall be to his Majeſty, his heirs and ſucceſſors, and the other moiety to the perſon or perſons aggrieved thereby, who ſhall ſue for the ſame in the proper court in ſuch colony or plantation; and for the ſecond offence, he ſhall forfeit his place, and be for ever after incapable of executing any office or employment in the cuſtoms.

Margin notes: and on the continent. — Comptrollers fees to be one third as much as the collector of the cuſtoms. — Remedy for recovering of the ſaid fees. — Penalty of exacting greater fees.

CAP.

CAP. XLVI.

An act for altering the ſtamp duties upon admiſſions into corporations or companies; and for further ſecuring and improving the ſtamp duties in Great Britain.

WHEREAS great frauds are committed in the ſeveral duties of one ſhilling reſpectively impoſed (among other duties) on admiſſions into corporations and companies, by an act of parliament made in the fifth and ſixth years of the reign of their late Majeſties King *William* and Queen *Mary*, intituled, *An act for granting to their Majeſties ſeveral duties upon vellum, parchment, and paper, for four years, towards carrying on the war againſt* France; and by another act of parliament made in the ninth and tenth years of the reign of his ſaid late Majeſty King *William* the Third, intituled, *An act for granting to his Majeſty, his heirs, and ſucceſſors, further duties upon ſtampt vellum, parchment, and paper*; owing to the ſaid duties being charged on the admiſſions, and not on the entries, minutes, or memorandums, made of ſuch admiſſions in the court books, rolls, or records, of ſuch corporations or companies: your Majeſty's moſt dutiful and loyal ſubjects the commons of *Great Britain* in parliament aſſembled, do therefore beſeech your Majeſty, that it may be enacted, and be it enacted by the King's moſt excellent Majeſty, by and with the advice and conſent of the lords ſpiritual and temporal, and commons, in this preſent parliament aſſembled, and by the authority of the ſame, That from and after the fifth day of *July*, one thouſand ſeven hundred and ſixty five, the ſeveral duties upon admiſſions into corporations and companies, granted by the ſaid acts, ſhall ceaſe and determine.

Preamble.

Act 5 and 6 Will. and Mary,

and 9 and 10 Will. 3.

From and after 5 July, 1765, the duties upon admiſſions into corporations, granted by the recited acts, are to ceaſe; and the following duties to take place in lieu thereof; viz.

II. And be it further enacted by the authority aforeſaid, That from and after the ſaid fifth day of *July*, one thouſand ſeven hundred and ſixty five, in lieu thereof, the duty herein after mentioned, be charged, impoſed, and paid, throughout the the kingdom of *England*, dominion of *Wales*, and town of *Berwick upon Tweed*; that is to ſay,

For and upon every ſkin or piece of vellum or parchment, and for every ſheet or piece of paper, upon which ſhall be ingroſſed, written, or printed, in the court book, roll, or record of any corporation or company, any entry, minute, or memorandum, of any admiſſion into any corporation or company, the ſum of two ſhillings.

Upon entry in the court book, of every ſuch admiſſion, 2s.

And if any town clerk, or other proper officer, ſhall neglect or refuſe to make ſuch entry, or minute, or memorandum, of ſuch admiſſion, upon the proper duty, in the court book, or on the roll or record of any ſuch corporation or company, within one month after any perſon ſhall be admitted into ſame, he ſhall, for every ſuch offence forfeit the ſum of ten pounds.

Officer neglecting or refuſing for one month to make ſuch entry, forfeits 10l.

III. And whereas it has been a common practice to make one policy

From and after 5 July, 1765, where the properties of more than one person, &c. in a ship, or cargo, or both, shall be assured for upwards of 100l. in the same policy, the policy is void, and the premium remains to the insurer; and in like manner, in case of any additional assurance not duly stampt.

policy of assurance on ships, cargoes, or both serve for several and distinct purposes, to the great diminution of his Majesty's revenue; to prevent which for the future, be it further enacted by the authority aforesaid, That from and after the fifth day of *July*, one thousand seven hundred and sixty five, if the properties of more than one person in any ship, cargo, or both, or of more than a particular number of persons in general partnership or of more than one body politick or corporate, to a greater amount in the whole than the sum of one hundred pounds in any ship, cargo, or both, be assured on the same policy, such policy shall be void, and the premium paid thereon shall remain the property of the assurer; and that if any risque or adventure distinct from the risque or adventure mentioned in the original policy, and upon which any further premium shall be given, shall be by any writing or declaration not duly stamped, added to the said original policy, such additional assurance shall be void, and the premium paid thereon shall remain the property of the assurer.

Any number may be assured on 1 policy, with 5 stamps of 5s. each.

IV. Provided always, That it shall and may be lawful to assure, or cause to be assured, the properties of any number of persons whatsoever, in any ship, cargo, or both, by one policy stamped with five stamps of five shillings each; any thing herein contained to the contrary notwithstanding.

The former allowance of 6l. per cent. on prompt payment of the duties, to cease;

V. And be it further enacted by the authority aforesaid, That the allowance after the rate of six pounds in the hundred pounds *per annum* for six months, directed to be made by several acts of parliament passed in the first, ninth, tenth, and twelfth years of the reign of Queen *Anne*, and in the twelfth year of the reign of King *George* the First, and in the thirtieth year of the reign of his late majesty King *George* the Second, to every person who shall at one time bring to be stamped, or buy of the commissioners for managing the stamp duties, paper or parchment, the duties whereof shall amount to ten pounds and upwards, after the rate of six pounds in the hundred pounds *per annum* for six months, upon the present payment of the said duties, shall, from and after the said fifth day of *July*, one thousand seven hundred and sixty five, cease and determine.

and from and after 5 July, 1765, 4l. per cent. only to be allowed in lieu thereof.

VI. And it is hereby further declared and enacted by the authority aforesaid, That from and after the said fifth day of *July*, one thousand seven hundred and sixty five, instead and in lieu of such allowance, there shall be allowed and paid in *Great Britain* to every person who shall at any one time bring to be stamped, or buy of the said commissioners, parchment or paper, the duties whereof shall in the whole amount to ten pounds or upwards, after the rate of four pounds in the one hundred pounds, *per annum* for six months, upon the present payment of the said duties, at the head office for marking or stamping of vellum, parchment, and paper.

Act 10 Anne.

VII. And whereas by an act of parliament made in the tenth year of the reign of her late majesty Queen *Anne*, intituled, *An act for laying several duties upon all soap and paper made in* Great Britain

Britain, *or imported into the same; and upon chequered and striped linens imported; and upon certain silks, callicoes, linens, and stuffs, printed, painted, or stained; and upon several kinds of stamped vellum, parchment, and paper; and upon certain printed papers, pamphlets, and advertisements; for raising the sum of eighteen hundred thousand pounds by way of lottery towards her Majesty's supply; and for licensing an additional number of hackney chairs; and for charging certain stocks of cards and dice; and for better securing her Majesty's duties to arise in the office for the stamp duties by licences for marriages and otherwise; and for relief of persons who have not claimed their lottery tickets in due time, or have lost exchequer bills, or lottery tickets; and for borrowing money upon stock (part of the capital of the* South sea *company) for the use of the publick*; a stamp duty of two shillings and three pence, among other duties, is laid on every skin or piece of vellum or parchment, or sheet or piece of paper, upon which should be ingrossed or written any surrender of, or admittance to, any copyhold land or tenement, within those parts of *Great Britain* called *England*, *Wales*, and the town of *Berwick upon Tweed*; or any grant or lease by copy of court roll, or any other copy of the court roll of any honour or manor within the same parts of *Great Britain*, or any of them other than and except the original surrender to the use of a will and the court roll or book wherein the proceedings of the court are entered or inrolled; and whereas great frauds have been committed in the said duty by stewards and others receiving the same, together with their own fees, without ever making out or delivering the said copies; for preventing the same for the future, be it further declared and enacted by the authority aforesaid, That from and after the said fifth day of *July*, one thousand seven hundred and sixty five, if any steward or other officer of any copyhold court shall demand, take, or receive, from any person whatsoever, any fee or fees for any such surrender, admittance, grant, or lease, or any other copy of any court roll, without at the same time demanding and receiving the stamp duty due thereon, and delivering such surrender or admittance, grant or lease, or copy to the person entitled thereto; then, and in every such case, every such steward or other officer shall, for every such offence, forfeit and pay the sum of ten pounds.

Stewards of copyhold courts, at the time of taking the fees for surrenders admittances, grants, or leases, &c. are to demand the stamp duty and deliver such surrenders, &c. on penalty of 10l.

VIII. And whereas by the said act of the tenth of Queen *Anne*, and also by an act of parliament made in the thirtieth year of the reign of his late Majesty King *George* the Second intituled, *An act for granting to his Majesty several rates and duties upon indentures, leases, bonds, and other deeds; and upon news papers, advertisements, and almanacks; and upon licences for retailing wine; and upon coals exported to foreign parts; and for applying, from a certain time, the sums of money arising from the surplus of the duties on licences for retailing spirituous liquors; and for raising the sum of three millions, by annuities, to be charged on the said rates, duties and sums of money; and for making perpetual an act made in the second year of the reign of his present Majesty, intituled,* An act for the better regulation of attornies and solicitors; *and*

Clause in act 10 Annæ.

and for enlarging the time for filing affidavits of the execution of contracts of clerks to attornies and solicitors; and also the time for payment of the duties omitted to be paid for the indentures and contracts of clerks and apprentices; the printers and publishers only, and not the proprietors, of news papers, and other papers and pamphlets, are made subject and liable to the duties imposed on advertisements, whereby great losses happen to the revenue; be it therefore further enacted by the authority aforesaid, That from and after the said fifth day of *July*, one thousand seven hundred and sixty five, neither the commissioners of the stamp duties, nor any officer to be appointed by them for distributing stamped vellum, parchment or paper, shall sell or deliver any stamped paper for printing any pamphlet, or any publick news, intelligence or occurences, to be contained in any one sheet, or any lesser piece of paper, unless the person applying for the same shall first give security to his Majesty for the payment of the duties for the advertisements which shall be printed therein or thereupon.

No stamps to be delivered out for pamphlets or news papers, till security be given for the duties for the advertisements to be printed thereon.

IX. And whereas great frauds and abuses are committed in the duties imposed, by several acts of parliament, on playing cards in *Great Britain*; for preventing whereof, be it further enacted by the authority aforesaid, That from and after the said fifth day of *July*, one thousand seven hundred and sixty five, every maker of playing cards in *Great Britain*, shall send to the commissioners for the stamp duties on vellum, parchment, and paper, or to their officers, a sufficient quantity of paper, in order to have as many several aces of spades marked or impressed thereon as such maker shall desire; and that no pack of playing cards made for play in *Great Britain*, or for exportation, shall be used in play, or exported, without one of such aces of spades marked or impressed, as herein after is mentioned and directed; and that the said commissioners for the stamp duties shall, instead of the present mark or stamp impressed on the ace of spades cause a new stamp, mark, or plate, to be prepared, with such device as they shall think proper, to denote the said ace of spades as well in every pack of cards made for use or play in *Great Britain*, as in every pack of cards made for exportation, so as that in such device there shall be some distinguishing mark between cards for home, and cards for foreign consumption; and that the said commissioners shall, from time to time, renew, alter, or add to, such device as they shall think proper.

Card makers to send paper to the stamp office, in order to have a sufficient number of aces of spades marked.

one of which is to be put in each pack,

and a new stamp is to be made for the purpose,

with a distinguishing mark between cards for home, and cards for foreign consumption;

X. And be it further enacted by the authority aforesaid, That every maker of cards shall, from and after the said fifth day of *July*, one thousand seven hundred and sixty five, send to the said commissioners of the stamps, or their officers, jews or wrappers made for inclosing cards for use or play in *Great Britain*, with his name, and any other particular word or thing printed thereon, as the said commissioners shall direct, in order that the same may be stamped, and delivered again, from time to time, to such maker, as occasion shall require; and that from and after the said fifth day of *July*, one thousand seven hundred and sixty five, the said commissioners of the stamp duties shall and

and they are also to send to the office wrappers for inclosing the cards, with their names &c. printed thereon.

which are to be stampt with one of

and may denote one of the six penny duties charged on playing cards in *Great Britain* on such jew or wrapper.

the six penny duties charged on cards;

XI. And be it further declared and enacted by the authority aforesaid, That from and after the said fifth day of *July*, one thousand seven hundred and sixty five, separate and distinct accounts shall be kept by the proper officer of the stamp duties with every card maker of the cards made by him for use or play in *Great Britain*, and of those made for exportation; the charges in which said several accounts shall be made out against him from the number of aces of spades, lavels, and jews or wrappers, delivered; and every such card maker shall, once in every twenty eight days, attend at the stamp office, or on the distributor of stamps next adjacent to the place where he shall make cards, and adjust, settle, and sign the same; and in case any difference shall arise in settling such accounts, then such card maker shall immediately, or within one week after, if he carries on his trade within ten miles of *London*; and, if at a greater distance, then within twenty days, apply to the said commissioners of the said duties to settle the same, whose determination shall be final; and if any such card maker shall neglect or refuse to apply as aforesaid, then such accounts, whether signed or not by him, shall be deemed conclusive, and be admitted in evidence against him.

And separate accounts are to be kept with each card maker, of the cards made for home, and of those for exportation; which are to be settled once a month, and any difference arising thereupon, is to be settled by the commissioners.

XII. And be it further enacted by the authority aforesaid, That in case any pack of playing cards, or part of any pack of playing cards, shall be damaged, defaced, or spoiled, in making the same, so as to be rendered unfit for play; then, on oath made thereof by the maker (which oath the said commissioners of the stamp duties, or any three of them, are hereby impowered to administer) such maker shall be allowed by such commissioners another ace of spades, instead of the ace so damaged, defaced, or spoiled, with any such pack, or part of any such pack, of playing cards, on producing and delivering to the said commissioners such damaged, defaced, or spoiled ace.

Where cards shall be spoiled in the making, the commissioners are to allow another ace of spades for the damaged one.

XIII. And be it further enacted by the authority aforesaid, That if any maker of cards shall use, in the making up any pack of cards, any ace of spades, jew, or wrapper, that has been used before; then every such card maker shall, for every such offence, forfeit the sum of twenty pounds.

Maker making up any ace of spades, or jew, used before forfeits 20 l.

XIV. And be it also enacted by the authority aforesaid, That if any person shall, from and after the passing of this act, sell or buy any such ace of spades, jew, or wrapper, in order to be made use of in, about, or for the inclosing, any pack or parcel of cards; every person so offending shall, for every such offence, forfeit the sum of twenty pounds.

and the seller or buyer of any such ace of spades, or jew, in order to be so made use of, forfeits also 20 l.

XV. Provided always, and be it enacted by the authority aforesaid, That if either the buyer or seller of any such ace of spades, jew, or wrapper, shall inform against the other party concerned in buying or selling such ace of spades, jew, or wrapper; the party so informing shall be admitted to give evidence

but either party informing, shall be admitted to give evidence, against the party informed against, and ſhall be indemnified againſt the penalties ſo by him or her incurred. *and be indemnified.*

Penalty on fraudulently re-landing cards for exportation,

XVI. And be it further enacted by the authority aforeſaid, That if any perſon whatſoever ſhall re-land, or cauſe or procure to be re-landed, any parcel of cards, after the ſame ſhall be entered and ſhipped for exportation in any port or place, other than the port or place to which ſuch cards are conſigned, every ſuch perſon ſhall, for every ſuch offence, forfeit the ſum of fifty pounds. *is 50 l.*

and any of the parties informing ſhall be admitted to give evidence, and be indemnified.

XVII. Provided always, and be it enacted by the authority aforeſaid, That if any perſon concerned in the re-landing of ſuch exportation cards, ſhall inform againſt any other party concerned, the perſon ſo informing ſhall be admitted to give evidence againſt the party informed againſt, and ſhall be indemnified againſt the penalties ſo by him or her incurred.

Clauſe in act 9 Annæ.

XVIII. And whereas by an act of parliament made in the ninth year of the reign of her late majeſty Queen *Anne*, intituled, *An act for the laying certain duties upon candles; and certain rates upon monies to be given with clerks and apprentices, towards raiſing her Majeſty's ſupply for the year one thouſand ſeven hundred and ten*, the duty, rate, or ſum of ſix pence, for every twenty ſhillings of every ſum of fifty pounds or under; and the duty, rate, or ſum of one ſhilling, for every twenty ſhillings of all and every ſum and ſums amounting to more than fifty pounds, which ſhould be given, paid, contracted, or agreed for, with, or in relation to, every clerk, apprentice, or ſervant, which ſhould be, within the kingdom of *Great Britain*, put or placed to or with any maſter or miſtreſs, to learn any profeſſion, trade, or employment, and proportionably for greater or leſſer ſums, was charged and impoſed on the ſaid maſters or miſtreſſes reſpectively: and whereas great inconveniencies ariſe in collecting the ſaid duties, for want of proper entries being made and kept by the chamberlain and other proper officers of cities and corporate towns, and companies, of the names of the maſter or miſtreſs, and clerk, apprentice, or ſervant; the place of abode of ſuch maſter or miſtreſs; the date of the indenture, covenant, articles, or contract; the ſum of money given, paid, contracted, or agreed for, and the profeſſion, trade, or employment, which ſuch clerk, apprentice, or ſervant, is to learn: for remedying whereof, be it further enacted and declared by the authority aforeſaid, That from and after the ſaid fifth day of *July*, one thouſand ſeven hundred and ſixty five, every chamberlain and other proper officer of every city and corporate town, and company, within the kingdom of *Great Britain*, where any clerk or apprentice, or ſervant, obtains his freedom by ſervitude, ſhall fairly write and enter in ſome book or books to be kept for that purpoſe, the names of all ſuch clerks, apprentices, and ſervants, as ſhall be put or placed out within the juriſdiction of ſuch city or town corporate, and alſo the names and places of abode of the maſters or miſtreſſes, and the ſums of money given, paid contracted, or agreed for, with, or in relation to, ſuch clerks

Where the freedom of any city or company is obtained by ſervitude, the chamberlain, or other proper officer, is to enter the names of all perſons put out clerks, apprentices,

apprentices, or servants, and the profession, trade, or employment, which they are respectively to learn; and the dates of the indentures, covenants, articles, or contracts, by which such clerks, apprentices, or servants, are respectively put and placed out; and if any chamberlain or other proper officer shall neglect or refuse to make any such entry, in manner as above set forth, he shall, for every such offence, forfeit the sum of twenty pounds.

or servants, with the names and abode of the masters, the apprentice fees, and dates of the indentures, &c. on forfeiture of 20 l.

XIX. And be it further declared and enacted by the authority aforesaid, That all printed indentures, covenants, articles, or contracts, for binding clerks or apprentices in *Great Britain*, after the said fifth day of *July* one thousand seven hundred and sixty five, shall have the following notice or memorandum printed under the same; *videlicet*,

and the following notice to be printed under all printed indentures, &c.

The notice.

THE *indenture, covenant, article, or contract, must bear date the day it is executed; and what money or other thing is given or contracted for with the clerk or apprentice, must be inserted in words at length; and the duty paid to the stamp office, if in* London, *or within the weekly bills of mortality, within one month after the execution, and if in the country, and out of the said bills of mortality, within two months, to a distributor of the stamps, or his substitute; otherwise the indenture will be void, the master or mistress forfeit fifty pounds, and another penalty, and the apprentice be disabled to follow his trade, or be made free.*

And if any printer, stationer, or other person or persons, shall sell, or cause to be sold, any such indenture, covenant, article, or contract, without such notice or memorandum being printed under the same; then, and in every such case, such printer, stationer, or other person or persons, shall, for every such offence, forfeit the sum of ten pounds.

on forfeiture of 10 l.

XX. And whereas by an act of parliament made in the twenty ninth year of the reign of his late majesty King *George* the Second, intituled, *An act for granting to his Majesty a duty upon licences for retailing beer, ale, and other exciseable liquors; and for establishing a method for granting such licences in* Scotland; *and for allowing such licences to be granted at a petty session in* England, *in a certain case therein mentioned*; it is, amongst other things, enacted, That from and after the feast of *Easter*, one thousand seven hundred and fifty six, there should be, throughout the kingdom of *Great Britain*, raised, levied, collected, and paid, to his said then Majesty, his heirs, and successors, for the purposes therein mentioned, a duty of twenty shillings for every piece of vellum, or parchment, or sheet or piece of paper, on which should be engrossed, written, or printed, any licence for selling ale or beer, or other exciseable liquors, by retail, over and above all other duties chargeable thereupon: and whereas several provisions are therein and thereby made, for the duly raising, levying, collecting, and paying, the same duty: and whereas it is found, by experience, that the said provisions are not sufficient

Clause in act 29 Geo. 2.,

for that purpose, in that part of *Great Britain* called *England*, the dominion of *Wales*, and town of *Berwick upon Tweed*; and that, by divers frauds and other ill practices, the crown has been, from time to time, defrauded of a great part of the said duty, and it is rendered difficult to convict the offenders: for remedy whereof, and for the further and better securing the raising, levying, collecting, and paying, of the said duty for the future, and for preventing such frauds and ill practices, and for rendering the conviction of the offenders more easy in that part of *Great Britain* called *England*, the dominion of *Wales*, and town of *Berwick upon Tweed*, be it enacted by the authority aforesaid, That from and after the said fifth day of *July*, one thousand seven hundred and sixty five, every victualler, or alehouse keeper, and every person selling ale, or beer, or other exciseable liquors, by retail; and every person permitting or suffering any ale, or beer, or any other exciseable liquors, to be sold by retail, in his, her, or their house, outhouse, or yard, garden, orchard, or other place, in that part of *Great Britain* called *England*, the dominion of *Wales*, and town of *Berwick upon Tweed*, do and shall, on demand to him or her made by any officer appointed by the commissioners for the time being to manage the duties charged on stamped vellum, parchment, and paper, produce and shew to such officer or officers, so demanding the same, his or her licence to sell ale, or beer, or other exciseable liquors, by retail; and shall permit such officer, at his own expence, to take and have a copy thereof on demand: and in case any such victualler, or alehouse keeper, or other person selling ale, or beer, or other exciseable liquors by retail, or other person or persons so permitting or suffering any ale, beer, or other exciseable liquors, to be sold by retail in his, her, or their house, or outhouse, yard, garden, orchard, or other place as aforesaid; shall refuse or neglect so to do, then every such victualler, or alehouse keeper, or person selling ale, or beer, or other exciseable liquors, by retail; or so permitting or suffering any ale, beer, or other exciseable liquors, to be sold by retail in his, her, or their house, or outhouse, yard, garden, orchard, or other place as aforesaid, shall, for every such offence, forfeit the sum of forty shillings.

Retailers of beer, and other exciseable liquors, to exhibit, on demand, their licence to the officer appointed by the commissioners for stamps, and to permit him to take a copy thereof; on forfeiture of 40s.

XXI. And be it further enacted by the authority aforesaid, That for the better detecting of such frauds and ill practices, and preventing the same for the future, every clerk of the peace of or for each county, riding, or division, in each county in that part of *Great Britain* called *England*, and the dominion of *Wales*, and town of *Berwick upon Tweed*, or his deputy, or person acting as such; and every clerk of the peace, or town clerk, or common clerk, or person acting as such, of or for every city, town, and liberty, in that part of *Great Britain* called *England*, and the dominion of *Wales*, and the town of *Berwick upon Tweed*, where licences to sell ale or beer, or other exciseable liquors, are, pursuant to the said act, to be granted by the justices or magistrates of or for such city, riding, division, town, or liberty, and of the said town of *Berwick upon Tweed*, or his deputy, or person acting as such, do and shall, on demand to him made by any officer of the

Clerks of the peace, town clerks, and common clerks, or their deputies, are to deliver, upon demand, to the officer of the stamp duties, lists of the several persons licensed to retail beer or other exciseable liquors,

the ſtamp duties for that purpoſe, or within the ſpace of three days next after ſuch demand ſhall be ſo made, deliver, or cauſe to be delivered, to ſuch officer a true liſt of the names and places of abode of all the victuallers, alehouſe keepers, and other perſons then licenſed to ſell ale or beer, or other exciſeable liquors, by retail, within every ſuch county, riding, diviſion, city, town, or liberty; and that on the delivery thereof, ſuch officer of the ſtamp duties ſhall pay to ſuch clerk of the peace, or his deputy, or perſon acting as ſuch, or to ſuch town clerk, or common clerk, or his deputy, or perſon acting as ſuch, for the making out and writing every ſuch liſt, after the rate of one farthing for every licenſed perſon whoſe name ſhall be therein inſerted; all which monies ſo paid ſhall, from time to time, be allowed to every ſuch officer of the ſtamp duties in his account; and in caſe any ſuch clerk of the peace, or his deputy, or perſon acting as ſuch, or any ſuch town clerk or common clerk, or his deputy, or perſon acting as ſuch, ſhall refuſe or neglect ſo to do by the ſpace of three days next after ſuch demand ſhall be ſo made, or ſhall not inſert in ſuch liſt a full, true, and perfect account of the names and places of abode of all the perſons the ſame ought to contain; that then, and in every ſuch caſe, every perſon ſo offending ſhall, for every ſuch offence, forfeit the ſum of five pounds.

he paying for ſuch body 1q. for each licenſed perſon inſerted in ſuch liſt.

If ſuch liſt ſhall be refuſed, or delayed, or be given in imperfect,

the offender forfeits 5 l.

XXII. And whereas by the laws now in force in that part of *Great Britain* called *England*, dominion of *Wales*, and town of *Berwick upon Tweed*, perſons ſelling ale or beer, or other exciſeable liquors, by retail, without licence, are liable and ſubject by different laws to different penalties and puniſhments, which has occaſioned much confuſion, and an ill and improper uſe has been made thereof in many inſtances: for the prevention whereof, be it further enacted by the authority aforeſaid, That from and after the fifth day of *July*, one thouſand ſeven hundred and ſixty five, every perſon lawfully convicted of ſelling ale or beer, or other exciſeable liquors, by retail, after that day, in that part of *Great Britain* called *England*, the dominion of *Wales*, or the town of *Berwick upon Tweed*, without being duly licenſed ſo to do, ſhall, for every ſuch offence, forfeit and undergo the ſeveral penalties and puniſhments herein after mentioned and provided in that behalf, inſtead and in lieu of the ſeveral pecuniary and corporal puniſhments which they are now liable or ſubject to by any law now in force; that is to ſay, for the firſt offence the ſum of forty ſhillings, and alſo the coſts and expences of convicting ſuch offender; and in caſe ſuch ſum, together with the charges and expences of convicting ſuch offender, ſhall not be paid within the ſpace of fourteen days next after ſuch conviction, that then the offender ſhall ſuffer impriſonment for the ſpace of one month, unleſs he or ſhe ſhall ſooner pay ſuch penalty, and the coſts, charges, and expences of ſuch conviction, and executing the ſame: and for the ſecond offence, the ſum of four pounds, and alſo the coſts and expences of convicting ſuch offender; and in caſe ſuch ſum, together with the charges and

Inſtead of the pecuniary and corporal puniſhments inflicted by former acts, on retailers of beer, &c. not being duly licenſed,

they are to forfeit, for the firſt offence, 40 s. and coſts of conviction; and, on nonpayment, are to be committed for one month; for the ſecond offence 4 l. and coſts; and, on nonpayment, to be committed for two months; and expences of convicting ſuch offender the ſecond time, ſhall not be paid within the ſpace of one week next after ſuch ſecond conviction, that then the offender ſhall ſuffer impriſonment for the ſpace of two months, unleſs he or ſhe ſhall ſooner pay ſuch penalty of four pounds, and the coſts, charges, and expences of ſuch ſecond conviction, and executing the ſame: and for the third offence, the ſum of ſix pounds, and alſo the coſts and expences of convicting ſuch offender; and in caſe ſuch ſum of ſix pounds, together with the charges and expences of convicting ſuch offender the third time, ſhall not be paid within the ſpace of three days next after ſuch third conviction, that then the offender ſhall ſuffer impriſonment for the ſpace of three months, unleſs he or ſhe ſhall ſooner pay ſuch penalty of ſix pounds, and the coſts, charges, and expences of ſuch third conviction and executing the ſame; and the like penalty and puniſhment for every other offence after the third offence and conviction thereof, as for the ſaid third offence; all which ſaid coſts and expences ſhall be aſſeſſed, ſettled, and aſcertained by the juſtice or juſtices of the peace before whom ſuch offenders ſhall reſpectively be convicted; any law, ſtatute, or cuſtom, to the contrary thereof in any wiſe notwithſtanding: all which penalties and forfeitures ſhall go and be paid, the one moiety thereof to his Majeſty, his heirs and ſucceſſors, and the other moiety thereof, and alſo all ſuch coſts, charges, and expences, to be aſſeſſed or aſcertained as aforeſaid, to the proſecutor or proſecutors of every ſuch offender or offenders.

for the third offence 6l. and coſts, and, on non-payment, to be committed for 3 months; and the like penalty and puniſhment as the third, for every ſubſequent offence. The coſts are to be ſettled by the juſtices; and the penalties to be applied, one moiety to the crown, and the other moiety and coſts to the proſecutor.

XXIII. And be it further enacted by the authority aforeſaid, That it ſhall and may be lawful to and for any one or more juſtice or juſtices of the peace, for the time being, of the county or place where any of the ſaid offences againſt this act, or the ſaid former act, ſhall be committed, to hear and determine the ſame offences in a ſummary way; which ſaid juſtice and juſtices of the peace are hereby authorized and required, upon any information exhibited, or complaint made, in that behalf, to or before him or them, to ſummon the party or parties accuſed, and alſo the witneſſes on either ſide (if they ſhall be required to ſummon any ſuch witneſſes) and upon the appearance, or contempt of the party or parties accuſed by not appearing, to proceed to examine and hear the matter in a ſummary way; and alſo to examine ſuch witneſſes on oath as ſhall be produced therein (which oath ſuch juſtice and juſtices reſpectively is or are hereby impowered to give and adminiſter) and to give his or their judgement thereon; and in caſe he or they ſhall convict the party or parties ſo accuſed or complained againſt, of the offence laid to his, her, or their charge, and ſuch party or parties ſhall refuſe or neglect to pay the penalty or penalties for which he, ſhe, or they, ſtand convicted, within the time herein before mentioned for that purpoſe, together with the coſts of ſuch conviction or convictions, to be aſſeſſed, ſettled, and aſcertained, as aforeſaid; that then, and in every ſuch caſe, it ſhall and may be lawful for every ſuch juſtice and juſtices, and he and they, and

The juſtices are authorized to hear and determine the ſaid offences in a ſummary way.

and each of them, is and are hereby authorized and required to iſſue his or their warrant or warrants under his or their hand and ſeal, or hands and ſeals, for the apprehending and committing to priſon every ſuch offender, for ſuch time, and in ſuch manner, as the nature of the offence ſhall require, according to the true intent and meaning of this act.

XXIV. And be it further enacted by the authority aforeſaid, That if any perſon or perſons ſhall be ſummoned as a witneſs or witneſſes to give evidence before any ſuch juſtice or juſtices of the peace, touching any of the matters aforeſaid, either on the part of the proſecutor, or of the perſon or perſons accuſed, and ſhall neglect or refuſe to appear at the time and place to be for that purpoſe appointed, without a reaſonable excuſe for ſuch his, her, or their neglect or refuſal, to be allowed of by ſuch juſtice or juſtices of the peace; or, appearing, ſhall refuſe to be examined on oath, and give evidence before ſuch juſtice or juſtices of the peace before whom the proſecution ſhall be depending; that then, every ſuch perſon ſhall forfeit, for every ſuch offence, the ſum of twenty ſhillings, to be levied and paid in ſuch manner, and by ſuch means, as are herein before directed as to other penalties.

Witneſſes being duly ſummoned, neglecting or refuſing to appear (without reaſonable cauſe ſhewn) or to give evidence, forfeit 40 s.

XXV. And be it further enacted, That if any perſon or perſons ſhall think himſelf, herſelf, or themſelves, aggrieved by the judgement or conviction of any juſtice or juſtices of the peace, for any of the offences aforeſaid, and ſhall give ſecurity to the ſatisfaction of ſuch juſtice or juſtices of the peace for the payment of the penalty, coſts, and expences, to be expreſſed in the warrant or warrants of diſtreſs on ſuch conviction; that then, and in every ſuch caſe, after ſuch ſecurity given, and not otherwiſe, it ſhall and may be lawful to and for ſuch offender and offenders to appeal from and againſt ſuch conviction or convictions, to the juſtices of the peace aſſembled at the next quarter ſeſſions of the peace to be held for ſuch county, riding, diviſion, liberty, city, town, or place, unleſs ſuch ſeſſions of the peace ſhall be held within ſix days or leſs next after ſuch conviction or convictions ſhall be ſo had or made; and in that caſe to the juſtices of the peace to be aſſembled at the next ſeſſions after ſuch ſeſſions, and not afterwards; and that the juſtices of the peace aſſembled at ſuch ſeſſions, ſhall thereupon proceed to hear and determine the matter of every ſuch appeal, and their judgement thereon ſhall be final and concluſive to all intents and purpoſes whatſoever; and in caſe the juſtices of the peace ſo aſſembled at ſuch ſeſſions, ſhall find and adjudge any ſuch appeal to be frivolous or vexatious, it ſhall and may be lawful to and for them to give and adjudge to the party or parties grieved by ſuch appeal, his or their reaſonable coſts and charges occaſioned thereby, not exceeding in the whole the ſum of five pounds on any one appeal.

Perſons aggrieved by the judgement or conviction of a juſtice, and giving ſecurity, may appeal to the quarter ſeſſions, who are to hear and determine the matter finally; and if they adjudge the appeal to be frivolous, or vexatious, may award coſts, not exceeding 5 l.

XXVI. And, in order to prevent frivolous and vexatious appeals, be it further enacted by the authority aforeſaid, That a conviction in the form or to the effect following, *Mutatis mutandis*,

Form of conviction.

tandis, as the caſe ſhall happen to be, ſhall be good and effectual to all intents and purpoſes whatſoever, without ſtating the caſe, or the facts or evidence in any more particular manner (that is to ſay)

Middleſex ſſ. BE *it remembered, That on this day of in the year* A. B. *of*, &c. *was duly convicted before me* C. D. *one of his Majeſty's juſtices of the peace for the county of* Middleſex, *or before us* C. D. *and* E. F. *two of his Majeſty's juſtices of the peace for the ſaid county of* Middleſex (as the caſe ſhall happen to be) *for ſelling ale or beer, or other exciſeable liquors* (as the caſe ſhall happen to be) *without being duly licenſed ſo to do, according to the ſtatutes in ſuch caſe made and provided, whereby he, ſhe, or they, has or have forfeited the ſum of this being the firſt, ſecond, or third offence* (as the caſe ſhall happen to be) *beſides the coſts and expences of this conviction; which coſts and expences I the ſaid juſtice of the peace, or we the ſaid juſtices of the peace* (as the caſe ſhall happen to be) *do hereby aſcertain and aſſeſs, at the ſum of purſuant to the ſtatute in ſuch caſe made and provided.*

Given under my hand and ſeal, or our hands and ſeals (*as the caſe ſhall happen to be*) the day and year above written.

Where the juſtices of the peace in Scotland ſhall not attend to admit and licenſe retailers of beer, and other exciſeable liquors, purſuant to act 29 Geo. 2.

the clerks of the peace, and of the royal boroughs may iſſue ſuch licences.

XXVII. And whereas the ſaid laſt mentioned act of parliament, made in the twenty ninth year of the reign of his ſaid late majeſty King *George* the Second, has not been duly carried into execution by the juſtices of peace, the magiſtrates of royal boroughs, in that part of *Great Britain* called *Scotland*, and in other reſpects hath been found defective and ineffectual, in that part of the united kingdom: for remedy whereof, be it enacted by the authority aforeſaid, That from and after the fifth day of *July*, one thouſand ſeven hundred and ſixty five, in caſe the juſtices of peace of any ſhire or ſtewartry, or the magiſtrates of any royal borough, in that part of *Great Britain* called *Scotland*, ſhall in this, or any ſucceeding year, neglect to aſſemble upon the days, and at the time and places, mentioned in the aforeſaid act, in order to admit and licenſe for the year then next enſuing, ſuch and ſo many perſons as they ſhall think meet and convenient, to keep ale houſes, tippling houſes, victualling houſes, or to ſell ale, beer, or other exciſeable liquors, by retail, within their reſpective ſhires, ſtewartries, and boroughs, according to the directions of the aforeſaid act; then, and in that caſe, it ſhall be lawful to the clerk of the peace of any ſuch ſhire or ſtewartry, or his lawful deputy, and to the clerk of any ſuch royal borough, or his lawful deputy reſpectively, and they are hereby

hereby required, after making an entry or record, that the juſtices of peace, or magiſtrates aforeſaid, had neglected to aſſemble in purſuance of the aforeſaid act, to deliver, or cauſe to be delivered, to every perſon living or reſiding within ſuch ſhire or ſtewartry, or royal borough or liberties thereof reſpectively, who ſhall apply for the ſame, (unleſs ſuch perſon ſhall be diſqualified to have a licence by this or any former act) a licence ingroſſed, written, or printed, upon a piece of vellum, parchment, or paper, ſtamped as by the aforeſaid act is directed, with a ſtamp denoting the payment of the duty of twenty ſhillings, ſigned by the clerk of the peace of ſuch ſhire or ſtewartry, or the clerk of ſuch royal borough, or their lawful deputies reſpectively; for each of which licences there ſhall be paid and payable the ſums mentioned in the aforeſaid act, and no more; and which licences ſo ſigned and delivered by the clerk of the peace of any ſhire or ſtewartry, or the clerk of any royal borough, or their lawful deputies reſpectively, ſhall be, to all intents and purpoſes, as good and effectual to the receiver or receivers thereof, as if the ſame had been allowed, granted, and ſigned, in a meeting of the juſtices of peace of ſuch ſhire or ſtewartry, or of the magiſtrates of ſuch royal borough; any thing in the aforeſaid act to the contrary notwithſtanding.

being firſt duly ſtampt with the 20s. duty; and they are thereupon intitled to the cuſtomary fees.

XXVIII. And be it enacted by the authority aforeſaid, That in caſe the juſtices of the peace of any ſhire or ſtewartry, or the magiſtrates of any royal borough, aſſembled, upon the days appointed by the aforeſaid act for executing the powers thereby committed to them, ſhall find it neceſſary, it ſhall and may be lawful for them to continue or adjourn their meeting to the next lawful day, and no longer; and in caſe the juſtices of peace of any ſhire or ſtewartry, or the magiſtrates of any royal borough, ſhall not upon one or other of theſe days, compleatly execute the powers committed to them by the aforeſaid act, by allowing or refuſing the petition or claim of every perſon within their ſeveral diſtricts, who ſhall apply to them for a licence to ſell ale, beer, or other exciſeable liquor by retail; then, and in that caſe, it ſhall be lawful to the clerk of the peace of ſuch ſhire or ſtewartry, or his lawful deputy, and to the clerk of ſuch royal borough, or his lawful deputy reſpectively, and they are hereby required, after making an entry or record that the ſaid juſtices of peace, or magiſtrates, had not compleatly executed the powers committed to them by the aforeſaid act, to deliver, or cauſe to be delivered, to every perſon who ſhall have ſo applied to the juſtices of peace, or magiſtrates aforeſaid, and upon whoſe application no deliverance or order ſhall have been made as aforeſaid, a licence duly ſigned by ſuch clerk as above directed; which ſhall be as good and effectual to the receiver thereof, as if the ſame had been allowed, granted, and aſſigned, in a meeting of the ſaid juſtices or magiſtrates reſpectively; any thing in the aforeſaid act to the contrary notwithſtanding.

Where it ſhall be neceſſary, the juſtices meeting for the purpoſes of the ſaid act, may continue, or adjourn their meeting to the next lawful day; and ſuch of the buſineſs as ſhall not be then compleated, the clerks of the peace, &c. are to finiſh; and the licences ſo granted are valid;

XXIX. Provided always, That no clerk of the peace, or of any royal borough, or their deputies, ſhall grant any licence under

but all ſuch licences muſt be granted

within 3 days after the times appointed for the justices issuing the same.

under this act, at any other time than within three days following the days appointed by this, or any former act, for the justices of peace, or magistrates of royal boroughs, to grant the same.

Clerk of the peace, &c. refusing to sign and deliver such licences, forfeit 10l. to the party, with full costs of suit.

XXX. And be it enacted by the authority aforesaid, That in case any clerk of the peace, or of any royal borough, or their deputies, shall, in either of the cases above expressed, refuse to sign and deliver such licence to any person applying for the same as aforesaid, each of them so offending shall forfeit and pay to each and every person to whom, or for whose behoof, such licence ought to have been delivered as aforesaid, the sum of ten pounds, with full costs of suit, to be sued for and recovered before the sheriff or stewart court of the shire or stewartry within which the person so offending shall reside, in manner herein after directed.

They are to make up, annually, lists of the persons licensed within their respective districts;

which are to be kept upon record, and signed by them;

and they are to transmit an attested copy thereof, before 1 Dec. annually, to the collector of the stamp duties at Edinburgh,

on forfeiture of 10l.

and if any person shall be wilfully omitted

or wrongfully inserted in such lists, the clerk is to forfeit 40s. for such omission,

XXXI. And be it further enacted by the authority aforesaid, That the clerk of the peace of each shire or stewartry, and the clerk of each royal borough respectively, shall be holden and obliged annually to make up a true and exact list, in a book or register to be kept for that purpose, of the names, additions, and places of abode, of all persons within their respective districts, to whom licences for retailing ale, beer, or other exciseable liquors, shall be delivered in pursuance of this or the aforesaid act; which list shall be signed in the book or register aforesaid, by the clerk of the peace of each shire or stewartry, or clerk of each royal borough, or their lawful deputies respectively, and shall be carefully preserved with the other records under their care; and the clerk of the peace of each shire or stewartry, and the clerk of each royal borough, and their deputies respectively, shall be holden and obliged, on or before the first day of *December* in this and every year, to transmit to the collector of the stamp duties at *Edinburgh*, an exact copy of such list, taken from the said book or register, duly attested and signed by such clerk or his deputy; and in case any clerk of the peace, or of any royal borough aforesaid, or their deputies, shall neglect or fail to make up and sign such list, in a book or register as above directed, or shall neglect or fail to transmit an exact copy of such list, as entered in the said book or register, to the collector of the stamp duties at *Edinburgh*, as above required, the person or persons offending shall, for every such offence, forfeit and pay the sum of ten pounds; to be sued for and recovered before the sheriff or stewart court of the shire or stewartry within which the person so offending shall reside, in manner herein after directed; and in case any clerk of the peace, or clerk of any royal borough, or their deputies, shall wilfully omit to insert in the aforesaid register, or in the copy thereof to be transmitted as aforesaid, the name of any person who shall be licensed to retail ale, beer, or other exciseable liquors, within their several districts; or shall wilfully insert in such register, or copy thereof to be transmitted as aforesaid, the name of any person as licensed, who shall not have been so licensed; such clerk shall, for every such offence, forfeit and pay the sum of forty shillings for each

each person licensed, whose name shall be omitted to be inserted in the said register, or copy thereof to be transmitted as aforesaid; and five pounds for each person not licensed, whose name shall be inserted in such register, or copy thereof; to be sued for and recovered before the sheriff or stewart court of the shire or stewartry within which the person so offending shall reside, in manner herein after directed.

and 5l. for such wrong insertion.

XXXII. And whereas persons may presume to keep ale houses, tippling houses, or victualling houses, or to sell ale, beer, or other exciseable liquors, by retail, without such licence as is hereby and by the above recited act required; be it enacted by the authority aforesaid, That every person in that part of *Great Britain* called *Scotland*, who, after the tenth day of *November*, one thousand seven hundred and sixty five, shall keep an ale house, tippling house, or victualling house, or shall sell ale, beer, or other exciseable liquors, by retail, except in fairs, without being licensed thereunto, according to the directions of this and the former act above recited, and shall be thereof convicted in manner herein after-mentioned; every such offender shall forfeit and pay, for the first offence, the sum of thirty shillings; for the second offence, the sum of forty shillings; and for the third, or any subsequent offence, the sum of five pounds; and shall, after the said third offence, be incapable of keeping an ale house, tippling house, or victualling house, or of selling ale beer, or other exciseable liquors, by retail, or of having any licence for such purpose thereafter; all which respective penalties and forfeitures, for selling ale, beer, or other exciseable liquors, by retail, without licence, shall and may be sued for and recovered before the sheriff or stewart court, or before any two or more justices of the peace of the shire or stewartry, or the baillie court of any royal borough, within whose jurisdiction respectively the offender or offenders shall reside, by any person who shall inform, and sue, or prosecute, for the same.

Persons in Scotland selling ale, or other exciseable liquors, by retail, not being duly licensed,

forfeit, for the first offence, 30s. for the second, 40s. and for the third, or any subsequent offence, 5l. and are disqualified;

XXXIII. And be it further enacted by the authority aforesaid, That any person or persons sued or prosecuted for retailing ale, beer, or other exciseable liquors, without licence, may and shall be legally convicted thereof on their own confession, or on the oath of one credible witness, or upon evidence by the stock book, or other accounts kept by the gauger or officer of excise, which he is required to produce, attested by the oath of such gauger or officer, that the person so sued or prosecuted has been charged or surveyed as a victualler or retailer, and has been charged with the same duties of excise that victuallers and retailers are usually charged with, and pay, for ale, beer, and other exciseable liquors, within the period mentioned in the information or complaint.

Method of conviction in such cases.

XXXIV. And be it enacted by the authority aforesaid, That all penalties and forfeitures inflicted by this act, not otherwise provided for, may be sued for or prosecuted before the respective courts above appointed, within six months after committing the offence, and shall be payable, one moiety thereof to his Majesty,

General method of recovery, and distribution of the penalties and forfeitures in Scotland, where not otherwise provided for.

jesty, his heirs, and successors, and the other moiety thereof to any person or persons who shall sue or prosecute for the same; and may be recovered and levied either by the usual execution of the law of *Scotland*, or by distress and sale of the goods and chattles of the offender (rendering to him or her the overplus, after the charges of the said distress and sale shall be deducted) by a warrant signed by the judge or magistrate before whom such offender shall be convicted, and which warrant shall contain power to enter houses, and break open doors, in order to make such distress effectual, and may be carried into execution without necessity of any previous intimation of the conviction; any any thing in the aforesaid act to the contrary notwithstanding.

Limitation as to the time of execution of warrants for distress, upon conviction of offenders. The grounds of such warrants to be preserved on record.

XXXV. Provided always, That no such warrant for distress shall be carried into execution, till after the expiration of six days after the conviction of every such offender; and the clerk or clerks of the respective courts aforesaid, before whom any conviction for any of the offences aforesaid shall proceed, shall, and they are hereby required, carefully to preserve the whole grounds and warrants of every such conviction amongst the other records of such court; and shall not be obliged to return or certify the same to any other court; any thing in the aforesaid act to the contrary notwithstanding.

Appeals to be made to the barons of the exchequer at Edinburgh;

XXXVI. And whereas the appeal to the quarter sessions allowed by the aforesaid act, has been found inconvenient and improper, be it enacted by the authority aforesaid, That from and after the tenth day of *November*, one thousand seven hundred and sixty five, it shall and may be lawful to any person or persons who shall think him, her, or themselves, aggrieved, by the sentence or decree of any judge or magistrate convicting him, her, or them, of any of the offences aforesaid described in this act, within three days after the date of such decree or sentence, to appeal to the barons of his Majesty's court of exchequer at *Edinburgh*; which appeal shall either be taken in open court in the presence of the judge or magistrate who shall have pronounced the decree or sentence appealed from, by a writing signed by the appellant or his procurator, or at the office of the clerk of such court, by a writing signed as aforesaid;

and are to be lodged with the original proceedings. Appellant to give in his reasons of appeal, and bond to prosecute, &c.

all which appeals, the clerk of such court shall carefully lodge and preserve along with the proceedings in the original suit; and the person or persons so appealing, shall, within six days after lodging such appeal, give in to the clerk of the said court his reasons of appeal, and a bond with a sufficient surety to prosecute the said appeal with effect, and to pay such costs as shall be awarded against him, her, or them, in case the appeal shall be dismissed, or the sentence or decree appealed from, be affirmed; and which reasons of appeal and bond, shall likewise be lodged and preserved by the said clerk along with the proceedings in the original suit;

otherwise the judgment to stand good.

and in case the person or persons so appealing, shall neglect to give in his reasons of appeal and bond to prosecute the same as above required, the appeal shall be holden as passed from, and the sentence or decree against which

which the appeal was taken, ſhall to all intents and purpoſes become final, and be carried into execution according to the directions of this act; and in caſe the reaſons of appeal and bond for proſecuting the ſame, ſhall be duly lodged as aforeſaid, the clerk of the court appealed from, ſhall, and is hereby required within fourteen days after the date of ſuch appeal, to tranſmit to the ſolicitor of the ſtamp duties at *Edinburgh*, a full extract of the whole proceedings in the original ſuit, and of the decree or ſentence following thereupon, and of the appeal, and reaſons of appeal, and bond for proſecuting the ſame, duly ſigned by him or his lawful deputy, for which he ſhall be intitled to receive the ordinary fees of an extracted decree; and which extract the ſolicitor of the ſtamp duties ſhall immediately lodge in the office of the King's remembrancer in the court of exchequer; and ſo ſoon as ſuch extract ſhall be ſo lodged, it ſhall and may be lawful to either party, appellant or reſpondent, to apply to the barons of the ſaid court, or any one of them, as well out of term as in term time, in order to have a day appointed for hearing and determining ſuch appeal; and the ſaid barons, or any of them, ſhall accordingly appoint ſuch day as they ſhall think proper, of which due notice ſhall be given by the party who applied for ſuch day, to the other party in the ſaid appeal, ten days at leaſt before the day appointed for hearing and determining ſuch appeal.

Where the reaſons of appeal ſhall be duly lodged, &c. the clerk of the court is to tranſmit a copy of the original proceedings and ſentence to the ſolicitor of the ſtamp duties at Edinburgh, with the reaſons of appeal, and the bond, &c. to be lodged in the office of the King's remembrancer, &c. and the barons are thereupon to appoint a day for hearing;

XXXVII. And be it enacted by the authority aforeſaid, That the ſaid barons, or any one of them, ſhall, and he or they is or are hereby impowered, as well out of term time as in term time, to hear and determine ſuch appeal, and to give ſuch judgement thereupon, as to them or him ſhall ſeem juſt; and to award full coſts of ſuit, in caſe the appeal ſhall be diſmiſſed, or the ſentence or decree appealed from ſhall be affirmed; which judgement ſhall be final to all intents and purpoſes, and ſubject to no other review whatſoever; and the ſaid barons, or any one of them, who ſhall give ſuch judgement, may and ſhall grant warrant for levying the ſum or ſums awarded by ſuch judgement, by diſtreſs and ſale of the goods and chattels of the perſon or perſons againſt whom ſuch judgement ſhall be given, and his, her, or their ſurety or ſureties, and for ſuch other execution of the law in the ſame way and manner as the inferior judge or magiſtrate, before whom the original ſuit was brought, might have done for levying any of the penalties inflicted by this act.

and ſuch appeal may be heard in or out of term.

Full coſts to be allowed if the appeal is diſmiſſed, or the ſentence affirmed; to be levied by diſtreſs and ſale.

XXXVIII. And be it further enacted by the authority aforeſaid, That all publick officers in *Great Britain*, who ſhall, from time to time, have in their cuſtody any books, papers, files, records, remembrances, dockets, or proceedings, the ſight or knowledge whereof may tend to the ſecuring any of his Majeſty's ſtamp duties, or to the proof or diſcovery of any fraud or omiſſion in relation thereto, or to any of them, ſhall, at any ſeaſonable time or times, permit and ſuffer any officer and officers thereunto authorized by the commiſſioners for the time being appointed to manage thoſe duties, or the major part of them, to

Publick officers having in their cuſtody any books or papers, which may tend to ſecure the ſtamp duties, or diſcover any fraud therein, are to permit the officer authorized for the purposes to inspect, and take notes gratis; on penalty of 50 l.

to inspect and view all such books, files, records, remembrances, dockets, papers, and proceedings, and to take thereout such notes and memorandums as such officer or officers shall see necessary for the purposes last mentioned, without fee or reward; upon pain that every such publick officer who shall refuse or neglect to permit or suffer such view and inspection, shall, for every such refusal and neglect, forfeit the sum of fifty pounds.

Stamps spoiled before the writings are executed,

and for which no consideration has been paid to the attorney or solicitor;

may be exchanged for other stamps of like value.

XXXIX. And be it further enacted and declared by the authority aforesaid, That from and after the said fifth day of *July*, one thousand seven hundred and sixty five, it shall be lawful for all persons who shall at any time have in their custody or possession any stamped vellum, parchment, or paper, written or ingrossed upon, which shall be inadvertently and undesignedly spoiled, obliterated, or by any other means rendered unfit for the purpose intended, before the same is executed by any party or parties, and which, in either case, shall not have been used for any other purpose, or in any other manner whatsoever, nor any money, or other consideration, paid or given to the attorney, solicitor, or other person employed to transact the business intended to have been carried into execution by such writing or ingrossment, or to the writer or ingrosser thereof, for the duty or duties marked, stamped, or impressed thereon, to bring or send such stamped paper, vellum, or parchment, unto the said commissioners of the stamp duties at their head office in *London* or *Westminster*; and upon oath made to the satisfaction of the said commissioners (which oath the said commissioners, or any three or more of them, are hereby authorized to administer) that such stamped vellum, parchment, or paper, so written or ingrossed upon, or spoiled, obliterated, or by any other means rendered unfit for the purpose intended, hath not been executed by any party or parties, or used for any other purpose, or in any other manner whatsoever; and that no money, or other consideration, hath been paid or given for the duty or duties marked, stamped, or impressed thereupon (save and except the money first paid for such duty or duties to the said commissioners, or the receiver general of the stamp duties, or other proper officer appointed to collect and receive the same) the said commissioners are hereby required to stamp and mark, or cause to be stamped and marked, for the several persons who shall so bring and deliver any quantity of stamped vellum, parchment, or paper, so written or ingrossed upon, spoiled, obliterated, or by any other means rendered unfit for use or service, the like quantity of vellum, parchment, or paper, with the several and respective duties stamped, marked, or impressed on the vellum, parchment, or paper, so written or ingrossed upon, spoiled, obliterated, or by any other means rendered unfit for use or service, without demanding or taking, directly or indirectly, for the same, any sum of money or other consideration whatsoever.

Penalty of counterfeiting

XL. And be it further enacted by the authority aforesaid, That if any person or persons shall counterfeit or forge, or cause or procure to be counterfeited or forged, any seal, stamp, mark,

mark, plate, or device, which ſhall be provided, made, or uſed, in purſance of this act; or ſhall counterfeit or reſemble the impreſſion of the ſame upon any vellum, parchment, or paper, or upon any cards, or ace of ſpades, or jew, or wrapper, or any thread or paper incloſing any pack or parcel of cards, with an intent to defraud his Majeſty, his heirs, or ſucceſſors, of any of the ſaid duties on vellum, parchment, or paper, or upon cards; or ſhall utter, vend, or ſell, any vellum, parchment, or paper, or any cards, ace of ſpades, or jew, or wrapper, with ſuch counterfeit ſeal, ſtamp, mark, plate, or device thereupon, knowing the ſame to be counterfeit; or if any perſon whatſoever ſhall privately and fraudulently uſe any ſeal, ſtamp, mark, plate, or device, provided or uſed, or to be provided or uſed, in purſuance of this or any former act or acts of parliament, relating to the duties upon ſtamped vellum, parchment, and paper, and upon cards, ſo as thereby to defraud his Majeſty, his heirs, or ſucceſſors, of any duty payable by this or any ſuch former act or acts of parliament; then every ſuch perſon ſo offending, and being thereof convicted in due form of law, ſhall be adjudged a felon, and ſuffer death as in caſes of felony, without benefit of clergy.

any of the ſtamps, or vending the ſame, or fraudulently uſing the legal ſtamps to defraud the King of the duty, is felony.

XLI. And be it further enacted by the authority aforeſaid, That all penalties and forfeitures inflicted, impoſed, or to incur, by this act, not herein before otherwiſe diſpoſed of, ſhall go and be paid, the one moiety thereof to his Majeſty, his heirs and ſucceſſors, and the other moiety thereof to the perſon or perſons who ſhall inform and ſue for the ſame, in any court of record, with his or their full coſts of ſuit, by action of debt, bill, plaint, or information, wherein no eſſoin, protection, or wager of law, or any more than one imparlance ſhall be allowed.

Diſtribution of the penalties and forfeitures not otherwiſe diſpoſed of; to be recovered with full coſts.

XLII. And be it further enacted by the authority aforeſaid, That all powers, proviſions, articles, clauſes, diſtribution of penalties and forfeitures, and all other matters and things, preſcribed or appointed by any former act or acts of parliament relating to the duties on vellum, parchment, and paper, on which any admiſſion into any corporation or company, or policy of aſſurance, ſhall be ingroſſed, written, or printed, and not hereby altered, ſhall be in full force and effect, with relation to the duties hereby impoſed, and ſhall be applied and put in execution, for the raiſing, levying, collecting, and ſecuring, the ſaid new duties hereby impoſed according to the true intent and meaning of this act, as fully, to all intents and purpoſes, as if the ſame had ſeverally and reſpectively been hereby enacted with relation to the ſaid new duties.

Powers, &c. granted by former acts relating to ſtamp duties on admiſſions, and policies of aſſurance, extended to theſe duties.

XLIII. Provided always, and it is hereby enacted by the authority aforeſaid, That all the money ariſing by the ſaid duty by this act charged and impoſed, upon the entry, minute, or memorandum, of any admiſſion into any corporation or company, ſhall be iſſued and applied to ſuch and the ſame uſes as the ſaid former duties were made applicable; and that all the money ariſing

Duties upon entries of admiſſion into corporations or companies, and the additional duty of 20 s. on policies of assurance, to be applied as the former duties. arising by the additional duty of twenty shillings by this act charged and imposed on policies of assurance, by which the properties of any number of persons in any ship, cargo, or both, not exceeding in the whole the sum of one hundred pounds, shall be assured; shall be issued and applied to such and the same uses, as the former duties upon policies of assurance are applicable.

XLIV. And be it further enacted by the authority aforesaid, That in case any action, suit, or other prosecution, shall be had, brought, or prosecuted, against any person or persons, for or by reason of any act, matter, or thing, by him, her, or them, done or committed, by virtue or in pursuance of this act; that then, in every such case, the action, suit, or prosecution, shall be laid and prosecuted in the county or city where the fact was committed, and not elsewhere; and that, in every such action, suit, or prosecution, the defendant or defendants may plead the general issue, and give this act, and any other act or acts of parliament, and any other matter or thing, in evidence; and in case there shall be a verdict or verdicts therein for the defendant or defendants, or judgement therein shall be given for the defendant or defendants, or the plaintiff or plaintiffs, prosecutor or prosecutors, shall become nonsuit, or the plaintiff or plaintiffs, prosecutor or prosecutors, shall discontinue such action or suit; that then, and in every such case, the defendant and defendants, in every such action, suit, or prosecution, shall recover his, her, or their, treble costs.

General issue.

Treble costs.

CAP. XLVII.

An act for encreasing the fund for payment of the sums of money directed, by an act made in the thirty second year of the reign of his late majesty King George *the Second, to be applied in augmentation of the salaries of the puisne judges in the court of* King's Bench, *the judges in the court of* Common Pleas, *the barons of the coif in the court of* Exchequer *at* Westminster, *and the justices of* Chester, *and the great sessions for the counties in* Wales, *for the time being; and for applying certain sums in augmentation of the salaries of the said judges and justices, and of the judges in the courts of* Session *and* Exchequer *in* Scotland, *for a certain time previous to the commencement of the augmentations established by the said act.*

Preamble, reciting clause in act 32 Geo. 2.

WHEREAS *by an act made in the thirty second year of the reign of his late majesty King* George *the Second, intituled,* An act for augmenting the salaries of the puisne judges in the court of *King's bench*, the judges of the court of *Common Pleas*, the barons of the coif in the court of *Exchequer* at *Westminster*, the judges in the courts of session, and exchequer in *Scotland*, and justices of *Chester*, and the great sessions for the counties in *Wales*;

it

was set forth, That the salaries of the said judges and justices were inadequate to the dignity and importance of their offices; and therefore in order to establish, in the first place, a proper fund for the augmentation of the salaries of the said judges in the courts at Westminster, *and justices of* Chester, *and the great sessions for the counties in* Wales, *certain stamp duties were thereby granted, and appropriated to the payment of the several and respective sums of money directed by the said act to be applied in augmentation of the salaries of the said last-mentioned judges and justices; and certain sums were directed to be paid yearly out of the duties and revenues therein mentioned, in augmentation of the salaries of the said judges in* Scotland: *and whereas by an act made in the second year of his present Majesty's reign, intituled,* An act for better securing the payment of the sums of money directed by an act made in the thirty second year of the reign of his late majesty King *George* the Second, to be applied in augmentation of the salaries of the puisne judges in the court of *King's bench*, the judges in the court of *Common Pleas*, the barons of the coif in the court of *Exchequer* at *Westminster*, and the justices of *Chester* and the great sessions for the counties in *Wales* for the time being; *it was set forth, That the fund provided by the said act of the thirty second year of the reign of his late majesty King* George *the Second, for payment of the sums thereby granted in augmentation of the salaries to the said judges and justices in* England *and* Wales, *had proved insufficient to make good and answer the same; and therefore certain other stamp duties were, by the said last-mentioned act, granted, appropriated, and made one joint fund with the duties arising by virtue of the said former act, for answering and paying, in such manner and proportions as are in the said former act directed and appointed with respect to the duties thereby granted, all such sums of money as should become due and payable from and after the fifth day of* July, *one thousand seven hundred and sixty two, in pursuance of the said former act, to the said judges and justices in* England *and* Wales: *and whereas the said joint fund so established and provided for payment of all such sums of money as should become due and payable from and after the said fifth day of* July, *one thousand seven hundred and sixty two, in pursuance of the said act made in the thirty second year of the reign of his late Majesty, to the said judges and justices in* England *and* Wales, *hath also proved insufficient to make good and answer the same:* we, your Majesty's most dutiful and loyal subjects, the commons of *Great Britain* in parliament assembled, in order to make the said joint fund effectual to answer the said purposes, do give and grant unto your Majesty the duties hereinafter mentioned; and do therefore most humbly beseech your Majesty, that it may be enacted; and be it enacted by the King's most excellent Majesty, by and with the advice and consent of the lords spiritual and temporal, and commons, in this present parliament assembled, and by the authority of the same, That from and after the fifth day of *July*, one thousand seven hundred and sixty five, there shall be throughout *England* the dominion of *Wales*, and town of *Berwick upon Tweed*, raised, col-

and 2 Geo. 3.

From and after 5 July, 1765, the following additional stamp duties to take place; viz.

collected, levied, and paid, unto and for the use of his Majesty, his heirs, and successors, for every piece of vellum, parchment, or paper, on which the matters and things herein after mentioned shall be ingrossed or written at any time or times after the said fifth day of *July*, over and above the rates and duties charges and sums of money, now due and payable to his Majesty for or in respect of the same, the further rates, duties, charges, and sums of money; that is to say,

On admissions into the four inns of court, 4l.

For every piece of vellum or parchment, or sheet or piece of paper, upon which any admission into the four inns of court shall be ingrossed or written, an additional stamp duty of four pounds.

On testimonials of the degree of utter barrister 6l.

For every piece of vellum or parchment, or sheet or piece of paper, upon which shall be ingrossed or written any register, entry, testimonial, or certificate, of the degree of utter barrister taken in any of the said four inns of court, an additional stamp duty of six pounds.

These duties to be under the management of the commissioners for the former duties on stamps.

II. And be it further enacted by the authority aforesaid, That for the better and more effectual raising, levying, collecting, and paying, the said additional rates and duties herein before granted, the same shall be under the government, care, and management, of the commissioners for the time being appointed to manage the duties payable to his Majesty, his heirs, and successors, and charged on stamped vellum, parchment, and paper, by former acts of parliament in that behalf made; who, or the major part of them, are hereby required and impowered to employ such officers under them for that purpose, as they shall think proper; and to use such dies and stamps, to denote the stamp duties hereby charged, as they shall think fit; and to repair, renew, or alter, the same, from time to time, as there shall be occasion; and to do all other acts, matters, and things, necessary to be done, for putting this act in execution, with relation to the said rates and duties hereby granted, in the like, and in as full and ample manner, as they, or the major part of them, are authorized to put in execution any former law concerning stamped vellum, parchment, or paper.

One new stamp may be provided for denoting all the duties.

III. Provided always, and be it further enacted by the authority aforesaid, That, to prevent the multiplication of stamps for and in respect of the additional rates and duties hereby granted, it shall and may be lawful for the said commissioners, instead of distinct stamps, to ascertain the duties granted by former acts, and this act, to cause one new stamp to be provided for denoting all the said duties, from time to time, as shall, by the said commissioners, be thought proper or necessary.

Such former stampt paper, vellum or parchment, as shall be used after the said 5 July, for the purposes a-

IV. And be it further enacted by the authority aforesaid, That all vellum, parchment, and paper, charged by this act with any of the stamp duties hereby granted, which hath been, or shall, before the said fifth day of *July*, be stamped or marked in pursuance of the former acts of parliament relating to his Majesty's stamp duties, or any of them, shall, before any of the matters or things, in respect whereof any rate or duty is hereby made payable, shall be ingrossed or written thereupon (such ingrossing or writing being, at any time after the said fifth day of *July*) be brought to the head office for stamping or marking of vellum, parchment, and paper, to be stamped or marked with another mark or stamp, over and besides the marks or stamps put, or to be put, thereupon, in pursuance of the said former acts, or any of them; and that all vellum, parchment, and paper, which hath not been, or shall not, before the said fifth day of *July*, be stamped or marked in pursuance of the said former acts, or any of them, shall, before any of the matters or things in respect whereof any stamp duty is payable hereby, and by the said former acts, or any of them, shall be thereupon ingrossed or written (such ingrossing or writing being after the said fifth day of *July*) be brought to the said head office, and there marked and stamped with the proper marks or stamps, or mark or stamp, provided, used, or appointed, or to be provided or appointed, in pursuance of the said former acts, or of this act, to denote the respective duties hereby and hereby respectively charged thereupon; and if any of the said matters and things, so to be ingrossed or written as foresaid, shall be ingrossed or written, contrary to the true intent and meaning hereof, upon vellum, parchment, or paper, not appearing to have been duly marked or stamped according to this act; that then, and in every such case, there shall be due, answered, and paid (over and above the stamp duties payable hereby, and by the said former acts, or any of them) for or in respect of every such matter or thing, the sum of five pounds; and that no such matter or thing shall be available in law or equity, or be given in evidence, or admitted in any court, unless as well the said duty hereby charged in respect thereof, as the said sum of five pounds, shall be first paid to the receiver general for the time being of the stamp duties, or his deputy or clerk, and until the vellum, parchment, or paper, upon which such matter or thing is so ingrossed or written, shall be marked or stamped according to the tenor and true meaning hereof; and the said receiver general, and his deputy or clerk, are hereby enjoined and required, upon payment or tender of the said duties, and of the said sum of five pounds, and such other sums as by the said former acts are payable in that behalf, to give a receipt for such monies; and the other proper officers are thereupon required to mark or stamp such matters or things with the proper marks or stamps, or mark or stamp, required in that behalf; which said sum of five pounds is to be applied to the same uses and purposes as the duties hereby granted are to be applied.

foresaid, is to be brought to the office, to be stamped with the duties granted by this act;

but all unstamped paper &c. is to be marked with the general stamp for all the duties.

Penalty of not using the proper stamps, is 5l. besides the duties;

and the instrument deemed unavailable, until these duties, as well as the penalty, are paid.

Receipt to be given for the said duties.

Penalty to be applied as the duties.

V. And be it further enacted by the authority aforesaid, That the rates and duties herein before granted shall be paid, from time to time, into the hands of the receiver general for the time being of the duties on stamped vellum, parchment, and paper, who shall keep a separate and distinct account of the rates and duties arising by virtue of this act; and pay the same (the necessary charges of raising, paying, and accounting for, such rates and duties being deducted) into the receipt of the exchequer,

duties to be paid over to the receiver general.

and by him into the exchequer.

for the purpoſes herein after expreſſed, at ſuch time and in ſuch manner, as any former duties on ſtamped vellum, parchment, or paper, are directed to be paid; and that in the office of the auditor of the ſaid receipt, ſhall be provided and kept a book or books, in which all the monies ariſing from the rates and duties hereby granted and paid into the ſaid receipt as aforeſaid, ſhall be entered ſeparate and apart from all other monies paid and payable to his Majeſty, his heirs, and ſucceſſors, upon any account whatſoever, and ſhall be applied in ſuch manner as is herein after mentioned.

and to be entered ſeparate and apart from all other monies.

Officers to obſerve the rules preſcribed them by the treaſury.

VI. And be it further enacted by the authority aforeſaid, That the ſaid commiſſioners, and all other officers who ſhall be employed in the collection or management of the ſaid rates and duties herein before granted, ſhall, in the execution of their offices, obſerve and perform ſuch rules and orders as they reſpectively ſhall, from time to time, receive from the high treaſurer or the commiſſioners of the treaſury, or any three or more of them, for the time being; and that no fee or reward ſhall be taken or demanded by any ſuch commiſſioners or officers from any of his Majeſty's ſubjects, for any matter or thing to be done in purſuance of this act; and in caſe any officer employed in the execution of this act, in relation to the ſaid rates and duties, ſhall refuſe or neglect to do or perform any matter or thing by this act required or directed to be done or performed by him, whereby any of his Majeſty's ſubjects ſhall or may ſuſtain any damage whatſoever, ſuch officer ſo offending ſhall be liable, by any action to be founded on this ſtatute, to anſwer to the party grieved all ſuch damages, with treble coſts of ſuit.

No fees to be taken by them.

Officer neglecting his duty, liable to pay damages, with treble coſts.

Penalty on officers guilty of a breach of truſt;

or miſapplying any of the monies.

Powers, &c. granted by former acts, extended to this act.

VII. And be it further enacted by the authority aforeſaid, That the ſaid commiſſioners and their officers ſhall be ſubject to ſuch penalties and forfeitures, for any breach of the truſt in them repoſed, or for diverting or miſapplying the money received in purſuance of this act, as by any former law relating to ſtamped vellum, parchment, or paper, are inflicted; and that all powers, proviſions, articles, clauſes, penalties, forfeitures, diſtribution of penalties and forfeitures, and all other matters and things preſcribed, inflicted, or appointed, by any former act or acts of parliament relating to the ſtamp duties on vellum, parchment, and paper, and not hereby altered, ſhall be in full force and effect, with relation to the rates and duties hereby impoſed; and ſhall be applied, and put in execution, for the raiſing, levying, collecting, and ſecuring, the ſaid rates and duties, according to the true intent and meaning of this act, as fully to all intents and purpoſes, as if the ſame had ſeverally and reſpectively been herein enacted with relation to the rates and duties hereby impoſed.

Penalty of counterfeiting or forging any of the ſtamps,

VIII. And be it further enacted by the authority aforeſaid, That if any perſon, from and after the ſaid fifth day of June, ſhall counterfeit or forge, or procure to be counterfeited or forged, any ſeal, ſtamp, or mark, to reſemble any ſeal, ſtamp, or mark, directed or allowed to be uſed by this act for the purpoſe of denoting the duties hereby granted; or ſhall counterfeit or reſemble

resemble the impression of the same with an intent to defraud his Majesty, his heirs and successors, of any of the said duties; or shall utter, vend, or sell, any vellum, parchment, or paper, liable to any such stamped duty, with such counterfeit stamp or mark, knowing the same to be counterfeit; or shall privately or fraudulently use any seal, stamp, or mark, directed or allowed to be used by this act, with intent to defraud his Majesty, his heirs, and successors, of any of the said duties; every person so offending, and being thereof lawfully convicted, shall be adjudged a felon, and shall suffer death as in cases of felony, without benefit of clergy.

or vending forged stamps, or privately or fraudulently using the real seal, to defraud his Majesty, is felony.

IX. And be it further enacted by the authority aforesaid, That the duties hereby granted, and the duties arising by virtue of the said former act made in the thirty second year of his late Majesty's reign, and in the second year of his present Majesty's reign, shall be and are hereby made one joint fund for answering and paying, in such manner and proportions as are in the said several acts directed and appointed with respect to the duties thereby granted, all such sums of money as shall become due and payable from and after the said fifth day of *July*, in pursuance of the said several acts, to the puisne judges in the court of *King's Bench*, the judges in the court of *Common Pleas* at *Westminster*, the chief and other barons of the coif in the court of *Exchequer* at *Westminster*, the chief and second justices of *Chester*, and the justices of the great sessions for the counties in *Wales*, for the time being respectively; and if any surplus shall remain of the produce of the said fund, the same shall (except the money herein after authorized to be paid thereout) be reserved for the disposition of parliament, in such manner as any surplus of the duties granted by the said several acts are thereby respectively directed to be reserved.

The several former duties, and those hereby granted, made a joint fund for paying the augmentation to the judges salaries established by the recited acts of 32 Geo. 2 and 2 Geo. 3.

Surplus money to be reserved for the disposition of parliament;

X. And be it further enacted by the authority aforesaid, That out of any of the surplusses which shall arise upon the said funds established for payment of the said augmentation, and upon the said additional stamp duties hereby granted, after the payments charged thereupon are, from time to time, satisfied, a sum not exceeding three thousand six hundred and twenty five pounds, shall be paid and applied in augmentation of the salaries of the said judges and justices, from the fifth day of *January*, one thousand seven hundred and fifty nine, to the fifth day of *July*, in the same year, according to the proportions appointed by the said act of the thirty second year of the reign of his said late Majesty, with respect to the augmentation therein mentioned.

first paying thereout 3,625l. in augmentation of the said salaries from 5 Jan. to 5 July, 1759.

XI. And be it further enacted by the authority aforesaid, That out of any of the duties and revenues in that part of *Great Britain* called *Scotland*, which by an act made in the tenth year of the reign of Queen *Anne*, were charged or made chargeable with the payment of the fees, salaries, and other charges, allowed, or to be allowed, by her Majesty, her heirs, or successors, for keeping up the courts of session and justiciary, and exchequer court in *Scotland*, a sum not exceeding two thousand one

2,100l. to be paid out of the funds established by act 10 Annæ, in Scotland, one hundred pounds, ſhall be paid and applied, in augmentation of the ſalaries of the judges in the ſaid courts of ſeſſion and exchequer, from the ſaid fifth day of *January*, to the ſaid fifth day of *July*, one thouſand ſeven hundred and fifty nine, according to the proportions appointed by the ſaid act made in the thirty ſecond year of the reign of his ſaid late Majeſty, with reſpect to the augmentation thereby granted of the ſalaries of the ſaid judges.

in augmentation of the judges ſalaries there, from 5 Jan. to 5 July, 1759.

XII. And it is hereby enacted by the authority aforeſaid, That if any perſon or perſons ſhall, at any time or times be ſued or proſecuted for any thing by him or them done or to be done or executed in purſuance of this act, or of any matter or thing in this act contained, ſuch perſon or perſons ſhall and may plead the general iſſue, and give the ſpecial matter in evidence for his or their defence; and if, upon the trial, a verdict ſhall paſs for the defendant or defendants, or the plaintiff or plaintiffs ſhall become nonſuited, then ſuch defendant or defendants ſhall have treble coſts to him or them awarded againſt ſuch plaintiff or plaintiffs.

General iſſue.

Treble coſts.

CAP. XLVIII.

An act for prohibiting the importation of foreign manufactured ſilk ſtockings, ſilk mitts, and ſilk gloves, into Great Britain *and the* Britiſh *dominions; and for rendering more effectual an act paſſed in the third year of the reign of his preſent Majeſty, for explaining, amending, and rendering more effectual, an act made in the nineteenth year of the reign of King* Henry *the Seventh, intituled,* Silk Works.

Preamble.

WHEREAS *the importation of foreign manufactured ſilk ſtockings, ſilk mitts, and ſilk gloves, into* Great Britain, *and the* Britiſh *dominions, is greatly prejudicial to the trade and manufactures of this kingdom, and tends to the depriving of his Majeſty's ſubjects of the means of ſupporting themſelves and their families*; for remedy whereof, may it pleaſe your Majeſty that it may be enacted; and be it enacted by the King's moſt excellent majeſty, by and with the advice and conſent of the lords ſpiritual and temporal, and commons, in this preſent parliament aſſembled, and by the authority of the ſame, That if any foreign manufactured ſilk ſtockings, ſilk mitts, or ſilk gloves, ſhall from and after the twenty fourth day of *June*, one thouſand ſeven hundred and ſixty five, be imported, brought, or conveyed, into this kingdom, or any part of the *Britiſh* dominions, the ſame ſhall be, and are hereby declared to be, forfeited, and ſhall be liable to be ſearched for and ſeized, in like manner as other prohibited and uncuſtomed goods are, and ſhall be diſpoſed of as is herein after mentioned; and every perſon or perſons who ſhall bring, convey, or import, or ſhall cauſe to be brought, conveyed, or imported, into this kingdom, or any part of the *Britiſh*

Foreign manufactured ſilk ſtockings, ſilk mitts, or ſilk gloves, are prohibited to be imported after 24 June, 1765. on penalty of forfeiture,

British dominions, any such silk stockings, silk mitts, or silk gloves, or shall be aiding, abetting, or assisting therein, or being a vender or venders, retailer or retailers, of any kind of silk stockings, mitts, or gloves, in whose custody or possession any such foreign manufactured silk stockings, silk mitts, or silk gloves, shall be found, or who shall sell, or expose to sale, any such silk stockings, silk mitts, or silk gloves, or who shall conceal any such silk stockings, silk mitts, or silk gloves, with intent to prevent the forfeiture or seizure of the same, shall, over and above the forfeiture and loss of such silk stockings, silk mitts, and silk gloves, and all interest which he, she, or they, may have therein, for every such offence, forfeit and pay the sum of two hundred pounds, together with costs of suit.

and the persons assisting, therein or dealers in whose custody such goods shall be found or exposing them to sale, &c.

forfeit also 200l.

II. Provided always, and be it further enacted by the authority aforesaid, That if any such silk stockings, silk mitts, or silk gloves, shall be found and seized in that part of *Great Britain* called *England*, out of the cities of *London*, and *Westminster*, and the limits of the weekly bills of mortality, and the same shall not exceed in value the sum of twenty pounds; it shall and may be lawful for two or more of his Majesty's justices of the peace for such county, city, borough, or place, where the same shall be so found and seized, upon information before them that such silk stockings, silk mitts, or silk gloves, were seized as silk stockings, silk mitts, or silk gloves, unduly brought into, and not manufactured within this kingdom, to hear and determine the same, and to proceed to condemnation or discharge thereof, as shall seem just, any thing herein before contained to the contrary notwithstanding.

Where such goods shall be found, and seized out of London, or weekly bills not exceeding 20l. in value; two justices for the county or place may proceed to condemnation or discharge thereof.

III. And be it further enacted by the authority aforesaid, That forthwith after the seizure of any such silk stockings, silk mitts, or silk gloves, as aforesaid, the same shall be deposited in one of the King's warehouses belonging to the custom-house, in case such seizure happens to be within the cities of *London* or *Westminster*, or the weekly bills of mortality, where the same shall be received and admitted at all times by the proper officer or officers there, who is and are hereby impowered and required to receive and preserve the same; and in case such seizure shall be made out of the said cities of *London*, and *Westminster*, and the weekly bills of mortality, then the same shall be deposited in the hands of the chief magistrate of such city, town, or place where the same shall be seized, or in the hands of the constable of the next adjacent village, who is and are impowered and required to receive and preserve the same; and all and every such silk stockings, silk mitts, and silk gloves, may, from time to time, be viewed and inspected by any person or persons, on behalf of the prosecutor or prosecutors, or of the person or persons interested in or claiming the said silk stockings, silk mitts, and silk gloves, with the leave of the court, officers, judges, or justices, where, or before whom any prosecution or suit shall be carried on, for condemnation thereof, or for recovery of any penalty by this act inflicted, who are and is hereby required to make and give such

Seizures, if made within London or Westminster, or weekly bills to be deposited in the King's warehouses; if made elsewhere, to be deposited with the chief magistrate, or constable.

and to be viewed with leave;

orders, from time to time for that purpoſe, as may be juſt and reaſonable; and after condemnation thereof in due courſe of law, all and every ſuch ſilk ſtockings, ſilk mitts, and ſilk gloves, ſhall be publickly ſold to the beſt advantage for exportation by the candle; and one moiety of the produce, or money ariſing by the ſale of ſuch ſilk ſtockings, ſilk mitts, and ſilk gloves, ſhall be to the uſe of his Majeſty, his heirs, and ſucceſſors, ; and the other moiety thereof to the uſe of the officer or officers who ſhall ſeize and ſecure the ſame; and no ſuch ſilk ſtockings, ſilk mitts, or ſilk gloves, ſhall be conſumed or uſed in this kingdom, but ſhall be exported again to ſome port or place, not being any part of his Majeſty's dominions, and ſhall not be ſold otherwiſe than on condition to be exported as aforeſaid; and ſuch ſilk ſtockings ſilk mitts, and ſilk gloves, ſhall not be delivered out of the ware-houſe or place wherein the ſame ſhall have been ſecured, until ſufficient ſecurity be firſt given to the King's majeſty, his heirs, and ſucceſſors, which the commiſſioners of his Majeſty's cuſtoms are hereby impowered and required to take, that the ſame, and every part thereof, ſhall be exported as aforeſaid, and not land-ed again in any part of his Majeſty's dominions; which ſecuri-ties ſhall be diſcharged without fee or reward, upon certificate returned under the common ſeal of the chief magiſtrate in any place or places beyond the ſeas, and out of his Majeſty's domi-nions, or under the hands and ſeals of two known *Engliſh* mer-chants upon ſuch place, that the goods were there landed; or upon proof by credible perſons, that ſuch goods were taken by enemies, or periſhed in the ſeas; the examination and proof thereof being left to the judgement of the ſaid commiſſioners; which commiſſioners are hereby impowered, from time to time to call upon the perſon or perſons who have entered into ſuch ſecurity, to produce ſuch certificate or proof as aforeſaid.

and after con-demnation, to be publickly ſold for ex-portation to foreign parts, not being any of his Majeſ-ty's domini-ons; for which ſe-curity is to be given, to be diſcharg-ed upon cer-tificate of the due landing thereof, or proof made of their being taken by the enemy, or that they pe-riſhed at ſea.

IV. And, for the better diſcovering and detecting any offen-der or offenders againſt this act; be it enacted by the authority aforeſaid, That upon an information in writing, made upon oath before any two or more of his Majeſty's juſtices of the peace for the reſpective county or place (which information ſhall be ſigned by the party or parties making the ſame) that there is good ground and reaſon to ſuſpect that ſuch ſilk ſtockings, ſilk mitts, or ſilk gloves as aforeſaid, have been imported into this kingdom, and are concealed by, or are in the poſſeſſion or cuſ-tody of, any retailer or ſeller of any kind of ſilk ſtockings, ſilk mitts, or ſilk gloves, contrary to the true intent of this act; it ſhall and may be lawful for ſuch juſtices reſpectively, to iſſue their warrant or warrants to any conſtable or conſtables, or other peace officer or officers, within the ſaid county or place, impow-ering him or them to ſearch in the day-time the houſe or houſes out-houſe, or out-houſes, ware-houſes, ſhops, cellars, rooms, and other places, belonging to, or hired, employed, or made uſe of by, ſuch retailer or ſeller who ſhall be ſuſpected to con-ceal or have in his, her, or their poſſeſſion or cuſtody any ſilk ſtockings, ſilk mitts, or ſilk gloves, not being made or manu-factured

Where there ſhall be grounds for ſuſpicion, and information upon oath be made and ſub ſcribed before a juſtice, of any ſuch goods being import-ed and con-cealed by the retailer, he is to iſſue his warrant for ſearching for and ſeizing the ſame.

factured within *Great Britain*; and if any such silk stockings, silk mitts, or silk gloves, not being made or manufactured within *Great Britain*, shall be found, to seize and carry away the same, for the purpose of carrying this act into execution, and and to dispose thereof as is herein before directed.

V. And be it further enacted by the authority aforesaid, That if any action or suit shall be commenced against any person or persons, for any thing done in pursuance of this act, the defendant or defendants in such action or suit may plead the general issue, and give this act and the special matter, in evidence, at any trial to be had thereupon, and that the same was done by the authority of this act; and if it shall appear to have been so done, then the jury shall find for the defendant or defendants; and if the plaintiff shall be nonsuited, or discontinue his action after the defendant or defendants shall have appeared; or if judgement shall be given upon any verdict or demurrer against the plaintiff, the defendant or defendants shall recover treble costs, and have the like remedy for the same as defendants have in other cases by law.

General issue.

Treble costs.

VI. Provided always, and be it further enacted, That in every such action, it shall and may be lawful for the defendant or defendants, by leave of the court where such action shall be depending, at any time before issue joined, to pay into court such sum of money as he or they shall see fit, as amends for the matter or cause complained of in such action; whereupon such proceedings, orders, and judgements, shall and may be had, made, and given, in and by such court, as in other actions where the defendant is allowed to pay money into court.

Defendant allowed to pay money into court.

VII. And be it further enacted by the authority aforesaid, That if any such silk stockings, silk mitts, or silk gloves, shall be seized by virtue and in pursuance of this act, and any doubt or question shall afterwards arise where the same were manufactured, the proof shall lie upon the person or persons in whose custody or possession the same were found, and not upon the prosecutor or prosecutors, plaintiff or plaintiffs; and in case no proof shall be given that such silk stockings, silk mitts, or silk gloves, were manufactured within *Great Britain*, then the same shall, without any further proceeding, be taken and held to have been manufactured out of *Great Britain*, and contrary to, and in violation of, this act; any law or custom to the contrary notwithstanding.

If any doubt arise with respect to the place of manufacture of such goods, proof to lie on the defendant.

VIII. Provided always, and be it further enacted, That if any person or persons in whose custody or possession any such silk stockings, silk mitts, or silk gloves, shall be seized, by virtue and in pursuance of this act, such person or persons not importing or concealing the same, shall discover upon oath, before any one or more justice or justices of the peace, the person or persons who sold such silk stockings, silk mitts, or silk gloves to such person or persons in whose custody or possession the same shall be seized, so as that such person or persons, so selling the same, shall or may be prosecuted and convicted according to the

Person in whose custody such goods shall be found, not importing or concealing the same,

discovering the seller,

the intent of this act, as the seller thereof, in case the same shall be, or be taken and held to be, within the intent and meaning of this act, manufactured out of *Great Britain*; such person or persons so discovering, as aforesaid, shall be, and is and are hereby freed and discharged of and from all and every the penalties and forfeitures by this act inflicted upon all and every person and persons being a vender or venders, retailer or retailers, having in his, her, or their custody or possession any such silk stockings, silk mitts, or silk gloves, not made or manufactured, in *Great Britain*; and of and from any proof that the same so seized, as aforesaid, were manufactured in *Great Britain*.

is discharged from all penalties.

Recovery and application of the pecuniary penalties and forfeitures.

IX. And be it further enacted by the authority aforesaid, That all pecuniary penalties and forfeitures by this act imposed, shall and may be sued for and recovered in any of his Majesty's courts of record at *Westminster*, or in the court of exchequer at *Edinburgh*, respectively, by action, bill, plaint, or information, in the name of his Majesty's attorney general, or in the name of his Majesty's advocate in *Scotland*, or in the name or names of some officer or officers of the customs; and that one moiety of every such penalty and forfeiture shall be to his Majesty, his heirs, and successors, and the other moiety thereof to the officer or officers of the customs who shall inform and prosecute for the same.

Wearer of such goods not subject to any forfeiture or penalty.

X. Provided also, and be it further enacted by the authority aforesaid, That nothing in this act contained shall extend, or be in any wise construed to extend, to subject any person or persons who shall wear or make use of such silk stockings, silk mitts, or silk gloves, as aforesaid, as part of his, her, or their apparel, or dress only, to any forfeiture, or to any pecuniary penalty or penalties inflicted by this act, or to any proof that the same were manufactured within *Great Britain*.

Penalties inflicted by act 19 Hen. 7. on persons importing ribbands, laces, or girdles, of foreign manufacture, and upon the aiders therein, and the venders, or concealers thereof, deemed insufficient.

XI. And whereas by an act passed in the third year of the reign of his present majesty, for explaining, amending, and rendering more effectual, an act made in the nineteenth year of the reign of King *Henry* the Seventh, intituled, *Silk Works*, certain penalties are thereby inflicted upon any person or persons, who shall import, bring, or convey, or cause to be imported, brought, or conveyed into this kingdom, any ribbands, laces, or girdles, not made and manufactured in *Great Britain* whether the same be wrought of silk alone, or wrought of silk mixed with any other materials: or who shall be aiding, abetting, or assisting, in the bringing and conveying, or importing into this kingdom any such ribbands, laces, or girdles, as aforesaid; and also upon every person and persons being a vender or venders, retailer or retailers, of any kind of ribbands, laces, or girdles, respectively, in whose custody or possession any such ribbands, laces, or girdles, or any of them, shall be found; or who shall sell or expose to sale, any such ribbands, laces, or girdles, as aforesaid; or who shall conceal any such ribbands, laces or girdles, with intent to prevent the forfeiture or seizure of the same; which penalties, by reason of the smallness thereof, have

have be found insufficient to answer the good intention of the said act; be it therefore further enacted by the authority aforesaid, That all and every person and persons, who shall be guilty of any of the offences aforesaid, shall, for every such offence, forfeit and pay the sum of two hundred pounds, together with costs of suit; and shall and may be sued for and recovered in any of his Majesty's courts of record at *Westminster*, or in the court of exchequer at *Edinburgh* respectively, by action, bill, plaint, or information, in the name of his Majesty's attorney general, or in the name of his Majesty's advocate in *Scotland*, or in the name or names of some officer or officers of the customs; and that one moiety of every such penalty and forfeiture shall be to his Majesty, his heirs and successors; and the other moiety thereof, to the officer or officers who shall inform and prosecute for the same.

and persons for the future guilty of any of the said offences, to forfeit 200l. with costs of suit;

One moiety to the King, and the other to the prosecutor;

XII. Provided always, and it is hereby further enacted by the authority aforesaid, That nothing in this act contained shall extend, or be in any wise construed to extend, to subject any person or persons whatsoever, who shall wear or make use of such ribbands, laces or girdles, as aforesaid, as part of his, her or their apparel or dress only, to any forfeiture, or to any pecuniary penalty or penalties inflicted by the said recited act, or this act; or to any proof that such ribbands, laces or girdles, were manufactured in *Great Britain*.

but the wearer is not to be subject to any forfeiture or penalty.

XIII. And whereas in and by the said recited act it is enacted, That all and every such ribbands, laces and girdles, after condemnation thereof, shall, by order of the court, judge or judges, or justices, where or before whom such condemnation shall be had, be publickly burnt and intirely destroyed: and whereas the intention of the said act might be more effectually answered, if such ribbands, laces and girdles, were sold and disposed of in manner herein after mentioned, instead of being burnt and destroyed as aforesaid; be it therefore further enacted by the authority aforesaid, That all such ribbands, laces and girdles, shall be only seized and secured, in pursuance of the powers granted by the said act, by some officer or officers of his Majesty's customs, and shall, after condemnation thereof in due course of law, be publickly sold for the best advantage for exportation, by the candle; and one moiety of the produce or money arising by the sale of such ribbands, laces and girdles, shall be paid to the use of the King's majesty, his heirs and successors, and the other moiety thereof to the use of such officer or officers of the customs who shall seize and secure the same as aforesaid; and no such ribbands, laces or girdles, shall be consumed or used in this kingdom, but shall be exported again to some port or place, not being any part of his Majesty's dominions, and shall not be sold, otherwise than on condition to be exported as aforesaid; and such ribbands, laces and girdles, shall not be delivered out of the warehouse wherein the same shall have been secured, until sufficient security be first given to the King's majesty, his heirs and successors, (which the commissioners of his Majesty's

Such ribbands, laces, and girdles, instead of being burnt, pursuant to the recited act, are to be publickly sold,

and exported to foreign parts, not being part of the King's dominions; for which security is to be given,

customs are hereby impowered and required to take) that the same, and every part thereof, shall be exported as aforesaid, and not landed again in any part of his Majesty's dominions; which said securities shall be discharged without fee or reward, upon certificate returned under the common seal of the chief magistrate in any place or places beyond the seas, and out of his Majesty's dominions, or under the hands and seals of two known *English* merchants of such place, that the goods were there landed, or upon proof by credible persons that such goods were taken by enemies, or perished in the seas, the examination and proof thereof being left to the judgement of the said commissioners; which commissioners are hereby impowered, from time to time, to call upon the person or persons who have entered into such security to produce such certificate or proof as aforesaid.

and a certificate returned of the due landing thereof accordingly, or proof made of their being taken by enemies, or of their perishing in the seas.

XIV. Provided always, and it is hereby further enacted, That if any officer or officers of the customs shall neglect or refuse, for the space of one month after such condemnation as aforesaid, to prosecute to effect any person or persons for any pecuniary penalty or forfeiture by this act inflicted upon offenders against the same; that then it shall be lawful for any person or persons whomsoever, to sue for, prosecute and recover the respective pecuniary penalties and forfeitures by this act inflicted, in like manner as is herein before directed with regard to the officers of the customs; and one moiety of the said pecuniary forfeitures, when recovered, shall, in such case, go and be applied to the use of his Majesty, his heirs and successors, and the other moiety to the person or persons who shall sue or prosecute for the same respectively.

Officer neglecting, for one month after condemnation, to sue for the penalties, any other person may sue for, and recover the same, &c.

CAP. XLIX.

An act to prevent the inconveniencies arising from the present method of issuing notes and bills by the banks, banking companies and bankers, in that part of Great Britain *called* Scotland.

Preamble.

WHEREAS *a practice has prevailed in that part of* Great Britain *called* Scotland, *of issuing notes, commonly called* Bank Notes, *for sums of money payable to the bearer on demand, or in the option of the issuer or granter, payable at the end of six months, with a sum equal to the legal interest, from the demand to that time: and whereas notes, with such option as aforesaid, have been and are circulated in that part of the united kingdom to a great extent, and do pass, from hand to hand, as specie, whereby great inconveniencies have arisen:* for remedy whereof, may it please your Majesty that it may be enacted; and be it enacted by the King's most excellent majesty, by and with the advice and consent of the lords spiritual and temporal, and commons, in this present parliament assembled, and by the authority of the same, That from and after the fifteenth day of *May*, one thousand seven hundred and sixty six, it shall not be lawful for any person or persons whatsoever, bodies politick or corporate, to issue or give,

From and after 15 May, 1766, no notes to be issued in Scotland, and

give, or cause to be issued or given, within that part of *Great Britain* called *Scotland*, any note, ticket, token or other writing, for money, of the nature of a bank note, circulated, or to be circulated, as specie, but such as shall be payable on demand, in lawful money of *Great Britain*, and without reserving any power, or option of delaying payment thereof for any time or term whatsoever; and that from and after the said fifteenth day of *May*, one thousand seven hundred and sixty six, all notes, tickets, tokens, or other writings, for money, of the nature of a bank note, issued previous to the said day, and circulated as specie in that part of the united kingdom, shall, and they are hereby declared and adjudged to be payable, on demand, in lawful money aforesaid; any option, condition, or other clause therein contained to the contrary notwithstanding.

circulated as specie, but what shall be payable on demand; and notes issued, and circulated as specie, previous to the said day, shall be payable on demand, notwithstanding any optional clause to the contrary;

II. Provided always, That nothing contained in this act shall prevent any person or persons, bodies politick or corporate, from issuing post bills, payable seven days after sight, in the same manner as they are at present issued by the bank of *England*.

Post bills, payable at seven days sight, excepted:

III. And be it further enacted by the authority aforesaid, That all and every person and persons whatsoever, bodies politick or corporate, and the legal administrators of such person or persons, bodies politick or corporate, who shall, after the said fifteenth day of *May*, one thousand seven hundred and sixty six, issue or cause to be issued, any note, ticket, token or other writing, for money, of the nature of a bank note, circulated, or to be circulated, as specie, contrary to the directions of this act before-mentioned, and to the true meaning and intent thereof, shall, for every such offence, forfeit and pay to the person or persons who shall inform or prosecute for the same, five hundred pounds sterling, with full costs of suit; to be sued for and recovered, by way of complaint, before the court of session, upon fifteen days notice to the person or persons, bodies politick or corporate, complained of; which complaint the said court of session is hereby authorized and required summarily to determine, without abiding the course of any roll.

and persons acting contrary hereto, forfeit 500l. with full costs of suit.

IV. And for rendering the payment of all notes, accepted bills, post bills, tickets, tokens, or other writings, for money, of the nature of a bank or banker's note, circulated, or to be circulated, as specie, in that part of the united kingdom, more effectual, be it further enacted by the authority aforesaid, That from and after the passing of this act, summary execution shall proceed upon every such note, accepted bill, post bill, ticket, token or other writing, at the instance of the holder thereof, against the person or persons, bodies politick or corporate, and the legal administrators of such person or persons liable in payment of the same, not only for the sum or sums therein contained, but also for the interest thereof, from the time of demanding payment; and that a protest, taken at the office of the person or persons, bodies politick or corporate, liable, in payment of the same, between the hours of nine in the morning and three in the afternoon, for not payment, or for not marking of any

Summary execution may proceed upon every such note, in order to enforce payment of the principal and interest.

Method of protesting where payment is denied, &c.

any ſuch note, accepted bill, poſt bill, ticket, token, or other writing, ſhall be regiſterable in the courts of ſeſſion, or other competent judicatories, at any time within ſix months after the date of ſuch proteſt; that letters of horning, upon a charge of ſix days, and the other uſual execution of the law of *Scotland*, may paſs thereupon, in the ſame manner as is competent by the law of *Scotland*, upon proteſts of bills of exchange and inland bills duly regiſtered.

No ſuſpenſion to paſs, but upon a diſcharge of the note, or tender made,

V. And be it further enacted by the authority aforeſaid, That no ſuſpenſion or liſt of ſuch charge, or other execution, ſhall paſs, but upon a diſcharge by the holder of the note or notes, accepted bills, or poſt bills, ſo proteſted; or upon an offer or tender made to him or her, in the form of an inſtrument, duly ſigned by a notary publick and two witneſſes, of the full contents of ſuch note or notes, bill or bills, with the legal intereſt thereof from the date of the proteſt, and alſo of the expences of the proteſt, regiſtration, and ſuch diligence as ſhall have followed thereupon, to be certified by an account under the hand of the holder of ſuch note or notes, accepted bills, poſt bills, or other writings, aforeſaid, all in lawful money of *Great Britain:* ſaving and reſerving always to the perſon or perſons, bodies politick or corporate, who ſhall make ſuch payment, their action at common law, before any competent court, for repetition of any overcharge in ſuch account of expences; and to the perſon or perſons who ſhall have proteſted ſuch note or notes; his, her or their action, before any competent court, for what further damages he, ſhe or they, may have incurred by the undue delay of payment.

with all charges.

Overcharge in the account of expences may be ſued for at common law; as may alſo the damages ariſing from an undue delay of payment of the note.

Proteſt may be made of ſeveral notes jointly.

VI. And for preventing the unneceſſary expence and delay of proteſting each note, accepted bill, poſt bill, ticket, token, or other writing aforeſaid, ſeparately, be it enacted by the authority aforeſaid, That the holder of ſuch notes, accepted bills, poſt bills, tickets, tokens, or other writings, after prefixing to his or her proteſt the full tenor and contents of any one note, accepted bill, poſt bill, ticket, token, or other writing aforeſaid, iſſued by the perſon or perſons, bodies politick or corporate, againſt whom ſuch proteſt is to be taken, may and ſhall ſubjoin thereto the dates and numbers of all other notes or writings aforeſaid, of the ſame tenor and contents whereof he or ſhe ſhall then demand payment; which proteſt, being duly regiſtered as aforeſaid, ſhall be ſufficient warrant for iſſuing letters of horning, and all other execution of the law for payment of the contents of the whole notes, accepted bills, poſt bills, tickets, tokens, or other writings aforeſaid, ſo ſpecified in the proteſt; any law, uſage, or cuſtom, to the contrary notwithſtanding.

VII. And whereas a practice has of late prevailed in that part of the united kingdom, of iſſuing and circulating notes as ſpecie, of the nature of bank notes, for ſmall ſums, leſs than twenty ſhillings lawful money of *Great Britain*, whereby great inconveniencies have ariſen: for remedy whereof, be it further enacted by the authority aforesaid, That from and after the first day of *June*, one thousand seven hundred and sixty five, no note, accepted bill, post bill, ticket, token or other writing, circulated, or which may be circulated, as specie, in the manner of a bank or banker's note, shall be issued, re-issued, or given out, as specie, by any person or persons, bodies politick or corporate, their servants or agents, in that part of the united kingdom, for any sum or sums of money less than twenty shillings lawful money of *Great Britain*; any law, usage or custom to the contrary notwithstanding: and that the person or persons, bodies politick or corporate, their servants or agents, who shall, after the said first day of *June*, issue, re-issue, or give out, any note, accepted bill, post bill, ticket, token, or other writing aforesaid, for any sum less than twenty shillings, shall, for every such offence, forfeit and pay the sum of five hundred pounds sterling, with full costs of suit, to the person or persons who shall inform or prosecute for the same; to be sued for and recovered by way of summary complaint, before the court of session; to be proceeded in, in manner before directed.

From and after 1 June, 1765, no note to be issued, and circulated as specie, for a less sum than 20s. ster.

on forfeiture of 500l. with full costs of suit.

VIII. Provided always, That nothing herein contained shall be interpreted to prevent the holders of all such notes, accepted bills, post bills, tickets, tokens, or other writings aforesaid, for sums less than twenty shillings, from passing the same in payment until the first day of *June*, one thousand seven hundred and sixty six, or from demanding payment thereof from the person or persons, bodies politick or coporate, who issued the same, at any time.

Holders of small notes not prevented hereby from passing the same, until 1 June, 1766, or from demanding payment thereof at any time.

CAP. L.

An act to enlarge the powers of, and to render more effectual, the several acts, passed in the second, third and fourth years of his present Majesty's reign, for paving, cleansing, lighting and otherwise regulating the squares, streets and other places, within the city and liberty of Westminster, *and other parts in the said acts mentioned; and for extending the provisions of the said acts to the* Surrey *side of* Westminster Bridge; *and for enlarging the powers of the said acts with respect to squares.*

Preamble.

WHEREAS *an act was made in the second year of the reign of his present Majesty, intituled,* An act for paving, cleansing, and lighting the squares, streets and lanes, within the city and liberty of *Westminster*, the parishes of Saint *Giles in the Fields*, Saint *George* the Martyr, Saint *George Bloomsbury*, that part of the parish of Saint *Andrew's Holbourn* which lies in the county of *Middlesex*, the several liberties of the *Rolls* and *Savoy*, and that part of the duchy of *Lancaster* which lies in the county of *Middlesex*, and for preventing annoyances therein, and for other purposes there mentioned: *and whereas another act was made in the third year of the reign of his present Majesty, to explain, amend, and render more effectual, the said last mentioned act: and whereas*

an-

another act was made in the last session of parliament, to explain, amend and render more effectual, the said two last mentioned acts: and whereas the commissioners for putting the said three several acts in execution, have made some further progress in the trusts thereby reposed in them, but find that all the said acts are defective with respect to some of the powers thereby given, and that the said several acts cannot be effectually put in execution, so as to answer the good purposes thereby intended, unless some new powers are granted, and the said several acts in other respects amended, and made more effectual: may it therefore please your Majesty, that it may be enacted; and be it enacted by the King's most excellent majesty, by and with the advice and consent of the lords spiritual and temporal, and commons, in this present parliament assembled, and by the authority of the same, That when and so often, after the passing of this act, as it shall happen, that any pipe or pipes belonging to any of the water companies, who furnish the city and liberty of *Westminster*, and the parishes and places comprized within the said former act, or this act, or any or either of them, with water, break or burst in any of the squares, streets, lanes, courts, yards, alleys, passages or places, which shall be begun to be paved by virtue of the said former acts, or of this act, or any or either of them, it shall and may be lawful to and for the supervisor to the said commissioners for the time being, or any other person or persons the said commissioners, or any three or more of them, shall appoint for that purpose, to give immediate notice to the pavior of the water company to whom he apprehends such pipe or pipes does or do or may belong, acquainting him in what square, street or place, such pipe or pipes so burst or broke up lay, and requiring him to take up the pavement, and open the ground at or near the place where the water shall or may issue by reason of such pipe or pipes breaking or bursting, within two days next after notice given to such pavior, or left at his last or usual place of abode; and if, upon taking up the pavement and opening the ground, it shall appear, that the pipe or pipes so broke or burst do not belong to the water company whose pavior shall have taken up such pavement, and opened such ground; that then, and in such case, the supervisor to the said commissioners for the time being, or such other person or persons who shall be appointed for that purpose by the said commissioners in manner aforesaid, shall give notice to the pavior of that company to whom it shall appear that the said pipe or pipes belong; such notice to be given or left with such pavior, or at his last or usual place of abode; and the pavior of the company to whom such pipe or pipes shall belong, is hereby required to repair the same, and fill in the ground within six days after such notice given or left as aforesaid; and, within twelve hours after such pipe shall be repaired and the ground filled in, give notice to the person or persons contracting with the said commissioners to relay the pavement so broke or taken up for the reasons aforesaid, or to the supervisor to the said commissioners, or such other person or persons as

Where any of the water companies pipes shall break,

and notice be given thereof, by the commissioners supervisor, to the companies pavior, to whom he deems such pipe to belong, he is to open the ground within 2 days.

and if the pipe is found to belong to some other company, the supervisor is to give notice accordingly;

and such pavior is to repair the same, and fill in the ground within six days, and give immediate notice of having so done to the commissioners

as ſhall be appointed by the ſaid commiſſioners in manner aforeſaid, of ſuch pipe or pipes being repaired, and ſuch ground being filled in, ſuch notice to be given to ſuch contractor, ſupervisor, or other perſon, or left at his or their laſt or uſual place of abode: and in caſe it ſhall happen that the pavior who firſt receives notice to take up the pavement and open the ground for the purpoſes aforeſaid, ſhall take up ſuch pavement and open ſuch ground, and it ſhall then be diſcovered that the pipe or pipes which is, are, or ſhall be burſt or broke, doth or do not belong to the company to whom he is pavior; that then, and in ſuch caſe, the pavior of the company to whom ſuch pipe or pipes belong ſhall make ſatisfaction to the pavior who ſo took up ſuch pavement and opened ſuch ground for ſuch work: and in caſe the pavior to whom ſuch notice ſhall be ſo given to take up ſuch pavement and open ſuch ground, ſhall neglect or refuſe to do the ſame within the ſaid two days after notice given; he ſhall, for the firſt offence, forfeit and pay the ſum of twenty ſhillings; for the ſecond offence, the ſum of forty ſhillings; and for the third and every other offence the ſum of three pounds; and in caſe the pavior of the company to whom ſuch pipe or pipes ſo broke or burſt ſhall belong, ſhall neglect or refuſe to repair and amend ſuch pipe or pipes, and fill in the ground ſo taken up, for the ſpace of ſix days next after ſuch notice given, or ſhall neglect to give notice to the perſon or perſons contracting with the ſaid commiſſioners to relay the pavement ſo broke or taken up for the reaſons aforeſaid, or to the ſupervisor to the ſaid commiſſioners, or to ſuch other perſon or perſons as ſhall be appointed by the ſaid commiſſioners in manner aforeſaid; ſuch pavior ſhall, for the firſt offence, forfeit the ſum of twenty ſhillings; for the ſecond offence, the ſum of forty ſhillings; and for the third and every other offence, the ſum of three pounds: and if the perſon or perſons contracting with the ſaid commiſſioners to relay ſuch pavement ſo broke or taken up for the reaſons aforeſaid, ſhall neglect or refuſe to relay ſuch pavement in a good, ſufficient, and effectual manner, within two days after ſuch notice given to him as aforeſaid; or if the ſupervisor, or other perſon to whom ſuch notice ſhall be given, ſhall neglect to acquaint the contractor of ſuch notice; then and in every ſuch caſe, the perſon or perſons ſo offending ſhall, for the firſt offence, forfeit the ſum of twenty ſhillings; for the ſecond offence, the ſum of forty ſhillings; and for the third and every other offence, the ſum of three pounds.

contractor or ſupervisor.

The pavior in the firſt inſtance is to be ſatisfied for his trouble.

Pavior neglecting to open the ground within two days after notice, forfeits, for the firſt offence, 20s. for the ſecond, 40s. and for every ſubſequent offence 3l.

and neglecting to repair the pipes, and fill in the ground within ſix days, or to give the notice required; forfeits, for the firſt offence, 20s. for the ſecond, 40s, and for every ſubſequent offence, 3l.

Commiſſioners contractor not relaying the pavement within two days, or ſupervisor not giving him due notice, forfeit in like manner.

II. And be it further enacted by the authority aforeſaid, That he ſeveral and reſpective paviors now appointed, or hereafter o be appointed, by the ſaid ſeveral and reſpective water companies, ſhall, and they are hereby required, within the ſpace of hree days next after the paſſing of this act, or within the ſpace of three days next after he ſhall be appointed pavior, to ſuch

Paviors appointed by the water companies, not giving immediate notice to the commiſſioners ſupervisor of their names, places of abode, and respective districts; such company or companies, to give notice in writing to the supervisor for the time being to the said commissioners, or to such other person or persons as shall be appointed by the said commissioners, or any three or more of them, for that purpose, of his the said pavior's name, place of abode, to what company he is pavior, and in what district he has the care of such company or companies pipes; and in case any such pavior or paviors shall neglect or refuse to give such notice within the respective times aforesaid, every such pavior so offending in either of the said cases, shall, for the first offence, forfeit the sum of twenty shillings; for the second offence, the sum of forty shillings; and for the third and every other offence, the sum of three pounds.

forfeit, for the first offence, 20 s. for the second, 40 s. and for every subsequent offence, 3 l.

Sewers to be repaired and cleansed

III. And be it further enacted by the authority aforesaid, That when and so often as any sewer or drain, which is or shall be under the direction of the commissioners of sewers, shall require to be made new, repaired, altered, cleansed, or emptied, in any of the squares, streets, lanes, courts, yards, alleys, passages, or places, which have been or shall be begun to be paved by virtue of this and the said three former recited acts; that then, and in every such case, the said commissioners of sewers shall within six days after notice given to or left for their surveyor for the time being, at his last or usual place of abode, effectually repair, clean, and empty, such sewer or drain, as the case may require; and in default thereof, that it shall and may be lawful to and for the said commissioners appointed by the said three former acts, or this act, or any three or more of them, or their surveyor or surveyors for the time being, to cause such sewer or drain to be made new, repaired, altered, cleansed, or emptied, as the case may require, or so much thereof as shall remain unfinished; the charges and expences whereof shall be paid by the commissioners for putting the said three former acts, and this act, in execution, who shall be reimbursed the same by the clerk or treasurer for the time being to the said commissioners of sewers: and in case the said clerk or treasurer to the said commissioners of sewers shall neglect or refuse to pay what shall have been so paid and disbursed, within ten days next after notice thereof shall be left at the dwelling-house or last place of abode of such clerk or treasurer, which notice shall be in writing, and signed by the clerk to the commissioners for putting this and the said three recited acts in execution, and annexed to the bill, containing an account of such charges and expences; it shall and may be lawful to and for the said last mentioned commissioners, or any three or more of them, and they are hereby authorized and impowered to bring, or cause to be brought, any action or actions, in the name or names of their treasurer or treasurers for the time being, against such clerk or treasurer of the commissioners of sewers for the time being, for the recovery of such sum or sums of money, as they shall have so expended for the purposes aforesaid; in which action or actions, no essoin, protection, or wager of law, or more than one imparlance, shall be allowed.

within six days after notice given to the commissioners, or their surveyor; and in default thereof, the same may be repaired and cleansed by the commissioners under this act; the expence to be paid by the treasurer of the commissioners of sewers,

or an action for the money may be brought against him.

IV. And

IV. And be it further enacted by the authority aforesaid, That when and so often as any of the pavement or pavements, in any of the squares, streets, lanes, courts, yards, alleys, passages, or places, which shall be begun to be paved by virtue of this or the said three former acts, shall be taken up by the commissioners of sewers for the purpose of making new, altering, repairing, cleansing, or emptying, any sewer or sewers, drain or drains, under the direction of the commissioners of sewers, the surveyor for the time being to the said commissioners of sewers shall, so soon as such sewer or sewers, drain or drains, shall be made new, altered, repaired, cleansed, or emptied, as the case may be, give immediate notice to the person or persons contracting with the said commissioners to relay the pavement so broke or taken up for the reasons aforesaid, or to the supervisor to the said commissioners, or such other person or persons as shall be appointed by the said commissioners in manner aforesaid, in order that the pavement or pavements so taken up may be relaid and replaced under the direction of the said commissioners surveyor or surveyors, or such other person or persons as the said commissioners, or any three or more of them, shall appoint for that purpose; and in case such surveyor to the commissioners of sewers shall make default in giving such notice twelve hours after such sewer or sewers, drain or drains, shall be so made new, altered, repaired, cleansed, or emptied, as the case may be, the said surveyor to the said commissioners of sewers shall forfeit and pay the sum of forty shillings.

Where the sewers shall be repaired and cleansed, immediate notice thereof is to be given to the commissioners pavior, or supervisor, for relaying the pavement; on forfeiture of 40 s.

V. And whereas the clause in the said recited act of the fourth year of his present Majesty, which relates to the commissioners of sewers making new or additional, or repairing or altering any of the old grates belonging to the said commissioners of sewers, in any of the squares, streets, lanes, courts, yards, alleys, passages, or places, which had been or should be begun to be paved by virtue of that and the two former acts, has been found ineffectual; by reason there is no provision in the said clause to recover any money which shall be expended by the commissioners appointed by the said last recited act, or the two former acts, where the commissioners of sewers shall neglect or refuse to make new, repair, alter, or lay down, grates in the manner by the said clause directed, and also by reason that the meetings of the said commissioners of sewers are frequently intermitted for a considerable time; be it therefore enacted by the authority aforesaid, That the said commissioners of sewers shall, and they are hereby required, within the space of one month next after the passing of this act, to appoint some fit and proper person to receive all such notice or notices which the said commissioners, or any three or more of them, or their surveyor or surveyors, shall have occasion to send, from time to time, for the making new or additional, or for repairing or altering any of the old grates belonging to the said commissioners of sewers, in any of said squares, streets, lanes, courts, yards, alleys, passages, or places, which have been or shall be begun to be paved

Commissioners of sewers to appoint a person to receive notices occasionally sent them from the commissioners under this act;

by virtue of this and the ſaid three former acts; and in caſe of the death of ſuch perſon, or removal from his office, to appoint another in his ſtead at their firſt meeting next after ſuch death or removal; and in default of ſuch appointment, from time to time, that then ſuch notice or notices ſhall be given to or left for the clerk or clerks for the time being to the ſaid commiſſioners of ſewers, at his or their uſual office, dwelling, or place of abode; and in caſe the perſon or perſons, to whom ſuch notice or notices ſhall be given or left in manner aforeſaid, ſhall neglect or refuſe to make new, repair, alter, and lay down, or cauſe or procure to be made new, repaired, altered, and laid down, ſuch grate or grates as ſhall be ſpecified in ſuch notice or notices, for the ſpace of ſeven days next after ſuch notice or notices ſhall be given or left in manner aforeſaid, it ſhall and may be lawful to and for the ſaid commiſſioners appointed by the ſaid recited acts, or this act, or any three or more of them, or their ſurveyor or ſurveyors for the time being, to cauſe ſuch grate or grates as ſhall be neceſſary to be made new, repaired, altered, and laid down, to be ſo made new, repaired, altered, and laid down; the expence whereof ſhall be paid by the perſon or perſons to whom ſuch notice or notices ſhall be given or left as aforeſaid; and in caſe of nonpayment thereof within four days next after notice in writing, to be ſigned by the clerk to the ſaid commiſſioners for paving, appointed by the ſaid recited acts, or this act, or by order of the ſaid commiſſioners, or any three or more of them, given or left at the office, or uſual dwelling, or place of abode, of ſuch clerk or clerks, perſon or perſons; it ſhall and may be lawful for the ſaid commiſſioners appointed as aforeſaid, or any three or more of them, to bring, or cauſe to be brought, any action or actions in the name of their treaſurer for the time being, againſt any clerk or clerks, perſon or perſons, for the recovery of the money ſo expended by the ſaid commiſſioners on the account aforeſaid; in which action or actions no eſſoin, protection, or wager of law, or more than one imparlance, ſhall be allowed.

In default of ſuch appointment, notices may be left with their clerk; and if the repairs ſpecified in ſuch notices ſhall not be made good within 7 days, the commiſſioners under this act may compleat the ſame, and charge the expence: and if not paid in 4 days, may bring an action for the money.

VI. And be it further enacted by the authority aforeſaid, That it ſhall and may be lawful to and for the ſaid commiſſioners, or any three or more of them, to cauſe to be dug and ſunk in ſuch place or places in any of the ſquares, ſtreets, lanes, courts, yards, alleys, paſſages, or places, which ſhall be begun to be paved by virtue of the ſaid former acts, and of this act, or in any ſquare, ſtreet, lane, court, yard, alley, paſſage, or place, adjoining to ſuch ſquare, ſtreet, lane, court, yard, paſſage, or place, which ſhall have ſo been begun to be paved (provided it does not exceed ten yards in diſtance) as they, or any three or more of them, ſhall think neceſſary and convenient, any well or wells; and alſo to erect any pump or pumps on or near the ſame, for the purpoſe of watering all or any part of the ſeveral ſquares, ſtreets, lanes, courts, yards, alleys, paſſages, or places, to be completed by virtue of the ſaid former acts, and of this act,

The commiſſioners may order wells to be dug in proper places, and pumps erected for watering the ſtreets;

act, or either of them, in such manner as the said commissioners, or any three or more of them, shall direct.

VII. And whereas several of the lanes, courts, yards, alleys, passages, and places, which lead out of or into the squares, streets, lanes, and other places, which have been or may be completed by virtue of the said recited acts, or of this act, are inhabited by poor persons; and several of the houses in such places are frequently let out in tenements, and the inhabitants and occupiers of such places, having no conveniency to lay or deposit their dust or ashes, the same is often thrown, cast, or laid in the lanes, courts, yards, alleys, passages, and places, which are not paved, cleansed, and lighted, under the direction of the said commissioners, and also in such squares, streets, lanes, and other places, out of or into which such lanes, courts, yards, alleys, passages, and places, lead, and which are paved under the direction of the said commissioners, to the great annoyance of the inhabitants and passengers: for remedy whereof, be it enacted by the authority aforesaid, That it shall and may be lawful to and for the said commissioners, or any three or more of them, to cause to be made or erected in any of the squares, streets, lanes, courts, alleys, passages, or places, which shall be begun to be paved by virtue of the said former acts, or of this act, or either of them, or in any of the lanes, courts, yards, alleys, passages, and places, which are not paved, cleansed, and lighted, under the direction of the said commissioners, as they the said commissioners, or any three or more of them, shall think necessary and convenient, such a number of moveable or fixed dust boxes, dust holes, or other conveniencies wherein dust and ashes may be deposited, until the respective scavenger or scavengers shall take and clear away the same.

and may also cause a number of dust boxes, or dust holes, to be erected where necessary, for depositing dust and ashes, till removed by the scavenger.

VIII. And be it further enacted by the authority aforesaid, That all and every the powers, authorities, directions, provisions, regulations, clauses, matters, and things whatsoever, contained in the said recited former acts, and this act, or either of them, shall extend to that part of the road adjoining to the abutments of *Westminster Bridge*, on the *Surry* side thereof, which now is paved with stone of any sort, as effectually, to all intents and purposes, as if the respective powers, authorities, directions, provisions, regulations, clauses, matters, and things, in the said acts, or either of them, contained, were herein repeated and specially enacted.

Powers, &c. of the former acts, and this act, extended to the Surry side of Westminster Bridge;

IX. Provided always, and be it enacted by the authority aforesaid, That nothing in the said former acts, or in this act, contained, shall extend, or be construed to extend, to *Westminster Bridge*, or the abutments thereof, or in any manner to affect, alter, or repeal, any of the powers, authorities, trusts, estates, or interests, given to, or vested in, the commissioners for building a bridge cross the river *Thames*, from the city of *Westminster* to the opposite shore in the county of *Surrey*, in or by virtue of any act or acts of parliament.

but so as not to interfere with the powers vested in the commissioners for the said bridge.

X. And whereas it frequently happens, by reason that the com-

commissioners do not at present pave, cleanse, or light, any courts, yards, alleys, passages, or places where the scavengers cannot come with their carts, which lead out of, into, or immediately communicate with, the several streets and places which have been hitherto paved, cleansed, and lighted, by and under the direction of the said commissioners, great inconveniencies have arisen to the several inhabitants of the said places which are not paved, lighted, and cleansed, under the direction of the said commissioners, by the parish scavenger frequently neglecting to come into those places to take away the dust, ashes, and other filth, from their respective houses, and to clean such places; be it therefore enacted by the authority aforesaid, That from and after the passing of this act, one or more rate or rates, assessment or assessments, shall, twice in every year, or oftener, if it shall be thought needful by the said commissioners, or any five or more of them, be made, laid, and assessed, by the said commissioners, or any five or more of them, upon all and every the lands, houses, shops, warehouse, cellars, vaults, or other tenements, within such courts, yards, alleys, passages, or places, as aforesaid, in such competent sum or sums of money as the said commissioners, or any five or more of them, shall yearly and every year, order and direct, so as such rates or assessments do not exceed in the whole the sum of three pence in the pound in any one year of the yearly rent of such lands, houses, shops, warehouses, cellars, vaults, or other tenements, as the same shall have been ascertained and rated towards the relief of the poor in such parish or place respectively, for each preceding year, in order to defray the expence of carrying away such dust, ashes, and other filth, and cleansing such places; which rate or rates, assessment or assessments, shall be paid quarterly, by such person and persons, and in such proportion, manner, and form, as the rates towards the relief of the poor are now paid; and with such powers and authorities as are directed by the said several recited acts for the recovery of the rates and assessments to be levied and raised for paving, cleansing, and lighting, the squares, streets, lanes, courts, yards, alleys, passages, and places, comprised in said recited acts, and this act, or any or either of them; and the person or persons paying such rate or rates, shall be and are hereby discharged from the payment of the parochial scavengers rate; any thing in this or any former act to the contrary notwithstanding.

Rates to be made by the commissioners upon the lands, houses, and other tenements, in courts and passages where scavengers cannot come with their carts, so as not to exceed 3d. in the pound of the rent, as assessed to the poor rate, in order to defray the expence of removing the dust, and cleansing such places; the rates to be paid quarterly as the poor rates; and the persons paying the same are discharged from the parochial scavengers rate.

XI. And whereas several houses, and other buildings, are very frequently erected, and so far finished as to have the roofs covered in, and others so much further finished as to be fit for tenants to dwell therein; but for want of being let or tenanted, through the negligence of the owners, and for other causes, are not rated to the poor, and therefore cannot be charged with any rate or assessment by virtue of any of the said recited acts; be it therefore enacted by the authority aforesaid, That until such houses, or other buildings, shall be rated to the poor, it shall and may be lawful to and for the said commissioners, or any five

Commissioners impowered to assess new buildings covered in, or five or more of them, and they are hereby required, when and at such time and times as the rates and assessments hereby, and in the said recited acts, or either of them, are directed to be made, to rate and assess all such houses, and other buildings, situate, standing, lying, and being, within the said parishes and places comprised within the said recited acts, or this act, or either of them, which are or shall be erected and covered in, or are fit to be inhabited, at a rate not exceeding six pence for every square yard of land or ground belonging to the fronts or sides of such house, or other building, to be laid, received, recovered, and applied, in such manner as other rates and assessments are directed to be laid, received, recovered, and applied, by the said former acts, or this act, or either of them.

finished though untenanted, not exceeding 6 d. per yard of the fronts or sides of such buildings.

XII. And whereas the clause in the said first recited act, which relates to the inflicting penalties on persons who shall set out, lay, drive or carry, or cause or procure, permit or suffer, to be set out, laid, drove or carried, any coach, cart, dray, waggon, or other carriage, wheels, timber, stones, or any other material, matter, or thing, which may occasion any annoyance, nuisance, or obstruction whatsoever, and also suffering any cart, waggon, or other carriage, to remain longer than is needful and proper, for the loading or unloading thereof respectively, has been found ineffectual: be it therefore enacted by the authority aforesaid, That from and after the passing of this act, it shall and may be lawful to and for the person already appointed by the said commissioners, or for any other person or persons hereafter to be appointed by the said commissioners, or any three or more of them, to supervise and inspect nuisances, obstructions, and other annoyances, found in any of the squares, streets, lanes, courts, yards, alleys, passages, or places, which have been or shall be begun to be paved by virtue of this and the said three former acts, to give notice to the person or persons who shall set out, lay, drive, or carry, or cause or procure, permit or suffer, to be set out, laid, drove, or carried, any coach, cart, dray, waggon, or other carriage, wheels, timber, stones, or any other material, matter, or thing, which may occasion any annoyance, nuisance, or obstruction whatsoever, in any of the squares, streets, lanes, courts, yards, alleys, passages, or places, which have been or shall be begun to be paved by virtue of this and the said three former acts, to remove the same within the space of six hours next after such notice given; and in case the person or persons who shall so set out, lay, drive, or carry, the same, or cause the same to be so set out, laid, drove, or carried, shall not remove, or cause the same to be removed, within the space of six hours, every such person and persons so offending shall, for the first offence, forfeit the sum of ten shillings; for the second offence, the sum of twenty shillings; and for the third and every other offence, the sum of forty shillings.

All obstructions and nuisances in the streets, and other places, to be removed within six hours after notice given by the commissioners supervisor; on forfeiture, for the first offence, of 10 s. for the second, of 20 s. and for every subsequent offence, 40 s.

XIII. And whereas the terrasses and steps on the west side of Saint *James's Street*, are very incommodious and inconvenient to foot passengers and sedan chairs, and accidents frequently happen thereby: and whereas the porch fixed or adjoining to a certain houſe on the eaſt ſide of the ſaid ſtreet, and commonly called or known by the name of *Arthur's* chocolate houſe, breaks in upon the foot pavement: and whereas the ſhops or ſheds built againſt and adjoining to the ſouth ſide of *Exeter* exchange in the *Strand*; and alſo the porch belonging to the ſaid exchange on the ſouth ſide thereof, cauſe that part of the *Strand* to be very narrow and incommodious to paſſengers, both in carriages and on foot: be it therefore enacted by the authority aforeſaid, That upon payment of ſuch ſum or ſums of money as ſhall be agreed to be paid for the premiſſes above mentioned, or ſuch part or parts thereof as ſhall be thought neceſſary by the ſaid commiſſioners, or any five or more of them, to be pulled down, removed, and taken away, for the purpoſe of making the ſaid ſtreets and places more ſafe and commodious to the publick; or if no agreement or contract ſhall be made, then upon making ſatisfaction, in manner herein after mentioned, to the owner or owners of, and perſon or perſons intereſted in, ſuch premiſſes, it ſhall and may be lawful to and for the ſaid commiſſioners, or any five or more of them, to take down, or cauſe or procure to be taken down, the ſaid terraſſes and ſteps, and to fill up and diſcontinue the cellars, vaults, and other buildings, under the ſame; and alſo to take down and remove the ſaid porch, and the rails, ſteps, and fences, belonging thereto, in Saint *James's Street* aforeſaid; and likewiſe the ſaid ſhops or ſheds built againſt or adjoining to the ſouth ſide of *Exeter* exchange aforeſaid, and the porch erected againſt or adjoining to the ſaid exchange on the ſouth ſide thereof, or any part or parts of ſuch premiſſes reſpectively, as ſhall be neceſſary for the purpoſes aforeſaid; and cauſe the materials thereof to be removed and taken away, or ſold, and the money ariſing from ſuch ſale to become the property of the commiſſioners, and to be diſpoſed of for the before mentioned purpoſes: and this act ſhall be ſufficient to indemnify the ſaid commiſſioners, and all perſons authorized by them, againſt the heirs, executors, adminiſtrators, or aſſigns, of any of the ſaid owners or occupiers, as if the ſame had been ſold by deed of feoffment, bargain and ſale, or other aſſurance in the law, or by fine and recovery, or by any other conveyance whatſoever.

> The commiſſioners are impowered, upon making ſatisfaction to the proprietors, to remove the terraſſes and ſteps on the weſt ſide of Saint James's Street, the porch at Arthur's chocolate houſe, and the ſheds and porch at Exeter exchange; and to ſell the materials;

XIV. And be it further enacted by the authority aforeſaid, That if any body politick, corporate, or collegiate, corporation aggregate or ſole, feoffees in truſt, executors, adminiſtrators, guardians, committees, or other truſtees, femes-covert, or any other perſon or perſons whomſoever, in any wiſe intereſted in any of the ſaid premiſſes, upon ten days notice to them given, or left in writing at the houſe or houſes, place or places of abode, of ſuch perſon or perſons, or of the treaſurer, ſecretary, clerk, or other officer officiating as ſecretary, clerk, or treaſurer, of ſuch body politick, corporate, or collegiate, or aggregate or ſole, or at the houſe, ſhop, ſhed, or other place, of the tenant in poſſeſſion of ſuch premiſſes, ſhall neglect or refuſe to treat, or ſhall

> And if the parties intereſted ſhall refuſe to treat for the ſale of the premiſſes, after notice given, or ſhall not agree about the price,

shall not agree for the sale of any such premisses, or any part or parts thereof, or for their interest therein; then, and in every such case, the said commissioners, or any five or more of them, shall cause the value of the premisses to be inquired into and ascertained, by and upon the oath of a jury of twelve indifferent men of the city and liberty of *Westminster*, or county of *Middlesex*, as the case shall require (which oath the said commissioners, or any five or more of them, are hereby impowered and required to administer) what damages will be sustained by, and what recompence and satisfaction shall be made to, such owners, occupiers, or proprietors, or other person or persons interested in the premisses before mentioned, or any part or parts thereof, which the said commissioners shall want to remove, pull down, or take away, for their respective interests therein; and in order thereunto, the said commissioners, or any five or more of them, are hereby impowered and required, from time to time, as there shall be occasion, to summon and call before the said jury, and examine upon oath all persons whatsoever, who shall be thought necessary or proper to be examined as witnesses touching or concerning the premisses; which oath the said commissioners, or any three or more of them, are hereby impowered and required to administer; and if any of the parties interested shall request the same, or the said commissioners, or any five or more of them, shall think it necessary, shall also cause the said jury to view the place or places in question, and shall use all other lawful ways and means, as well for their own as for the said jury's better information in the premisses, in such manner as they the said commissioners, or any five of them, shall think fit; and after the said jury shall have so inquired of, ascertained, and settled, such damage and recompence, they the said commissioners, or any five or more of them, shall thereupon order and adjudge the sum or sums of money so assessed by the said jury for such premisses as aforesaid, to be paid to the persons interested in the said premisses, or any part or parts thereof, according to the verdict or inquisition of the said jury; which said verdict and inquisition, and the order and adjudication so had and made, shall be final and conclusive to all intents and purposes, against all parties or persons whatsoever, claiming in possession, reversion, remainder, or otherwise, their heirs, executors, or administrators, and successors respectively, as well absent as present, infants, femes-covert, lunaticks, ideots, and persons under any other disability whatsoever, bodies politick, corporate, or collegiate, aggregate or sole, as well as all other person or persons whomsoever; and all and every such owners, occupiers, and proprietors, and all and every person and persons in any wise interested in the premisses, or any part or parts thereof, shall thereby be, from and after the money so assessed and adjudged as aforesaid, shall be paid, tendered, or left, as herein after directed, to all intents and purposes, divested of all right, title, claim, interest, or property, of, in, to, or out of, the same.

the commissioners may cause the value and damages to be inquired into, and assessed by a jury;

and may examine upon oath such witnesses as shall be necessary touching the premisses,

and order the jury to view the places in question, &c.

Commissioners to adjudge the money assessed to be paid to the parties interested;

and such verdict and adjudication is to be final and conclusive;

and the parties thereupon to be divested of the premisses.

XV. And be it further enacted by the authority aforesaid, That

Commiſſioners to iſſue warrants to the high bailiff or ſheriff, for ſummoning and returning ſuch jury;

That for the ſummoning and returning of ſuch jury or juries, the ſaid commiſſioners, or any five or more of them, are hereby impowered, from time to time, to iſſue their warrant or warrants to the high bailiff of *Weſtminſter*, or to the ſheriff of the ſaid county, thereby requiring him or them to impanel, ſummon, and return, an indifferent jury of twenty four perſons to appear before the ſaid commiſſioners, or any five or more of them, at ſuch time and place as in ſuch warrant ſhall be appointed, of which time and place all parties intereſted ſhall have ten days notice given or left in manner herein laſt before mentioned; and the ſaid high bailiff or ſheriff, or his deputy or deputies, is and are hereby required to impanel, ſummon, and return, ſuch twenty four perſons accordingly, and out of the perſons ſo impanelled, ſummoned, and returned, or out of ſuch of them as ſhall appear according to or upon ſuch ſummons, the ſaid commiſſioners, or any five or more of them, ſhall cauſe to be ſworn twelve, who ſhall be the jury for the purpoſes aforeſaid; and for default of a ſufficient number of jurymen, the ſaid high bailiff or ſheriff, or his or their deputy or deputies, ſhall return ſo many of the ſtanders-by as ſhall be neceſſary to make up the number of twelve to ſerve on ſuch jury.

who are to ſummon and return ſuch jury accordingly; and for want of a ſufficient number appearing, any of the ſtanders-by may be returned.

Jury may be challenged.

XVI. Provided always, and be it further enacted by the authority aforeſaid, That all perſons concerned ſhall, from time to time, have their lawful challenges (but not to challenge the array of the pannel) againſt any of the ſaid jurymen when they come to be ſworn; and the ſaid commiſſioners, or any five or more of them, acting in the premiſſes, ſhall have power from time to time, to impoſe any reaſonable fine or fines on ſuch high bailiff or ſheriff, his or their deputy or deputies, bailiffs, or agents, making default in the premiſſes, and on any of the perſons that ſhall be ſummoned and returned on ſuch jury, and ſhall not appear or refuſe to be ſworn on the ſaid jury, or to give their verdict, or in any manner wilfully neglecting their duty therein, contrary to the true intent and meaning of this act; and on any of the perſons who, being required to give evidence touching the premiſſes, ſhall refuſe to be examined or to give evidence, and from time to time to levy ſuch fine or fines, in ſuch manner as any penalties in the ſaid recited acts are directed to be levied and received, ſo as that no ſuch fine ſhall exceed the ſum of ten pounds upon any one perſon for any one offence.

Commiſſioners impowered to fine the high bailiff and ſheriff, or their deputies, making default in the premiſſes; as likewiſe the jury and evidences not doing their duty.

Where the parties intereſted cannot be found, or diſputes ſhall be depending in the courts, &c.

XVII. And be it further enacted by the authority aforeſaid, That in caſe ſuch perſon or perſons, to whom ſuch ſum or ſums of money ſhall be ſo aſſeſſed or due as aforeſaid, cannot be found, or if, by reaſon of diſputes depending in any court of law or equity, or for default of evidence, or otherwiſe, it ſhall not appear to the ſaid commiſſioners what perſon or perſons is or are intitled, or if any mortgagee or mortgagees ſhall refuſe to take in his, her, or their mortgage money due on the premiſſes after notice given him, her, or them for that purpoſe; then, and in all and every ſuch caſe or caſes, it ſhall and may be lawful to and for the ſaid commiſſioners, or any five or more of them, to order

the ſums aſſeſſed, &c. for the premiſſes,

der the sum or sums so assessed and awarded as aforesaid, or as shall be due on such mortgage, to be paid into the bank of *England* in the name of the treasurer of the said commissioners for the time being, and of any three or more of the said commissioners, for the use of the parties interested in the said premisses, to be paid to them, and every of them, according to their respective estates and interests in the said premisses as the said commissioners, or any five or more of them, shall, by any order to be made by them, direct.

may be paid into the bank, for the use of the said parties.

XVIII. And whereas frequent applications have been made to the commissioners by the inhabitants of particular squares, streets, and places, requesting them to new pave such squares, streets, and places, and take them under the direction of the said commissioners; and offering to lend money at interest upon the rates of such squares, streets, and places: and whereas it is apprehended, That if the inhabitants of particular squares, streets, and places, or others, would raise among themselves such competent sum and sums of money as would be sufficient to new pave such particular square, street, and place, or streets and places, it would be a means of greatly forwarding the several works under the direction of the said commissioners; be it therefore further enacted by the authority aforesaid, That it shall and may be lawful to and for the inhabitants of any particular square, street, or place within the liberty, parishes, and places, comprised in the said former acts, or this act, or any or either of them, or any other person or persons whatsoever, to raise from time to time such competent sum or sums of money as shall be sufficient to new pave such particular square, street, or place, so as three fourths of the owners and occupiers of houses in such particular square, street, or place, shall be willing and consenting to the new paving, and putting the same under the direction of the commissioners; and such sum and sums of money, when so raised, shall be paid to the said commissioners, or any three or more of them, or to their treasurer or treasurers for the time being, or to such other person or persons as the said commissioners, or any three or more of them, shall direct and appoint; and which money, when so paid and received, shall be deposited in the bank of *England*, and thence issued and applied by the said commissioners, or any three or more of them, for new paving such particular square, street, or place: and it shall and may be lawful to and for the said commissioners, or any five or more of them, by any writing or writings under their hands and seals, to assign over and convey the rate or rates, assessment or assessments, of such particular square, street, and place, and as a security for the repayment of the sums so raised and received for the purposes aforesaid, with legal or lower interest for the same; and also to lay such further rate as may be necessary for the purposes of cleansing, lighting, and keeping in repair, such particular square, street, or place; and the treasurer or treasurers for the time being to the said commissioners shall, from time to time, keep the accounts of receipts and disburse-

Where the inhabitants, &c. of any particular square or street shall raise a competent sum for the new paving thereof, and shall consent to put the same under the direction of the commissioners, and pay in the money accordingly; the commissioners may assign over the rates as a security for repayment of such sums, with interest.

Treasurer to keep a separate account

of the receipts and disbursements, and other transactions relating to such square or place. bursements, and other business and transactions relating to such particular square, street, or place, separate and distinct from the other accounts and transactions of the commissioners: and if any sum or sums of money shall at any time remain, over and above what shall be sufficient to new pave such square, street, or place, and pay the interest of the sums raised and received, such sum or sums shall be applied towards paying off the sum or sums of money so borrowed as aforesaid; and for that purpose may be placed out at interest on government securities, in the name of any three or more of the commissioners for the time being, at such times and in such manner as the said commissioners, or any three or more of them, shall direct or appoint, till the same shall amount to a competent sum for paying one or more creditor or creditors lending money on such particular square, street, or place.

Surplus money to be placed out at interest, till it amount to a competent sum for paying one or more creditors.

The inhabitants to be previously convened, in order to give their assent or dissent to such measure.

XIX. Provided always, and be it further enacted by the authority aforesaid, That nothing in this act contained shall extend, or be construed to extend, to authorize or impower the said commissioners to new pave any such particular square, street, or place, upon application to them by the inhabitants thereof as aforesaid, unless one month's notice at the least of such application shall be published in the *London Gazette*, requiring the owners and occupiers of houses in such particular square, street, or place, to meet at the time and place in such notice to be mentioned, to signify their assent to, or dissent from, the new paving such particular square, street, or place, as shall be specified in such notice; and also unless notice in writing shall be left at every house, then occupied in such particular square, street, or place, one month at the least before the time of such meeting; and also unless three fourths of the owners and occupiers of houses in such particular square, street, or place, shall consent thereto in writing under their respective hands; and in case any owner or occupier shall neglect to attend such meeting, according to such respective notices, he or she so neglecting, shall be deemed to have given his or her assent to the new paving such particular square, street, or place as aforesaid.

Persons neglecting to attend, deemed to assent.

Where the occupier shall have a term of 7 years, or more, unexpired, his assent only is necessary; but where he shall not have such term, the person under whom he holds may give his assent or dissent to the new paving.

XX. Provided always, That where the occupier of any house within any such particular square, street, or place as aforesaid, shall have at least a term of seven years unexpired therein at the time such notices shall be given as aforesaid, or any longer term, that then, and in every such case, the assent of the owner of such house shall not be necessary to be had or obtained for the purpose aforesaid; and where the occupier of any house within any such particular square, street, or place, as aforesaid, shall not have such term therein, at the time such notices shall be given as aforesaid, that then, and in every such case, the person under whom such occupier holds shall be deemed to be the owner thereof for the purposes aforesaid; and every such person may, as well as the occupier of such house, attend the meetings pursuant to such notices aforesaid, and give his, her, or their assent to, or dissent from, the new paving such particular square, street,

street, or place, as shall be expressed in such notices respectively.

XXI. And be it further enacted by the authority aforesaid, That copies of assignments and conveyances made in or by virtue of and in pursuance of this act, shall be entered in a book or books to be kept for that purpose by the treasurer or clerk to the said commissioners; and all and every person and persons to whom any such assignment or conveyance shall be made as aforesaid, is and are hereby impowered, from time to time, by assignment under his, her, or their hand or hands, and to be indorsed on the back of his, her, or their security, or by any other writing or writings, which shall be executed in the presence of two or more credible witnesses, to assign over or transfer his, her, or their right to the principal or interest money thereby secured to any person or persons whomsoever; all which assignments or transfers shall be produced and notified to the said treasurer or clerk within thirty days after the date thereof, who shall cause an entry of such assignment or assignments, containing the date, names of the parties, and sums of money therein mentioned to be assigned and transferred, in the said book or books to be kept for entering the said original assignments and conveyances, for which the treasurer or clerk shall be paid the sum of two shillings and six pence, and no more; and which said book or books shall and may at all seasonable times be perused and inspected without fee or reward by any person or persons interested in such security or securities, assignment or assignments; and after such entry made, such assignment and transfer shall intitle such assignee, his, her, and their executors, administrators, and assigns, to the benefit thereof, and payment thereon, and such assignee may in such manner assign or transfer again, and so *toties quoties*; and it shall not be in the power of any persons who shall have made such assignment or transfer, to make void, release, or discharge the same, or any monies thereon due.

Entry to be made of all assignments and conveyances.

Method of assigning and transferring.

Assignments to be produced and notified within 30 days to the treasurer or clerk, and an entry to be made thereof, upon paying 2s. 6d.

Books of entry may be inspected *gratis*;

and assignments may be made *toties quoties*.

XXII. Provided always, and be it enacted, That nothing in the said former acts, or this act, contained, shall extend, or be construed to extend, to any place or places which are paved, cleansed, and lighted, under any particular act or acts of parliament.

These acts not to extend to places paved, cleansed, or lighted, under any particular act.

XXIII. And be it enacted by the authority aforesaid, That when any defective or bad pavement shall be mended, altered, or repaired, by the order or direction of the said commissioners, or any three or more of them, by virtue of the powers given by the act passed in the third year of his present Majesty's reign, and which shall adjoin to, or belong to, any lands, houses, shops, warehouses, cellars, vaults, or other tenements, or any part or parts thereof, within the said city and liberty, parishes and places, comprized in the said last recited act, which shall, at any time from and after the passing this act, be occupied or held by any ambassador or minister from any foreign prince or state, or other person or persons not liable by law to pay the charges and expences of such amending, altering, or repairing; that then,

The charges of repairing pavements belonging to houses occupied by ambassadors or foreign ministers, then, and in every ſuch caſe, the charges and expences thereof ſhall be paid by the ſaid commiſſioners, who ſhall be reimburſed and paid the ſame by the owner or owners, proprietor or proprietors, of ſuch lands, houſes, ſhops, warehouſes, cellars, vaults, or other tenements reſpectively; and in caſe of non-payment thereof, within ten days next after notice in writing to be ſigned by the clerk to the ſaid commiſſioners for the time being, by order of the ſaid commiſſioners, or any three or more of them, and annexed to a copy of the bill, containing an account of the expence of ſuch repairs, given or left at the laſt or moſt uſual place of abode of ſuch owner or owners, proprietor or proprietors, to pay the ſame; or in caſe ſuch reſpective place of abode ſhall not be known, then within ten days next after ſuch notice in writing, ſigned as aforeſaid, ſhall be affixed on ſome conſpicuous part of ſuch land, or left for ſuch owner or owners, proprietor or proprietors, with any perſon or perſons in ſuch houſe, ſhop, warehouſe, cellar, vault, or other tenement reſpectively, the ſaid commiſſioners, or any three or more of them, ſhall and may, if they think proper, bring, or cauſe to be brought, any action or actions, in the name of their treaſurer for the time being, againſt any ſuch owner or owners, proprietor or proprietors, for ſuch charges and expences; in which action or actions no eſſoin, protection, or wager of law, or more than one imparlance ſhall be allowed.

are to be paid by the commiſſioners, who are to be reimburſed by the owners; and they may bring an action for the ſame.

Commiſſioners may order monies for the charges of ſuch works to be iſſued accordingly.

XXIV. And be it further enacted by the authority aforeſaid, That from and after the paſſing of this act, it ſhall and may be lawful to and for the ſaid commiſſioners, or any three or more of them, to iſſue money, or cauſe the ſame to be iſſued, for payment of bills for any work or works that has or have been ordered to be done and performed by ſuch a number of commiſſioners as is directed by any of the ſaid former acts, upon ſuch work or works being ſo done and performed.

All writings to be tax-free.

XXV. And be it further enacted by the authority aforeſaid, That no nomination, appointment, order, contract, bond, warrant, precept, judgement, conviction, aſſignment, indorſement, transfer, or other writing whatſoever, under the hand and ſeal, or hands and ſeals of, or only ſigned by, any commiſſioner or commiſſioners, or juſtice or juſtices of the peace, or exhibited before them, or under the hand and ſeal, or hands and ſeals of, or only ſigned by, any other perſon or perſons whatſoever, relating to the execution of this act, or the ſaid two laſt recited acts, ſhall be charged or chargeable with any duty whatſoever.

Commiſſioners recovering in any action brought by them, are to have double coſts.

XXVI. And be it further enacted by the authority aforeſaid, That if any action or actions ſhall be brought by order of the ſaid commiſſioners, or any three or more of them, againſt any perſon or perſons whatſoever, for the recovery of any money or monies laid out or expended by the ſaid commiſſioners, by virtue of the ſaid three former acts, or of this act; and a verdict ſhall be had and given againſt ſuch perſon or perſons againſt whom ſuch action or actions ſhall be brought; ſuch perſon or perſons ſhall pay double coſts; and the plaintiff or plaintiffs in ſuch

such action or actions, shall have such remedy and remedies for recovering the same, as any plaintiff or plaintiffs may have for his, her, or their costs, in any other cases by law.

Persons aggrieved may appeal to the quarter sessions,

XXVII. Provided always, and be it further enacted by the authority aforesaid, That if any person shall think himself aggrieved by any thing done in pursuance of this act, and for which no particular method of relief hath been already appointed, such person may appeal to the justices of the peace at any quarter sessions of the peace to be held for the county or place wherein the cause of complaint shall arise and within three months after the cause of such complaint shall have arisen; such appellant first giving, or causing to be given, twenty one days notice at the least in writing, of his or her intention to bring such appeal and of the matter thereof, to the clerk or treasurer to the said commissioners; and within two days after such notice, entering into recognizance before some justice of the peace for such county or place, with two sufficient sureties, conditioned to try such appeal at, and abide the order of, and to pay such costs as shall be awarded by the justices at such quarter sessions: and the said justices at such sessions, upon due proof of such notice being given as aforesaid, and of the entering into such recognizance, shall hear and finally determine the causes and matters of such appeal in a summary way, and award such costs to the parties appealing or appealed against, as they the said justices shall think proper; and the determination of such quarter sessions shall be final, binding, and conclusive, to all intents and purposes.

giving notice of such intention, and entering into a recognizance. Justices to hear and determine appeals in a summary way.

Penalties and forfeitures how to be recovered and applied.

XXVIII. And be it further enacted by the authority aforesaid, That all penalties and forfeitures by this act imposed (the manner of levying and recovering whereof is not hereby otherwise particularly directed) shall be levied and recovered by distress and sale of the offenders goods and chattels, by warrant under the hand and seal of such justice of the peace for the said county of *Middlesex*, or the city and liberty of *Westminster*, as the case may be, which warrant such justice is hereby impowered and required to grant, upon the confession of the party or parties, or upon the information of any one or more credible witness or witnesses upon oath (which oath such justice is hereby impowered to administer) and the penalties and forfeitures when recovered, after rendering the overplus (if any be) upon demand, to the party or parties whose goods and chattels shall be so distrained and sold (the charges of such distress and sale being first deducted) shall be paid to the treasurer to the said commissioners for the time being, and be applied towards the purposes of this act.

Proceedings not to be quashed for want of form; nor removeable by *Certiorari*.

XXIX. And be it further enacted by the authority aforesaid, That no proceeding to be had touching the conviction of any offender or offenders against this act, or any order made, or other matter or thing to be done or transacted in or relating to the execution of this act, shall be vacated or quashed for want of form, or be removed by *Certiorari*, or any other writ or process

2 what-

whatſoever, into any of his Majeſty's courts of record at *Weſtminſter*; any law or ſtatute to the contrary notwithſtanding.

Limitation of actions,

XXX. And be it further enacted by the authority aforeſaid, That no action or ſuit ſhall be commenced againſt any perſon or perſons for any thing done in purſuance of this act, until twenty one days notice ſhall be thereof given in writing to the clerk or treaſurer to the ſaid commiſſioners, or after ſufficient ſatisfaction or tender thereof hath been made to the party or parties aggrieved, or after ſix calendar months next after the fact committed, for which ſuch action or actions, ſuit or ſuits ſhall be ſo brought; and all ſuch actions and ſuits ſhall be laid and tried in the county or place where ſuch matters and things reſpectively ſhall be committed or done, and not in any other county or place; and that the defendant or defendants in ſuch actions and ſuits, and every of them, may plead the general iſſue, and give this act and the ſpecial matter in evidence, at any trial or trials which ſhall be had thereupon; and that the matter or thing for which ſuch action or actions, ſuit or ſuits ſhall be ſo brought; was done in purſuance and by the authority of this act: and if the ſaid matter or thing ſhall appear to have been ſo done, or if it ſhall appear that ſuch action or ſuit was brought before twenty one days notice thereof given as aforeſaid, or that ſufficient ſatisfaction was made or tendered as aforeſaid, or if any ſuch action or ſuit ſhall not be commenced within the time before for that purpoſe limited, or ſhall be laid in any other county or place than as aforeſaid; then the jury or juries ſhall find for the defendant or defendants therein; and if a verdict or verdicts ſhall be found for ſuch defendant or defendants, or if the plaintiff or plaintiffs in ſuch action or actions, ſuit or ſuits, ſhall become nonſuited, or ſuffer a diſcontinuance of ſuch action or actions; or if, upon any demurrer or demurrers in ſuch action or actions, judgement ſhall be given for the defendant or defendants therein; then, and in either of the caſes aforeſaid, ſuch defendant or defendants ſhall have treble coſts, and ſhall have ſuch remedy for recovering the ſame, as any defendant or defendants may have for his, her, or their coſts, in any other caſes by law.

General iſſue

Treble coſts.

CAP. LI.

An act for repealing ſeveral laws relating to the manufacture of woollen cloth in the county of York, *and alſo ſo much of ſeveral other laws as preſcribes particular ſtandards of width and length of ſuch woollen cloths; and for ſubſtituting other regulations of the cloth trade within the weſt riding of the ſaid county, for preventing frauds in certifying the contents of the cloth, and for preſerving the credit of the ſaid manufacture at foreign markets.*

Preamble reciting act, 7 Anne.

WHEREAS *an act was made in the ſeventh year of the reign of her late majeſty Queen* Anne, *intituled*, An act for the better aſcertaining the lengths and breadths of the woollen cloth made

made in the county of *York*: *and whereas another act of parliament was made and passed in the eleventh year of the reign of his late majesty King* George *the First, intituled,* An act for the better regulating the manufacture of cloth in the west riding of the county of *York*: *and whereas another act of parliament was made and passed in the seventh year of the reign of his late majesty King* George *the Second, intituled,* An act to explain and amend an act passed in the eleventh year of the reign of his late majesty King *George* the First intituled, *An act for the better regulating the manufacture of cloth in the west riding of the county of* York: *and whereas another act of parliament was made and passed in the fourteenth year of the reign of his late majesty King* George *the Second, intituled,* An act for continuing an act passed in the seventh year of the reign of his present Majesty, *To explain and amend a former act passed in the eleventh year of the reign of his late majesty King* George *the First, for the better regulating the manufacture of cloth in the west riding of the county of* York, and for making the said acts more effectual; *which said several acts of parliament, notwithstanding the many good provisions and directions therein contained, have nevertheless been found by experience not to be effectual for the preventing the frauds, abuses, and deceits, which are frequently used and practised in the manufacture of woollen cloth within the west riding of the said county of* York, *particularly in the unreasonable stretching and straining the said cloths*; which ill practices tend very much to the debasing, undervaluing, and discrediting of the said manufacture, both at home and in foreign parts beyond the seas, where great part thereof hath been usually vended; be it therefore enacted, by the King's most excellent majesty, by and with the advice and consent of the lords spiritual and temporal, and commons, in this present parliament assembled, and by the authority of the same, That the said several recited acts of parliament of the eleventh year of his late majesty King *George* the First, and of the seventh and fourteenth years of his late majesty King *George* the Second, and every clause, matter, and thing, therein respectively contained, and so much of all and every other act or acts heretofore made as relate to the ascertaining the length, breadth, or weight, of woollen cloths, within the said west riding of the county of *York*, shall, from the twenty fourth day of *June*, one thousand seven hundred and sixty five, be repealed.

11 Geo. 1.

7 Geo. 2.

& 14 Geo. 2.

The said recited acts repealed.

II. And, for preventing frauds, deceits, and abuses, for the future, be it enacted by the authority aforesaid, That the justices of the peace for the said west riding of the county of *York*, (not being dealers in woollen cloth, or occupiers of any fulling mill) at their next quarter sessions of the peace, to be holden for the said riding, next after the twenty fourth day of *June*, one thousand seven hundred and sixty five, or at some adjournment of the same, and at their general quarter sessions of the peace, to be holden next after *Easter* yearly, shall and may, and they are hereby authorized and required to choose and appoint so many men, of good character and repute, within the said riding,

Justices to appoint searchers and measurers.

ing, (being persons following, or having been brought up in the manufacture of woollen cloth in the said riding, and being under the age of sixty years) as they shall think convenient, to be searchers and measurers of cloth within the said riding, and to appoint and station such measurers and searchers so to be chosen, at such mills and other places, and in such manner as to the said justices, at their general or adjourned sessions, shall seem meet and convenient; and shall and may assign, allow, and appoint, to the said searchers and measurers, so appointed, such yearly salaries, as the said justices, at their said general or adjourned sessions, or the major part of them, shall think proper.

When the searchers shall measure and seal,

III. And it is hereby further enacted, That such of the said searchers and measurers as shall be appointed to, or stationed at, any mill or mills within the said riding, shall and may, and they are hereby authorized and directed, at their respective fulling mills, where they shall respectively be stationed or placed, to measure all the cloths, and ends or half cloths, which shall be there milled respectively, at the respective times, and in manner herein after mentioned; that is to say, such cloths or ends as shall be streamed or washed in the goit or mill stream of the said mills respectively, shall be measured within six, and not sooner than four hours after the same shall be streamed or washed; and such cloths or ends as shall not be so streamed or washed, shall be measured within four hours after the same shall come out of the stock; and every such searcher and measurer shall affix, or cause to be affixed, on one end of every such cloth, before it shall be carried from the mill, a seal of lead, to be furnished and provided by the maker of such cloth, and shall rivet the seal, so to be affixed by him on every such cloth, and stamp, in words and figures, plainly to be read and distinguished, upon the seal or rivet, his name, and the length and breadth of every such cloth, together with the number of each of such cloths, milled at such fulling mill successively, beginning at the time of his entering to his said office with number one, and proceeding progressively, until the twenty fifth day of *March* then next ensuing; and on the said twenty fifth day of *March* then next ensuing, and on every succeeding twenty fifth day of *March*, beginning again with the same number one, and proceeding progressively in numbers, during the year then ensuing; and immediately after the said cloth shall be measured, sealed and stamped as aforesaid, the said searcher and measurer, measuring and stamping the same, shall enter in a book, to be provided by the treasurer, and kept by such searcher or measurer for that purpose, the name and place of abode of the maker of every such cloth, and the colour or sort of such cloth, together with the length, breadth, and number on the seal; and shall give, at the least once in every month, to the supervisor within whose district the said mill shall be situate, an account of all the cloths milled, measured, and stamped at such mill during such month; and the owner or maker of such cloth shall pay to the said

said searcher and measurer, for measuring and sealing of such cloth, the respective sums following; *videlicet*,

For the seal of every whole or long cloth, containing in length thirty five yards or upwards, the sum of six pence.

and what shall be paid for the same, and how applied.

And for every end or half cloth, containing less than thirty five yards, and more than thirty yards in length, the sum of four pence.

And for every end or half cloth, containing less than thirty yards in length, the sum of three pence.

Which said sums shall be accounted for and paid by such searcher or measurer, to the treasurer of the west riding for the time being, to be applied for such purposes as are herein after directed.

IV. And it is hereby further enacted by the authority aforesaid, That if any searcher or measurer shall neglect or refuse to measure and stamp any such cloth, end or half cloth or to give such monthly account, or give a false or fraudulent account of the cloths by him measured and stamped as aforesaid, such searcher or measurer, being thereof legally convicted on the oath of one or more credible witness or witnesses, before any such justice or justices of the peace as aforesaid, shall, for the first offence, forfeit and pay the sum of twenty shillings, one moiety whereof shall be paid to the informer or informers, and the other moiety to the treasurer for the said riding; and for the second offence shall forfeit or lose his office or place, and be for ever after rendered incapable of being appointed a searcher or measurer of woollen cloth.

Penalty on searchers neglect.

V. And be it further enacted, That no cloth maker shall take away his cloth from any such fulling-mill, in case the same hath been streamed or washed, before the same hath laid six hours after it hath been so streamed or washed, or before such cloth hath lain four hours after it has come out of the stock (in case it shall not be washed or streamed) unless such cloth shall be sooner measured and stamped in manner hereby directed, by the searcher or measurer, at the mill where such cloths shall respectively be milled or fulled; and if any cloth maker shall take away his cloth from the mill before the same shall be so measured and stamped, or before the sum of money, hereby directed to be paid for the measuring, sealing, and stamping thereof, be duly paid and satisfied, or shall take away his cloth after nine of the clock in the evening, or before five of the clock in the morning, unless the same shall be measured and stamped; every person so offending in any of the said cases, and being thereof convicted upon the oath of such searcher or measurer, or of the inspector or supervisor herein afterdirected to be appointed, or of any other credible witness, before one or more justice or justices of the peace for the said riding, or any corporation within thesame (such justice or justices not being traders or dealers in the woollen manufacture, or farmers or occupiers of a fulling-mill) every per-

Makers not to take cloths from thr mills before they are measured and stamped.

ſon ſo offending, ſhall, for every ſuch offence, forfeit and pay the ſum of twenty ſhillings, to be levied and recovered in ſuch manner as is herein after mentioned, and to be applied and diſpoſed of in manner following; that is to ſay, one moiety thereof to the informer, and the other moiety to the treaſurer of the weſt riding of the county of *York*.

Cloths to be ſealed before they are put upon the tenters.

VI. And it is hereby further enacted by the authority aforeſaid, That every maker of cloth, commonly called *Broad Cloth*, within the ſaid riding, after every cloth, end or half cloth, ſhall be brought from the fulling mill, and before the ſame ſhall be put upon the tenter, ſhall meaſure the ſame, and ſhall affix, or cauſe to be affixed, on the other end of every ſuch cloth, one other ſuch ſeal of lead, and ſhall rivet the ſame, and ſtamp upon ſuch ſeal or rivet, in figures plainly to be ſeen and diſtinguiſhed, the length and breadth of every ſuch cloth.

Juſtices to appoint inſpectors of fulling mills,

VII. And be it further enacted by the authority aforeſaid, That the juſtices of the peace for the ſaid weſt riding of the county of *York*, (not being dealers in woollen cloth, or occupiers of any fulling mill) at their quarter ſeſſions of the peace to be holden for the ſaid riding next after the twenty fourth day of *June*, one thouſand ſeven hundred and ſixty five, or at ſome adjournment of the ſame, and at their general quarter ſeſſions of the peace to be holden after *Eaſter* yearly, ſhall and may, and they are hereby authorized and required to chuſe and appoint ſo many men, of good character and repute, within the ſaid riding, not exceeding twelve in number, to be inſpectors of all cloths, called *Broad Woollen Cloths*, and the workſhops, tenters, tenter grounds, and warehouſes of the merchants or dreſſers where any ſuch cloths, made and milled within the ſaid riding, ſhall be dreſſed or tentered, and to appoint and ſtation the ſaid inſpectors to inſpect and examine ſuch and ſo many work-ſhops, tenter grounds, tenters, and warehouſes, and in ſuch diſtricts, towns, pariſhes, or places, and in ſuch manner, as to the ſaid juſtices, at their general or adjourned ſeſſions, or the major part of them, ſhall think proper; and alſo the ſaid juſtices, at their ſaid ſeſſions, ſhall and may, and they are hereby directed to chuſe and appoint ſuch and ſo many men of good repute, within the ſaid riding, not exceeding four in number, to be ſupervisors of the ſeveral fulling mills within the ſaid riding, and of the conduct and behaviour of the ſeveral ſearchers and meaſurers appointed and ſtationed at ſuch mills reſpectively, and of all cloths called *Broad Woollen Cloths*, and the workſhops, tenters, tenter grounds, and warehouſes, of the merchants or dreſſers where any ſuch cloths made and milled within the ſaid riding, ſhall be milled, dreſſed, or tentered, and of the conduct and behaviour of the ſeveral inſpectors ſo to be choſen and appointed as aforeſaid; and to appoint and ſtation the ſaid ſupervisors reſpectively in ſuch diſtricts, towns, pariſhes, or places, in ſuch manner as to the ſaid juſtices, at their general or adjourned ſeſſions, or the major part of them, ſhall think proper, in order to prevent the falſe ſtamping and undue ſtretching of woollen cloths,

who are to conform to the rules of the general quarter ſeſſions, and to take an oath.

cloths, and to enforce the due observation of this act; and shall and may assign, allow, and appoint, to the said inspectors, such yearly or other salaries as the said justices, at their quarter sessions to be held next after the twenty fourth day of *June*, one thousand seven hundred and sixty five, or at the said general or adjourned sessions to be held yearly after *Easter*, or the major part of them, shall think proper; provided that no such salary shall be less than twenty pounds for one year, nor less in proportion for part of a year; and also shall and may, at the same times, assign, allow, and appoint, to the said supervisors, such yearly or other salaries, as they shall think proper and convenient; provided that no such salary shall be less than forty pounds, and ten pounds more if their duty require them to keep a horse, to one supervisor for one year, nor less in proportion for part of a year; and all and every such searcher and measurer, inspectors and supervisors, before he or they shall enter upon the duty of his or their said office, shall severally and respectively take the following oath, before one or more justice or justices of the peace for the said riding; that is to say,

The oath.

I A. B. *do swear, That I will well and truly, to the best of my skill and power, execute the office of a searcher and measurer, or an inspector or supervisor* (as the case may be) *of woollen cloth, within the west riding of the county of* York.

So help me GOD.

Supervisors to visit mills and tenter grounds.

VIII. And be it further enacted by the authority aforesaid, That the said supervisors so to be chosen and appointed shall, and they are hereby required to be daily employed in visiting the several and respective mills, tenters, tenter grounds, work shops, and places, within the respective districts allotted to them as aforesaid, where any such cloths shall be milled, dressed, or tentered, and shall, out of the number of cloths which shall come under their several and respective inspections, measure and mark with a seal of lead, whereon shall be impressed or stamped the name of such supervisor, so many of such cloths as they conveniently can, or their time will allow, and shall keep a regular and distinct account of such cloths as they shall severally examine, measure, and mark, and shall transmit the same, together with the accounts by them respectively received from the searchers and measurers at the several mills within their respective districts, to the justices of the peace, at every quarter sessions held for the said riding; and if any of the said inspectors or supervisors shall be negligent or remiss in his duty, or shall transmit a false account of the cloths by him or them respectively measured and marked as aforesaid, such inspector or supervisor shall forfeit and lose his office.

How inspectors are to act if they find cloth falsly stamped.

IX. And be it further enacted, That if any of the said inspectors or supervisors shall find any cloth or cloths falsly stamped by any of the measurers or searchers, above two inches in breadth, or above one yard in length, such inspector or supervisor shall, within seven days after the same shall be discovered, give information thereof to one of his Majesty's justices of the peace within the said riding (not being a dealer in woollen cloth, or occupier of any fulling mill) and on conviction of such measurer or searcher, before any such justice of the peace as aforesaid, such searcher or measurer shall forfeit and pay, for every such offence, the sum of ten shillings, to be recovered as any other penalty is hereby directed to be recovered; one moiety whereof shall be paid to the informer, and the other moiety to the treasurer for the said riding.

How inspectors shall be appointed, in case of death, &c.

X. Provided always, and be it further enacted by the authority aforesaid, That if any person, who shall be so appointed, to be a searcher and measurer, or an inspector or supervisor of cloth, shall happen to die, during the year in which he is so appointed, or shall be removed or displaced from his said office, or shall by sickness, or any other accident, be rendered incapable of executing the said office, that then, and in any of the said cases, it shall and may be lawful for any one of such justices of the peace as aforesaid, living near to the place where such searcher and measurer, inspector or supervisor, did or shall reside, to appoint some other proper person, properly qualified, to supply tho place of such searcher and measurer, inspector or supervisor, until the next *Easter* sessions, to be there, by the major part of such justices present, confirmed, or another person appointed in his place; or in case of sickness, or other accident, during the sickness or incapacity of such searcher and measurer, inspector or supervisor; and the person so confirmed or appointed shall take the same oath, and be invested with the same powers, and liable to the same penalties for any breach or neglect of duty, as the searchers and measurers, inspectors or supervisors, respectively elected or to be elected at the *Easter* sessions, by virtue of this act, are or ought to be.

Inspectors to enter shops where they shall suspect any undue stamped or stretched cloths.

XI. And be it further enacted by the authority aforesaid, That it shall and may be lawful for every such inspector or supervisor, from time to time, as occasion shall require, in the daytime, to enter into any shop or shops, out-house or out-houses, tenter grounds or ware-house, of any merchant or merchants, dresser or dressers, or any other dealer in cloth, or any fulling mill, or any out-house or out-houses, or other places belonging thereto respectively, within the said riding, to search for any woollen cloth, which he shall suspect to be falsely or unduly stamped, or be stretched or strained more than is allowed by this act, or any alteration made in the seal or seals, contrary to the direction, true intent and meaning of this act; and for the better discovering of such abuse, to measure, or cause to be measured, any such cloth; and in case of resistance or refusal by any person, to permit and suffer such inspector or supervisor to enter the said places, or any of them, for the purposes aforesaid, the person so resisting or refusing shall forfeit the sum of ten pounds, on conviction thereof before any such justice of the peace; and if such inspector or inspectors shall at any time find any

any woollen cloth, after the times herein directed for sealing the same, without the seal or seals hereby directed to be put thereon, or such seal or seals defaced, counterfeited, or altered, except it shall appear that such seal or seals was or were accidentally lost or maliciously taken off, or that any of such cloths appear, by the lowest of the marks, stamps, or seals, to be over stretched or strained, either in breadth or length, beyond the dimensions allowed of and provided for by this present act, or that the name and place of abode of the maker of such cloths shall be cut out or altered; in such case the owner of such cloth, or the person in whose custody such cloth shall be found, shall, for every such offence, forfeit not exceeding the sum of five pounds, nor less than forty shillings.

Penalty on offenders.

XII. Provided nevertheless, That nothing herein contained shall extend, or be construed to extend, to give any power or authority to such inspector or inspectors, to be appointed pursuant to this act, to search and examine such cloths as shall be pressed and packed up for exportation.

Proviso.

XIII. And be it further enacted by the authority aforesaid, That it shall and may be lawful to and for the justices of the peace for the said west riding, or the major part of them, at their general quarter sessions of the peace to be held yearly after *Easter*, and they are hereby impowered to make and issue such further orders and directions, to the several officers to be appointed by virtue of this act, for the more effectual execution thereof, as to them shall seem meet; all which regulations, orders, and directions, the several searchers, measurers, inspectors, and supervisors, so to be appointed, shall, and they are hereby required to obey and perform.

Justices to make regulations.

XIV. Provided always, and it is hereby further enacted by the authority aforesaid, That if the merchant or buyer of any such cloth shall have cause to suspect the real and true lengths and breadths of such cloth not to be the same as stamped upon such seal or seals, such merchant or buyer shall and may, for proof thereof, have the liberty, within six weeks next after his buying the same (if such cloth shall not before then have been raised, dressed, or dyed) and upon two days notice given in writing to all the parties, who measured and stamped the said cloth, to put such cloth into cold water, for any time not exceeding four hours, and, immediately after the same shall be taken out of the water, to cause the same to be measured by some sworn inspector or supervisor of cloth in and for the said riding; and if, upon such admeasurement last-mentioned, there shall be found a less or smaller quantity of cloth in length or less or smaller quantity in breadth, in more than one half part of the length thereof than is mentioned on any of the seals affixed to such cloth; in every such case the searcher, measurer, or supervisor, who measured and stamped the said cloth, being convicted of having wilfully and knowingly affixed such false and fraudulent seals to such cloth, upon the oath of the inspector or supervisor who last measured the said cloth as aforesaid, or of

Where merchants suspect frauds, they may wet the cloths, and have them measured by the inspector.

any other credible witness, before one or more such justice or justices of the peace for the said riding, or any corporation within the same (not being dealers in woollen cloth, or occupiers of any fulling mill) shall, for every such offence, forfeit and pay the respective penalties and sums following; that is to say,

Penalty on conviction.

For two inches in breadth, or one yard in length, that such cloth shall fall short of the measure stamped and marked on the seals thereto affixed, the sum of five shillings; and

For every other inch in breadth, or yard in length, so overstamped, the sum of ten shillings.

The said penalties, after deducting thereout the costs and charges of such prosecution and conviction, to be paid and applied as follows; *videlicet*, one moiety to the informer, and the other moiety to the treasurer of the west riding of the said county of *York*, for the purposes herein after-mentioned.

Where false seals are found, the inspector is to fix new seals, which are to be the rule of payment for the cloths.

XV. And be it enacted by the authority aforesaid, That in all such cases, upon such second admeasurement of any such clothes as aforesaid, where any of the seals affixed shall be found not to contain the just lengths and breadths of such cloths, then, and in every such case, the inspector or supervisor, who, upon such information and complaint as aforesaid, measured the same, shall affix on every such cloth new seals, to be made and fixed as aforesaid, which shall contain the true lengths and breadths of the said cloth, and that the length and number of yards, by such inspector or supervisor so stamped on such seals as aforesaid, shall be the rule of payment for such cloth by the merchant or buyer thereof, save only that such merchant or buyer (in order to discourage the vending or exposing to sale of any such cloth with such defective and fraudulent seals) shall and may, and he is hereby authorized and impowered, to deduct and retain to himself, out of the price of such cloth, upon which the maker, searcher, measurer, or supervisor thereof shall have fixed such defective and fraudulent seals as aforesaid, the value or amount of so many yards thereof, out of the number of yards in length so stamped upon such seals by such inspector or supervisor who last measured and stamped the same as aforesaid, as the said cloth shall fall short in inches of breadth, or yards in length, of the length and breadth respectively expressed on the former fraudulent seal so affixed by the maker.

Treasurer to deduct money forfeited out of inspectors salaries.

XVI. And it is hereby enacted and declared, That it shall and may be lawful to and for the said treasurer to deduct and detain the sums of money to be forfeited by the searchers and measurers, inspectors and supervisors respectively, out of the yearly salaries of such searchers and measurers, inspectors and supervisors respectively, as such salaries respectively shall become due and payable.

Persons charged with frauds may examine the cloths in the merchant's hands, &c.

XVII. And be it further enacted, That every offender or offenders, against whom such information shall be made as aforesaid, shall and may, and are hereby authorized and impowered, within two days after notice of such information to him or them given, to go to the house of the merchant, buyer, or owner

owner of the cloth in ſuch information mentioned, and requeſt to ſee the ſaid cloth, to examine that the crimes and facts ſo charged upon them be juſt, and that no frauds have been committed by the merchant, buyer, or owner of the ſame; and that upon the merchant, buyer, or owner of ſuch cloth refuſing to permit and ſuffer ſuch offender or offenders to ſee or examine ſuch cloth as aforeſaid, ſuch proſecution, ſo intended to have been made againſt ſuch offender or offenders, ſhall be at an end and ceaſe; and any conviction to be made thereupon ſhall be void, and of none effect.

XVIII. And be it further enacted by the authority aforeſaid, That every clothier and maker of ſuch cloth ſhall, at the time of making thereof, weave or ſew into the head of the cloth, in diſtinct letters or words, plain to be read, at length, the name and place of abode of ſuch clothier and maker; and if any clothier or maker of ſuch woollen cloth ſhall, after the twenty fourth day of *June*, one thouſand ſeven hundred and ſixty five, expoſe to ſale any cloth without ſuch ſeals as before directed, or without ſuch name and place of abode ſo woven and ſewed into ſuch cloth, in words at length, plainly to be ſeen and read, ſuch clothier or maker, ſo offending, and being thereof lawfully convicted upon the oath of any one or more credible witneſs or witneſſes, made before any ſuch juſtice or juſtices of the peace for the ſaid riding, or any corporation within the ſame (he being no dealer in cloth, or occupier of any fulling mill) who is hereby authorized to adminiſter the ſaid oath, ſhall forfeit the ſum of twenty ſhillings for every ſuch piece of cloth ſo by him expoſed to ſale without ſuch ſeals as aforeſaid, and the ſum of forty ſhillings for every piece of cloth ſo by him expoſed to ſale without ſuch name and place of abode ſo ſewed or woven into the ſame as aforeſaid; and if any perſon or perſons whatſoever ſhall willingly take off, alter, or counterfeit, deface, obliterate, or cut out, any of the aforeſaid ſeal or ſeals of lead ſo fixed and riveted to ſuch end or half cloth, or to ſuch long or whole cloth, or the figures, letters, and words thereon ſtamped, made, or ſet, or therein woven or ſewed, before the cloth be taken off the tenters and brought to the preſs, every perſon or perſons ſo offending, and every perſon in whoſe cuſtody any ſuch cloth without ſeals, or with the ſeals defaced, cut out, or obliterated, as aforeſaid, ſhall be found, being thereof legally convicted; for every ſuch offence ſhall forfeit not exceeding the ſum of five pounds, nor leſs than forty ſhillings.

Clothiers to weave their names and places of abode in the heads of their cloths.

Penalty on perſons defacing or counterfeiting ſeals, &c. before cloth taken from the tenters.

XIX. And be it further enacted, That for every yard of cloth, exceeding the length of fifty eight yards, whether in one cloth, or in two ſhort cloths or ends, which ſhall be milled in one ſtock, at one and the ſame time; the owner of ſuch cloth or cloths ſhall pay to the miller of ſuch cloth or cloths, the ſum of one half-penny *per* yard, for every yard ſuch cloth (whether conſiſting of one cloth only, or of two ſhort cloths or ends) ſhall exceed the length of fifty eight yards, over and above the uſual price for milling a ſtockful, or fifty eight yards of cloth.

Payments for milling long cloths.

XX. And

Justices to settle disputes between clothiers and millers.

XX. And be it further enacted by the authority aforesaid, That all disputes and demands which shall hereafter arise between the makers of such cloths as aforesaid, and the occupiers of such fulling mills, or their agents or servants, relating to the wages for fulling, milling, or scouring, of any such woollen cloths as aforesaid; shall, in case such occupiers, agents, or servants, desire the same, and the matter in dispute shall not exceed the sum of two pounds, be heard and determined by one or more justice or justices of the peace for the county, division, or place, where such disputes or demands shall arise (such justice or justices not being traders or dealers in the woollen manufacture, farmers or occupiers of a fulling mill) who is and are hereby required and authorized, upon complaint to him or them made, to summon the parties, and to hear and examine upon oath, and adjudge such damages, and give such costs, not exceeding ten shillings, to the party so aggrieved, as in his or their discretion shall seem reasonable; and to issue his or their warrant or warrants, to levy such costs and damages by distress and sale of the goods and chattels of such person or persons who shall refuse, for the space of ten days, to pay such costs or damages by him or them so adjudged.

Penalty on stretching or straining cloths.

XXI. And it is hereby further enacted by the authority aforesaid, That if any person whatsoever, after the twenty fourth day of *June*, one thousand seven hundred and sixty five, shall stretch or strain, or cause or procure to be stretched or strained, any whole or long cloth, or end or half cloth, more than one yard in length, in every twenty yards of the length thereof, or more than one inch in every twelve inches of the breadth thereof (the whole yard in breadth containing thirty six inches only) and so in proportion for cloths that are more or less in lengths and breadths, above or beyond the length or breadth of such cloth, upon the lowest of such stamps or seals, marked, set down, and expressed; then, and in such case, every person so offending, and being thereof convicted by the oath of one or more credible witness or witnesses, before one or more such justice or justices of the peace as aforesaid, shall, for every quarter of a yard in length such cloth shall be overstretched, forfeit and pay the sum of ten shillings; and for every inch in breadth such cloth shall be overstretched, forfeit and pay the sum of twenty shillings; which said sums shall be recovered and applied in the same manner as the other penalties are herein directed to be recovered and applied.

Owners of tenters to measure and mark the lengths of their tenters.

XXII. And, for the better and more easy discovery of the undue stretching and straining of cloth, be it further enacted by the authority aforesaid, That every owner or proprietor of any tenter or tenters, in the said west riding of the said county of *York*, shall, and he is hereby required, to measure such tenter or tenters as shall be made use of for tentering of cloth, and to mark or number in figures plain and fair to be seen, the true length of yards (computing thirty seven inches to each yard) of each tenter or tenters, beginning at number one, and so continuing it to the end thereof, marking and numbering each yard distinctly, plainly, and fairly to be seen, upon the top bar belonging to each tenter, on the foreside thereof; and if any such tenter or tenters shall, after the twenty fourth day of *June*, one thousand seven hundred and sixty five, be found not to be measured, and truly marked and numbered as aforesaid, the occupier of such tenter or tenters shall forfeit and pay the sum of five pounds for each tenter that shall be found not so numbered and marked as aforesaid; such penalty to be levied and recovered as any other penalty is hereby directed to be recovered and levied.

Penalty on using cards made with wire or wire teeth.

XXIII. And whereas the using of cards made with wire, or with wire teeth, in dressing of cloth, hath by experience been found to be very prejudicial to the said woollen manufacture: now, to the end the said woollen manufacture may be improved as much as possible, be it enacted by the authority aforesaid, That if any person or persons, within the said west riding of the said county of *York*, shall, from and after the twenty fourth day of *June*, one thousand seven hundred and sixty five, use, or cause to be used, in dressing of cloth, any cards made with wire, or with teeth of iron, or any other metal whatsoever; every such person or persons so using the same, shall, for every such offence, forfeit forty shillings.

How offences shall be prosecuted, and forfeitures applied.

XXIV. Provided always, and it is hereby further enacted, That information upon oath shall be given of the offences mentioned in this act, within the space of twenty days next after such offence shall be discovered; and all and every the offences in this act mentioned (except such for which any other remedy is hereby provided) shall be enquired of and determined, and convictions thereon made upon oath of one or more credible witness or witnesses, by any one or more justice or justices of the peace (not being a dealer in woollen cloth, nor occupier of any fulling mill as aforesaid) notice being first given of the charge to the person or persons therewith charged; and that all such penalties and forfeitures as shall or may happen by reason of this act, shall go and be disposed of, one half to the person or persons who shall give information of the offence on which the conviction shall be made, and the other half to the treasurer of the said riding; and if any offender or offenders shall, by the space of ten days next after he or they shall be convicted of any of the offences aforesaid, and have notice thereof to him, her, or them given, at his, her, or their dwelling house, or place of abode, refuse or neglect to pay any forfeiture by him, her, or them incurred, by reason of this act, or shall not appeal, as is herein after provided, to the quarter sessions, then, and not before, it shall and may be lawful to and for the justice or justices of the peace, before whom such conviction shall be made, or any other justice or justices of the peace for the said riding, or any corporation within the same (not being a dealer in woollen broad cloth, or occupier of any fulling mill) upon a certificate of such conviction sent to him or them, from the justice

ſtice or juſtices before whom ſuch conviction was made; and he or they is or are hereby authorized and required to iſſue out one or more warrant or warrants, under his or their hand and ſeal, or hands and ſeals, to the conſtable of the town or place, or bailiff or bailiffs of the liberties, wapentakes, or limits, where ſuch offender or offenders doth or ſhall inhabit, thereby commanding him or them to levy the ſame by diſtreſs and ſale of the offender's goods and chattels, returning the overplus (if any be) after paying likewiſe the charges of ſuch diſtreſs and ſale, to the offender or offenders demanding the ſame; and where no ſufficient diſtreſs can be found, to commit the offender or offenders to the houſe of correction, for any time not exceeding three months.

Appeal to the quarter ſeſſions.

XXV. Provided always, and it is hereby further enacted by the authority aforeſaid, That if any perſon or perſons ſhall find him, her, or themſelves, aggrieved by any order or warrant made by any juſtice or juſtices, or upon any conviction before him or them, in purſuance of this act, ſuch perſon or perſons may appeal to the next general quarter ſeſſions to be held for the ſaid weſt riding of the ſaid county of *York*, which ſhall not be held within fourteen days next after the cauſe of appeal ſhall ariſe, giving ten days notice of ſuch appeal to the perſon or perſons diſcovering the offence on which the conviction was made; and if the juſtices at the ſaid quarter ſeſſions either confirm or diſannul the orders or proceedings of the ſaid juſtice or juſtices, they ſhall allow ſuch coſts and charges to the party aggrieved thereby, as they ſhall think reaſonable; to be levied and paid in ſuch manner, as is uſual in caſes of appeal from any order of the juſtices of the peace to the ſeſſions, whoſe order herein ſhall be final.

Juſtices, &c. to tranſmit to the quarter ſeſſions accounts of convictions, &c.

XXVI. And it is hereby enacted and declared, That the ſeveral juſtices of the peace before whom any conviction ſhall be made by virtue of this act, as alſo the ſeveral ſearchers, meaſurers, inſpectors, and ſupervifors, ſo to be appointed, ſhall, and they are hereby required at the four general quarter ſeſſions of the peace in and for the ſaid riding, held quarterly in every year, to return and tranſmit to the juſtices of the peace aſſembled at ſuch general quarter ſeſſions, a true and perfect account in writing, of all the convictions to be made purſuant to this act that ſhall happen within their knowledge, and of all the penalties and forfeitures inflicted or levied by means or on account thereof, which, by virtue of this act, are made payable to the ſaid treaſurer for the time being; and ſhall, at the ſame time, pay or cauſe to be paid to the treaſurer for the time being, all and every ſum and ſums of money by them, or any of them, or for their or any of their uſe, had or received, for, or on account of any ſuch conviction or convictions, and which by this act are made payable to the ſaid treaſurer; and every perſon and perſons neglecting or refuſing to return and tranſmit ſuch account, or to pay, or cauſe to be paid, ſuch ſums of money ſo by them received, or in their hands, or any part thereof, for the space of twenty days next after any of the said sessions, and being thereof convicted upon the oath of one or more credible witness or witnesses, before any two justices of the peace of and for the said riding (not being dealers in cloth, or occupiers of any fulling mill) shall forfeit and pay the sum of ten pounds, over and above the several sums by him or them received, or being in his hands as aforesaid, to be recovered, paid, and applied, in such manner as the other penalties inflicted by this act are directed to be recovered, paid, and applied.

This act shall extend to all woollen cloths, except such narrow cloths as are described in act 11 Geo. 2.

XXVII. And be it further enacted by the authority aforesaid, That this act, and all the penalties and clauses therein contained, shall extend to all woollen cloth which shall be made and milled in the west riding of the county of *York*; except such narrow woollen cloths as are mentioned and described, and for which provision is made in and by one act made in the eleventh year of the reign of his said late majesty King *George* the Second, intituled, *An act for the better regulating of narrow woollen cloths in the west riding of the county of* York.

Application of money now in the hands of the treasurer of the west riding.

XXVIII. And whereas there is now in the hands of the treasurer of the west riding of the county of *York* a considerable sum of money, which hath arisen by and out of the duties granted by the said former acts for the stamping and measuring of cloth; now it is hereby further enacted by the authority aforesaid, That the said treasurer of the said west riding for the time being, shall, out of the money remaining in his hands, and which shall hereafter be received by him on account of the duties herein before directed to be paid to such treasurer as aforesaid, in the first place, pay the charges and expences attending the passing this act, and shall afterwards pay and apply the said duties and penalties, as the same shall come in and be received, to the payment of the salaries of the searchers or measurers, inspectors and supervisors of cloth, herein before directed to be chosen and appointed as aforesaid, in such proportions, and in such manner, as the justices of the peace of and for the said riding, at their general quarter sessions yearly to be held next after *Easter*, shall direct and appoint.

When justices may increase or diminish the rates.

XXIX. And it is hereby further enacted by the authority aforesaid, That after all the money to be expended in and about the obtaining this act, shall be totally paid off and discharged, it shall and may be lawful to and for the justices of the peace for the said west riding, at their general quarter sessions held next after *Easter* yearly, to make orders for the increasing or diminishing the rates or duties to be paid for measuring, stamping, and sealing of cloth, so as the same shall never exceed six pence for every such whole cloth, and three pence for every such end or half cloth as aforesaid.

Limitation of actions.

XXX. And be it further enacted by the authority aforesaid, That if any suit or action shall be commenced or prosecuted against any person or persons for any thing done or to be done in pursuance of this act, every such suit or action shall be commenced within six calendar months next after the fact committed,

ted, and not afterwards; and ſhall be laid, brought, and tried, in the county of *York*, and not elſewhere; and the defendant or defendants in ſuch ſuits or actions ſhall and may plead the general iſſue, and give this act, and the ſpecial matter, in evidence, at any trial to be had thereupon; and that the ſame was done in purſuance of, and by the authority of, this act; and if it ſhall appear to be ſo done, or if any ſuch ſuit or action ſhall be brought after the time before limited for bringing the ſame, or ſhall be brought in any other county or place; that then the jury ſhall find for the defendant or defendants: and upon ſuch verdict, or if the plaintiff or plaintiffs ſhall become nonſuit, or diſcontinue his, her, or their action, after the defendant or defendants ſhall have appeared; or if, upon demurrer judgement ſhall be given againſt the plaintiff or plaintiffs; the defendant or defendants ſhall and may recover treble coſts, and have the like remedy for the ſame as any defendant or defendants hath or have for coſts in other caſes by law.

General iſſue.

Treble coſts.

XXXI. And it is hereby further enacted and declared, That this act ſhall be deemed, and taken to be, a publick act; and all judges, juſtices, and other perſons, are to take notice thereof as ſuch, in all courts and places whatſoever, without ſpecially pleading the ſame.

Publick act.

CAP. LII.

An act for repairing and widening the road leading from the town of Wadhurſt *in the county of* Suſſex, *to the turnpike road at* Lamberhurſt Pound *and* Pullen's Hill, *in in the county of* Kent; *and from the top of* Pullen's Hill, *through the pariſhes of* Horſmonden, Marden, Yalden, *and* Weſt Farley, *to* Weſt Farley Street, *in the ſaid county of* Kent.

CAP. LIII.

An act for continuing the terms of ſeveral acts, and for giving further powers for repairing the road from Chatteris Ferry, *to* Hammond's Eau *and* Somerſham Bridge, *and for amending and widening the road from* Somerſham Bridge *to the* Sheep Market *in* Saint Ives; *and alſo the road branching out of the ſaid road near* Stocks Bridge *through* Needingworth, *to* Earith *in the county of* Huntingdon.

CAP. LIV.

An act for repairing and widening the road from Dunham Ferry, *to the ſouth end of* Great Markham Common, *in the county of* Nottingham.

CAP. LV.

An act to continue the term, and to vary and enlarge the powers,

powers, of an act passed in the twenty fifth year of his late Majesty, for repairing the road from Wallingford *in the county of* Berks, *to* Wantage, *and from thence to* Faringdon, *and also from* Wantage *to* Idson, *in the said county, so far as the same relate to the road leading from* Wallingford *to* Wantage, *and from thence to* Faringdon; *and for discontinuing the said term and powers, so far as the same relate to the road leading from* Wantage *to* Idson, *and for repairing the road leading from the north east corner of* Nuffield Common, *by the parish church of* Nuffield, *otherwise* Tuffield, *in the county of* Oxford, *to the commencement of the said turnpike road leading from* Wallingford *to* Wantage.

CAP. LVI.

An act for repairing and widening the road leading from Porthaethwy Ferry, *to* Holyhead *in the county of* Anglesey.

CAP. LVII.

An act for continuing the term, and altering and enlarging the powers of an act passed in the thirtieth year of the reign of his late Majesty, for amending, widening, and keeping in repair, the roads leading from the village of Milford *in the county of* Surrey, *through* Petworth, *to the top of* Dunckton Hill, *and from* Petworth *to* Stopham Bridge, *in the county of* Sussex.

CAP. LVIII.

An act for repairing, widening, and keeping in repair, several roads in and near Great Torrington, *in the county of* Devon.

CAP. LIX.

An act for repairing and widening several roads leading from the quay at Limington, *in the county of* Southampton.

CAP. LX.

An act for continuing and rendering more effectual, two acts, passed in the twelfth year of King George *the First, and the twentieth of his late Majesty, for repairing the several roads therein mentioned, in the counties of* Essex *and* Suffolk; *and for repairing and widening several other roads in the counties of* Essex *and* Hertford.

CAP. LXI.

An act for repairing, widening, and keeping in repair, several

ral roads leading to and from Crewkerne, *in the county of* Somerfet.

CAP. LXII.

An act for enlarging the term and powers of two acts of the thirteenth of George *the First, and of the sixteenth of his late Majesty, for repairing several roads leading from the town of* Warminster, *in the county of* Wilts; *and for amending several other roads near the said town; and for repealing so much of an act made in the first year of the reign of his present Majesty, for repairing several roads therein mentioned, in the said county, as relates to the road within the town of* Heytesbury; *and for other purposes therein mentioned.*

CAP. LXIII.

An act for repairing and widening the roads leading from the turnpike road at Kipping's Crofs *in the parish of* Brenchley, *in the county of* Kent, *through the parishes of* Brenchley, Horfmonfden, *and* Goudhurft, *by the left hand side of* Iden Green, *to the turnpike road on* Wilfley Green, *in the parish of* Cranbrooke; *and from a place near* Goudhurft Gore, *through the parish of* Marden, *to* Stile Bridge, *in the said parish, and from* Underden Green, *in* Marden *aforesaid, to* Wanfhutt's Green, *in the county of* Kent.

CAP. LXIV.

An act for repairing, widening, and keeping in repair, the road leading from the turnpike road on Hurft Green, *in the county of* Suffex, *through* Etchingham *and* Burwafh, *to the extent of the said parish of* Burwafh, *in the said county.*

CAP. LXV.

An act for rebuilding the parish church of Alhallows on the Wall, *in the city of* London; *and for rebuilding the house belonging to the rector of the said parish; and for purchasing several pieces of ground and tenements thereon, to render the passages to and from the said church and house more commodious.*

CAP. LXVI.

An act to continue the term, and enlarge the powers, of an act passed in the Second year of the reign of his present Majesty, for repairing and widening the road from Mullen's Pond

Pond, *in the county of* Southampton, *to the eighteen mile stone from the city of* Salisbury, *and several other roads in the said act mentioned; and also for repairing and widening several other roads, leading out of the said roads, and for other purposes therein mentioned.*

CAP. LXVII.

An act for amending the road from the Pinfold *in* Balby, *in the county of* York, *to* Workſop, *in the county of* Nottingham.

CAP. LXVIII.

An act for repairing, widening, and keeping in repair, the road leading from the turnpike road at Wrotham Heath, *in the county of* Kent, *to the turnpike road leading from* Croydon *to* Godſtone, *in the county of* Surry.

CAP. LXIX.

An act for repairing and widening the roads from the south end of Newton Abbott *to the passage way in* Kinſwear, *opposite* Clifton Dartmouth Hartneſs, *and from the end of a lane leading out of the turnpike road between* Newton Abbott *and* Totnes, *towards* Abbotts Kerſwell, *to* Five Lanes; *and from* Langvers Barn *to the said turnpike road, between* Newton Abbott *and* Totnes; *and from* Galmpton Warborough *to* Monks Bridge *and* Brixham Quay; *and from* Langvers Barn *to the north end of* Paington *town, all in the county of* Devon.

CAP. LXX.

An act for repairing and widening the roads from Keyberry Bridge *to the passage at* Shalldon; *and from the said bridge to the pier or harbour of* Torkey, *in the county of* Devon.

CAP. LXXI.

An act for repairing and widening the road from Tonbridge *to* Maidſtone, *and from* Watt's Croſs *to* Cowden, *in the county of* Kent.

CAP. LXXII.

An act for amending and widening the road from the sign of the Coach and Horſes *in* Birſtol, *to the turnpike road at* Nunbrook; *and from* Bradley Lane *to the town of* Huddersfield, *in the west riding of the county of* York.

CAP. LXXIII.

An act for repairing and widening the road from Great

Grimsby Haven, *at or near a place called the* Upper Sand End, *to* Wold Newton Church; *and from* Nuns Farm *to the* Mill Field, *in the parish of* Irby, *in the county of* Lincoln.

CAP. LXXIV.

An act for enlarging the powers of several acts for repairing the road from Stump Cross *to* Newmarket Heath *and the town of* Cambridge, *and from* Foulmire *to* Cambridge, *and other roads adjoining thereto, so far as the same relate to the road from* Foulmire *to* Cambridge, *and the said other roads adjoining thereto.*

CAP. LXXV.

An act for enlarging the term and powers of so much of an act made in the twenty seventh year of the reign of his late Majesty, for repairing several roads in the counties of Dorset *and* Devon, *as relates to the road from* Penn Inn, *in the county of* Dorset, *to the work-house at the east end of the town of* Honiton, *in the county of* Devon, *and to the road from the intrenchment on* Askerwell Hill *to* Penn Inn, *and from* Bridport *to* Beamister; *and for repairing and amending several other roads therein mentioned in the counties of* Dorset *and* Devon.

CAP. LXXVI.

An act for repairing, widening, and keeping in repair, several roads, leading from Kidwelly, *in the county of* Carmarthen; *and also several roads leading from* Llandilo, *in the said county.*

CAP. LXXVII.

An act for enlarging the terms and powers of several acts of the ninth and twelfth years of Queen Anne, *and of the thirteenth of King* George *the First, and of the fourteenth of his late Majesty, for repairing the highways leading from* Royston, *in the county of* Hertford *to* Wandsford Bridge, *in the county of* Huntingdon, *so far as relates to the middle and south divisions of the road comprized in the said acts; and for amending the road from the town of* Huntingdon *to the causeway at or near the west end of the town of* Somersham, *in the said county of* Huntingdon.

CAP. LXXVIII.

An act for repairing, widening, and keeping in repair, the road from Welford Bridge, *in the county of* Northampton, *through* Husband's Bosworth *and* Great Wigston, *to* Milston Lane, *in the town of* Leicester.

CAP. LXXIX.

An act to continue the term, and alter and enlarge the powers of an act passed in the third year of his present Majesty, for repairing, widening, turning and keeping in repair, the road from the town of Cambridge *to* Ely, *and from thence to* Soham; *and for building a bridge cross the river* Ouze, *at or near a place called* Stretham Ferry, *in the county of* Cambridge; *and for repairing and widening, and making several other roads, adjoining to the roads directed to be repaired and widened by the said act.*

CAP. LXXX.

An act for continuing the terms of several acts, and for giving further powers for repairing the road leading from Chapel on the heath, *in the county of* Oxford, *to* Bourton on the Hill, *in the county of* Gloucester.

CAP. LXXXI.

An act for cleansing and lighting the streets, lanes, and passages, within the towns of Manchester *and* Salford, *in the county palatine of* Lancaster; *and for providing fire engines and fire-men; and for preventing annoyances within the said towns.*

CAP. LXXXII.

An act to enlarge certain powers granted by an act passed in the twenty second year of the reign of King George *the Second, intituled,* An act for enlarging and maintaining the harbour of *Ramsgate*, and for cleansing, amending and preserving the haven of *Sandwich*.

CAP. LXXXIII.

An act for amending the road from Chatteris Ferry, *through* Chatteris *and* Marsh, *to* Wisbech Saint Peter's; *and from thence to* Tid Gote *in the* Isle of Ely; *and from* Wisbech *aforesaid, through* Outwell, *to* Downham Bridge *in the county of* Norfolk; *and for repealing the several acts for repairing the said road between* Wisbech *and* Marsh.

CAP. LXXXIV.

An act for repairing and widening the road from Newcastle under Line *to* Hassop; *and from* Middle Hills *to the*

Macclesfield *turnpike road, near* Buxton; *and also the road branching out of the said first mentioned road at* Cobridge, *to* Burslem; *and to the* Uttoxeter *turnpike at* Shelton, *in the county of* Stafford.

CAP. LXXXV.

An act for repairing and widening the roads from Bawtry Bridge, *in the county of* Nottingham, *to* Hainton, *in the county of* Lincoln; *and from* North Willingham *to the north end of the lane betwixt* Dexthorpe *and* Langton, *and from* West Raisin *to* Pilford Bridge *and from the great road near* Bishop Bridge *to* Bishop Norton Common; *and from the hamlet of* Morton *to* Epworth; *and from* Haxey Field, *to the* Trent *at* Kinnald Ferry, *in the county of* Lincoln.

CAP. LXXXVI.

An act for enlarging the term and powers of an act made in the twenty fifth year of the reign of his late Majesty, for repairing the high road from the town of Shrewsbury *through* Cressage, Harley, Much Wenlock, *by* Muckley Cross, *and through* Morville, *to* Bridgenorth, *in the county of* Salop; *and for amending several other roads near or adjoining thereto.*

CAP. LXXXVII.

An act to amend several acts passed in the fourth and sixth years of King George *the First, and in the eleventh and twenty fourth years of King* George *the Second, for repairing several roads from the* Stone's End *in* Kent Street, *and* Bermondsey Street, *Southwark, to* Dartford, *and to the extent of the parish of* Lewisham, *next* Bromley *and* Beckenham, *in the county of* Kent; *and for extending the said acts to the repair of the roads leading from the end of the present turnpike to the west end of* Stroud Green, *and to* Farnborough Well, *and to the* Stone's End *in* London Street, Greenwich, *and to the north end of* Burnt Ash Lane, *in the parish of* Lee, *and from the west end of* Greenwich Park Wall *to* Woolwich Warren; *and for making an allowance out of the tolls arising by the said acts to the trustees for putting in execution an act of the twenty second year of King* George *the Second,* for opening and making a new road from the east end of *New Street*, in the parish of *Saint John, Southwark*, to and through the several places therein mentioned; and for keeping the said road in repair for the future.

CAP.

CAP. LXXXVIII.

An act for repairing and widening the road from Barton Waterſidehouſe, *to* Riſeham Hedge Corner, *and ſeveral other roads in the county of* Lincoln, *therein mentioned.*

CAP. LXXXIX.

An act for the building a bridge over the river Tay, *at or near the town of* Perth, *in the county of* Perth.

CAP. XC.

An act for repairing and widening the road from the Alfreton *turnpike road, near a place called* Little Robbins, *in the pariſh of* Mansfield, *in the county of* Nottingham, *through* Woolley Moor, *to the* Nottingham *turnpike road, near* Tanſley, *in the county of* Derby, *and from* Woolley Moor, *to the* Cheſterfield *turnpike road at* Kelſtidge, *in the county of* Derby.

CAP. XCI.

An act for veſting certain glebe lands, belonging to the rectory of the pariſh church of Saint Chriſtopher, *in the city of* London, *in the governor and company of the bank of* England; *and for making a recompence to the rector of the ſaid pariſh, and his ſucceſſors, in lieu thereof; and for obviating certain doubts in an act paſſed in the thirty third year of the reign of his late Majeſty, for widening certain ſtreets, lanes, and paſſages, within the city of* London.

CAP. XCII.

An act for explaining and amending, and likewiſe for enlarging the term and powers granted by a certain act of parliament, paſſed in the twenty fifth year of the reign of his late majeſty King George *the Second, intituled,* An act for amending ſeveral roads leading from the town of *Taunton*, in the county of *Somerſet*.

CAP. XCIII.

An act for repairing, widening, turning, altering, and keeping in repair, the roads leading from the port town, and borough of Minehead, *through* Dunſtan *and* Timberſcombe, *to* Hele Bridge, *and through the town of* Dulverton, *and by the river and* Bruſhford Green *to* Exbridge, *in the county of* Somerſet, *and from thence to* Batham Bridge, *in the town of* Bampton, *in the county of* Devon; *and alſo the road leading from the ſaid port town and borough of* Minehead, *through* Carhampton *and*

Billbrooke *to* Harrow Gate, *in the parish of* Stogumber, *in the county of* Somerset; *and also the road leading from* Carhampton *aforesaid, through the town of* Watchet, *in the parish of* Saint Decumans, *in the county of* Somerset, *to or near the village of* Rydon, *and by* Long Cross Barn, *to the end of the* Bridgewater *turnpike road, in the town of* Nether Stowey, *in the county of* Somerset; *and also from the said town of* Watchet *to* Tower Hill, *in the village of* Williton *in the parish of* Saint Decumans, *and from the said town of* Watchet, *by way of* Five Bells *to* Fair Cross, *and from thence to* Stickle Path, *over* Brendon Hill, *to* Robery Lane, *and to* Bampton *in the said county of* Devon.

CAP. XCIV.

An act for repairing the church of the united parishes of All Saints *and* Saint John, *in the town of* Hertford.

CAP. XCV.

An act for repairing and widening the road, leading from a street called The Hundred, *at* Romsey, *through* Chilworth, *to the river at* Swathling, *in the county of* Southampton, *and for connecting the same with the road leading from the city of* Winchester, *through* Hursley, *to* Chandler's Ford; *and from* Hursley *aforesaid, to the turnpike road at* Romsey *aforesaid; and also for repairing and widening the road leading from the river at* Swathling *aforesaid, through* Botley, *to the turnpike road at* Sherril Heath, *in the said county of* Southampton.

CAP. XCVI.

An act for repairing and widening the road from Alford *to* Boston, *and from thence to* Cowbridge, *in the county of* Lincoln.

CAP. XCVII.

An act for the better relief and employment of the poor, in the hundreds of Loes, *and* Wilford, *in the county of* Suffolk.

CAP. XCVIII.

An act to enlarge the term and powers of an act made in the twenty fourth year of his late Majesty, for repairing the road from Crossford Bridge *to* Manchester, *and for amending the road from* Crossford Bridge *aforesaid, to a certain place in* Altrincham, *in the county palatine of* Chester.

CAP. XCIX.

An act for amending and widening the road, from the city of York,

York, *by* Grimston Smithy, *to* Kexby Bridge, *and from* Grimstone Smithy *aforesaid, to a certain gate, at the upper end of* Garraby Hill, *in the county of* York.

CAP. C.

An act for repairing and widening the road from Stockport, *in the county of* Chester, *to* Saxon's Lane End, *in the county of* Lancaster, *and from the cross, in* Ashton-Under-Line *in the said county of* Lancaster, *to* Doctor's-Lane-Head, *in the county of* York; *and also the road branching out of the first-mentioned road, in the township of* Bredbury, *to* Mottram, *in the said county of* Chester.

CAP. CI.

An act for repairing and widening the roads from the Little Bridge, *over the end of the drain, next* Wisbeach River, *lying between* Roper's Fields, *and the* Bell Inn *in* Wisbeach, *in the* Isle of Ely, *to the sign of the* Bear *in* Walsoken, *in the county of* Norfolk; *and from* Walsoken Bridge, *lying over the same drain, to the said sign of the* Bear, *and to* Lord's Bridge, *in* Islington, *and from thence to the west ends of* Maudlin Bridge *and* German's Bridge, *in the county of* Norfolk; *and from the east of* German's Bridge *aforesaid, to the west end of* Long Bridge, *in* South Lynn, *in the borough of* King's Lynn, *in the said county of* Norfolk; *and from* Islington *aforesaid, to* Cross Keys Wash *in the said county.*

CAP. CII.

An act for repairing and widening several roads, leading from between the second and third mile stones, on the turnpike road between the town and county of Coole, *and* Winborn Minster, *in the county of* Dorset, *to* Bratton Corner, *in the county of* Somerset.

CAP. CIII.

An act to enlarge the term and powers of an act made in the twenty seventh year of his late Majesty, for opening, making, widening, and keeping in repair, a road from Ratcliffe Highway, *through* Cannon Street, *in the county of* Middlesex, *and other roads in the said act mentioned; and for lighting, watching and watering the said roads.*

CAP. CIV.

An act for enlarging the term and powers granted by an act passed in the twenty sixth year of his late Majesty's reign, intituled, An act for repairing and widening the roads therein

therein mentioned, leading to and from the towns of *Shepton Mallet* and *Ivelchester*, in the county of *Somerset*, and for repairing the roads from *Shepton Mallet* to *Leighton*, and from *Shepton Mallet* to *Long Cross Bottom*.

CAP. CV.

An act for repairing and widening the road, from the turnpike road in Banbury, *in the county of* Oxford, *through* Daventre, *and* Cottesbach, *to the south end of* Mill Field, *in the parish of* Lutterworth, *in the county of* Leicester.

CAP. CVI.

An act to continue the term and render more effectual an act passed in the thirtieth year of the reign of his late Majesty, for repairing and widening the roads leading from Spalding High Bridge, *through* Littleworth, *and by* Frognall, *and over* James Deeping Stone Bridge, *in the county of* Lincoln, *to* Maxey Outgang, *in the county of* Northampton, *adjoining to the high road there.*

CAP. CVII.

An act for repairing and widening the road from the Great Bridge, *in the borough of* Warwick, *through* Southam, *and* Daventry, *to the town of* Northampton.

CAP. CVIII.

An act for amending and widening the road, from the north end of Old Malton Gate, *in the town and borough of* New Malton; *to the town of* Pickering, *in the county of* York.

The END *of the Twenty-Sixth Volume.*

www.ingramcontent.com/pod-product-compliance
Lightning Source LLC
Chambersburg PA
CBHW022127020426
42334CB00015B/794
* 9 7 8 3 7 4 2 8 9 9 4 5 3 *